ITALIAN RIVIERA
& PIEDMONT

*'Against these deeply coloured coves and cliffs
rise villages of weathered pastels, silvery groves of
olives and striped terraces, gazing out over fleets
of fishing craft and sleek white yachts.'*

Dana Facaros & Michael Pauls

About the Guide

The **full-colour introduction** gives the authors' overview of the region, together with suggested **itineraries** and a regional **'where to go' map** and **feature** to help you plan your trip.

Illuminating and entertaining **cultural chapters** on local history, art, architecture, food, wine, culture and everyday life give you a rich flavour of the region.

Planning Your Trip starts with the basics of when to go, getting there and getting around, coupled with other useful information, including a section for disabled travellers. The **Practical A–Z** deals with all the **essential information** and **contact details** that you may need while you are away.

The **regional chapters** are arranged in a loose touring order, with plenty of public transport and driving information. The author's top **'Don't Miss'** 🟊 sights are highlighted at the start of each chapter.

A **language and pronunciation guide**, a **glossary** of cultural terms, ideas for **further reading** and a comprehensive **index** can be found at the end of the book.

Although everything we list in this guide is **personally recommended**, our authors inevitably have their own favourite places to eat and stay. Whenever you see this **Author's Choice** 🟊 icon beside a listing, you will know that it is a little bit out of the ordinary.

Hotel Price Guide (*see also* p.73)

Luxury	€€€€€	€230 and above
Very expensive	€€€€	€150–230
Expensive	€€€	€100–150
Moderate	€€	€60–100
Inexpensive	€	under €60

Restaurant Price Guide (*see also* p.77)

Very expensive	€€€€	€45 and above
Expensive	€€€	€30–45
Moderate	€€	€20–30
Inexpensive	€	under €20

About the Authors

Dana Facaros and Michael Pauls have written over 30 books for Cadogan Guides. They have lived all over Europe with their son and daughter, and are currently ensconced in a old farmhouse in southwestern France with a large collection of tame and wild animals.

5th Edition published 2008

INTRODUCING THE ITALIAN RIVIERA & PIEDMONT

01

Vermouth in Turin and wine in Barolo; snow-covered mountains; the sea in Rapallo; walking the Cinque Terre, in a landscape of dreams: these are just a few of our – everyone's – favourite things in Liguria, Piedmont and the Valle d'Aosta. Yet there aren't as many favourite things as there would be if people knew Italy's northwest better. Set apart from the Italian mainstream, much of it is *terra incognita*.

Blame altitude. Some 60 per cent of the land here is seriously mountainous, isolating the northwest then dividing it further into a mosaic of landscapes and cultures. If variety, as they say, is the spice of life, then these three regions add up to a pretty hot curry of rice paddies, glaciers and subtropical gardens. In the relatively compact Valle d'Aosta, people speak Italian and French, Occitan or even medieval German. Piedmont is packed with wonderful nooks, nearly all tucked under the mass-tourism radar: Saluzzo, the 'Siena of the Alps'; little Lake Orta; the gourmet havens in the hills of Le Langhe and Monferrato; the lakes and castles of the Canavese, and much more. The gilded fleshpots of the Italian Riviera, where a climate similar to the Bay of Naples attracted the first sun-starved Britons two centuries ago, are only a short hairpinning drive away from the *entroterra*, where quiet villages lost in time seem to grow organically from wooded hills – even Italians are surprised to learn that Liguria is the most densely forested region in Italy.

History, too, has shaped the land. Liguria is bony under its pretty frock of palms, olives and flowers, forcing its inhabitants to go to sea to seek their fortunes. Feisty medieval Genoa became a bold and wealthy maritime republic rivalled only by Venice, then went one better in the late 16th century by becoming the financial centre

Previous page: Cinque Terre, pp.196–200

Above: Camogli, pp.180–2

Top: Cenobio dei Dogi hotel, Riviera di Levante, pp.181–2

Above: Portofino, Riviera di Levante, p.184

Opposite: Coastline, Riviera di Levante, pp.175–212

of Europe, sucking up the gold and silver of the Spanish treasure fleet. Even humble fishing villages found the wherewithal to finance a Baroque or rococo fantasy by the sea, the best resembling big *semifreddo* desserts, good enough to eat.

Piedmont and the Valle d'Aosta danced to a different tune. The mountains are higher here, and for centuries their passes were used by pilgrims and merchants from northern Europe. Barons in castles charged them tolls and monks sheltered them in hostels (one monk even developed a breed of large dog to rescue travellers lost in the snow). In the mid-1500s, in the twilight of the Renaissance in the rest of Italy (it didn't quite make it up here), Piedmont's rulers, the Dukes of Savoy, moved over the Alps from Chambéry to Turin, the new capital of what the major powers in Europe saw as a useful buffer state. When they became kings, Turin became their 'Little Paris'.

Post-Napoleonic politics united Liguria and Piedmont, and united the very different personalities of Garibaldi, Mazzini, Cavour and Vittorio Emanuele II, who would go on to create the kingdom of Italy in the 19th century. It was a head start that helped to make Genoa and Turin two corners of Italy's industrial triangle (along with Milan), a fact that also shunted them off many travellers' itineraries. This is changing: Genoa (2004 Cultural Capital of Europe) and Turin (host to the 2006 Winter Olympics) have worked hard to remake themselves into savvy, hip cities of art and culture. Genoa is particularly proud of its aquarium, now the third most visited attraction in Italy. The rest of the Riviera is as delightful as ever, especially if you go outside of the summer rush, and the rest of Piedmont and Aosta wait patiently to be discovered. They may not fit many Italian stereotypes, but that's the whole point.

Where to Go

Liguria resembles a big rainbow, and we follow it west to east, beginning on the French border with the voluptuous **Riviera di Ponente**, the coast of the setting sun. Genoa divides it from the wilder Riviera di Levante, where the Apennines in many places bathe their toes in the sea. The often scenic, often slow Via Aurelia (S1) follows the coast – that is, where it can, side by side with the railway – while the remarkable mountain-piercing, viaduct-straddling *autostrada* is handy for speedy hops along or over the rainbow. Ideally base yourself somewhere for a few days, and explore from there, at least once venturing into the lush mountainous *entroterra*. Otherwise trains, buses and boat services along the coast are frequent and spare you the stress of trying to find a place to park – in season a serious problem nearly everywhere.

The landmarks of the Riviera di Ponente begin smack on the frontier: the prehistoric caves of Balzi Rossi and the botanical gardens at Villa Hanbury, near Ventimiglia, a fine town in its own right. The Riviera's first capitals of sun and fun, Bordighera and San Remo, make splendid bases, especially for jaunts up to the medieval hill villages of Dolceacqua and Taggia. The best olive oil in Italy, or so they claim, comes from the groves around Imperia; beyond it lies the delightful coral fishers' village of Cervo, the wide beach at lively Alassio, and early medieval Albenga, near the Riviera's most beautiful caves at Toirano. Towards Savona wait the fine beaches at Finale, picturesque little Varigotti and the mini-maritime republic of Noli. Beyond Savona, you'll find Liguria's ceramics capital, Albisola, and, lying in the embrace of the Genoese metropolitan area, Pegli, with the romantic gardens of Villa Durazzo-Pallavicini.

Italy's busiest port, **Genoa**, shares the startling vertical geography of the Rivieras. There's more to see and do than you might expect: noble palaces and churches packed with art, an evocative medieval quarter – one of the largest in Europe, crockery from the Last Supper, an extravagant cemetery, and all the more recent attractions of the Porto Antico, starting with the biggest aquarium in Europe.

East of Genoa on the **Riviera di Levante** are more villas and gardens at Nervi, followed by the Gulf of Paradise, framed by the promontory of Monte di Portofino. Here are places straight out of picture postcards – the fishing village of Camogli, the ancient abbey of San Fruttuoso, the resorts of Santa Margherita Ligure, Rapallo, ultra-chic Portofino, and Sestri Levante with its twin bays, followed by the Cinque Terre – five extraordinary villages set amid sheer mountains striped with vines and stone terraces. On the Gulf of Poets (famous residents included Shelley and Byron) are La Spezia, a big naval port with excellent museums, beautiful old Portovenere, and Lerici with its grand castle. The high coast over the Val di Magra closes off the

Top: San Remo, pp.95–101

Above: Palazzo Ducale, Genoa, p.159

Chapter Divisions

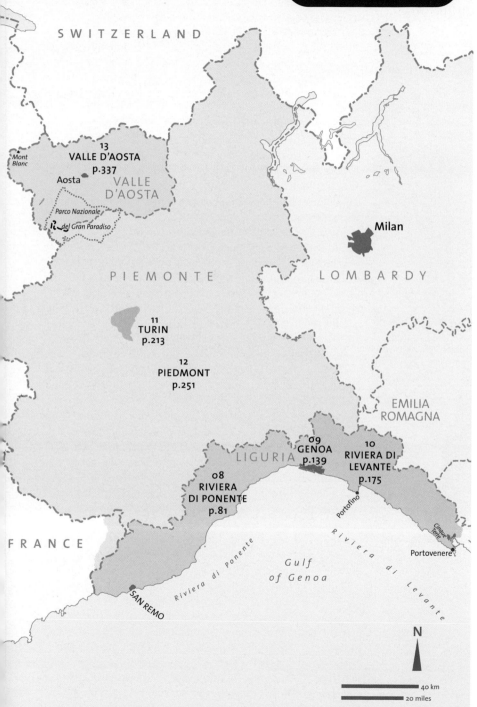

SWITZERLAND

Mont Blanc

13 VALLE D'AOSTA p.337

Aosta

VALLE D'AOSTA

Parco Nazionale del Gran Paradiso

Milan

PIEMONTE

LOMBARDY

11 TURIN p.213

12 PIEDMONT p.251

EMILIA ROMAGNA

09 GENOA p.139

LIGURIA

10 RIVIERA DI LEVANTE p.175

08 RIVIERA DI PONENTE p.81

Portofino

Cinque Terre

FRANCE

Portovenere

Gulf of Genoa

Riviera di Ponente

Riviera di Levante

SAN REMO

N

40 km

20 miles

region by Tuscany. Here, too, are the ruins of Roman Luni and the castles and churches of its medieval successor, Sarzana.

In Piedmont we start with **Turin**, for four centuries the royal capital of the Savoys, with great museums, the Holy Shroud, staggering Baroque churches, a garland of remarkable palaces and Italy's most elegant cafés and liveliest music scene. It was also the host city for the 2006 Winter Olympics, and the city has been rejuvenated during the past few years.

The next chapter, **Piedmont**, starts west of Turin with three remarkable abbeys – Sant'Antonio Ranverso, the Sacra di San Michele and Novalesa. Further west the skiing events of the 2006 Olympics took place in the 'Milky Way' of winter resorts around Sestriere. To the south, atmospheric Saluzzo has beautiful courtly art and Alpine valleys, one leading up the source of the Po. Southern Piedmont, in particular Le Langhe and Monferrato, with their beautiful hills, fairytale castles, Italy's most prestigious vineyards (Barolo, Barbaresco), chic *agriturismi* and fabulous restaurants, are now familiar to discerning, food-loving travellers. Alba is the capital of wine, white truffles and hazelnuts. Jaunty medieval Asti, its rival, holds a *palio* older than Siena's and has a lot more going for it than its world famous Spumante. The whole area is packed with interest, extending into Piedmont's southeast corner around Alessandria.

North of the Po, the venerable art cities of Novara and Vercelli are surrounded by the flat lands of Piedmont, where rice paddies reflect the drifting clouds. Next comes fabled Lake Maggiore, all villas, subtropical gardens and exquisite islands, and the seldom visited Ossola Valleys. Charming little Lake Orta has its own island and great Romanesque basilica; west in Varallo you can visit the original Sacro Monte, Piedmont's curious contribution to piety. Biella, an old mill town, is full of cashmere factory outlets and lies near the biggest Marian sanctuary in the Alps, at Oropa. Lastly, due north of Turin, are the pretty glacier-sculpted hills and lakes of the Canavese, with a few 10th-century surprises up its sleeve.

The highest Alps of all surround the pocket autonomous region of the **Valle d'Aosta**. Here a string of minor valleys twists into the mountains, often ending at ski resorts such as Gressoney-la-Trinité, Champoluc or Breuil-Cervinia, under the Matterhorn. Besides grandiose scenery, there are fascinating castles, several with delightful frescoes (Issogne and Fénis). To the west, Aosta, the regional capital, has striking Roman and medieval relics, and a thousand-year-old fair. It lies at the crossroads of the Great Saint Bernard (with the dogs) and Little Saint Bernard passes, as well as the roads to Cogne, the gateway to the majestic Gran Paradiso National Park. Last to the west is the swish resort of Courmayeur under Mont Blanc, where in summer you can take a truly awesome five-stage cable-car ride all the way to Chamonix in France.

Top: An elegant house in Turin, pp.213–250

Above: Sacra di San Michele, Piedmont, p.256

Top: Santa Margherita, Riviera di Levante, p.183

Above: Portofino, Riviera di Levante, p.184

Glowing All Over

Fly away from the grey skies of home and, as you drive out of Genoa airport, like Dorothy you'll know you aren't in Kansas anymore: the world here comes in deep, glossy Technicolor tones. Squeezed between the Mediterranean and the Maritime Alps, the Italian Riviera not only looks like a rainbow on the map, but has the sun, the rich light, and a dry summer subtropical microclimate that lends it the colours to match. With the Ligurian Alps to shield it from the cold and rain to the north, it's both vertical and fertile. Wildflowers poke out of every crevice, whether rock or medieval church wall. Pines, cypresses and olives cloak the slopes of the *entroterra* in a rich, variegated green. In the markets, bunches of intensely green basil, the Riviera's totem herb, are piled high by tomatoes blazing red. The Ligurians, for their part, hardly take this drenching in colour lying down: their tall ochre, red, yellow, orange and salmon-pink houses cluster under gaily painted churches and *campaniles*, sharply set in focus against the clear blue skies – so intense some afternoons, they verge on black – looking over each other's shoulders down to a sea of constantly changing aquamarine, turquoise and sapphire blue.

A Tale of Two Cities

The two great cities in this guide, separated not by distance so much as by history and attitude, could scarcely look more different. Steep, long and narrow Genoa, one of the Mediterranean's greatest port cities, earned its spurs in the early Middle Ages as one of Italy's four great maritime republics, before settling into a profitable mid-life career as banker for the kings of Spain. As a result, it preserves one of the biggest medieval centres in the world, a unique 17th-century millionaires' row, plus scores of palatial villas and gardens on its fringes. On the other hand, there's Turin, set where the Alps end on a plain along the Po, formally designed in an elegant hierarchical grid to match the ambitions of the House of Savoy – counts, dukes and later kings of Italy. When they moved to Rome after the Risorgimento, Turin became one of Italy's industrial locomotives. Both Genoa and Turin do, however, have one thing in common: after difficult postwar decades, they've used major international events – a world's fair in Genoa in 1992 and the Winter Olympics in Turin in 2006 – to launch their latest roles, as beautifully restored art cities topped up with a host of new attractions.

Top left: Hazelnuts

Top right: Garlic

Above: Caffé Torino, Turin, p.245

Previous page: Palazzo Spinola dei Marmi, Genoa, p.155; Turin palazzo

Truffles and Pesto

Say 'Piedmont' to an Italian, and like Pavlov's dog they begin to salivate with visions of culinary treats. Central headquarters of the now worldwide Slow Food movement, it is legendary among gastronomes who come on eating tours, especially in the autumn and winter, to feast on the famous white truffles of Alba, homemade *agnolotti* and *risotti*, rich stews, mountain cheeses, hazelnuts and chocolate, and the most prestigious wines in Italy, beginning with Barolo, 'the king of wines'. Yet Liguria hardly takes a back seat in the kitchen; although until recently dubbed *cucina povera*, its Mediterranean-style dishes based on fresh vegetables and olive oil are healthy and delicious (and rather less fattening then the classics of Piedmont). This is the home region of pesto, chard-filled ravioli and *trenette*, *focaccia* and above all, fresh seafood, which is especially lovely washed down with the Riviera's own wine – delicate white Vermentino.

Above: Palazzo Podestà, Genoa, p.155

Opposite: Duomo di San Lorenzo, Genoa, p.160

Stripes and Curls

While central Italy and Lombardy blossomed during the Renaissance, our corner of northwest Italy was playing Sleeping Beauty. But don't think that Liguria, Piedmont and the Valle d'Aosta are going to let you off the hook when it comes to art: they were wide-awake for the Romanesque, Gothic, Baroque and Rococo eras, thank you very much, periods that give them a distinctly different look from the rest of Italy. Churches and monasteries dating back to Carolingian times stand in isolated Alpine splendour. Majestic cathedrals rise in the heart of cities such as Casale Monferrato, Albenga, Asti, Vercelli and Novara, while Genoa boasts a trove of black and white striped churches and *palazzi* in the heart of its *centro storico*. When the money began rolling in again in the mid-16th century, the Genoese lavished it on sumptuous mansions, suburban villas and gardens, and frothy stucco-dripping churches that resemble ballrooms. The Savoy dynasts who created Turin not only acquired hordes of art, but also hired three of Italy's most inventive architects – Juvarra, Guarini and Vittone – to design Turin's astonishing churches and its unique ring of *palazzi* (including the newly reopened Versailles of Piedmont, the Venaria Reale) and make them into a dazzling Baroque showcases.

Romantic Mountains, Romantic Lakes

Europe's tallest and most fabled mountains fringe Piedmont and the Valle d'Aosta. Think Mont Blanc and the Matterhorn and the Great St Bernard, complete with big booze-toting dogs, or Hannibal and Napoleon marching armies and even elephants over the high passes. Down below, cows with bells the size of saucepans graze in the sweet emerald meadows, next to old chapels and picturesque wooden huts. Their snows feed the rivers that feed the great lakes of northern Italy, gouged out by primordial glaciers: two, Maggiore and Orta, are in Piedmont, and act like giant solar panels surrounded by lush gardens. South of the lakes lie the great rice paddies of Vercelli, cradle of a million *risotti*, reflecting passing clouds in a giant mosaic of watery mirrors.

Top: Alps, Piedmont, pp.253–64

Above left: Isola Madre, Lake Maggiore, p.306

Above right: Rice field near Vercelli and Monte Rosa, Piedmont

Itineraries

Western Riviera and Southwest Piedmont in Two Weeks

Days 1–3 **Genoa** and its medieval quarter, Baroque *palazzi* and art museums, its **Aquarium** and **Porto Antico**.

Day 4 In the morning, visit the splendid gardens of the **Villa Durazzo-Pallavicini** in **Pegli**, then head west to **Albissola Marina** for a look at Liguria's biggest ceramics centre, then stop in **Savona** to see its cathedral and rococo Sistine Chapel. Overnight in **Noli**.

Day 5 Have a look at pretty **Varigotti**, then carry on to **Toriano** and its beautiful caves. In the afternoon see the sights of medieval **Albenga**. Overnight in lively **Alassio**.

Day 6 Continuing west, have a look at **Cervo**'s church of the coral fishers, visit the **Museo dell'Olivo** in **Imperia**, and spend the rest of the day and night in **San Remo**.

Day 7 Backtrack to **Arma di Taggia** with its lovely beach, then loop inland to the medieval villages of **Taggia**, **Montalto**, **Triora**, **Pigna** (with its frescoes by Giovanni Canavesio), **Apricale** and **Dolceacqua**. Overnight in **Bordighera**.

Day 8 Visit the Principality of **Seborga**, just for fun, and the **Hanbury Gardens** and **Balzi caves** just west of **Ventimiglia**. Overnight in **Bordighera** or **Ventimiglia**.

Day 9 Head north up the **Gorges de Saorge** (in France, but once part of Liguria) stopping at **Notre Dame des Fontaines** near La Brigue to see Canevesio's superb fresco cycle. Rejoin Italy at **Limone Piemonte**. Overnight in **Saluzzo**.

Day 10 Visit **Saluzzo** and the lovely **Castello di Manta**, then drive east to **Bra**. Overnight in **Cherasco**.

Days 11–12 Splendid food, wine and scenery: tour around **Santa Vittoria Alba**, **La Morra**, **Barolo**, **Grinzane Cavour**, **Alba** and **Barbaresco**.

Day 13 **Asti**: its churches and art.

Day 14 Visit **Nizza Monferrato** and **Aqui Terme**, then return to the coast via **Sassello** (stopping for some *amaretti*) to **Sestri Ponente**, home of Genoa's airport.

Above: Genoa, pp.139–74

Below: San Remo, pp.95–101

Above: San Remo,
pp.95–101

Below: Sacra di San
Michele, Piedmont, p.256

A Week on the Riviera di Levante

Day 1 Start in **Genoa** and head east to **Nervi** to see the Magnascos in the **Museo Giannettino Luxuro**, then carry on to **Camogli** and take a walk in the **Parco Naturale di Portofino** or a boat ride to **San Fruttuoso**. Overnight in **Santa Margherita Ligure**.

Day 2 **Portofino** and **Rapallo**. Overnight in **S. Margherita**.

Day 3 Head east to **Chiavari**, **Lavagna** (see the **Basilica di San Salvatore dei Fieschi**). Overnight in **Sestri Levante**.

Day 4 Visit **Levanto**, then take the *autostrada* to **La Spezia**. See the **Museo Amadeo Lia**, and have dinner in **Portovenere**. Overnight there or in **La Spezia**.

Day 5 Visit the **Cinque Terre** by train or boat.

Day 6 Tour around **Lerici** and the **Gulf of Poets**, **Ameglia** and ancient **Luni**. Overnight in **Ameglia** or **Sarzana**.

Day 7 Return to **Genoa** on the *autostrada*.

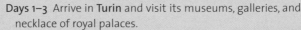

Ten Days in Piedmont and Aosta

Days 1–3 Arrive in **Turin** and visit its museums, galleries, and necklace of royal palaces.

Day 4 Go south to **Saluzzo** to see the courtly frescoes at the castles of **Manto** and **Lagnasco**. Overnight in **Saluzzo**.

Day 5 North to **Pinerolo** to see its museum and parrots. After lunch, have a look at the great walls at **Fenestrelle**, then drive to **Susa** to see its Roman monuments and cathedral and overnight.

Day 6 Head down the **Susa Valley** – visit the striking **Sacra di San Michele** and the frescoes at **Sant'Antonio di Ranverso**. In the afternoon take the A5 north into the **Valle d'Aosta**.

Days 7–8 Visit **Aosta** and its medieval churches, and **Courmayeur** for a funicular ride over **Mont Blanc**.

Day 9 You have to go out the way you came in to the Valle d'Aosta – then turn east and take the scenic Strada Panoramica Zegni to see the **Sacro Monte** chapels at **Varallo**; overnight in **Orta San Guilio** on Lake Orta.

Days 10–11 Visit the beauty spots on the lake and **Isola San Giulio** and its church. Then drive from **Omegna** to **Lake Maggiore**; stay in a mid-lake resort and visit the islands.

Day 12 Head south, with a look at the giant statue of Charles Borromeo in **Arona**, and head to **Vercelli** – see the **Basilica di Sant'Andrea**, the cathedral and treasure and the **Pinacoteca Borgogna**. Overnight.

Day 13 South to the lovely countryside and medieval churches in and around **Casale Monferrato** and the **Abbazia di Vezzolano**.

Day 14 Back to **Turin** and home.

CONTENTS

**01 Introducing
the Italian Riviera
& Piedmont 1**
Where to Go 6
Itineraries 15

02 History 19
Early Days: Mysterious
Ligurians and Inevitable
Romans 20
400–961: a Teutonic
Interlude 21
961–1500: Genoa and
the Savoys 22
1500–1796: Profiting from
Italy's Decline 24
1796–1830: Napoleon,
Restoration and Reaction 25
1830–1915: the Risorgimento
and United Italy 26
1915–1945: War, Fascism
and War 28
1945–the Present 29

**03 Art and
Architecture 31**
Prehistoric, Roman and
the Dark Ages 32
Middle Ages and the
Renaisssance 32
Baroque, Rococo and
Beyond 34

04 Tales of Tenacity 37
Just Who Was Christopher
Columbus? 38
Liguria's Idealists: Mazzini
and Garibaldi 42
The Italian Village Model 48
Under the Sign of the
Snail 49

05 Food and Drink 51
Restaurant Generalities 52
Specialities of the Riviera,
or the Marriage of Popeye
and Olive Oyl 53
Specialities of Piedmont
and Aosta 55

Wines and Spirits of
Piedmont and Aosta 58
Italian Menu Reader 60

06 Planning Your Trip 63
When to Go 64
Climate 64
Calendar of Events 64
Festivals 65
Tourist Information 65
Embassies and
Consulates 66
Entry Formalities 66
Passports 66
Customs 66
Disabled Travellers 67
Disability Organizations 67
Insurance and EHIC Cards 67
Maps and Publications 67
Money and Banks 67
Getting There 68
By Air 68
By Train 69
By Coach 69
By Car 69
Getting Around 70
By Train 70
By Coach 71
By Car 71
By Motorcycle or Bicycle 72
Where to Stay 72
Hotels and Guesthouses 72
Hostels and Budget
Accommodation 73
Agriturismo and Bed and
Breakfast 73
Camping 73
Villas and Flats 74
Tour Operators and Special-
interest Holidays 74
Self-catering Operators 74

07 Practical A–Z 75
Conversion Tables 76
Crime 77
Eating Out 77
Electricity 77
Health and
Emergencies 77

National Holidays 77
Opening Hours 78
Post Offices 78
Shopping and Markets 78
Sports and Activities 79
Street Numbers 80
Telephones 80
Time 80

The Guide
08 Riviera di Ponente 81
The Riviera dei Fiori:
Ventimiglia to
Bordighera 84
Ventimiglia 85
Bordighera 91
Around Bordighera 92
San Remo 95
Up the Valle Argentina 101
The Riviera degli Olivi 104
Imperia 105
Inland from Imperia 108
The Gulf of Diano: Beaches
East of Imperia 110
The Riviera delle Palme 113
Alassio 113
Albenga 116
Around Albenga 117
Toirano, Loano and Pietra
Ligure 121
Up the Coast: Finale Ligure
to Savona 125
Savona 129
On to Genoa 134

09 Genoa 139
Genoa's West End 151
Stazione Principe, Palazzo
del Principe and the
Lanterna 151
Via Balbi to Via Garibaldi 152
19th-century Genoa 155
Via XX Settembre and
Around 156
Into the Old City 157
Piazza Matteotti: the Palazzo
Ducale and Duomo di San
Lorenzo 159

Contents

Contents

Piazza San Matteo 160
The Northern Historic
    Centre 161
Porto Antico 163
Behind Genoa: Hills, Walls
    and a Boneyard 164
West of Genoa: to Pegli
    and Voltri 166
Pegli and its Parks and
    Museums 167
Eastern Genoa to Nervi 168
Genoa's *Entroterra* 173

10 Riviera di Levante 175
The Gulf of Paradise 178
The Promontory of Portofino
    and Golfo del Tigullio 182
The Golfo del Tigullio: Santa
    Margherita, Portofino and
    Rapallo 183
Chiavari, Lavagna and
    Sestri Levante 188
The Val di Vara 192
Sestri Levante to La Spezia
    and the Cinque Terre 193
The Cinque Terre 196
La Spezia and
    Portovenere 201
The Gulf of Poets and the
    Val di Magra 205
Up the Val di Magra 207

11 Turin 213
The New Turin 220
Piazza Castello 223
The Duomo and the Cappella
    della Sacra Sindone 226
West of Piazza Castello 228
The West End 230
East of Piazza Castello 231
Towards the River 232
On the Right Bank 233
South of Piazza Castello 234
GAM – Galleria
    d'Arte Moderna e
    Contemporanea 237
East of Porta Nuova 238
Lingotto and the Pinacoteca
    Giovanni e Marella
    Agnelli 239
Northeast of the Centre:
    Superga 240
Chieri and Martini 241

Around Turin: a Garland of
    Pleasure Domes 246
Stupinigi and Carignano 247
Rivoli and the Museo d'Arte
    Contemporanea 248
Really Big Pleasure
    Palaces 248

12 Piedmont 251
West of Turin into the
    'Olympic Mountains' 253
Southwest Piedmont: the
    Marquisate of Saluzzo 264
Carmagnola to Stroppo 265
Cuneo and the Alpi
    Marittime 271
Mondovì and the
    Monregalese 274
South of Turin: Roero
    and Le Langhe 276
Bra, Slow Capital of the
    Universe, and the Roero 277
Alba: World Capital of White
    Truffles 279
Asti and Monferrato 285
Piedmont's Far Southeastern
    Corner 294
Northeast of Turin: Vercelli,
    Novara and Rice 298
Vercelli 299
Novara 300
Lake Maggiore 302
From the South: Arona
    to Baveno 303
Verbania and Maggiore's
    Northwest Shore 308
North of the Lakes: the
    Lower Ossola Valleys 312
Domodossola and the
    Upper Ossola Valleys 314
Lake Orta 318
West of Lake Orta: Varello
    and Biella 322
North of Turin: Valli di Lanzo
    and the Canavese 328

13 Valle d'Aosta 337
The Eastern Valleys 340
Aosta: the 'Rome of
    the Alps' 345
The Western Valleys 351

Maps and Plans

Italian Riviera & Piedmont
    inside front
Chapter Divisions 7
Riviera di Ponente 82–3
Riviera dei Fiori and Riviera
    degli Olivi 84
Imperia to Albenga 107
Albenga to Savona 118
Savona to Genoa 136
Genoa 140–41
Around Genoa 174
Riviera di Levante 176–7
Genoa to Sestri Levante 178
Sestri Levante to
    La Spezia 194
Central Turin 214–15
Turin and Around 221
Piedmont 252
The 'Olympic Mountains'
    West of Turin, Southwest
    and Southeast
    Piedmont 254–5
Lakes Orta and
    Maggiore 305
Varallo, Biella, the Valli
    di Lanzo and the
    Canavese 324
Valle d'Aosta 338–9
Touring maps *end of guide*

Reference

14 Language 357
15 Glossary 360
16 Further Reading 361
17 Index 362

History

*Early Days: Mysterious Ligurians
and Inevitable Romans* 20
400–961: a Teutonic Interlude 21
961–1500: Genoa and the Savoys 22
*1500–1796: Profiting from Italy's
Decline* 24
*1796–1830: Napoleon, Restoration
and Reaction* 25
*1830–1915: the Risorgimento and
United Italy* 26
1915–1945: War, Fascism and War 28
1945–the Present 29

02

Early Days: Mysterious Ligurians and Inevitable Romans

Some of the first known Europeans had the good taste to settle on the Riviera. Just over the border in France near Menton, in the Grotta del Collonet, are signs of human habitation going back as long as 900,000 years. Jump ahead 700,000 years, to a time when the Alps were covered by ice and the low level of the Mediterranean made Italy a much wider peninsula than it is now, and we find the Neanderthals gracing the Italian side of the Riviera with their low-browed presence, notably in the Balzi Rossi caves. The Middle Palaeolithic (80,000 BC) Neanderthals at Balzi Rossi were succeeded in 30,000 BC by their better-looking Cro-Magnon rivals, who left Italy its very first works of art – lumpy fertility goddesses or 'Venuses'.

By the 8th century BC, a group of powerful, distinct tribes with related languages inhabited the peninsula: the 'Italics'. Everything north of the fabled Rubicon (a little stream near Rimini) was the classical Cisalpine Gaul, the stomping ground of Celts and **Ligurians** or Ligures, who made their debut on the scene some time around 1800 BC, occupying not only present-day Liguria but parts of northern Tuscany and southern Piedmont.

Just who were the Ligurians? No one is really sure – the Phoenicians and Greeks traded with them, most notably at Genoa, but by the time the first Roman historians posed the question, the Ligurians themselves had forgotten. No one is even sure if they were Indo-European or pre-Indo-European. A Phoenician legend declared they were the offspring of Albione and Ligure, sons of the sea god Poseidon, who were overcome at the Foce del Rodano by a mighty hail of pebbles. Curiously enough, a version of the story appears in Hercules' Tenth Labour, where Zeus sent him a hail of stones to throw at his Ligurian enemies. Even curiouser, an ancient Lapp tradition has it that the Lapps were cousins of the Ligurians, who fled north following a cataclysm of some nature, pebble or otherwise.

To add to the confusion, there were several tribes of Ligurians. Most seemed to have mingled with their Celtic neighbours, while others are believed to have fled into the mountains to avoid them. Those who stayed on the Riviera, at least, built villages called *castellari*, surrounded by a ring of stone walls, on crags or on other easily defensible sites, which developed into small trading and religious centres (in some atavistic way, they may also be behind the hundreds of sanctuaries dedicated to the Madonna that more recent Ligurians have built in similar locations). The ancients were primarily shepherds, although they apparently did little hunting and even less fishing, proving that from the first the Ligurians were landlubbers. Mont Bégo (in the upper Val Roja, now part of France) was an important holy site, followed by Monte Beigua west of Genoa, where the Ligurians (or Celto-Ligurians) left rock etchings from *c.* 1800 BC–1000 BC. Mont Bégo has them by the thousands – spirals, stick figures, animals and scenes of war. At the opposite end of Liguria, around the Lunigiana, they left their distinctive statue steles – menhirs with faces.

The one thing that's certain is that the Ligurians were among the toughest nuts the Romans had to crack. In 207 BC, Hannibal's brother Hasdrubal recruited them, along with the Celts, Celtiberians and Numidians, to fight for Carthage; a third brother, Mago, landed in 203 but was pinned down by the Romans. This support was enough to earmark the Ligurians for later conquest, besides the fact that they stood square in the way of Rome's plans to build an overland road to Spain. In 177 BC the Romans founded the colony of *Portus Lunae* (Luni) at the far east end of Liguria, and, not long after that, *Albintimilium* (modern Ventimiglia) at the far west. Sandwiched between the legions, the Ligurians were sufficiently subdued by the time of Augustus for Rome to build the Via Julia Augusta. At about the same time (23 BC), the legions finally crushed some other tough hombres, the Salassian Gauls, who lived in the highest Alps, and they founded *Augusta Praetoria* (Aosta) to keep them in line.

The Romans were clever in managing their conquests, maintaining most of the tribes and cities as nominally independent states, while planting colonies everywhere between the sea and mountains – *Genua*, *Vada Sabatia* (Savona), *Albium Ingaunum* (Albenga), *Segusium* (Susa), *Augusta Taurinorum* (Turin) and others. For the most part, what is now northwest Italy shared the fate of the rest of the country in the Imperial centuries, a quiet backwater where little ever happened. In the late Empire, from the 3rd century AD onward, as Rome decayed and Milan increased in importance, Genoa tagged along, assuming the role as Milan's port that it still holds today.

400–961: a Teutonic Interlude

The barbarian invasions of Italy in the 5th century were not quite as cataclysmic as the schoolbooks would have it. Italy, including the northwest, ended up in a strong Gothic kingdom, and even saw a modest revival in cities and culture. The real disaster came in 536, with the Eastern (Byzantine) Emperor Justinian's attempt at reconquest. The bloody Greek-Gothic wars that followed lasted three decades, and though the Byzantines ultimately prevailed, in 563, the damage to an already stricken society and economy was incalculable.

Italy's total exhaustion was exposed in 568, when the **Lombards**, a Germanic tribe that worked hard to earn the title of barbarian, overran most of Italy. A new pattern of power appeared, with semi-independent Byzantine dukes and exarchs defending the coasts, and Lombards ruling most of the interior. The repercussions were felt in Liguria, where Roman fortifications along the coast were shored up and garrisoned by the Byzantines. Albenga, the powerful bishopric created on the Riviera di Ponente, would remain a force until the 14th century. The Byzantines saw their Riviera holiday come to an end in 641, when the Lombards, under their chief, Rotharis, chased them out and welcomed the coast into the Dark Ages. Their legacy was more to the gene pool than to the stream of culture: surnames ending in *aldo* or *aldi* (like Grimaldi) are Lombard, and it may not be too far-fetched to say they contributed a tough chromosome or two to the DNA of the already fibrous Ligurian stock.

With trade and culture at their lowest ebb, the 7th century marks the rock bottom of Italian history. The Lombards held on in northern Italy until the 8th century, when they succumbed to an alliance of the Papacy and the new Carolingian dynasty in France, under Pepin and Charlemagne. Carolingian control in Italy was never much more than a claim and a fond hope. With the real power now in the hands of local barons, dukes and the occasional battling bishop, this part of Italy joined the rest of Europe in feudal anarchy. There was also a new invader to deal with – the Arabs. In the 8th century, their raiders established a permanent base in Provence at Fraxinet (above St Tropez). They made their first recorded incursion into Liguria in 901, raiding the coast and marching up the Alpine valleys; one of their towers still stands just over the border in Piedmont, between Ormea and Garessio. Besides sacking and raiding, the Saracens also introduced a number of useful things, such as pears and *grano saraceno* (buckwheat), water mills and irrigation, and economic innovations, reflected in Arabic words that found their way into Italian such as *dogana* (customs) and *darsena* (arsenal).

Elsewhere, in less precarious parts of Italy, life was slowly beginning to change; the first precocious maritime cities – Venice, Pisa and Amalfi – were freeing themselves from Byzantine or feudal overlordship. Genoa lagged behind; one of the few records pertaining to it from the period was the report of an early 10th-century Imperial envoy, who described it as primarily a farming community. But it obviously differed from other farming communities in one important aspect: it knew how to build ships and sail them. Even in the 800s, there was enough money around for the reviving town to build itself a wall.

961–1500: Genoa and the Savoys

A big break for Italy came in 961 with the invasion of the German **Otto the Great**, heir to the imperial pretensions of the Carolingians; he was crowned the first Holy Roman Emperor the following year. Not that any of the Italians were happy to see him, but the strong government of Otto and his successors helped to control the great nobles, and allowed trade and cities to expand. A pattern was set: Germanic emperors would be meddling in Italian affairs for centuries, not powerful enough to establish total control, but usually able to keep out other powers. Playing off the emperors with the local feudal lords, the growing cities were able to set themselves up as *comuni*, or free cities; Milan, in 1024, was the first.

It was during this period that the Ligurians found the wherewithal to free themselves and their sea of the Saracens, with enough momentum left over to catapult Genoa into the thick of Mediterranean affairs – just in time for the **First Crusade** (1097–1130). For Italy, and especially for Genoa and Pisa, the cities with sufficient boats to ship the Crusaders, the affair meant nothing but pure profit. In 1099 Genoa became a *comune* or, to be precise, a *Compagna comunis*, an association of citizens' groups bound to support the city's maritime adventures. From the beginning, these expeditions would be dominated by bold, ambitious men who were hungry and clever enough to seize the main chance when they saw it; Genoa's chameleon nobility could change roles from sea captain to merchant to warlord at a moment's notice.

Cities were booming, though political trouble was never far off. Emperor Frederick I Hohenstaufen, known to the Italians as **Barbarossa**, was strong enough in Germany to try to reassert imperial power in Italy. Beginning in 1154, he crossed the Alps five times, molesting free cities that asked nothing more than the right to fight one another eternally. Genoa had grown so quickly that it had to build a new 'Barbarossa' wall to protect itself, but the emperor's main target was Milan, which he demolished in 1161. For over two centuries, the endless Italian factional wars would be defined by Ghibellines (supporters of the emperors) and Guelphs (supporters of the popes and the *comuni*). In the end, Genoa learned to get along much better with the Germans. Frederick I and his grandson Frederick II confirmed the city's rights over the empire it had gradually built for itself, stretching from Monaco to Tuscany and including the island of Corsica.

By the 13th century, Genoa's traders were known across the Mediterranean and far into the Black Sea. Once Genoa had been a possession of Byzantium, now the city ran the trade of the whole empire from its colony within Constantinople. Its only serious rivals were Pisa and Venice. Genoa put an end to Pisa's power at the Battle of Meloria in 1284, and it would spend another three centuries battling the Venetians, usually coming out second best.

Venice's secret weapon was its strong system of government, restraining the ambitions of the powerful merchant clans for the good of the city. Genoa never managed the trick, even though it copied the Venetians by electing a *doge* after 1339. Like most Italian cities, the Genoese spent all the time and energy they could spare from fighting their enemies in fighting each other. Here the conflict was particularly ugly. The four most powerful families controlled factions and pursued vendettas on a scale that left the other Italians in awe, with the Doria and Spinola on the Ghibelline side and the Grimaldi and Fieschi on the Guelph. All had lands elsewhere on the Riviera; the Grimaldi even aced a principality in 1297, when one of their scions, Francesco the Spiteful, disguised himself and his followers as monks, gained entrance into the Ghibelline fortress at Monaco, and knifed the proprietors (the Grimaldi later officially purchased it from Genoa, and of course still hold it today).

Outside the Genoese lands, people were totally dependent on their lords, who busily fought their own little wars, against each other, against Genoa and against the other power in the region, the counts of Savoy, who constantly made incursions from their mountain fortresses in an effort to control their essential trading routes, or 'salt roads', to the coast. This period, in fact, marks the debut of the House of Savoy on the greater Italian stage, although it would be centuries before they landed a proper speaking part. As guardians of the French and Swiss Alpine passes, the dynasty got its first break when Umberto Biancomano ('of the White Hands'), based in Chambéry, vassal of Duke Rudolph III of Burgundy, obtained for its loyalty a vast tract of land stretching from Aosta to the north of Vienne, and was made count in 1032 by Conrad II 'the Salician' in gratitude for his help in obtaining the imperial crown; in 1052, Umberto's son Otto (Odone) married Adelaide, heiress of Marches of Turin and Ivrea. A branch of the Savoys known as the princes of Acaia built a castle in Turin, and during the 13th century the name Savoia Piemonte (Savoy Piedmont; 'foot of the mountains') came to describe the patchwork of transalpine fiefs, marquisates and free *comuni* that were ploddingly added to the growing state by marriage, political savvy and conquest.

The Savoys quietly expanded their boundaries all through the 1300s and 1400s, especially the 'Green Count' Amedeo VI (d. 1383), who added Aosta, Geneva and Lausanne, and his son, the 'Red Count' Amedeo VII, who grabbed a useful seaport, Nice. His son, Amedeo VIII, famed for his justice, piety and wisdom, was created Duke by Emperor Sigismund in 1416, and promulgated a *Statuto*, an early attempt at constitutional law, before retiring in 1434 to a monastery and rather daftly letting the Council of Basle elect him antipope Felix V. His son, Ludovico, picked up some more fancy titles when he married Anne of Lusignan, heiress to the kingdoms of Jerusalem, Cyprus and Armenia – still part of the many titles of the head of the House of Savoy.

1500–1796: Profiting from Italy's Decline

While the rest of Italy was enjoying its artistic Renaissance, the Savoys maintained the old medieval spirit in Piedmont and Aosta, while Genoa's nasty little money-making oligarchy made it the only major Italian city entirely indifferent to the arts. Genoa found the 15th century the occasion for more intramural warfare in the good old Guelph and Ghibelline style, while working hard to beat down rebellious nobles along the Riviera. The Genoese would later look upon this difficult time as a period of preparation for their Republic, a time of *reculer pour mieux sauter*.

If Genoa cared little for the finer things, however, it could not avoid Renaissance politics – the momentous, protracted scrum between Spain, France, the Papacy and the host of minor local powers for mastery of Italy. Genoa and the Savoys found themselves in multiple crosshairs, caught between the ambitions of the French, who sent an army over the Alps whenever they could afford it, and the Spanish – under Charles V (1516–56), the House of Habsburg had united Spain, the Netherlands and Germany, and they saw this corner of Italy as the key to maintaining communications between their far-flung domains. Genoa was brutally sacked in 1522 by Spanish troops; in 1527, the French were defeated at Naples by the treachery of their Genoese ally Andrea Doria. France would soon get back at Genoa by making alliances with Turkish corsairs, and setting them to prey on Liguria, while the Genoese drifted into what would prove a long-standing alliance with Spain. Up in the mountains, Savoy Piemonte (Piedmont) went into near total eclipse under a series of weak dukes, as the Swiss and the French nibbled away and occupied their lands.

Credit for the resurrection of Savoy fortunes goes to young Duke Emanuele Filiberto 'the Iron Head', who had served Philip II as Governor of the Netherlands and defeated the French in the important Battle of Saint-Quentin (1557). The Savoys were back with a few new lands, helping them serve as a useful buffer between France and Spain's Italian possessions. But the Iron Head had ideas of his own; one of his first moves was to relocate his capital from Chambéry to the more defensible Turin, and make Italian the official language of his court. He used the fortune he had earned from the ransoms of French prisoners to build his first navy and a modern army, and set up an absolutist state on the French-Spanish model, asserting his control over civic, feudal and Church powers, encouraging agriculture and education, and promoting religious tolerance (quite rare in those fanatical times), protecting the Waldensian dissenters in the valleys, and inviting Jews into Piedmont to help revive trade.

Back on the Mediterranean, the Genoese found themselves fitting increasingly snugly into the Imperial Spanish system. They helped the combined Christian forces turn back the newest foreign threat, the Ottoman Turks, at sea in the battles of Malta (1566) and Lepanto (1571), and their banks had the cleverness or good fortune to cash in magnificently from Spanish imperialism in the New World. Renting ships and floating loans, they snatched up most of the gold and silver arriving from America. The Genoese nabobs in their new golden age built a whole new city district of palaces, and this time they even spent a little on frescoes to decorate them.

While Genoa wallowed in lucre, after 1600 nearly everything started to go wrong for the rest of the Italians. Textiles and banks, long the engines of their economy, both withered in the face of foreign competition. Port towns began to look half-empty, and as Spain slipped into decadence through the century, even Genoa started to suffer. In Piedmont, Emanuele Filiberto's extravagant son, Carlo Emanuele, nearly sabotaged his promising little state by wasting all its resources trying to regain Geneva, leaving his own son, Vittorio Amedeo I (d. 1637) little more than a title. The latter's wife, Christine, however, was very conveniently the daughter of Henri IV of France, and all was made well again. Later on, pressure from the popes led Emanuele Filiberto's descendants to abandon his tolerance towards the Waldensians, reaching a nadir with the massacres in 1655 under Carlo Emanuele II.

Italy in the 18th century hardly has any history at all; with Spain economically and militarily on the ropes, the great powers decided the futures of Italy's states. The end of the War of the Spanish Succession (France and Spain versus Austria and England) in 1713 gave Austria control of the old Spanish possessions in the north. Duke Vittorio Amedeo II, who had adroitly changed sides in mid-war, earned himself the title of King of Sicily from a grateful Habsburg emperor in the Treaty of Utrecht. Six years later, the powers compelled him to trade it for the crown of Sardinia, which was closer, but had a much lower tax base. It mattered little. The real prize was the title; the Dukes of Savoy were now Kings. In 1738, Carlo Emanuele III continued his predecessor's habit of lucky guesses and chose the winners in the wars of the Polish and Austrian Successions, and was rewarded with the western bits of Lombardy (Novara, Vercelli and half of Lake Maggiore). The infant kingdom was backward in many ways, but as the only strong and independent state in Italy it would come to play the leading role in the events of the next century.

1796–1830: Napoleon, Restoration and Reaction

Napoleon, that greatest of Italian generals, arrived in the country in 1796 on behalf of the French revolutionary Directorate, sweeping away the Austrians and sending King Carlo Emanuele IV hightailing it to Sardinia, where he abdicated in 1802 (by a curious twist, he later became the head of the Stuart dynasty in 1807 on the death of the pretender King Henry IX, Cardinal Duke of York). Italy woke with a start from its Baroque slumbers, and local patriots gaily joined the French cause. Perhaps because he only just missed being born Genoese (Genoa had sold Corsica to France, and the French occupation force arrived the day he was born), Napoleon had a soft spot for the old Republic; he obliged it to change its name to the Republic of Liguria, looted it as thoroughly as he did every other region of Italy, and imprisoned the recalcitrant Pope in Savona (see p.132), but otherwise left much of the old Genoese constitution written by Andrea Doria intact, including the office of doge. The Ligurians, among the most enthusiastic revolutionaries in Italy, also added some highly radical laws on human rights and duties and the right to an education.

Although Napoleonic rule lasted only until 1814, in this busy period important public works were begun. Liguria's coastal highway, the Via Aurelia, was laid out, along with the road from Domodossola over the Simplon Pass and the carriage road over the Monginevro Pass. Society was reformed after the French model, and immense Church properties were expropriated. At the same time, the French implemented high war taxes and conscription (some 25,000 Italians died in the invasion of Russia), and brutally repressed a number of local revolts, systematically exploiting Italy for the benefit of the Napoleonic élite and the crowds of speculators who came flocking over the Alps. The Republic of Liguria went into a long depression caused by the Continental blockade. When the Austrians and English came to chase all the little Napoleons out, no one was sorry to see them go.

The experience, though, had given Italians a taste of the opportunities offered by the modern world, as well as a dawning sense of national feeling. The 1815 Congress of Vienna tried to stifle them by putting the political clock back to 1789; reactionary King Vittorio Emanuele I officially repealed every new law. Liguria, which found itself unwillingly annexed to the Savoy Kingdom, was livid. Almost immediately, there emerged revolutionary agitators and secret societies like the Carbonari that would keep Italy convulsed in plots and intrigues. Piedmont was eventually fortunate enough to find a reforming king, Carlo Alberto (1831–49). He encouraged the spread of the French July Revolution of 1830 to Italy, but once more the by-now universally hated Austrians intervened. In Liguria, the disappointment was made worse by a cholera epidemic; discouraged by the political situation and disease, hundreds of thousands from both regions emigrated to Argentina.

1830–1915: the Risorgimento and United Italy

After the failure of the Italy-wide revolts of 1830, conspirators of every colour and shape, including Genoa's **Giuseppe Mazzini**, had to wait another 18 years for their next chance. Mazzini (*see* pp.42–7) agitated frenetically all through the years 1830–70, inspiring all (fellow Ligurian Giuseppe Garibaldi was one of his first converts) but accomplishing little. It was typical of the times, and the disarray among republicans, radicals and those who simply wanted a united Italy set the stage for the stumbling, divisive process of the Risorgimento.

The idea that Piedmont would be the 'warrior province' leading the way to union was set out in 1843 in the widely read *Moral and Civil Supremacy of the Italians* by a Piedmontese abbot in exile, Vincenzo Gioberti; by now it was clear to everyone that both the revolutionaries and the Piedmontese would have a role in the struggles ahead. The big chance came in the revolutionary year of 1848, when uprisings in Palermo and Naples anticipated even those in Paris itself. Soon all Italy was in the streets. Carlo Alberto, the shining hope of most Italians for a war of liberation, marched against the Austrians, but his bungled campaigns allowed the enemy to re-establish control and forced Carlo Alberto's abdication in favour of his son Vittorio Emanuele II. Rome, led by Mazzini and Garibaldi, still held out, along with Venice, but by 1849 the Pope and the Austrians were back, with help from Louis Napoleon of France, the new leader who would soon make himself Napoleon III.

Despite failure on such a grand scale, at least the Italians knew they would get another shot. To fend off Mazzini and Garibaldi, moderates wanted the Piedmontese to do the job, ensuring a stable future by making Vittorio Emanuele II King of Italy. **Vittorio Emanuele**'s minister, the polished, clever Count Camillo Cavour, spent the 1850s getting Piedmont in shape for the struggle, building its economy and army, participating in the Crimean War to earn diplomatic support, and plotting with the French for an alliance against Austria.

War came in 1859, and French armies did most of the work in conquering Lombardy. Tuscany and Emilia revolted, and Piedmont was able to annexe all three. The price, secretly negotiated between Cavour and Napoleon III, was a piece of Liguria and Savoy, what is now the *département* of the Alpes-Maritimes, including Nice (represented in the Piedmontese parliament by Garibaldi himself). A blatantly rigged plebiscite was set up in 1860: the official result: 24,449 pro-France to 160 against.

In May 1860, hearing that the south was ripe for revolt, Garibaldi and his ragtag red-shirted 'Thousand' sailed from Genoa. Cavour almost stopped them at the last minute, but they landed in Sicily and electrified Europe by beating the Bourbon army all the way to Naples by September, where Garibaldi proclaimed himself temporary dictator on Vittorio Emanuele's behalf. The king and the Piedmontese army joined Garibaldi on 27 October, and after finding out what little regard the Piedmontese had for him, the least self-interested leader modern Italy has known went off to retirement on the Sardinian islet of Caprera.

The first decades of the Italian Kingdom, installed in Rome after 1870, were just as unimpressive as its wars of independence. A constitutional monarchy was established, but part of the problem was a Savoy attitude that tended to regard Italy as an annex to Piedmont; Vittorio Emanuele II reigned mostly from Turin until he was succeeded by his son Umberto I, in 1878, who finally took the fiercely loyal Savoy court to Rome. Parliament decomposed into cliques and political cartels. Finances started in disorder and stayed there, while a rapidly growing rural population faced worse poverty than ever, and corruption became widespread. Like the other European powers, Italy felt it necessary to snatch up some colonies to relieve domestic pressure. The attempt revealed the new state's limited capabilities, with embarrassing military disasters at the hands of the Ethiopians at Dogali in 1887, and again at Adowa in 1896. The protests and strikes that followed were brutally repressed, and Umberto I, almost universally detested, was assassinated in 1900, and succeeded by his son Vittorio Emanuele III.

Meanwhile, something unexpected but momentous was happening along the Riviera: an English invasion, but a peaceful one. It began with a book: Giovanni Ruffini, from Taggia near San Remo, had emigrated to England and, feeling homesick, he wrote a novel in English called *Doctor Antonio* (1855), the story of Sir John Davenne and his daughter Lucy who come to San Remo and are swept away by the sensuous Mediterranean climate and beauty (Lucy also gets swept away by the local doctor). It was very much the *A Year in Provence* of its day: the Brits under Queen Victoria, busily covering up the limbs of their pianos, read Ruffini and flocked down to the Riviera in droves, especially to San Remo and Bordighera, the two warmest towns on the coast. They were followed in short order by other cold

Europeans with money, and more than a few crowned heads from Germany, Holland, Sweden and Russia.

Turin, no longer a capital, found a new job for itself. Partly thanks to Cavour's economic mercantilism, the city had already built up an industrial base in textiles. Machinery followed, and the founding of Fiat in 1899 and Lancia in 1906 launched Turin on its career as the 'Detroit of Europe'. There was more to it than just cars. Major industries in electronics, food and chemicals grew up, not to mention typewriters; Olivetti got its start in Ivrea in 1908. Turin also became the first centre of Italian cinema. Piedmont, a traditionally poor and backward region, had rapidly and unexpectedly transformed itself into a modern industrial powerhouse.

That also meant social troubles, and the rise of a strong Socialist movement; as elsewhere in Italy, strikes, riots and police repression often occupied centre stage in politics. Even so, important signs of progress showed that at least the northern half of Italy was becoming a fully integral part of the European economy, and going on holiday, too. The 15 years before the First World War came to be known by the slightly derogatory term *Italietta*, the 'little Italy' of modest bourgeois happiness, an age of sweet Puccini operas, the first motor cars, blooming Liberty-style architecture and Sunday afternoons at the beach.

1915–1945: War, Fascism and War

Italy could have stayed out of the First World War, but let the chance go by for the usual reasons – a hope of grabbing some new territory. Also, a certain segment of the intelligentsia found the peace and prosperity of the *Italietta* boring and disgraceful: irredentists of all stripes, some of the artistic Futurists, and the followers of the perverse, idolized poet Gabriele D'Annunzio. These groups, along with Vittorio Emanuele III, the self-styled 'soldier king', who didn't like Germans, helped Italy leap blindly into the conflict in 1915, with a big promise of boundary adjustments dangled by the beleaguered Allies. Italian armies fought at first with their accustomed flair, masterminding an utter catastrophe at Caporetto (October 1917) that any other nation but Austria would have parlayed into a total victory. No thanks to their incompetent generals, the poorly armed and equipped Italians somehow held firm for another year, until the total exhaustion of Austria allowed them to prevail (at the battle of Vittorio Veneto you see so many streets named after), capturing some 600,000 prisoners in November 1918.

In return for 650,000 dead, a million casualties, severe privation on the home front and a war debt higher than anyone could count, Italy received only Trieste and Gorizia. The end of the First World War found the Italian economy in shambles, and the population disillusioned over what had been a very bloody and very pointless conflict. Revolution was in the air, and nowhere more than in industrial Turin, where a highly organized working class and a group of active intellectuals including the Socialist philosopher Antonio Gramsci made that city a flash point of the struggle.

In the national economic crisis of 1919–20, Turin's auto workers formed themselves into 'workers' councils' on the pattern of the Soviets in the Russian Revolution. They raised the red flag over the Fiat plants, fomented a mighty wave of strikes and demonstrations, and in so doing frightened the daylights out of the Italian upper and middle classes.

The threat of revolution had encouraged extremists of both right and left, not only in Turin, and many Italians became convinced that the liberal state was finished. The situation was made in heaven for a certain **Benito Mussolini**, a professional intriguer in the Mazzini tradition (and former anti-war Socialist) with bad manners and no fixed principles. The Italian industrialists and their political allies had already taken great pains to crush the auto workers after their failed general strike in 1920, but they remained frightened enough to finance Mussolini's new movement and grease his way into power. Not only the industrialists: the catastrophic Vittorio Emanuele III worked behind the scenes for Mussolini, and notably failed to intervene to stop Mussolini's March on Rome in October 1922.

Afterwards, Fascist gangs, the *squadri*, saw to it that things settled down. The northwest spent a moderately prosperous and rather uneventful two decades under Fascist rule, though the Reds of Turin never really gave up the fight. Reorganized under the new Communist Party, they kept their unions and their clandestine press alive all through Mussolini's rule, and even managed to mount the occasional strike.

Strikes, in fact, occurred even during the Second World War. Though northwest Italy avoided major battles in this conflict, the war was never far away. Turin, Genoa and La Spezia suffered major bombings (Genoa was even once bombarded from the sea by the Royal Navy). After the Allied invasions in 1943, Piedmont spawned some of the strongest and most resourceful Resistance bands in Italy, who took control of some of the Alpine valleys months before the end of the war.

At the end of the war, the bilingual Valle d'Aosta in northern Piedmont, which had suffered under Mussolini's Italian-only imperialist policies and contributed a disproportionate share of partisans against him, was granted regional autonomy. National territorial concessions, however, were relatively slight; France, always careful to snatch up little bits of territory when it can, demanded one last piece of Liguria – Mont Bégo and its valley.

1945–the Present

Under the Allied occupation, a plebiscite on the now discredited monarchy in June 1946 made Italy a Republic, but only by a narrow margin, putting an end to the reign of Europe's oldest ruling house; Umberto II went into exile, and a law was passed forbidding any male member of the House of Savoy from ever returning to Italy (a law relaxed in 2002, however; in September 2003 Rome hosted the royal wedding of Emanuele Filiberto, the young pretender, who is also a jet-ski champion).

As elsewhere in the north, post-war recovery was swift and solid. Turin went back to work; by the mid-1960s Fiat was cranking out hundreds of thousands of those cute *cinquecentos* and putting the average Italian behind the wheel for the first time. The vast expansion of the auto industry brought the city a wave of immigrants from the south, amplifying a trend that had begun in the 1920s; northern bigotry towards the newcomers caused considerable social friction, although this has since much subsided. Genoa kept its place as Italy's leading port. After decades as a slightly bedraggled, workaday city, it started to come alive again, sprucing itself up for the 500th anniversary of native son Christopher Columbus's big trip in 1992. The momentum of this effort, which included a big redevelopment of the city's waterfront around the Porto Antico, continued in 2004, when Genoa became the 'European Capital of Culture', and shows little sign of abating.

Along the way, Genoa played host to the infamous G8 summit in July 2001, when 200,000 anti-globalization demonstrators stole all the headlines, and for the first time one was shot dead by police, along with 231 wounded. The brutal police attacks reminded many of the days of Mussolini, and provided a big black eye for the right-wing government of Silvio Berlusconi. Behind the headlines, the big news in Liguria and Piedmont is an often difficult economic adjustment, as old-time industries are fading (Fiat) or just plain gone (Olivetti) while others follow the rest of the West to the low-wage underdeveloped world. Yet on the whole Piedmont and Liguria are doing quite well. Hi-tech, service industries and tourism are all a part of it; Genoa and Turin have packaged themselves as snazzy weekend break cities, and the latter went through a massive process of restructuring and refurbishment in order to host the 2006 Winter Olympics, which brought a real feel of enthusiasm and an international atmosphere into town. Following the big event, the strategy to re-qualify the sabaudian capital in order to transform it into a more metropolitan and tourism-oriented hub still goes on, including the reassessment and recovery of dismissed industrial areas, re-opening important historic sites and a continuous programme of sport, cultural and artistic events to keep and enhance the reputation acquired during the international happenings.

Elections held in the spring of 2005 put the northwest regions – along with all the other regions except for Lombardy and the Veneto – into the moderate left-wing camp. Yet the ever-resilient Berlusconi reshuffled his cabinet and survived again, becoming the longest-lasting premier in postwar Italian history until, in April 2006, the political polls assigned victory to a coalition of the moderate left wing, thanks to the slightest prevalence ever seen – contested as usual by Berlusconi who tried to call for the annulment of the electoral results. The campaign preceding the elections took place under the *par condicio* catchword, including an even number of debates and conferences by the main leaders of the two groups. The Unione, led by Romano Prodi – who at the time of writing is still the premier – carries on amongst contrasts and continuous debates involving its various components, yet so far the coalition has survived. The Italian economy, however, is still in trouble. The premier believes that in the next few years there will be signs of recovery, and meanwhile he tries to give credibility to the image of a nation revising their fiscal strategy and projecting a positive international image – especially before the European Union.

Another part of the story here is a kind of anti-globalization-inspired return to the countryside's deepest agricultural roots and talents, promoted with brio by the likes of the Piedmont-based Slow Food movement and endeavours such as the recently opened University of Taste in Pollenzo. This corner of Italy knows what it is about; it seems to have both the talent and the right instincts to make its way in a strange post-industrial world.

Art and Architecture

Prehistoric, Roman and the
  Dark Ages 32
The Middle Ages and the
  Renaissance 32
Mannerism 33
Baroque, Rococo and Beyond 34

03

Prehistoric, Roman and the Dark Ages

The Riviera was popular even in the Palaeolithic times, back when the first artists made the first stubby little fertility 'Venuses' in c. 40,000 BC, now in the museums at Balzi Rossi, Toirano and Finaleborgo. Skip ahead 38,000 years or so to the Neolithic era and the first Ligurians, who left two enigmatic art forms: rock engravings in the upper Val Roja above Ventimiglia (there are casts in the Museo Bicknell in Bordighera), and the statue steles in eastern Liguria, in the castle museum in La Spezia.

The Romans followed, and as usual built to last: sturdy gates and towers remain at Turin, Susa and Aosta. On the east end of the Riviera you can visit ancient Luni, an important Roman garrison town and marble port that died on the vine in the early Middle Ages. Perhaps the most fitting legacy of antiquity's crack engineers is the dozen or so ancient bridges along the Riviera, some of which are perfectly intact; in Donnaz in Aosta a section of Roman road is preserved, cut into the living rock.

Although Liguria was nominally protected by Byzantium, the Dark Ages were pretty gloomy outside Albenga, seat of a bishopric, which preserves an evocative 5th-century baptistry with mosaics. Other rare survivors are the 5th-century baptistry at Novara, and the treasures in the museum at Susa and the Vercelli Cathedral Treasury.

The Middle Ages and the Renaissance

The lights came on again around the turn of the first millennium. Pilgrims tramped over the Alps, the Saracens were chased off the coast and trade and confidence revived. Romanesque churches and abbeys went up all over the place, their architects in this part of the world synthesizing French and Lombard styles: some of the best are the cathedral and SS. Pietro e Orso in Aosta, the basilica of San Giulio at Orta, the abbey at Novalesa, San Giusto at Susa and the unique Sacra di San Michele above Avigliana; on the Riviera the best Romanesque church is San Paragorio at Noli.

Genoa was the big news in the 12th and 13th centuries; its *centro storico* is one of the largest surviving medieval neighbourhoods in Europe. Stripes were in, for Genoese town houses and the Romanesque-Gothic churches of Santo Stefano, San Matteo and the Cathedral San Lorenzo. As for the art, 'the inhabitant of Liguria was proverbial among Italians for his contempt of higher culture' according to Burckhardt, but not quite – there are beautiful things to see in the San Lorenzo cathedral treasury and Museo di Sant'Agostino, and the frescoes and paintings of Barnaba da Modena, who worked in Genoa from c. 1350–80. Other fine Ligurian churches of the period are San Pietro at Portovenere and the Basilica di San Salvatore dei Fieschi above Lavagna, and the little gems with marble lace rose windows in the Cinque Terre; there's a great horde of medieval art, reliquaries and manuscripts in the Museo Lia in La Spezia.

Up in Piedmont, the Basilica of Sant'Andrea at Vercelli is one of the earliest Gothic buildings in Italy. Two important abbeys likewise went up on the cusp of the Gothic period, at Vezzolano and Sant'Antonio di Ranverso just west of Turin, the latter with lofty gables over the doors that became all the rage. Brick was a favourite building material, as in Asti's two Gothic jewels, San Secondo and the Cathedral. And Gothic continued to rule in Piedmont well into the 15th century, when the great cathedrals of Chieri and Saluzzo were built, without a hint of the Renaissance in full flow in Tuscany. Castles went up on every hill, especially in Le Langhe, Monferrato and the Canavese, where they punctuate the vineyards today. The Valle d'Aosta, thanks to its cultured rulers, the Challants, is something of a castle showcase: the castles come in all shapes and sizes, from fairy-tale models to big cubes, some with frescoes.

The best of these frescoes (at Fénis) were inspired by **Giacomo Jacquerio** of Turin (d. 1453), the elegant court painter and one of the great masters of International Gothic art in northern Italy, who left his best work on the walls of Sant'Antonio di Ranverso. His follower **Guglielmetto Fantini** frescoed the baptistry in Chieri in the 1430s; another anonymous master – long believed to be Jacquerio himself – painted the delightful frescoes based on a chivalric poem in the Castello di Manto near Saluzzo. The marquises of Saluzzo also patronized the Burgundian **Hans Clemer** (d. 1508) who left his masterpiece, a tremendous *Crucifixion*, in the parish church of Elva. Other talented Piedmontese painters of the period, such as **Gandolfino da Roreto** and **Defendente Ferrari**, also have a touch of Gothic elegance in their style; the great exception was the polymath **Gaudenzio Ferrari** (d. 1546), who was influenced by Leonardo da Vinci and his Milanese circle, and painted powerful, highly charged works of character, but is little known outside the region because his works are often in remote areas; some of the best are in Varallo, where he left a whole wall of paintings in Santa Maria delle Grazie and helped invent Piedmont's unique contribution to devotional art, the Sacro Monte (*see* p.319).

Between 1435 and 1515, a number of itinerant painters worked up and down the Riviera di Ponente and into what is now the Côte d'Azur. Their favourite theme was the *Golden Legend*, by Ligurian Jacopo da Varagine, especially his accounts of the *Last Judgement*, the cycles of *Life and Death* and the *Passion of Christ* – colourful didactic paintings for illiterate parishioners, inspired as much by the Flemish school as the Italian. A native of Pinerolo, **Giovanni Canavesio** (*c*. 1420–1500), stands head and shoulders above the others, thanks to his bright palette, exquisite stylized draughtsmanship and ability to put genuine religious feeling in his frescoes, as at San Bernardo in Pigna. Another refined artist to look for in churches along the coast is **Ludovico Brea** (1450–1522) from Nizza (Nice), who favoured a rich shade of wine-red that French artists still call *rouge brea*; some of this best work is in Dolceacqua and Taggia.

Mannerism

The Italian Renaissance was in its strange twilight when Andrea Doria, the 'Saviour of Genoa', also rescued his philistine city's low reputation in the arts by hiring **Perino del Vaga** (d. 1547), a pupil of Raphael, to design and fresco his Palazzo del Principe. The year was 1527 and Perino was available because he had just fled Charles V's brutal Sack of Rome, a calamity that had turned the world upside down in Italy. The Mannerism that Perino practised, in its own way, turned the Renaissance upside down. It had begun with Michelangelo in Florence, where his fellow Florentines had the intellect and background to understand its virtuoso, equivocating artiness; transplanting it to Liguria, as Perino did, was like exporting bowler hats to Bolivia – out of context, it became pure decorative fashion.

Perino was a major influence on the founder of the Genoese school, **Luca Cambiaso** (1527–85), a painter known for his innovative draughtsmanship and monumental decorative frescoes, which would become the hallmark of the local style. He often worked with **Giovanni Battista Castello** from Bergamo (1509–69), who spent most of his career in Genoa, decorating interiors and façades. Cambiaso's work increasingly reflected the ideas of the Counter-Reformation, and earned him an invitation from Philip II to become the court painter at the Escorial. In the 1550s **Galeazzo Alessi** of Perugia designed the Villa Cambiaso Giustiniani at Albaro, inventing what was to become the standard Genoese *palazzo* with its interior courtyard atrium or *cortile*.

Baroque, Rococo and Beyond

In the 17th century the obscenely wealthy old and *nouveau riche* families of Genoa required a large number of fluent painters to decorate their new palaces and villas with portraits and allegories that did credit to their families. Artists from all across Italy (the Bolognese **Guido Reni**, **Domenichino**, **Orazio Gentileschi**, **Barocci** and the innovative **Giulio Cesare Procaccini** from Milan were especially popular) either came to Genoa to seek their fortune in person or sent their paintings to eager patrons there. The one who was to exert the most formative influence, however, was **Peter Paul Rubens**, who arrived in 1606 and painted a number of portraits in the new grand and vibrant style he had evolved during his Italian sojourn, combining his native Flemish realism with vibrant Venetian colours and scintillating brush strokes. He loved Genoa and, convinced that its new stately palaces were paragons of beauty and architecture, made sketches of them, later published as *The Palaces of Genoa* (1622); he designed his own home in Antwerp with numerous Genoese echoes. A second key influence was Rubens' protégé **Antony Van Dyck**, who came and left the city a number of portraits during his stays in 1621–2 and 1626–7, and was the chief inspiration for the popular aristocratic portraitist **Giovanni Battista Carlone** (1614–83).

Rubens' grand style and Van Dyck's more sensitive, refined techniques combined in the work of the greatest Genoese painter of the first half of the century, **Bernardo Strozzi** (1581–1644); his style, however, was distinctively his own, characterized by bold brushstrokes and light-filled colours, although he later moved on to Venice and left his best work outside Genoa. His contemporary, and the most popular painter among the Genoese nobility, was the dull-as-toast **Domenico Fiasella** (Il Sarzana, 1589–1669); the best was **Gioacchino Assereto** (1600–49), who could equal Strozzi, although most of his work is in private collections. The greatest Baroque architect working in Genoa was **Bartolomeo Bianco** (*c.* 1590–1657), designer of Via Balbi and its great Palazzo della Università (1630), where he used the steep grade of the terrain to create one of the most stunning Baroque buildings in northern Italy.

The last half of the *seicento* saw the full flowering of the Genoese school, with its bravura and bold handling inspired by Rubens and influenced by Velázquez, who visited Genoa in 1629 and 1649. One major figure, **Giovanni Benedetto Castiglione** (Il Grecchetto, d. 1665), spent much of his career in Rome and Mantua; in his unusually versatile career he was always open to change and went through a variety of styles, as Rudolph Wittkower explains it, 'torn between a philosophical scepticism and an ecstatic surrender' that was typical of his generation. Castiglione produced some magnificent etchings, inspired by Rembrandt, and prints in monotype, a technique that he invented (Blake would later adapt the process).

Castiglione inspired the two greatest Genoese fresco painters, **Domenico Piola** (1628–1703) and **Gregorio De Ferrari** (1647–1726), both masters of fluid rhythms and superbly decorative frescoes, where life is a grand, hedonistic holiday, overflowing in fantasy settings of Bolognese-style *quadratura* (trompe-l'œil architectural settings); the two painters often worked side by side in friendly rivalry, as in the Palazzo Rosso. De Ferrari, generally considered the superior artist, spent four years in Parma, where he discovered Correggio and adopted his *sfumato* technique. A third painter, **Valerio Castello** (1624–59), a student of Fiasella, reacted against Baroque classicism, and in his brief career left dramatic, highly sophisticated canvases of dissolving forms.

Valerio Castello's spiritual heir was one of the most original painters of the day, **Alessandro Magnasco** (1667–1749). Magnasco had a reputation for his ability to paint *piccole figure*, distinctive wraith-like people used to populate the landscapes of Antonio Francesco Peruzzini and scenes of imaginary ruins by Clemente Spera. He worked in Florence for the Grand Duke Ferdinand di Medici, where he saw prints of Jacques Callot's *Misères de la Guerre*, which affected him deeply, leading him to a sombre *chiaroscuro* colouring and phantasmagorical subjects, often demonic or grotesque – beggars and friars, wars and the Inquisition were favoured subjects, painted quickly and nervously as if infected by the distemper of the times. At the end of his career he returned to Genoa, where he painted two of his greatest works: the *Reception in a Garden* (in the Palazzo Bianco) and the *Supper at Emmaus* (at San Francesco in Albaro). He had no followers, but his proto-Impressionistic technique influenced 18th-century painters in Venice, especially the Guardi brothers.

It was also in the late 17th century that Genoa's sculptors found their stride. A long residency in the 1660s by **Pierre Puget** (1620–94) from Marseille motivated the locals, especially **Filippo Parodi** (1630–1702), a student of Bernini, who found a kindred spirit in Puget and added a certain French rococo grace to the High Roman style of his master: see the *St Martha in Ecstasy* in Santa Marta, in Genoa. One of his Genoese pupils, Angelo de' Rossi, went on to a successful career in Rome; other pupils were his son, **Domenico Parodi**, and the brothers **Bernardo** (1678–1725) and **Francesco Schiaffino** (1689–1765). Another important Genoese sculptor of the period, **Anton Maria Maragliano** (1664–1739), a student of Domenico Piola, became one of the few Baroque masters with the ability to sculpt expressively in wood, adroitly combining ecstatic attitudes with a rococo charm; many churches along the Riviera contain his work. But, as often as not, the most delightful works of 18th-century Liguria are the minor churches: Cervo, Laigueglia and Bogliasco are prime examples.

Turin, made capital of the dukes of Savoy in 1563, had a lot of catching up to do, and the Savoys were leaving nothing to chance with their carefully planned streets and royal squares. Three exceptional Baroque architects left their mark on the city and on the ring of pleasure palaces that surround Turin: the most startling, original was **Guarino Guarini** of Modena (1624–83), a Theatine priest and mathematician who moonlighted as an architect and came to work for Carlo Emanuele II in 1668, seeking God in geometry and leaving the city three of the Baroque era's most audacious buildings – the Chapel of the Holy Shroud, the Royal Chapel of San Lorenzo and the undulating brick Palazzo Carignano. The Sicilian **Filippo Juvarra** (1678–1736), whose grand theatrical vision of classical forms had an irresistible appeal to up-and-coming royalty, was granted the prestigious title of 'first architect to the king' by Vittorio Amedeo II and spent 22 years in Turin, apparently without sleep as he recreated the city: he designed the city extension towards Porta Susa, and built the Basilica di Superga, the magnificent rococo palace at Stupinigi, the façade and stair of Palazzo Madama, and the church of the Carmine, while contributing to a score of other churches and royal residences in and around Turin, and working on countless other projects in the rest of Europe. The third architect, his head full of Guarini and Juvarra, was the Turinese **Bernardo Vittone** (1705–70), who, like painter Gaudenzio Ferrari, would be much better known had he worked in large cities: although he has one fine church in Turin (Santa Maria in Piazza) his best works are in Bra, Villanova, Mondovì and Carignano.

Although Turin lost its royal capital status with the Reunification of Italy, it didn't lose its momentum. **Alessandro Antonelli** of Ghemme (1798–1888) challenged the laws of gravity with the city's unique landmark, the Mole Antonelliana, as well as with his remarkable tower on Novara's church of San Gaudenzio. Tourism on the Riviera and the Italian Lakes led to the creation of a monumental, eclectic but festive style of holiday architecture in hotels and villas, which effortlessly took on board the florid *Belle Epoque* and Liberty (Italian Art Nouveau) styles that followed – **Charles Garnier** of Paris Opéra fame also worked around San Remo and Bordighera. Of special note, in Pegli near Genoa, are the remarkable romantic gardens of the Villa Durazzo-Pallavicini, laid out in 1840 by an opera set-designer and recently restored.

Much of the Riviera's recent building is concentrated in Genoa, although much of this is in the state-of-the-art restoration of historic buildings. One exception is the Bigo, or Crane, by Genoa's superstar architect **Renzo Piano** (b. 1937), which rises like a bouquet of giant ships' masts high above the Porto Antico – the vortex of the newly reinvented, fun Genoa.

In the 19th and early 20th centuries, Turin held a series of international exhibitions as it went through its great industrial expansion – factories that today are finding a range of new uses, beginning with the conversion of the once avant-garde Fiat plant at Lingotto by Renzo Piano. Turin was also the first city in Italy to open a museum of modern art (GAM) and remains the best place in Italy to see it – especially works of its own home-grown movement, Arte Povera, which developed in the 1960s in the wake of Polish playwright Jerzy Grotowsky's Impoverished Theatre. As opposed to the Minimalist art coming out of the United States, Arte Povera artists (**Mario Merz, Giuseppe Penone, Michelangelo Pistoletto, Giovanni Anselmo, Gilberto Zorio, Giulio Paolini, Pier Paolo Calzolari, Luciano Fabro** and **Alighieri Boetti** are the big names) reused humble everyday and natural materials to magically transform their reality and find new meanings: the huge museum of contemporary art at the Castello di Rivoli just outside Turin has one of the most extensive collections of their works.

Tales of Tenacity

Just Who Was Christopher
  Columbus? 38
Liguria's Idealists: Mazzini and
  Garibaldi 42
The Italian Village Model 48
Under the Sign of the Snail 49

04

Just Who Was Christopher Columbus?

The Genoese are not Neapolitans, so if you ask this question you won't get a theatrical gesture of despair or an imploring glance up to heaven to please preserve the cosmic order from such ignorant ninnyhammers. This being the new kinder, gentler Genoa, you won't even get knifed. Instead, expect a gentle sigh, and the polite reply that what you learned in school was correct: the great Admiral of the Ocean Sea was from Genoa. Christopher Columbus, who should have known, said so himself.

So why do people keep trying to prove that he was something else, or from some other place, that he was Jewish and/or from Mallorca, or from Calvi, Corsica (part of Genoa at the time) or Cogoleto (between Savona and Genoa), or Cuccaro in Piedmont? The one person responsible for all the enigma, of course, is Columbus himself. He went out of his way to shroud himself in mystery, and the clues he left behind are so tangled that a sci-fi writer could easily cast him as a bungling alien from outer space. So much of his private life is unexplained that even the ponderous Italian documentation doesn't convince. In fact, it contradicts Columbus' own words and his first biographers'. A renowned 19th-century criminal psychologist, studying the case, concluded that the great discoverer was a paranoid nut.

When was he born, for instance? In his own writings, Columbus suggests birth dates ranging between 1447 and 1469. Bartolomé de Las Casas and Columbus' son, Fernando, who were his earliest biographers, who knew him intimately and had all his papers, never mention a date. All right then, who were his parents? Christopher never told anyone, not even his own son, the name of his father.

Christopher and his first biographers all claim that he went to sea as a lad – traditionally a Genoese would start off as a deckhand at age 14. But documents in Savona dated 1472 say that he was an apprentice wool carder at 12 and a weaver at age 21. To add to the confusion, once he left Genoa (that much, at least, everyone agrees on!) he used a variety of aliases – Colon, Colonus, Colomo – but never his presumed Genoese name, Cristoforo Colombo, or the Latinized Columbus.

The names Cristovam Colón and Christovao Colom are first recorded when he moved to Portugal. According to two sources (Las Casas and Christopher himself), he arrived there in 1470, already a well-known navigator, with credentials that impressed the Crown with his vision of sailing west to the Indies. The notarial deeds in Genoa and Savona, however, have it that he didn't even go to sea until 1473, most likely as a trade representative; that his experience at sea was that of a passenger; and that he didn't arrive in Portugal until 1476, and then only by grasping an oar and floating to shore after his ship sank. His Portuguese biographer João de Barros (1496–1571) describes how he was injured, cared for by the locals, then later moved to a Genoese neighbourhood in Lisbon. If true, and it seems to be, Christopher had chutzpah on a truly heroic scale, among all his other qualities; not every shipwrecked Italian salesman in his mid-20s (presumably) could pass himself off as a great mariner to the Kings of Portugal and the Catholic Kings of Spain.

In Lisbon Christopher found his young brother, Bartolomé, a gifted cartographer, who helped him get a job making maps. According to Christopher and his first biographers, he made up a globe in 1474 (note, two years before he apparently arrived in Portugal) and sent it the Florentine astronomer Paolo Dal Pozzo Toscanelli, who sent him an encouraging note and a nautical chart showing the westward approach to Japan (a sketch of this was found in the 19th century among Toscanelli's papers in Florence). Christopher took the chart along with him in 1492.

No documents survive that begin to explain just when and where the Colombo brothers learned the art of map-making, which has led to the speculation that our man may have been Jewish. The most accurate maps of the day were made in Mallorca, by Jewish cartographers, and in the dawn of the Age of Exploration were treated as state secrets. One theory, proposed by Salvador de Madariaga in his *Vida del muy magnifico señor Don Cristobal Colón*, is that Christopher was the son of a Jewish family who had moved to Genoa from Spain, fleeing the growing bigotry, and that he completely recreated himself when he was shipwrecked in Portugal in 1476. De Madariaga's evidence is mostly circumstantial, but intriguing: after all, Colombo is among the recorded surnames of Italian Jews, one of whom had served as a rabbi in Livorno in the 19th century.

Whatever his previous experience at sea or lack thereof, Christopher soon proved to be a bold and able mariner. In 1477 he convinced Prince João to give him a ship to sail to Iceland, where he made observations on tides that were confirmed in 1497 by another Genoese-born explorer, Giovanni Caboto (John Cabot). He voyaged down the west coast of Africa. He also married Doña Filipa de Perestrello y Moniz, who gave him his first son, Diego, in 1479, and died a few years later.

Most historians agree that Christopher the widower and little Diego moved from Portugal to Spain in late 1484 or 1485, after King João II refused to sponsor his vision of sailing west to reach the east. They travelled in secret, perhaps one step ahead of the law; a letter from the King dated March 1488, addressed to Cristovam Colón, says that the King was willing to re-examine his plans and that he could return to Portugal without fear of persecution.

The rest of the famous story falls into place from here: Christopher arrives in Spain, destitute, at Palos de La Frontera, and seeks help at the Franciscan monastery of Santa María de La Rábida where he meets Friar Juan Pérez, a confessor of Queen Isabella, and Friar Antonio de Marchena, who agreed to work to obtain him an audience with the Catholic Kings of Spain. Christopher left Diego in the care of the friars, met the Queen in 1486, and made an impression; a document from 1487 refers to a payment to Cristobal Colomo in regards to some service rendered. In that same year Christopher met Beatriz Enríquez in Córdoba; she became his mistress and in 1488 gave birth to his second son, and biographer, Fernando.

It was not until 1492, after completing the Reconquista, that Ferdinand and Isabella were ready to give ear seriously to the Genoese. On 17 April 1492, at Villa de Sancta Fe de La Vega de Granada, the *Capitulaciones* were spelled out between the Spanish sovereigns and their Admiral Don Cristobal Colón. The *Capitulaciones* stated that if he reached the Indies by sailing westward, he would be given the titles of Admiral of the Ocean Sea, Viceroy and Governor General of all lands that he discovered, and get a 10 per cent cut of all merchandise acquired there; and that these entitlements, upon the death of Don Cristobal Colón, would be passed to his successors in perpetuity. After all his years of waiting, Christopher had become wary and suspicious of kings.

Rightly so. By the time he returned from his second voyage (of 1493–6) the Spanish were already arguing that the *Capitulaciones* were only a draft for an agreement and withdrew the first of his privileges. Occasionally the Crown granted him a few 'mercies' to keep him from claiming the whole thing was a fraud. For the rest of his life, Christopher would find himself falling deeper into debt, scorned by the Spanish court, surrounded by detractors and indifference. His only reliable income turned out to be the 10,000 *maravedis* granted to him by the Crown as a life pension in 1493.

But discouragement that would have driven a lesser man to despair was water off a duck's back to Christopher. After two years of poverty, confinement and abuse in Spain, he set sail again in 1498 and discovered the continent of South America. He left behind his Will, a *Mayorazgo*, a strange document in which he made the point repeatedly that his name and that of his heirs is Colón, and that he was a true Colón born in Genoa, and that his successors should 'always endeavour for the honour and welfare of the city of Genoa'. He then goes on to say how Diego and his heirs should sign their papers: they must imitate him, and never use any family name, identifying themselves only by their first name (in Christopher's case, Xpo FERENS, a Latinization of his name) or simply as 'the Admiral' under a cabalistic pyramid of letters:

.S.
.S.A.S.
X M Y
El Almirante

On 20 November 1500 Christopher returned from his third voyage – in chains, charged with badly administering the new territories, after he had been unable to put down a rebellion of the first colonists on Hispaniola. Humiliated, all of his privileges revoked and fearing that his two sons would never receive a *peso*, the Admiral collected copies of all the promises on paper made to him by Spain, and sent them for safekeeping to the most reliable institution in Genoa: the Bank of St George. Which brings up another Columbian mystery: why did he always write in Castilian Spanish (using many Portuguese spellings) even when writing home to Genoa? But he could presumably read his native tongue – all the letters from the bank addressed to 'Our beloved fellow citizen Christopher' were written in Italian.

Despite ill health, poverty, dispiriting ingratitude and outright scorn, Christopher managed to get together four tiny decrepit caravels, and set sail with his 14-year-old son Fernando on his fourth and final voyage. He discovered Central America during his two years there, and was shipwrecked on Jamaica where he was left to die, unaided and unsought, even after Governor Ovando of Hispaniola knew he had survived. He came home against all odds, sick with gout and, having no home to go to, lodged in a boarding house in Valladolid until he died in 1506.

Who was that guy? The question arose while he was still warm in the grave. A Genoese Dominican, Agostino Giustiniani, came out with a book claiming that Christopher was of plebeian origin and had been a manual labourer. This was enough to offend the honour of Fernando, who went to Italy in a futile search of noble kin. When he replied to Giustiniani by writing his father's biography, he reluctantly conceded the plebeian origins, but denied the manual labour – no man so well-read and learned in cartography could have been a humble worker. As for his father's name, Fernando had to admit, 'with respect to the truth about such a name and last name it did not come about without some mystery'.

His older brother, Diego, had gone to court to claim his rights, and had won the title of Admiral and governor of Hispaniola. Diego's son Luis had to go to court as well, and reached a settlement with the Crown: in exchange for giving up claims to the ten per cent in the *Capitulaciones*, he and his heirs would have the honorary title of Admiral of the Ocean Sea, two noble titles, Duke of Veragua and Marquis of Jamaica, and an annuity of 1,000 gold doubloons, all in perpetuity (which lasted until 1830, when by Royal Order the 1,000 gold doubloons were reduced to 23,400 pesos).

In 1578 the identity issue flared up again when there appeared to be no direct male heir. It was duly confirmed that the names Colón and Colombo were one and the same, and two hundred potential Colombos were located. Curiously, although some of these were Genoese and the reward was great, not a single one of them petitioned the Spanish crown (the rights eventually passed to a great-great-nephew in Spain). Genoa, naturally prudent, remained out of the fray, but by 1618 a Genoese school of scholars emerged to root out the truffle of truth.

One was Filippo Casoni, who studied Christopher's genealogy in 1708 and whose results were published posthumously in Genoa in 1799 as the *Annali della Repubblica di Genova*. Here we learn at last that the Colombos were a respected family in Liguria, from a place near Nervi and Fontanabuona, where a tower called the Colombi is still located. Christopher's father, Domenico, a weaver, was a Genoese citizen from the parish of Santo Stefano, and his mother was Susanna Fontanarossa; she and Domenico had 'lived together for many years' and their 'first fruit' was Cristoforo.

Casoni's work has largely stood up to further researches by generations of Columbian scholars in Genoa. Their efforts were published by the state in 15 volumes in three multilingual editions in 1892–6, complemented by a prodigious publication of the city of Genoa called *Colombo* (1932) with copies of all pertinent deeds and documents (many only discovered in the 19th century). Both establish beyond any reasonable doubt that a Christopher, son of Domenico, was born in Genoa or nearby in 1451. As the Mayor Eugenio Broccardi wrote in the preface:

> *To reject the documents here assembled in their authentic and legitimate form is to deny the light of the sun; their acceptance signifies the freeing of truth from the infinity of idle words that are increasing every day in vain attempts to find outside Genoa the origin of the discoverer of America.*

So there. But the question remains: why did Christopher go to such extremes to cover up his tracks? In *The Discovery of North America*, Maurizio Tagliattini comes up with a plausible answer: that Christopher may have been the first-born of Susanna, but not of Domenico Colombo. Tagliattini bases his theory on two important pieces of evidence. The first is in Fernando's biography of Christopher. Fernando spends an entire chapter inconclusively musing about the names of his father's parents, but further along states that the Admiral's brother and lieutenant Bartolomé was the founder of the city of Santo Domingo, which he named in memory of his father, whose name was Domenico. His father, this is, not Christopher's.

The second is a notarized Latin document of 1473 from Savona, in which Susanna, wife of Domenico, agrees to the sale of rights to Domenico's house. With her as witnesses are her two sons, Christopher and Giovanni (who is never mentioned elsewhere) with the surname of Pelligrino. In the document the notary described them also as the sons of Domenico, but then crossed it out. Tagliattini surmises that, while living in Genoa, Christopher only pretended to be the son of Domenico Colombo to hide the disgraceful fact that his true father, Pelligrino, had abandoned him and his mother – hence the change of name once he left Genoa, and his frequent references to Moses, born out of wedlock and abandoned by his father. Of course, Tagliattini has found that Pelligrino is a Jewish surname in Italy... See Tagliattini's website – *http://muweb.millersville.edu/~columbus/tagliattini.html* – for more information.

Typically, no one is quite sure where Christopher is buried (both Seville and Santo Domingo claim his bones) or whether or not his ghost suffers over the ambivalence of his legacy; it seemed as if the general consensus that came out of the review of his career in 1992 was that he should have stayed in Genoa and left the New World alone. The greatest mystery of all is just where he found the heart and courage to carry on; his resilience seems almost superhuman. He wrote: 'And the sea will grant each man new hope, as sleep brings dreams of home.' Which, in his own case, in spite of everything, must have been dreams of the Genoa he knew as a child.

Liguria's Idealists: Mazzini and Garibaldi

Proud, stubborn tenacity must always have been a characteristic of the Ligurians for them to survive on their rocky, vertical homeland. Tenacity kept Columbus going when the chips were down, and it kept the leading families of the Genoese Republic embroiled in feuds and vendettas for generations. Even after Andrea Doria put Genoa under Spanish protection, tenacity kept him from surrendering to Spanish pressure to change the Republic into a principality. This enabled Genoa to maintain at least the illusion of being a free agent, with its own constitution. No region in Italy was more democratically minded in the early 19th century, and when the kings in Turin inherited the Republic by treaty in 1815, they were pleased to have a port but very wary of the political hot potato that came with it. One of their first acts was to spend buckets of money on fortifications around Genoa, as if they could bottle up the genie.

Fortunately for Italy, a tenacious Ligurian love of independence had already taken root in two young souls, one a dreamer and schemer, the other a man of action, both of whom also possessed a (very non-Genoese) disinterested idealism of staggering proportions. Without the generous and unflagging spirits of Giuseppe Mazzini and Giuseppe Garibaldi, the Risorgimento and Italian unification would have been a different thing altogether, a patched-together political answer to questions about 'a geographical expression' as Metternich disdainfully called Italy in 1847. Mazzini and his impossibly lofty aims and romantic failures contributed mightily to the idea that there was indeed a nation called Italy that could be governed by Italians, inspiring Garibaldi to lead the fight that galvanized the world and give the people of Italy a genuine sense of unity for the first time since the Romans, defying Dante's famous line:

Oh servile Italy, house of suffering
a ship without a pilot in a great tempest
not mistress of provinces, but a brothel!

Act I: Birth of an Idea

Mazzini was born in Genoa in 1805, the son of a doctor enamoured of the French Revolution and a mother who, even more than the typical Italian mamma, thought her son was the Messiah. Although physically frail, he was a precocious child, and could read before he could walk. At age 16 he witnessed a tide of refugees pouring though Genoa, hoping to escape to Spain after their failed revolution against the reactionary Piedmont of 1821. The sight of people suffering for political ideals moved him deeply. He started wearing black, as if in mourning for freedom, and dressed that way for the rest of his life. He devoured the writings of humanist philosopher Johann Gottfried Herder, who believed that empires were monsters and that a people who shared a common language naturally shared a past and organically made up a nation, and that if all states were so composed, a peaceful world would inevitably result.

Mazzini briefly followed his father's career as a doctor, but fainted at his first operation, then obeyed his parents' wishes and studied law. His real vocation, as an agitator, began in 1827 when he joined the Carbonari, a hierarchical secret society that planned armed revolution in Italy. Mazzini was not one to take orders blindly, however, and in 1830 he was betrayed to the police by the leader of his cell and sent to prison for three months. Like St Francis, Mazzini used his time in the clink to reflect and change his life, developing a philosophy that distilled Herder to the purest essences. He believed in God, not the Christian God, but a God incarnate in the will of the people: Mazzini's religion was pure democracy. His bedrock beliefs were in the equality of humanity (radically including women and workers in that number) and in its ability to progress with education. Every individual was born with equal rights, but that alone was not enough, as everyone learned from the French Revolution:

The theory of Rights may suffice to arouse men to overthrow the obstacles placed in their path by tyranny, but it is impotent where the object in view is to create a noble and powerful harmony... With the theory of happiness as the primary aim of existence, we shall only produce egoists who will carry the old passions and desires into the new order of things, and introduce corruption into it a few months after. We have, therefore, to seek a Principle of Education superior to any such theory... This principle is DUTY... to struggle against injustice and error (wherever they exist), in the name and for the benefit of their brothers, is not only a right but a Duty; a duty which may not be neglected without sin; the duty of their whole life.

Essay on the Duties of Man Addressed to Workingmen (1844)

From exile in Switzerland, Mazzini founded his own semi-secret society called La Giovane Italia, 'Young Italy', with the goal of instilling a sense of national identity in the Italian people and educating them to lead a revolution from within, one that would make Italy a democratic republic and a model for Europe. One of his first recruits was a sailor named Garibaldi, who participated in Mazzini's first insurrection in 1834. This was botched before it began, when Mazzini's commander lost all of Giovane Italia's funds in the gambling dens of Paris. Garibaldi and Mazzini were both sentenced to death in Genoa, but fled – Garibaldi to Marseille and Mazzini to London.

In London (where the only thing he loved was the fog) Mazzini kept the flame alive by making contacts and writing endless letters. There are accounts of him giving most of his meagre income from journalism to beggars, who knew that the affable, otherworldly Italian in black could never say no. He lived in a cramped, book-filled room, smoking cigars (his one self-indulgence) while his canaries flew about everywhere because he could not bear to keep them in cages. He founded and taught in a free evening school to teach poor Italian immigrants to read and write. He charmed all who met him, especially Thomas Carlyle, who thought Mazzini was an impossible dreamer, but adamantly refused ever to hear anyone speak ill of him.

Giuseppe Garibaldi, the impossible doer, was born in Nice in 1807, his father a sailor from Chiavari. He loved the sea from an early age, and was hired as a cabin boy at the age of 15, travelling all over the Mediterranean and Black Sea, having bloodcurdling adventures from the start. He later wrote that the influential event in his life was a visit to Rome in 1825 with his father. The ancient monuments thrilled him, and inspired him to imagine that the city could one day again be the capital of a united Italy; it became, as he wrote: 'the dominant thought and inspiration of my whole life'.

Garibaldi got his first commission as a captain in 1832, just before the Mazzinian debacle, and afterwards carried on from Marseille. Discouraged and weary of his life in exile, he joined tens of thousands of other Ligurians and Piedmontese who left for South America. Garibaldi had taken to heart Mazzini's notions on one's duty to fight oppression wherever it existed, and at once got involved in local wars of independence. From his very first conflict he showed extraordinary personal courage, disregard for danger, and leadership, using imaginative guerrilla tactics and brutal (but effective) bayonet charges. Garibaldi's battles in South America were nearly all defeats – most were suicide missions from the start – but they were popular moral victories.

When Garibaldi was put in charge of the Italian Legion at Montevideo, he was wounded by disparaging remarks about Italian military prowess. To help make his ragtag band into a serious fighting force, he absconded with a shipment of red shirts intended for slaughterhouse workers and made them into a uniform, creating the first *garibaldini*, who defied all the nay-sayers by acquitting themselves with courage and distinction. But the politicians of Uruguay found the Red Shirts expendable, and in 1847 Garibaldi and some 70 *garibaldini* returned to Genoa, where they received a tumultuous welcome, thanks to accounts of their bold exploits in the papers.

Act II: 1848 and the Roman Republic

By this time, however, Garibaldi regarded Mazzini's dreams for an Italian revolution without outside help as impossible and, although he hated the monarchy, he, like many others, believed that a unified Italy required the support of Carlo Alberto in Turin. With his usual forthrightness, Garibaldi went to the King, demanding an army to fight the Austrians in Lombardy. Carlo Alberto, already wary of Garibaldi and his popular support, refused, so Garibaldi gathered together a band of volunteer *garibaldini* and went about it in the name of Lombardy. When the king's blundering armies went down to defeat at Custoza, Garibaldi and his volunteers fought on, impressing all Europe with their guerrilla tactics. Carlo Alberto ordered Garibaldi's arrest, but his Legion, reduced to 500, only gave up the fight after they were surrounded by 5,000 Austrian troops, and escaped after a daring bayonet charge. Garibaldi returned to the Riviera, disappointed that so few Italians had rallied to the cause.

But an unexpected second chance fell into his lap: the people of Rome, furious that Pius IX, in spite of his liberal talk, had failed to send troops to help the Piedmontese, rose up against him. Garibaldi was made a general of the newly proclaimed Roman Republic, and Mazzini became the natural leader of the governing triumvirate, and gave Rome the most tolerant, enlightened government it ever had – while working for no pay and dining in a workers' canteen. Meanwhile, Garibaldi laboured day and night to organize the Roman defence – needed soon enough when President Louis Napoleon of France sent an expeditionary force to Rome to restore papal power. An argument erupted in the Assembly: Mazzini hoped to reach a peaceful accommodation, while Garibaldi wanted no appeasement at all, and won the day.

The usually world-weary Romans, aided by not a few foreigners (one was the American political cartoonist Thomas Nast), put up a gallant defence of the Republic. On 1 July 1849 the Roman assembly passed the most liberal and advanced constitution in Italian history. Two days later, after a three-month siege, the French entered Rome. Just before leaving, Garibaldi gave his famous speech: 'Whoever wishes to continue the war against the foreigner, let him come with me. I offer neither pay nor quarters nor provisions. I offer hunger, thirst, forced marches, battles and death.'

Act III: Discouragement and Failures

After barely escaping from Rome with his life, then watching his beloved wife die in the subsequent hardship, Garibaldi found himself all but abandoned. Writing bitterly that 'the name of Italian will be a laughing stock for foreigners in every country. I am disgusted to belong to a family of so many cowards', he made candles in a factory on Staten Island for four years and applied for American citizenship.

While he sulked, Mazzini was back in London, scheming away. When Garibaldi couldn't bear to stay away and returned to Italy by way of England, Mazzini was anxious to discuss an incursion into Sicily, but Garibaldi avoided him, blaming him for the failure of the Roman Republic. He took no part in the romantic republican insurrections supported by Mazzini (then secretly living in Genoa) in 1853, 1856 and

1857, all of which went down to tragic defeat; instead, he bought Caprera, an island off the north coast of Sardinia, and bided his time farming. After 1857, however, he was summoned to Turin to discuss the evolving situation with the new, pro-unification King Vittorio Emanuele II and his prime minister, Count Camillo Cavour.

Act IV: The Unification of Italy

In 1860, Mazzini's idea of a Sicilian expedition, followed by a battle of liberation up the peninsula, persuaded *émigré* Sicilians to propose it themselves to Garibaldi, assuring him that the people, oppressed by the backward Bourbon kings in Naples, would rise up with him. But Sicily was poor, and far away, and didn't fit in at all with the plans of Cavour, who was busily cutting secret deals with Louis Napoleon (now Emperor Napoleon III) and who dreamed of a modern state with an economy based on northern European models; besides, Piedmont was at peace with Naples, and Cavour didn't want to get into hot water with all the European governments he had been cultivating to his cause. When he refused to support the Sicilian expedition, Garibaldi took matters into his own hands and sailed south with a thousand volunteers. Cavour attempted to stop the popular hero, whom he regarded as a loose cannon, but as the Italians say, Garibaldi's *stellone* (his lucky star) was on the rise.

What Cavour had hoped would be just another hopeless Mazzini-style insurrection succeeded beyond anyone's dreams. Garibaldi and his Thousand Red Shirts electrified Europe by taking Sicily from the regular Bourbon army, and declaring himself dictator in the name of Vittorio Emanuele (unlike Mazzini, Garibaldi didn't concern himself too closely about the social aspects of revolution). When the *garibaldini* crossed the Straits of Messina, their ranks had swelled to 20,000; when they captured Bourbon Naples, Garibaldi learned that Cavour had outmanœuvred him in the north and closed off his dream of marching on to French-held Rome. In disgust, Garibaldi refused all honours and rewards and retired to his farm, taking only a sack of seed, coffee, sugar, dried fish and a bag of macaroni, as poor as he was when he started.

Act V: To the Bitter End

Although their dream of Italian unification was accomplished, it was controlled and compromised by their adversaries, and both Giuseppes, the doer on Caprera and the dreamer in exile, could not help but feel disillusioned. Nevertheless, both agitated for the annexation of Rome and Venetia to complete the Italian state. Garibaldi, a true Cincinnatus, passed his time planting crops and talking to his cows and goats. Elected Senator, he rarely took his seat, until 1861, when feeling his *garibaldini* were being hard done by, he went to Turin and launched a vicious attack on Cavour, who had in fact fought against the Piedmontese generals on his men's behalf. Although furious at Garibaldi's remarks, Cavour kept his cool, but was never the same, and died soon afterwards. Garibaldi, for his part, always kept his hand in, offering to lead the Union armies in the American Civil War (Lincoln politely refused). Against the will of the French generals, he went to France to lead more *garibaldini* against the Prussians in 1870, only to suffer again the ingratitude of politicians. Declaring to the bitter end that he would rise up to do war with Italy if she ever oppressed any people, the old warrior died in Caprera in 1882.

Mazzini, for his part, declared that the Italy of Vittorio Emanuele II was not the real Italy, the tolerant democracy of his dreams, and refused to live in it. With his close contacts with English workers, he helped to organize the First International in London, but his beliefs in private property and insistence on a social as well as a political revolution meant that he was soon eclipsed by Marx and Bakunin, especially after he failed to support the Paris Commune in 1871 (because French republicans had destroyed his Republic of Rome, he could not bring himself to trust them again). In 1872, sad and lonely and sensing the end was near, Mazzini returned clandestinely to Italy, to Pisa, under the alias of John Brown, the American abolitionist, and died. His chief memorial is the nice big tomb in Genoa's Staglione Cemetery, with its angry epitaph by the greatest Italian poet of the day, Giosuè Carducci:

THE LAST

OF THE GREAT ANCIENT ITALIANS

AND THE FIRST OF THE NEW

THE THINKER

WHO FROM THE ROMANS FOUND HIS STRENGTH

FROM THE COMMUNES HIS FAITH

FROM OUR TIMES HIS IDEAS

THE POLITICAL MAN

WHO THOUGHT, AND WILLED, AND MADE ONE THE NATION

WHILE MANY JEERED AT HIS GREAT PURPOSE

WHO NOW ABUSE HIS ACHIEVEMENT

THE CITIZEN

TOO LATE HEEDED IN 1848

REJECTED AND FORGOTTEN IN 1860

LEFT IN PRISON IN 1870

WHO ALWAYS AND ABOVE ALL LOVED

THE ITALIAN FATHERLAND

THE MAN

WHO SACRIFICED EVERYTHING

WHO LOVED MUCH

AND NEVER HATED

GIUSEPPE MAZZINI

AFTER FORTY YEARS OF EXILE

TODAY PASSES FREELY ON ITALIAN SOIL

NOW THAT HE IS DEAD

O ITALY

SUCH GLORY AND SUCH BASENESS

AND SUCH A DEBT FOR THE FUTURE

The Italian Village Model

Medieval Italians, even in isolated villages, had a near-perfect instinct for creating streets and squares with a maximum of delight, a sense of urban design that depended not on paper plans and geometry, but on arranging buildings and monuments to form a composition, as a painter would. The result was asymmetrical, seemingly haphazard townscapes that always seem somehow 'right'; to explore their subtleties, walk through a village or town and see how the composition changes every few steps. Unexpected perspectives and angles, and carefully planned surprises as you turn a corner, are all part of their art. With the passion for geometry and order that began with the Baroque – Turin's plan is a prime example – they slowly lost the knack. Now, rather belatedly, in a reaction to the dull dystopian sameness of modern cities and sprawling suburbs, some planners are beginning to look towards the 'Italian village model' for ideas that might recapture some of the visual delight that draws people to be out and about, and create a sense of community, while leaving the surrounding countryside open for agriculture and recreation.

Although the hill towns of Tuscany hog most of the attention, many villages in Liguria, clinging tenaciously to the mountains or coastal rocks, have arranged their buildings in a tiny space with the eye of a Michelangelo; visit a few, and you will soon notice how urbane a place of 300 souls can be, closely knit but never dull, with narrow lanes and steps, vaults and archivolts. Bell towers double as defensive towers – in Lingueglietta the church itself, with nice economy, moonlighted as a castle. By the sea, houses are painted intense colours – ochres, reds and pinks – so sailors and fishermen could spot them from afar, but also to beautify the village. Many of the villas and palaces that seem rather austere in comparison originally had trompe-l'œil frescoes on their façades imitating architectural features.

There's a whole Ligurian vocabulary for streets: *carrugio, carera, chu, ciassa, chibo* (a shadowy side street), *capitoli* (steep vaulted stairs, easy to defend) up to a *crosa* (a boulevard designed for fancy villas). A favourite technique for building on hills is in concentric rings crisscrossed by narrow *chibi*; two examples are the medieval quarter of San Remo and a hill town above Bordighera, both called La Pigna (pine cone). One town, Varese Ligure, was planned by its feudal lords in a circle in 1300.

In the early days, separate baptistries and churches offered an opportunity to create architectural ensembles in a piazza, the idea that created so many great city centres in Tuscany, reflected in small Ligurian towns like Albenga. The late 16th century brought a new fad for building oratories near the church, creating a sacred area (*sagrato*), which was set apart with a *risseu*, a black-and-white pebble mosaic – one spectacular example is in Moneglia. Space, however, was often very tight, leading to imaginative solutions – a prime example is Montalto Ligure's complex of church and oratory built on different levels. Other villages achieve remarkable theatrical effects, such as tiny Buggio's unique *piazzetta principale*, which includes a stone bridge. Arcola's Piazza della Parrocchiale could be an opera set, with its grand stair and balustrade; Apricale's main square is so perfect that it is used as a stage for a summer theatre festival.

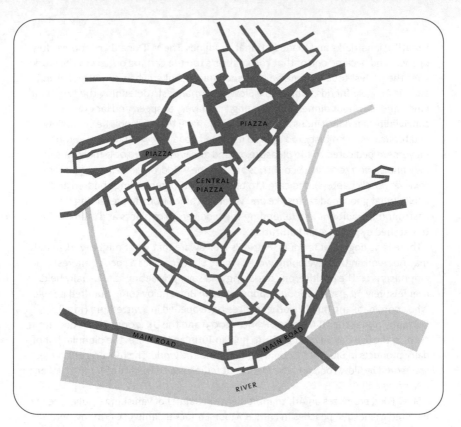

Best of all, unlike the *villages perchés* on the Côte d'Azur, Liguria's villages have not been converted into arty trinket shopping malls. Although emigration and the lure of easy money on the coast have led to a decline in population over the past 150 years, and a few villages, inevitably, have become clusters of second homes, the hill towns are still places where people live as they have for centuries. They could have all moved down to the coast, or to the cities, but then they would be leaving too much behind.

Under the Sign of the Snail

I came to understand that those who suffer for others do more damage to humanity than those who enjoy themselves. Pleasure is a way of being at one with yourself and others.

Carlo Petrini

Eat well and save the world. It started as a joke back in 1986, when Carlo Petrini, a left-wing journalist from Bra in Piedmont and member of the Italian gastronomical society Arcigola, was provoked by the announced opening of a McDonalds in Rome's Piazza di Spagna. 'What better weapon to battle fast food than slow food?' thought Petrini. He and his friends protested the violation of one of Italy's most beautiful landmarks and made national headlines. The McDonalds, of course, duly opened, and became one of that corporation's top ten earning outlets in the world.

Yet the protest touched a nerve, and encouraged, but still half-seriously, Petrini and his Arcigola friends published a Slow Food manifesto defending the two-hour lunch and four-hour dinner, condemning the slavery of speed and lack of conviviality in modern industrial society. They made their symbol the snail, slow and tenacious – and tasty, too. And so it started. Today, Slow Food, a non-profit movement dedicated to the pleasure of food and wine, has 40,000 members in Italy and some 77,000 in 48 countries around the world, organized into 700 local *convivia* (local chapters), dedicated to teaching and/or reminding children and adults what good food tastes like and where it comes from, to preserving gastronomic traditions and defending the biodiversity of plants and animals threatened by global standardization.

There is no dogma or formula; Petrini is well aware that what might work in Italy may not work in the developing world, where Slow Food has a special interest. The emphasis is on the positive, on cherishing and saving. Meetings are usually held over leisurely meals. Slow Food headquarters in Bra employ some hundred people who coordinate and publish; other offices have opened in Switzerland (1993), Germany (1992), the USA (2000), France (2003) and the UK (2005). Slow Food events such as the five-day *Salone del Gusto* held in Turin and 'Cheese', the biennial fair of dairy products in Bra, draw people from around the world. The most recent project sponsored by Slow Food and the Piedmont region is a University of Taste in Pollenzo (*see* pp.277–8).

Slow Food promotes an 'Ark' of ingredients in danger of vanishing (mullet roe in Italy, red Manosque peaches in France, Moorschnucken lamb in Germany, heritage turkeys in the USA), in the hope that once people get to know them they will demand them in their local shops and restaurants, and thus preserve them through market forces. This includes microbes. Generations and generations of wisdom went into finding just the right little bugs to make the tastiest cheese and cured meats; but 'hyper-hygienist' homogenizing, pasteurizing laws tend to ban them. Slow Food helps small traditional producers of cheese, meats (and microbes) deal with the daunting paperwork required by the EU and US governments to carry on.

The Slow Food philosophy of good food produced and sold by rural artisans in a healthy environment is hard to resist, but already in Italy, as Pertini has noted, a threat has been spawned by the movement's own success. Goliath agribusinesses, scenting profits, are attempting to co-opt the positive attitudes that Slow Food has created towards 'traditional local products' by opening factories in their particular areas, to be able to use their often protected (DOP) name, while compelling small producers to become mere 'pieceworkers' to survive, which usually means cutting corners to make bigger profits and losing that essential loving care on the farm; to keep posted (or to join up), visit *www.slowfood.com*.

Food and Drink

Restaurant Generalities 52
Specialities of the Riviera,
  or the Marriage of Popeye
  and Olive Oyl 53
Specialities of Piedmont
  and Aosta 55
Wines and Spirits of
  Piedmont and Aosta 58
Italian Menu Reader 60

05

Food and wine are a star attraction of Liguria and Piedmont, yet it's hard to imagine two more different regional cuisines: cross the Maritime Alps and *presto!* the Riviera's seafood, pesto, *focaccia* and white wine turn into truffles, cheeses, breadsticks and slowly stewed dishes that complement Piedmont's full-bodied red wines.

Restaurant Generalities

Breakfast (*colazione*) in Italy is no lingering affair, but an early-morning wake-up shot of caffeine to the brain: a foamy *cappuccino* or a *caffè latte*, accompanied by a croissant-like *cornetto* or *brioche*. This can be consumed in any bar and repeated as often as necessary before noon, and can be better than breakfast in a hotel.

Lunch (*pranzo*), served around 1pm, is traditionally the most important meal of the day, although nowadays many people have too far to commute home and get by with considerably less: in the cities you'll find restaurants and bars offering a range of lighter options such as sandwiches (*panini*), hot buffets (*tavola calda*), one- or two-course lunch menus, or pizza by the slice (*al taglio*) and other snacks.

If a traditional lunch is on the cards, there will be a minimum of a first course (*primo piatto* – any kind of pasta dish, broth or soup, or rice dish), a second course (*secondo piatto* – a meat dish, accompanied by a *contorno* or side dish – a vegetable, salad, or potatoes usually), followed by cheese (in Piedmont and Aosta), fruit or dessert and coffee. To go the whole hog, begin with *antipasti* – the appetizers Italians do so brilliantly, ranging from warm seafood delicacies, to raw ham (*prosciutto crudo*), salami in a hundred varieties, lovely vegetables, savoury toasts, olives, pâté and many, many more. There are restaurants that specialize in *antipasti*, and if you want you can just forget the pasta and meat and nibble on these (although in the end it may very well cost more than a full meal). Most Italians accompany their meal with wine and mineral water – *acqua minerale*, with or without bubbles (*gasata* or *naturale*), which supposedly aids digestion – concluding their meals with a *digestivo* liqueur.

Dinner (*cena*) is usually eaten around 8pm, or later in summer. This for many people has replaced *pranzo* as the big family meal with *primo* and *secondo* etc. If not, it's the favourite time to tuck into a pizza – often pizzerias only stoke up their wood-fuelled oven (*forno a legna*) at night.

The various terms for types of **restaurants** – *ristorante*, *trattoria* or *osteria* – have been confused. A *trattoria* or *osteria* can be just as elaborate as a *ristorante*, though rarely is a *ristorante* as informal as a *trattoria*. Unfortunately the old habit of posting menus and prices in the windows has fallen from fashion, but, as a rule, the fancier the fittings, or prettier the view, the fancier the **bill** or *conto*, though neither of these points has anything to do with the quality of the food. Although some restaurants offer a set budget *menu turistico*, the new trend is for a French-style *menu a prezzo fisso* (fixed-price menu), which offers a choice between several starters, main courses, and desserts. Fancier chefs offer a *menu degustazione* – a set-price gourmet meal featuring their specialities, often with a different wine with each course.

Specialities of the Riviera, or the Marriage of Popeye and Olive Oyl

Liguria, with its fresh seafood, sun-ripened vegetables (including Popeye's favourite spinach, chard and other greens – the very things craved by a sailor nation when it returns from sea, and the few things an anxious sailor's family could afford) and its delicious olive oil, has one of the healthiest of all Italian cuisines, the one that nearly perfectly matches all the criteria of the vaunted Mediterranean diet: olive oil as its main source of fat, lots of greens, wild herbs, legumes, pulses and fresh vegetables, but very little meat; little milk, butter or cream, but a discreet amount of cheese, and wine in moderation.

Although it's now the prize item on restaurant menus, seafood played a surprisingly small role in the traditional diet of Liguria; after all, one's garden, especially in this climate, was always much more reliable, especially in the centuries of pirates. Among the many herbal sauces, the most celebrated is **pesto**, that tangy, rich sauce of basil, pine nuts, garlic, olive oil, pecorino and parmesan cheese, ground with a mortar and pestle (which gave it its name) with the addition of green beans and boiled potatoes (according to some, especially if it's for a main course). Forget those jars of ready-made in your supermarket – try the real McCoy, with Ligurian olive oil and fresh-picked basil from Prà west of Genoa, both now proud to have DOP (AOC) status from the EU.

The special **pasta** forms of Liguria are *trenette* (short linguine) and *trofie*, simple twists that resemble worms, made of wheat or chestnut flour, with sauces that combine fresh vegetables, herbs and wild mushrooms in season. More elaborate forms include *pansotti*, filled with spinach and herbs, served with a delicious walnut sauce; and ravioli, invented in Nice (back when it was still Nizza). On the Riviera it comes in a hundred varieties, including *ravioli di magro*, 'lean ravioli', filled with chard or herbs, egg, *grana padano* cheese and marjoram, and served with melted butter and fresh thyme. For feast days, you would get ravioli with *tuccu*, a thick meat sauce. Lasagne, baked with vegetables or seafood, is another favourite.

Minestrone and other vegetable soups on the Riviera often come with *bigareli*, tiny pieces of home-made pasta. Around La Spezia try *lattughe ripiene in brodo* (stuffed lettuce in broth) and *mesciua*, made of spelt, cannellini beans and chickpeas, from a recipe handed down by the Romans at Luni. The Ligurians aren't big eaters of rice and *risotti*, as it was an expensive import, but in Genoa you may find *riso arrosto alla genovese* – rice baked with sausage, mushrooms, artichoke hearts and cheese.

Genoa is the birthplace of some of Italy's most elaborate **cold dishes** – *cima alla genovese*, breast of veal stuffed with minced sweetbreads, pistachios, veal, egg, dried mushrooms, artichoke hearts, peas and various herbs. Another, *cappon magro*, is a salad of cold fish, shellfish, hard-boiled eggs and vegetables, served with a garlicky sauce made with anchovies, oil and vinegar. During Easter (and at other times) don't pass up a chance to try *torta pasqualina*, the king of pies, traditionally made of 33 sheets of pasta, one for each year that Jesus lived, filled with ricotta, artichoke hearts, spinach, chard, courgettes, onions and hard-boiled eggs.

For all that, in many Riviera restaurants **seafood** is lord and master, which is great if you love fish and not so great if you don't. Anchovies, long one of Liguria's chief exports, are a common *antipasto*; sometimes you may even see *cotolette di acciughe*, anchovy 'cutlets' (stuffed and fried anchovies). Seafood stars in a wide variety of pasta dishes, soups and stews, including *burridà*, a soup made of white fish served with garlic sauce, not unlike Provençal *bourride*, although *burridà* may include cuttlefish and peas. *Zimino* is another favourite, a stew made of a mixture of fish with fennel, onion, celery, tomatoes, olive oil and parsley.

The now rare *datteri del mare* (*Litophaga litophaga*) are a speciality of the Ligurian coast: date-shaped little mussel-like shellfish with such a long life-cycle that a very elderly person may be described as 'older than a date clam'. Now their fishing is strictly regulated, and you'll be very lucky to find the legendary *zuppa di datteri*, which is like *moules marinières*, only much finer. The more common *mitili*, the local mussels, are often stuffed and baked, as are *arselle* (clams). Cockles (*tartufi di mare*) are common, while octopus (*polpo*) is a favourite in the Gulf of Poets (in salads, or boiled and placed in a mould, and served in slices as an *antipasto*). Squid (*totani*) is often stuffed with a mix of breadcrumbs, parmesan, mortadella and tomatoes. Then there are oysters, scampi and scampi's 'poor' cousin, the mantis shrimp or squill (*cicale*). Pricier offerings (usually priced by weight on the menu) include Mediterranean lobster (*aragosta*), sea bass (known either as *branzino*, *spigola* or *lupo di mare*), and *orata* or *dorata* (varieties of sea bream). For special occasions, there's *triglie all'imperatrice*, red mullet cooked with tomatoes, cream, onions, capers, white wine and cognac.

It may seem a bit odd for a coast, but salt cod and the more prestigious wind-dried cod (*baccalà* and *stoccafisso*, respectively) have been big favourites ever since they were introduced by English merchants in the Middle Ages. The Genoese like to eat either one in the form of light fritters, or as *stoccafisso accomodato* (stewed with wine, potatoes, mushrooms and olives), while a prize dish in many seafood restaurants is *baccalà mantecato* (puréed and flavoured with garlic).

Among the few **land food** specialities, you'll find stewed rabbit in various forms, snails – either *bagioi*, in a mint-flavoured tomato sauce, or *lumache alla genovese*, served with anchovies, garlic, oil, basil and white wine – guinea fowl and chicken *fricassea* or *fritto alla stecco* – a mix of sweetbreads and mushrooms, dipped in egg and breadcrumbs and fried on a skewer. Lamb prevails over beef and pork, although you may find *brasato di manzo alla genovese*, braised beef with vegetables and mushrooms in red wine. Look for steak prepared *s'a ciappa*, grilled on a slab of slate.

French influences have seeped over the border to the Riviera di Ponente, in dishes such as *brandacüyun* (dried cod with potatoes, similar to *brandade*). Other dishes are idiosyncratic, for instance *ü marò*, a sauce of ground fava beans and anchovies, invented by sailors to prevent scurvy and now used to accompany boiled meats; and the *gran pistau* from Pigna, grain boiled with bacon then fried with leeks and garlic, a genuinely old recipe because it uses animal fat instead of olive oil (olive cultivation only began in earnest under the Benedictines, in the 13th century). In higher altitudes the chestnut was for a long time just as important as the olive, supplying the flour for bread (*pattona*) and pasta; *porcini* mushrooms grow in chestnut forests and hold a prime place on autumn restaurant menus, served with pasta or polenta.

Liguria is a specialist in finger food and other **snacks**. *Focaccia*, soft inside and crispy golden on the outside, can be bought in stands along the street like slices of pizza: the classic is made with white cheese from Recco that is well-nigh irresistible when it comes hot from the oven, but you'll also see it with onions or olives, spinach, cheese and ham, or simply sprinkled with rosemary and salt. Even simpler, and sometimes sold in *focaccerie* and *pizzerie*, is *farinata*, made of chickpeas ground into flour and olive oil, baked in a hot wood oven or sometimes fried.

Each town in Liguria seems to have its special **pastry** or **sweet**: the best-known cake is the Genoese *pandolce*, filled with raisins, pine nuts and candied fruits. In Ventimiglia you'll find *castagnola*, a pastry made of chestnuts, sugar, cinnamon and cloves; Sassello is famous for its airy *amaretti*; elsewhere there are also *crostoli*, light anise-flavoured fritters served with warm *zabaglione*; *millesimi al rhum*, the delicious chocolates from Millesimo; *gobelletti* (or *cobbelletti*), shortcrust biscuits made in Genoa, often with cherry, pear or fig jam; the *spongata* or *spungata*, a pastry filled with jam and topped with sugar; *buccellato*, a festive cake, often with pine nuts, raisins or nuts; and *castagnaccio*, a flat cake made of chestnut flour, covered with pine nuts, scented with rosemary, and eaten with creamy fresh ricotta.

Liguria, like any self-respecting Italian region, produces **wine**, although very little, owing to its topography. Most are whites – good ones to try include **Pigato** from Albenga, named for its grape, which produces a fine, full-flavoured wine with a slightly bitter almond taste that can quickly make you tipsy, but compares very favourably with **DOC Cinqueterre**, made in that lovely zone (where it tastes best). Another white wine, which many people consider Liguria's best, is straw-yellow **Vermentino**, a crisp dry fruity wine made from the local malvasia grape produced around Diano Castello just east of Imperia; **Vementino dei Colli di Luni**, grown on the Tuscan frontiers of the Riviera, has recently been accorded DOC status.

The Cinque Terre also produces a famous sweet white wine called **Sciacchetrà**, made from grapes that grow by the sea and are left to dry in the sun. Formerly used only as a medicine, or to celebrate a wedding, it is now a prized dessert wine.

Liguria's best red wine is **DOC Rossese di Dolceacqua**, which is vinified either to be drunk young and ruby red or to take a few years' ageing, when it becomes a fine structured deep garnet wine, aromatic and soft, perfect with chicken or rabbit.

Specialities of Piedmont and Aosta

The pleasures of the table are taken very seriously in Piedmont; even before the birth of the Slow Food Movement, it was hard to find a town that didn't have a festival or market dedicated to some gastronomic delight. Piedmont's bracing Alpine climes (cheeses and game), rolling hills (wheat and maize), woodlands (truffles and mushrooms), soggy paddies (rice and frogs) and the micro-regions in between produce a veritable cornucopia of specialized products: sweet peppers for instance, thrive at Carmagnola, while just a few kilometres away at Pancalieri, it's mint. Cuneo takes great pride in its high-altitude beans. Snails hold pride of place at Cherasco and Borgo San Dalmazzo, as do tench (*tinca*) in the lakes of Poirino. This sacrosanct localism has led to an endless number of dishes and variations, although on the whole cooking styles are rarely elaborate. Turin has its own urban, slightly Frenchified style, while dishes in the mountains tend to be simple, wholesome and rich.

What makes Piedmontese cuisine unique is its use of **white truffles** (*tartufi bianchi* or *trifola d'Alba*; botanical name *Tuber magnatum pico*), named after Alba, in the centre of the growing area. White truffles are extremely rare outside Piedmont, but, unlike black truffles, they grow not only around oaks but around other trees as well; their musky erotic perfume, lumpy shape and aphrodisiac reputation have led to their nickname, the 'testicles of the earth'. They are at their pungent best when freshly dug up by a *trifolau* and his faithful truffle hound. The season is from October to February (although December is best) when gastronomes from around the world flock to Le Langhe and Monferrato.

A favourite way **to start** a Piedmontese feast is with a couple of *grissini* or breadsticks. You'll notice two types in the bakeries, the familiar long thin *stirati*, or the fat striped *rubatà*, which can come in a range of flavours, from cheese and onion to walnut and curry. They are especially good if two-thirds of the stick is coated with a paste of butter, garlic and white truffles, wrapped in a thin slice of prosciutto. Truffles also appear in a speciality unique to Piedmont: *bagna cauda* (literally 'hot bath'), a dip made with butter, olive oil, garlic, anchovies and sliced white truffles, served in heated bowls, into which one dips raw *cardi* (cardoons), artichoke-like edible thistles, and also raw carrots and other crudités with a piece of bread to collect the juices; the dish grew up along the medieval Salt Roads, along which Liguria sent Piedmont anchovies, salt and olive oil in exchange for wine. White truffles also appear in *insalata d'Alba* (with white lettuce, celery and asparagus tips) and *fonduta* (melted fontina cheese from the Valle d'Aosta, mixed with milk and egg yolks) served on a plate or poured over slices of polenta, potatoes, salami, onions or cucumber in vinegar.

The classic Piedmontese **pasta** is *agnolotti* – envelopes of egg pasta, similar to ravioli, stuffed with beef, pork or rabbit, flavoured with sausage, parmesan, eggs, nutmeg or herbs (no two recipes are alike), served in roast meat juices; the best are *agnolotti al plin* – little handmade sacks pinched closed with a gadget called a *plin*. *Taiarin* are narrow tagliatelle often topped with truffles. *Tagliatelle alla piemontese* are served with a meat sauce and truffles. As Italy's top producer of rice, Piedmont also has good *risotti*, which can get the truffle treatment, too; in Vercelli the classic dish is *panissa*, a one-dish meal of rice, beans and mortadella or *salam d'la doja* (*see* right). Stuffed onions, peppers and mushrooms are also popular.

Traditional **secondi** include hearty dishes such as *brasato al Barolo* (beef braised in Barolo, often a rather salty dish) and *bollito misto* (boiled pork, veal, turkey, beef and vegetables) accompanied by sweet and savoury sauces, including *salsa verde*, made from parsley, garlic and breadcrumbs drenched in vinegar, hard-boiled eggs, olive oil and pepper. Not a few restaurants serve the 19th-century classic *finanziera*, a rich stew made of veal, sweetbreads, cocks' combs and *porcini* mushrooms, cooked in butter and wine, named after the financiers in Turin who loved it. Piedmont's beef is among the finest in Italy (try the excellent *bresaola della Val d'Ossola*); in the

Alpine valleys west of Saluzzo, they raise a unique race of lamb, *sambucano*, tasty yet lean. Pork goes into a wide variety of *salume* and sausages including *salam d'la doja*, popular in rice-growing areas (pork with spices, garlic and red wine, left to dry for ten days, then preserved in its own lard in a terracotta jug for a few months or even a year and then eaten, sliced or in dishes such as *panissa*). Another traditional dish, popular in the Canavese and Biella, is *salame di patate*: pork mixed with boiled potatoes and garlic, and served either fried or on bread; the Canavese also produces the unique *salampatata* – a delicate tasty spud, good in omelettes. Its most famous sausage is *turgia* – made from old cows.

Piedmont makes some of Italy's best **cheeses**, usually served on a board with a selection of jams and *mostarda* (a sweet, spicy relish more like chutney than mustard). Nine have DOP status (the food equivalent of DOC for wines): the cows' milk *castelmagno*, the Barolo of cheese, aged at high altitudes in the Grana valley; the well-known *gorgonzola* and *grano padano*; goat and sheeps' milk *robiola di roccaverano*; *toma piemontese*, a heavy cheese, soft inside with a thin pale yellow crust, sometimes conserved with oil and herbs; little white cow's milk rounds, *tomino di melle*; *bra*, another cows' milk cheese, can be mild and soft (*tenero*) or aged and sharp (*duro*). *Murazzano* is a tasty ewes' milk cheese from the Alte Langhe. Thanks in part to Slow Food, local traditional cheeses in danger of extinction such as *toma di lanzo, acceglio, boves, bruss, testun, caprino presamico, escarun, nostrano, ormea, paglierina, sola, valcasotto, roccaforte, tomino di Chiaverano* and *valcavera* are being revived by small producers, celebrated in the biennial Cheese fair in Bra and well worth a try.

The **pastries** are among the best in Italy: the *Bocca di Leone* is a sinfully rich calorific heavyweight, *torta di nocciole* a divine hazelnut cake made in Le Langhe, which claims to be the best in the world. Chocolate was produced in Turin even before Switzerland: its iconic dessert is *gianduiotto*, chocolate with crushed hazelnuts, invented during the Napoleonic blockades when the city couldn't get enough of its beloved cocoa – only to find that the combination was divine.

The **Aosta valleys** are too steep and cold to grow many crops, but they are famous for game and meats, honey, butter and lovingly-made cheeses, most famously Fontina. Traditionally the *Valdostani* eschew all the *antipasti* beloved of the Piedmontese, and tuck right in – many dishes are full meals in themselves. Classic *fontina* dishes include *seupa vapellenentse*, made with layers of country bread, boiled cabbage, *fontina*, hot butter and *bouillon*, then baked in the oven; *fonduta* (fondue); *costoletta di vitello con fontina*, a breaded veal chop with a wedge of *fontina* melted in the centre; *risotto mantecato alla fontina* (creamy cheesy risotto); and *polenta grassa* (baked with lots of butter and *fontina*). Cheese even appears in a tasty green salad with a cream sauce (*insalata di verdure al fromazdo*). There are good hams, and wind- and salt-dried beef (*mocetta*) which is popular in *carbonade* – a stew invented by charcoal burners – with bacon, garlic, white wine, cinnamon, cloves and pepper, served with polenta. Be sure to try a *pierrade* – various meats and vegetables that diners cook on a hot stone at the table, then dip them in sauce. Although ibex and marmots are protected by law, some secretly find their way into the pot; an invitation to a *civet di marmotte* is a signal, for an outsider, that they've been accepted into the local community. The classic dessert is *montebianco*, of course, made with chestnut purée.

Wines and Spirits of Piedmont and Aosta

Bun pi bun fa bun (good with good becomes very good), the Piedmontese like to say when describing what happens when the region's wines accompany its wonderful cuisine – for these are nearly all unabashedly 'food wines', not made for quaffing on their own. The vast majority are red, either named after their place of origin (Barolo, Barbaresco, Asti and Grattinara) while others (Dolcetto, Nebbiolo, Barbera, Erbaluce and Cortese) are named after their grape. To promote them, the region has ten regional wine shops (*enoteche regionali*) in historic castles and buildings along the wine roads. The finest, made from the indigenous Nebbiolo grapes (a name that suggests mist, although no one seems quite sure why; perhaps because the mornings are often foggy during the harvest) have been grown along the banks of the River Tanaro, around Alba, first documented in 1300; the variety isn't at all a big yielder, but produces high-quality wines with a hint of violet and wild roses. The 1990, '93, '95, '97, '99, 2000 and '01 vintages are rated as exceptional – and very individual.

Barolo, the 'king of wines and the wine of kings' is full-bodied, profound, mellow and velvety. It's also the most tannic of Italian wines, requiring a minimum of two or three years in oak, and sometimes as many as seven, followed by ten or twelve additional years in the bottle. Yet it wasn't always so: until the mid-19th century, Nebbiolo wines were sweet and unstructured. Enter Count Cavour who, when he wasn't orchestrating the Risorgimento, was busy modernizing Piedmont, and invited French oenologist Louis Oudart to the region to improve its wines. Oudart at once recognized the great potential of Nebbiolo, introduced the French techniques to bring out its best, and the Barolo we know today was born.

Elegant **Barbaresco**, 'the prince of wines', is also made of Nebbiolo and grown south of the Tanaro in an even smaller area than Barolo. For years, in fact, all the Nebbiolo grapes grown here were sold to make Barolo – until 1894 when Domizio Cavazza, a resident of Barbaresco and the head of the Royal Oenological School of Alba, decided the difference in the grapes grown in the two zones was distinct enough for Barbaresco to be sold under its own label. Cavazza founded the first cooperative or *Cantine Sociali* of nine growers and, although the Fascists closed it down in the 1930s as not conforming to the rules of the corporate state, it was revived in 1958 as the *Produttori del Barbaresco*, which now has some 60 members and has been praised as a model in Robert Parker's *Wine Advocate* 'for setting some of the highest standards of wine making for any cooperative in the world'; in exceptional years, the *Produttori* also produces nine single vineyard wines from classic growing areas. Grapes that don't measure up to Barbaresco go into a lighter, less complex (and less expensive) Nebbiolo Langhe DOC, which is released earlier on the market. Barbaresco is generally less powerful than Barolo (which can reach 16% alcohol) and is generally drinkable after three or four years; it's recommended for rich dishes, roasts and liver dishes.

Third on the list of giants is **Nebbiolo** (11.5–13.5%), grown north of the Tanaro, dry and a bit lighter again and recommended for white meats, grills or fondues. In between these three growing areas comes Barbera (12–14%), made from the greater-yielding Barbera grape; it's also grown near Asti and in Alessandria province. A full-bodied wine, it takes four years in wood, and can be drunk shortly thereafter; try it with roasts, game and strong cheeses. Further south, where altitudes are higher, the grape is **Dolcetto**, the 'little sweetie', a quick ripener, although the red wine it makes is dry, dark red and lighter bodied, good with roasts, cold meats and chicken. The sixth variety grown near the Tanaro is white **Moscato d'Asti**, a golden dessert wine made from muscat; the *frizzante* version is the well-known **Asti Spumante**.

There are good wines from other pockets of Piedmont, many of which are making a comeback after decades of neglect. From Monferrato come ruby-red **Freisa**, with a raspberry aftertaste (good with first courses) and the slightly nutty garnet **Grignolino** (excellent with *bollito misto*); velvety, tannin-filled **Gattinara**, made from Nebbiolo grapes north of Novara, is also best when aged and served with meats with strong sauces. **Ghemme** is its lighter version, a mix of Nebbiolo and Bonarda, recommended with game dishes. **Carema**, these days a rather fashionable wine grown in a tiny area north of Ivrea, is a Nebbiolo that can have a good deal of finesse and reach 13.5% – it comes either Classico, Riserva or Barricato (in the cask); rarer, tannic **Bramaterra** needs 18 months in the cask; **Brachetto** is a sweet rose-scented red dessert wine from near Turin. Nebbiolo grapes are grown in Aosta's sunnier valleys as well; the best-known wine is **Donnaz**, popular with pasta dishes. And there's **Vin de l'Enfer**, Hell's wine, grown towards Mont Blanc at 3,800ft – named not for its taste, but the heat reflected from the rocks that enables the grapes to ripen.

There are a few **white wines**, too: dry, slightly effervescent **Erbaluce** ('light of grass'), good with soups and *antipasti,* and the sweet, aged dessert wine **Passito di Caluso** of the Canavese; **Gavi di Gavi** and **Cortese**, grown south of Alessandria, both light wines good with fish, and the punchier **Roero Arneis**, which can reach 13%.

Much of the neutral white wine grown in Piedmont (and in Sicily, Emilia-Romagna and Puglia) are destined for a special fate. In 1786, Benedetto Carpano changed the history of drink when he invented Italian **vermouth** ('wormwood' in German) in Turin, and the city, with its access to Alpine herbs, remains Italy's top producer: Carpano still bottles the popular bittersweet Punt e Mes (its name was born when a financier in Turin, exhausted by his day's work, flopped into his seat in a café and shouted out 'Point and a half!' instead of 'vermouth'). The competition, Martini & Rossi and Cinzano, are known around the world for their classic dry *bianco* and popular reddish elixir (made red not from the grapes, but from caramelized sugar).

Aosta makes its own excellent **grappa** and *genepì*, an 80% grappa steeped in the herby yellow flowers of *Artemisia genipi* and *Artemisia glacialis*. Add a good shot of both of these to coffee, orange peel and sugar and heat, and you have the Valdostano classic winter warmer, the 'cup of friendship' or *Coppa dell'Amicizia*, served in a traditional wood-carved, multi-spouted *grolla*, which they say is named and modelled after the Holy Grail, hidden in Aosta's mountains.

Italian Menu Reader

Antipasti

These before-meal treats can include almost anything; the most common include:

antipasto misto mixed *antipasto*
bruschetta garlic toast (often with tomatoes)
carciofi (sott'olio) artichokes (in oil)
frutti di mare seafood
funghi (trifolati) mushrooms (with anchovies, garlic and lemon)
gamberi ai fagioli prawns (shrimps) with white beans
mozzarella (in carrozza) cow or buffalo cheese (fried with bread in batter)
prosciutto (con melone) cured ham (with melon)
salsicce sausages

Minestre (Soups) and Pasta

These dishes are the principal first courses (*primi*) served throughout Italy.

agnolotti ravioli with meat
cacciucco spiced fish soup
cappelletti small ravioli, often in broth
crespelle crêpes
fettuccine long strips of pasta
frittata omelette
gnocchi potato dumplings
minestra di verdura thick vegetable soup
minestrone soup with meat, vegetables and pasta
orecchiette ear-shaped pasta
panzerotti ravioli filled with mozzarella, anchovies and egg
pasta e fagioli soup with beans, bacon and tomatoes
pastina in brodo tiny pasta in broth
penne all'arrabbiata quill-shaped pasta with tomatoes and hot peppers
polenta cake or a kind of savoury pudding of corn semolina
risotto (alla Milanese) risotto (served with saffron)
spaghetti all'Amatriciana with spicy sauce of salt pork, tomatoes, onions and chilli
spaghetti alla Bolognese with minced/ground meat, ham, mushrooms, etc.
spaghetti alla carbonara with bacon, eggs and black pepper
spaghetti al pomodoro with tomato sauce
spaghetti al sugo/ragù with meat sauce
spaghetti alle vongole with clam sauce
stracciatella broth with eggs and cheese
tagliatelle flat egg noodles
tortellini al pomodoro/panna/in brodo small pasta parcels filled with meat and cheese with tomato sauce/with cream/in broth

Carne (Meat)

abbacchio milk-fed lamb
agnello lamb
anatra duck
animelle sweetbreads
arista pork loin
arrosto misto mixed roast meats
bocconcini veal fried with ham and cheese
bollito misto stew of boiled meats
braciola chop
brasato di manzo braised beef with vegetables
bresaola dried raw meat
capretto kid
capriolo roebuck
carne di castrato/suino mutton/pork
carpaccio thin slices of raw beef served with a piquant sauce
cassoeula winter stew with pork and cabbage
cervello (al burro nero) brains (in black butter sauce)
cervo venison
cinghiale boar
coniglio rabbit
cotoletta (alla milanese/alla bolognese) veal cutlet (fried in breadcrumbs/with ham and cheese)
fagiano pheasant
faraona guinea fowl
fegato alla veneziana liver (usually of veal) with filling
involtini sliced, stuffed slices of meat
lepre (in salmi) hare (marinated in wine)
lingua tongue
lombo di maiale pork loin
lumache snails
maiale (al latte) pork (cooked in milk)
manzo beef
osso buco braised veal knuckle with herbs
pajata calf's or lamb's intestines
pancetta rolled pork
pernice partridge
petto di pollo (sorpresa) boned chicken breast (stuffed and deep-fried)
piccione pigeon
pizzaiola beef steak with tomato and oregano sauce
pollo (alla cacciatora/alla diavola/alla Marengo) chicken (with tomatoes and mushrooms, grilled/fried with garlic and wine)
polpette meatballs
ragù meat sauce
rane frogs
rognoni kidneys
saltimbocca veal escalope with prosciutto, sage, wine, butter
scaloppine thin slices of veal sautéed in butter
spezzatino beef or veal pieces, usually stewed
spiedino meat on a skewer or stick

stracotto slow-cooked beef with wine, herbs and vegetables
stufato beef in white wine with vegetables
tacchino turkey
uccelletti small birds on a skewer
vitello veal
zampone pig's trotter

Pesce (Fish)

acciughe or *alici* anchovies
anguilla eel
aragosta lobster
aringa herring
baccalà dried salt cod
bonito small tuna
branzino sea bass
brodetto fish stew
calamari squid
cappesante scallops
cefalo grey mullet
coda di rospo angler fish
cozze mussels
dorato gilthead
fritto misto mixed fried delicacies, mainly fish
gamberetto shrimp
gamberi prawns
gamberi di fiume crayfish
granchio crab
insalata di mare seafood salad
lampreda lamprey
merluzzo cod
nasello hake
orata bream
ostriche oysters
pesce azzurro various small fish
pesce di San Pietro John Dory
pesce spada swordfish
polipi/polpi octopus
rombo turbot
sarde sardines
seppie cuttlefish
sgombro mackerel
sogliola sole
squadro monkfish
stoccafisso wind-dried cod
tonno tuna
triglia red mullet (rouget)
trota trout
trota salmonata salmon trout
vongole small clams
zuppa di pesce mixed fish in sauce or stew

Contorni (Side Dishes, Vegetables)

aglio garlic
asparagi alla fiorentina asparagus with fried eggs
broccoli broccoli
capperi capers
carciofi (alla giudea) (deep-fried) artichokes

cardi cardoons/thistles
carote carrots
cavolfiore cauliflower
cavolo cabbage
ceci chickpeas/garbanzo beans
cetriolo cucumber
cipolla onion
fagioli white beans
fagiolini French (green) beans
fave broad beans
finocchio fennel
funghi (porcini) mushrooms (boletus)
insalata (mista/verde) salad (mixed/green)
lattuga lettuce
lenticchie lentils
melanzane aubergine/eggplant
patate potatoes
patate fritte chips, French fries
peperoncini hot chilli peppers
peperoni sweet peppers
peperonata stew of peppers, onions, etc.
piselli (al prosciutto) peas (with ham)
pomodoro(i) tomato(es)
porri leeks
radicchio red chicory
radice radish
rapa turnip
rucola rocket
sedano celery
spinaci spinach
verdure greens
zucca pumpkin
zucchini courgettes

Formaggio (Cheese)

Bel Paese a soft white cow's cheese
cacio/caciocavallo pale yellow, sharp cheese
caprino goat's cheese
fontina rich cow's milk cheese
gorgonzola soft blue cheese
groviera mild cheese (gruyère)
mozzarella soft cheese
parmigiano Parmesan cheese
pecorino sharp sheep's cheese
provolone sharp, tangy; *dolce* is less strong
ricotta creamy white cheese
stracchino soft white cheese

Frutta (Fruit, Nuts)

albicocche apricots
ananas pineapple
arance oranges
banane bananas
ciliege cherries
cocomero watermelon
datteri dates
fichi figs
fragole (con panna) strawberries (with cream)
lamponi raspberries

limone lemon
macedonia di frutta fruit salad
mandarino tangerine
mandorle almonds
melagrana pomegranate
mele apples
more blackberries
nocciole hazelnuts
noci walnuts
pera pear
pesca peach
pesca noce nectarine
pinoli pine nuts
pompelmo grapefruit
prugna/susina prune/plum
uva grapes

Dolci (Desserts)

amaretti macaroons
cannoli crisp pastry tubes filled with ricotta, cream, chocolate or fruit
coppa gelato assorted ice cream
crema caramella caramel-topped custard
crostata fruit flan
gelato ice cream
granita water ice, usually lemon or coffee
panettone sponge cake with candied fruit
panforte dense cake of chocolate, almonds and preserved fruit
saint honoré meringue cake
semifreddo refrigerated dessert
sorbetto sorbet/sherbet
spumone a soft ice cream
tiramisù layers of sponge, mascarpone, coffee and chocolate
torrone nougat
torta cake, tart
torta millefoglie layered pastry and custard cream
zabaglione hot dessert made with eggs and Marsala wine
zuppa inglese trifle

Bevande (Beverages)

acqua minerale mineral water
   con/senza gas sparkling/still
aranciata orange soda
birra (alla spina) beer (draught)
caffè coffee
caffè freddo iced coffee
caffè macchiato espresso with a drop of milk
cioccolata calda hot chocolate
cioccolata con panna chocolate with cream
gassosa lemon-flavoured soda
ghiaccio ice
granita iced drink (with fruit or coffee)
latte milk
latte macchiato milk with a drop of coffee
latte (intero/scremato) milk (whole/skimmed)

limonata lemon soda
spumante sparkling wine
succo di frutta fruit juice
tè tea
tè freddo tea (sweet, iced)
tonica tonic water
vino (rosso/bianco/rosato) wine (red/white/rosé)

Snacks

biscotti biscuits
caramelle sweets, candy
cioccolato chocolate
grissini bread sticks
patatine crisps/potato chips
pizzetta small pizza with cheese and tomato

Cooking Terms (Miscellaneous)

aceto (balsamico) vinegar (balsamic)
affumicato smoked
aglio garlic
alla brace on embers
bicchiere glass
burro butter
cacciagione game
conto bill
coltello knife
cucchiaio spoon
forchetta fork
forno oven
fritto fried
griglia grill
in bianco without tomato
magro lean meat/pasta without meat
marmellata jam
menta mint
miele honey
mostarda candied mustard sauce
olio oil
pane bread
pane tostato toasted bread
panini sandwiches (in rolls)
panna cream
pepe pepper
piatto plate
prezzemolo parsley
ripieno stuffed
rosmarino rosemary
sale salt
salmì wine marinade
salsa sauce
senape mustard
tartufi truffles
tavola table
tazza cup
tovagliolo napkin
umido cooked in sauce
uovo egg
zucchero sugar

Planning
Your Trip

When to Go 64
  Climate 64
  Festivals 65
Tourist Information 65
Embassies and Consulates 66
Entry Formalities 66
Disabled Travellers 67
Insurance and EHIC Cards 67
Maps and Publications 67
Money and Banks 67
Getting There 68
  By Air 68
  By Train 69
  By Coach 69
  By Car 69
Getting Around 70
  By Train 70
  By Coach 71
  By Car 71
  By Motorcycle or Bicycle 72
Where to Stay 72
Tour Operators 74

06

When to Go

Climate

Protected from winds and cold by the Maritime Alps, Liguria enjoys the mildest **winter** climate in Italy, with the warmest temperatures in sheltered Alassio and Bordighera. While the coast gets moderate rain, the mountains just behind get buckets of water and snow. This is a good time to visit Genoa, with music and opera seasons in full swing.

Winters are considerably colder up in Piedmont and Aosta: in a normal year the Alpine ski resorts operate from December to April. Snow is not unusual in Turin but, as in Genoa, winter is a good time to visit for the museums and cultural life: just be sure to bundle up. The truffles at Le Langhe and Monferrato are at their best in December and attract knowing gourmets. Carnival in February is another reason to come, especially to orange-slinging Ivrea (*see* pp.331–2).

Spring, especially April to June, is a lovely time to visit – warm but not too crowded: the famous gardens in Liguria and on Lake Maggiore are at their best; walking and cycling are a delight; the mountain meadows are covered with wild flowers in May and June, and it's warm enough to swim or at least sunbathe on the Riviera.

Summer is high season on the Riviera and the Lakes. Accommodation is at a premium, and the traffic on the few roads, especially the Via Aurelia, tends to get bottled up. There are lots of music festivals and fireworks, and the beaches are packed, especially in August, when most Italians take their holidays; the cities can seem deserted (and their best restaurants tend to close). Temperatures can stay in the high 30s °C (90s °F) for days, even in Aosta. It's cooler in the mountains, where many resorts, especially Courmayeur, have a summer season for walkers and cyclists.

Autumn can be lovely, and it is the high season in southern Piedmont's Le Langhe and Monferrato regions, for the colours of the vines, festivals and delicious specialities. The weather is mild, places aren't crowded, and you can swim off the coast into September. In recent years, however, Liguria has been subject to tempestuous autumn rains and floods. By December, mountain villages only 16km from the sea can be snowed in.

Calendar of Events

January

Jan–July Opera and ballet season: Genoa and Turin.

Closest Sun to 20 San Sebastiano, ancient processions at Dolceacqua.

Late Feb–early Mar Festival of Italian Popular Song, San Remo; also parade of floats covered with flowers in *San Remo in fiore*.

31 Sant'Orso Fair Aosta.

February

Early Feb *Festa dei Furgari*, in Taggia, celebrating the town's near-miraculous escape from the Saracen invaders with a heady mixture of fireworks, bonfires and historical costumes. Mimosa festival, Pieve Ligure.

Carnival Historic carnival and battle of oranges in Ivrea; masked balls in the historic palaces along Via Garibaldi, Genoa; also the ancient Baio in Sampeyre and villages in the Saluzzo valleys.

March

March–April Holy Week celebrations, with processions, especially in Genoa and Savona: on Good Friday marchers bear floats of heavy sculptured figures of the Passion dating from the 17th century.

Easter Week Antique market in the streets, Sarzana.

19 San Giuseppe street fair, La Spezia.

April

End month Sword dancing, San Giorio.

May

All month *Città delle Donne*, women's month-long festival, with sports, theatre, culture and more dedicated to women, Varazze.

2nd week Turin International Book Fair

2nd Sun *Sagra del Pesce*, fish festival at Camogli, including an enormous fry-up in a giant frying pan, served to all-comers.

4th Sun *Focaccia* festival, Recco.

Pentecost *Festa della Barca*, Baiardo.

June

Historical Regatta of the Four Ancient Maritime Republics (Pisa, Venice, Amalfi and Genoa), in Genoa every four years (next one 2008). Battle of Flowers, Ventimiglia. Festival of ethnic music, Alassio. Eating races, Cavour.

Mid-month Re-enactment of the Battle of Marengo, in even-numbered years.

23–4 St John's Day celebrations in Genoa, Celle Ligure, Laigueglia and Turin, with an enormous bonfire and lights on the sea.

29 Festival of the Sea, Alassio, including a procession of boats decked with flowers.

Corpus Domini *Infiorate* – patterns in the streets made with flowers – at Diano Marina, Monterosso and Sassello.

July

Ballet festival, Nervi. International harp festival, Isolabona. *Sagra delle Rose*, Pogli (Ortovero, near Albenga). *Festa del Marchesato*, Finale. Mediterranean festival, Porto Antico, Genoa. Jazz festival, in Turin and the towns of the Golfo di Paradiso.

July and Aug International Chamber Music Festival, Cervo. Arts festival, Villa Faraldi (above San Bartolomeo al Mare). Cabaret, Loano. Classical music concerts, San Fruttuoso.

Early July Garlic festival, Vessalico. Re-enactment of a pirate attack, with music, flowers and dancing, Ceriale.

2 Procession of the Madonna, Loano.

3rd Sun Festival of Mary Magdalene, complete with a Dance of Death, Taggia; *Autani dei Sette Fratelli*, age-old procession, Cheggio.

Last Sun Festivals of lights on the sea, Arma di Taggia. Landing of the Saracens, Laigueglia.

August

All month *Agosto medievale*, Ventimiglia, with costumes, medieval music and other events. Bathtub races, Diano Marina. Election of Miss Muretto, Alassio. Festival of classical ballet in the caves, Toirano. International piano competitions, Finale Ligure.

1st Sat Festival of little fish, wine and bread, all in abundance, Ospedaletti.

1st Sun Festival of the Sea, La Spezia. *Stella Maris* nautical procession, Camogli.

2nd Sun Historical regatta, Ventimiglia. *Palio del Golfo* rowing regatta, La Spezia.

14 *Torta dei Fieschi*, Lavagna: historical re-enactment of a 13th-century wedding, featuring a massive cake.

15 Sea festival, Diano Marina. Big traditional festival at the Madonna della Costa, San Remo. Huge fireworks over the bay, Alassio.

Last week Sept Big musical festival, Stesa. Festa di San Vito, with fireworks, Omega.

September

Antique yacht and sailboat regatta, every other year, Imperia. *Regatta dei Rioni*, Noli. Humour festival, Bordighera. Classical music festival, 'Settembre musica', Turin.

7–8 Fire festival, Recco.

2nd–3rd weekend *Douja d'Or* food festival and Palio in Asti (*see* p.285–6).

October

The *Rassegna Tenco*, international festival of songwriters who sing, San Remo. Finals of the *Batailles des Reines*, Aosta.

1st weekend *Man in the Iron Mask* celebrations, Pinerolo. Donkey palio, Alba, beginning of a month-long truffle festival.

3rd week Huge boat show, Genoa.

November

International Film Festival and *Luci d'Artista* illuminations, till mid-Jan, both in Turin.

December

Rassegna della ceramica, big exhibition of ceramics, at Albisola. National pianists' competition, Albenga.

13 Santa Lucia, Savona.

Mid-Dec Ligurian crafts fair, Genoa.

Festivals

Liguria, Piedmont and Aosta are festival mad and hold events throughout the year, including some that are of ancient origin; only the most important of these are listed above or this book would be as fat as a phone directory.

Every *comune* has at least one festival honouring a patron saint, and a relaxed little village *festa* can be just as enjoyable as (or more so than) the big national crowd pullers. Historic re-enactments are big everywhere (any excuse to dress up in those gorgeous costumes), and Piedmont in particular holds festivals dedicated to food, especially in autumn. **Always check tourist offices for precise dates.**

Tourist Information

Italian tourist offices usually stay open from 8am to 12.30 or 1pm, and 3–7pm, possibly longer in summer. Few of them are open on Saturday afternoons or Sundays; smaller ones close down altogether out of season.

UK: 1 Princes St, London W1B 9AY, t 800 0048 2542, *www.italiantouristboard.co.uk.*

USA: 630 Fifth Ave, Suite 1565, New York, NY 10111, t (212) 245 4822; 12400 Wilshire Blvd, Suite 550, Los Angeles, CA 90025, t (310) 820 1898; 500 N. Michigan Ave, Suite 2240, Chicago 1, IL 60611, t (312) 644 0996.

Australia: Level 4, 46 Market Street, Sydney, NSW 2000, t (02) 92 621 666.

Canada: 175 Bloor St E, Suite 907, Toronto, Ontario, M4W 3R8 t (416) 925 4882, *www.italiantourism.com.*

Embassies and Consulates

Foreign Embassies in Italy

UK, Via San Paolo 7, Milan, t (02) 723 001 (consulate); Via XX Settembre 80/a, Rome, t (06) 42 20 001 (embassy).

Ireland, Piazza di Campitelli 3, Rome, t (06) 697 9121 (embassy).

USA, Via Principe Amedeo 2/10, Milan, t (02) 290 351 (consulate); Via V. Veneto 121, Rome, t (06) 46 741 (embassy).

Canada, Via Vittor Pisani 19, Milan, t (02) 67581 (consulate); Via Zara 30, t (06) 445 981, Rome (embassy).

Australia, Via Borgona 2, Milan, t (02) 777 041 (consulate); Via Alessandria 215, Rome, t (06) 852 721 (embassy).

New Zealand, Via Guido d'Arezzo 6, Milan, t (02) 4801 2544 (consulate); Via Zara 28, Rome, t (06) 441 7171 (embassy).

Italian Embassies Abroad

UK: 38 Eaton Place, London SW1X 8AN, t (020) 7235 9371; 14 Three Kings Yard, London W1K 4EH, t (020) 7312 2200; 32 Melville St, Edinburgh EH3 7HA, t (0131) 226 3631, *www. embitaly.org.uk.*

Ireland: 63–5 Northumberland Rd, Dublin, t (01) 660 1744, *www.ambdublino.esteri.it*; 7 Richmond Park, Belfast, t (02890) 668 854.

USA: 690 Park Ave, New York, NY, t (212) 439 8600, *www.italconsulnyc.org*; 12400 Wilshire Boulevard, Suite 300, Los Angeles, CA, t (310) 820 0622.

Canada: 1100–510 West Hastings St, Vancouver V6B 1L8, t 1-604 684 7288, *http://consvancouver.esteri.it.*

Australia: Level 45, The Gateway Building, 1 Macquarie Place, Circular Quay, Sydney 2000, NSW, t (02) 9392 7939, *www. conssydney.esteri.it.*

New Zealand: PO Box 463, 34 Grant Rd, Thorndon, Wellington, t (04) 473 5339, *www. italy-embassy.org.nz.*

Entry Formalities

Passports

EU nationals with a valid passport can enter and stay in Italy as long as they like. Citizens of the USA, Canada, Australia and New Zealand need only a valid passport to stay 90 days.

By law you should register with the police within eight days of your arrival in Italy. In practice this is done automatically when you check into your first hotel. Don't be alarmed if the owner of a self-catering property proposes to 'denounce' you to the police when you arrive – it's just a formality.

Non-EU citizens who mean to stay longer than 90 days have to get a *permesso di soggiorno.* For this you will need to state your reason for staying and be able to prove a source of income and medical insurance. After a couple of exasperating days at some provincial Questura office filling out forms, you should walk out with your permit.

Customs

Those over the age of 17 arriving from another **EU country** do not have to declare goods imported into Italy for personal use if they have paid duty on them in the country of origin. In theory, you can buy as much as you like, provided you can prove the purchase is for your own use and not for other purposes (e.g. selling on to friends). In practice, customs will be more likely to ask questions if you buy in bulk, e.g. more than 3,200 cigarettes or 400 cigarillos, 200 cigars or 3kg of tobacco; plus 10 litres of spirits, 90 litres of wine and 110 litres of beer. Travellers caught importing any of the above for resale will have the goods seized along with the vehicle they travelled in, and could face imprisonment for up to seven years.

Travellers from **outside the EU** must pay duty on goods worth more than €175 that they import into Italy.

Travellers from the USA are allowed to bring home, duty-free, goods to the value of $400, including 200 cigarettes or 100 cigars; plus one litre of alcohol. For more information, call the US Customs Service. You're not allowed to bring back absinthe or Cuban cigars. Canadians can bring home $300 worth of goods in a year, plus their tobacco and alcohol allowances.

Disabled Travellers

Although things are steadily improving, the geography of Liguria and many Alpine villages will always make large areas difficult for wheelchairs, although the coastal resorts and most of Genoa, Turin and the larger towns in Piedmont and Aosta should pose few problems. The Italian tourist office can also advise on hotels, museums with ramps

Disability Organizations

In the UK

RADAR, 12 City Forum, 250 City Rd, London EC1V 8AF, **t** (020) 7250 3222, *www.radar.org.uk*. Information/books about travelling abroad.
Holiday Care Service, 7th floor, Sunley House, 4 Bedford Park, Croydon, CR0 2AP, **t** 0845 124 9971, *www.holidaycare.org.uk*. A charity that disseminates information to holiday-makers.
Can be Done, **t** (020) 8907 2400, *www. canbedone.co.uk*. Specialist holidays.

In the USA and Canada

See also *www.disabilitytravel.com*.
Alternative Leisure Co, 165 Middlesex Turnpike, Suite 206, Bedford, MA 01730, **t** (781) 275 0023, *www.alctrips.com*. Specialist in vacations for disabled people.
Mobility International USA, PO Box 10767, 132 E. Broadway, Suite 343, Eugene, OR 97401, USA, **t**/TTY (541) 343 1284, *www.miusa.org*. International educational exchange programmes as well as volunteer service overseas for the disabled.
SATH (Society for Accessible Travel and Hospitality), 347 5th Avenue, Suite 605, New York NY 10016, **t** (212) 447 7284, *www.sath.org*. Provides travel and access information.
Emerging Horizons, *www.emerginghorizons. com*. An online travel newsletter.

and so on. Once in Italy, call the CO. IN. Sociale, **t** 800 271 027 (freephone), *www.coin sociale.it* for advice on accommodation and travel, or see *www.italiapertutti.it/english/ regioni.asp* or *www.accessibleeurope.com*.

Insurance and EHIC Cards

You can insure yourself against almost any mishap – cancelled flights, stolen or lost baggage and ill health. Check policies you hold to see if they cover you while abroad, and judge whether you need a special **traveller's insurance** policy.

The E111 forms for EU nationals have been replaced by the **European Health Insurance Card** (EHIC) that will give the bearer access to the state health care scheme and public hospitals in all EU countries. Like the old system, the card is available for UK residents for free at post offices or online at *www. ehic.org.uk*. Unlike the E111 forms, you'll need to apply for a card for every member of the family (you'll need passports and national insurance numbers). The EHIC must be stamped and signed to be valid, and the card must be renewed every five years.

Australia has a reciprocal health care scheme with Italy, but New Zealand, Canada and the USA do not. If you already have health insurance, a student card or a credit card, you may be entitled to some medical cover abroad.

Maps and Publications

In addition to the maps in this guide, motorists in particular may want to invest in a regional map of Liguria and Piedmont/ Aosta. The green Touring Club Italiano maps (1:200,000) are excellent. In the UK, you can buy them online at *www.stanfords.co.uk*; in the US through *www.globecorner.com*.

Money and Banks

The wide acceptance of credit cards and ATM machines (*Bancomats*) make them by far the most convenient option, although there are a few things to note. Although it's always wise to have some cash on hand, you'll probably come out ahead by using your card to pay when you can, rather than taking out loads of cash from the machine and paying the percentage/commission charges. On the other hand, note that some British credit cards may lack the microchip required to work automatic machines such as petrol station pumps. Also note that, to prevent fraud, your credit card company may (much to your embarrassment!) refuse payment in an Italian shop because it's an 'unusual' purchase that deviates from your normal buying habits; it may be wise to let your bank know that you are travelling abroad and may be doing some 'unusual' purchasing.

Getting There

By Air

The international airports serving the region are Cristoforo Colombo in Genoa, t 010 601 5461, www.airport.genova.it, and Sandro Pertini/Caselle in Turin, t 011 5676 362,

www.aeroportoditorino.it, served on direct flights by Ryanair, easyJet and British Airways. In general the earlier you book, the cheaper the flight.

If you're visiting the western Riviera or western Piedmont, also consider Nice (t 33 (0) 4 89 88 98 28), served by a wide variety of charter and scheduled flights **from the UK and Ireland**; besides the frequent coastal trains you can also pick up the scenic train over the Maritime Alps to Cuneo. For Lake Maggiore and eastern Piedmont, Milan Malpensa (t 02 74 8522 00) has direct links to UK airports and is connected to Genoa and Turin by frequent trains. Neither is Pisa airport far (t 050 849300), with plenty of scheduled flights and charters if you plan to visit the eastern end of the Riviera.

Charter flights are available to popular destinations; check listing at www.charter-flights.co.uk. You may find cheaper fares by

Airline Carriers

UK and Ireland
Alitalia, t 0870 544 8259, www.alitalia.co.uk.
British Airways, t 0870 850 9850, www.britishairways.com.
Aer Lingus, reservations t 0818 36 50 00 (Ireland); t 0870 87 65 000 (UK), www.aerlingus.com.
easyJet, t 0905 821 0905, www.easyjet.com.
Ryanair, t 0871 246 0000 (UK); t 0818 30 30 30 (Ireland), www.ryanair.com.

USA and Canada
Alitalia, (USA) t 800 223 5730, www.alitaliausa.com; (Canada) t 800 361 8336, www.alitalia.ca.
Continental, t 800 231 0856, www.continental.com.
Delta, t 800 241 4141, www.delta.com.
Air Canada, t 888 247 2262, www.aircanada.com.
American, t 800 433 7300, www.aa.com.

Charters, Discounts, Students and Special Deals

UK and Ireland
Budget Travel, 134 Lower Baggot St, Dublin 2, t (01) 631 1111, www.budgettravel.ie.
Club Travel, 30 Lower Abbey St, Dublin 1, t (01) 500 5555, within Eire, www.clubtravel.ie.

Europe Student Travel, 6 Campden St, London W8, t (020) 7727 7647. A small travel agent catering to non-students too.
STA, 52 Grosvenor Gardens, London SW1W, www.statravel.co.uk, t 0871 2300 040, with 51 branches throughout the UK.
Trailfinders, 194 Kensington High St, London W8, t 0845 050 5945, www.trailfinders.com.
United Travel, 2 Old Dublin Rd, Stillorgan, County Dublin, t (01) 215 9300, www.unitedtravel.ie.

Websites (UK and Ireland)
www.aboutflights.co.uk (t 0870 330 7311)
www.cheapflights.co.uk
www.ebookers.com
www.expedia.co.uk
www.flyaow.com
www.lastminute.com
www.majortravel.co.uk
www.opodo.co.uk
www.sky-tours.co.uk
www.traveljungle.co.uk
www.travellersweb.com
www.travelocity.com
www.travelselect.com

USA and Canada
If you're resilient, flexible and/or youthful and prepared to shop around for budget deals on stand-bys or even courier flights (you can usually only take hand luggage on the latter), you should be able to get yourself some rock-bottom prices. Check the Yellow Pages for courier

companies. For discounted flights, try the small ads in newspaper travel pages (for example, *New York Times*, *Chicago Tribune*, and *Toronto Globe and Mail*). Numerous travel clubs and agencies also specialize in discount fares, but they may require you to pay an annual membership fee. See *www.traveldiscounts.com* and *www.smartertravel.com*.

Airhitch, *www.airhitch.org*. Last-minute discount tickets to Europe.

Last Minute Travel Club, (USA/Canada), t 800 442 0568, *www.lastminutetravel.com*. Annual membership entitles you to cheap stand-by deals, special car rental rates in Europe and deals on train passes.

STA, *www.statravel.com*, with branches at most universities and at 2871 Broadway, New York, NY, t (212) 865 2700, and ASUC Building, 1st Floor, Berkeley, CA 94720, t (510) 642 3000.

Travel Cuts, 187 College St, Toronto, Ontario ON M5T 1P7, t (888) FLY CUTS (toll free) or t (416) 979 2406 from the USA, *www.travelcuts.com*. Canada's largest student travel specialists, with six offices plus one in New York.

Websites (USA and Canada)
www.eurovacations.com
www.expedia.com
www.flights.com
www.orbitz.com
www.priceline.com (bid for tickets)
www.smartertravel.com
www.traveldiscounts.com
www.travelocity.com

combing the ads in the travel pages of Sunday papers. Take good travel insurance, however cheap your ticket is.

The main air gateways for direct flights **from North America** are Milan Malpensa and Nice (*see* above): Alitalia, American, Delta and Continental fly from a number of cities. From Canada, Air Canada and Alitalia operate from Toronto and Montreal. Trawl the internet well in advance and you may pick up a good deal. For discounted flights, check the small ads in newspaper travel pages.

By Train

A train journey to Italy used to be something of a nightmare, involving ferries and station changes, and taking around 16 hours. Today, taking a Eurostar to Paris your journey time could be reduced by as much as four hours depending on your destination. It may well be worth looking into the bewildering variety of discounts and passes on offer, though if you are just planning to visit Liguria and Piedmont, inclusive **rail passes** are a waste of money. Fares on Italy's trains are among the lowest in Europe. For domestic rail passes available in Italy, see 'Getting Around', p.70.

Rail Europe, UK t 08708 371 371, *www.raileurope.co.uk*; USA t 1 888 382 7245, *www.raileurope.com*; Canada t 1-800 361 7245, *www.raileurope.com/canada*.

Rail Choice, UK t 0870 165 7300, *www.railchoice.com*.

By Coach

Eurolines coaches are booked in the UK through National Express, t 08705 80 80 80, *www.nationalexpress.com*. There are regular services to Turin and Genoa. Needless to say, the journey is long: 21 hours to Turin, 25 to Genoa. Book in advance, though, and you may get a good deal, such as £71–92 return to Genoa or Turin.

By Car

Driving from London is a rather lengthy and expensive proposition. If you're only staying for a short period, check costs against fly-drive schemes. Liguria is the best part of 20 hours' driving time from the UK, even if you stick to fast toll roads. On the other hand, now that the Mont Blanc tunnel has reopened, it's only 850km from Calais to Courmayeur, on a scenic and fairly hassle-free route. If you pass through Switzerland, expect to pay for the privilege (around £17 for motorway use); neither are the big tunnels under the Alps cheap (one-way tolls range from about €22–62 per car). You can avoid some of the driving by putting your car on the train, though this is expensive too. Express Sleeper Cars run to Milan from Paris or Boulogne.

To bring a GB-registered car into Italy, you need a vehicle registration document, full driving licence and insurance papers – these must be carried at all times. Non-EU citizens should preferably have an international driving licence. A red triangular hazard sign is obligatory; also recommended are a spare set of bulbs, a first-aid kit and a fire extinguisher. Foreign-plated cars are no longer entitled to free breakdown assistance from the Italian Auto Club (ACI), but their prices are fair. For more information on breakdown cover in Italy contact the **AA, t** 0800 085 2840, *www.theaa.com*, or **RAC, t** 0800 015 6000, *www.rac.co.uk*.

Getting Around

Italy has an excellent network of railways, highways and byways, and you'll find getting around fairly easy – until one union or another takes it into its head to go on strike. There's talk about passing a law to regulate strikes, but it won't happen soon, if ever. Instead, learn to recognize the word in Italian: *sciopero* (SHO-per-o), and do as the Italians do – quiver with resignation. There's always a day or two's notice, and strikes usually only last a day (long enough to throw a spanner in the works if you have a plane to catch). Keep your ears open and watch for notices posted in the stations – rail strikes are so well organized that schedules for reduced services will be posted in advance.

To encourage the use of public transport, the Piedmont region has a toll-free number, **t** 800 333 444 (daily 7am to 9pm), and a website, *www.regione.piemonte.it/ptplweb/index.do*, waiting to tell you how to get from A to B.

By Train

Trenitalia information from anywhere in Italy: **t** 89 20 21; *www.trenitalia.com*.

Italy's national railway, Trenitalia, is well run, inexpensive and often a pleasure to ride. There are also several private rail lines; these may not accept Interail or Eurail passes. Possible unpleasantnesses you may encounter, besides a strike, are delays, crowding (especially at weekends), and crime on overnight trains, where someone goes through your bags while you sleep. The crowding, at least, is less of a problem if you reserve a seat in advance (*fare una prenotazione*); the fee is small and can save you hours standing in a train corridor. Otherwise tickets are valid for two months from the day they're purchased.

There is a fairly straightforward hierarchy of trains. At the bottom of the pyramid is the humble *Regionale* which often stops even where there's no station in sight; it can be excruciatingly slow. When you're checking the schedules, beware of what may look like the first train to go to your destination – if it's a *Regionale*, it may be the last to arrive. A *Diretto* or *Interregionale* stops far less. The kings of the rails, Intercity, Intercity Plus and Eurostar Italia trains whoosh between the big cities. These services require a supplement – some 30% more than a regular fare. Reservations are free, but must be made at least five hours before the trip. Eurostars tend to be considerably more expensive than Intercity trains, which are almost as fast; note that travelling by 1st-class Intercity is nicer than going by 2nd-class Eurostar.

Tickets may be purchased not only in the stations, at counters and big yellow machines, but at travel agents in the city centres. For Intercity, Intercity plus and Eurostar Italia trains the easiest way to buy a ticket is via the Trenitalia website – you'll receive a reservation code number and details of your seat and reservation to print out and show the conductor, who will give you a receipt/ticket.

Local tickets (Genoa to Savona, say) can be bought at newsagents and tobacconists near the stations (ask for *biglietti a fascia chilometrica* and tell them your destination, and they'll know how much to charge). Be sure you ask which platform (*binario*) your train arrives at; the permanent boards in the stations are not always correct. Always stamp your ticket (*convalidare*) in the not-very-obvious machines at the head of the platform before boarding the train. Failure to do so could result in a fine. If you get on a train without a ticket you can buy one from the conductor, with an added 20% penalty. You can also pay a conductor to move up to first class or get a couchette if there are places available.

Trenitalia offers a range of discount cards (*see* their website), although for travelling in just Liguria, Piemonte and Aosta they are rarely worth bothering with. Other discounts, such as a Carta Verde for under-26s, a Carta Argento for over-60s, an Intercity card and a Club Eurostar card for frequent users of those lines, are only really worth looking into if you're spending several months in Italy and using a lot of trains.

Refreshments on routes of any great distance are provided by trolleys. Station bars often have a good variety of takeaway travellers' fare. Note that all domestic trains in Italy are now non-smoking.

Besides trains and bars, Italy's stations offer other facilities. Most have a *Deposito Bagagli*, where you can leave your bags for hours or days (when there isn't a terrorist alert) for a small fee. The larger ones have porters and some even have luggage trolleys; major stations have an *Albergo Diurno* ('Day Hotel', where you can take a shower, get a shave and a haircut), information offices, currency exchanges, accommodation services, etc. You can also arrange to have a rental car awaiting you at your destination.

Trenitalia may have its strikes and delays, its petty crime and bureaucratic inconveniences, but when you catch it on its better side it will treat you to a dose of the real Italy. Just try to avoid travel on Friday and Sunday evenings, when the major lines are packed.

By Coach

Inter-city coach travel is sometimes quicker than train travel, but it's also a bit more expensive; often you'll find regular coach connections between big towns only where there is no train to offer competition. For smaller towns and villages, the system is top class; you'll be able to reach more destinations conveniently by public transport in Italy than almost anywhere in western Europe.

Coaches almost always depart from the vicinity of the train station, and tickets usually need to be purchased before you get on. If you can't get a ticket before the coach leaves, get on anyway and tell the conductor or driver.

City buses are the traveller's friend; all charge flat fees for rides within the city limits and immediate suburbs. Bus tickets must always be purchased before you get on, at a tobacconist's or newspaper kiosk, in bars, or from ticket machines near the main stops. Once you get on, 'obliterate' your ticket in the machines in the front or back of the bus; controllers stage random checks to make

sure you've punched your ticket. Fines for cheaters are about €25.

By Car

The advantages of driving in Italy generally outweigh the disadvantages, but, before you bring your own car or hire one, consider the kind of holiday you're planning. If you're sticking to the Riviera or the big cities, you'll be better off not driving at all: parking and traffic are impossible, and one-way street systems, signals and signs can seem like an exercise in obfuscation to the uninitiated.

Third-party insurance is a minimum requirement in Italy. Obtain a Green Card from your insurer, which gives proof that you are fully covered. Also get hold of a European Accident Statement form, which may simplify things if you are unlucky. Always insist on a full translation of any statement you are asked to sign. Breakdown assistance insurance is a sensible investment (*see* p.70).

Petrol (unleaded is *senza piombo*, and diesel *gasolio*) is relatively expensive in Italy. Many petrol stations close for lunch and in the afternoon, and few stay open late, although there will always be a 'self-service' where you feed a machine a credit card. Motorway (*autostrada*) tolls are high. Rest stops and petrol stations along the motorways stay open 24 hours. The cuisine in these may be a treat, though the fuel prices can be a crime.

Italians are famously anarchic behind a wheel. The only way to beat the locals is to join them by adopting an assertive and constantly alert driving style. Always bear in mind the maxim that he/she who hesitates is lost (especially at traffic lights, where the danger of crashing into someone in front is less great than that of being rammed from behind). All drivers from boy racers to elderly nuns seem to tempt providence by overtaking at the most dangerous bend, and no matter how fast you hammer along the *autostrada* plenty of vehicles will whiz past you. In towns, watch out for scooters.

North Americans who are used to leisurely speeds and gentler road manners may find the Italian interpretation of the highway code stressful. Speed limits, which are generally ignored, are 130kph on motorways,

110kph on highways, 90kph on secondary roads and 50kph in built-up areas.

If you are undeterred, you may actually enjoy driving in Italy, at least away from the congested coast and cities. Roads are well maintained. Some are feats of engineering – notably the A10/A12 across the Ligurian coast, made up of alternating viaducts and tunnels. You won't appreciate it while you're stuck for an hour trying to get through Genoa – but then, that city's topography ensures that its traffic rivals Naples' as Italy's worst.

Buy a good map (the Italian Touring Club series is excellent). The **Automobile Club of Italy (ACI)** is a good friend to the motorist. They can be reached from anywhere by dialling t 803 116 – they can tell you where the nearest service station is or if you need major repairs, can make sure the prices charged are according to their guidelines.

Hiring a Car

Hiring a car, *autonoleggio*, is simple but not cheap – Italy has some of the highest car-hire rates in Europe; you'll nearly always save money if you book your car abroad or as party of a fly-drive scheme. The minimum age is usually 25 (sometimes 23), and the driver must have held their licence for over a year – this will have to be produced, along with the driver's passport, when hiring the car. Note that unless you specify (and pay a lot more) the car will be a manual stick shift. Major

Car Hire Companies

UK

Avis, t 0844 581 0147, *www.avis.co.uk*.
Budget, t 08701 56 56 56, *www.budget.com*.
easyCar, t 08710 500 444, *www.easycar.com*.
Europcar, t 0870 607 5000, *www.europcar.com*.
Hertz, t 08708 44 88 44, *www.hertz.co.uk*.
Thrifty, t 01494 751500, *www.thrifty.co.uk*.

USA and Canada

Auto Europe, t 1 888 223 5555, *www.autoeurope.com*.
Avis Rent a Car, t 800 331 1212 or t 800 331 2323 (hearing-impaired), *www.avis.com*.
Budget, t 800 527 0700, *www.budget.com*.
Europcar, t 877 940 6900, *www.europcar.com*.
Europe by Car, t 800 223 1516, *www.europebycar.com*.
Hertz, t 800 654 3131, *www.hertz.com*.

companies have offices in airports or at major train stations, though it may be worth-while checking prices of local firms.

By Motorcycle or Bicycle

Mopeds, Vespas and scooters are the vehicles of choice for many Italians. In the traffic-congested towns this is a ubiquity born of necessity. Many ride in as laid-back a style as possible: riding sidesaddle, while on the phone, holding a dog or child under one arm and so on. Despite the obvious dangers (especially if you choose to do it Italian-style), there are benefits to mopeds in cities and resorts – it's cheaper than car hire, easier to park, and is faster than any other means of transport. Nonetheless, only consider hiring a moped or scooter if you have ridden one before; Italian streets are no place to learn. Also, be warned, some travel insurance policies exclude claims resulting from scooter or motorbike accidents.

The less mountainous areas of Piedmont and Aosta are excellent for cycling tours; local tourist offices offer itineraries and addresses for hire and repair. However, if you're not training for the Tour de France, consider the steep topography of Liguria before pedalling there. If you bring your own bike, check the airlines to see what their policies are on transporting them. Bikes can be transported by train in Italy, either with you or within a couple of days of your arrival – apply at the baggage office (*ufficio bagagli*).

Where to Stay

All accommodation in Italy is classified by the Provincial Tourist Boards. After a period of rapid and erratic fluctuation, tariffs are at last settling down again to more predictable levels under the influence of market forces. Good-value, interesting accommodation in cities can be hard to find and you will need to book well in advance for some of the most desirable places. On the other hand, many city business hotels offer significant discounts at weekends.

Hotels and Guesthouses

Italian *alberghi* come in all shapes and sizes. They are rated as one- to five-star,

Hotel Price Categories

Note that prices listed here and elsewhere in this book are for a double room in high season.

luxury	€€€€€	€230 and over
very expensive	€€€€	€150–230
expensive	€€€	€100–150
moderate	€€	€60–100
inexpensive	€	under €60

depending on what facilities they offer. The star ratings are some indication of price levels, but for tax reasons not all hotels choose to advertise themselves at the rating to which they are entitled, so you may find a modestly rated hotel just as comfortable (or more so) than a higher-rated one. You can often get big off-season discounts and bargain last-minute offers by booking through internet portals.

Prices must be posted on the door of every room, along with any extra charges. Low-season rates may be a third lower than peak-season tariffs. Some resort hotels close down altogether for several months of the year. During high season you should always book ahead (by fax or through a hotel's website). If you have paid a deposit, your booking is valid under Italian law, but don't expect it to be refunded if you have to cancel.

If you arrive without a reservation, begin looking for accommodation early in the day. Also note that Italian hoteliers may legally alter their rates twice during the year, so printed tariffs may be out of date. If you feel you've been overcharged, contact the local tourist office. You will be asked for your passport for registration purposes.

Prices listed in this guide are for double rooms (*camera doppia*) with bath (*see* above). If you want a double bed, specify a *camera matrimoniale*. Expect to pay about two-thirds the rate for single occupancy (*camera singola*), although in high season you may have to pay the full double rate if no singles are available. Extra beds are usually charged at an extra third of the room rate, although most offer discounts for children sharing parents' rooms.

Breakfast is normally optional in hotels, and you can usually get better value by eating breakfast in a café. In high season you may be expected to take half-board in resorts, and one-night stays may be refused.

Hostels and Budget Accommodation

The **Associazione Italiana Alberghi per la Gioventù** is affiliated to the International Youth Hostel Federation and open to anyone, regardless of age; book online at *www.ostellionline.org*. A membership card enables you to stay in any of them. If you don't have one, purchase a card on the spot at hostels. You should generally expect to check in after 5pm, and to pay for your room before 9am. Most hostels close for the best part of the day, and many operate a curfew. In spring, be aware that noisy school parties often cram hostels for field trips.

Religious institutions, usually monasteries or sanctuaries, take in guests; some of the nicer ones are included in the text. Rates are usually €20–30, with breakfast.

Agriturismo and Bed and Breakfast

For a breath of rural life, Italians head for a **working farm**, in *agriturismo* accommodation (sometimes self-catering, but often B&B, so the classifications tend to blur). Often, the pull of such places is cooking by the hosts and the chance to sample home-grown produce. Half-board terms are usually offered. Quite a few newer *agriturismi* are quite stylish (and pricy, especially on fancy wine estates in Piedmont). Local tourist offices have information on *agriturismi*; full listings are compiled (in Italian) by **Agriturist**, *www.agriturist.it*, and **Turismo Verde**, *www.turismoverde.it*.

B&B accommodation has recently taken off in Italy, although prices are rarely a bargain. In northwest Italy, there are several umbrella organizations with detailed listings:
www.bbitalia.it
www.bed-breakfast.it
www.bbitalia.net

Camping

Campsites are particularly popular with holiday-making families in August, when you can expect to find many of them at bursting point. Many *agriturismi* also have a few spots for campers.

You can obtain a list of sites from any regional tourist office: many now have websites. Charges are generally about €8 per adult; tents and vehicles carry an additional cost of about €9–12. For information on sites and booking, see *www.camping.it*.

Tour Operators and Special-interest Holidays

Italy

The Italian Culinary Institute for Foreigners, in Costigliole d'Asti, **t** (+39) 0141 962 171, *www.icif.com*. In-depth courses in Italian cookery, in a lovely castle near Asti.

UK and Ireland

Acorn Family Adventure, t 0800 074 5149, *www.acornadventure.co.uk*. Family adventure holidays in Aosta.

Alternative Travel, t (01865) 315 678, *www.atg-oxford.co.uk*. 'Discover Italy' walking and gastronomic tours.

Arblaster & Clarke Wine Tours, t (01730) 26 31 11, *www.winetours.co.uk*. Wine tours taking in Piedmont's finest.

Brompton Travel, t (020) 8398 3672, *www.bromptontravel.co.uk*. Tailor-made and opera tours in Turin and Genoa.

Great Rail Journeys, t (01904) 52 19 36, *www.greatrail.com*. Scenic train excursions around Lake Maggiore.

HF Holidays, t (020) 8905 9558, *www.hfholidays.co.uk*. Walking in the Cinque Terre.

Inntravel, t (01653) 617 949, *www.inntravel.co.uk*. Walking tours in Liguria and Piedmont.

Kirker, t (020) 7593 2288, *www.kirkerholidays.com*. Portofino-based tours.

Kudu, t (01722) 716 167, *www.kudutravel.com*. Music, flower, walking and shopping tours around Lake Orta and in Turin.

Martin Randall Travel, t (020) 8742 3355, *www.martinrandall.com*. Cultural tours to Turin and the beautiful gardens of Lake Maggiore.

Ramblers, t (01707) 331 133, *www.ramblersholidays.co.uk*. Walking tours of the Cinque Terre.

Specialtours, t (020) 7730 2297, *www.specialtours.co.uk*. Guided cultural tours of Turin.

USA and Canada

Ciclismo Classico, t 800 866 7314, *www.ciclismoclassico.com*. Cycling tour of Le Langhe and around Mont Blanc.

Villas and Flats

The northwest of Italy isn't as well endowed with villas and self-catering properties as Tuscany, but there are quite a few. Some of the larger operators are listed in the box below.

La Dolce Vita, t (888) 746 0022, *www.dolcetours.com*. Wine and epicurean tours, Barolo and truffle tours, walking and cycling in Piedmont and walking in the Cinque Terre.

Mama Margaret Italian Cooking Holidays, t 800 557 0370, *www.italycookingtours.com*. Cuisine and wine in Piedmont and Liguria.

Rustico Culinary Tours, t 917 602 1519, *www.rusticocooking.com*. Cooking tours of Liguria.

www.actividay7.com. Internet-based company offering activity holidays: hiking the Cinque Terre, pesto-making and watching artisans at work in Liguria.

Self-catering Operators

Italy

Agenzia Immobiliare Martinelli, t +39 0183 650 707, *www.immobiliaremartinelli.com*. Villas on the Riviera di Ponente.

Northwest Way, t +39 0183 930244, *www.northwestway.it*. Flats in Turin, *agriturismi* and villas in Piedmont and Liguria.

UK and Ireland

Cottages to Castles, t (01622) 775 236, USA **t** (866) 687 7700, *www.cottagestocastles.com*.

Individual Traveller Co, t 08700 782 100, *www.indiv-travellers.com*. Villas on the Lakes and the Cinque Terre.

Inghams, t (020) 8780 4433, *www.inghams.co.uk*. Lake Maggiore and skiing.

Italiatour, t 0870 733 3000, Ireland **t** (01) 671 7821, *www.italiatour.co.uk*. Villas in Liguria.

Lakes & Mountains Holidays, t (01243) 792 442, *www.lakes-mountains.co.uk*. Lake Maggiore.

USA and Canada

Villa Escapes, t 888 214 2170, *www.villaescapes.com/villas/europe/italy*.

RentVillas.com, t 800 726 6702, or 800 3203136, *www.rentvillas.com*. Liguria and Piedmont.

Internet-based Companies

Holiday Rentals.com, *www.holiday-rentals.co.uk*.

Parker Villas, *www.parkervillas.co.uk*.

Vacanca, *www.vacanca.com*.

Practical A–Z

Conversion Tables 76
Crime 77
Eating Out 77
Electricity 77
Health and Emergencies 77
National Holidays 77
Opening Hours 78
Post Offices 78
Shopping and Markets 78
Sports and Activities 79
Street Numbers 80
Telephones 80
Time 80

07

Conversions: Imperial–Metric

Length (multiply by)
Inches to centimetres: 2.54
Centimetres to inches: 0.39
Feet to metres: 0.3
Metres to feet: 3.28
Yards to metres: 0.91
Metres to yards: 1.09
Miles to kilometres: 1.61
Kilometres to miles: 0.62

Area (multiply by)
Inches square to centimetres square: 6.45
Centimetres square to inches square: 0.15
Feet square to metres square: 0.09
Metres square to feet square: 10.76
Miles square to kilometres square: 2.59
Kilometres square to miles square: 0.39
Acres to hectares: 0.40
Hectares to acres: 2.47

Weight (multiply by)
Ounces to grams: 28.35
Grammes to ounces: 0.035
Pounds to kilograms: 0.45
Kilograms to pounds: 2.2
Stone to kilograms: 6.35
Kilograms to stone: 0.16
Tons (UK) to kilograms: 1,016
Kilograms to tons (UK): 0.0009
1 UK ton (2,240lbs) = 1.12 US tonnes (2,000lbs)

Volume (multiply by)
Pints (UK) to litres: 0.57
Litres to pints (UK): 1.76
Quarts (UK) to litres: 1.13
Litres to quarts (UK): 0.88
Gallons (UK) to litres: 4.55
Litres to gallons (UK): 0.22
1 UK pint/quart/gallon =
1.2 US pints/quarts/gallons

Temperature
Celsius to Fahrenheit:
multiply by 1.8 then
add 32

Fahrenheit to Celsius:
subtract 32 then multiply
by 0.55

°C	°F
40	104
35	95
30	86
25	77
20	68
15	59
10	50
5	41
-0	32
-5	23
-10	14
-15	5

Italy Information

Time Differences
Country: + 1hr GMT; + 6hrs EST
Daylight saving from last weekend in March
to end of October

Dialling Codes
Italy country code 39
To Italy from: UK, Ireland, New Zealand 00 /
USA, Canada 011 / Australia 0011 then dial 39
and the full number including the initial zero
From Italy to: UK 00 44; Ireland 00 353; USA,
Canada 001; Australia 00 61; New Zealand 00
64, then the number without the initial zero
Directory enquiries: 12
International directory enquiries: 176

Emergency Numbers
Police: 112/113
Ambulance: 118
Fire: 115
Car breakdown: 116

Embassy Numbers in Italy
UK: (06) 422 0001; Ireland (06) 697 9121;
USA: (06) 46 741; Canada (06) 854 441;
Australia (06) 852 721;
New Zealand (06) 441 7171

Shoe Sizes

Europe	UK	USA
35	2½ / 3	4
36	3 / 3½	4½ / 5
37	4	5½ / 6
38	5	6½
39	5½ / 6	7 / 7½
40	6 / 6½	8 / 8½
41	7	9 / 9½
42	8	9½ / 10
43	9	10½
44	9½ / 10	11
45	10½	12
46	11	12½ / 13

Women's Clothing

Europe	UK	USA
34	6	2
36	8	4
38	10	6
40	12	8
42	14	10
44	16	12

Crime

There is relatively little petty crime in Liguria and Piedmont. Pickpockets may strike in train stations, crowded buses or gatherings; try not to carry too much cash, and split it so you won't lose the lot at once if you're unfortunate enough to be targeted; if you are, grab hold of any vulnerable possessions or pockets and shout (passers-by will often come to your assistance if they realize what is happening). Put all your valuables in hotel safes, and park your car in a garage, guarded car park or lot, or a well-lit street, with portable temptations out of sight.

Purchasing small quantities of soft drugs for personal use is technically legal in Italy, though what constitutes 'small' is unspecified, and, if the police don't like you, it will be enough to get you into trouble.

The black-uniformed national police, the *carabinieri*, have barracks in most towns and their emergency number is 112. Local matters are usually in the hands of the *polizia urbana*; the nattily dressed *vigili urbani* concern themselves with traffic and parking.

Eating Out

For smokers the bombshell hit in 2005: a total **smoking ban in bars and restaurants** was put in effect, and is being enforced.

When eating out in Italy, mentally add a 15% service charge to the bill (*conto*). This is often included in the bill (*servizio compreso*); if not, it will say *servizio non compreso*, and you'll have to do your own arithmetic. Additional tipping is at your own discretion. Although it's going out of fashion, some restaurants also have a bread and cover charge (*pane e coperto*, between €1 and €3). For restaurant price categories in this guide, *see* above.

When you leave a restaurant you will be given a receipt (*scontrino* or *ricevuta fiscale*) which by law you must take with you out of the door and carry for at least 60m. If the tax police (*guardia di finanza*) stop you and you don't have a receipt, they could slap you with a heavy fine.

For more about eating in Italy, including local specialities and wines, *see* **Food and Drink**, pp.51–62.

Restaurant Price Categories

Price of a full meal for one, without wine.

very expensive	€€€€	€45 and above
expensive	€€€	€30–45
moderate	€€	€20–30
inexpensive	€	€20 and under

Electricity

Italy uses 220 volts. Travellers from some countries, including the UK, will need to take an adaptor; some Italian plugs and sockets are non-standard however. For details of which plug to use, see *www.kropla.com*.

Health and Emergencies

Fire t 115
Carabinieri **t 112**
Ambulance t 113

Many problems can be treated at a *Pronto Soccorso* (emergency/first aid department) at any hospital clinic (*ambulatorio*), or at a local health unit (*Unità Sanitaria Locale* – USL). Airports and main railway stations also have **first-aid posts**. If you have to pay for health treatment, always get a receipt.

Dispensing **chemists** (*farmacie*) are generally open 8.30–1 and 4–8. Pharmacists are trained to give advice for minor ills. Any city will have a *farmacia* that stays open 24hrs; others take turns (the rota is in the window).

Most Italian doctors speak rudimentary English, but if you can't find one contact your embassy or consulate for suggestions.

National Holidays

1 January New Year's Day
6 January Epiphany
Easter Monday
25 April Liberation Day
1 May Labour Day
2 June Republic Day
15 August Assumption, or *Ferragosto*, the heart of the Italian holiday season
1 November All Saints' Day
8 December Immaculate Conception
25 December Christmas Day
26 December Santo Stefano, St Stephen's Day

Opening Hours

Banks

Banking hours vary but basic times are Monday to Friday 8.30am–1pm and 3–4pm, closed weekends and on local and national holidays, as well as the afternoon before.

Churches

Italy's churches have always been a prime target for art thieves and as a consequence are usually locked when there isn't a care-taker to keep an eye on things. Nearly all churches, even the big cathedrals, close in the afternoon at the same times as the shops, and the little ones tend to stay closed. Always have coins on hand for the light machines, or whatever work of art you came to inspect may remain clouded in ecclesiastical gloom. Don't visit during services.

Museums and Galleries

Many of Italy's museums are magnificent, and many have been closed for years for 'restoration' with slim prospects of reopening in the foreseeable future. With two works of art per inhabitant, Italy has a hard time financing the preservation of its national heritage. Local tourist offices can tell you exactly what is open and when. Entrance fees vary (any over €5 is labelled 'exp' in the text). All EU citizens under 18 and over 65 get free admission to state-run museums.

Offices

Government-run dispensers of red tape stay open for limited periods, usually morn-ings, Monday to Friday. It pays to get there as soon as they open (or before) to spare your nerves in an interminable queue. Regardless, take something to read.

Shops

Shops usually open Monday to Saturday from 8am to 1pm and 3.30pm to 7.30pm, although hours vary according to season. In some large cities, hours are longer and super-markets and department stores tend to stay open throughout the day.

Post Offices

Dealing with *la posta italiana* has always been a risky, frustrating, time-consuming affair. Even buying the right stamps (*francobolli*) can be a challenge; you can buy them at tobacconists as well as in post offices, which tend to have long queues.

Post offices in Italy are usually open from 8am until 1 or 2pm (Monday to Saturday), or until 6 or 7pm in a large city. To have your mail sent *poste restante* (general delivery), have it addressed to the central post office (*Fermo Posta*) and expect to wait around three to four weeks for it to arrive. Make sure your surname is very clearly written in block capitals. To pick up your mail, present your passport and pay a nominal charge.

You can also have money telegraphed to you through the post office; if all goes according to plan, this can happen in a mere three days, but you can expect a fair propor-tion of it to disappear in commission.

Shopping and Markets

'Made in Italy' has become a byword for style and quality, especially in fashion (Biella, Italy's cashmere capital, is famous for factory outlets) but also in home design, ceramics (the biggest centres here are Albisola on the Riviera and Castellamonte in Piedmont), kitchenware (Lake Orta), jewellery (Valenza), lace (Rapallo), chocolates (Turin), hats, art books, engravings, bicycles, woodworking, just about anything in slate in the Maritime Alps above Lavagna, as well as food and drink – wines, liqueurs, aperitifs, olive oil, *pumate seche* (sundried tomatoes) or dried *porcini* mushrooms – and antiques. You'll find the best variety of goods in Genoa, Turin and San Remo, and designer boutiques in the resorts.

Non-EU citizens should save all receipts for customs on the way home; however, if you spend over a certain amount in a shop you can get a tax rebate at the airport; partici-pating shops have details. If you are looking for antiques, be sure to demand a certificate of authenticity – reproductions can be very, very good. To get your antique (or modern art) purchases home, you will have to apply to the Export Department of the Italian Ministry of Culture and pay an export tax as well; your seller should know the details.

Liguria and Piedmont have colourful **markets**: most towns have weekly outdoor food markets, open from 8am to 1pm, and

San Remo has the largest flower market in Europe. Organic food markets (*mercatini biologici*) are becoming increasingly popular. Many towns (Sarzana, Saluzzo, Turin) hold antique and bric-a-brac markets once or twice a month (tourist offices have details).

Sports and Activities

You can find any conceivable summer and winter sport in Liguria, Piedmont and Aosta, including parachuting (Albenga airport) and hot-air ballooning at Levaldigi.

Bocce and Pallone Elastico

As on the French side of the Riviera, *bocce* (*boules*) is a very popular game: it doesn't take up much space, doesn't require much energy, takes about five minutes to learn (if a lifetime to perfect) and you can bet on it. Some resorts even have indoor *bocciodromi*.

Pallone elastico, 'rubber ball', on the other hand, is a kind of rustic outdoors handball unique to the mountain valleys of Liguria and southern Piedmont, where space to play other sports is limited by the vertical geography. You can play against any old wall (next to a bar is good), whacking it with your fist and chasing after it. You can bet on it, too, and there are championship matches, which are covered assiduously in the local press.

Cycling

Liguria isn't amenable to cycling holidays unless you're very fit and ready to escape the busy coast for the quiet, steep mountain roads. Although a few Riviera hotels hire out bikes for pedalling around the resorts (a good idea, as parking is often at a premium), it's rare to find a bike good enough for longer forays, for which it is best to bring your own and spare parts (*see* **Planning Your Trip**, p.72).

Piedmont, on the other hand, has all kinds of landscapes, and is perfect for both road cycling (off the main routes) and mountain biking. Local tourist offices have detailed maps of mountain trails – the Zegna Natural Oasis near Biella and the Alpine valleys west and southwest of Turin are among the most beautiful places to aim for. You can combine cycling, wine and gastronomy in Le Langhe and Monferrato, while Novi Ligure, cradle of some of Italy's greatest racers, has a Museo

dei Campionissimi dedicated to their exploits, and circuits to whiz around.

Football

Soccer (*calcio*) is a national obsession. For many Italians its importance far outweighs tedious issues like the state of the nation, the government of the day, or any momentous international event – not least because of the weekly chance (slim but real) of becoming an instant millionaire in the *Lotteria Sportiva*. All major cities, and most minor ones, have at least one team. The sport was actually introduced by the English, but a Renaissance game, something like a cross between football and rugby, has existed in Italy for centuries.

Modern Italian teams (especially Juventus, *see* p.240) are known for their grace, precision and coordination, and rivalries are intense. Big-league matches are played on Sunday afternoons from September to May.

Golf

Italians have been slow to appreciate the delights of biffing a small white ball into a hole, but they're catching on fast, especially in Piedmont, which now has over 40 courses, detailed with a map at *www.piemonte golf.italy/index.htm*. Top courses are the Circolo Golf Torino and the Associazione Sportivi I Roveri, designed by Robert Trent Jones (for both, *see* p.242). There are five courses in Liguria and two in the Valle d'Aosta (*www.pmfgolfguide.com/it*). Turin's tourist office (*see* p.242) offers a discount package on nearby courses.

Mountains and Skiing

The highest Alps touch Piedmont and Aosta, and mountains sports have long been central to their appeal. Walking is generally practicable in high altitudes between May and October. Strategically placed **Alpine refuges** (*rifugi alpini*) open from the end of June to the end of September (so if you come earlier or later, carry camping gear). In July and August book a bed in advance. Many *rifugi* are owned by the Italian Alpine Club (CAI); others are privately owned, usually by ski resorts. All offer bed and board; nearly all require that you bring a sleeping sheet, or buy one on site. The higher and more difficult the access, the more expensive.

There are also custodian-less *baite* (wooden huts), *casere* (stone huts) and *bivouacs* (beds but no food) along some of the higher trails. For information, contact the **Italian Alpine Club**, *www.cai.it*, or local tourist offices.

Some of the most beautiful walks are in Gran Paradiso National Park and around Lake Maggiore. You can follow the path of medieval pilgrims to Rome on the Via Francigena, through the Susa valley, trace the ancient salt roads between Liguria and Piedmont or follow the 440km Alta Via dei Monti Liguri from Ventimiglia to Ceparana. If you prefer your mountains vertical, the cliffs at Finale Ligure attract free climbers from around Europe.

The 2006 Winter Olympics gave Piedmont's 45 ski resorts (*see* p.253) a big boost. The free, annually updated handbook *Skiing in Piedmont* is a mine of information, covering all the facilities on and off the pistes as well as the après-ski; request one from the regional tourist office or download it from *www.regione.piemonte.it/turismo*. Nearly all resorts have web pages with weather reports. Also check *www.ifyouski.com* for good resort deals.

Skiing is even more important up in Aosta, with its major resorts at Courmayeur and Cervinia and a dozen others; for complete information on resorts and packages and the Aosta ski pass, valid at all the resorts, check *www.regione.vda.it/turismo/*.

Prices are highest during the Christmas and New Year holidays, in February and at Easter. Most resorts offer *Settimane Bianche* ('White Weeks') at economical rates.

Riding Holidays

Riding holidays are on offer, often associated with *agriturismo* holidays (*see* p.73); most cities and resorts have riding stables.

Tennis

If soccer is Italy's most popular spectator sport, tennis is probably the game most people play. Every *comune* has public courts for hourly hire and hotel courts can often be used by non-guests for a fee.

Watersports

Riviera beaches are often beautiful, and a good many are pebbly. Most of the desirable sand is plagued or blessed, according to your point of view, by that peculiarly Italian phenomenon, the concessionaire, who parks lines of sunbeds and brollies all along the best stretches of coast, and charges all comers handsomely for the privilege of using them. No one bats an eye at topless bathing, though nudism requires more discretion.

The Italian Riviera is one of the prettiest regions for **sailing**, and the larger resorts, especially on the Riviera di Ponente, are well equipped with **windsurf** rentals (the sport is fairly tame in these sheltered parts) and **waterskiing** facilities. A few areas make for excellent **diving**, such as Alassio and its Isola Gallinaria. Resorts such as San Remo hire out **deltaplanes** if you want to soar over the sea.

Street Numbers

In Genoa and Savona, there is a complicated **street-numbering system**: any commercial establishment receives a red (r) number, but any residence a black or blue number.

Telephones

Most Italian public phones take either coins or phonecards (*schede telefoniche*), available in €1, €2.50, €3, €5, €7.50 and €10 amounts at tobacconists – snap off the corner to use them. If you bring your mobile, contact your provider before leaving to see what services are on offer, or see *www.0044.co.uk*, *www.SIM4travel.com*, *www.textbay.net* and *www.uk2abroad.com*. Some phones can make use of local providers by changing the SIM card, which requires 'unblocking' your phone.

If you're calling Italy from abroad, dial t 0039 and then the number, including the first zero for a land line (but you should omit the zero if calling a mobile number).

Time

Italy is on Central European Time, one hour ahead of Greenwich Mean Time and six hours ahead of Eastern Standard Time. From the last weekend of March to the last weekend of October, summer time (daylight saving time) is in effect.

Riviera di Ponente

Stretching between France and Genoa, the Riviera di Ponente is the coast of the setting sun, nightly kissed by that golden orb as it bids Italy sweet dreams. Less glamorous perhaps, but the more fertile and populous of Liguria's two rivieras, the Ponente is streaked with the silver of olives under emerald Alpine peaks, its coastal towns splashed with colour, its hill towns as spectacular as any.

08

Don't miss

⭐ **Caves and lush gardens**
Ventimiglia and Hanbury Gardens p.85–6

⭐ **A Liberty-style grand resort of the 1890s**
San Remo p.95

⭐ **A medieval village with an art-filled convent**
Taggia p.101

⭐ **A Romanesque cathedral**
Albenga p.116

⭐ **Whale watching**
Savona p.133

See map overleaf

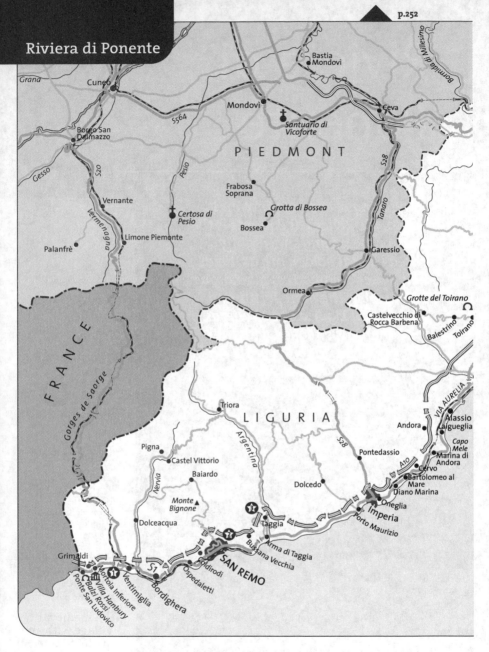

Don't miss

⭐ Ventimiglia and Hanbury Gardens **p.85–6**

⭐ San Remo **p.95**

⭐ Taggia **p.101**

⭐ Albenga **p.116**

⭐ Savona **p.133**

LIGURIA

Madonna
della Guardia

Millesimo

Bocchetta di
Cadibona

Albisola
Superiore

Celle Ligure
Albissola Marina

Savona

Vado Ligure

Spotorno

Noli

Capo di Noli

Grotta di
Valdemino

Borgio
Pietra Ligure
Loano

Borghetto Santo Spirito
Ceriale

Albenga

Isola Gallinara

Finale Ligure

Varazze

Cogoleto

Voltri Pegli
Sestri
Ponente

GENOA
(GENOVA)

A10

A6

A10

S1

SS9

Ajaccio

Cagliari/Porto Torres

Olbia/Arbatax/Palermo

Tunis/Bastia/Ile-Rousse

Civitavecchia

Riviera di Ponente

Gulf

of Genoa

N

10 km
5 miles

SWITZERLAND   AUSTRIA

SLOVENIA

CROATIA

FRANCE

Corsica

Sardinia

Sicily

San Remo, the biggest resort along the Riviera di Ponente, is larger than the provincial capital, Imperia; Savona, the Ponente's biggest city, was long a bitter rival of Genoa and outdid the bossy Republic in at least one respect – by producing a pair of Renaissance popes, including the calamitous Julius II.

In between you'll find plenty of surprises: a new independent principality, whose prince will sell you a sticker for your car; the 'Little Dolomites' by Buggio; perfect Roman bridges; a museum dedicated to songs and another to church-tower clocks; a shop that sells witches' philtres; and stalactite caves where our Stone Age ancestors got up to some very curious monkeyshines indeed.

The Riviera dei Fiori: Ventimiglia to Bordighera

The westernmost wedge of the Riviera di Ponente enjoys one of the mildest winter climates in Italy. Flowers thrive here even in February, and are cultivated in fields that dress the landscape in patchwork (albeit often shrouded in plastic), lending this stretch the name of the 'Riviera of Flowers'. Not surprisingly, when the first

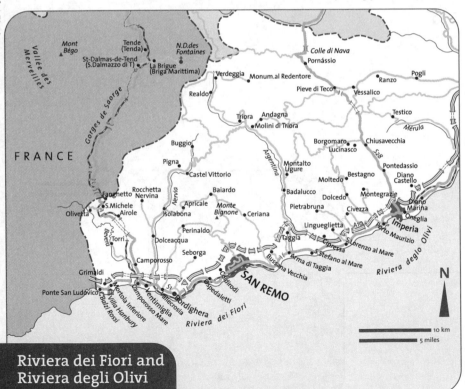

Riviera dei Fiori and Riviera degli Olivi

Getting around the Riviera dei Fiori

Trains run frequently along the coast. **Bus** no.1 goes near Balzi Rossi and La Mortola; bus no.2 runs along the coast to San Remo; bus no.7 goes up the Val Nervia to Dolceacqua, Isolabona, Pigna and Buggio.

---

pioneering Britons flocked down to winter here, this was their prime nesting ground; some of it is a bit faded now, but that's part of its old-fashioned appeal.

Ventimiglia

 Ventimiglia

The Maritime Alps meet the sea to form a natural border, but the first town in Italy, Ventimiglia, in spite of a lovely setting and climate, is having a hard time adjusting to the euro and post-Schengen era – now that people don't have to stop at customs or change money, Ventimiglia seems content to lure the French over the border with cheap booze (it has more liquor stores than any town in Italy). But it does have beaches, both pebble and lovely, sandy, wild Calandre, a pretty ten-minute walk west of Ventimiglia Alta, and cheap hotels in easy reach of Monaco and San Remo.

In Roman times Ventimiglia was **Albintimilium**, on the Via Julia Augusta. A kilometre east of town you can see a small 2nd-century AD **theatre**, the Provence Gate and traces of baths, houses and insulae (Roman apartment blocks); the finds are up in the **Civico Museo Archeologico**, in the Forte dell' Annunziata – worth a visit perhaps more for its tremendous views than its artefacts.

In the unstable 7th century, the locals took refuge in the dark, twisting cobbled lanes of **Ventimiglia Alta**, the old, refreshingly unsanitized town picturesquely crumbling on a hill west of the River Roja, where swans add a touch of class. The main street, Via Garibaldi, is lined with handsome *palazzi*, especially the **Palazzo Pubblico**, with its 15th-century Gothic Loggia dei Mercanti. Inside the atrium of the Teatro Civico, the **Civica Biblioteca Aprosiana** is Liguria's oldest public library, founded in 1648; it contains Italy's best collection of 17th-century books. Further along, the attractive 11th–12th-century **Cattedrale dell'Assunta** was built by the Counts of Ventimiglia, the lords of much of this coast at the time of the first millennium. It has a Romanesque façade and a Gothic porch added around 1222, a Byzantine font and a two-ton 17th-century wooden tabernacle; the cathedral's octagonal Baptistry has a magnificent 12th-century total immersion font. Isolated near the Renaissance walls, **San Michele**, with its warm-coloured stones, is another fine Romanesque church, founded by the local counts before the 10th century; its crypt has an altar made of Roman columns from a temple of Castor and Pollux and a milestone from the time of Caracalla, but you'll need a miracle to get in to see it.

Theatre
open Sat and Sun 3–6, but ask at the tourist office; free; for guided tours, contact Co-operative Omnia, **t** *0184 229 507*

Civico Museo Archeologico
Via Verdi 41, **t** *0184 351 181; open Tues–Sat 9–12.30 and 3–5, Sun 10–12.30; adm*

Civica Biblioteca Aprosiana
Via Garibaldi, **t** *0184 351 209; open Oct–May Mon, Wed and Sat 8.30–1.30, Tues and Thurs, Fri 2–7.30; June–Sept Mon–Sat 8.30–1.30*

Cattedrale dell'Assunta
t *0184 351 813*

San Michele
can be visited during weekdays by calling the Co-operative Omnia, **t** *0184 229 507*

08

Riviera di Ponente | The Riviera dei Fiori: Ventimiglia

From the *centro storico*'s **Porta Nizza**, a road climbs up to three forts west of Ventimiglia that tell of the many battles fought over this choice piece of real estate (claimed, at various times, by the Byzantines, the Provençals, the Angevins, the Grimaldi and the Republic of Genoa): the **Forte San Paolo**, the tower-gate **Canarda** (bearing the arms of Genoa's Bank of St George) and, uppermost, the ruins of the 12th-century **Castel D'Appio**, named after Consul Appio Claudio, who defeated the Ligurians here in 185 BC. The site was a Ligurian *castelliere*, and later a Roman *castrum*; the castle was the headquarters of the often-piratical Counts of Ventimiglia. On the east bank of the River Roja, modern (mostly postwar) Ventimiglia is lined with seaside promenades and adorned with palm gardens. Here the big event is the seafront **Friday market** offering a cornucopia of food, clothes and counterfeit luxury goods (be warned: police are cracking down on buyers as well as sellers). In June, come for the cheeky, exuberant 'Battle of the Flowers'.

Friday market
8am–4pm

Balzi Rossi

As far as we know, people lived here longer than elsewhere in Liguria, in the Balzi Rossi ('Red Cliffs') caves, located just a few feet from France below the village of Grimaldi. Here, *c.* 200,000 years ago, thrived *Homo erectus grimaldi* followed some 185,000 years later by Cro-Magnon tenants, who left traces of elaborate burials, with seashell finery; one cave, the **Grotta del Caviglione**, has an etching of a Przewalski horse, now common only on the Russian steppes. At the entrance, the **Museo Preistorico**, founded by Sir Thomas Hanbury in the 1890s, displays ornaments, tools, weapons and the bones of hippopotamuses, rhinoceroses, elephants – and reindeer from the last Ice Age. Here, too, are some of the earliest-known works of art: lumpy fertility soapstone 'Venuses'. Bring your swimming gear: Balzi Rossi also has a pretty **beach**.

Museo Preistorico
t 0184 38 113; museum and caves open Tues–Sun 9–1 and 2.30–6 in winter; 9–12.30 and 2–6 in summer; adm

Hanbury Gardens

Nearby at Mortola Inferiore, the Hanbury Gardens are the oldest botanical gardens on the Riviera, a paradise founded in 1867 by Londoner Sir Thomas Hanbury and his brother Daniel. Sir Thomas was a wealthy dealer in silks and spices, who fell in love with the spot during a holiday in 1867. He bought a villa and 30 acres, and during his travels brought back rare and exotic plants from Africa, Australia, the Americas and Asia, which he acclimatized to co-exist with native Mediterranean flora. Queen Victoria stopped by to visit in 1882; by 1912 the garden had some 6,000 species and a permanent staff of 45 gardeners. After Sir Thomas died, his daughter-in-law landscaped the garden, never suspecting that it would have two unwelcome guests in the 1930s: Mussolini (who had a soft spot for the English and their gardens) chose it as the

✪ Hanbury Gardens
t 0184 229 507; open daily last Sun Mar–14 June 10–5; 15 June–last Sun Sept 9–6; last Sun Sept–end Oct 10–6; Nov–last Sun Mar Thurs–Tues 10–4; adm

perfect spot to host Franco, who let his soldiers march over the plants in their jackboots. During the war, the estate fell into decay and in 1960 it was sold to the state. The gardens are now managed by green thumbs at the University of Genoa, and are back in shape – highlights include the Garden of Scents and the Japanese garden. The *palazzo* is now open as well.

Within the gardens there's a section of the ancient **Via Julia Augusta**, with a plaque alongside listing the famous who have passed this way, from St Catherine of Siena to Napoleon. The main road leads to the former customs post at **Ponte San Ludovico**, with its landmark castle, where Russian surgeon Count Serge Voronoff (d. 1951) performed his experiments, seeking the Fountain of Youth in monkey glands. He chose Ventimiglia because the sea here has the highest concentration of iodine in the whole Mediterranean; one of his famous patients was Eva Peron.

The Val Roja

Inland from Ventimiglia, the Val Roja cuts over to Cuneo and Piedmont through France, following a hoary trail through a wild landscape of white cliffs and crags to Mont Bégo, which was either an ancient Ligurian holy site or the early inhabitants' favourite outdoor art gallery. The more recent inhabitants of the upper valley voted in the plebiscite of 1860 to become French along with Nice – although a whopping 73 per cent of the electorate abstained – but their votes were ignored when Vittorio Emanuele II intervened; he may have been useless as a king, but as a hunter few crowned heads could match him, and he asked Napoleon III to let him keep the upper Val Roja as a hunting reserve. Another rigged plebiscite in 1947 made it France's last territorial acquisition.

You can make the journey up the valley from Ventimiglia to Cuneo by train, on a line that is something of an engineering marvel, threading through 81 tunnels and over 400 bridges. The Dutch have restored many of the old houses along the lower, still Italian part of the valley, especially around **Airole** and **Olivetta-San Michele**, two steep grey stone villages which resemble Tibetan monasteries, and were once notorious bases for smuggling people and goods over the border. A third village, **Torri Superiore**, at the top of the Val Bevera (a fork in the Val Roja), has been restored by an environmentalist group based in Turin, which takes in stressed-out urbanites and gives them useful things to do like building stone walls. North, **Fanghetto** is now the last village in Italy, and has a striking stone bridge for its landmark.

The Val Nervia

The next valley east, the Val Nervia, is linked by buses hourly from Ventimiglia. The lower part of the valley is now a wildlife oasis run by the WWF. Fertile farmland surrounds **Camporosso** near the bottom of the valley, an old town which has preserved little of its character, although it does have three 16th-century polyptychs in the church of **San Marco**, including one by Ludovico Brea.

Dolceacqua

In contrast, the valley's main town is as picturesque as you could wish. Dolceacqua, a 20-minute drive from Ventimiglia, occupies both banks of the Nervia – the older 'Terra' on the hill and 'Borgo' – linked by a singular, airy 110ft span of a 15th-century **Ponte dei Romani**, which was painted by Monet in 1884. The name means 'Sweetwater' (although it actually derives from a local Roman named Dulcius) but most people seek out something with a little more punch: the hillsides are terraced with vines producing Liguria's best red wine, **DOC Rossese**, of which Napoleon was so fond that he gave Dolceacqua the right to rename it after his imperial self.

Dolceacqua was the fief of some other bigwigs, the Doria. The founder of the dynasty, Oberto, who memorably led the Genoese victory over the Pisans at Meloria, picked it up in 1270 and his descendants held on to it through thick and thin. Their 16th-century and reputedly haunted **Doria Castle**, damaged in an earthquake in 1887, where the lords are said to have taken full advantage of their *droit de seigneur* with local brides, now stares down lugubriously from its rock. It was reopened in July 2007 after two years of restructuring. The Dorias' nasty habits (it's safe now; the local branch died out in 1902) and the resistance of a bride named Lucrezia to their claims are still remembered today, in a wacky fashion, in the **Sagra della Michetta** on the night of 15 August. A *michetta* is a kind of long brioche, and the young bloods of the town fill up their donkey panniers or carts with them, and, accompanied by musicians, stop under the balconies of unmarried girls and offer them a *michetta*; nowadays the girls can just say no.

Of the town's churches, **Sant'Antonio Abate** has fine stucco work and a beautiful polyptych of Santa Devota (1515) by Ludovico Brea, and the **Oratorio di San Sebastiano** has a figwood statue of the eponymous saint, attributed to Maragliano; the statue goes for an airing on his feast day (20 January). This Dolceacqua celebrates in another quaint way – a religious procession led by the 'tree man', who bears a huge branch hung with large, coloured communion hosts. After the procession the hosts are distributed to the inhabitants, who keep them for luck. The story is said to celebrate Sebastian's martyrdom; his gaolers refused to give him communion, so an angel came down and delivered a wafer when they weren't looking. Dolceacqua stays abreast of modern technology, too: its **Visionarium** offers a 3D virtual tour of the Val Nervia, with special effects and other documentaries.

Doria Castle
open daily 10–1 and 3.30–6.30

Visionarium
Via Doria 12 bis, t 0184 206 638, www.visionarium-3d.com; best to ring ahead; adm

Beyond Dolceacqua

A road runs northwest up to the Y-shaped village of **Rocchetta Nervina**, the attractions of which include little swimming lakes, two hog-backed bridges, a water mill and a dense fir forest. The main road, for its part, continues to **Isolabona**, which sits at the confluence of the Nervia and Merdanzo rivers and has a pretty octagonal fountain of 1486; its restored **Doria castle** hosts an international harp festival in July. On the main road, the **Santuario della Madonna delle Grazie** has a classical pronaos and is covered with frescoes by Giovanni Cambiaso.

From here you can make another windy road detour, northeast, to the remarkable medieval village of **Apricale**, 'open to the sun', cascading gracefully from its hilltop perch. Apricale preserves another Doria pile, the 'lizard castle', the **Castello della Lucertola**, with a fun museum of contemporary art and history, including a copy of the town's statutes, the oldest in Liguria (1267). It preserves three gates in its walls, and a perfectly charming **Piazza Principale**, which looks like a stage set – and is used as one on summer nights, when actors from Genoa's Teatro della Tosse put on shows in the narrow lanes. An annual 'Fresco Day' has left the *centro storico* covered with colourful murals; a bicycle (*La forza della non gravità*, 2000) poetically climbs the roof of the campanile.

Castello della Lucertola
t 0184 208 126; open May–June Tues–Sun 3–7; July–Aug Mon–Sat 4–7 and 8–10pm, Sun 10.30–12; Sept–April Tues–Sat 2–6, Sun 10.30–12 and 2–6; adm

Pigna and the Upper Val Nervia

Pigna, beautifully set in the lush foothills of the Maritime Alps, was founded by the Counts of Ventimiglia and looks like its name, 'pine cone', with its concentric porticoed lanes rising up the hill, where houses still bear medieval monograms and designs cut in the stone. It has some exceptional art and churches: below, just before the town, are the impressive ruins of **San Tommaso**. By the main square, **San Michele Arcangelo** (1450) has a lovely marble rose window by Giovanni Gagini, where spokes of salvation radiate from the central Agnus Dei to a ring of pretty floral motifs, with stained glass showing the Twelve Apostles. Inside, the polyptych of *St Michael and Other Saints* (1500) by Giovanni Canavesio is one of the greatest works of the 'Fra Angelico of the Maritime Alps'. The cemetery church of **San Bernardo** has more by Canavesio: earlier, excellent frescoes of the *Passion* and *Last Judgement* (1483). In Piazza XX Settembre is the **Museo Etnografico**. The drive from Pigna north up the lush **Gola di Gouta** is enchanting.

In the crazy territorial quilt of old Liguria, Pigna belonged to the Savoys. The village you see hanging among the trees 3km up the valley, **Castel Vittorio**, belonged to their rivals, Genoa, and has changed little since the 13th century when its thick walls defended it from predatory raids by Pigna. Some bravos from Pigna once managed to get in anyway and steal Castel Vittorio's bell from its

San Bernardo
t 0184 229 507; open daily 5–7; to visit the museo and frescoes at other times, call t 349 2847549

Museo Etnografico
t 0184 241 016; open daily 4–7

08 Riviera di Ponente | The Riviera dei Fiori: Ventimiglia

pretty tiled campanile; in revenge Castel Vittorio boldly made off with the paving stones from Pigna's piazza.

From here, drivers can circle back, by way of Baiardo (*see* p.98), to the coast at San Remo, or you can continue up to **Buggio**, at the foot of Monte Toraggio, a perfect example of an intact rural village, with a unique *piazzetta*, parish church and oratory and a little bridge. It is the base for visiting the **Parco Naturale Regionale Alpi Liguri**, where oak and fir and rhododendron take over and the mountains are known as the 'Little Dolomites' for their beauty. In the winter you can ski here; the **Rifugio Allavena** has rooms and can set you on the path up to the top of **Monte Toraggio**. A remarkably beautiful spot to aim for (especially if you have a jeep, or at least good walking shoes) is the **Colla di Langàn**, just above the Lago di Tenarda.

Rifugio Allavena
t 0184 241 155; closed Nov

Where to Stay and Eat in and around Ventimiglia

ⓘ **Ventimiglia >**
Via Cavour 61, t 0184 351 183

ⓘ **Dolceacqua >>**
Pro Loco, Via Doria 10, t 0184 20 68 99

★ **Locanda di Bricco Arcagna >>**

★ **Balzi Rossi >**

Ventimiglia ✉ 18039

***La Riserva di Castel d'Appio, Loc. Peidaigo, t 0184 229 533, *www.la riserva.it* (€€€). Up in the olive groves at Castel d'Appio, 5km west of the town, a fine family-run inn with magnificent views, garden, pool and comfortable rooms. *Open April–Sept and Christmas hols only.*

***Sea Gull, Via Marconi 24, t 0184 351 726, *www.seagullhotel.it* (€€€–€€). Comfortable and on the waterfront, with a bit of garden and own beach.

***Sole Mare, Via Marconi 22, t 0184 351 854, *www.hotelsolemare.it* (€€€–€€). Across from the Sea Gull, large rooms with internet portals. The popular restaurant, **Pasta e Basta** (€€), has imaginative pasta and a hilarious English menu. *Eves only; closed Mon.*

Balzi Rossi, Via Balzi Rossi 2, Frontiera San Ludovico, t 0184 38132 (€€€€). Long and still the class restaurant here, in a dining room hanging over the sea on the frontier at San Lodovico. The French-Ligurian cuisine includes a legendary *terrina di coniglio*, exquisite fresh fish and divine desserts. *Book. Closed Mon, Tues lunch and most of Nov.*

Baia Beniamin, Corso Europa 63, t 0184 38002, *www.baiabeniamin.it* (€€€€). Balzi Rossi's near-neighbour at

Grimaldi Inferiore, beautifully set in a lush garden; food and service are above average. It also has five lovely rooms (€€€) with access to the private beach. *Closed Mon, also Sun eve in winter, Nov and a week at Easter.*

Stella Marina, Passeggiata Marconi 1, t 0184 33897 (€€). Good seafood on the waterfront, with a fine pinot nero to wash it down. *Closed Mon.*

Dolceacqua ✉ 18035

Locanda di Bricco Arcagna, Località Arcagna, t 0184 31426, *www.terre bianche.com* (€€). An exceptional *agriturismo* lodging, with simple rooms on a farm, a pool, mountain bikes and horses for guests. The **restaurant** (guests and visitors, but by previous reservation only) serves up good, home-grown food. *Closed Nov.*

La Cantina del Rossese, Via Roma 33, t 0184 206 958 (€€). Good, honest trattoria with a huge wine cellar.

Apricale ✉ 18030

Locanda dei Carugi, Via Roma 12–14, t 0184 209 010, *www.locandadei carugi.it* (€€€). Lovely B&B, reeking of charm and authenticity.

***La Favorita, Strada San Pietro 1, t 0184 208 186, *www.hotelristorante lafavorita.com* (€€). Just before town, off the road from Isolabona, this family-run establishment on the hillside has great views. Try the home-made pasta followed by *coniglio al vino rossese*, and remember to leave room for the creamy *zabaglione*, a house speciality. If you don't feel like the drive back to the coast, there are six comfortable rooms upstairs. *Restaurant closed Tues eve and Wed all day; Jul on Wed only; Aug always open.*

Apricale da Delio, Piazza Vittorio Veneto 9, **t** 0184 208 008, *www. ristoranteapricale.it* (€€). Delio of Gastone's has relocated here, specializing in delicious inland Ligurian cuisine (boar, rabbit, etc.) and great cheeses. *Closed Mon eve and Tues (except Aug).*

Pigna ✉ 18037

****Grand Hotel Pigna Antiche Terme, Regione Lago Pigo, **t** 0184 240 010, *www.termedipigna.it* (€€€€€–€€€€). By Lake Pino east of Pigna, new spa

hotel built by a source rich in sulphur and popular in the 19th century. Now a beauty farm with Turkish baths, the spa offers traditional crenotherapy cures for skin disorders and all the latest treatments.

Terme, Loc. Madonna Assunta, **t 0184 241 046 (€). Simple hotel and well-known restaurant, serving traditional *entroterra* cuisine, with dishes such as kid and beans; *menu degustazione* (€€). *Closed 10 Jan–11 Feb.*

La Castellana, in the castle walls, **t** 0184 241 014 (€€). A memorable place to dine, with a singing proprietor. Try the beans, the *fagioli di Pigna*, which the renowned French chef Alain Ducasse orders specially. *Closed Mon and Nov.*

Bordighera

Once a favourite winter residence of Europe's pampered set, blessed with a good beach and regal promenades, Bordighera is one of the most jovial resorts on the Riviera, perhaps due to the lingering effects of its Festival of Humour. The British get all the credit for instilling Bordighera with the proper attitude for this annual September funfest, which does everything possible to make you laugh, with films, plays, comedy acts and more. As in Ventimiglia, the environs contain vast fields of cultivated flowers, but here the speciality is palms, especially date palms; ever since Sant'Ampelio brought the first seeds from Egypt in 411, Bordighera has supplied the Vatican with fronds during Easter week.

Around the Town of Palms and Mimosa

Compared to Ventimiglia, Bordighera is a baby. Its original nucleus, shoe-horned behind its gates above the Spianata del Capo, is only about 500 years old; from here you can continue up the flower-bedecked **Via dei Colli** for excellent views of the shimmering coast. Down by the sea, the Romanesque chapel of **Sant'Ampelio** stands on its little cape, above the grotto where St Ampelio lived and perhaps swam, as people do today, in clear turquoise waters. What looks like a rotunda is actually all that survives of a casino bombed during the war. From here you can walk west to the spa along the pleasant Lungomare Argentina (named after Evita came to visit in 1947), or east along the seaside Via Arziglia, past the port, with views of Charles Garnier's white asymmetrical villa, and further on to Bordighera's palm and mimosa plantations at the **Winter Garden** and the **Giardino Madonna della Ruota**, a 45-minute walk all told.

Back in the 19th century, the British outnumbered the native Bordigotti in the winter, and a large part of their elegant ghetto of villas and hotels remains intact, especially around Via Romana and Via Vittorio Veneto. In Via Shakespeare, the Tennis & Bridge Club was the first of its kind in Italy, founded in 1878, but has come down in the world to become a *carabinieri* barracks; the Anglican church in Via Regina Vittoria is now a cultural centre. The grandest of the grand hotels were along Via Romana, a lovely street lined with old trees and bougainvillea. Most of them have since been converted into condominiums, with the notable exception of the astonishing Hotel Angst. The Angst (it is the name of the owner!) was one of the showpieces of the Riviera until the Nazis occupied it and left it a wreck. And a haunted wreck the Angst sadly remains.

The most beautiful building, by contrast, is the **Villa Etelinda** (No.36), designed by Charles Garnier and purchased by Queen Margherita of Savoy, who died here in 1926; it now serves as a rest home. The **Istituto Internazionale di Studi Liguri** houses two museums: the **Museo and Library Bicknell**, containing casts of prehistoric Ligurian rock engravings from France's Valle delle Meraviglie, discovered by Rev Clarence Bicknell, his butterfly collection, and coins of Seborga (*see* p.93), and the **Quadreria Mariani**, with works by one of the world's great marine painters, Pompeo Mariani (1857–1927); Bicknell also planted the lovely English gardens. Claude Monet based himself in Bordighera for three months in 1884, enraptured by 'this brilliance, this magical light'. In summer, the tourist office organizes tours, pointing out the places that Monet sketched or painted.

Istituto Internazionale di Studi Liguri
Via Romana 39, t 0184 263 601, www.iisl.it

Museo and Library Bicknell
t 0184 263 694, www.iisl.it; open Mon–Fri 9.30–1 and 1.30–4.45

Quadreria Mariani
t 0184 263 601; open Mon–Fri 9.30–12 and 3.30–4.30; adm

Around Bordighera

Vallecrosia

Just west of Bordighera, new development merges with the seaside village of Vallecrosia. This has an older inland section: its original name, 'Vallechiusa' or Closed Valley, refers to the days when it was a Byzantine border town, 'closing' the valley against invaders, until its inhabitants were drawn to the coast by the presence of the railroad. Today the old steam engine and carriages have been converted to hold the Ristorante Erio's collection of all things musical, inaugurated in 1988, in the commanding presence of Pavarotti, as the **Museo che Canta**, full of records, gramophones, sheet music, and anything associated with Italian song.

Museo che Canta
Via Roma 108, t 0184 291 000, www.museodella canzone.it; visits by appointment

The Pint-sized Principality of Seborga

The valley behind Bordighera has a surprise as well. Seborga may look like any Ligurian hill village, but there's more here than meets the eye: in September 1995 it became a 14 square km democratic principality, having elected a flower gardener as Prince George I (304 votes for, 4 against). But Seborga is only picking up where it left off in the 19th century, after a history even longer and perhaps even more dignified than that of the Riviera's more famous principality. In 954, the Count of Ventimiglia gave it to the Benedictine monastery on the Iles de Lérins near Cannes. At the time, Seborga was a stronghold of the Cathars (or 'Bulgars': the Manichaean sect that started in Persia and made its way through the Balkans; Bulgarians brought it to northern Italy and southern France; Seborga's name comes from 'Castrum Bugrum').

Where there were Cathars, could Templars be far behind? In fact, the founders of the order may have started it all here, when they met in 1118 before sailing to Jerusalem. When they came back from the Holy Land it was to Seborga they returned, and they ordained their first Grand Master here. In the beginning, the Templars seem to have been closely allied to the Cistercians, the equally new monastic order founded by St Bernard of Clairvaux, and Bernard was related to the French nobles from up in Champagne who started the Templars. The Cistercians had been granted Seborga a few years earlier, and in 1118 its Abbot-Prince Edouard declared it the one and only sovereign Cistercian State.

A Templar archive discovered here talks of a 'great secret' Bernard and the Templars were guarding – as in Turin, people in Seborga are sure they have the Holy Grail lying around somewhere. After the fall of the Templars in 1309 Seborga carried on as a sleepy monastic backwater; until 1686 the principality even minted its own coins. It was sold in 1729 to the Savoys, but the act was drawn up so wrongly as to invalidate it. Seborga was so unimportant that it was over-looked at the 1815 Congress of Vienna, which defined the territories that made up Savoy-Piedmont, whose king would become the king of united Italy – but legally not the king of Seborga. They say they have an ironclad case under international law, though they are careful not to push those bureaucrats in Rome too far.

Prince George and his 2,000 contented subjects will be happy to sell you some stamps, a 'tourist passport', a sticker for your car, or some coin of the realm, which they began to mint again in 1995 (the 'Luigino': there's a bureau de change at the Bank of St Bernard's Knights). At the time of writing, the principality has ambassadors at Alassio, just up the coast, and in Scotland; for more information, see www.seborga.net.

Perinaldo

Perinaldo, further up the valley, is high on a ridge, way above all light and air pollution. Even before such things existed, however, it was the birthplace of astronomer Gian Domenico Cassini

Museo Cassiniano
open Mon–Fri 8.30–1,
Mon, Wed and Thurs
also 3–5, Sat 8.30–12

Osservatorio
Cassini
for schedules,
t 348 552 0554, www.
astroperinaldo.it; adm

(1625–1712), who discovered the first asteroid, Ceres; the first moons of Saturn; the space between Saturn's rings; and the speed at which Mars, Venus and Jupiter rotate on their axes. He spent much of his career in Paris, working for the Sun King, who understandably had a keen interest in the planets. The Palazzo Comune houses a **Museo Cassiniano** with exhibits on his life. You can have a look at the stars on astronomical evenings at the **Osservatorio Cassini**. Another Cassini legacy is the sundial on the parish house (formerly a Doria hunting lodge), made according to the specifications of Gian Domenico's astronomer grandson.

Ospedaletti and Coldirodi

Giardino
Esotico Pallanca
t 0184 266 347; open
winter Tues–Sun 9–5,
Mon 2–5; summer
Tues–Sun 9–12.30
and 2.30–7, Mon
2.30–7; booking
recommended; adm

Driving east of Bordighera on the Via Aurelia, right after a tunnel you'll find a surprising little patch of desert – the **Giardino Esotico Pallanca**. Considered one of the top succulent gardens in the world, built on a series of terraces in one of the most sheltered spots on the Riviera, cacti grow like crazy – one stands 21ft high. There are some 3,500 different kinds, and nearly all burst into bloom in March: not to be missed if you're in the area.

Just beyond is **Ospedaletti**, a quiet oasis between the worldly resorts of Bordighera and San Remo, shaded by pines, palms and eucalyptus and guarded by two medieval 'Saracen towers'. The town got its name from the Knights Hospitallers of Rhodes who shipwrecked here *c.* 1300 and built a pilgrims' hospice, which has long since vanished, and the surviving church of Sant'Erasmo. The biggest and grandest building in Ospedaletti, **Villa Sultana** on Corso Regina Margherita, was one of the first big casinos (1886), and in its day it offered some keen competition to the Grimaldi enterprise over in Monte Carlo. Katherine Mansfield stayed in Ospedaletti in the early 1900s, before moving on to Menton; her villa has since been replaced by the Hotel Madison.

Rambaldi
Art Gallery
t 0184 670 131; open
Tues, Thurs, Fri, Sat and
Sun 1–12, Fri and Sat
also 3.30–6

The Knights of Rhodes also bestowed their name on the nearby hill town of **Coldirodi**, to where the folk of Ospedaletti could hotfoot it if the Saracens showed up. Its church of **San Sebastiano** has good Baroque paintings, and there's more art in its **Rambaldi Art Gallery**, with some good paintings among the dross: a *Madonna col Bambino* by Tuscan Lorenzo di Credi and some very credible forgeries of Rembrandt, Veronese and Guido Reni.

ⓘ **Bordighera >**
Via Vittorio Emanuele
II 172, t 0184 262 322,
www.bordighera.it;
open in winter Mon–Fri
8–1, plus Tues and
Thurs 3–6; summer
Mon–Sat 8–1

Where to Stay and Eat in and around Bordighera

Bordighera ✉ 18012

★★★★**Grand Hotel del Mare**, Via Portico della Punta 34, t 0184 262 201, *www. grandhoteldelmare.it* (€€€€€–€€€€). For real elegance check in at this modern hotel in a beautiful panoramic position over the sea, with private beach, sea-water pool, gardens and tennis. *Closed Nov–Christmas.*

★★★**Villa Elisa**, Via Romana 70, t 0184 261 313, *www.villaelisa.com* (€€€–€€). An inviting villa above the town,

⭐ **La Reserve Tastevin** >>

⭐ **Via Romana** >

ⓘ **Ospedaletti** >>
Corso Regina Margherita 13, t 0184 689 085

❷ **San Remo**

standing in pretty gardens, with very attractive rooms.

***Britannique & Jolie, Via Regina Margherita 35, t 0184 261 464 (€€–€). A traditional favourite, set in a pretty park near the sea. Breakfast included. *Closed Oct and Nov.*

***Enrica, Via Noaro 1, t 0184 263 436 (€€). Sweet, family-run hotel with bright rooms and a roof garden, located near the train station.

**Rosalia, Via Vittorio Emanuele 429, t 0184 261 366, *www.hotelrosalia.it* (€€–€). Nice rooms, half with sea views, convenient to the station and the beaches.

**Lora, Via dei Bagni 1, t 0184 262 324, *www.albergolora.it* (€). Another bargain on the beach.

Via Romana, Via Romana 57, t 0184 266 681, *www.laviaromana.it* (€€€€). For a superb meal with all the frills book a table in the elegant Liberty-style dining room of the former Grand Hotel Londra. Refined, aromatic combinations of seafood and fresh produce are the speciality (*zuppa* of cuttlefish and artichokes, prawns *au gratin* with herbs). The desserts, dessert wines and *petits fours* are equally lovely. Excellent €45 lunch menu. *Closed Wed, and Thurs lunch.*

Carletto, Via Vitt. Emanuele 339, t 0184 261 725 (€€€€). Very elegant, intimate atmosphere, with a seafood-based menu and wines to match. *Closed Wed (except Aug) and 20 June–12 July, 5 Nov–20 Dec.*

La Reserve Tastevin, Via Aurelia 20, Capo Sant'Ampelio, t 0184 261 322 (€€€). The most spectacular place to eat in Bordighera, inserted in the cliffs. The views are fantastic and so is the food, a delightful combination of ingredients from the sea and the Valle Argentina. *Closed Mon and Sun.*

Le Chaudron, Piazza Bengasi 2, t 0184 263 592 (€€€€). Very elegant, tiny restaurant serving delicious spaghetti with artichokes, and the Ligurian speciality, *pesce al sale* (fish baked in salt). *Closed Mon.*

Osteria Magiargè, Piazza G. Viale, t 0184 262 946 (€€). Up in Bordighera Alta (*centro storico*), popular with the locals for its relaxed atmosphere and ever-changing menu. During the summer there are tables outside in the piazza. *Book. Closed all Mon and for lunch on Tues; open every day in July and Aug but for dinner only.*

Il Tempo Ritovato, Via Vittorio Emanuele 144, t 0184 261 207 (€€). Ligurian cooking and lots of seafood; also stewed boar and goat, and even paella. *Closed Sun in winter.*

Ospedaletti ✉ 18014

***Le Rocce del Capo, Lungomare Colombo 102, t 0184 689 733, *www.leroccedelcapohotel.it* (€€€ but special offers on website). Good value, with its own covered pool, private beach and well-equipped rooms that come in three floral themes: carnation, lily or rose.

08
Riviera di Ponente | San Remo

San Remo

San Remo is the opulent queen of the Italian Riviera, of grand hotels and villas as beautiful and out of date as antimacassars. Yet, even if the old girl isn't as fashionable as she once was, she's still a game corker with a Mae West twinkle in her eye. Other resorts may have more glamour, but few have more character.

Set on a huge, sheltered bay, San Remo first became a watering hole for British toffs (among them Edward Lear, who ended his travels through the Mediterranean here in 1888), then for the Russians, led in 1874 by Empress Maria Alexandrovna who arrived on the new railroad. Tchaikovsky found the place inspiring enough to compose *Eugene Onegin* and the *Fourth Symphony* in 1878. In 1887 Kaiser Frederick Wilhelm bunked over at Villa Zirio.

Getting to, around and from San Remo

The **train** station is at the west end of town near the casino; **buses** depart from the big station in Piazza Colombo: Riviera Trasporti, t 800 034 771, *www.rivieratrasporti.it*, will take you to Taggia or as far as Andora to the east. Piazza Colombo is also a good area to park.

For a **taxi**, call t 0184 541 454.

San Remo was also the home town of Italo Calvino (1923–85), who was born in Cuba but brought here as a small child by his parents, both avid botanists, who planted a beautiful garden by their villa in Via Meridiana. Calvino fought in the Resistance at Baiardo, but after the war moved to Turin and never returned, as the changes in San Remo made him too sad; only a tiny fraction remains of his parents' garden, now subdivided into second homes for the Torinese and Milanese. But, as he said in an interview, he never forgot the city of his childhood: 'San Remo continues to jump out in my books, in the most varied views and prospects, especially when viewed from on high, but most of all in many of the *Invisible Cities*.' In these dialogues between Marco Polo and Kublai Khan, Polo admits that all the stories he tells Kublai about cities are really about Venice – but for Calvino, they were about San Remo.

San Remo, the fourth largest city in Liguria, is made up of three distinct parts: the shopping district around Corso Matteotti, the steep old town called La Pigna and the smart west end where the grand hotels are situated. In no part, however, will you find a church or legend for Remo, an invisible saint in Calvino's invisible city; the closest anyone has found is a 7th-century hermit named Romolo, who lived nearby – a mystery Romulus for a mystery Remus. In fact, the locals prefer to see the name written Sanremo, just so people stop asking embarrassing questions.

Modern San Remo

To get the full flavour of San Remo, take a *passeggiata* down the seafront **Corso dell' Imperatrice**, named in honour of Tsarina Maria Alexandrovna who donated the first palms that line the street; here, springing out of luxuriant, tropical foliage, are San Remo's most prestigious hotels, the statue of *Spring*, symbol of the city's sweet climate, and the charming onion domes of the dainty jewel box **Russian Orthodox Church**, built in the 1920s by the exiled nobility. Members of the royal family of Montenegro are buried within. Along the Corso, you can visit the lush **Marsaglia Park** with its fat 'elephant foot' palms.

This west end of town reaches its zenith at the white, brightly lit, Liberty-style **Municipal Casino**, built in 1904, a legacy from those golden days of fashion and still the lively heart of San Remo's social life, with its roof-garden cabaret, and a celebrated restaurant with a live orchestra. According to the 1930s Baedeker to the Riviera, it

Russian Orthodox Church
t 0184 531 807; open Tues–Sun 9.30–12.30 and 3–6.30

Municipal Casino
Corso degli Inglesi 18, t 0184 5951; open to over-18s, 10am–2.30am; there's a dress code for some rooms, but you can borrow a jacket; free Mon–Thurs except holidays, adm Fri–Sun

had more class than Monte Carlo: 'There are people who really look like as if they want to be ruined by gambling, and prefer to stake their finances in San Remo rather than in Montecarlo. Yes, because if you lose in San Remo, you lose it elegantly, in a respectable way.'

Today one of the largest casinos in Europe, and the only active one on the Italian Riviera, it also has something that Las Vegas has never dreamed of: 'Literary Tuesdays', in its intimate Teatro dell'Opera, an institution founded in the 1920s by a local poet to amuse the wives of the gamblers and keep them from trying to stop their husbands from going broke. The discussions and debates here attract some of Italy's top scribes and journalists; musical evenings are held on the roof garden.

East of the casino begins **Corso Matteotti**, lined with designer boutiques. It also has a relic of the past, the handsome Renaissance-Baroque Palazzo Borca d'Olmo, now the **Museo Civico Archeologico**, which contains finds from the Palaeolithic caves in the region, especially the Grotta dell'Arma; one room is dedicated to Garibaldi, who moved to San Remo for a few years after his nemesis, Count Cavour, traded his home town of Nice to the French under Napoleon III; other rooms have 17th–19th-century paintings.

Museo Civico Archeologico
bus no.143, t 0184 531 942; open Tues–Sat 9–12 and 3–6

In February the Teatro Ariston on the Corso hosts the biggest event in the wonderland of Italian pop, the **Festival della Canzone**, an extravagant, five-day-long ritual of glitter and hype. The Festival once served as the prelims for the Eurovision Song Contest: now that Italy doesn't compete any more, it's the last word (and, best of all, an Italian always wins). In 1967, one hopeful contestant named Luigi Tenco committed suicide when he didn't make the cut; in his memory, the Rassegna Tenco takes place in October, drawing singer-songwriters from around the world.

La Pigna

La Pigna is San Remo's 'casbah', a tangled mesh of steep lanes and stairs weaving under archways and narrow tunnels, fortified around the year 1000 as a refuge against the Saracens, back when San Remo belonged to the bishops of Genoa. Get there by way of Piazza San Siro (back from Corso Matteotti) and its 12th-century **Cathedral of San Siro**, built by the Maestri Comacini and painstakingly stripped of its Baroque froufrou. Two side doors have bas reliefs, one with a 15th-century Madonna and two saints, the other from the 12th century, with motifs so unusual for the area that no one has a clue who might have carved them. Inside there's an unusual black 15th-century *Crucifix*, once believed to be miraculous, and a tabernacle by the Gagini family. The still Baroque **Oratorio dell' Immacolata Concezione** (1563) stands opposite; nearby, the large **market** in Piazza Eroi Sanremesi draws hundreds of Italian and French gourmets.

Market
Tues and Sat only 8–1

Inside La Pigna's tangled skein are a number of tiny piazzas, one hosting the 17th-century church of **San Giuseppe**, with a 12th-century door and a fountain topped with the quarter's pine cone symbol. From here you can wend your way up through the casbah to the **Giardini Regina Elena**, which is rather dull as Riviera gardens go but has fantastic views of the town and harbour.

Santuario Madonna della Costa
t 0371 487 404; regular buses from San Remo

Standing majestically at the top of La Pigna, at the head of a long lane and the largest polychrome pebble mosaic *sagrato* in all Liguria, is the **Santuario Madonna della Costa**, rebuilt in 1630. The Sanremesi pulled out all the stops in the interior; the Madonna on the high altar (1401) saved a local sailor, who donated the first gold coin to establish the shrine. On 15 August, the event is celebrated with fireworks and a feast.

Villa Nobel
open Tues–Sat 11–12.30, Sat 4–6.30 also, closed Sun and Mon

Lastly, to the east on Corso Cavallotti over the pleasure port, are the beautifully landscaped gardens of the **Villa Ormond**, planted by Swedish merchants and now a city park, and the **Villa Nobel** (1874), a Moorish-style confection. Alfred Nobel, the father of dynamite and plywood, and founder of the famous prizes, called this his 'nest'; you can look at his laboratory and library, and at the exhibit dedicated to his life; he died here in 1896. Flowers from San Remo always decorate the Nobel prize ceremonies in Stockholm.

San Remo Flower Market
Mon–Fri 4am–8am, www. sanremoflower market.it

Further east in the Valle Armea, just off Via Aurelia, early risers can take in the colour and scent of the **San Remo Flower Market** – a working, wholesale market, but fascinating nonetheless.

Above and Behind San Remo

Via Crucis
open daily 10–8

If you're driving, the road to take is the panoramic **Corso degli Inglesi** from the casino; at No.374 is a **Via Crucis** with life-sized bronze figures by Milanese sculptor Enrico Manfrini (1990) set in a beautiful shady grove by a car park. Although the funicular up to **Monte Bignone** (4,281ft), the highest peak in the amphitheatre around San Remo, is out of action, you can drive on Via Galileo halfway up to **San Romolo**, with a golf course, great views and one of the biggest chestnut trees in Europe, 18ft in diameter, a mere nut back in the year 1200 or so.

Further inland, **Baiardo** (or Bajardo) once spread over a conical hill once sacred to the Celto-Ligurians, with a backdrop of wooded mountains. Devastated by the great 1887 Ash Wednesday earthquake (*see* opposite), the town was rebuilt further down; its reputation for healthy air has now made it a modest resort. One relic of old Baiardo is the ruined church of **San Nicolò**, where two hundred people were killed when the roof crashed down on their heads. Its capitals are carved roughly with the heads of Mongols, perhaps representing some who accompanied the Saracens to Liguria. The views are especially lovely from the nearby **Terrazza sulle Alpi**.

In the year 1200, a Pisan employed by Ventimiglia (an ally of Pisa then) was felling trees here for ships and fell in love with the daughter of the Count of Baiardo. Her father, an ally of Genoa, was so adamantly opposed to their marriage that he cut off his daughter's head. Ever since then, Baiardo solemnly remembers her in the **Festa della Barca** ('of the boat') on Pentecost Sunday, when a large tree trunk topped by a smaller pine tree is erected in the piazza, around which the people dance slowly while singing the 44 verses of the 'Ballad of the Count's Daughter' in dialect. The ritual is so important to the villagers that they have performed it even during times of war and occupation. After Pentecost the tree is auctioned off: it, at least, brings good luck.

If you don't mind the narrow, spaghetti-like mountain roads that prevail here, you can circle back to the coast by way of **Ceriana**, another pretty hill town surrounded by terraces, its narrow lanes built in concentric rings, all crowned by a campanile. Pretty Baroque churches dot the lanes: **SS. Pietro e Paolo**, with its two bell towers, has some good 16th-century paintings and a beautiful altar in the sacristy, carved of linden wood.

East of San Remo: Bussana New and Old

A few kilometres down the coast from San Remo, Bussana is relatively new by Riviera standards, built in the late 19th century. The chief monument is the massive **Santuario del Sacro Cuore**, lavishly decorated inside; the sacristy contains an excellent *Birth of Christ* by Caravaggio's great follower, Mattia Preti.

The original Bussana, 2km inland and enjoying views of San Remo's greenhouses, is now the 'ghost town' **Bussana Vecchia**. On 23 February 1887, an earthquake killed thousands and turned the town into a ruin. The tremors knocked in the roof of the church (packed for the Ash Wednesday service), but nearly all the parishioners managed to escape into the side chapels; one survivor, Giovanni Torre detto Merlo, went on to invent the ice cream cone in 1902. The stucco decorations sprout weeds, trees grow in the nave, and cherubs smile down like broken dolls on a shelf.

It is a rather typical Italian contradiction that, although Bussana Vecchia officially no longer exists, it has inhabitants (mostly foreign artists) who are equally officially non-existent, but who have restored the interiors of the ruined houses, and been hooked up with water, lights and telephones. They make a living selling paintings and all sorts of arty dust magnets – disdainful Italian purists compare it to the 'French method' of managing their Riviera hill towns by turning them into quaint shopping malls. The village can be visited by leaving the car at the entrance and walking all around.

Sports and Activities in San Remo

There's no lack of things to do in San Remo. From May to September you can take a day trip by sea to Monte Carlo or go **whale watching** with the Riviera Line, Molo di Levante 35, **t** 0184 505 055. You can go **diving** with Polo Sub, in Arma di Taggia, **t** 0184 535 335; play **tennis** at a dozen spots; go **riding** nearby at the Società Ippica Sanremo, **t** 0184 660 770, or in Arma di Taggia at San Martino, **t** 0184 477 083, or shoot bogeys at San Remo's 18-hole Ulivi **golf course**, **t** 0184 557 093.

Where to Stay in San Remo

(i) **San Remo** >
Largo Nuvoloni 1,
t 0184 59059,
toll-free t 800 813012,
www.rivieradeifiori.org

San Remo ✉ 18038

*****Royal, Corso Imperatrice 80, **t** 0184 5391, *www.royalhotel sanremo.com* (€€€€€). Near the casino, and more of a palace than accommodation for rent. Surrounded by lush gardens, with tennis courts and an enormous heated sea-water pool, this turn-of-the-last-century grande dame has rooms that vary from imperial suites to more modest, refurbished doubles. True to tradition, the hotel orchestra serenades guests in the afternoon and gets them dancing in the evening.

****Grand Hotel Londra, Corso Matuzia 2, **t** 0184 65511 (€€€€€). If you prefer something with a Liberty-style touch, this hotel from the turn of the last century has a lovely garden and pool, and fine original interior details. *Closed Oct and Nov.*

****Nyala, Strada Solaro 134, **t** 0184 667 668, *www.nyalahotel.com* (€€€€€). Away from the bustle, a wonderfully welcoming hotel in the hills on the west edge of town. It has large bedrooms and suites with sun terraces where you can sit for hours gazing at the hillside views, a restaurant and bar, and a heated outdoor pool with pool-side bar in a tropical garden.

****Astoria West End, Corso Matuzia 8, **t** 0184 65541, *www.astoriasanremo.it*

(€€€€–€€€). One of the region's oldest hotels sits in all its confectionery elegance – grand chandeliers, stucco ceilings and carved lifts – opposite the sea. It also has a garden with a pool.

***Lolli Palace, Corso Imperatrice 70, **t** 0184 531 496, *www.lollihotel.it* (€€€–€€). A lovely hotel and decent restaurant. The sea-facing rooms are bright and airy with big bay windows and cute little balconies.

***Paradiso, Via Roccasterone 12, **t** 0184 571 211, *www.paradisohotel.it* (€€€–€€). Perfect if you seek peace and quiet, set just back from the seafront, and enveloped with flowers. It has a distinguished, glass-enclosed **restaurant** and a sunny breakfast room. *Closed Nov and first half Dec.*

***Bel Soggiorno, Corso Matuzia 41, **t** 0184 667 631 (€€). A Liberty-style hotel in the same area, renovated in 2000. The dining room has a gorgeous view over the gardens.

***Eletto, Via Matteotti 44, **t** 0184 531 548, *www.elettohotel.it* (€€). A very pretty 19th-century hotel in the centre, furnished with antiques. It also has a lush little garden.

*Terminus e Metropoli, Via Roma 8, **t** 0184 577 110 (€€–€). One of several cheaper options on Corso Matteotti, Via Roma, and Corso Mombello.

Corso, Corso Cavallotti 194, **t 0184 509 911, *corsohotelsanremo@virgilio.it* (€€–€). A quiet and simple hotel, located at the east end of town near the Villa Comunale and only a short walk from the beach by Porto Sole.

Sole Mare, Via Carli 23, **t 0184 577 105, *www.solemarehotel.com* (€€–€). Tiny, comfortable choice with eight rooms, especially popular with Italians. The **restaurant** is a big favourite with the locals.

Eating Out in San Remo

(★) **Paolo e Barbara** >>

Paolo e Barbara, Via Roma 47 (near the casino, in case you hit the jackpot), **t** 0184 531 653, *www.paolobarbara.it* (€€€€). Highly acclaimed restaurant, run by a couple dedicated to perfect contemporary Ligurian food. Paolo Masieri in the kitchen is a wizard of invention, which he deftly combines with Riviera traditions – home-made focaccia, famous *gamberoni San Remo* flambéed in whisky, and much more; the bill with a good wine can quickly come to €100. *Book. Closed Wed, Thurs, for ten days before Christmas and one week in Jan, July open Fri–Sun eve only.*

Da Giannino, Corso Trento e Trieste 23, t 0184 504 014 (€€€€). Exquisite dishes based on fresh ingredients, including speciality of the region *tagliolini al sugo di triglia* (pasta with red mullet sauce), polenta with cheese and vegetable sauce, and pigeon with ginger. *Closed Sun, Mon eve.*

Bagatto, Via Matteotti 145, t 0184 531 925 (€€€). One of the brightest and most relaxed restaurants in San Remo, with tempting *antipasti, risotti* and dishes using sun-ripened vegetables, as well as delicious seafood and lamb. *Closed Sun and July.*

Nuovo Piccolo Mondo, Via Piave 7, t 0184 509 012 (€). Atmospheric 1920s trattoria, with prices to match; includes simple seafood dishes such

as *baccalà* and octopus. *Book. No credit cards. Closed Sun, half of June and half of July.*

Entertainment and Nightlife in San Remo

At night in San Remo all roads lead to the **casino** (see below) and the **Disco Loco** to the right of it, also a cabaret-revue venue.

The **old port**, along Corso Nazario Sauro, Piazza Bresca and Via Nino Bixio, is a favourite place to hang out after dark, with tables to sit at outside watching the passing crowd; medieval La Pigna is also a popular hangout.

Baiardo ✉ 18031

Armonia, Via Roma 124, t 0184 673 283 (€€). A century-old inn, with wonderful views and superb food, offering some of the best-value fine dining on the Riviera. Be sure to book. *Closed Tues.*

Up the Valle Argentina

Arma di Taggia and Taggia

Just east of Bussana, at the mouth of the Valle Argentina, **Arma di Taggia** has one of the finest sandy beaches in the area, and is devoted to the pleasures of the sea. All hints of culture are kept 3km inland, in the lovely medieval village of **Taggia**, carefully preserved in its 16th-century walls. The biggest dose of culture, however, is outside, in the museum of **San Domenico**. Built between 1460 and 1490, this monastery was the wealthiest art patron in these parts for centuries: there are manuscripts and *incunaboli*, two polyptychs by Ludovico Brea, works by his sons Francesco and Antonio, paintings and frescoes by Giovanni Canavesio, and a beautiful *Epiphany* attributed to the great Mannerist Parmigianino. Other works are in the refectory, in the cloister with its black stone columns, and in the Sala Capitolare (Canavesio's superb fresco of the *Crucifixion*). As well as supporting the arts, the Dominicans also introduced the olive trees that made Taggia's fortune and took its name, *taggiasca*.

The walled town is a striking sight next to its remarkable, dogleg 16-arched medieval **bridge**. Within the walls, the lanes are lined with palaces, fountains, gateways and a beautiful Baroque church, **SS. Giacomo e Filippo**, built to a design by Bernini over a Romanesque church and containing works by Luca Cambiaso. Via Soleri and Via San Dalmazzo are lined with porticoes, sculpted architraves

 Taggia

San Domenico
t 0184 476 254; open Mon–Sat 9–12 and 3–6; adm

and noble houses with their coats of arms. Another church outside the walls, the **Madonna del Canneto,** has frescoes by Giovanni and Luca Cambiaso, including *The Resurrection*, one of the materpieces of their career. Next to it stands the Villa Ruffini; Taggia was the home of Giovanni Ruffini, the man most responsible for the tourist boom on the Riviera (*see* **History**, p.27). Come on the third Sunday of July for the ancient Festival of Mary Magdalene, a personage who, according to tradition, once paid Taggia a call. She is remembered by members of her red-capped confraternity with an eerie Dance of Death, performed by two men, one playing the role of 'the man', and the other that of Mary Magdalene, who dies and is brought back to life with a sprig of lavender.

Badalucco and Montalto Ligure

Attractive old villages dot the Valle Argentina. **Badalucco,** with another pretty bridge of two asymmetrical arches, has murals and ceramic works hidden in every alley. The powers that be in Badalucco weren't always so nice: the nearby village, **Montalto Ligure,** was founded by newlyweds fleeing the Count of Badalucco's insistence on his first-night *droit de seigneur* (the Ligurian nobles seem to have been real creeps in that regard). Half of Badalucco followed them in protest. Not long after, the Count regretted his ungentlemanly behaviour and invited his ex-subjects to a reconciliatory banquet, but their desertion had left him so poor he only had dried chestnuts to offer them. The good people of Montalto had a word with one another, went home, and returned with all the fixings of a sumptuous feast. And so they were reconciled – but the protestors never went back to Badalucco.

The village they built is one of the most impressive of Liguria's 'mini-cities'. This reaches an astonishing level of sophistication in the arrangement of Montalto's centrepiece, the 18th-century church of **San Giovanni Battista** and the older **Oratorio di San Vicenzo Ferreri**: the church is built over a vaulted passageway, its façade half hidden behind the bell tower, in turn half hidden beyond the oratory, also built over a portico, with stairs ascending and descending, all in a 'piazza' measuring only a few square metres. San Giorgio's polyptych by Ludovico Brea (1516) spent time in the Louvre after Napoleon pinched it, but the French had a change of heart (and better polyptychs) so they sent it back.

Further up, the villages take on a more mountainous character and have slate roofs over their bare stone walls. **Andagna** is a steep 3km off the main Argentina road, enjoying a fine panoramic view over the valley below. Another reason to visit is its **Cappella di San Bernardo**, with fine frescoes of 1436 showing the Passion, along with the Seven Virtues and Seven Vices. **Molini di Triora,** down in the valley, was named for the 23 watermills that made it an industrial centre in the Middle Ages; it was destroyed by the Piedmontese in the 17th century. But they missed the 15th-century **Santuario della Madonna della Montata** on the top of Molini.

Triora and its 'Witches'

Hill towns were relatively safe in those centuries of endless war, at least from passing armies. Fortified Triora was from 1216 onwards an outpost of the Republic of Genoa. In the 17th century it defied two major sieges by the Piedmontese; worse happened in 1944 when it became the victim of Nazi reprisals. Still, Triora looks much the same as it always did, defences and houses intact, a picture postcard village of just over 400 souls, its fountains trickling with water carried by the original 15th-century pipes.

Triora is best known, however, as the Salem of the Italian Riviera. The story goes that in the late 16th century witches, or *bagiue*, would gather at a now ruined house called **La Cabotina** outside the village to communicate with the devil. They were also expert herbalists and healers, but in 1588 famine struck, and the *bagiue* (13 women, four girls and a boy) were accused by some of their fellow citizens of having brought the hunger. In the collective neurosis of the Counter-Reformation they were hauled before the Inquisition. Five perished, but for the eight survivors their story had a rare happy ending – their condemnation was revoked and their accusers were excommunicated. In the old prison where they rotted on Corso Italia, the **Museo Etnografico e della Stregoneria** documents local life, witch hunts and archaeology.

Museo Etnografico e della Stregoneria
t 0184 94477; open Mon–Fri 2.30–6, summer 3–6.30; Sat and Sun 10.30–12 and 3–6.30; adm

Besides a modest amount of tourist tat spawned by the witches, Triora has some serious art, especially in the Romanesque-Gothic **Collegiata dell'Assunta**, with a beautiful *Baptism of Jesus* (1397) by Sienese master Taddeo di Bartolo and works by Luca Cambiaso. The nearby Baroque **Oratorio di San Giovanni** has a fine marble portal. Just outside Triora, the pretty church of **San Bernardino** is coated with *quattrocento* frescoes in the style of Canavesio, including a *Last Judgement*. Nearby, a stepped path leads up to the towers of the castle on top of the village. You may have seen loaves of flat round *pane di Triora* sold elsewhere in Liguria and Piedmont; it's good mountain bread, and stays fresh for a week.

Beyond Triora, the beautiful upper Valle Argentina approaches the highest peaks of Liguria and the stunning hamlet of **Realdo**, balanced on a sheer crag 3,500ft above sea level. **Verdeggia** is even higher up, if not quite as picturesque as Realdo, having been rebuilt after an avalanche in 1805. Quarrying slate is a big industry here, much in evidence in the houses. From Verdeggia a not very difficult path leads up in three hours to the **Passo della Guardia** (7,105ft) crowned by a statue of Christ; from here you can climb up Saccarello (7,216ft) and descend into France.

Where to Stay and Eat in the Valle Argentina

(i) **Arma di Taggia >**
Via Boselli 1,
t 0184 43733

(i) **Triora >>**
Corso Italia 7 (in witchcraft museum),
t 0184 94477

Arma di Taggia/Taggia ✉ 18011

★★★**Svizzera**, Via Lungomare 123, t 0184 43152 *www.hotelsvizzera.it* (€€). Family-run hotel, located in an ideal position for excursions along the coast and in the hinterland. The **restaurant** has a pleasant veranda and recipes are based on the best Ligurian tradition. *Closed Nov–Christmas.*

★★★**Roma**, Via Cornice 10, t 0184 43076 (€€–€). Just 300m from the sea, 14 clean, modern rooms and a good **restaurant/pizzeria**. *Closed mid-Oct to mid-Nov; restaurant closed Mon.*

La Conchiglia, Via Lungomare 33, t 0184 43169 (€€€€). Highly regarded restaurant serving Ligurian delights based on seafood, local cheeses and olive oil – the prawn and white-bean salad is delicious. *Book. Closed Wed, part June, part Nov.*

Germinal, Via Gastaldi 15b, up in Taggia, t 0184 41153 *www.osteria germinal.it* (€€). All you could want: vegetables from the family garden, fresh fish from the sea, and home-made pasta and desserts. Booking advisable. *Open Thurs–Sun eves only, Sun and hols lunch also; closed Mon.*

Badalucco ✉ 18010

Al Vecchio Frantoio, Bivio Vignal, t 0184 408 024 (€€). Delicious home-made breads accompany fine renditions of Ligurian meat and fish dishes. *Closed Tues and first two weeks of Jan.*

Il Ponte, Via Ortal 3, t 0184 408 000 (€€€). Good home cooking in an old olive press, with vegetables picked fresh from the garden and exquisite pesto. *Closed Wed and Nov.*

Molini di Triora/Triora ✉ 18019

Colomba d'Oro, Corso Italia 66, t 0184 94051, *www.colombadoro.it* (€€). Up in Triora, a convent converted into a hotel, with a **restaurant** – a sombre but atmospheric place to sleep with lovely views.

★★**Santo Spirito**, Piazza Roma 23, t 0184 94019, *www.ristorante santospirito.com* (€). The oldest hotel/restaurant in Molini (founded in 1897) and a good place to tuck into a steaming dish of home-made pasta and game dishes with mushrooms.

Angela Maria, Piazza Roma 26, t 0184 94021. Not a restaurant but a shop, and another good reason to stop. Run by a 'good witch' who sells her delicious home-made cheese, including Alpine *tome* and *brusso* (fermented ricotta) and a 'witch's philtre' made of Alpine herbs, a recipe handed down from Angela Maria's ancestor, Francesca Ciocheto, one of the women dragged before the Inquisition in 1588.

The Riviera degli Olivi

Imperia divides the 'Riviera of Flowers' from the more rugged 'Riviera of Olives' to the east. Olive-oil connoisseurs rate Liguria's top in Italy, although of course there are plenty of other regions ready to dispute this most slippery of crowns. This stretch of coast, especially the area around Imperia, also gets fewer tourists.

From Santo Stefano to Imperia

After San Remo, you can already see the olive groves taking over from the greenhouses. The first villages on the coast, **Santo Stefano** and **Riva Ligure**, have merged together, with fishermen's houses right on the sea. Just up the road, **Cipressa** was named after Cyprus by its founders – three shepherds who escaped from there. Devastated by Turkish pirates in the 16th century, the inhabitants

Getting around the Riviera degli Olivi

If you plan to rely on **buses**, Riviera Trasporti, **t** 800 036 771, offers a seven-day Travel Card, good for all destinations from Ventimiglia to San Bartolomeo al Mare, for €12.50.

survived by taking refuge in the mighty Torre Gallinara. Nearby, **Linguaglietta** in the olive groves has kept its medieval appearance and one of the most peculiar churches in Liguria: the 12th-century **San Pietro**, transformed into a fortress against these same pirates in the 1500s. Its little rose window is topped by machicolations (from where the defenders could drop boiling oil; in one corner is a watch tower, in the other a bell tower). Behind the church are the ruins of the castle of the Della Lengueglia, while off the road you can visit the picturesque ruins of the church of **San Sebastiano**.

San Lorenzo al Mare, back on the sea, is another small resort dominated by the railway, but with two tiny pedestrian centres and pebbly beaches that, for once, are free, if *stabilimenti balneari* drive you crazy. Inland, **Civezza**, lost in olive groves, was founded by exiles from Venice who left five towers (now all private houses) and dedicated a church to their patron, **San Marco**; in 1783 it was rebuilt by Tommaso Carrega.

Pietrabruna, up the San Lorenzo Valley, is another picturesque village, and one that used to cultivate lavender; since the mid-1980s the village has turned to greenhouse anemones. Remains of the old lavender distilleries and lavender fields lie along the pretty ring trail, a walk of three-and-a-half hours along the slopes of Monte Faudo, starting from the parking lot under the town.

Imperia

In 1923 two towns, Porto Maurizio and Oneglia, were married by Mussolini to form a new provincial capital with a name that warmed the cockles of his little fascist heart: Imperia. This marriage of towns had the longest possible engagement; by the year 1000 they were already distinct towns under different lords – Porto Maurizio belonged to Genoa, while Oneglia was an insignificant port of Albenga, only to become, after 1567, the only seaport of the Dukes of Savoy. The two towns were first 'introduced' in 1815 when both were part of the kingdom of Sardinia; in 1848 they were 'betrothed' by a bridge over the river Impero. When Nice was ceded to France in 1860, Porto Maurizio became a provincial capital. This began a building boom, interrupted in 1887 by the big earthquake. Relations with Oneglia, its bride, remain cool.

Imperia is one of the rare cities in Italy that fits Gertrude Stein's famous description of Oakland, California: 'there's no there there.'

While bits are very pleasant, Imperia remains estranged from itself and, no matter how often you go, you leave with a warm, fuzzy but ultimately anonymous feeling.

Porto Maurizio

Porto Maurizio itself has three distinct parts. Rather dull seaside **Borgo Foce** to the west, the aristocratic **Parasio** quarter on the acropolis in the centre, and, to the east, another maritime quarter, **Borgo Marino**, with a sandy beach. The latter was a port of call protected by the Byzantines after the fall of Rome, and later became important as the Vicarate of Liguria di Ponente, when the town's first fancy palaces were built. The Knights of St John used Borgo Marino as one of their ports to Jerusalem, Rhodes and then Malta; the little deconsecrated church of **San Giovanni** is all that remains of their passing. A pretty seaside footpath links Borgo Foce and Borgo Marino.

Halfway up the hill above Borgo Marino you can't miss the enormous neoclassical **Duomo di San Maurizio**, the biggest church in Liguria, built between 1781 and 1838 and full of nondescript 18th-century painting. More of the same fills the Pinacoteca Civica, while ships' models and nautical instruments wait in the small but excellent **Museo Navale del Ponente Ligure**. From Piazza Duomo, Via Acquarone will take you up to the **Parasio** (from *palatium*, an ancient keep used as a fortress and prison then demolished), its steep lanes and steps lined with the palaces and Baroque churches that make it such a grand sight from sea level. One is dedicated to Imperia's official patron, **San Leonardo**, and linked to his birthplace; another place to aim for is the **Convento di Santa Chiara**.

Pinacoteca Civica
Piazza Duomo, t 0183 61136; open Mon–Sat 9–12 and 3–6, closed Sun; in winter Wed 3.30–7.30, Sat 4.30–7.30

Museo Navale del Ponente Ligure
Piazza Duomo 11, t 0183 651 541; open summer Wed and Sat 9pm–11pm, other times Wed and Sat 3–7

Liguria's Liquid Gold

No one knows when the first olive trees were planted along the Riviera – whether by the Romans or Crusaders. In the early Middle Ages, at any rate, olive trees were mainly used to define the borders of the farms. The essential olive-pressing know-how was in the hands of the Benedictines at San Pietro in Triora, who over the decades taught farmers how to build the dry-stone terraces you see everywhere, how to plant and irrigate the young trees, and how to press the olives in the *frantoio*. The friars at San Domenico in Taggia are given credit for elevating Ligurian olive oil to the top of the class, thanks to the small black *taggiasca* olives they planted, which are also famous for the work they require – they are harder to pick and yield less oil per bushel, but from the 16th to the 19th centuries their golden-green nectar was in great demand across Italy. For many people in the *entroterra* olive oil was their major, and often only, source of income. But raising olives on these steep slopes is hard, hard work and when tourists first began to appear not a few people abandoned their groves and found new jobs along the coast.

Recently, of course, with the much-vaunted virtues of olive oil as a basis for a healthy diet, the Ligurians are finding it worthwhile to return to their terraces, to squeeze out their famous *extra vergine* and *spremuta d'oliva*, fresh olive juice. Although olives grow all along the coast, the Riviera di Ponente produces the finest and best; inland from Imperia, Taggia or Albenga you'll find *frantoii* to visit that sell their product. You won't find a better (or healthier) souvenir.

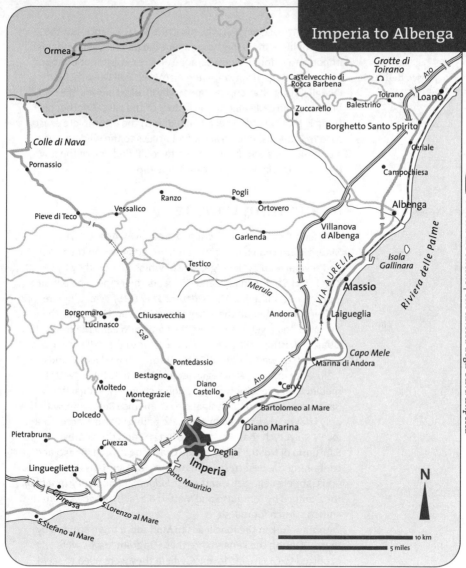

Ormea

Grotte di
Toirano

Castelvecchio di
Rocca Barbena

A10

Toirano

Loano

Zuccarello   Balestrino

Borghetto Santo Spirito

Colle di Nava

Ceriale

Pornassio

Campochiesa

Ranzo   Pogli

Vessalico   Ortovero   Albenga

Pieve di Teco

Villanova
d'Albenga

Garlenda

Testico   *Isola
Gallinara*

Merula   Alassio

VIA AURELIA

Borgomaro   Chiusavecchia   Andora   Laigueglia

Lucinasco

SS8

Capo Mele

Pontedassio   Marina di Andora

A10

Bestagno   Diano
Castello   Cervo

Moltedo

Montegrázie

Bartolomeo al Mare

Dolcedo

Diano Marina

Pietrabruna

Civezza

Oneglia

Linguaglietta   Imperia

Porto Maurizio

N

Cipressa

S.Lorenzo al Mare

S.Stefano al Mare

10 km

5 miles

Riviera delle Palme

Oneglia

East, the oil port (olive oil, that is) of Oneglia was sold by the
bishop of Albenga to the Doria in 1298. It saw the birth of two
famous men: Andrea Doria in 1466, and composer Luciano Berio in
1925. Its citizens tend to regard their town's marriage to Porto
Maurizio as a shotgun affair: when the Church declared that the
two halves of Imperia should unite behind one patron saint –
Leonardo, born in Porto Maurizio – Oneglia refused to go along and
still sticks stalwartly to St John, to his harmonious church of **San
Giovanni Battista** (1762), and especially to his big festival in July.

The centre of Oneglia is the theatrical Piazza Dante, but the centre of life is in the porticoes along the **port**. Fishing remains important: at four in the afternoon all the excitement is around the day's catch. The award-winning **Museo dell'Olivo**, behind Oneglia's train station, was opened by local oil barons, the Carli brothers, and dedicated to the history of the olive. Another nice thing is that cars have been banned from the incomplete coastal road to Diano Marino, to allow foot access to the wild beaches along **Galeazza Bay**; near Capo Berta you'll find one of the few places in Liguria where you can skinny-dip.

Museo dell'Olivo
Via Garessio 11, t 0183 295 762, www.museo dellolivo.com; open Mon–Sat 9–12.30 and 3–6.30; free

Inland from Imperia

Imperia's *entroterra* is a vast forest of olives. Above Porto Maurizio, **Dolcedo** has the most renowned groves in the region, and several medieval bridges, one of which was built by the Knights of St John in 1292 and still bears their cross. The parish church contains a fine *Martyrdom of St Peter of Verona* by Gregorio De Ferrari. Further up the valley, above Prelà and Pantsina, there are the expected lovely views from the **Santuario della Madonna della Guardia**. Further still, you can cross east into the Valle Argentina (*see* p.101) by way of **Colle d'Oggia**, through a wild rocky landscape.

Closer to Imperia, **Montegrazie** sits high on its hill, a typical medieval village with two exceptional churches: a regal late-Baroque parish church designed by Domenico Belmonte, with the only known work signed by Milanese painter Carlo Braccesco, a lovely polyptych that was painted in 1478; and the nearby **Santuario di Nostra Signora delle Grazie**, dedicated in 1450 and containing the best frescoes in the area, by Ligurians Pietro Guido and Gabriele della Cella, and a *Last Judgement* and *Punishment of the Damned* by Tommaso and Matteo Biazaci; the views from the church stretch for miles.

Another fork in the road leads to **Moltedo**, a town scented by myrtle. During the Renaissance these fragrant leaves were exported to Grasse in Provence, where they were used to scent fine leather used for gloves – before Grasse discovered perfume. Moltedo, too, has a regal Baroque church, with two good paintings, a *St Isidore* by Gregorio De Ferrari and the *Holy Family with an Angel* by Jan Roos. This for a long time was attributed to Anthony Van Dyck, who took refuge in Moltedo when he escaped from Genoa with his lover, noblewoman Paolina Adorno.

Above Oneglia, the main SS28 leads to pretty **Pontedassio**, home of the Agnesi pasta-making dynasty, whose first flour mill still stands in Via Garibaldi. Sadly their old spaghetti museum has

Frantoio Calvi
Via Nazionale 29,
t 0183 27 90 10,
www.oliocalvi.it; open
on weekends and hols
8.30–12.30 and
3.30–7.30

closed, but you can visit Pontedassio's **Frantoio Calvi**, home to Liguria's biggest olive-crushing millstones.

From Pontedassio you can make a loop to the west through **Bestagno**, under the ruins of a powerful medieval castle, or continue up the valley to **Chiusavecchia**, with its mighty stone bridge; a road from here twists up to Lucinasco, overlooking thousands of ancient olives in the valley below. **Lucinasco** has a small **Museo di Arte Sacra**, with seven statues from the 15th century, mourning the Dead Christ. The pretty 13th-century church **Santo Stefano** is just outside the village, reflected in a little lake. Another 3km up the road is the isolated 15th-century **Santuario della Maddalena**, a simple white church made from cut stone blocks – a national monument in a beautiful setting.

Museo di Arte Sacra
t 0183 651 541; open
mid-May–Sept Sun and
hols 10–11 and 4–6;
otherwise, visits by
request; adm

Continuing up the main Valle Impero from Chiusavecchia, **San Lazzaro Reale** has yet another medieval bridge, and is worth a stop if the church is open, to see the 16th-century anonymous triptych of the *Madonna*. **Borgomaro**, the most important village in these parts, has its work of art as well, a good polyptych of *SS Nazarino e Celso* from the 16th century; outside Borgomaro, the picturesque church dedicated to the same saints is in part from the 11th century. Further up the valley, the most impressive sight of all is the **oak tree** in Villa San Sebastiano, believed to be the biggest if not the oldest in Europe (follow the sign for *ruve de megu*).

(i) **Imperia >>**
Viale G. Matteotti 37,
Porto Maurizio,
t 0183 660 140,
www.turismoinliguria.it

Whale Watching West of Imperia

Blu West Imperia, t 0183 769 364, *www.whalewatch.it*, runs half- and full-day excursions out of Imperia and Andora.

Where to Stay and Eat West of Imperia

Santo Stefano al Mare ✉ 18010

La Riserva, Via Roma 51, **t** 0184 484 134 (€€€€). Prettily set in the old bishopric, serving fresh seafood and dishes including some French ones, using the owner's own olive oil. *Closed Sun eve and Mon; May–Sept Mon only.*

San Giacomo, Lungomare Colombo 19, **t** 0184 486 808 (€€€€). For a change of pace, tasty pasta and meat with truffles, as well as Ligurian seafood and vegetable dishes. *Closed Mon and two weeks in winter.*

Imperia ✉ 18100

****Residence Hotel Miramare, Via Matteotti 24, **t** 0183 667 120, *www. rhotels.it* (€€€–€€). Set in a 19th-century villa with its own park with century trees, a pool and all the amenities. The dining area offers great views of the *duomo* and sea.

***Corallo, Corso Garibaldi 29, **t** 0183 666 264, *www.coralloimperia.it* (€€€). Functional rooms, but a pretty garden and private beach, and special weekend rates.

***Croce di Malta, Via Scarincio 148, Porto Maurizio, **t** 0183 667 020, *www.hotelcrocedimalta.com* (€€–€). Comfortable seaside hotel in Borgo Marina with a pretty breakfast terrace and views.

***Robinia, Via Pirinoli 14, **t** 0183 62720, *www.rhotels.it* (€€–€). Pleasant, with its own beach, lovely terrace, and 55 rooms, most with sea view.

Lanterna Blù, Via Scarincio 32, Borgo Marina, in Porto Maurizio, **t** 0183 63859 (€€€€). Excellent dishes using

ingredients from two local farms. *Eves only summer.*
Hostaria, Via S. Antonio 7, t 0183 667 028 (€€). In the *centro storico* of Porto Maurizio, serving classics like *stoccafisso accomodato*. *Eves only summer; closed Mon.*

Beppa, Calata Cuneo 24, t 0183 294 286 (€€). In Oneglia, opposite the boats. Good, fresh, no-frills fish.
Sciabecco, Via Nizza 33, t 0183 61921, in Porto Maurizio (€). Prize-winning pizzeria. *Closed Wed.*

The Gulf of Diano: Beaches East of Imperia

East of Imperia, the coastal road skirts the rocky lump of Capo Berta, covered with Mediterranean *macchia* and Aleppo pines, and the inevitable watchtower dating from times when life on this coast was hardly a carefree holiday. Beyond lies a string of popular resorts, which, like about a thousand others, claim to enjoy the most mild climate on the Italian peninsula, although no one really wants to have a thermometer war to prove it once and for all.

Diano Marina

The first resort east of Capo Berta, Diano Marina, has a long sandy beach and palm trees, with a fertile coastal plain stretching behind, all sheltered from the cold and wind – but not, unfortunately, from earthquakes. Shattered by the big one of 1887, Diano had to be completely rebuilt, which gave the inhabitants a chance to forget their old job as an olive oil centre and port, and make their town into a purpose-built resort. They salvaged all the marble altars and paintings they could find and stuck them in the big new church, **Sant'Antonio Abate**.

The origin of the town's name goes back to ancient times, when Diano's hinterland was covered with a sacred oak forest, the *Lucus Bormani*, where the Ligurians worshipped their woodland gods Borman and Bormana. It was the Roman custom to promise an enemy's gods temples and offerings if they changed sides, and after the war they would take their cult images to Rome, and give the deity a Roman name, in this case the virgin goddess of the hunt, masculinized to Diano to suit Borman. The late 19th-century Palazzo del Parco contains the **Museo Civico**, with fossils, finds from a Bronze-Age necropolis, a 1st-century BC Roman shipwreck and other relics up to the 7th century. For Corpus Christi, Diano fills its streets with carpets of flowers; in August, it hosts one of the funniest events on the Riviera – Vascup, a regatta of bathtubs.

Diano's *entroterra* villages were spared by the quake and, like those to the west, are all surrounded by slopes striped laboriously by stone terraces planted with olives. When pirate sails were spotted on the horizon, the coastal population would flee 2km inland to **Diano Castello** (Roman *Castrum Diani*), which still bristles

Museo Civico
Corso Garibaldi 60, t 0183 497 621, www.palazzodel parco.it; open winter Mon–Sat 1–12.30 and 3–5.30; July–Aug Mon and Sat 9–12, Tues–Fri 9–12 and 8.30pm–10.30pm; adm

with towers. The **Municipio**, opposite the lavish Baroque church of San Nicola di Bari, has a 17th-century fresco which recalls Diano's participation in the Genoese victory over Pisa at Meloria in 1284. Another 2km up the valley, **Diano Borello** has a good 14th-century church, **San Michele**, with a Renaissance fresco in the lunette and a polyptych by Antonio Brea inside. Besides olives, this is the land of Liguria's white wine, Vementino, made from malvasia vines brought over long ago from Greece by way of Spain; try it at the Cantina Maria Donata Bianchi, Via delle Torri 16, in Diano Castello.

Next along the coast, modern development at **San Bartolomeo al Mare** has choked the two medieval hamlets of San Bartolomeo and Rovere. In Rovere, the age-old **Santuario della Madonna della Rovere** has a neoclassical façade and a statue of the Virgin, which she handed in person to some shepherds. San Bartolomeo's church, also much altered over the centuries, contains a polyptych by Cristoforo Pancalino, the Betty Crocker of painting in the respect that he never existed; the name was invented by art historians to attribute 16th-century works by Ligurian painters influenced by the Tuscans. Another polyptych by 'Pancalino' is in the church in lovely **Villa Faraldi**, a medieval village lost in the olive groves, 8km above San Bartolomeo. This holds an arts and music festival in summer, and usually has an exhibition of some kind or another going on, thanks to the initiative of a Norwegian sculptor named Fritz Roed.

The east end of the Golfo di Diano is occupied by **Cervo**, a curl of white, cream and yellow houses sweeping up from the sea on to a small promontory, forming one of the most beautiful townscapes on the Riviera. At the top of the curl stands the pretty San Giovanni Battista, better known as the **Chiesa degli Corallini** (of the coral fishermen), designed by Giovanni Battista Marvaldi in 1686, with a distinctive concave façade emblazoned with stuccoes and a stag, or *cervo* in Italian. It was built with money raised by the fishermen themselves, whose life is recorded in the chapel dedicated to their patron saint, Erasmus. It forms a lovely backdrop for Cervo's July and August **Chamber Music Festival**, founded in 1964 by Hungarian violinist Sandor Vegh, featuring internationally known pianists and violinists.

Chamber Music Festival
www.cervo.com

The old town has a delightful, sunny, vaguely Moorish atmosphere. Until the 12th century, Cervo was the fief of the Clavesana family, whose castle, above the church, combines the medieval structure with a Baroque manor house, now seat of the **Museo Etnografico del Ponente Ligure**, with exhibits on costumes and customs, daily life and seafaring. Cervo has just three small hotels near its shingle beach, none good.

Museo Etnografico del Ponente Ligure
Piazza Santa Caterina 1, t 0183 408 197; open 9–12.30 and 3.30–7.30

East of Cervo, **Andora** is a small resort on the torrent Merula (and a departure point for whale watching excursions), encompassing medieval **Andora Marina** and its Genoese watchtower. The ten-

08

Riviera di Ponente | The Riviera degli Olivi: The Gulf of Diano arched bridge over the Merula is medieval but called the Ponte Romano; it was, however, used on the **Roman road** (pedestrians only, or you can drive up the back way on Via al Castello) up to isolated, stunning **Andora Castello**: an egg-shaped fortified hamlet built by the Clavesana around the year 1000 and sold to Genoa in 1252, and all but abandoned after a flood of the Merula caused the inhabitants to relocate to Laigueglia. It makes an impressive sight: a tower gate with Ghibelline crenellations leads into the lovely Romanesque-Gothic church of **SS. Giacomo e Filippo**, built in 1100. The church itself was part of the defences; today it is used as one of the venues for the *Musica nei Castelli di Liguria* (July –Sept).

You can continue up the 'Strada Romana' on foot (or drive from Laigueglia) to **Colla Micheri**, a pretty little rural hamlet restored by Thor Heyerdahl, the Norwegian ethnologist who sailed the *Kon Tiki*. 'I have spent my life exploring the world,' he wrote. 'But when I arrived in this place, I did not hesitate: my own house would be here in this little paradise.' Beyond this little paradise, Andora's *entroterra* is very sparsely populated, with approximately one inhabitant per thousand olive trees; if you want to go exploring, one place to aim for is **Testico**, once a possession of the Doria. The road above Testico has lovely views over the Maritime Alps.

On the other side of Capo Mele lies the lively, attractive old town of **Laigueglia**. Like Cervo, it was a coral fishing village, and has taken on the postwar demands of tourism more graciously than some. Also like Cervo, it has a majestic Baroque church for a centrepiece: **San Matteo** (1754) with two bell towers at angles, crowned with cupolas covered in majolica tiles, their crosses oriented to the prevailing sea winds, the *maestrale* and the *libeccio*; inside there's an *Assumption* by Bernardo Strozzi. The coral fishermen paid for the nearby Oratorio di Santa Maria Maddalena.

Where to Stay and Eat on the Gulf of Diano

ⓘ Diano Marina ›
Corso Garibaldi 60 (Palazzo del Parco), t 0183 496 956

Diano Marina ✉ 18013

****Grand Hotel Diana Majestic**, Via Oleandri 15, t 0183 402 727, *www.dianamajestic.com* (€€€€). Set amid olive groves, this comfortable hotel with a lovely terrace supplies the oil used in the **restaurant** overlooking the pool and beach. *Closed mid-Oct to mid-Dec.*

****Bellevue & Méditerranée**, Via Generale Ardoino 2–4, t 0183 4093, *www.bellevueetmediterranee.it* (€€€). One of the nicest on the beach; pool and garden.

***Sasso**, Via Biancheri 17, t 0183 494 319, *www.hotelsassoresidence.com*

(€€–€). Well-run hotel 200m from the sea (guests have free use of the hotel's beach cabins), and a good bet for families; rooms are modern and functional, and apartments with kitchenettes sleep up to six. Excellent breakfast buffet. There are big off-season discounts to be had. *Closed Oct–mid-Dec.*

***Caprice**, Via Roma Est 25, t 0183 495 061 (€). A classy (for this price) family-run place, with a garden and beach, and **restaurant** (€€) with fresh fish and wonderful desserts (open to non-guests, but get there early).

*De La Ville**, Via Garibaldi 1, t 0183 494 655, *www.fradiavolo.it* (€). The main attraction, aside from the six comfortable rooms, is that just downstairs waits the **Fra Diavolo**, t 0183 495 583 (€€), proud holder of three world championship titles for pizza, with engraved silver cups and news clippings on the walls to prove it. They also do seafood. *Closed Tues.*

Candidollo, Corso Europa 23 in Diano Arentino, frazione Borello, t 0183 43401 (€€). Authentic country inn serving delicious snails and other traditional Ligurian specialities. *No credit cards. Closed Tues and Nov–Mar.*

Cervo ✉ 18010

Porteghetto, Via Aurelia 9, t 0183 400 047 (€€€). Bar with its own beach and a restaurant with a lovely terrace overlooking the sea. Traditional Mediterranean cuisine. *Closed Wed.*

San Giorgio, Via Volta 19, up in the old town, t 0183 400 175 (€€€€). Well-prepared Ligurian specialities like *trenette al pesto* or *verdure ripiene* (stuffed vegetables) in an intimate, arty setting. The prawns are divine. Lovely views. *Book. Closed Tues and part of Jan and Nov.*

Serafino, Via Matteotti 8, t 0183 408 185 (€€€€). With only the freshest fish on offer (the owner claims not to open if the fishermen don't fish), the menu varies daily. Try the prickly pear sorbet, which is a house speciality. *Closed Tues (except summer) and Nov.* The owner also has three **apartments**, with incredible sea views, for rent by the night or the week.

Andora ✉ 17020

★★★Moresco, Via Aurelia 96, t 0182 89141, *www.hotelmoresco.com* (€€). A comfortable hotel not far from the sea, with extras like satellite TV, a **restaurant** with a children's menu, and bike hire, and great views from the solarium on top.

Casa del Priore, Via al Castello 34, t 0182 87 330 (€€€€). An old stone manor house converted into a romantic **restaurant**. The dishes have a decidedly French touch, and there is often live music in the bar downstairs to add to the atmosphere. *Book. Closed Mon and mid-Jan to mid-Feb.*

Laigueglia ✉ 17053

★★★★Splendidmare, Piazza Badarò 3, t 0182 690 325, *www.splendidmare.it* (€€€–€€). For something a bit special, book a room in this 18th-century monastery, which has been elegantly refurbished with antiques. The rooms are light and airy, some have sea views, and there's a small pool, too. The monastic lifestyle clearly had its benefits. *Closed Oct–April.*

★★★Mediterraneo, Via A. Doria 18, t 0182 690 240, *www.hotelmedit.it* (€€). Peacefully set back among the olives, although the beach is only a short walk away from this charming little place. *Closed Oct–Christmas.*

Baia del Sole, Piazza Cavour 8, t 0182 690 019 (€€). Pretty place with brick vaults, sea views and imaginative cuisine; seafood reigns supreme, with *taglioni* tossed with fresh scampi, and lovely dishes such as baked fish with artichokes. *Closed Mon and Wed (except summer), mid-Oct–mid-Dec and Jan–Easter.*

ⓘ **San Bartolomeo al Mare**
Piazza XXV Aprile 1,
t 0183 400 200

ⓘ **Cervo** >
Piazza Santa Caterina 2,
t 0183 408 197

ⓘ **Laigueglia** >>
Via Roma 2,
t 0182 690 059

⭐ **Splendidmare** >>

ⓘ **Andora** >
Via Aurelia 122/a,
t 0182 681 004

08 Riviera di Ponente | The Riviera delle Palme: Alassio

The Riviera delle Palme

After the Riviera dei Fiori and the Riviera degli Olivi comes the Baia del Sole and the Riviera delle Palme, where the big-time seaside resort action picks up again at Alassio.

Alassio

A suntrap with 3km of beaches of sugar-fine sand, tucked well away from the busy Via Aurelia, Alassio, according to some, is named after Aldelasia, the daughter of the 10th-century Holy Roman Emperor Otto the Great, who eloped here with her lover

Arelamo. Back then it was a fishing village belonging to the Benedictines; in 1541 the Republic of Genoa took over. In the 19th century the Hanburys (of the garden fame, in Ventimiglia) were the pioneers who first saw Alassio's potential as a winter resort, and to this day the surrounding hills are dotted with English-built villas and gardens. Alassio's destiny underwent its most recent twist when summer tans became the rage, thanks to Coco Chanel, who dared to go brown on the French Riviera in 1923.

Of pre-resort Alassio, little remains other than a defence tower, some old *palazzi* and the pretty church of **Sant'Ambrogio** (1597), with a Romanesque campanile, a Renaissance portal and a statue of St Michael stabbing the devil.

Sant'Ambrogio
t 0182 640 573

Back in the 1930s, when Alassio's **Caffè Roma** was *the* celebrity rendezvous, owner Mario Berrino looked across at the little wall of the garden opposite and said to Ernest Hemingway, 'Caro Ernesto, wouldn't it be something if all the famous people who ever sat in the café left their autographs there?' Papa agreed and contributed his John Hancock, which Berrino made into a ceramic plaque, starting a custom that endures to this day, making the **Muretto** (off Via Cavour, near the train station) the Riviera's Hollywood Boulevard; in August there's even a 'Miss Muretto' beauty contest. Alassio's main Via XX Settembre (better known as the *Budello*) crosses here and runs parallel to the beach, or at least next to the houses that give directly on to the sands. A 15th-century convent at Via S. Giovanni Bosco 12 houses the **Museo di Scienze Naturali** with embalmed animals, minerals, fossils and a new botanical section.

**Museo di
Scienze Naturali**
*t 0182 640 309; open
winter Sat 5–7, Sun
and hols 9.30–11.30;
summer Tues and
Thurs 9pm–11pm, Sat,
Sun and hols 4–8*

In summer, excursion boats (contact the tourist office for arrangements) sail to the private **Isola Gallinara**, a mile off the coast between Alassio and Albenga. Once populated by wild hens (*gallinas*), the islet provided sanctuary for St Martin of Tours in the 4th century when Arian heretics were persecuting him. For more than a thousand years afterwards, Gallinara hosted a wealthy Benedictine abbey, with properties all over the Riviera and Provence; its ruins stand next to a villa. Today the islet is a nature reserve, the last place on the coast to preserve its original *macchia*; it is also a popular destination for divers. From Alassio you can also go up to the 13th-century church of **Santa Croce**, once a dependent of Gallinara and one of the best viewpoints in the area, then follow the ancient Roman Via Julia down to Albenga.

Where to Stay in Alassio

ⓘ **Alassio >**
*Viale Gibb 26,
t 0182 647 11*

Alassio ✉ **17021**
★★★★ Diana Grand Hotel, Via Garibaldi 110, t 0182 642 701, *www.hoteldiana*

alassio.it (€€€€€–€€€€). Alassio's finest, with its own beach, beach bar and restaurant, free bikes, heated indoor pool and spa. The seafront rooms are nice and large, with balconies, and four excellent **restaurants**.

****Al Saraceno**, Corso Europa 64, t 0182 643 957, *www.alsaraceno group.com* (€€€). One of the more popular hotels; comfortable rooms and a classy **restaurant**.

***Beau Sejour**, Via Garibaldi 102, t 0182 640 303, *www.beausejour hotel.it* (€€€€€). On the beach, with well-furnished rooms, a terrace and garden. *Closed Oct–Mar.*

***Ligure**, Passeggiata Grollero 25, t 0182 640 653, *www.ligurealassio.it* (€€€€). In the heart of the old town but with sea views and modern rooms; good **restaurant** offering local and international cuisine. *Closed mid-Oct–mid-Dec.*

***Milano**, Piazza Airaldi Durante 11, t 0182 640 597, *www.milanohotel.info* (€€€). Excellent hotel on the beach; rooms are well equipped, with balconies and sea views. There's also a very nice **restaurant** serving some of the usual Ligurian specialities. *Closed Nov–mid-Dec.*

*Italia**, Via XX Settembre 126, t 0182 644 108, *www.hotelitaliaalassio.com* (€€). Centrally located hotel, with satellite TV and kitchenettes in every room, and a **restaurant** serving local fish dishes and a kids' menu.

****Kon Tiki**, Viale delle Palme 11, t 0182 640 928, *www.hotelkontiki-alassio.com* (€€). Offers a great breakfast included in the fare, and two kitchen-dining rooms to cook your own meals if you wish to. Small pets admitted.

****Bel Air**, Via Roma 40, t 0182 642 578, *www.belairhotel.it* (€). Wonderful value; its rooms are modern, the **restaurant** is good and inexpensive (open to non-guests) and it has its own beach.

Monti e Mare, Via F. Giancardi 47, t 0182 643 036, *www.mmapartments. it* (€). Overlooking the sea 2km from the town, fully equipped flats sleeping up to six, let by the week in a tranquil lush setting with friendly owners.

Eating Out in Alassio

Palma, Via Cavour 11, t 0182 640 314 (€€€€). What Alassio may lack in grand hotels it makes up for with this gourmet palace, where you can choose between two *menus degustazione*, one highlighting basil, the totem herb of Liguria, and the other Provençal-Ligurian specialities, with an emphasis on seafood. *Book. Closed Wed, Nov.*

Le Nuove, Passeggiata Italia 7, t 0182 640 693 (€€€). An atmospheric old restaurant in the heart of the old town, serving typical Ligurian cuisine like *trofie al pesto* and fish soups. *Book. Closed Wed.*

La Prua, Passeggiata Baracca 25, t 0182 642 557 (€€€€). Ligurian classics, such as *branzino alla ligurie* are second to none at this stylish restaurant. *Book. Menu degustazione €42 and €55. Closed Thurs and Nov.*

El Galeon, Largo Beniscelli 7, t 0182 642 732 (€€€). This is something altogether more casual. Good pizza and pasta, and frequent live music from the piazza. *Closed Thurs (except in summer).*

I Matetti, Viale Hanbury 132, t 0182 646 680 (€€). *Osteria* serving traditional *entroterra* dishes – lots of chickpea dishes, pesto, and some seafood for *secondo. Closed Mon (except in July and Aug) and Jan.*

Entertainment and Nightlife in Alassio

During the summer season this area is one of the liveliest on the coast. From July to September the **Musica nei Castelli di Liguria** festival takes place, in which the many castles of the region host a series of classical concerts by Italian and international ensembles, mostly in the open air under the stars.

Alassio at nighttime attracts a fairly hip crowd, who start meeting up from about 10pm in the seafront bars. The clubs and discos generally get going about midnight and close at 4 or 5am.

Zanzibar, Via Vittorio Veneto 143. Lots of loud music and 1950s memorabilia.

Sandon, Passeggiata Cadorna 134. All ages can bend an elbow here, with a maritime theme and photos of Hemingway, who came here for his *centenario*, and a concoction of rums.

Albenga

 Albenga

Swinging Alassio's neighbour, Albenga, has more history than any town on the Riviera del Ponente, owing its centuries of good fortune and prestige to the River Cento and its tributaries, which formed the most fertile alluvial plain in all Liguria. The settlement dates back at least to the 6th century BC, when it was *Albium Ingaunum*, port of a Ligurian tribe called the Ingauni. Once in Roman hands, the name was elided into *Albingaunum* and the town was rebuilt in the typical *castrum* grid.

Destroyed by Goths and Vandals, Albenga was rebuilt in the 5th century by Constantius, the husband of Galla Placidia and future emperor of the west at Ravenna. During the dark years of Lombard and Saracen invasions, Albenga endured it all as the capital of the Byzantine Marca Arduinica. By the 11th century it was a *comune*, and joined in the First Crusade on the same footing as Genoa, thereby obtaining trade privileges for itself in the Middle East.

After the 12th century, however, Albenga fell prey to typical Ligurian intramural quarrels. Powerful families took control (the Clavesana, followed by the Del Carretto) and by the 15th century, weakened and strife-torn, Albenga lost its freedom altogether to the Republic of Genoa. At this point, however, it didn't really matter. Albenga's harbour shifted away with the course of the Cento river, and the port became a malarial marsh. Nowadays the town stands a kilometre from the sea, and grows asparagus and other vegetables in the fertile soil of its old river bed.

The Medieval Centre

Albenga's evocative, urbane centre retains its *castrum* layout from Roman times. Via Enrico d'Aste was the *decumanus* and Via Medaglie d'Oro the *cardus*; and the beautiful main **Piazza San Michele** was for centuries the seat of civil and spiritual authority, all in the shadow of an impressive collection of 13th-century brick towers from the days when Albenga was a free *comune*. All Italian cities used to have these proto-skyscrapers, but few have preserved so many (a dozen, of which seven are perfectly intact) in such a small area, most of them leaning, due to the marshy soil. Three stand like slightly tipsy bridesmaids around the elegant campanile (1391) of the 11th-century **Cattedrale di San Michele**, rebuilt on the palaeochristian original; inside you can see the Carolingian crypt.

The tower (*c.* 1300) of the Palazzo Vecchio del Comune in Via Nino Lamboglia now houses the **Museo Civico Ingauno**, with Roman and medieval finds, mosaics and frescoes and lovely views over Albenga from the top floor. Steps from the nearby **Loggia Comunale** (1421) lead down to the street level of Albenga 1,500 years ago, and to the 5th-century **baptistry**. It was Emperor Constantine who set the fashion for geometrical baptistries when he built the first one, in

Museo Civico Ingauno
t 0182 51215, www.iisl.it; open Tues–Sun winter 10–12.30 and 2.30–6; summer 9.30–12.30 and 3.30–7.30; adm

Baptistry
same ticket as the Museo Civico

an octagon, at St John Lateran in Rome, and Albenga's is a minor *tour de force* of the genre, its architects combining an unusual ten-sided exterior with an octagonal interior. Some of the niches inside have windows covered with lovely sandstone transennas, carved with stylized motifs; there are granite columns from Corsica, topped with ancient Corinthian columns. The original cupola was dismantled by confused 19th-century restorers, who thought it was from the Renaissance. The interior contains early-medieval tombs carved with Lombard-style reliefs, and a total immersion font. One niche contains rare 5th-century mosaics, depicting a pair of lambs, a cross and 12 doves, symbols of the Apostles.

Museo Navale Romano
t 0182 51215, www.iisl.it; same hours as the Museo Civico; adm

A third tower was joined in the 17th century to the Palazzo Peloso Cipolla ('Hairy Onion Palace'), with a Renaissance façade and frescoes. It contains the recently rearranged **Museo Navale Romano**, with amphorae and other items salvaged from a 1st-century BC Roman shipwreck discovered near the Isola Gallinara, 16th–18th-century blue-and-white pharmacy jars from Albisola and prehistoric finds from the Val Pennavaira.

Just north of the cathedral's rounded apse, Piazzetta dei Leoni is named after the three 17th-century stone lions brought here from Rome by the wealthy Costa family to show off their **Palazzo Costa Del Carretto di Balestrino** (1525). This is now the residence of Albenga's bishop; the Costa also owned the piazza's medieval house and tower, with Ghibelline swallow-tail crenellations.

From Piazza San Michele, Via Bernardo Ricci (the continuation of the *decumanus*) is lined with medieval porticoes and houses and the grandiose 17th-century Palazzo d'Aste. Opposite, the **Palazzo Vescovile**, decorated with black and white stripes and frescoes attributed to Giovanni Canavesio, now houses the **Museo Diocesano**, containing a handsome collection of 17th-century tapestries, paintings, reliquaries and illuminated manuscripts. Where Via Bernardo Ricci meets Via Medaglie d'Oro, the 13th-century **Loggia dei Quattro Canti** marks the centre of the Roman town, where three more towers stand, or rather tilt.

Museo Diocesano
t 0182 50288; open Mon–Sat 10–12 and 3–6; adm

A short walk east along Viale Pontelungo will take you to ancient Via Julia and the 495ft **Ponte Lungo**, built in the 13th century to span the Cento; apparently it only did the job for a few years before the river changed course. Along the road, note the ruins of the 4th-century basilica of San Vittore, one of the oldest in Liguria.

Around Albenga

Villanova, Garlenda and Campochiesa

Besides asparagus, artichokes and Pigato wine, the plain of Albenga is the site of **Villanova d'Albenga**, laid out in the 13th

Albisola
Superiore •

Bocchetta di
Cadibona

A6

Savona

A10

• Vado Ligure

Calizzano

Colle di Melogno

S1

Spotorno

Nuovo

Noli

Bardineto

Bardino

Capo di Noli

Varigotti

Perti

Finaleborgo

Grotta di Valdemino Ω

Colle di Caprazoppa

Giustenice

Borgio

Finale Ligure

Grotte di
Toirano Ω

Pietra Ligure

Castelvecchio di
Rocca Barbena

Toirano

Loano

Balestrino

• Zuccarello

Borghetto Santo Spirito

A10

Ceriale

Riviera di Ponente

S1

Campochiesa

N

Villanova
d'Albenga

Albenga

10 km

5 miles

Around Albenga

Villanova, Garlenda and Campochiesa

Besides asparagus, artichokes and Pigato wine, the plain of
Albenga is the site of **Villanova d'Albenga**, laid out in the 13th
century as a new town in a polygonal plan to form an outer
defence for Albenga, back when the town still dreamed big.
Although now minus most of its walls, Villanova has kept all of its
medieval charm, augmented by a fondness for potted plants that
cascade in every nook and cranny. Just outside town stands a
round Renaissance church, **Santa Maria della Rotonda**, the kind of

church of **San Giorgio**: a *Last Judgement*, based on the description of the *Divine Comedy*, complete with figures of Dante and Virgil.

Albenga's *Entroterra*: Roads into Piedmont

Two historic mountain roads converge at Albenga: the S453 towards Pieve di Teco and the S582 to Garessio. It's easy to see both by way of a circular route, if you continue up the S28 from Pieve di Teco to Ormea, drive east to Garessio, and from there return to Albenga. The term *vie del sale* (salt roads) is still used for these old routes of exchange between the people of the sea and the people of the Padana, or greater Po Valley. One other Riviera export in great demand was anchovies, which became an integral part of Piedmontese cuisine, especially in its *bagna cauda*.

The S453 follows the *via del sale* to Piedmont, up the River Arroscia up the plain to **Ortovero** and **Pogli**, the latter an important rose-growing centre, with a rose festival in July. Further up, **Ranzo** (just before Borghetto d'Arroscia) is the site of the church of San Pantaleo, with a pre-Romanesque apse and a 15th-century carved portal with frescoes. Continuing up the valley, **Vessalico** is the garlic capital of the Riviera, and honours its fragrant little bulbs in a garlic festival, also in July, making it possible to celebrate both roses and garlic in the same valley on the same holiday.

The key town in these parts is **Pieve di Teco**, its name derived from a Byzantine fort (*teichos*). Its feudal bosses, the Clavesana, rebuilt the castle here, of which a few bits remain, in the 12th century; a more impressive citadel, destroyed in the 17th century, was the family's stronghold until 1385, when Genoa took it over and made it the seat of a captain, who had to constantly deal with the Piedmontese threat to the town and salt road. Pieve continues to make its bread and cheese the old-fashioned way; workshops line the main Corso Ponzoni. The oldest houses are near the parish church, Santa Maria della Ripa, while the 18th-century Collegiata San Giovanni Battista has a *Last Supper* by Domenico Piola and a *San Francesco di Paola* by Luca Cambiaso.

The scenery becomes increasingly pretty on the way up to **Pornassio**, which has another castle and a pretty 15th-century frescoed church, San Dalmazzo, in the hamlet of Villa; this area produces good Rossese wine. From here the road winds up to the meadows of the **Colle di Nava** (2,952ft) where fields of lavender and bees combine to make a famous honey. From here you can turn west, taking narrow mountain roads eventually to **Monesi**, Liguria's highest ski resort.

The second road from Albenga, the S582, follows the River Neva, which is guarded by two medieval castle villages. **Zuccarello** was founded in 1248 by the Clavesana, who lost it to another powerful family, the Del Carretto, who liked to tease, for in the 17th century they ceded their rights, half to Genoa and half to Piedmont. Both, of course, wanted the whole shebang, and their quarrel erupted in the so-called War of Zuccarello, which ended in 1625 with a Genoese victory. The amazing thing about Zuccarello is that nothing at all has happened there since; it is so well preserved that history students come to examine it, with its perfect porticoed medieval street, with gates on either end. Its ruined castle was the birthplace of Ilaria del Carretto, whose beautiful tomb by Jacopo della Quercia is the jewel of the cathedral at Lucca.

Further up the valley, the even older **Castelvecchio di Rocca Barbena** sits high on a crag, its castle dating from the 11th century, encircled by the walled village, with magnificent views down the valley. During another war between Genoa and Savoy in 1672, the castle here was the base of the deliciously named Bastian Contrario, the 'Piedmontese Robin Hood' (but not so well dressed, the Italians hasten to add), who fought against the wicked Genoese, and eventually lost.

Sports and Activities in and around Albenga

Garlenda's **golf club** has 18 holes, t 0182 580 012, *www.garlendagolf.it*; it also has a riding stable, a football field, tennis courts, a rollerskating rink, a gym and *bocci* courts. Albenga's **airport** at Villanova has scheduled flights to Rome (t 0182 582 033, *www.rivierairport.it*), and is the local base for parachuting and gliding.

Where to Stay and Eat in and around Albenga

ⓘ Albenga >
Piazza del Popolo,
t 0182 558 444,
www.inforiviera.it

Albenga ✉ 17031

***Ca' di Berta, 6km east of Albenga at Salea, t 0182 559 930, *www. hotelcadiberta.it* (€€€). If you have a car, this is a lovely place to stay, a complex of stone buildings in the countryside by a pool. Rooms are well equipped, and there's a good restaurant, the **Carlotta** (€€€), serving up home-made pasta and Ligurian specialities using ingredients grown in the owner's garden. *Open to non-guests; closed Wed and Nov.*

***La Gallinara, Via Piave 66, a kilometre south of the historic centre, t 0182 53086, *www.hotellagallinara.it* (€€€–€€). The modern airy rooms all have internet portals and there are

ⓘ Garlenda >>
Via Roma 4, t 0182 582
114, www.inforiviera.it

discounts at the bathing concession. Pets admitted.

***Sole Mare, Lungomare Colombo 15, t 0182 51817 (€€€–€€). Simple but pleasant rooms and beach views.

*Italia, Viale Martiri della Libertà 8, t 0182 50405, *faustocarrara@libero.it* (€). Take a trip back to the 1930s, and dine well in the same classy old atmosphere.

Pernambucco, Viale Italia 35, t 0182 53458 (€€€€). Welcoming, romantic restaurant with impeccable service. Classic Ligurian fish and seafood.

Antica Osteria dei Leoni, Via Avarenne 1, t 0182 51937 (€€€€). Offers a change, giving Ligurian seafood a Neapolitan touch – try the lasagne with aubergines and clams. *Closed Tues.*

Sutta Cà, Via Enesto Ricci 10, t 0182 53198 (€). In the *centro storico*, big portions of pasta, fish and meat, just like mamma makes. *Closed Thurs eve and Sun.*

Puppo, Via Torlaro 20, t 0182 51853, *www.dapuppo.it* (€). Join the crowds for pizza and the best *farinata* in Albenga. *Closed Mon 15 Sept–15 Jun; always open in summer but eves only.*

Garlenda ✉ 17033

*****La Meridiana, Via ai Castelli 11, t 0182 580 271, *www.lameridiana resort.com* (€€€€€). A *Relais &*

Châteaux golfer's paradise, built next to the course, amid olive groves, ancient oaks and vineyards. There are two restaurants – **Rosmarino** (€€€€) is open for dinner only and offers local cuisine (book); **Bistrot** (€€€) is more

informal and open at both lunch and dinner. *Open May–Nov.*
★★★Golf Club, Bra, Via del Golf 7, t 0182 580 012 (€€). Simple but nice rooms near the links, for golfers with more modest budgets.

Toirano, Loano and Pietra Ligure

Up the coast from Albenga you'll find the most beautiful caves on the Riviera at Toirano, where the evidence suggests our distant ancestors liked to hang out with bears, as well as the popular resorts of Loano and Pietra Ligure.

Toirano and its Grottoes

Next up the coast east of Albenga, Ceriale is a small resort with a long beach, palm trees, camp sites, and the aqua-park Le Caravelle for serious wet fun. Just beyond Ceriale, Borghetto Santo Spirito is the junction (and bus pick-up point) for Toirano.

Le Caravelle
Via Sant'Eugenio 51, t 0182 931 755, www.lecaravelle.com; open June–Sept; adm exp

Toirano was originally Varatelia, an outpost of Byzantine Albenga. In the 9th century its fortunes improved when Charlemagne founded a Benedictine abbey, **San Pietro dei Monti**, on a crag above town. Although only a few ruins remain, this was, until it closed in 1495, a major power in the area, and its monks were pivotal in promoting the cultivation of the olive. In 1385 Toirano was annexed by Genoa. Some of the walls and towers remain – one of the latter was converted into a campanile for the church of **San Martino** in the charming piazza. In Toracco, the oldest part of Toirano, tall medieval houses loom over the lanes; a stone bridge from the 1100s crosses the River Varatella. In the old stables of the Palazzo del Marchese in Via Polla, you can visit the Museo Etnografico della Val Varatella.

Museo Etnografico della Val Varatella
t 0182 989 968; open daily 10–1 and 3–6; adm, or free with a ticket for the caves

All of this seems spanking new, however, after a visit to the **caves** in the limestone cliffs just up from Toirano. In the Middle Ages these 50 or so caverns were believed to be entrances to hell, guarded by ocellated lizards, Europe's largest, which can grow up to two feet long if you measure to the tip of their tails. The secrets they guard are rather older than hell, however, especially in the three Grotte di Toirano open to visits, that in c. 80,000 BC were inhabited by Palaeolithic Italians. Even back then they chose the loveliest caves, designed by Mother Nature with draperies and pastel stalactites.

Grotte di Toirano
t 0182 98062, www.toiranogrotte.it; open daily 9.30–12.30 and 2–5, summer till 5.30; adm exp

The most intriguing cave is the **Grotta della Bàsura** ('of the witch'), where they kept some interesting company: one section is called the **Bear Cemetery**; here masses of bear bones (the extinct *Ursus spelaeus*) were found. Another is the **Corridor of the Imprints**, where bears and humans left foot-, hand- and knee-prints, claw

Dances with Bears

Have you ever wondered why children respond so viscerally to teddy bears? One possible answer may be sheer atavism: way back in the Middle Palaeolithic or Mousterian culture (120,000–35,000 BC) bears often occupied the same caves as our ancestors, and perhaps not always as dangerous rivals for shelter.

Toirano's Grotta della Basura is one of the most intriguing examples of possible cohabitation, but it's not the only one. In the 1950s, in the Grotte de Regourdou (next to the famous but much later cave of Lascaux in southwest France) a bear cemetery from the same era as Basura was found; unlike Basura, where bones were just massed together willy-nilly, some 20 bears were laid out in proper tombs, their bones carefully arranged around their skulls, sprinkled with red ochre, and covered with a slab. Around them were the fossilized remains of smaller animals, presumably funerary gifts for the bear to enjoy in the afterlife. Much later, in the vivid mural art of the Upper Palaeolithic period (c. 20,000–12,000 BC) in southwest France, bears (like people) are rarely depicted among the favourite bison, horses, mammoths and reindeer; there's a fine one engraved in the Grotte du Pech Merle in the Lot, where bears lived for thousands of years; there's another at Lascaux, hidden in the body of a bull, almost as if it were part of a find-the-hidden-picture game. Other drawings and etchings in the caves are often accompanied by bear claw marks. These decorated caves were not for day-to-day living, however; they seem to have been holy places, with an important if unknowable religious or ritual meaning. The bears were there, though. Perhaps the most suggestive of all are carvings found on bone throwing-staffs found at the Upper Palaeolithic shelters at La Madeleine (in the Dordogne) and Massat (in the Ariège). Few other works of the period are as explicitly, and mysteriously, sexual; they apparently show the bears licking disembodied human male and female genitalia. Then of course there are the statuettes made by the Old Eskimo, from a culture technologically similar to the Upper Palaeolithic, and demonstrating a sexual intimacy with bears that is shocking, at least by the standards set by Christopher Robin and Winnie the Pooh.

Judging by the bear cults that survived into historical times, our ancestral relationship with bears was limited to hunting cultures. A famous example comes from the Ainu people of northernmost Japan, who according to their own legends were descended from the son of a woman and a bear. Ainu hunters would apologize profusely if they slew one, and set up bear skulls (where the animal's spirit resides) in a place of honour. If a cub was captured, it would be suckled by an Ainu woman and raised with her children until its own strength made it a dangerous playmate; then for two or three years it would be put in a cage and pampered with delicacies, in preparation for the Bear Festival. Then the bear would be given a huge last meal in a show of sorrow, as the Ainu apologized and explained to the bear their reasons for sending it to its ancestors, before it would be strangled, and eaten.

marks and torch marks, all helter-skelter, as if from some mad prehistoric boogie woogie. Then there's the so-called **Room of Mystery**, where the Homo Sapiens Sapiens (the 'smart smarts', because the Cro-Magnons had bigger brain pans than us) hurled balls of clay at the wall. Although this is inevitably interpreted as having some religious significance, it's just as easy to imagine the smart smarts doing it for the fun of watching them stick. Maybe they bet mastodon steaks on the outcome.

The next cave, the **Grotta di Santa Lucia**, became a holy place in the Middle Ages; the spring behind the altar is credited with curing eye diseases, hence the dedication to Lucy, whose luminous name made her the patroness of sight. Her sanctuary is built into the cliff, next to two needley cypresses. The third cave, the **Grotta del Colombo**, is a beautiful natural hypogeum. A **Prehistoric Museum** on site contains remains found in these and other caves in the valley, and a reassembled bear skeleton.

Another road from Toirano passes the two-hour path up to the ruined monastery of **San Pietro dei Monti** (*see* p.121) before reaching **Balestrino**, defended by a picturesque sunbleached Del Carretto castle-residence, built in the 16th century.

Above Toirano: a Circular Route through the Forests

This route, which passes through the *entroterra* to Calizzano and back to the coast at Pietra Ligure, is especially lovely, passing through deep beech and chestnut woods at Colle di Melogno. The road from Toirano rises up the Val Varatella to cheese-making **Bardineto** and the mountain village of **Calizzano**, both former Del Carretto properties. Head back to the coast from here, through the enchanting **Colle di Melogno**: lush green and cool in the summer, and golden in the autumn, when the woods echo with the tramp of *porcini* mushroom hunters.

On the way back down to the Riviera, don't miss **Bardino Nuovo**, site of the G.B. Bergallo Museum of Tower Clocks, which houses numerous examples and is dedicated to a local family who made them until 1980.

G.B. Bergallo Museum of Tower Clocks Piazza San Sebastiano 10, t 019 648 545; currently closed for restoration

Loano and Pietra Ligure

If you've ever spent time reading all the inscriptions on the Arc de Triomphe in Paris you'll recognize **Loano** as the site of Napoleon's first victory in Italy. An attractive, palm-shaded town with a long beach, Loano was a hot property throughout history. It originally belonged to the bishop of Albenga, who sold it to Oberto Doria in 1263; the Fieschi took it briefly, and then Milan, but in 1547 it was bestowed back on the Doria by Emperor Charles V in gratitude for services rendered by Admiral Andrea.

The entrance to the old town is through a clock tower gate, built in honour of King Vittorio Amedeo III, who picked up Loano for Piedmont in 1795. Among the town's 16th-century palaces, the biggest is naturally the **Palazzo Doria** (now the Palazzo Comunale); pop in to see the beautiful 3rd-century AD Roman mosaic pavement kept here. Opposite, the 17th-century church of **San Giovanni** has a dodecagonal central plan and a peculiar copper cupola cap, added after the earthquake of 1887. The oldest part of town, Borgo Castello, surrounds a castle that the Doria converted into a magnificent villa in the 18th century. They also founded, in 1608, the **Monte Carmelo** convent in a panoramic spot in the hills; the church contains numerous Doria tombs.

Another old seaside town and modern beach resort, **Pietra Ligure**, was inhabited back in Neolithic times when the caves of Monte Trabocchetto were *the* place to stay. In Roman times it was an important stop along the Via Julia Augusta; the Byzantines, feeling rather less secure, built their *Castrum Petrae* high up, where a ruined Genoese castle now stands. Pietra has a mix of medieval buildings and 18th-century palaces; in central Piazza del Mercato, the **Oratorio dei Bianchi** was redone in Baroque and has a campanile crowned by a bronze St Nicholas who, according to legend, rang the bell in 1525 to announce the end of a plague. Here, too, is the late 18th-century church of **San Nicolò di Bari**, dedicated to Pietra's patron (also known as Santa Claus), containing two noteworthy paintings: *St Nicholas Enthroned* by Giovanni Barbagelata ('Frozen Beard') (1498) and *SS. Anthony Abbot and Paul the Hermit* by Domenico Piola (1671).

High above Pietra, **Giustenice** (from *Jus tenens*, 'where one obtains justice') has magnificent views. It once had a proud Del Carretto castle, which, after standing up to a long siege, was razed to the ground by Genoa in 1448. In July, the villagers re-enact the battles, serve a 15th-century banquet and play Renaissance football, similar to the *calcio storico* in Florence, with no rules whatsoever, much less justice.

Next up the coast, **Borgio Verezzi** is a shade calmer as beach resorts go, but it's less attractive, too. It has two medieval nuclei: one, Verezzi, is set 700ft over the sea. But the main site is underground: the 'most colourful caves in Italy', the **Grotte di Verezzi**, a labyrinth of colourful stalactites that goes on and on.

Grotte di Verezzi
t 019 610150, www. grottediborgio.it; open Oct–May Tues–Sun; guided tours on the hour 9.30–11.30 and 3–5; June–Sept open daily 9.30–11.30 and 3–5.30; adm

Where to Stay and Eat around Toirano, Loano and Pietra Ligure

Calizzano ✉ 17057

***Miramonti, Via Cinque Martiri 6, t 019 79604 (€€–€). A cosy place to sleep, but also a great place to eat, which draws in weekend diners around Liguria for its delicious selection of *porcini* mushroom dishes in season; well-prepared *salame*, fresh pasta, game and poultry, and home-made comfort desserts of the order of *budino della nonna*, 'Grandma's pudding'. *Closed Mon (except in summer), Dec–Mar.*

Loano ✉ 17025

****Garden Lido, Lungomare N. Sauro 9, t 019 669 666, *www.gardenlido.com* (€€€€€–€€€€). Overlooking the little port; ugly, kitsch 1960s building, with exceptionally well-furnished rooms and a wide range of facilities – private beach, pool, gym, bicycles, and a baby-sitting service. *Closed Oct–mid-Dec.*

***Iris, Viale Martiri Libertà 14, t 019 669 200, *www.hotelvillairis.it* (€€–€). Set in a lush garden of rhododendrons, azaleas and palms, Iris offers tranquillity, proximity to the old town and beach, and parking. *Closed Oct–Nov.*

***Villa Beatrice, Via S. Erasmo 6, t 019 668 244, *www.panozzohotels.it* (€€€–€€). Peaceful rooms in an early 19th-century villa, with a pool, fitness room, jacuzzi, sauna and beach. *Closed Oct–mid-Dec.*

Pietra Ligure ✉ 17027

****Hotel Paco, Via F. Crispi 225, t 019 615 715, *www.hotelpaco.it* (€€). Two swimming pools, tennis, lounge rooms, private beach and bikes to rent at this hotel, located in a quiet area of the town.

Borgio Verezzi ✉ 17022

***Ideal, Via XXV Aprile 32, t 019 610 438, *www.idealhotel.com* (€€). Economical choice near the sea, with its own beach and renovated rooms. *Closed mid-Oct–mid-Dec.*

ⓘ **Pietra Ligure** >>
Piazza S. Nicoló, t 019 629 003, www.inforiviera.it

ⓘ **Loano** >
Corso Europa 19, t 019 676 007, www.inforiviera.it

ⓘ **Borgio Verezzi** >>
Via Matteotti 158, t 019 610 412, www.inforiviera.it

DOC, Via Vittorio Veneto 1, t 019 611 477, *www. ristorantedoc.it* (€€€€). A romantic place in a villa, with the emphasis on fresh fish and delicious pasta with garden-fresh vegetables. *Menu degustazione* €65 without wine. *Closed Mon and Tues.*

Da Casetta, Via XX Settembre 12, t 019 610 166 (€€€). Justly celebrated for excellent Ligurian cuisine – *torta di verdura, cappon magro*, stuffed courgette blossoms, homemade bread at kind prices. *Eves only exc Sat and Sun; closed Tues.*

Up the Coast: Finale Ligure to Savona

Beyond bulky Capo di Caprazoppa ('Lame Goat Cape') begins the territory of Finale Ligure. Thirty million years ago, this was under the sea, where zillions of molluscs turned into a popular building stone, reddish limestone *pietra di Finale*, much of which can be found in cliffs and caves, magnets not only for prehistoric types looking for a place to hang their hats, but also for modern rock-climbers.

Finale Ligure

Throughout history, Finale has been on the edge: its name comes from when it marked the border between two Ligurian tribes, the Ingauni (west of Caprazoppa), and the Sabazi. In Roman times it was the end (*ad fines*) of the *municipium* of Vada Sabatia. Under the Lombards, it separated the March of Arduinica from the eastern March of Aleramica. The Del Carretto, Marquises of Arduinica, were the dominant force at Finale and at Noli, two Ghibelline needles in the side of Guelph Genoa.

This lively resort, like so many Riviera towns, has more than one frock in its closet, and actually consists of three Finales, like some very long opera where the fat lady refuses to die. The resort action and nightlife are concentrated in **Finale Marina**, with its wide swathes of fine pebble beaches framed by Caprazoppa. The town of Finale Ligure itself grew up in the mid-15th century, when the coast was clear; its castle changed hands several times between the Del Carretto and the Genoese.

Finale Pia, across the River Sciusa, is older, built around the 12th-century church of **Santa Maria di Pia**, with a Romanesque-Gothic campanile. In the 16th century, the church was joined by a Benedictine abbey, and later given a rococo façade; it has a beautiful 15th-century tabernacle inside. The monks keep bees, and a shop sells their honey and sweets, wax and royal jelly.

The medieval village of **Finaleborgo**, 2km inland, is one of the most beautiful along this coast. Founded in 1100 as *Burgus Finarii* by the Del Carretto and destroyed in their ongoing tussle with Genoa, it was rebuilt in the 15th century by Enrico II Del Carretto. Their impressive if derelict castle remains, while the walled town has a splendid ornament, the 13th-century octagonal campanile of **San Biagio**, built over a defensive tower. The church itself has fine works in marble, including a magnificent pulpit sculpted in 1765 by Pasquale Bocciardo, and a polyptych dated 1540 by 'Cristoforo Pancalino'. In 1359 the Del Carretto founded the convent of **Santa Caterina**, which had the sad fate of serving as a penitentiary for a century, until 1965; its restoration revealed a cycle of 15th-century Tuscan-inspired frescoes in the Cappella Oliveri. Its cloisters house the **Museo Archeologico del Finale**, housing pottery, an early-Christian sarcophagus, Palaeolithic Venuses, Neolithic tools, a huge bear skeleton and other items from Finale's prehistoric caves, most famously the **Grotta delle Arene Candide**.

Museo Archeologico del Finale
t 019 690 020, www. museoarcheofinale.it; open Tues–Sun July–Aug 10–12 and 4–7, Sept–June 9–12 and 2.30–5; adm

Just above Finaleborgo, before the *autostrada*, **Perti** is an interesting old place in the limestone heights. Its 14th-century church, Sant'Eusebio, has a pretty campanile and Romanesque crypt; a bit further on, in an olive grove, there's **Nostra Signora di Loreto**, a Renaissance gem known as the 'church of five bell towers'. Also near Perti stands all that remains of the **Castel Gavone**, built by Enrico II Del Carretto in the 1180s, destroyed by Genoa, rebuilt by Giovanni Del Carretto, and re-destroyed by Genoa in 1713, leaving only the picturesque 'Diamond Tower', containing some original frescoes. A pretty path leads up from Finale, beginning at the Spanish castle of San Giovanni.

The lofty patch of *entroterra* between Finale Pia and Noli is now protected as the **Parco delle Manie**, a high-altitude meadow crisscrossed by paths through the pines and Mediterranean flora. You can make your way along the ancient Via Julia Augusta, which weaves through the Parco delle Manie and the Val Ponci (near Finale Pia), traversing five Roman bridges built in 124 AD, when the locals improved the road; one, the **Ponte delle Fate** (Fairies' Bridge), is in perfect nick.

The next spot up the coast, tucked under the limestone cape on Saracen Bay, **Varigotti** is about as picturesque as a seaside village can get, its houses painted in rich shades of ochre and pink giving directly on to a wide sandy beach and turquoise sea. This was the Byzantine *Varicottis*, destroyed in 643 by those heavy metal barbarians, Rotharis and the Lombards, and only rebuilt in the 14th century by the Del Carretto. Ernest Hemingway was very fond of it, and modern painters find it a very attractive subject. The castle – what remains of the Byzantine *castrum* and the Del Carretto fort – can be seen over Punta Crena, while a lone watchtower stands on the summit of the cape. The Via Aurelia, carved out of the bleached cliffs between Varigotti and Capo Noli, is one of the most scenic stretches of road on the Ponente; rare plants grow on the cliffs, and peregrine falcons often soar high overhead.

Noli

Lying under **Monte Ursino** (an impressive pale bulk, which some say inspired Dante's idea of Purgatory), Noli resembles a mini Genoa, with its narrow lanes, or *carrugi*, and tall houses. Of its original 72 medieval skyscrapers, eight remain, including the 125ft **Torre del Canto** and the perfectly intact 13th-century **Torre Comunale**, topped with Ghibelline crenellations. This is on **Corso Italia**, which once had a portico that sheltered both people and boats; a part of this remains, encompassing the Loggia del Comune. Noli's 13th-century **Cattedrale di San Pietro** was covered with a Baroque skin, and contains a polyptych by the school of Ludovico Brea.

Noli's most important monument, however, is off the south end of Corso Italia: the beautiful 11th-century church of **San Paragorio**, one of the finest Romanesque monuments in Liguria. Founded in the 8th century (the date of the sarcophagi that line its left flank) and restored in the 19th century, the façade is decorated with blind arches; inside, there's a 13th-century bishop's throne, an ambon, and a 12th-century crucifix called a *Volto Santo*, because it's said to be a true portrait of Christ. Other medieval buildings in Noli are secular: **Casa Repetto**; the 14th-century gate of **San Giovanni**, preserving its original door; and the **Palazzotto Trecento**. If you have enough puff, there's also a path up to the scenographic 12th-century **castle** draped on Monte Ursino, built by the Del Carretto. The views are lovely, but you may find Dante's description of Purgatory ('rugged and difficult of access') more than apt on a hot day.

There's a good beach at Noli, and an even better one nearby at **Spotorno**, which has grown into a large resort, but keeps a 14th-century castle tucked in the back. Off rockbound Capo Maiolo, closing off Spotorno from Savona, is the little islet of **Bergeggi**, now a nature reserve and future marine park but used at various times in the past as a monastic retreat and outer defence. The little village of the same name has one of the most famous restaurants

Bergeggi
to visit, enquire at the Alassio tourist office, t 0812 647 11, or IAT tourist office at Bergeggi, t 019 859 777

Noli: the Fifth Republic

Every Italian schoolchild learns of the four great maritime Republics of medieval Italy: Genoa, Pisa, Amalfi and Venice. But in Liguria they learn that there were really five; at least if you count the not-so-great maritime republic of Noli. Noli's independent spirit goes way back; stories tell how its first inhabitants, unlike the other Ligurians, joined the Romans against the Carthaginians. The Byzantines made it their *castrum* Neapolis ('new town'), which was shortened to Noli by the time the Marchese Del Carretto led it in the First Crusade in 1097. Like Genoa, Noli fought well enough in the Holy Land to jump-start its career back home. When Savona threatened in the 12th century, Noli allied itself with Genoa and remained an independent republic for 600 years, from 1192 to 1797, when Napoleon wiped it off the map. It's not a bad record, however, and Noli commemorates its centuries of independence with regattas that pit its four quarters, or *rioni*, against one another every September.

Pinacoteca Civica
t 019 886 350; open Tues, Sat and Sun 6–7 (winter 3–6), Thurs and Fri 9.30–12.30; adm

on the Riviera (*see* p.129); the diving's good, too. In **Vado Ligure**, the last town before Savona, the Renaissance Villa Groppallo at Via Aurelia 72 contains the **Pinacoteca Civica** with artworks awarded the *Premio Vado* and a room dedicated to Arturo Martini.

(i) **Finale Ligure**
Via San Pietro 14, t 019 681 019; in summer, also at Piazza Porta Testa in Finaleborgo, t 019 680 954, www.inforiviera.it

Sports and Activities up the Coast from Finale Ligure

Diving is big here. In Finale contact Peluffo Sport, Via Molinetti 6, t 019 601 620; in Spotorno, the Bergeggi Diving School at the Bagni Cormorano, t 019 859 950, *www.bergeggidiving.it*. The Lega Navale, in Finale's Porto Capo San Donato, t 019 600 440, *www.leganavale.it/finaleligure*, hires out **sailing boats**. The *entroterra* of Finale, especially around Pia Finale with its cliffs, is a **rock-climbing** mecca: the fantastical Rocca di Corno in the Parco Naturale delle Manie is a favourite. Contact the CAI Finale, Piazza del Tribunale, t 019 215 4211.

Where to Stay and Eat up the Coast from Finale Ligure

Finale Marina ✉ 17024
****Grand Hotel Moroni**, Lungomare San Pietro 38, t 019 692 222, *www.hotelmoroni.com* (€€€). On the promenade of palms, big air-conditioned, renovated rooms without sea views, or smaller ones with views. *Three-day minumum stay; full-board terms.*
***Park Hotel Castello**, Via Caviglia 26, t 019 691 320, *www.parkhotelcastello.com* (€€€). Near the top of the town, with more character than most, and a garden; rare in that it remains open all year.
***Medusa**, Lungomare di Via Concezione, t 019 692 545, *www.medusahotel.it* (€€). Good base, with family rooms and special facilities for small children; they also cater for cyclists. *Half-board terms.*
***Colibri**, Via Colombo 57, t 019 692 681, *www.colibrihotel.it* (€€). Very efficiently run, modern place in the

old town, 30m from the sea; rooms have views of the hills. There is also a sun roof and a good **restaurant**. *Full-board terms.*
***Conte**, Via Genova 16, t 019 680 234, *www.residenceconte.it* (€€). In an 18th-century building, apartments rented by the week, sleeping from two to six in a secluded garden in a lovely setting.
***San Marco**, Via Concezione 22, t 019 692 533 (€). Fairly basic hotel, with a good **restaurant**, right on the seafront.
Pasticceria Ferro, Via Garibaldi 10. For a sweet pick-me-up; renowned for almond *chifferi*.

Finaleborgo ✉ 17024
Villa Piuma, Via Cappelletto Nuova 8, Loc. Perti, t 019 687 030, *www.agrisport.com/liguria.htm* (€). *Agriturismo* amid the olive groves in a lovely restored manor of 1703, up in the hills, 3km from the beaches. *Open Mar–Dec.*
***Vecchie Mura**, Via delle Mura 1, t 019 691 268 (€€–€). Located just outside the medieval town, a comfortable family-run hotel. During the winter it is particularly popular with the rock-climbing fraternity.
Ai Torchi, Via dell'Annunziata 12, t 019 690 531 (€€€€). Warm *antipasti*, herb-filled ravioli and a couple of meat dishes as well as good fish dishes in a 15th-century olive oil press. *Closed Tues except in Aug.*
Osteria del Castel Gavone, Via Penti Alto 8, t 019 692 277 (€€€). Above Finale at Perti Alto (follow the signs for Calice Ligure). A varied menu that includes dishes rarely seen in Liguria, including wild boar. *Closed Tues in winter.*

Finale Pia ✉ 17024
***La Gioiosa**, Via Manie 53, t 019 601 306, *www.lagioiosahotel.it* (€€). Stunning views of the sea from the seven beautiful rooms, plus a restaurant and a large terrace with

ⓘ **Spotorno** ››
Piazza Matteotti 6,
t 019 741 5008,
www.inforiviera.it

ⓘ **Varigotti** ›
Via Aurelia 79,
t 019 698 013,
www.inforiviera.it

ⓘ **Noli** ›
Corso Italia 8, t 019 749
9003, www.inforiviera.it

⭐ **Claudio** ››

loungers. The only thing that will force you to budge is the lack of a pool.

Varigotti ✉ 17029

Muraglia-Conchiglia d'Oro, Via Aurelia 133, **t** 019 698 015 (€€€€).The menu changes daily and the food is authentic and true; try *fazzoletti* (Ligurian pasta with scampi) and mouthwatering *grigliata. Book. Closed Tues and Wed (in summer Wed only) and 15 Jan–15 Feb.*

Noli ✉ 17026

***Miramare, Corso Italia 2, **t** 019 748 926 (€€€). An old seaside fort converted into a hotel. All rooms have sea views and a touch of class; there's also a garden and breakfast buffet, and a **restaurant** also open to non-guests. *Closed Nov–Dec.*

***El Sito, Via La Malfa 2, **t** 019 748 107, *www.elsito.it* (€€). Set back in a garden, a peaceful and pleasant family-run place with modern rooms and a delicious terrace. *Half-board terms. Closed Nov.*

Ines, Via Vignolo 1, **t 019 748 086 (€€). In the heart of the old town, comfortable rooms in a 17th-century *palazzo* overlooking the main square. The friendly **restaurant** serves Ligurian classics.

Pino, Via Cavalieri di Malta 37, **t** 019 7490 065 (€€€€). Noli's best seafood restaurant. *Closed Mon.*

Lilliput, 4km up in Frazione Voze, regione Zuglieno 49, **t** 019 748 009 (€€€€). Not small, but out of the way, and worth finding for well-executed dishes – even *minestrone alla genovese* takes on a new quality here. There's land food as well as seafood, and a summer garden. *Closed Mon,*

lunch Tues–Fri; 10–31 Jan; early Nov–early Dec.

Spotorno ✉ 17028

****Acqua Novella, 1km from the centre at Via Acquanovella 1, **t** 019 741 665, *www.hotelacquanovella.it* (€€€). Has a lovely garden and pool, Turkish bath, fitness centre and private beach reached by a lift.

***Miramare, Via Aurelia 70, **t** 019 745 116, *www.miramarespotorno.com* (€€€). Good amenities, a private beach and balconies plus an impressive breakfast buffet open till midday. *Open mid-Mar–early Nov.*

Bergeggi ✉ 17042

***Claudio, Via XXV Aprile 37, **t** 019 859 750, *www.hotelclaudio.it* (€€€€). Award-winning hotel, with luminous rooms furnished with antiques; terraces, a pretty pool and beach, and good breakfast. *Open Mar–end Nov.* The **restaurant** (€€€€) is one of the best: you won't find dreamier seafood, accompanied by perfect wines and desserts in magical surroundings; bookings essential. *Closed Jan and Mon. Open eves only, except during hols.* Claudio's latest venture, the **Hosteria Borgo S. Sebastiano** at Via XXV Aprile, **t** 019 859 361, is more affordable; traditional dishes on a €27 menu with wine, plus a boutique and wine shop.

Vado Ligure ✉ 17047

***La Fornace di Barbablu, Via Lazio 11A, above Vado in Fraz. Sant' Ermete, **t** 019 888 535 (€€€€). Romantic spot, serving beautifully presented, tasty food (mainly fish) in an atmospheric stone building, used as a furnace in Roman times. *Book. Closed Mon.*

Savona

🔆 **Savona**

Liguria's second city, Savona, offers a change of pace, and more than one surprise. It is the bitter orange (*chinotto*) capital of the Riviera, thanks to a Savonese sailor who brought the tree back from China in 1500; once popular in *digestivos*, the fruit fell from favour but is currently being revived, with the blessing of the Slow Food movement. Some 200 cruise ships a year call here, but this is still very much a working town, not a resort, and one of Italy's

Getting around Savona

Savona is one of the main ports for Corsica, with Corsica Ferries-Sardinia Ferries, *www.corsicaferries.com*.

busiest ports; if you have small children, it's fun to hang around the docks and watch the aerial cable cars unload coal for the iron works at San Giuseppe di Cairo. Savona was always a rival of Genoa; if Genoa was Milan's natural port, Savona plays a similar role with Turin. In Roman times there were two towns here: Savo on the rock Priamar, founded over a Ligurian *castellari*, and Vada Sabatia down by the sea. The Byzantines fortified Savo; it grew up to become an independent city, which Genoa only put under its thumb in 1528.

Around the Port

Savona's old port, now filled with pleasure craft, is the most picturesque corner of the city, with its collection of medieval towers. One, its landmark, the **Torre di Leon Pancaldo**, dates from the 13th century, but was renamed to honour Magellan's pilot, born nearby; Pancaldo was one of the four survivors on the *Trinidad* to return to Spain after their epic journey around the world. A niche near the top holds a statue of the Madonna della Misericordia, the patroness of local sailors. Another tower, the 12th-century **Torre del Brandale**, has a great big bell called A Campanassa, which summoned the Savonesi in times of emergency.

Merchants built their houses around the portside Piazza Salinera, where they only had to glance out of the window to see if their ship had come in. The most important of these, the 16th-century Palazzo Lamba-Doria, is now the **Camera di Commercio**; if they let you in, look at the frescoes along the grand stair, by Ottaviano Semino, inspired by the work of Perino del Vaga in Genoa.

Behind the Torre di Leon Pancaldo, portico-lined **Via Paleocapa** is Savona's main shopping street; it has a pretty Liberty-style address, the **Palazzo dei Pavoni** (1912) at No.3, designed by Alessandro Martinengo, and the 18th-century church of **Sant'Andrea**, which contains in the sacristy an icon of St Nicolas from the Hagia Sofia. The nearby **Oratorio del Cristo Risorto** was rebuilt in 1604 and covered with frescoes, including a mighty *Triumph of God* around the altar. It has fine choir stalls from the late 1400s, made by German sculptors, as well as two small German Gothic paintings. A third church, **San Giovanni Battista**, was built by the Dominicans after the Genoese destroyed their church on Priamar, and is replete with Baroque frescoes and paintings. The large processional scenes often stored in these churches are used in Savona's Good Friday procession, in even-numbered years.

Sant'Andrea
open mornings only

Oratorio del Cristo Risorto
*open during Heritage Days, **t** 010 203 1043*

Just north, in Piazza Diaz, is the monumental **Teatro Chiabrera** (1850), dedicated to Savona's 17th-century poet Gabriello Chiabrera, who composed a fawning epic called the *Amedeide* in honour of the Savoy dukes; the theatre's tympanum depicts the poet presenting his opus to a grateful Duke Carlo Emanuele I in all its provincial glory. The Palazzo Pozzombello, behind the theatre at Via Montegrappa 5, contains the **Raccolta di Scienze Naturali**, with fossils, including those of a one-of-a-kind beast called an Athracotherium.

Via Paleocapa intersects with narrow **Via Pia**, Savona's medieval high street. Just off this crossroads, in Piazza Chabrol, the

Pinacoteca Civica
t 019 811 520; open Mon, Wed and Fri 8.30–1, Tues and Thurs 2–7, Sat 8.30–1 and 3.30–6.30, summer 8.30pm–11.30pm, Sun 10–1, summer 8.30pm–11.30pm; adm

Pinacoteca Civica houses a golden 13th-century *Madonna col bambino* by Taddeo di Bartolo, Foppa's *Pala Fornari* and three 15th-century *Crucifixions* by Donato De Bardi, Ludovico Brea and Giovanni Mazone. There's plenty of local talent from the 17th and 18th centuries from Savona's churches, but then comes a surprise: a collection by Picasso, De Chirico, Man Ray, De Pisis, Fontana, Capogrossi, Mirò and Magritte, donated by Savonese writer Milena Milani in memory of her companion Carlo Cardazzo; one room is devoted to portraits of Milena by some of the greats.

Savona of the Popes

Savona gave Rome two Della Rovere popes: Sixtus IV, who built the Sistine Chapel in the Vatican, and his nephew, Julius II, who hired Michelangelo to paint its ceiling. Sixtus and Julius left their mark on Savona, too, but more discreetly; their **Della Rovere Palace** on Via Pia (No.28, now the law courts) was designed for Julius while he was still a cardinal by one of the architects of St Peter's, Giuliano da Sangallo. This was lavishly decorated inside, until it became a convent and the nuns plastered over the walls; only the part of the palace housing a post office retains some of its original frescoes.

In the street behind the Della Rovere palace rises the 16th-century **Duomo di Santa Maria Assunta**, hiding behind an 18th-century façade. This contains a 6th-century Byzantine baptismal font, big enough for adult immersions, a 15th-century marble *Crucifix*, from Savona's first cathedral, and a pulpit with symbols of the Evangelists (1522). The chapel on the far right has a great Hallowe'en altar with praying skeletons and the *Madonna Enthroned Between Saints*, which is considered the masterpiece of Alberto Piazza, a Lombard painter. In the apse, note the magnificent carved choir stalls (1515).

Cathedral Treasury
t 019 825 960; open on request if the sacristan is there, or by appointment; adm

Sistine Chapel
same adm as treasury, or most Sundays at 4pm when there are guided tours to Duomo, Capella Sistina and carved choir

There are more goodies tucked away in the Cathedral Treasury, with a fine *Assumption and Saints* by Ludovico Brea, an *Adoration of the Magi* by the Hoogstaeten master, 14th-century English alabaster statues, intarsia work, and religious items donated by the popes. Through the cloister, Savona's own Sistine Chapel was built

08 Riviera di Ponente | Up the Coast: Savona

The Savonese Captivity

A third pope spent, or rather did, time in Savona, in an affair that marks the nadir of the papacy's prestige. Petrarch labelled King Philip le Bel's corralling of the 14th-century papacy in Avignon as the 'Babylonian Captivity', but it took an even more brazen French agent named Napoleon to arrest a pope to try to bend him to his will.

Napoleon, declaring himself the new Charlemagne, had forced his *Code Napoléon* on the papal states in 1801, along with a Concordat that made the Gallican Church practically autonomous. Pius VII had no choice but to go along or risk losing the papal states altogether, but he balked when the new Charlemagne ordered him in 1808 to expel all British ministers from Rome and not to allow British ships into his ports. Napoleon responded by invading the papal states and revoking the pope's rights to a temporal state; Pius, a mild-mannered liberal, replied by excommunicating Napoleon. Napoleon ordered his police to keep this a secret (they failed), and had Pius arrested and imprisoned in Savona's bishop's palace.

Napoleon did all he could to browbeat Pius, even taking away the Pope's pen and ink when he discovered that he had secretly sent out letters ordering the Church not to accept the Napoleon-appointed bishops. When the chips were down and Napoleon wanted to negotiate with the Pope to appease the Allies, he had his prisoner brought to Fontainebleau in a journey that nearly killed him. After being treated extremely rudely by Napoleon for a week, the Pope signed a new Concordat that gave him everything he wanted, except the papal states; in 1813, when the Allies were invading France, Napoleon offered to give these back to the Pope as well. Pius replied that no treaty was necessary for the return of stolen property – a remark that earned him a return ticket to Savona to cool his heels.

He was only released and allowed to return to Rome in March 1814, when the Allies had reached the outskirts of Paris, and the papal states, 'so awful that even the earth refuses to swallow them up' as Goethe put it, limped on until 1870.

Oratorio Nostra Signora di Castello
open Sun 8–10am

Civico Museo Storico Archeologico
t 019 822 708, www.museoarcheo savona.it; open mid-Sept–May Tues–Fri 9.30–12.30 and 3–5, Sat 10–12 and 3–5, Sun 3–5; June–mid-Sept Tues–Sat 10–12 and 5–7, Sun 5–7; adm

Museo Sandro Pertini
t 019 801 908; open Mon–Sat 8.30–12.30; adm

Museo Renata Cuneo
currently closed, but for information call Servizi Museali t 019 8387 391

by Sixtus for his parents, and frosted with charming rococo decorations and stucco oaks (*rovere*) by another member of the clan, the Genoese Doge Francesco Maria della Rovere; it contains the Renaissance tomb of Sixtus' mum and dad, with a relief of their papal son introducing them to the Virgin.

Behind the cathedral, the **Oratorio Nostra Signora di Castello** contains the finest painting in Savona: a polyptych of the *Madonna and Saints* from the late 1400s, begun by Vincenzo Foppa and completed by Ludovico Brea.

Fortezza di Priamar and its Museums

Savona once had a dense medieval core on its promontory, with most of its houses and a cathedral, but in 1542 the Genoese, who really knew how to bear a grudge, razed it all to erect their fortress, **Priamar** – not to protect Savona, but to keep it in its place after clobbering it in 1528. After serving as a prison (Mazzini was here in 1830–31), Savona now uses the no-nonsense pile for exhibitions and three museums, including the **Civico Museo Storico Archeologico** with Greek and Etruscan ceramics, a Roman relief of a hunt, and bits of medieval Savona. The **Museo Sandro Pertini** has modern art (by De Pisis, Guttuso, Manzù) given to Savona native Sandro Pertini, 'the best-loved Italian president' (1978–85); the **Museo Renata Cuneo** is in the Bestione di San Bernando. It is dedicated to the sculptress of some of Savona's Good Friday floats.

Don't miss the Liberty building covered with nymphs and bees near Priamar, at the corner of Corso Mazzini and Via Manzoni. To the west stretches Savona's blue flag beach.

For an encore, carry on 6km above Savona (take the road from Piazza Aurelio Saffi), where a theatrical piazza in a pretty wooded setting holds the striking Mannerist **Santuario di Nostra Signora della Misericordia**, begun in the 1550s and completed in 1610 by Taddio Carlone. Inside, there's a *Nativity of the Virgin* by one of Caravaggio's best followers, Orazio Borgianni and, in the third chapel on the left, a superb marble relief of the *Visitation*, probably by Bernini. The **treasury** has as its most precious relic a piece of the Virgin's veil, bejewelled donations and sailors' *ex votos*.

Treasury
t 019 879 025,
www.santuario
savona.eu

Savona's *Entroterra*

Thick forests mark Savona's hinterland, which also has the traditional boundary between the Alps and the Apennines at **Bocchetta di Altare di Cadibona**. The trees were used to build ships and fuel the furnaces of **Altare** (on the SS29), famous for hand-blown glass since the 12th century at least, an art learned from artists from Flanders, who changed their names from Bousson and Raquette to Buzzone and Racchetti. Their work is displayed in the **Museo del Vetro**, in the Villa Rosa in Piazza del Consolato, one of several Liberty-style mansions in town. The collection includes engraved glass, and some of the biggest single pieces of hand-blown glass ever made.

Museo del Vetro
t 019 584 734,
www.museodel
vetro.org; open winter
Wed–Sun 3.30–7;
summer Wed–Sun 4–7;
adm

Beyond this, **Millesimo** is a charming, fortified hill town with a ruined Del Carretto castle of 1206, where even the 15th-century bridge has a watch tower. It has a fine 11th-century Romanesque church, **Santa Maria Extra Muros**, and a neoclassical **Santuario della Madonna del Deserto**, frescoed and full of *ex votos* (1725). The town, with a clutch of artisans' workshops, is a popular excursion destination, not least for its scrumptious rum chocolates called *millesimini*. Above, on the Colle di Millesimo, there's a rare menhir and a few incisions, similar to the Vallée des Merveilles.

Santuario della Madonna del Deserto
open April–Oct
Mon–Sat 9–6.30,
Sun and hols 8.30–7;
Nov–Mar Mon–Sat
9–5.30, Sun 9–6

The best scenery is north of Dego (backtrack a bit and turn north at Carcare) in the little **Parco Regionale di Piana Crixia**, where the rocky landscape is eroded into peculiar forms, including one in the shape of a giant mushroom near the hamlet of Borgo.

(sidebar)
08
Riviera di Ponente | Up the Coast: Savona

Whale Watching in Savona

① Savona >>
Corso Italia 157/r,
t 019 840 2321,
www.inforiviera.it

Whale Watch Liguria, **t** 010 265 712, *www.whalewatchliguria.it*, have excursions departing from Savona and Varazze.

Where to Stay and Eat in Savona

Savona ✉ 17100

★★★★Mare, Via Nizza 89/r, **t** 019 264 065, *www.marehotel.it* (€€€–€€). By the sea, with every comfort and an exquisite seafood **restaurant** (€€€€)

with the funny name **A Spurcacciun-A** (open to non-guests). The seven-course menu is a seafood-lovers' heaven, each course served with its own wine; other simpler menus are also available. Leave room for the bitter chocolate soufflé. *Closed Wed and Christmas.*

★★★Riviera Suisse, Via Paleocapa 24, **t** 019 850 853, *www.rivierasuisse hotel.it* (€€–€). Downtown, in a historic building, with good standard rooms.

L'Arco Antico, Piazza Lavagnola 26/r, **t** 019 820 938 (€€€€). Family-run trattoria, serving tasty *bagna cauda*,

lasagnette with lobster and artichokes. *Closed Sun, some of Jan, two weeks in Sept and at lunch.*

Vino e Farinata, Via Pia 15/r, no phone (€). A city institution, serving not only *farinata* but authentic pasta with pesto, *ceci e fagioli*, etc. *Menu degustazione* €22. *Closed Sun, Mon and July.*

Quiliano ✉ 17040

Il Respiro del Tempo B&B, Via Don Peluffo 8, **t** 019 887 8728, *www.ilrespirodeltempo.com* (€€). Seven km from Savona and linked by city bus 9, a B&B of character in an early 19th-century setting.

On to Genoa

There are good beaches along this coast, before you strike greater Genoa, that long, long tapeworm of a city that has swallowed up fishing towns and villas in its wake. Near both Savona and Genoa, these resorts are favourites for a lazy day by the sea.

Villa Durazzo Faraggiana
t 019 480 622, www.villafaraggiana.it; open Mar–Sept Tues–Sun 3–7; adm

Fabbrica Casa-Museo Giuseppe Mazzotti
Viale Matteotti 29, t 019 489 872, www. gmazzotti1903.it; open Mon–Sat 8.30–12.30 and 2.30–7.30, Sun 9.30–12.30 and 3.30–7.30

Museo Villa Jorn
t 019 400 29 ext 280–281; visits by appointment only

Museo della Ceramica Manlio Trucco
Corso Ferrari 195, t 019 482 741; opening hours vary according to the exhibitions – for information, call the Ufficio Culture of the Commune, t 019 482 295 ext 257–226

Albisola, Albissola and Ceramics

Like many Riviera towns, 'Le Albisole' (from the Latin *AlbaDocilia*) has a split personality, but in this case the two sides have been separate *comuni* since the 16th century: the seaside **Albissola Marina** and the upper **Albisola Superiore**. Together they form Liguria's most important ceramics centre, using their rich red clay to make plates, pots and decorative tiles since the mid-15th century. Although production plummeted in the 19th century, Le Albisole began to revive in 1891, when Nicolò Poggi began to create Liberty art pieces. Later, Tullio di Albisola made Albissola Marina a centre of Futurist ceramics, and the town hasn't looked back since. Even if you're just passing through, you can't miss the town's vocation, not only in the many shops, but in the panels and mosaic pavements that decorate the seaside **Passeggiata degli Artisti**.

There are permanent exhibits as well: the 18th-century **Villa Durazzo Faraggiana**, set behind a stately exedra in a lovely garden on Via Salomoni in Albissola Marina, has its original furnishings, a gallery paved in majolica, and a museum on the history of ceramics; the **Fabbrica Casa-Museo Giuseppe Mazzotti** in a Futurist factory of 1903, with pieces by top contemporary ceramicists; **Museo Villa Jorn** has works by the great Danish ceramicist Asgar Jorn, who used to live here; and the **Museo della Ceramica Manlio Trucco** in a villa in Albisola Superiore, with works by Manlio Trucco, Arturo Martini (*St George and the Dragon*), Francesco Messina, archaeological finds and frequent temporary exhibitions.

There's more. A Roman Imperial **villa** was discovered in Albisola's plain, an enormous agricultural estate from the time when small landowners were being taxed into selling themselves into serfdom. There's a beautiful risseu pebble mosaic in front of the church of **Nostra Signora della Concordia** in Albissola Marina, and, up in Albisola Superiore, the 15th-century **Palazzo Gavotti**, which the last Doge of Genoa, Francesco Maria della Rovere, refurbished as a sumptuous residence (1739–53). It can be seen from the outside or by guided tour.

Palazzo Gavotti
booking required,
t 010 27181

The *Entroterra*: Sassello and Monte Beigua

Up in the Ligurian Apennines on the S334 from Albisola, **Sassello** is a summer resort that always remains fresh and cool; in winter people come here from the coast to play in the snow. It still looks pretty much as it did in the 18th century, although only the memory remains of its old iron manufacturers, who combined ore shipped up from Elba with their abundant water power and forests to keep the furnaces ablaze. Paths in the woods are filled with mushroom hunters in the autumn and roadside stands wait to sell you not only bags of dried *porcini*, but also grappa and Sassello's golden brown *amaretti*, a speciality for over a century and among the best in Italy. On Good Friday the streets are decorated with 'paintings' made of flowers.

From Sassello you can follow a scenic circular route further into the Apennines by way of **Urbe**. This area was owned by the Cistercian abbey at **Tiglieto**, founded in 1120 – one of the first in Italy, although it was later converted into a private residence. There's a pretty stone bridge, and a swimming hole just below. From Tiglieto or Urbe you can head back south through the wooded **Parco Naturale del Monte Beigua** (4,221ft), encompassing the striking rocky outcrop of Beigua which, like that mountain of similar name, Bego in the Val Roja, provided a canvas for shepherds to scratch their thoughts from prehistoric times up to the Middle Ages. These mountains are rich in titanium, although so far the ecologists have won the battle to keep Beigua unscarred by gaping pits. Another road from Urbe leads to the **Passo del Faiallo**, with a fantastic view as far as Corsica; if you continue east to the Passo del Turchino, the S456 will take you back to the coast at Voltri, in the suburbs of Genoa.

Celle Ligure and Varazze

In spite of its popular sandy beach, **Celle Ligure** has maintained its integrity as a colourful old seaside town, backed by hills to keep it snug. In the centre, a theatrical stair leads up to the church of **San Michele**, with a 12th-century campanile and, inside, a polyptych of *SS Michele, Pietro and Giovanni* by Perino del Vaga (1535) and a

Map labels: Urbe, Sassello, Passo di Faiallo, Dego, Parco Regionale del Beigua, Eremo del Deserto, Alpicella, Pegli, Millesimo, Arenzano, GENOA (GENOVA), Cogoleto, Albisola Superiore, Varazze, Celle Ligure, Bocchetta di Cadibona, Albissola Marina, Gulf of Genoa, Giustenice, Savona, N, 10 km, 5 miles

Ages. These mountains are rich in titanium, although so far the ecologists have won the battle to keep Beigua unscarred by gaping pits. Another road from Urbe leads to the **Passo del Faiallo**, with a fantastic view as far as Corsica; if you continue east to the Passo del Turchino, the S456 will take you back to the coast at Voltri, in the suburbs of Genoa.

Celle Ligure and Varazze

In spite of its popular sandy beach, **Celle Ligure** has maintained its integrity as a colourful old seaside town, backed by hills to keep it snug. In the centre, a theatrical stair leads up to the church of **San Michele**, with a 12th-century campanile and, inside, a polyptych of *SS Michele, Pietro and Giovanni* by Perino del Vaga (1535) and a peculiar *Crucifixion* in the shape of a tree. The *comune* has an extremely pretty pine grove to the west, the **Pineta Bottini**, the perfect place for a picnic, perhaps with a bottle of Celle's own dry white wine, Lumassina, and a plate of *lumasse* (snails), the food that goes so well with it that it gave the wine its name.

Varazze, the biggest resort in these parts, has always had shipyards; its Roman name, *Ad Navalia*, evolved into Varagine in the 13th century, when it produced Jacopo da Varagine. A Dominican who became an archbishop, Jacopo wrote the medieval bestseller, the *Golden Legend*, the inspiration for the popular Discovery of the

St Catherine of Siena by Anton Maria Maragliano. At the west end of Varazze, Romanesque **SS. Nazario e Celso** hides behind a Baroque façade, with a 1902 mosaic. A third church, **San Domenico**, has the tomb of the local 'saint' Jacopo da Varagine as well as a cannonball embedded in its façade, fired by a French ship in 1746.

Inland, a favourite trip is up to the Franciscan convent, the **Eremo del Deserto**, with walking and riding paths radiating into the Parco Naturale del Beigua (*see* p.135). There's a small archaeology museum in **Alpicella** with local prehistoric finds; it also has a picturesque bridge, built by the Saracens.

Alpicella
*Piazza IV Novembre,
t 019 93901 or 019
95210; open May–Oct
Sun 3–6, other times
by request*

Last Stops before Genoa: Cogoleto and Arenzano

A pretty seaside path, the 5km **Lungomare Europa**, replaces the old railway line from Varazze to **Cogoleto** where there are fantastic views and no traffic. According to one tradition, Cogoleto was the birthplace of Columbus. At least everyone in the village thinks so, and they have erected a statue to him in the main piazza. Their conviction is based on a Latin document dated Cogoleto, 23 August 1449, which states: 'Maria, wife of Domenico daughter of Jacobi Justi de Lerdra in Cogoleto resides in Cogoleto, with three sons, Christophor, Bartholomé et Jacopo recently born.' If true, it would make Christopher older than his accepted birthdate of 1450. Nevertheless, a house in Cogoleto has a venerable history as Columbus' birthplace, and in 1650 a priest named Antonio Colombo living in the house wrote three inscriptions on the façade. One says: *Unus erat mundus; duo sunt ait iste, fuere.* ('There was but one world; let there be two said he, and it was so.')

Arenzano is another resort with villas and a Grand Hotel, its *lungomare* planted with palms in the late 19th century. It has the **Golf Tennis Club della Pineta** west of town, and there's a pretty park to laze about in, by the 16th-century hilltop **Villa Pallavicini-Negrotto-Cambiaso**, now the town hall. For all that, the main draw in Arenzano is the modern Sanctuary of the Christ Child of Prague.

**Golf Tennis Club
della Pineta**
t 010 911 1817

Riviera di Ponente | On to Genoa

08

Where to Stay and Eat from Albissola to Genoa

ⓘ **Albissola >**
*Piazzo Wifredo Lam,
t 019 400 2525*

Albissola Marina ✉ 17012

****Garden**, Viale Faraggiana 6, t 019 485 253 www.hotelgardenalbissola.com (€€€). Tranquil and packed full of modern art; all of the bright, air-conditioned rooms have terraces, and most have sea views. Pool.

****Splendor**, Via Repetto 108, t 019 481 796 (€€–€). Though not as grand as the name would suggest, rooms are well equipped and functional. Mother/daughter owners very helpful. *Closed last week Nov to mid-Dec.*

Gianni ai Pescatori, Corso Bigliati 82, t 019 481 200 (€€). A pretty, light-filled setting, where land food and seafood are prepared with a refined touch; great crème brûlée. *Closed Tues out of season, and 15 days in autumn.*

La Familaire, Piazza del Popolo 8, t 019 489 480 (€€€). Sit and watch the chefs prepare a seafood extravaganza, including a classic spaghetti with clams. *Closed Mon.*

(i) **Celle Ligure**
Via Boagno,
t 019 990 021

(i) **Arenzano >>**
Lungomare Kennedy,
t 010 912 7581

Varazze ✉ 17019

****Torretti**, Viale Nazioni Unite 6,
t 019 934 623, *www.hoteltorretti.it*
(€€€–€€). In the same family since
1874, a classy and charming hotel
close to the sea.

****Cristallo**, Via F. Cilea 4, t 019
97264, *www.cristallohotel.it* (€€€–€€).
Very well-equipped rooms, plus playground, gym and private beach.

***Coccodrillo**, Via N. Sardi 16,
t 019 932 015, *www.coccodrillo.it* (€€).
Rooms and flats with a pool, a good
restaurant and a garden atmosphere,
200m from the sea. Special weekend
deals out of season.

***Doria**, Piazza Doria 6, t 019 930
101 (€). Worthy of at least two stars;
rooms in a 19th-century *palazzo*. Both
the train station and the sea are
within walking distance.

Antico Genovese, Corso Colombo 70,
t 019 96482 (€€€€). In business since
1910, where succulent variations on
Ligurian seafood will not disappoint:
the *cuscus di gamberi* is a delicious
starter, and there are so many wines
on the list it's hard to choose. *Closed
Sun, and Christmas week.*

Cavetto, Piazza Santa Caterina 7, t 019
97311 (€€€€). Very popular restaurant,
offering meat and fish dishes,
including great home-made pasta
with pesto. *Closed Tues and Wed lunch.*

Arenzano ✉ 16011

****Grand Hotel**, Lungomare Stati
Unite, t 010 91091, *www.grandhotel
arenzano.it* (€€€€€). Majestic neo-
Renaissance hotel that was built in
the 1920s, with 110 stylish rooms; pool
and beach, and a fitness salon to work
away any excess calories you may
have consumed in the hotel's
restaurant, **La Veranda** (*closed Tues*).

***Poggio**, Via di Francia 24, t 010
913 5320, *www.poggiohotel.it* (€€€).
Another good choice, near the train
station and sea, with a pool and
comfortable rooms.

Genoa

There is always a tingling air of excitement and chaos in real port cities, where sailors, merchants, travellers and vagrants of all nationalities fill the streets, and the sea itself is ever present, ready to make or break a fortune and tempt you to sail off to distant shores. But of the country's four ancient maritime republics (Venice, Amalfi and Pisa are the others), only Genoa has retained its salty tang and thrill.

09

Don't miss

⭐ **The 'Golden Way'**
Via Garibaldi **p.154**

⭐ **Fabulous fishes**
Aquarium **p.163**

⭐ **A black and white cathedral**
Duomo di San Lorenzo **p.160**

⭐ **16th century splendour**
Palazzo del Principe **p.151**

⭐ **A grand Spinola palace**
Galleria Nazionale di Palazzo Spinola **p.162**

See map overleaf

CORSO FIRENZE

CORSO DOGALI

VIA S. UGO

Castello d'Albertis/
Museo delle Culture del Mondo

Albergo
dei
Poveri

SALITA D.
PROVVIDENZA

Stazione
Principe

PIAZZA
ACQUAVERDE

CORSO

PIAZZA D.
PRINCIPE

VIA A. DORIA

Commenda

S. Giovanni
di Prè

Palazzo
dell'Università

V. BRIGNOLE DE FERRARI

VIA S. BENEDETTO

Palazzo del
Principe

VIA ADUA

VIA DI PRÈ

VIA BALBI

SS.
Annunziata
del Vastato

Palazzo
Reale

PIAZZA
BANDIERA

FUNICOLARE AL EIGHI

to Lanterna,
Museo di Genova

Stazione
Marittima

VIA ANTONIO GRAMSCI

PIAZZA D.
NUNZIATA

CALATA ZINGARI

Galata-Museo
del Mare

Porta dei
Vacca

LARGO D.
ZECCA

S. Filippo
Neri

VIA LOMELLINI

VIA CAIROLI

PONTE
ANDREA
DORIA

PONTE
DEI MILLE

PONTE
PARODI

PONTE
MOROSINI

VIA SOTTO RIPA

VIA D. CAMPO

Casa di
Mazzini

S. Siro

VIA D. MADDALENA

PONTE
CALVI

Galleria Nazionale
di Palazzo Spinola

PIAZZA
DI PELLICCERIA

VIA S. LUCA

Bacino
Porto Vecchio

Porto
Antico

Aquarium

ℹ

PIAZZA
CARICAMENTO

VIA AL
PONTE
REALE

PIAZZA
DELLE FESTE

PIAZZA
BANCHI

Palazzo
Imperia

Ex-Magazzini del Cotone

Bigo

Palazzo
S. Giorgio

Duomo di
S. Lorenzo

VIA S. LORENZO

Città dei
Bambini

Molo Vecchio

Antarctic
Museum

Porta Siberia/
Museo Luzzati

VIA MOLO

San
Marco

San
Giorgio

VIA TURATI

VIA S. BERNARDO

MURA D. GRAZIE

PIAZZA
CAVOUR

CORSO AURELIO SAFFI

S. Maria di
Castello

Torre degli
Ebriaci

STR. S. AGOSTINO

N

VIA S. CROCE

PIAZZA
SARZANO

CORSO M. QUADRIO

250 metres
250 yards

Int

Don't miss

① Via Garibaldi p.154

② Aquarium p.163

③ Duomo di San Lorenzo p.160

④ Palazzo del Principe p.151

⑤ Galleria Nazionale di Palazzo
Spinola p.162

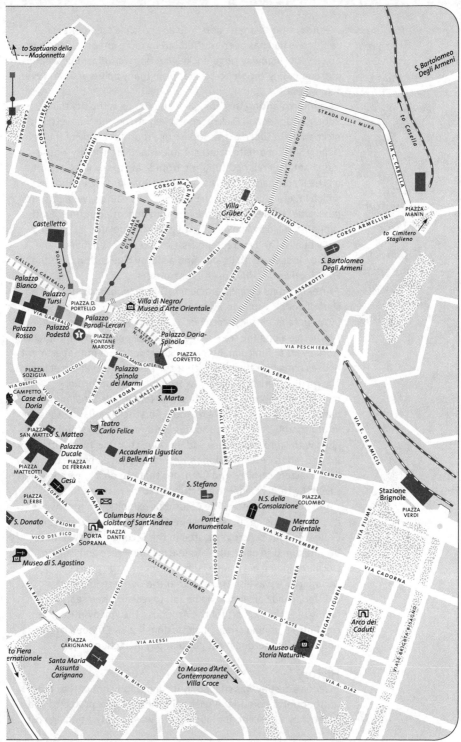

to Santuario della Madonnetta

S. Bartolomeo Degli Armeni

CORSO FIRENZE

CORSO PAGANINI

CARBONARA

STRADA DELLE MURA

to Casella

VIA C. CABELLA

SALITA DI SAN ROCCHINO

CORSO MAGENTA

CORSO SOLFERINO

CORSO ARMELLINI

PIAZZA MANIN

to Cimitero Staglieno

Villa Grüber

VIA CAFFARO

FUNICOLARE DI S. ANNA

VIA A. BERTANI

VIA G. MAMELI

VIA PALESTRO

S. Bartolomeo Degli Armeni

VIA ASSAROTTI

Castelletto

GALLERIA GARIBALDI
LEVATOIO

Palazzo Bianco

Palazzo Tursi

VIA GARIBALDI

Palazzo Rosso

Palazzo Podestà

PIAZZA D. PORTELLO

Palazzo Parodi-Lercari

Villa di Negro/ Museo d'Arte Orientale

GALLERIA N. BIXIO

Palazzo Doria-Spinola

PIAZZA CORVETTO

VIA PESCHIERA

PIAZZA FONTANE MAROSE

SALITA SANTA CATERINA

PIAZZA SOZIGLIA

VIA LUCCOLI

VIA OREFICI

VICO CASANA

Palazzo Spinola dei Marmi

VIA XXV APRILE

VIA ROMA

VIA XXII OTTOBRE

VIA SERRA

VIALE IV NOVEMBRE

VIA GALATA

VIA E. DE AMICIS

CAMPETTO

Case dei Doria

GALLERIA MAZZINI

S. Marta

PIAZZA SAN MATTEO

S. Matteo

Teatro Carlo Felice

Palazzo Ducale

PIAZZA DE FERRARI

Accademia Ligustica di Belle Arti

VIA S VINCENZO

Stazione Brignole

PIAZZA MATTEOTTI

VIA P. SOPRANA

Gesù

V. DANTE

VIA XX SETTEMBRE

S. Stefano

N.S. della Consolazione

PIAZZA COLOMBO

PIAZZA VERDI

PIAZZA D. ERBE

S. D. PRIONE

S. Donato

Columbus House & cloister of Sant'Andrea

PORTA SOPRANA

PIAZZA DANTE

Ponte Monumentale

Mercato Orientale

VIA FIUME

VIA XX SETTEMBRE

VICO DEL FICO

V. RAVECCA

Museo di S. Agostino

GALLERIA C. COLOMBO

CORSO PODESTÀ

VIA FRUGONI

VIA CESAREA

VIA CADORNA

VIA RAVASCO

VIA FIESCHI

Arco dei Caduti

VIA BRIGATA LIGURIA

VIALE BRIGATA BISAGNO

to Fiera ernationale

PIAZZA CARIGNANO

Santa Maria Assunta Carignano

VIA ALESSI

VIA N. BIXIO

VIA CORSICA

VIA J. RUFFINI

to Museo d'Arte Contemporanea Villa Croce

Museo di Storia Naturale

VIA A. DIAZ

For various days I lived in real ecstasy... Paris and London, in the face of this divine city, look insignificant, as simple agglomerations of houses and streets without any form.

Richard Wagner, 1825

Genoa is the queerest place in the world.

Henry James, *Italy Revisited*, 1877

Genoa is Italy's largest port, and any possible scenic effect it could have had has been snuffed out by more important concerns: an elevated highway, huge docks, warehouses, unloading facilities and cranes hog the shore, so that from many points you can't even see the sea.

Counterbalancing this busy, working Genoa is the city that Rubens, Wagner and Dickens marvelled at, the one that Petrarch nicknamed *La Superba*, the Superb or 'Proud' (as in one of the Seven Deadly Sins), of ornate palaces, gardens and art; the city whose merchant fleet reigned supreme from Spain to the Russian ports on the Black Sea, the city that gave the Spaniards Columbus but which in return controlled the contents of Spain's silver fleets until it became the New York of the late 16th and 17th centuries, proto-capitalist, ruled by bankers and oligarchs, populated by rugged individualists and entrepreneurs. Genoa even left a mark in the fashion industry with its silks and a sturdy blue cotton cloth the French called *de Gênes*, useful for trousers.

After lazy days on a Riviera beach, Genoa (pop. 640,000) is like a shot of double espresso. Even its topography is exciting: squeezed by mountains, the city stretches in a narrow belt for over 33 kilometres along the sea – and there are people who commute to work by lift or funicular. Tunnels bore under the centre; apartment houses hang over the hills so that the penthouse is at street level. The medieval quarter is a vast warren of alleys, or *carrugi* – miniature canyons under eight-storey tenements, streaming with banners of laundry. Elsewhere, you'll find the famous aloofness of 'multi-marbled Genoa', as Thomas Hardy called it, in stately streets lined with late-Renaissance and Baroque churches filled with great art and *palazzi*, even the doge's, decorated with elaborate trompe l'œil pilasters, cornices and froufrous that put on a brave show and saved the thrifty Genoese a fortune in stone masons.

And now there's more. The Columbus exhibition in 1992, while itself not a rousing success, inspired a new razzmatazz spirit in Genoa: historic buildings blasted in the Second World War have been restored, in particular the Teatro Carlo Felice and Palazzo Ducale, bringing big league culture back into the heart of La Superba. It was also the year that the Genoese followed Baltimore and Barcelona and began to reclaim their seafront, taking over the old port for the Americas, the Porto Antico, and creating a stunning range of attractions, led by Europe's largest Aquarium, the second most popular pay attraction in Italy.

History

Genoa's destiny was shaped by its geography, not only as the northernmost port on the Tyrrhenian Sea, but one protected and isolated by a crescent of mountains. It was already a trading post

Getting to and around Genoa

By Air

Genoa's airport, t 010 60151, *www.airportgenova.it*, is 6km from the city in Sestri Ponente. A taxi from the airport to the centre is about €18; shuttle buses (*Volabus*) depart every hour from Stazione Brignole, Stazione Principe and Piazza De Ferrari. The €4 ticket includes a bus, train or metro transfer within Genoa.

By Sea

You can sail away to exotic lands – Corsica, Sardinia, Sicily, Tunisia – on a ferry. Nearly any travel agency in Genoa can sell you a ticket, or book through the Genoa-based website, *www.fun.informare.it*.

Departing from Calata Zingari, the **Cooperativa Battellieri**, t 010 265 712, *www.battellierigenova.it*, sail to most main destinations between Savona and La Spezia.

By Rail

Train information: t 800 89 20 21.

Genoa has two main stations: **Stazione Principe**, in Piazza Acquaverde, t 010 274 111, just northwest of the centre, and **Stazione Brignole**, to the southeast. Principe in general handles trains from the north and France, while Brignole takes trains from the south, although most long-distance trains call at both. Bus no.37 links the two – or just catch a passing train.

By Coach

Intercity services depart from Piazza della Vittoria, south of Stazione Brignole, or from Piazza Acquaverde, in front of Stazione Principe; ring the tourist office for information. For buses in Genoa province, ring ALI, t 010 5467 4410, *www.ali-autolineeliguri.it*.

By Public Transport

Genoa is long and narrow, and trains run frequently from one end to the other, stopping at the city's 20 stations, and convenient for places like Nervi or Pegli. A metro line is now almost finished, although the Brignole and Corretto stations are expected to be completed between 2010 and 2012; useful central stations are at Dinegro, Principe, Darsena, San Giorgio and Sarzano. Genoa's public transit is run by AMT, t 010 558 114, *www.amt.genova.it*; a ticket, valid for 90 minutes' travel on **buses**, **trains** and **lifts** in the city is €1.20 (€2 if bought on board); there are also day tickets for €3.50. Tickets are available from tobacco shops or AMT kiosks.

The **funiculars** run from Piazza Portello and Largo della Zecca and ascend the city's upper residential quarters. An Art Nouveau lift from Piazza Portello will also take you up to the belvedere at Castelletto.

Piazza Manin is the base for visiting the hills above Genoa, and the terminus for the very narrow-gauge **Trenino di Casella**, pulled by the oldest working electric locomotive in Italy (built in 1924); the scenery and trattorias along the way are reason enough to go (departures roughly every two hours; t 010 837 321, *www. ferroviagenovacasella.it*, for information).

Genoa can seem daunting. One way to get a handle on it is the two-hour **Girocittà bus tour**, followed by a walking tour, both with an English-speaking guide (Macramè Viaggi, t 010 595 9779, to book). Buses depart from Piazza Verdi, by Stazione Brignole (or major hotels, through prior arrangement) at 9.30am; the third Saturday of each month it takes place at 8.30am. Tickets are €13, children 6–12 €5, under-5s free.

By Car and Taxi

Driving in Genoa is not fun. The old quarter is closed to traffic, the street plan is chaotic and signs are rare. If it gets too horrible, the *Sopraelevata*, the ugly elevated A10 motorway along the harbour, is never hard to find.

Car parks convenient for the Old City are by the Porta Soprana/Casa di Colombo and Piazza Caricamento, by the Porto Antico and in Piazza della Vittoria (*open 8am–8pm*). **Taxis** are plentiful. For a radio taxi, call t 010 5966.

---

in the 6th century BC, when the Phoenicians and Greeks bartered with the Ligurians, 'as indomitable as they are proud', according to Diodorus Siculus, who admired their sheer physical strength. The city became a stalwart outpost of Rome, and as such suffered the wrath of Hannibal's brother, Mago Barca, in 205 BC; rebuilt after his sacking, it remained relatively happy until the Lombards arrived in 641, initiating a dark, troubled period. While Amalfi, Pisa and Venice were busy creating their maritime republics in the 10th and 11th centuries, Genoa was still a backwater, its traffic dominated by Pisa, its coasts prey to Saracen corsairs.

Adversity, more than anything, formed the Genoese character. Once she rallied to defeat the Saracens, the city began a dizzily rapid rise to prominence in the 12th century. She captured Corsica, and joined forces in the First Crusade with the Norman Prince Bohemond of Taranto, helping him to conquer Antioch and asking as her reward the right to establish trading counters in the Near East. The Genoese took to trade like ducks to water, and by the next century they had established trading counters and colonies stretching from Syria to Algeria, including the whole district of Pera in Constantinople. The walls had to be enlarged in 1155, and as the city grew, so did the bravado of the Genoese. At the siege of Acre, Richard the Lionheart was so impressed by their courage that he placed England under the protection of Genoa's patron, St George, taking the red cross of Genoa and making it the national flag of England.

It wasn't long before business competition with Pisa grew into a battle. Genoa lost the first round at Meloria in 1241, but the turning point came in 1284, at the same location. Both cities were willing to risk all, and according to the chroniclers of the day every able-bodied man on their respective coasts was on board to do battle on nearly equal fleets; but luck (in the form of a strong wind) was with Genoa. Five thousand Pisans perished, and another 11,000 were taken captive and held in ransom for the island of Sardinia, which Genoa coveted; the Pisans preferred to die in prison.

With Pisa out of the way, Genoa's only rival in the east was Venice. In 1293, an accidental encounter between their galleys off Cyprus started a vicious war. This time Genoa won the first round: Admiral Lamba Doria crushed the Venetians at the Curzolani Islands in 1298, burning 66 galleys and bringing 7,000 prisoners (including Marco Polo) in triumph back to Genoa. The Genoese were acclaimed as the bravest of mariners; the city's trade counters spread even further afield, from the Black Sea to Spain, and her captains were the first to sail to the Canaries and the Azores.

Medieval Genoa was one of the most densely populated cities in Europe. Her patricians constructed the characteristic tower houses that seemed so 'superb' to visitors. Her fame was so widespread that Genoa appeared in the *Arabian Nights*; she was the only Western city to earn a mention. At the same time, one of the most popular fairy tales told in Genoa was called 'Money Can Do

Everything' and goes about proving just that: who needs goodness or magic, when you have money and cleverness?

Punch and Judy, and Simone Boccanegra

Party conflicts here assumed so fierce a character, and disturbed so violently the whole course of life, that we can hardly understand how, after so many revolutions and invasions, the Genoese ever contrived to return to an endurable condition.

Jacob Burckhardt,
The Civilization of the Renaissance in Italy

What Genoa singularly failed to do, unlike Venice or Pisa, was govern herself. Genoa's first golden age was marred, as all subsequent ones were to be, by civic strife and turmoil that were disgraceful even by Italian standards. The individualistic, stubborn Genoese never developed a sense of community; every enterprise was privately funded, including most of the city's military expeditions. Like Pisa and Venice, Genoa's merchant-captains brought fabulous treasures and relics back from the east but they failed to translate their achievement on to any higher plane. Genoa has no Field of Miracles to match Pisa, no Basilica of San Marco to rival Venice. It was a Republic not by virtue of its institutions but by default. Even Dante found Genoa lacking: 'Sea without fish, hills without wood, men without honour, women without shame.' The Genoese achievement, in fact its miracle, is how such a weak and fragmented state not only survived, but actually prospered.

The Republic itself was divided into factions based on hereditary enmity: prominent Guelphs (the Grimaldi and Fieschi) against prominent Ghibellines (the Doria and Spinola); nobles against the mercantile classes; the merchants against the artisans or *popolano*. Each faction dominated its own quarter of the city, forming brotherhoods, or *alberghi*, of their partisans, running their own prisons and armies. For two centuries, Genoese history is a chronicle of one faction after another gaining political control, while the others did all they could to undermine it. In times of danger, however, these same irksome families, especially the Doria, produced the brilliant admirals whom the Genoese relied on. In admiration for their heroes, the *popolano* would join in their blood feuds until they became sick of them again.

The arrival in 1311 of Emperor Henry VII made things worse. At first he was greeted as a saviour by all Genoa's factions, who declared him absolute sovereign of their Republic for 20 years in the hope that he would enforce the peace that they were always breaking. The Emperor, however, alienated the Genoese by demanding a 'gift' of 60,000 florins for his services. Life quickly became precarious for the imperial party, and Henry was glad when a Pisan fleet arrived in 1312 to take him away, leaving Genoa's Guelphs and Ghibellines to melt down on their own.

In 1339, the *popolano* won a victory by excluding all nobles from the government. Admiring the Venetian system, they elected Genoa's first doge, Simone Boccanegra (1301–63), who, five hundred years later, would become the hero of Verdi's opera. A lover of liberty, Boccanegra didn't use his position to take more

The Famous Insult to the Genoese

In 1316 occurred one of the most beloved anecdotes of Genoese history, a story the Genoese like to tell for its evocation of their proud, stubborn character: a Genoese merchant, Megollo Lercari, was the guest of the Byzantine emperor at Trebizond, when he disagreed with one of the emperor's pages, who slapped him. The emperor refused to let the Genoese strike back, though he apologized for the youth's arrogant behaviour. It was not enough. Seething, Megollo returned to Genoa, got up a private fleet, sailed to Trebizond, and demanded the page. When the emperor refused, the Genoese besieged the city, capturing whoever they could and sending them back, minus their ears or noses. Finally his subjects' despair made the emperor give in. He handed over the youth and watched, first in trepidation and then amazement, as Megollo made the page stoop over, then gave him a smart kick in the seat of the pants. Honour thus regained, the merchant returned the page to the emperor, lifted the siege and sailed back to Genoa.

power, but like most Italian politicians he used it to take more money and raised taxes so high that the nobles exiled him to Pisa and invited in the Visconti of Milan. The Visconti, as was their wont, behaved badly, driving Genoa to revolt a few years later; Boccanegra returned and was re-elected doge in 1356, but died suddenly seven years later. Although the idea had been to elect doges 'in perpetuity', as in Venice, Boccanegra was one of only four to die while in office. It was far more common for a Genoese doge to be forced to resign on the day of his election.

Meanwhile, rivalry with Venice was heating up again into a fourth hot war for Eastern Mediterranean trade. In 1378 the Venetians sided with the Cypriots in their quarrel with the Genoese and defeated them in a battle fought in a raging tempest. The Genoese sent Admiral Lucian Doria to exact revenge, and when the two fleets met again at Pola, Doria was slain, which infuriated the Genoese sailors into fighting so fiercely the Venetian fleet was nearly annihilated. Scenting blood, the Genoese appointed Pietro Doria to finish off the kill. He started by besieging Chioggia, the southernmost port of the Venetian lagoon; Pietro Doria declared he would not leave until he had 'bridled the horses of St Mark with his own hand'.

This time luck was on Venice's side. Her fleet from the east arrived in the nick of time to save the day, and blockaded the Genoese at Chioggia; Genoa sent a new fleet to succour them, but the trapped and starving Genoese were unable to escape, and surrendered with honour. Chioggia marked the end of Genoa's leading role in the east, a blow followed by the loss of most of its trading colonies to the Ottomans.

In the aftermath, in 1382, new Genoese families – the Adorni for the Guelphs, the Fregosi for the Ghibellines – arose to contest the authority of the established power brokers. As soon as they took control, however, they behaved as obstreperously as the Doria or Spinola, who remained excluded from power. The Fregosi alone contributed 13 doges; when one, Domenico Fregoso, deposed

Gabriel Adorno in 1370, the republic was plunged into civil war. Life hit such a nadir that both families threw up their hands and on several occasions gave the lordship of the Republic to foreigners, in the hope that they could ease the city's heartburn – Savoy for periods in 1382 and 1390, France in 1396, Monferrato in 1409, Milan in 1463, and France again in 1499.

Bankers to the Rescue

The real power turned out to be a bank. During the wars with Venice, the city's creditors – Genoa's oligarchs – formed a syndicate, the Casa di San Giorgio, to guarantee their increasingly precarious loans. This the bank did by gradually assuming control of the city's overseas territories, castles, towns, and even its treasury. By the 15th century Genoa, for all practical purposes, was run as a business – once, in 1421, when the bank had a cash-flow problem, it sold Livorno to Florence for a tidy sum. One writer in the 19th century aptly described the Banco di San Giorgio as the Bank of England combined with the East India Company, with the added responsibility of collecting taxes. The Genoese never had the slightest reason to identify with their government, but, as Machiavelli noted, they were very loyal to their bank.

By forcing the Genoese to transform their economy from the mercantile to the financial, the defeat at Chioggia was actually a blessing in disguise. The opening up of new sea routes around the Horn of Africa and discoveries in the New World by two Genoese, Christopher Columbus and Giovanni Caboto, were quickly making its old Mediterranean sphere of influence obsolete. But with the Bank of St George and its exquisite accounting methods (necessary to avoid the sin of usury), no place in Europe was better poised to deal with the great influx of wealth brought over the Atlantic in Spain's treasure fleet.

Andrea Doria, the 'Saviour of Genoa'

After the exclusion of the old nobility from power, the Doria, the proudest clan in Genoa, had chafed in their compound in Piazza San Matteo. Their attempts at re-taking the city were notable failures, until the advent of Andrea Doria (1468–1560). He began his career in the guard of Pope Innocent VIII, and served several states as a mercenary. When the Wars of Italy between the Habsburg Emperor Charles V and Francis I of France broke out, Doria was employed by France, Genoa's traditional ally.

Unfortunately for Genoa, the war began during one of her periodic lapses in self-government, when the doges had placed the Republic under the rule of France. This was sufficient reason for Imperial troops to sack it brutally in 1522. Under Cesare Fregoso, the Genoese recaptured the city for the French (1527), but in the meantime, the French made a fatal miscalculation: they granted commercial privileges to Savona at Genoa's expense. Getting funny with money was the one act a Genoese could never forgive, and Andrea Doria at once offered Charles V his services, in return for assurances that Genoa would have its 'liberty' under Spanish-Austrian protection. Charles agreed, and Doria and his men drove the French from Genoa and Savona in 1528. Doria used the occasion to write a new Republican constitution institutionalizing the shared rule of the 28 *alberghi*, and in effect created an oligarchy of plutocrats of both the old and new nobility, even though he made sure that the plums of office, including the dogeship, went to the old. The constitution provided for the annual election of five senators, and punters would wager on the five names in what they called the *lotto* – the origin of our modern lottery.

Charles V rewarded Doria for screwing the French by making him Prince of Melfi and Admiral of the Empire's Mediterranean fleet. Nor was it long before other Genoese were seen taking prominent posts throughout the Habsburg lands. At home, Doria's aloof neutrality in city politics and near-dictatorial powers did much to cool the feuding, although many Genoese were deeply humiliated by the realpolitik terms that bound them to Charles V. One was Gian Luigi de' Fieschi, who in 1547 formed a conspiracy with his partisans and vassals in the name of Genoese liberty. Andrea Doria fled, and the revolutionaries succeeded in taking the city – only they couldn't find de' Fieschi, who, when no one was looking, had fallen overboard in his armour and drowned. Without their leader, the conspirators haplessly surrendered, promised an amnesty by Doria, who immediately executed them. Charles, sensing that his protégé was floundering, made a bold attempt to intimidate Doria into surrendering the title of Republic for Genoa, but the old man stalwartly refused, and the motto *Libertas* remained proudly on the city's escutcheon.

Andrea Doria, at the age of 91, gained the Republic's last territorial acquisition when he led an expedition to reconquer Corsica. He was also Genoa's first great patron of the arts, introducing the High Renaissance to a city that had formerly managed to do without. In his footsteps, the wealthy abandoned their medieval palaces to build grander ones further up on new marble streets, each more sumptuous than the next.

At the same time, a number of prominent families went bankrupt, their fleets attacked by the Ottomans and their sometime allies, the French, who were keen to get back at the treacherous republic. Counter-Reformation policies, in line with the Spaniards and papacy, saw Genoa's expulsion of the Jews – another setback for the economy. Spanish taxes were so onerous that the Genoese tried to reopen negotiations with the Ottomans and France, to no avail. Under Andrea Doria's nephew and heir, Gian Andrea Doria (d. 1606), disputes between the ever-prickly old and new noble families flared up yet again. Doria asked the Spaniards to intervene for the old nobility, and a Spanish-papal force arrived on the scene. Its leaders at last did the one thing the Genoese were incapable of: they made peace. They eliminated the *alberghi* and all distinctions between the old and new nobility, and inscribed 170 families from both sides into the Golden Book (the list of those eligible to serve on the Republic's council). Now at relative peace, with a constitution that would survive until 1797, Genoa was ready to get its money back from Spain – with interest.

The 'Genoese Century'

This extraordinary city, devouring the world, is the greatest human adventure of the 16th century. Back then Genoa seemed like the city of miracles.

Fernand Braudel

Isabella and Ferdinand may have bilked Columbus and his heirs out of a tenth of all the profits from the New World (*see* pp.38–42), but Genoa got it instead. Historians have labelled the years between 1528 and 1630 the 'Genoese Century'; while the rest of Italy (except Venice) wilted under Spanish rule, the Bank of St George and its directors (the Pallavicini, Sauli and Spinola) became increasingly fat through worldwide banking manipulations, financing the wars in the Low Countries for Charles V and Philip II, processing Spain's silver, and stealing the international money markets away from Besançon and Antwerp: millions of *scudi* passed through Genoa every year.

Chivalrous, warlike, religion-crazed Spain would have been even more lost without the acumen of Genoa's bankers. In return, the treasure fleet from the Americas found its way into Genoese stucco and gilt, frescoes and paintings. Her mercantile nobility grew ever more exclusive and aped Spain's grandees, going about with large bands of bodyguards and assassins. They had their reasons. In 1628, Julius Caesar Vachero, member of a great family excluded from the Golden Book, plotted a coup d'état with an army of bravos. They planned to capture the Palazzo Pubblico, massacre the nobles and take over Genoa, with the support of the Duke of Savoy. The plot was only revealed the night before, and Vachero and his co-conspirators were executed.

In 1644 the English traveller John Evelyn visited Genoa and wrote that 'this beautiful city is more stained with horrid revenges and murders than any one place in Europe, or haply the world.' A devastating cholera outbreak struck Genoa in 1657, but it barely caused a blip in the city's financial statements; far more damaging, in 1684, was a bombardment by the fleet of Louis XIV, who took it amiss that Genoa had refused to allow the French to establish a military depot at Savona. After taking 14,000 bombs in three days, the doge agreed to go to Paris and apologize to the king, to keep the French from destroying the city altogether.

Decline and Unification, and the New Genoa

The sovereign nobility, prodigal and voracious, created by their pomp wants beyond their resources; accordingly, they stooped to the most disgraceful depredations to obtain money. The state could make no contract without being robbed... every place was an object of sale, and justice was venal in the tribunals...

Sismondi, *A History of the Italian Republics*

Genoa's 18th century may sound uncannily like our own times, but its days of easy money were numbered. Spain's bankruptcies came too frequently; Atlantic commerce overtook Mediterranean trade, leading to the decline of the city's bread and butter. In 1734, Genoa chose the wrong side in the War of the Austrian Succession, and in 1746, when an Austrian army appeared at the gate, the city could only let the soldiers in. The Austrians demanded that the Republic fork out over nine million imperial florins as they began to cart away everything they could grab; the Genoese were even compelled to haul their own cannons down to the Austrian ships, where the Austrians brutally beat the haulers. This led to a spontaneous revolt in the narrow medieval streets, pitting armed Austrians against unarmed, rock-throwing Genoese, who destroyed them. It was the last victory of an Italian republic over a foreign tyrant. Corsica, Genoa's last colony, was in revolt, too, and the Bank of St George could do nothing but sell it to France in 1768. Napoleon was born the next year.

The Genoese tried to stay neutral in Napoleon's wars, but failed, and under French rule found themselves compelled to change the name of their republic to the Republic of Liguria, meaning that everyone had a share in the government. Although the city underwent the usual Napoleonic looting, the *popolano* found much to admire in their new constitution, and soon became among the most radicalized population in Italy. Genoa, however, suffered grievously. In 1800, a French army was blockaded there by the Austrians and British, causing the deaths of an estimated 30,000 from famine and disease. The doge threw the desperate city at Napoleon's feet, and after the war the Republic was snuffed out by the powers and annexed to Piedmont, an act the Genoese regarded as wholly unfair and unjustified.

For Piedmont, gaining Genoa turned its attention to the Mediterranean, and led to Turin's greater involvement in the Italian peninsula. For Genoa, the absolutist rule of the Savoy kings was enough to put it in the revolutionary camp once and for all. The former self-centred city of plutocrats rose to the occasion by giving Italy Giuseppe Mazzini, a beacon to other patriots from Liguria: Nino Bixio, Goffredo Mameli, the Ruffini brothers and, of course, Garibaldi himself (*see* pp.42–7).

Unification with Italy brought Genoa its first speculative building, a railroad and a return of its status as Italy's chief port. The same brought US bombs on its head in the Second World War – the Teatro Carlo Felice and the ducal palace were among the many casualties. They languished in ruins until Columbus came to the city's rescue again, or at least the celebrations of the 500th anniversary of his discovery of America. The impetus to remake the city continues apace. As a cradle of capitalism, Genoa was a natural to host the G8 summit in July 2001, accompanied by riots it prefers to forget; its moment as Europe's 2004 Capital of Culture saw a major sprucing-up and the beginning of an enormous ten-year project – a tunnel to bury the nasty elevated highway, the *Sopraelevata*, that divides the city from the seafront.

Genoa's West End

Stazione Principe, Palazzo del Principe and the Lanterna

Both of Genoa's main train stations are palatial – **Stazione Principe** on the west end of the centre could easily host a fancy-dress ball. Outside in Piazza Acquaverde, visitors are greeted by a statue of Columbus and a view of the port. Just below the Piazza is a medieval institution: **La Commenda**, Genoa's first hotel, founded in the 11th century to shelter pilgrims waiting to sail to the Holy Land, and now used to shelter temporary exhibitions instead. In 1180 the Knights of St John added the adjacent two-storey church, **San Giovanni di Prè**, with a spire-clustered campanile.

Via Andrea Doria leads to the Piazza and **Palazzo del Principe**, the only 'Royal' palace built during the Republic and the most important 16th-century monument in Liguria. The royal in this instance was Andrea Doria, Prince of Melfi, who in 1528 commissioned Raphael's pupil Perino del Vaga to decorate the interior of his new palace and introduce the joys of art to his fellow oligarchs. Perino designed the grand portal, golden galleries and on the walls frescoed stories of the kings of Rome, the Loggia degli Eroi, featuring the greats of the Doria family and that favourite Mannerist subject, the *Fall of the Giants*. There's a famous portrait of *Andrea Doria* by Sebastiano del Piombo (1526) but the most affectionate is an anonymous portrait of the old admiral and his cat, who resemble each other. His descendants, in fact, still live here. Originally the gardens covered the entire hill and ran down to the waterfront, marked by once gracious **Loggia a Mare** (now used as an office); from there the palace is at its most impressive, with its prospect of terraces and a fountain by Michelangelo's pupil, Giovanni Angelo Motorsoli, beautifully illuminated at night.

In the 1930s, the Doria's private quay below the Loggia was made into the **Stazione Marittima**; the next quay, the **Ponte Andrea Doria**, has been redesigned for cruise ships. A wooden 800m promenade leads from the Ferryboat Terminal to the park surrounding Genoa's slender landmark, the 386ft lighthouse or **Lanterna**, first built in the 12th century and last worked in 1543; originally open fires on top welcomed home the city's fleet,

Palazzo del Principe
t 010 255 509, www.palazzodel principe.it; open Tues–Sun 10–5, closed Easter, 1 May, 15 Aug and 1 Jan; adm; book ahead to arrive by sea on a reconstructed 16th-century frigate, from the Porto Antico – included in the adm

Lanterna
t 010 910 001; open weekends and hols 10–7; adm

superseded by a massive olive oil-fuelled lamp, now replaced by a beam of electric light extending 33km. You can climb up to the first terrace to admire the views. Admission includes a **museum** in the surrounding Savoy fortifications of 1830, dedicated to the lighthouse but also to the port, the city and the Genoese.

Via Balbi to Via Garibaldi

In front of the Principe station begins aristocratic **Via Balbi**, a street laid out in 1606 and named for one of the city's wealthiest families by Genoa's top Baroque architect, Bartolomeo Bianco. Bianco also designed many of Via Balbi's residences, including the remarkable **Palazzo dell'Università**, begun as a Jesuit college in 1630; the vestibule and *cortile* are a *tour de force*, allowing the eye to take in four levels all at once, with two tiers of airy arcades and two staircases that divide twice. Ask to visit the Aula Magna upstairs, with frescoes by Giovanni Andrea Carlone and six large bronzes on the Theological and Cardinal Virtues by Giambologna.

Galleria Nazionale di Palazzo Reale
t 010 271 0236, www.palazzoreale genova.it; open Tues–Wed 9–1.30, Thurs–Sun 9–7; adm exp

Opposite, the massive yellow and red **Galleria Nazionale di Palazzo Reale** was built for the Balbi and in 1824 was purchased by the Savoys, who later donated the whole shebang to the State. This offers a fine introduction to the style to which Genoa's oligarchs had become accustomed in 'their' century: hanging gardens and superb mosaic pavements; *quadratura* (architectural trompe-l'œil) frescoes by Angelo Michele Colonna of Bologna and Valerio Castello; a hyper-decorated 18th-century ballroom; a Gallery of Mirrors (with a marble *Metamorphosis* group by Filippo Parodi); rooms hung with Gobelin tapestries and sprinkled with paintings by Veronese, Guercino and Van Dyck, and sculpture, including an 18th-century *Pluto and Proserpina* by Francesco Schiaffino.

Bartolomeo Bianco also designed Via Balbi's **Palazzo Durazzo-Pallavicini** (No.1), and **Palazzo Balbi-Senarega** (No.4), both of which have been altered, their austere façades offering no hint of their once lavish trompe-l'œil frescoes. The first palace is the last one on the street still in private hands, while the latter now holds the university's department of humanities. All Genoa's Baroque masters had a hand in its frescoes, especially Valerio Castello, Gregorio De Ferrari, Domenico Piola and Andrea Sighizzi, another master of *quadratura*. The street's church, **SS. Vittore e Carlo** (1632), has sculptures in the right transept by Alessandro Algardi, who introduced Roman Baroque to Genoa, and in the left by Bernini's pupil Filippo Parodi (*Virgin and Child*).

Via Balbi gives on to Piazza della Nunziata, a traffic inferno under the brooding presence of the 16th-century **Basilica della SS. Annunziata del Vastato**, hiding an insanely voluptuous interior. This was redone, beginning in 1591, by the Lomellini, a family as fervently Catholic as they were wealthy, who insisted that every square inch be covered over with frescoes, paintings, marbles and statues; even the stuccoes were covered with gold. Only the façade was neglected, to be given a controversial outsize neoclassical pronaos in 1867 that has nevertheless become an urban landmark.

An even more staggering landmark built by the Lomellini (who owned, among other things, the Tunisian island of Tabarka) is behind the church, at the top of Via Brignole De Ferrari: the 17th-century **Albergo dei Poveri**, theatrically rising over twin stairs, rivalling the one in Naples as the biggest and most pompous poorhouse in Italy. Built when the insatiable demands of the wealthy forced Genoa's poor onto the streets and into crime, this monster has four courtyards with a church in the centre, housing a sculpture by Pierre Puget, who designed a similar project, the Charité, in his native Marseille. Today the building is part of the university.

From Via P. Bensa, the wide street just east of Piazza della Nunziata, a little detour south leads to the **Casa di Mazzini**, at Via Lomellini 11, where the prophet of Italian unification was born in 1805 and is remembered in the **Museo del Risorgimento**. While on Via Lomellini, note the church of **San Filippo Neri**, with a Roman-Baroque concave façade, a style later reflected in some of the prettiest Riviera churches, such as Cervo; if open, pop in to see the charming 18th-century rococo oratory.

From the next crossroads, the **Largo della Zecca**, you have several options, including a quick fix of upward mobility: a thrilling ride up to **Righi**, where the astronomical observatory is located, on a century-old funicular that rises some 900ft in under a mile. Here you can have a coffee with a view over the Riviera, and make your way back towards Genoa's 17th-century walls, linked by a footpath; the fort at Sperone is only 15 minutes away by foot.

The high road of art and culture, however, continues round on Via Cairoli. Just off this, on Via San Siro, is the important church of **San Siro**, Genoa's cathedral in the 4th century, rebuilt after a fire in the late 1500s by the Theatines. Although the main façade was redone in 1821, the south face still preserves a grand 17th-century portal over the stair. A double row of columns creates an illusion of space in the interior, richly decorated with marbles, frescoes by Giovanni Battista Carlone, and altars with paintings by Orazio Gentileschi, Il Pomarancio and Aurelio Lomi, all culminating in the high altar, a confection in black marble and gilded bronze by Pierre Puget.

Via Cairoli then continues around to Piazza della Meridiana, named after a sundial on its 16th-century palace, built for the Grimaldi and decorated with Mannerist mythological frescoes. Beyond lies Genoa's most famous street, Via Garibaldi.

Albergo dei Poveri
can be visited by request t *010 272 218*

Museo del Risorgimento
t *010 246 5843,*
www.istituto
mazziniano.it; open
Tues–Fri 9–1, Sat
10–7; adm

San Filippo Neri
open Sat 3.30–6.30

Righi astronomical observatory
www.osservatorio
righi.it

09

Genoa | Genoa's West End

Via Garibaldi

🕐 Via Garibaldi

Gold was born in America, died in Spain, and was buried in Genoa.
A popular saying

This, the former *Strada Nuova* or Via Aurea, 'Golden Way', was laid out in 1558 and at once became Genoa's Millionaires' Row. It has now been declared a World Heritage site by UNESCO. The street's exquisite late 16th-century *palazzi* put on a solid front of sombre elegance, their façades decorated with red and golden frescoes by the likes of Cambiaso; most had exotic gardens and aviaries of rare birds. Rubens, besotted by their dignity and understated wealth, drew them in 1622 (the originals are now at the London Royal Institute of British Architects). In the 20th century many were converted into banks and offices, but the street's unique character has been carefully maintained (*see www.stradanuova.it*). Two *palazzi*, with collections of Grand Masters still in the settings they were commissioned for, are now museums.

Palazzo Bianco
t 010 557 2193, www.museopalazzo bianco.it; open Tues–Fri 9–7, Sat and Sun 10–7, closed Mon and hols; adm

The first, **Palazzo Bianco**, at No.11, was another residence of the Grimaldi and has the best paintings in the city: Filippino Lippi's *Madonna with Saints*, Pontormo's *Florentine Gentleman*, Veronese's *Crucifixion*, and works by the great Lombards, Caravaggio and Giulio Cesare Procaccini. There's an even more impressive collection of Flemish art, which was much admired in Genoa: Hans Memling's *Christ Blessing* and Gerhard David's sweetly domestic *Madonna della Pappa*; an overripe *Venus and Mars* by Rubens, with the war god in the guise of a Counter-Reformation captain; and Jan Matsys' *Portrait of Andrea Doria* with remarkable hands. Other paintings are by Cranach, Van der Goes, Van Dyck, the Dutch artists Steen and Cypt, Simon Vouet from France, and Spanish masters, especially Murillo, and a fine *San Bonaventura* by Zurbarán. Another section features the Genoese: Luca Cambiaso, Strozzi, Giovanni Andrea De Ferrari, Gregorio De Ferrari, Gioacchino Assereto and Alessandro Magnasco; the latter's *Trattenimento in un giardino d'Albaro*, painted at a villa east of Genoa, is an elegant, twilit work that sums up the end of Baroque. The museum also keeps one of Genoa's more exotic treasures, an embroidered purple silk pallium, given in 1261 by Byzantine Emperor Michael VIII to thank the city for helping him regain Constantinople from the Frankish Crusaders.

Palazzo Rosso
t 010 247 6351, www.museopalazzo rosso.it; same hours as the Palazzo Bianco; adm

Opposite, at No.18, the **Palazzo Rosso** was built in 1671 by the Brignole Sale family and donated to the city in 1874 by their last descendant, the Duchessa di Galliera. Named for the reddish tint of its stone, the palace was bombed in the war, but after restoration has regained its position as the apotheosis of Genoese domestic Baroque, with its gilt stucco and woodwork, hall of mirrors designed by Filippo Parodi, and rooms frescoed with allegories of the Four Seasons by Domenico Piola (*Autumn* and *Winter*) and Gregorio De Ferrari (*Spring* and *Summer*), who wielded their brushes here in friendly competition. The Brignole family produced more than one doge, and are remembered in their excellent family portraits by Van Dyck. There are other portraits by Pisanello and Dürer, a *Christ Bearing the Cross* by Rubens, works by Caravaggio's followers and a *Judith* by Veronese; here, too, is *La Cuoca*, a favourite work by Genoa's own Bernardo Strozzi, and a *Cleopatra* by Guercino. The gallery also includes an excellent collection of drawings, and ceramics made in Genoa, Savona and Albisola.

Palazzo Doria-Tursi
t 010 557 2193, www.museopalazzo tursi.it; same hours

Near the Palazzo Rosso at No.9, the grandest palace on the block, the **Palazzo Doria-Tursi** was built by Rocco Lurago in 1568 for Nicolò Grimaldi, banker to Philip II; his nickname was 'the Monarch' and his palace was built to measure, but it was purchased soon after by Giovanni Andrea Doria and now serves as Genoa's city hall. It has a beautiful *cortile* and stairway, and contains a collection of decorative art, ceramics, Genoese coins, weights and measures and municipal treasures such as Paganini's famous Guarneri del Gesù violin (rumoured to have been made by the devil himself) and three letters from Columbus. If you get married in Genoa, however, the civil ceremony will be held in a splendid Baroque room of antiques and tapestries over in the **Palazzo Doria** (No.6). At No.14, the **Palazzo Podestà** has an elegant façade by Mannerist Giovanni Battista Castello; the door is often open so you can peek into the Baroque *cortile*. You can step inside the **Palazzo Carrega Cataldi** (No.4, now the Chamber of Commerce), built in 1558 with a golden rococo gallery added on the upper floor in the 1700s. The façade of No.3, the 16th-century **Palazzo Parodi-Lercari**, was built by the heirs of Megollo Lercari, who recalled the 'Insult to the Genoese' at Trebizond with earless and noseless caryatids.

Castelletto
open every day 6.40am–midnight; one-way ticket €0.60 or bus ticket €1.20, valid for 90 minutes

Via Garibaldi ends at romantic **Piazza delle Fontane Marose**, which is a pedestrian island encased in more palaces, including the 15th-century **Palazzo Spinola dei Marmi**, embellished with black-and-white bands, and statues of the Spinola family. Just up Via Interiano, Piazza del Portello offers the visitor another chance to get above the city, thanks to its venerable Liberty-style lift up to **Castelletto** and its Belvedere Montaldo.

19th-century Genoa

Museo d'Arte Orientale
t 010 542 285, www.museochiossone genova.it; open Tues–Fri 9–1, Sat and Sun 10–7; adm

In the 19th century, after Genoa was joined to Piedmont, an architect named Carlo Barabino was appointed to give the old city some breathing space. He started above Piazza del Portello with a park, the **Villetta di Negro**, a once private oasis built over the 16th-century bastions, taking full advantage of Genoa's crazy topography, with cascades and grottoes. At the top of the park, however, waits a surprise: the **Museo d'Arte Orientale**, Italy's finest hoard of Oriental art, donated by Edoardo Chiossone (1833–98), who served the Imperial government in Tokyo as one of its *oyatoi gaikokujin* (hired foreigners) in charge of setting up the new finance ministry. Chiossone sent home statues, paintings, theatre masks and an extraordinary set of samurai armour, all displayed in a sun-filled building designed by Mario Labò in 1971.

Below, **Piazza Corvetto** is a busy roundabout with a statue of Vittorio Emanuele II in the centre. One side of Piazza Corvetto is anchored by the **Palazzo Doria-Spinola**; this, built in 1543 by Antonio Doria, admiral of the papal fleet, is now the Prefecture, and still bears the exterior frescoes once common in Genoa. Within, there's a lovely *cortile*, frescoes by Luca Cambiaso and his father Giovanni, and views over the city from the upper loggia. Here, too, is the church of **Santa Marta**, embellished by Genoa's choice interior decorators, Domenico Piola and Valerio Castello, with a passionate marble *St Martha in Ecstasy* by Filippo Parodi in the choir. On the corner of Via Roma, you can stop for a history-imbued coffee break at the early 19th-century **Caffè Mangani**.

Parallel to Via Roma runs the elegant **Galleria Mazzini**, with its glass roof, cafés and boutiques, leading into tumultuous **Piazza De Ferrari**, where the central fountain is a favourite Genoese meeting point. Under Carlo Barabino, this became an important address in Genoese cultural life, beginning with the construction of the neoclassical **Teatro Carlo Felice** in 1829. After 1944 only the façade remained, crumbling away until 1992, when it was restored and given state-of-the-art acoustics; it has flourished ever since and now holds a year-round programme of opera, dance and theatre. In spite of the lyrical associations of his name, Carlo Felice was an unpopular, reactionary king, and the Genoese placed an equestrian statue of Garibaldi in front of the theatre to neutralize the sour aftertaste of his name. Adjacent, the **Museo dell'Accademia Ligustica di Belle Arti** is a good place to learn about the evolution of the Genoese school of art, with paintings from the 14th–19th centuries, among them Perino del Vaga's *Polyptych of St Erasmus*, Luca Cambiaso's night scenes of *Christ before Caiaphas* and *Madonna and Child*, and Bernardo Strozzi's *St Augustine Washing Christ's Feet*.

Museo dell'Accademia Ligustica di Belle Arti
Largo Pertini 4, t 010 560 131, ticket office t 010 5601 327, www.accademia ligustica.it; open Tues–Fri 2.30–6.30, closed Sat–Mon; adm but included in the Genoa card

Across the piazza, and separating it from Piazza Matteotti below, is the giant black-and-white mass of the 16th-century **Palazzo Ducale** (*see* p.159).

Via XX Settembre and Around

East of Piazza De Ferrari awaits yet another side of La Superba. Porticoed **Via XX Settembre**, the main thoroughfare of 19th-century Genoa, is still the city's chief shopping street, adorned with Liberty-style flourishes and good old-fashioned neon. The **Ponte**

Monumentale carries Corso A. Podestà overhead, near another striped church, **Santo Stefano**, consecrated in 1217, with a beautiful apse decorated with blind arcading and an octagonal tribune. Not much in Genoa recalls the Lombards, but Santo Stefano's base was a Lombard defensive tower and its crypt, discovered during post-war restoration, may be theirs as well. The church contains an excellent *Martyrdom of St Stephen* (1524) by a less flamboyant than usual Giulio Romano.

Genoa's market, the **Mercato Orientale** (1889), perfumed by piles of fresh basil just waiting to be turned into pesto, occupies the former cloister of the 18th-century church **Nostra Signora della Consolazione**; its name comes not from Chinese vegetables but its location east of the centre. Under the Ponte Monumentale, the avenue continues to **Piazza della Vittoria**, a large Fascist-era square presided over by a War Memorial Arch of 1931. Nearby is the Giacomo Doria Museum of Natural History, a collection gathered by 19th-century Genoese noblemen in their travels.

Giacomo Doria Museum of Natural History
Via Brigata Liguria 9, t 010 564 567, www.museodoria.it; open Tues–Fri 9–7, Sat and Sun 10–7; adm

Carignano, the 19th-century residential neighbourhood south of here, has two attractions: at the highest point, the four-square church of **Santa Maria Assunta** in **Carignano**, one of the landmarks of Genoa, built between 1552 and 1602 and topped by a cupola; it has fine statues by Pierre Puget in the alcoves and a *Pietà* by Luca Cambiaso. Then there's the **Museo d'Arte Contemporanea di Villa Croce**, a beautiful neoclassical villa housing 20th-century works by Italian and foreign artists.

Museo d'Arte Contemporanea di Villa Croce
Via J. Ruffini 3, t 010 580 069, www.museovillacroce.it; open Tues–Fri 9–7, Sat and Sun 10–7; adm

Into the Old City

...if you bring peace, you are permitted to stop within this gate; if you ask for war, you will fall back deluded and defeated.
From the inscription on the Porta Soprano

Casa di Colombo, *t 010 246 5346; open Sat and Sun 9–12 and 2–6; adm*

From Piazza De Ferrari you can descend into the skein of medieval Genoa. The classic introduction is by way of Via Dante to **Piazza Dante** (with its skyscraper by Marcello Piacentini, Mussolini's favourite architect) and through the **Porta Soprana** (also known as Porta di San Andrea), built in 1155 as part of the **Barbarossa walls** designed to repel the emperor of that name. By the gate you'll find the **Casa di Colombo**, owned by a certain Domenico Colombo, giving rise to the notion that this was Christopher's 'boyhood home'. Although the Genoese were long ambivalent about their great admiral (in a mid-16th-century list of great men he didn't make the grade) they thought enough of him by 1684 to reconstruct this house after it was shattered by a French bomb; there's little to see inside. Here, too, stands the ruined 12th-century **Cloister of Sant'Andrea**, set out on the lawn amid the olive trees.

Genoa's medieval centre, now mostly restored after war damage, is one of the most extensive in Europe. In some ways it's like Venice, only built on a slope; the six- and seven-storey houses are sliced by corridor-like alleys, or *carrugi*, instead of canals, some so narrow that they live in perpetual shade – pots of geraniums catch any ray of sun, while laundry flaps overhead. Portals striped with white marble and black slate denote families who performed a good deed for Genoa. Corners are decorated with *aedicolae* called *madonnette* for their statuettes of the Madonna, erected by corporations, merchants and individuals for grace granted; over 400 still survive.

To see the highlights, take Via di Ravecca down from the Porta Soprana to the 13th-century Gothic church of **Sant'Agostino**, with a bell tower dressed up in majolica. The church and its monastery are now used by the innovative Teatro della Tosse, while the unusual triangular cloisters have been converted into the Museo di Sant'Agostino, containing sculptures and architecture salvaged from demolished churches. One of the finest works is the fragment of the tomb (1312) of Margherita of Brabant, wife of Emperor Henry VII, sculpted by Giovanni Pisano. Margherita died suddenly in Genoa *en route* to Rome for her husband's coronation, and Henry, whom Dante and others had hoped would be able to end the feud between Italy's Guelphs and Ghibellines, died in Siena two years later, many believe of sorrow; his last request was that his heart be taken to Genoa to be interred with his wife. There are also Roman works, Romanesque sculpture, frescoes, Barnaba da Modena's mid-14th-century *Crucifixion* decorated with Islamic motifs, and the 14th-century wooden *Christ of the Caravan*. Later sculptures are by the Gagini, Parodi, Pierre Puget and Antonio Canova.

Museo di Sant'Agostino
Piazza Sartano 35/r, t 010 251 1263, www.museosant agostino.it; open Tues–Fri 9–7, Sat and Sun 10–7; adm

Sant'Agostino gives onto elongated, lively **Piazza Sarzano**, the largest square in the medieval walls. Once it saw tournaments, jousts and its share of Genoa's intramural donnybrooks; at other times it served as a place for ropemakers to stretch out their wares. The city stored its water beneath the square, in enormous cisterns located under a little temple built in the 1600s. In the 1990s, many of the buildings here were converted into a home for Genoa University's school of architecture, a move that started a revival in local nightlife, in bars opened by the students themselves.

From Piazza Sarzano, Stradone di Sant'Agostino leads to the 12th-century church of **San Donato**, with a lovely octagonal campanile, portal and interior, combining a mix of Roman and Romanesque columns. A short walk up Via S. Donato takes you to Piazza delle Erbe, and the atmospheric (and very crowded, on Friday and Saturday evenings) **Bar Berto**, founded in 1904 and covered with tiles from Albisola.

If you walk in the opposite direction down Via San Donato, you'll reach **Via San Bernardo**, one of the few straight streets in the old city, laid out by the Romans and used by mule caravans to bring goods up through the Porta Soprana. The Roman castle (reached by way of a striking 12th-century tower house, the 135ft **Torre degli Ebriaci**, the tallest in town) provided, in the 4th or 5th century, the foundations for Genoa's oldest church and the first of a zillion dedicated to the Virgin in Liguria, Romanesque **Santa Maria di Castello**, which has Roman columns and stones in its structure. The crusaders used this complex as a hostel, and when the Dominicans took over in the 15th century, they added a friary and three cloisters, all paid for by the Grimaldi, who are glorified on the sacristy portal. Fairest of its decorations is the 15th-century fresco of the *Annunciation* by Giusto d'Alemagna in the cloister, while the strangest is the *Crocifisso Miracoloso* near the high altar – miraculous in that the Christ's beard is said to grow whenever Genoa is threatened with calamity. It also has a **museum** of art accumulated over the years.

Museum
t 010 254 9511; church, cloister and museum open daily 9–12 and 3.30–6.30

The seafront here has kept its 16th-century walls. If you follow Piazza Cavour up two streets, you'll regain Via San Bernardo, and just here, in Vico San Cosima, is the church of **SS. Cosma e Damiano**, dedicated to the patron saints of doctors and barbers; close by, at Vico Caprettari 7, you can get a haircut at Italy's most beautiful Art Deco **barber's shop**, now a historic monument. Another node in this area is Piazza San Giorgio, site of the church of Genoa's patron, **San Giorgio**, built in the 10th century and rebuilt in the 16th in a circular plan; it has paintings of St George by Luca Cambiaso. In the Middle Ages Pisan merchants were based in the square, and had their own church, **San Torpete** (St Tropez), rebuilt in 1730 in a rococo oval by the Cattaneo family.

Piazza Matteotti: the Palazzo Ducale and Duomo di San Lorenzo

An alternative entrance into the medieval centre from Piazza De Ferrari is by way of the huge monumental stair, used for the Republic's most theatrical processions to Piazza Matteotti, overlooked by the **Palazzo Ducale**. Built in the late 16th century on a design by the Lombard Andrea Vannone, the *palazzo* was altered in the following century to serve as Genoa's law courts. Like the Carlo Felice, it was bombed in the war, abandoned, then beautifully refurbished for 1992, and now you can walk through its *cortiles*, and sample restaurants, bars, shops, cultural spaces and exhibitions. Guided tours take in the Grimaldi tower, prisons, the council chambers, the doge's apartments and ducal chapel, frescoed by Giovanni Battista Carlone with scenes of Genoese conquests in the name of God, including one of Columbus planting a cross in the New World. A recent addition is the **Museo del Jazz**, with rare recordings and videos of the greats of jazz and a research centre on Afro-American music. The management also organizes school courses for jazz musicians.

Palazzo Ducale
guided tours t 010 557 4000, www.palazzo ducale.genova.it; open Tues–Sun 10–7; adm

Museo del Jazz
entrance at Via T. Reggio 34, t 010 585 241, www.italianjazz institute.com; open Mon–Sat 4–7

09

Genoa | Into the Old City

Sharing the square is the Baroque church of the **Gesù** (or Sant'Ambrogio and Andrea), designed in the 17th century by Jesuit Giuseppe Valeriani. Open the door and walk into a Baroque jewel box, all lavish stuccoes, frescoes and trompe-l'œil stage effects that highlight its frothy treasures: a *Circumcision* (1607) on the high altar and *St Ignatius Exorcizing the Devil* (1622), both by that great Catholic convert, Peter Paul Rubens, an *Assumption* by the 'Divine' Guido Reni and a *Crucifixion* by Simon Vouet.

🎟 Duomo di San Lorenzo

Just off Piazza Matteotti stands the jauntily black-and-white-striped **Duomo di San Lorenzo**, begun in the 12th century and modified several times; the façade was last restored in 1934. Odds and ends from the ages embellish the exterior – two kindly 19th-century lions by the steps, a 'knife-grinder' (said to be a saint holding a sundial), and a carving of St Lawrence roasting on his grill, above the central of three portals. These doors were among the very first Gothic works in Italy, built by French architects in the early 1200s. The pretty **Portal of San Giovanni** (1160) decorates the north side; Hellenistic sarcophagi, another Romanesque portal and a 15th-century tomb the south. The rather gloomy interior also wears jailbird stripes, and keeps, in the first chapel on the right, a marble *Crucifixion* of 1443 and a British shell fired from the sea five hundred years later that hit the chapel but miraculously failed to explode, while the last chapel has an altarpiece by Federico Barocci (1597). On the left, note the sumptuous Renaissance **Cappella di San Giovanni Battista**, with sculptures and marbles by Domenico and Elia Gagini (1451), and a 13th-century sarcophagus that once held the Baptist's relics.

Museo del Tesoro della Cattedrale
t 010 254 1250, www.museosan lorenzo.it; open Mon–Sat 9–12 and 3–6, every first Sun of the month 3–6; adm

In the subterranean vaults to the left of the nave, the **Museo del Tesoro della Cattedrale** is an Ali Baba cavern of holy treasures, acquired during the heyday of Genoa's adventures in the Holy Land: a bowl that was part of the dinner service of the Last Supper (said to be the Holy Grail, in which Joseph of Arimathea gathered the blood of Christ), the blue chalcedony dish on which the Baptist's head was served to Salome, an 11th-century arm reliquary of St Anne, the jewel-studded Byzantine *Zaccaria Cross*, and a 15th-century silver casket holding John the Baptist's ashes. There's more: the 12th-century cloister of the Canons of San Lorenzo (Via Tommaso Reggio 20) now holds the **Museo Diocesano**, with art from the 14th century onwards: gold-ground works by Barnaba da Modena, Pier Francesco Sacchi, Luca Cambiaso, Perino del Vaga and Gregorio De Ferrari.

Museo Diocesano
t 010 254 1250, www.diocesi.genova.it/ museodiocesano; open Tues–Sun 3–7, Tues and Sat also 10–1; adm

Piazza San Matteo

The Salita del Fondaco follows the back of the Palazzo Ducale from Piazza De Ferrari, then veers right for Piazza San Matteo, a beautiful little square completely clothed in the black-and-white bands of illustrious benefactors – and it's no wonder, for this was the foyer of the Doria, address of their proud *palazzi* and their 12th-century church of San Matteo, inscribed with their deeds. One of the most important of these happened in this very square: in 1528 Andrea Doria convinced Genoa's nobles to rise up against the French. One palace was donated by the Republic in 1298 to Lamba Doria, victor at Curzola; No.17, with a florid Gothic loggia, was bestowed on Andrea, while No.14, with a beautiful portal and St George and the Dragon, belonged to Branca Doria (d. 1325), who invited his father-in-law to dinner and murdered him, and whose soul, according to Dante (*Inferno XXXIII*), went to hell while his body lived on, inhabited by a devil, occasioning the famous remark of a Tuscan still sore over the defeat of Pisa in 1284:

O all you Genovese, you men estranged from every good, at home with every vice, why can't the world be wiped clean of your race?
(Translation by Mark Musa)

The square also has the Doria's private **cloister** (early 1300s), designed by Maestro Marco Veneto, with charming capitals on twinned columns. Zebra-striped **San Matteo**, the family church, was founded in 1125 but rebuilt in the early 14th century along with the rest of the piazza. The interior was given a complete Renaissance facelift commissioned by the admiral Andrea Doria, whose tomb is within.

San Matteo
t 010 247 4361;
open daily 7.30–12
and 4–6.30

The Northern Historic Centre

The northern section, built up mostly in the Renaissance, has survived in somewhat better nick than the area around Porta Soprana. Get there from Piazza Fontane Marose by descending **Via Luccoli**, a lively shopping street, or from Piazza San Matteo and the **Campetto**, a lovely square adorned with the down-at-heel 16th-century Mannerist **Palazzo Imperiale**, with frescoes and stuccoes inside by Luca Cambiaso and Giovanni Battista Castello – all subject of a recent restoration. Within are antique shops and the **Museo Fabrorum della Filigrana**, dedicated to gold, silver and filigree work, for which this quarter of Genoa was famous. Adjacent, the **Palazzo Casareto De Mari** from the same period is known as the 'pomegranate palace' for the tree by the entrance; the *cortile* has a statue of Hercules and fountain by Filippo Parodi. In nearby Piazza Soziglia two coffeehouses have been serving java since the early 1800s: **Klainguti** and **Romanengo**.

From Piazza Soziglia and the Campetto, the pretty Via degli Orefici (meaning 'of the goldsmiths') meanders down past the most beautiful of the *centro storico's aedicolae*, commissioned by the goldsmiths from the Gagini family with a sculpture of the *Magi*, and a *Madonna and Saints* (originals now in the Accademia

Museo Fabrorum della Filigrana
t 010 247 3536,
www.museofiligrana.
org; currently closed
for restoration

09 Genoa | Into the Old City

Ligustica) by a young painter, Pellegro Piola, who took his fee on the day it was hung, invited his friends on a spree and was murdered out of jealousy that evening. Via degli Orefici continues down to the very core of old Genoa, **Piazza Banchi**, where the bankers and merchants met in the late 16th-century Renaissance **Loggia dei Mercanti**, under a single, daring vault. This square saw a good amount of the murder and mayhem of old Genoa, and the bankers and their church, **San Pietro della Porta** (founded in the 9th century), were often victims. In the 1500s, the Senate rebuilt the church, this time directly over the bankers' stalls; their rents financed its upkeep.

From here, Via al Ponti Reale descends to harbourside Piazza Caricamento (now relieved of its traffic snarls thanks to a tunnel) lined with the ancient, evocative arcades of **Via Sotto Ripa**, reminiscent of a souk and filled with seafood restaurants and snack bars; in the Middle Ages the sea lapped at its feet. Here the massive, gaudily frescoed **Palazzo di San Giorgio** was built in 1260 for the Capitani del Popolo, using masonry hijacked from Venetian galleys. In 1298, at the battle of Curzola, the Genoese also snatched Marco Polo and imprisoned him here, where he met romance writer Rustichello of Pisa. Marco whiled away the time telling of his adventures, and Rustichello became the ghostwriter of his book, *Il Milione* ('The Million', i.e. tall tales; in English it's simply *The Travels*) of which Columbus possessed a well-thumbed copy. In 1408 the palace was taken over (like so many things in Genoa) by the Bank of St George, whose directors required a headquarters from where they could scrutinize the comings and goings of the port. The palace now belongs to the Harbour Board, but you can ask the guard to see rooms refurbished in their original 13th-century style.

Galleria Nazionale di Palazzo Spinola

Behind the Palazzo di San Giorgio, off Piazza Banchi, runs **Via San Luca**, the former 'Caruggio Dritto' or straight street, wide enough for double-laden mules. This was the turf of another prominent family, the Spinola, who shared it in an uneasy arrangement with their Guelph enemies, the Grimaldi. The Spinola's church of **San Luca** is one of the best family chapels in Genoa, rebuilt in 1626 with a palatial interior, entirely frescoed in the ballroom style by Domenico Piola, and endowed with Castiglione's magnificent altarpiece of the *Nativity* (1645) and sculptures by Filippo Parodi.

One of the grandest Spinola palaces, just off Via San Luca in Piazza di Pellicceria, now houses the **Galleria Nazionale di Palazzo Spinola**, arguably the best of all Genoa's *palazzo* museums, with its lavish 16th- to 18th-century décor and hall of mirrors, and paintings still arranged as in a private residence. Highlights include Antonello da Messina's sad, beautiful *Ecce Homo*, Joos Van Cleve's

✪ **Galleria Nazionale di Palazzo Spinola**
t 010 246 7786, www. palazzospinola.it; open Tues–Sat 8.30–7.30, Sun 1.30–7.30; adm

magnificent *Adoration of the Magi*, works by Van Dyck (*Portrait of a Child* and the *Four Evangelists*), and another fragment of Margherita di Brabante's tomb. There are excellent works by Genoa's masters (Cambiaso, Strozzi, Valerio Castello, Domenico Piola and Gregorio De Ferrari) and the dramatic equestrian *Portrait of Giovanni Carlo Doria* by Rubens. Don't miss the terrace, with its orange and lemon trees and views over Genoa's slate roofs.

Porto Antico

Seawards from Piazza Caricamento, Genoa's scabrous old port was redeveloped as the showcase for the 1992 celebrations. Having fun by the sea proved to be just what Genoa needed, and the Porto Antico has been expanding ever since as the city's favourite playground, hosting a number of events over the year (*see www.portoantico.it*). Renzo Piano (born in Genoa, in 1937) has been responsible for much of it, and has kept up the port theme throughout: its landmark is his **Bigo**, the 'Crane', which towers over the quay; a revolving lift at the end of a tentacle will take you up 130ft for the view. His glass **Bolla**, or 'Bubble', anchored to the sea floor contains rainforest plants and insects; nearby you can visit the picturesque *Galeone Neptune*, the sailing ship used in Roman Polanski's 1986 film *Pirates*.

Other attractions include a marina, an ice-skating rink, an outdoor swimming pool, and in the former cotton warehouses a ten-screen cinema complex, congress centre, and the Città dei Bambini, a vast play area, designed for ages 3–14 and full of climbing frames, giant plastic insects, and a building site where children can dress up in hard hats and push plastic wheelbarrows full of sand. Behind this, the gateway, the **Porta Siberia**, was designed by Galeazzo Alessi in 1553 and hints at the former opulence of the Molo Vecchio, the main quay of old Genoa, considered in the 1600s the greatest of all La Superba's wonders. The Porta Siberia was reworked by Renzo Piano to house the delightful, child-friendly **Museo Luzzati** dedicated to set designer Emanuele Luzzati (born in Genoa in 1921, died 2007) with drawings, models, animation films and cartoons. The thumb-shaped district by the gate, the **Quartiere del Molo**, has, curiously, a church of **San Marco**, founded in 1173 (perhaps in the hope of luring Mark away from Venice); it also has the 13th-century **Palazzo del Boia**, where criminals were hanged over the quay until 1852.

The Porto Antico's big attraction, however, is Europe's largest **Aquarium**, which Piano designed to resemble a container ship, filled with different marine environments, hosting seals, dolphins, sharks, penguins, guitar fish, reconstructions of coral reefs, a 3D

Città dei Bambini
*t 010 247 5702,
www.cittadei
bambini.net; open
1 Jul–23 Sept 11.30–7.30,
last entry 6.15; Oct–June
Tues–Sun 10–6, last
entry 4.45; closed last
week of Sept and first
week of Oct; adm*

Museo Luzzati
*t 010 253 0328,
www.museoluzzati.it;
open Tues–Thurs and
Sun 11–1 and 3–7, Fri
and Sat 11–1 and
3–11pm; adm*

Aquarium
*t 010 234 5678,
www.acquario.ge.it;
opening times change
slightly every month –
see www.acquario.
ge.it/orari_anno.asp –
entry every half hour
starting from the
opening time; adm
exp, under-3s free*

Museo Nazionale dell'Antartide
Antarctic Museum,
t 010 254 3690,
www.mna.it; open
Tues–Sun 10.30–6.30,
winter 9.45–5.30; adm

Galata-Museo del Mare
t 010 234 5655,
www.galatamuseo delmare.it; open
Mar–Oct Tues–Sun 10–7.30; Nov–Feb Tues–Fri 10–6, Sat and Sun 10–7.30; last entry one and a half hours before closing time; adm exp

movie, restaurants, and a new special hummingbird room (extra admission); allow at least three hours to see it all – note that end times here are last admissions, 90 minutes before closing. In an old warehouse nearby, the **Museo Nazionale dell'Antartide** is the only one in Europe devoted to the South Pole, in particular an Italian research expedition of 1985.

In 2005, Genoa's ongoing reclamation of its seafront moved north to take on the massive grain docks along **Ponte Parodi** with a new Piazza del Mediterraneo project, adopting a design won by Dutch architect Ben van Berkel; it will be dedicated to sports, music, travel and leisure, and should be ready by 2008. Already in place next to it, in the old Darsena, the shiny new **Galata-Museo del Mare** opened in 2004 and boasts of being the biggest museum in the Mediterranean, dedicated to 500 years of ships, shipbuilding and seafaring from reconstructed galleys to modern cruise liners.

Behind Genoa: Hills, Walls and a Boneyard

Thanks to centuries of shipbuilding, the hills around Genoa are the least forested in Liguria. Not only are they naked, but vulnerable, and here the Republic built its first outer walls and forts in the early 14th century. When the rouble was rolling in the 17th century, Genoa decided, mostly for show, to construct a new system of fortifications, designed by Bartolomeo Bianco. This stretches for 13km, forming a boundary which the Genoese boast is surpassed only by the Great Wall of China. It also adds a dramatic touch to Genoa's upper rim. The easiest way to visit is a drive along the panoramic **Strada della Mura** from Piazza Manin, north of Stazione Brignole (take Via C. Cabella). **Piazza Manin** is the site of one of the odder fortifications, the early 20th-century **Mackenzie Castle**, a folly with more teeth than a school of sharks.

Piazza Manin is also the base of the wonderful narrow-gauge **Trenino di Casella** (*see* p.143) up to **Casella**. The train was built in the 1920s and much used during the war to bring provisions into the city. It still makes its 25km journey in about an hour, and is a favourite weekend jaunt, when the trattorias along the way do a brisk trade (highly recommended and moderately priced: **Caterina**, at Cortino).

Caterina
t 010 967 7146

Piazza Manin is the point of departure for an inner ring road through the hills, too, the panoramic **Circonvallazione a Monte**, which skirts the villa-encrusted slopes, a route best taken by bus no.33, from Stazione Brignole or Piazza Manin. If you're driving (beware the dense traffic) the *Circonvallazione* starts at Corso Armellini, address of the church of **San Bartolomeo degli Armeni**, famous for its relic: the *Santo Volto* or *Mandylion*, a 'true' portrait of Jesus, painted on linen. Tradition has it that King Abgar V of Edessa (Urfa, Turkey), a contemporary of Christ, suffered from leprosy and sent ambassadors (perhaps the 'Greeks' mentioned in the gospel of St John) to meet Jesus, and he gave them the imprint of his face on a small cloth, an *acheiropoietos* 'image not made by human hands', which Agbar touched and was healed. Not long afterwards, the *Mandylion* disappeared when one of Agbar's heirs began to persecute Christians; one supposes it was hidden by a believer, who took the secret to the grave.

In 544, however, the *Mandylion* resurfaced, found by accident in a niche behind a stone in a city gate. Tellingly, there is a sudden change in Christian art: the earliest depictions of Christ often show him as a beardless, almost Apollo-like figure; after 544 the portrait of Jesus as a bearded man become current everywhere. In the 8th-century iconoclastic disputes that rocked Byzantium, the Christ of Edessa was the main evidence used by pro-icon factions to prove that images go back to Jesus' time. When Edessa was captured by Muslims, they kept the *Mandylion* on display and did a roaring pilgrim trade, until 944, when Constantine VII Porphyrogenitus' army besieged Edessa, and offered its emir a large sum of money, 200 hostages and perpetual immunity in exchange for the *Mandylion*, and it was transferred to Constantinople (on 4 May, a date still celebrated in the Orthodox liturgy).

Until that point, it seems that what the Greeks called the *Mandylion* was really the Shroud now in Turin, and that several portraits (also known as *Mandylions*) were made of the head. In 1204, during the Fourth Crusade, one of these was sold to the French, who kept it in the Sainte Chapelle in Paris, where it was destroyed during the Revolution. The Genoese version (identical to one in Rome and recently dated to the 13th century) remained in Constantinople until 1362, when Genoese Captain (later Doge) Leonardo Montaldo received it as a gift for military aid from Emperor John V Paleologus. Montaldo deposited the relic in this church, and there it has remained – except in 1507, when it was stolen by the troops of Louis XII and taken to France; it was soon returned thanks to pressure from Genoa's bankers. The frescoes tell the story.

Villa Grüber
t 010 816 737; open Tues–Sat 9.30–12 and 3–5.30; in summer until 7pm

Presepe
t 010 272 5308; open by request

Further east, you can visit the English gardens of the 17th-century Villa Grüber. The *Circonvallazione* continues east towards Corso Firenze, passing the route up to the **Santuario della Madonnetta** (1696) with a pretty pebble mosaic, a 15th-century Madonna by the Gagini family, an *Annunciation* attributed to Ludovico Brea in the sacristy and, in the crypt, a famous 17th-century **Presepe** (Christmas crib). Further west at Corso Dogali 18 is the imposing

Museo delle Culture del Mondo
t 010 272 3820; open Tues–Fri 10–5, Sat and Sun 10–6, April–Sept til 6; last entry one hour before closing; adm

Castello d'Albertis, rebuilt in the 19th century by the eclectic Genoese sailor, writer and Columbus scholar Captain Alberto d'Albertis (1836–1932) and, after 14 years of restoration, now reopened as the **Museo delle Culture del Mondo**, with items d'Albertis gathered from the Americas, Oceania, New Guinea and Southeast Asia; one section is dedicated to music.

Staglieno Cemetery and Around

Staglieno Cemetery
open daily 7.30–5, closed 1 Jan, 6 Jan, Easter Monday, 1 May, 24 June, 15 Aug, 8 Dec, 26 Dec, Christmas closes 12.30; bus no.34 from Piazza Acquaverde or Piazza Corvetto

Below Piazza Manin is the last port for the Genoese, **Staglieno Cemetery**. Founded in 1844, this covers 160 hectares, and even has its own internal bus system. The Genoese have a reputation for being tight-fisted, but when it comes to post-mortem self-indulgence they have few peers: Staglieno is a crumbling surreal city of miniature cathedrals, medieval chapels, Egyptian temples and Art Nouveau palaces. In the centre, Mazzini lies in a simple tomb behind two massive Doric columns and inscriptions by Tolstoy, Lloyd George, D'Annunzio, Carducci and others. Mrs Oscar Wilde is buried in the Protestant section. But it's not only the rich and famous vying for attention: one lavish tomb belongs to a nut-seller, who squirrelled away her savings her whole life to pay for it.

On the east bank of the Bisagno, you'll find the stadium L. Ferraris in **Marassi**; in **San Fruttuoso**, completely engulfed by modern buildings, is the **Villa Imperiale di Terralba** (now a public library) and a centuries-old park. The villa was built in 1502, and was used by Lorenzo Cattaneo to host Louis XII in courtly style (note the *fleur de lys* in the vaults of the atrium); within, the villa was given a Mannerist remodelling, and has excellent frescoes on the *Rape of the Sabines* by Luca Cambiaso.

West of Genoa: to Pegli and Voltri

Genoa has no suburbs, as it will tell you; its surroundings have all been hooked into the metropolis. Its business end lies west of the city and the residential areas to the east, although there are exceptions. Just west of the Lanterna, for instance, is **Sampierdarena**, a city within the city, but one that has always played an important role in Genoa; the Republic's earliest galleys were beached on its long sandy strand. The Doria were big shots here, too, and rebuilt the oldest church in Sampierdarena, **Santa Maria della Cella** (1206), around a cell where St Augustine's remains were kept in the 8th century, before going to Pavia. Santa Maria's Gothic interior has Baroque stuccoes, Doria tombs and an altarpiece by Castiglione. Although now swamped by industry, three villas from the 16th century still haunt Via Dottesio and Via D'Aste, known as **Bellezza, Fortezza e Semplicità** (Beauty, Strength and Simplicity), each packed full of frescoes. Only traces remain of their once-splendid gardens, along with a charming rustic grotto (Via D'Aste 9). The **Villa Centurione-Carpaneto**, Piazza Montano 4, has Genoa's only surviving frescoes by Bernardo Strozzi.

Further west, you'll find other villas woebegone in industrial zones; one of these is a grand rococo summer residence of the Savoys in **Cornigliano**. Others, including a magnificent Spinola spread, are in **Sestri Ponente**, site of Genoa's airport and the Cantiere Cadenaccio shipbuilding yard, but also an excellent restaurant (Baldin; *see* p.171). Beyond is **Multedo**, of wasted landscapes; here the 16th-century Villa Lomellini Rostan, with its loggias and watch tower, frescoes and bits of the gardens that were once celebrated for elegant parties, is a wistful reminder that it wasn't always so.

**Villa Lomellini
Rostan**
t 010 532 586

Pegli and its Parks and Museums

West of the Villa Lomellini lies **Pegli**, and although there's new building here, too, the character of this longtime retreat of the Genoese has not been totally lost, especially in the parks of the two princely villas. One belongs to the 16th-century **Villa Centurione Doria**, built by Giovanni Andrea Doria and his heir, the fabulously wealthy banker Adamo Centurione. Decorated with excellent Mannerist mythological frescoes by Nicolosio Granello and Lazzaro Tavarone, the villa holds the **Museo Navale di Pegli**, with a portrait of Columbus attributed to Ridolfo del Ghirlandaio, models of his three caravelles, and a famous *View of Genoa*, a copy of the late 15th-century original, and other nautical bits. The park still contains a lake and 'fairy island' laid out by Galeazzo Alessi in 1548, although the gardens are in need of restoration.

**Museo Navale
di Pegli**
*Piazza C. Bonavino 7,
t 010 696 9885,
www.museonavale.it;
open Tues–Fri 9–1, Sat
and Sun 10–7; adm*

The second park, the magnificent **Villa Durazzo-Pallavicini**, is even more full of fancy, although located directly over an *autostrada* tunnel. In the 1840s Michele Canzia, set designer at the Teatro Carlo Felice, created 'a drama in three acts' in which the visitor is the hero, beginning at a Triumphal Arch, passing through hell and ending at 'Paradise Regained' (a map-guide explains the story in English) by way of a temple of Diana on a lake, a beautiful old cedar of Lebanon and *Cinnamonum camphor*. The gardens are at their best in spring, when the ancient camellias burst into bloom. In 2002 the Botanical Gardens of 1794 reopened as well. The highest part of the villa, on the other hand, is being restored and is not currently open to the public. The villa contains the **Museo di Archeologia Ligure**, with pre-Roman and Roman finds from Genoa, Luni and Libarna, and from the Palaeolithic caves to the west of Genoa. The star exhibit is the 'Young Prince' from the Grotta delle Arene Candide at Finale Ligure, buried with a seashell headdress, *c.* 20,000 years ago. Another highlight is the bronze *Tabula*

**Villa Durazzo-
Pallavicini**
*entrance next to Pegli's
train station in Via
Pallavicini 13, t 010 698
2776; open Tues–Sun
April–Sept 9–7,
Oct–Mar 10–5; adm*

**Museo di
Archeologia
Ligure**
*t 010 698 1048; open
Tues–Fri 9–7, Sat and
Sun 10–7; adm*

Villa Duchessa di Galliera
t 010 561 401; entrance at Via Da Corte; take the train to Voltri, or bus no.1 from Piazza Caricamento; open summer 8am–7.30pm, till dusk at other times

Polcevera (117 BC), an account of Roman judgements in Liguria, found in the Val Polcevera in 1527.

Voltri, on the western edge of Genoa, is famous for its *focaccia* and the grounds of the 18th-century **Villa Duchessa di Galliera**, with Italian and romantic gardens, and a deer and Tibetan goat park.

Eastern Genoa to Nervi

The best way to visit Genoa's genteel eastern districts and beaches is along the coast-hugging Corso Italia, which begins at the **Fiera Internazionale**, the setting for Genoa's annual seafaring extravaganza, the Salone Nautico. **Albaro**, the first town to the east, was a favourite resort in the 14th century and has remained a residential area, although now its villas are engulfed in flats. It was the last home of Alessandro Magnasco, who painted the *Supper at Emmaus* for the church and convent of **San Francesco**, in Albaro's *centro storico*. The park at the crossroads of Via Albaro and Via

Villa Cambiaso Giustiniani
entrance on Via Montallegro

Montallegro belongs to the **Villa Cambiaso Giustiniani** (1548), the masterpiece of Galeazzo Alessi and the prototype for all subsequent Genoese palaces, with its tripartite façade and airy loggia. Today the Villa is home to the Faculty of Engineering and the park is open to the general public. Just up Via Albaro, the 16th-

Villa Saluzzo Bombrini
visit by appointment, t 010 576 791

century **Villa Saluzzo Bombrini**, or 'Paradise', is still private and intact, down to its fine Renaissance gardens, where Magnasco painted *Reception in a Garden in Albaro*, now in the Palazzo Bianco.

Other villas line the sea, one of which, the **Villa Bagnarello**, hosted Dickens while he wrote *Pictures from Italy* (1843). Genoa, incidentally, met Boz's approval ('I would never have believed that the time would come when I would be attracted even by the stones of Genoa's streets...'). Next east is **Boccadasse**, a bijou fishing port with good restaurants. **Quarto dei Mille**, from where Garibaldi and his Thousand set sail to Sicily and glory before Cavour could stop them, has a dramatic monument to the heroes.

Nervi
bus no.15 or 17 from Piazza Caricamento

Parchi di Nervi
open till dusk

Galleria d'Arte Moderna e Collezione Wolfson
t 010 372 6025, www.gamgenova.it and www.wolfsoniana.it; open Tues–Sun 10–7, closed during official hols; adm

Raccolte Frugone
t 010 322 396, www.raccoltefrugone.it; open Tues–Fri 9–7, Sat and Sun 10–7; adm

Beyond lies **Nervi**, an old resort with a lovely path, the **Passeggiata Anita Garibaldi**, along its wild and rocky shore. Just inland, on Via Capolungo, the gardens of three 17th- and 18th-century villas are now the **Parchi di Nervi**, the scene of Nervi's prestigious summer international ballet festival. Two villas are museums; the Villa Saluzzo Serra is now the **Galleria d'Arte Moderna e Collezione Wolfson** with an excellent collection of 19th- and 20th-century Italian art. Further east at Via Capolungo 9, Villa Grimaldi is the home of the **Raccolte Frugone**, featuring figurative paintings by Italian and other artists of the *Belle Epoque*; its lovely rose garden doubles as an outdoor cinema in summer. Further east, at Via Malfalda di Savoia 3, the

Museo Giannettino Luxoro
t 010 322 673, www.museoluxoro.it; open Tues–Fri 9–1, Sat 10–1; adm

Museo Giannettino Luxoro is in another lovely park. It, too, has a modern art collection and paintings by Magnasco, and an array of decorative arts: clocks, Christmas crib figures and furniture. It is possible to buy a joint ticket allowing entry to the Wolfsoniana, Raccolte Frugone and Museo Luxoro.

Tourist Information in Genoa

ⓘ **Genoa >**
Via Sottorife 5, t 010 557 4372; www.turismo inliguria.it

Stazione Principe, t 010 248 2633; open daily 9.30–1 and 2.30–6

Airport, t 010 601 5247; open Mon–Sat 9.30–1.30 and 2.30–5.30, Sun 10–1 and 2.30–5

There are IaT offices at Via Sottorife, Piazza Matteotti and Porto Antico; also at **Stazione Principe**, at the **airport**, t 010 601 524, and at the **Stazione Marittima**, when cruise ships arrive in summer.

Genoa's two-day **Card Musei** (€20) (see *www.museigenova.it/card*) includes admission to 22 museums, transport and discounts to the aquarium and theatres. You can pick one up at participating museums and AMT ticket offices.

Genoa has an unnecessarily complicated **street-numbering system**: any commercial establishment receives a red number, but any residence a black or blue number.

Shopping in Genoa

Antiques are a speciality in the streets around Via Garibaldi. The Palazzo Ducale hosts frequent antique shows and has some of the city's better bookshops and fashion boutiques.

The **Mercato Orientale**, Via XX Settembre, is a great place to experience the cornucopia of seafood and vegetables that help make Liguria Liguria. For more exotic items, try the evocative bazaar-like **Sottoripa** by the port.

For **English books**, try Bozzi, on Via Cairoli 2.

The **Antica Drogheria Torielli**, Via San Bernardo 32/r, t 010 246 8359, is the last medieval grocer's in Genoa. *Closed Wed pm.*

Sports and Activities in Genoa

Tours of Genoa's port are run by the Cooperativa Battellieri (*see* p.143), and by Alimar, t 010 256 775, *www.alimar.*

ge.it; both depart from the Aquarium (with further stops at Calata Zingari and Genoa Pegli; booking required) and offer **whale watching excursions**, trips to Portofino etc.; the Battellieri sail to Palazzo del Principe (*see* p.151).

Genoa has two **football** teams: Sampdoria and Genoa, both in the First Division. Both play at the Stadio Luigi Ferraris, in walking distance of Brignole station; tickets are sold at *tabacchi*.

For something a bit different, from December to March you can don blades at the **ice-skating rink** in the Piazza delle Feste in the Porto Antico.

Where to Stay in Genoa

Genoa ✉ 16100

Luxury (€€€€€)
****Starhotel President**, Via Corte Lambruschini 4, t 010 5727, *www. starhotels.com*. Luxurious sleek design, part of a complex in front of Brignole Station built for the 1992 Columbus celebrations, with 192 rooms, suites, a fitness room and a gourmet restaurant.

****Jolly Hotel Marina**, Molo Ponte Calvi 5, t 010 25391, *www.jollyhotels.it*. Spanking new and superbly positioned opposite the Aquarium in the Porto Antico. The 140 elegant rooms have all mod cons including dual phone lines and internet access.

****Villa Pagoda**, Via Capolungo 15, Nervi ✉ 16167, t 010 372 6161, *www.villapagoda.it*. Beautifully set in its own park near the sea, with 17 spacious and tastefully decorated rooms in an 18th-century villa, and a big buffet breakfast.

Locanda di Palazzo Cicala, Piazza S. Lorenzo 16, t 010 251 8824, *www. palazzocicala.it*. New hip, elegantly minimalist boutique hotel with high fancy-stuccoed ceilings in an 18th-century *palazzo* near the cathedral.

09

Genoa | Where to Stay in Genoa

⭐ **Torre Cambiaso** >

Very Expensive (€€€€)

****Torre Cambiaso**, Via Scarpanto 49, just west in Pegli ✉ 16157, **t** 010 698 0636, *www.antichedimore.com/torre cambiaso*. Beautiful antique-furnished rooms in a *palazzo* built around a medieval tower, set in a beautiful park with a heated pool, woods and grotto; a popular venue for weddings.

****Bristol Palace**, Via XX Settembre 35, **t** 010 592 541, *www.hotelbristol palace.it*. Near Brignole Station, full of 19th-century atmosphere with sumptuous furnishings in the rooms and an English bar. Hitchcock filmed some of *To Catch a Thief* here.

****Soglia Hotel**, Via Balbi 38, **t** 010 26991, *www.sogliahotels.com*. Near Stazione Principe; slick, if rather garish black and red. The top-floor rooms enjoy fantastic views, and although there's no restaurant it does have a café, gym, billiard room and garage.

Expensive (€€€)

****Astor**, Viale delle Palme 18, Nervi ✉ 16167, **t** 010 329 011, *www.astorhotel. it*. Fashionable and elegant hotel and restaurant in an enchanting garden near the sea, far from the hurly-burly of the city centre. Parking.

****Savoia**, Via Arsenale di Terra 1, **t** 010 261 1641, *www.hotelsavoia genova.it*. Near Stazione Principe, a historic Liberty *palazzo* built in 1897 with marble bathrooms and parquet floors. Can creep into the very expensive/luxury category in season. The restaurant offers Ligurian dishes.

***Veronese**, Vico Cicala 3, **t** 010 251 0771, *www.hotelveronese.com*. In the heart of the old town, with comfortable, if oddly decorated, rooms.

Cristoforo Colombo, Via di Porta Soprana 59, **t** 010 251 3643, *www.hotelcolombo.it*. Full of funky character, with a roof terrace where breakfast is served.

Moderate (€€)

***Agnello d'Oro**, Via Monachette 6, **t** 010 246 2084, *www.hotelagnello doro.it*. In a 17th-century property of the Doria family, near Via Balbi. Although most of the old-fashioned charm of the place is in the lobby, the bedrooms are very comfortable.

***Boccascena**, Via Carlo Barabino 62r, **t** 010 532 148, *www.hotel boccascena.it*. Out by the International Fair in a 19th-century building, the hotel is in walking distance of a free pool and beach; there's internet access and a shuttle into the centre is available.

***La Capannina**, Via T. Speri 7, **t** 010 317 131, *www.lacapanninagenova.it*. Out to the east, by the fishing port of Boccadasse, with a delightful breakfast terrace and tranquil rooms (cheaper in the *dipendenza*). During the summer season, the hotel's boat goes out on diving expeditions.

***Vittoria & Orlandini**, Via Balbi 33, **t** 010 261 923, *www.vittoria orlandini.com*. A charming, slightly eccentric hotel with an inner garden, comfortable bedrooms and a pretty breakfast room with good views.

Bel Soggiorno, Via XX Settembre 19/2, **t** 010 542 880, *www.belsoggiorno hotel.com*. The friendliest hotel in this category, in an excellent position near the centre, 5 minutes from the Aquarium; can be slightly noisy.

Cairoli, Via Cairoli 14/4, **t** 010 246 1454, *www.hotelcairoligenova.com*. Very central, with sparkling, modern rooms and a relaxed, friendly and personal atmosphere.

Della Posta, Via Balbi 24, **t** 010 246 2005. The best of several *pensioni* in the same building near Brignole.

Villa Bonera, Via Sarfatti 8, Nervi, **t** 010 372 6164, *www.villabonera.com*. Attractive option with 26 charming rooms in a 17th-century villa surrounded by a pretty garden.

*Balbi Family Hotel**, Via Balbi 21/3, **t** 010 2759 288, *www.hotelbalbi genova.it*. En-suite rooms in a *palazzo* 200m from Principe Station, with frescoed ceilings, parquet floors, satellite TV.

B&B Flowers, Via Lomellini 1, **t** 010 246 1918, *www.bbflowers.it*. Well-furnished rooms with air conditioning on the top floor of a 15th-century *palazzo*; the owner is English-speaking.

Inexpensive (€)

*Major**, Vico Spada 4, **t** 010 247 4174, *www.hotelmajorgenova.it*. Just inside the *centro storico*, by Piazza De Ferrari.

The rooms are clean and modern; a real bargain.

*Argentina, Via Gropallo 4/4, **t** 010 839 3722, *www.albergoargentina genova.it*. Near Stazione Brignole; clean and friendly. If it's full, there's another good one in the same building (*see* below).

*Carola, Via Gropallo 4/12, **t** 010 839 1340, *www.pensione carola.com*.

*Carletto, Via Colombo 16/4 (signposted off Via XX Settembre), **t** 010 588 412. Not far from Brignole, with good rooms and lots of *focaccia* stands nearby.

Eating Out in Genoa

The Genoese hate spending money but love good food, which means you can eat better for less here than any city in northern Italy.

Very Expensive (€€€€)

(★) Baldin >

Baldin, Piazza Tazzoli 20, in Sestri Ponente, **t** 010 653 1400. Rated by some as the finest restaurant in all Liguria, where young chefs Luca Collami and Maria Medaglia prepare marvels with seafood and other Genoese classics, with just the right touch of invention. For a treat, try the '25 tastes from raw to cooked'. *Closed Sun and Mon.*

La Bitta nella Pergola, Via Casaregis, 52, **t** 010 588 543. Superb Neapolitan chef and a cushy romantic setting for well-prepared seafood (the scampi is exquisite), but lamb dishes too, followed by fine desserts, home-made chocolates and the house's own *limoncello*. *Book. Closed Sun eve and Mon and first 10 days in Jan and Aug.*

Gran Gotto, Viale Brigata Bisagno 69/r (near Piazza della Vittoria), **t** 010 564 344. A Genoese classic which first opened in 1939, and seems to be getting better all the time, featuring imaginative and delicately prepared seafood like turbot in radicchio sauce, warm seafood antipasti, famous *rognone* (kidney) dishes and delectable desserts. *Closed Sat lunch and Sun and three weeks in Aug.*

Torre dei Greci, Vico dei Lavatoi 2/r, **t** 010 251 8851. By the Molo Vecchio, stylish cuisine based on the best of what the market provides, with forays into the exotic (baby squid stuffed with green curry in coconut broth). *Closed Sat lunch and Sun and 10 days at beginning of Jan.*

Zeffirino, Via XX Settembre 20, **t** 010 591 990. A Genoese institution since 1939, Frank Sinatra often made a special trip from Monte Carlo just to tuck into the perfect pasta and pesto and grilled seafood in a dining room that has changed little since.

Saint Cyr, Piazza Marsala 4/r, **t** 010 886 897. The menu is by no means extensive, but what they do they do well. The food is always beautifully presented and the staff are charming. Try their *minestrone genovese*, with pesto. *Closed Sat lunch and Sun.*

Antica Osteria del Bai, Via Quarto 12 in the eastern district of Quarto dei Mille, **t** 010 387 478. Former fishing shack, now a seductive gourmet haven where owner chef Gianni Malagoli creates fresh dishes with Ligurian basics. *Closed Mon, Sun lunch and some of Jan and Aug.*

Vittorio al Mare, Belvedere Edoardo Firpo 1, east of centre at Boccadasse, **t** 010 376 0141. The most elegant seafood restaurant in the bijou fishing port at Boccadasse, with views over the sea – or dine for a lot less in the adjacent pizzeria. *Closed Mon and weekday lunches and all of Jan.*

Expensive (€€€)

Da Rina, Mura delle Grazie 3/r, **t** 010 246 6475. The perfect example of why a book should not be judged by its cover. Run by the same family since 1946, Rina is still popular with politicans and film stars thanks to simple, good food served in a refurbished warehouse by the port. Great *antipasti* and *branzino* in *salsa di asparagi*, positively to die for. *Book. Closed Mon and Aug.*

Da Vittorio, Via Sottoripa 59, **t** 010 247 2927. If the beautiful display of seafood isn't enough to entice you in, then the knowledge that half a lobster with *linguine*, wine and coffee will be under €25 should be. *Book or be prepared to wait. No credit cards.*

Mannori, Via Galata 70/r, **t** 010 588 461. Excellent home cooking: the pots simmer all morning to create hearty soups and other dishes. *Closed Sun and Aug.*

Genio, Salita San Leonardo 61/r, off Via Fieschi, t 010 588 463. Another popular restaurant, near Piazza Dante, serving great traditional Ligurian food (the house speciality is *stoccafisso*) but also offering a wider choice than usual for non-seafood fans. *Closed Sun and Aug.*

Antico Osteria della Castagna, Via Romana della Castagna 20r, in Quarto dei Mille, t 010 399 0265. When the Genoese hanker for traditional Ligurian seafood, they make a special trip out to sit on this big veranda. *Closed Sun eve, Mon and mid-Aug–early Sept.*

Moderate (€€)

Antica Cantina Dei Tre Merli, Vico dietro il coro della Maddalena 26, t 010 247 4095. Handsome brick *osteria* in a former stable, just off Via Garibaldi; good food and plenty of wines, even a red wine ice cream. *Open till 11pm; closed Sat lunch and Sun.*

 Patrone >> **Sola Enoteca**, Via Barabino 120/r, t 010 594 513. Elegant wine-bar restaurant serving tasty classics such as *cima alla genovese* and *stoccafisso accomodato. Closed Sun and Aug.*

Da Maria, Vico Testadoro 14,t 010 581 080. Wonderful old-fashioned trattoria just off Via XXV Aprile, serving up two huge courses with wine on communal tables. *Book. Closed Sun, and Mon evening.*

Ostaria Da U Santu, Via al Santuario delle Grazie 33, west of Genoa at Voltri, t 010 613 0477. Good Genoese home cooking and beautiful views from the pergola, up near Volti's hilltop sanctuary. *Closed Sun eve, Mon and Tues, but do ring ahead.*

Osteria San Matteo/Enoteca Migone, Piazza S. Matteo, t 010 247 3282. In a *palazzo* in one of the *centro storico*'s prettiest squares, friendly wine bar with creative dishes based on what looked good in the market. *Closed Sun, Mon lunch and 15 days in Aug.*

Inexpensive (€)

Antica Osteria della Foce, Via Ruspoli 72/r, t 010 553 3155. Not a long menu, but appreciated for its excellent

Genoese soul food – *minestrone, stoccafisso*, and *farinata* in the evenings. *Book. Closed Sat lunch, Sun and Aug, Christmas and Easter.*

Capitan Baliano, Piazza Matteotti 11/r, t 010 265 299. Excellent traditional dishes next to the Ducal palace with tables on the pavement. *Closed Sun.*

Antica Osteria di Vico Palla, Vico Palla 15/r, t 010 246 6575. Authentic old Ligurian *osteria* near the Porta Siberia, famous for its *stoccafisso. Closed Mon.*

Genoese Snacks

Focaccia, topped with olive oil and salt in its simplest form, is sold throughout the city, in bakeries and pizzerias; follow your nose to find it fresh from the oven, when it's at its best. *Farinata* (made of chickpea meal, olive oil and water, and baked) and *panissa* (similar, only fried) are a bit more specialized.

Panificio Mario, Via S. Vincenzo 61/r, t 010 580 619. Near Brignole station, with an infinite variety of *focaccia* (cheese, onion, tomato). *Open from 5.50am–7.40pm.*

Patrone, Via Ravecca 72/r, t 010 251 1093. Near Porta Soprana, the best *focaccia* in Genoa.

Friggitoria Corege, Via Sottoripa 113/r, t 010 382 671. For classic *farinata* and *panissa, frisceu di baccalà* (salt-cod croquettes) and fried fish.

Tumioli, Via Gramsci 37/r, t 010 246 5956. First-class *focaccia* made with olive oil, as it should be.

Cafés/Pasticcerie/Gelaterie

Genoa has had a very long love affair with sweets. The technique for making the candied fruit that plays such a prominent role in the city's *confetterie* was originally brought back from Syria, while the orange-flower water in the city's classic cake, *pandolce*, comes from Sidon in Lebanon.

Romanengo, Via Soziglia 74/r, t 010 247 4574. Since 1814, legendary for candied fruit, chocolates. *Closed Sun pm and Mon am.*

Zuccotti, Via di S. Zita 36/r, t 010 589 594. A big favourite for hazelnut creams and chocolates. *Closed Sun.*

Caffè degli Specchi, Salita Pollaiuoli 43/r, t 010 246 8193. Atmospheric black-and-white Liberty-style café, where Dino Risi filmed *Profumo di Donna*. *Closed Sun.*

Pasticceria Traverso, Via Pastorino 116–118/r, **t** 010 740 3747. Founded in 1893 and renowned for its cakes, the Pasticceria has also created a gluten-free line of delicacies.

Klainguti, Piazza di Soziglia 98/r, **t** 010 247 4552. Verdi spent his winters in Genoa and passed much of his time in the rococo salons of this elegant *caffè/pasticceria* of 1826; try their unique *klaingutino* (their version of *pandolce*) and the *torta sacripantina*.

Caffè Gelateria Balilla, Via Macaggi 84/r, **t** 010 542 161. Turn-of-the-last-century café, a favourite for luscious ice creams.

Entertainment and Nightlife in Genoa

For entertainment and events listings, check Genoa's daily paper, *Il Secolo XIX*.

In Paganini's home town there is plenty of music – including the **Paganiniana**, a violin fest which takes place from mid-Sept to mid-Oct. The dynamic **Genoa Opera** in the Teatro Carlo Felice sponsors the prestigious summer **Ballet Festival** in the park in Nervi (book tickets online at *www.carlofelice.it*; or book Tues–Fri 2–5 with a credit card, **t** 010 570 1650).

Teatro della Corte, Via E.F. Duca d'Aosta 19, **t** 010 570 2472, shows **classic and avant-garde theatre**. The Teatro della Tosse, Piazza Negri 6/2, **t** 010 248 7011, *www.teatrodella tosse.it*, is dedicated to **alternative and underground performances**.

Every year Genoa competes with Venice, Pisa and Amalfi in the **Regatta of the Ancient Maritime Republics**. Genoa's premier event is its annual **Salone Nautico Internazionale**, held in the second week of October. Each year half a million people come to look at over 2,000 boats at the Fiera di Genova.

Café and bar life in Genoa is concentrated around the Porto Antico's Via del Molo and also in the medieval city, around Piazza S. Donato. You may prefer to avoid the seamier places located around Via San Luca. Ask for *aperitivi* with your drink and you'll get tapas-sized saucers of goodies.

Rosa dei Venti, on Via del Molo. A summer bar with an outdoor pool by the Porto Antico. *Open until 3am.*

Bruschetta e Vino, Via Mascherona 30. Wine and snacks served up till late in the heart of the *centro storico*, next to the Architecture Faculty. *Closed Sun.*

Bar Le Corbusier, Via San Donato 36–38/r. An atmospheric place to bend an elbow.

Genoa's *Entroterra*

Genoa has sucked most of the juices out of its hinterland, leaving few reasons to delve inland. Since the building of the *Via Postumia* (148 BC), the main roads to Milan and the Po Valley go up the busy **Val Polcevera**. Close to **Bolzaneto**, just off the *autostrada*, there's a surprise: the **Villa Serra**, a Tudor-style mansion in an English garden created by painter Carlo Cubandi. To the west is the queen of Ligurian hilltop sanctuaries, the **Madonna della Guardia**. In the old days the Genoese (especially sailors) would walk up here to deposit their *ex votos*; today people drive up to enjoy the view and have lunch. Further north, **Ronco Scrivia** has an impressive triple-arched medieval bridge that seems to be going nowhere.

To the east of the Val Polcevera, **Sant'Olcese** is famous for its smoky-flavoured salami. **Casella**, further up, is a favourite excursion

Villa Serra
t 010 715 577,
www.villaserra.it;
open last Sun Oct–Feb
Tues–Sun 10–5; last Sun
of Mar–May Tues–Sun
9–7; June–Sept
Tues–Sun 9–8; Mar and
Oct until last Sat of
month 10–6; on Mon all
year the park opens at
2pm; adm; guided
tours available

10 km

5 miles

PIEDMONT

Ronco Scrivia

Castello della Pietra

Vobbio

Monte Antola

S45

N

Val Polcevera

Casella

S226

Parco dell'Antola

Montebruno

A26

Madonna della Guardia ✝

Sant'Olcese

LIGURIA

Villa Serra 🏛 Bolzaneto

Val Bisagno

San Siro di Struppa ✝

Doria

S45

S225

A10

VIA AURELIA Voltri

Pegli

Arenzano

Sestri Ponente

GENOA (GENOVA)

Nervi

A12

Riviera di Ponente

Recco

Camogli

Penisola di Portofino

San Fruttuoso

Santa Margherita

Portofino

Rapallo

Gulf of Genoa

Riviera di Levante

Ajaccio/I. Canarias

Barcelona/Palma

Cagliari/Porto Torres

Olbia/Arbatax/Palermo

Tunis/Bastia/Ile-Rousse

Castello della Pietra

t 010 944 175; open April–Oct Sat from 2.30 each hour until 5.30, except in Oct, Sun and hols 10.30–5.30

destination thanks to its *trenino* (*see* p.143). Even further north at **Vobbia** stands the striking 13th-century Spinola **Castello della Pietra** sandwiched between the rocks. This area is now a *Parco Regionale*, encompassing 'Genoa's sacred mountain', **Antola**.

In the Valle Scrivia, just below Antola, **Torriglia** (reached by bus or car) is Genoa's 'Little Switzerland'; it has an impressive, derelict medieval castle and pretty artificial lake. **Montebruno**, 9km east, was owned at various times by Genoa's big families; it has a small museum of country culture and, in the church across the bridge, pieces of hawsers from Andrea Doria's galleys, donated as an *ex voto* for his victories.

Closer to Genoa, above Staglieno in the Val Bisagno, **San Siro di Struppa** (near Doria) was built in *c.* 1000 to honour Genoa's bishop saint, a famous 4th-century persecutor of the Arians. The church has been restored to its original pre-Romanesque form and boasts a wonderful polyptych of 1516, attributed to Pier Francesco Sacchi, showing Siro confronting a benign-looking and smartly decked-out basilisk, a symbol of heresy.

Riviera di Levante

East of Genoa, the coast becomes a creature of high drama and romance. The beaches on this Coast of the Rising Sun, the Riviera di Levante, aren't as prominent, nor the climate quite as mild, but there are compensations. From Nervi and the Golfo Paradiso, past Monte di Portofino to the Cinque Terre and in and out of the nooks and crannies of the Gulf of Poets, the mountains and sea tussle and tumble in a voluptuous chaos of azure, turquoise and piney green.

10

Don't miss

★ Home of the world's biggest frying pan
Camogli p.180

★ An exquisite town and its promontory
Portofino p.184

★ A clifftop chapel
Bonassola p.195

★ Cliff-hanging villages
Cinque Terre p.196

★ A zebra church
Portovenere p.203

See map overleaf

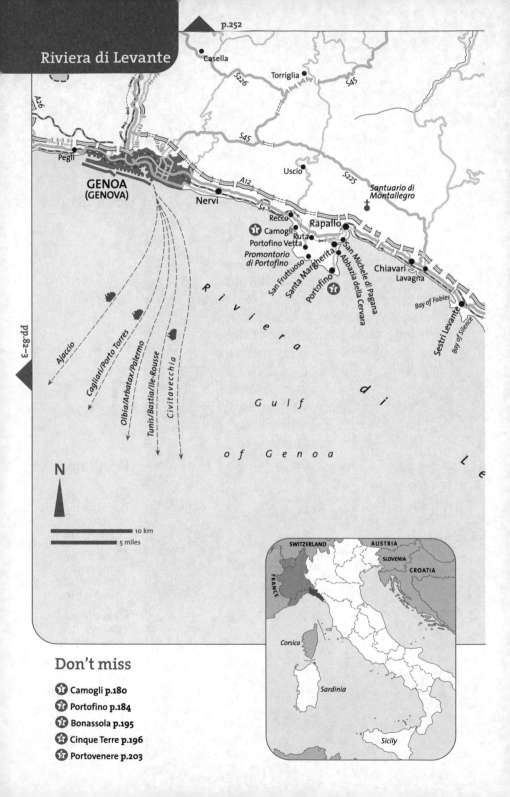

p.252

Riviera di Levante

pp.82–3

Casella

Torriglia

S226

S45

Pegli

A26

S45

Uscio

Santuario di
Montallegro

GENOA
(GENOVA)

A12

S225

Nervi

S1

Recco

Rapallo

Camogli

Ruta

Portofino Vetta

San Michele di Pagana

Promontorio
di Portofino

Abbazia della Cervara

San Fruttuoso

Santa Margherita

Portofino

Chiavari

Lavagna

Bay of Fables

Sestri Levante

Bay of Silence

R i v i e r a

Ajaccio

Cagliari/Porto Torres

Olbia/Arbatax/Palermo

Tunis/Bastia/Ile-Rousse

Civitavecchia

d i

G u l f

o f   G e n o a

L e

N

10 km

5 miles

SWITZERLAND

AUSTRIA

SLOVENIA

FRANCE

CROATIA

Corsica

Sardinia

Sicily

Don't miss

- ⭐ Camogli **p.180**
- ⭐ Portofino **p.184**
- ⭐ Bonassola **p.195**
- ⭐ Cinque Terre **p.196**
- ⭐ Portovenere **p.203**

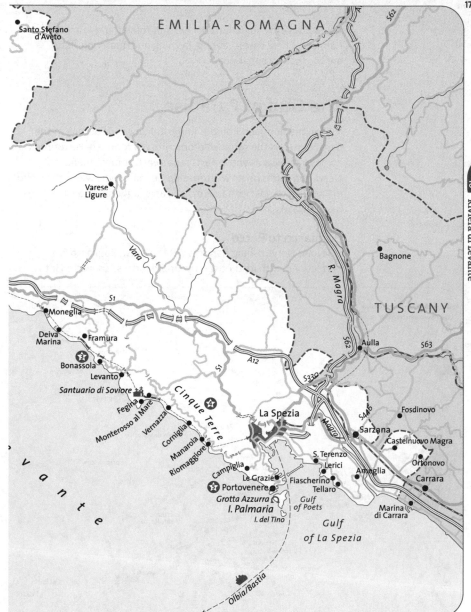

Against the deeply coloured coves and cliffs of the coast rise villages of weathered pastels, silvery groves of olives, and striped terraces, gazing out over fleets of fishing craft and sleek white yachts. Everyone has heard of Portofino, but there are other lovely if less glittering places to anchor yourself – Camogli, Portovenere, Santa Margherita. The Apennines of the *entroterra* offer another world altogether, of luxuriant chestnut forests and modest hamlets, where sheep-rearing, farming and quarrying slate are the main occupations.

The Gulf of Paradise

Of all the nubs and notches in the Italian coastline, one of the best beloved is the squarish promontory of Monte di Portofino. It comes into view as you leave Genoa's easternmost toehold at Nervi, and forms on its western side Genoa's own Riviera, the Golfo di Paradiso – and if its name may be an exaggeration, well, we've heard worse.

Bogliasco to Recco

Beyond Nervi, fishing hamlets dot the coast: **Bogliasco** is a perfect one, with its thousand-year-old fortress converted into

Getting around the Gulf of Paradise

The Genoa–Pisa **railway** hugs the coast here, passing through tunnel after tunnel. **Buses** use the scenic old coastal road, Via Aurelia (S1). From Camogli a **boat** service, which is run by the Battellieri del Golfo Paradiso, Via Scalo 2, **t** 0185 772 091, *www.camogli.it/va_tras.htm*, sails frequently to San Fruttuoso, and runs excursions from Recco, Nervi, Genoa Porto Antico and Pegli to the Cinque Terre and Portovenere.

pastel-washed apartments by the sea, with laundry flapping and the delightful oval rococo church of the Natività (1731). Next comes **Pieve Ligure**, hemmed in by Monte Santa Caterina and its olive terraces. Pieve is proudest of another tree, however: as the mimosa capital of the Riviera, it fills up with little yellow pompom blooms in January and early February. **Sori**, next in line, has a fine sandy beach tucked in a pretty inlet and a curvaceous confectionery church, the pink Santa Margherita (1711). Unfortunately it also has a few too many holiday homes.

Recco, at the crossroads to Camogli, was bombed in the war but has come back to life as the gastronomic capital of the Riviera di Levante thanks to its many restaurants and legendary cheese *focaccia*. On 7–8 September the town explodes with a superb display of fireworks, the *Sagra del Fuoco*. One thing the bombs couldn't hurt, however, is the perfect pebble beach at **Mulinetti**, set among villas and gardens.

A Detour into Columbus Country

A twisting road from Recco leads up steeply to **Avegno**, the village of bell-makers, where that foundry has been in business since 1594; the nearby church of Santa Margherita at **Tesana** has a remarkable 16th-century Flemish wooden relief of the *Crucifixion*. A by-road leads to **Terrile**, an even smaller hamlet, where craftsmen since 1824 have made everything else a fashionable campanile needs – the bell supports and clocks. **Uscio**, the main village here, was a Lombard stronghold, and has a 12th-century Romanesque church restored to its original appearance. Mostly, however, Uscio is renowned for its refreshing climate and one of the first health farms in Italy. Its chestnut forests supply the flour to make the local pasta, *trofie*, and make for lovely walks and drives – the high road back to Genoa, by way of **Monte Fasce** (2,736ft), the bald mountain that looms east of the city, is especially grand at sunset, taking in views as far as Corsica, Elba and the Apuan Alps.

Another road above Uscio writhes to **Gattorna**, a toy-making and flower-growing town in the **Val Fontanabuona** that runs parallel to the coast to Chiavari; the valley's river, the Lavagna, was one of the few things in Liguria that met Dante's approval (he called it a *fiumana bella*). This quiet vale of slate quarries was the cradle of the Columbus family; Christopher's grandfather Giovanni, a woolworker, hailed from tiny **Terrarossa Colombo** and, with his son

Terrile
to visit call the Uscio tourist office, **t** 0185 91101

Domenico, was one of many who migrated to Genoa to seek a better living. You can follow their presumed path from here to Nervi, the **Itinerario Storico Colombiano**, beginning at the sculpture (1982) by Antonio Leveroni. **Neirone**, up a valley north of Gattorna, holds a festival in August in honour of one of the greatest gifts of the New World: spuds. The local lord introduced the potato in the 18th century, in the face of charges of witchcraft by the locals, who suspected it of being as poisonous as its cousin, the deadly nightshade; they changed their minds when famine struck in 1795 and have fêted the potato ever since.

The biggest settlement of the Fontanabuona Valley is **Cicagna**, famous for good bread, for a bridge built by the Fieschi, and for slate, the subject of the **Museo dell'Ardesia** that will take you all around the area to historic workshops and quarries. Cicagna was also famous for the reactionary *Viva Maria* revolt that its priests and peasants led against the Napoleonic Republic of Liguria in 1797. Afterwards, many residents followed the Columbian itinerary all the way to the Americas, so many, in fact, that there's a rather sweet *Monument to the Italian Emigrant* in **Favale di Malvaro**, up the road from Cicagna. In exchange for the potato, Favale gave the New World the parents of Amedeo Pietro Giannini, the founder of what was for a long time the biggest bank in the world, the Bank of America. The Giannini homestead, now the **Museo dell' Emigrante**, has documents on his career and immigration.

Museo dell'Ardesia
t 0185 971 091; open weekends and hols, guided tours 10 and 3; adm exp

Museo dell' Emigrante
Loc. Acereto 16, t 0185 975 067; open by request

Camogli

⓱ Camogli

Returning to the coast, salty Camogli, tucked down on the promontory, was luckily spared the bombs that flattened its neighbour. Unabashedly picturesque, the town has a proud maritime tradition: this was the home port of a renowned republican fleet that rivalled Genoa's, which fought with Napoleon, and its vessels were all along the Riviera in the 19th century. Its nautical school produces many of the country's merchant marines. Its name derives from *Casa Mogli* (house of wives), since the menfolk were almost always at sea. Many of them still are.

The harbour, piled high with huge, faded houses, is the scene of Camogli's famous *Sagra del Pesce*: spectacular fireworks on the second Sunday in May are followed by a fish fry in Italy's largest frying pan (14ft across). Thousands of sardines are distributed free to all comers – a display of generosity that carries the hope that the sea will provide the same in the coming year. A small promontory separates Camogli's pebble beach from its port, and wears like a hat the bijou **Dragonara Castle**, built against the Saracens and now serving as a multimedia centre. Nearby, the neoclassical Basilica di Santa Maria Assunta has an interior rich with gilded stuccoes and frescoes, with funds donated by sailors.

Sagra del Pesce
www.sagradelpesce.it

Museo Marinaro
Via Gio Bono Ferrari 41,
t 0185 729 049; open
Mon, Thurs and Fri
9–12, Wed, Sat and
Sun 9–12 and 3–6

Camogli recalls its days as a rough-and-tumble sea power in the **Museo Marinaro** with models, more than a hundred 'ships' portraits' (including one of the semi-clipper *Narcissus*, owned by a local *armateur*, on which Joseph Conrad served as second mate, inspiring *The Nigger of the Narcissus*), nautical instruments, votive offerings, diaries and other salty memorabilia, including items telling of the blood link between Camogli and the British South Atlantic island of Tristan da Cunha.

Sports and Activities on the Gulf of Paradise

The **B&B Diving Centre**, Lungomare di Camogli, **t** 0185 772 751, mobile **t** 3477 154 616, *www.bbdiving.it*. Offers diving tours in the Portofino Natural Reserve area; also hires out boats. *Open all year.*

Where to Stay and Eat on the Gulf of Paradise

ⓘ Bogliasco >
Via Aurelia 106,
t 010 3470429

Bogliasco ✉ 16031

Nuovo Hotel Villa Flora, Via Aurelia 5, **t 010 347 0013, *www.hotelvilla flora.it* (€€). A little hotel, the only one in town.

Tipico, Via Poggio Favaro 20 up at San Bernardo, **t** 010 347 0754 (€€€€). Restaurant providing lovely views as well as excellent seafood *antipasti* and home-made pasta. In the spring, don't miss the *pansotti* with asparagus tips. Follow it with grilled fish, and home-made desserts. *Closed Mon, also mid-Jan and mid-Aug.*

ⓘ Uscio >>
Via IV Novembre 1,
t 0185 91319

Pieve Ligure ✉ 16063

Hobbit's Folly B&B, Via delle Chiappe 14, **t** 010 346 0695 (€). English-owned rooms with a view in an 18th-century *palazzo* with a beautiful garden and olive groves. Minimum stay two nights. *Open mid-May–mid-Sept. No credit cards.*

ⓘ Recco >
Via Ippolito d'Aste 2/a,
t 0185 722 440

ⓘ Camogli >>
Via XX Settembre 33,
t 0185 771 066

Recco ✉ 16063

Besides cheese *focaccia*, Recco is celebrated for its *trofie* with pesto and *pansotti*.

***Da ö Vittorió, Via Vastato 5, **t** 0185 74029, *www.daovittorio.it* (€€€). Deservingly renowned, this restaurant is more than 100 years old, and has added comfortable rooms to its repertoire. Specialities include *minestrone di verdura alla Genovese* and *trofie al pesto. Closed Tues.*

****La Villa, Via Roma 274, **t** 0185 720 779, *www.manuelina.it* (€€€–€€). A Genoese pleasure villa with modern extension, gym and sun terrace, set in a garden with pool; the bigger rooms are in the annexe. The hotel loans out mountain bikes, and has an excellent *enoteca* with theme tastings. Predating the hotel is its restaurant, **Manuelina**, **t** 0185 720 779 (€€€€), where you can try exquisite *focaccia*, *trofie* with pesto, and a variety of seafood for *secondo. Closed Wed.*

***Elena, Corso Garibaldi 5, **t** 0185 74022, *www.hotelelena.it* (€€€–€€). On the seafront, offering comfortable, modern rooms with great views of Monte Portofino.

Vitturin, Via dei Giustiniani 50, **t** 0185 720 225, *www.vitturin.it* (€€€). Owned by the same family since 1860. Nibble on cheese *focaccia*, while choosing from the market-based menu; good lamb as well as prawns in cognac and other fish. *Closed Mon.*

Uscio ✉ 16030

****Centro Arnaldi Uscio, **t** 0185 919 406 (€€€€–€€€). Founded back in 1906 to make clients feel better. Phytotherapy (including a secret herbal potion), beauty and relaxation treatments, tailor-made diet, a pool and tennis are part of the cure.

Camogli ✉ 16032

****Cenobio dei Dogi, Via Cuneo 34, **t** 0185 7241, *www.cenobio.it* (€€€€€–€€€€). A former ducal palace at the water's edge, with fantastic views – on a clear day you can see the winking of Genoa's Lanterna. The bedrooms are airy and decorated in white and wood. There are sun terraces, a flower-filled park, private beach, heated pool, tennis and two excellent **restaurants**, open to the public.

****Portofino Kulm**, Viale Bernardo Gaggini 23, Portofino Vetta, t 0185 7361, *www.portofinokulm.it* (€€€€–€€€). Built in 1905, this sumptuous, Liberty-style hotel ('*kulm*' is German for summit) is set in a peaceful forest on top of Monte di Portofino, overlooking Camogli. There's a fitness centre, indoor pool, and **restaurant** run by Zefferino.

***Casmona**, Salita Pineto 13, t 0185 770 015, *www.casmona.com* (€€€–€€). A quiet, tidy place with a **restaurant** and shady patio.

La Camogliese, Via Garibaldi 55, t 0185 771 402, *www.lacamogliese.it* (€€). Family-run hotel by the sea,

with access to a pool and gym. Its restaurant (*closed Wed*) serves good, reasonably priced fish dishes.

Rosa, Largo Casabona 11, t 0185 771 088 (€€€). Gorgeous sunset views from the restaurant terrace and delicious pasta and fresh seafood. *Closed Tues, and Wed lunch, mid-Jan–early Feb, mid-Nov–early Dec.*

Nonna Nina, Loc. S. Rocco, Via Molfino 126, t 0185 773 835 (€€€). Sit down in the garden and indulge in Ligurian classics; including exceptional *pansotti* in walnut sauce. *Book. Evenings only; closed Wed.*

Vento Ariel, Calata Porto 1, t 0185 771 080, *www.ventoariel.it* (€€). Tasty fish freshly plucked from the nearby sea is served at this friendly place in the bustling port. Try the anchovies, their speciality. *Closed Wed.*

The Promontory of Portofino and Golfo del Tigullio

The steep, emerald Promontory of Portofino, covered with lush Mediterranean vegetation and kissed by the transparent turquoise waters of the Gulf of Paradise, is encompassed by the **Parco Naturale di Portofino**, one of the loveliest spots on the Riviera, crisscrossed by well-marked paths that are hard to resist. One point of departure is **Ruta**, just above Camogli, where you can park near the church of **San Rocco** (with a statue of man's best friend, honoured every 16 August with an International Prize of Canine Fidelity and Goodness); from here a path descends to the pretty 12th-century church of **San Nicolò di Capodimonte** and **Punta Chiappa**, which is a tiny fishing hamlet on a rocky toe in the sea, famous for the changing colours of the water.

You can also drive up to **Portofino Vetta**, with its famous hotel; the views from here are simply stunning. An hour's walk will take you to the summit of **Monte di Portofino** (2,001ft), or you can walk down in two hours to San Fruttuoso (alternatively, a two-hour hike from Portofino village, or catch a boat from Camogli or Portofino).

San Fruttuoso, a minute seaside hamlet with a beach, enveloped in palms, flowers and olives, is named after its delightful Benedictine abbey, its arches partly buried in the sand. The abbey was founded in 711 by the bishop of Tarragona as he fled Spain from the Moors, carrying with him the bones of the 3rd-century martyrs St Fructuosus and two deacons in his bag, and was later owned by the Doria; in 1562, Andrea Doria built the **Torre dei Doria**

Abbey
t 0185 772 703; open Mar, April and Oct Tues–Sun 10–4; May–Sept daily 10–6; Dec–Feb Sat, Sun and hols only 10–4; closed Nov; adm

Getting to and around Portofino

For Portofino, leave your car at Santa Margherita; **buses** (no. 82) from the station make the journey every 20 minutes or so. From Santa Margherita the **Servizi Maritimo del Tigullio**, t 0185 284 670, *www.traghettiportofino.it*, has daily boats to San Fruttuoso, Portofino and Rapallo, and in summer to the Aquarium in Genoa, the Cinque Terre and Portovenere.

to defend it from Turkish corsairs. In 1983 the family donated the abbey to the FAI (the Italian National Trust); you can visit the pretty 11th-century church, with its Byzantine-style cupola and the tiny cloister housing black and white striped vaults where seven members of the Doria family were buried from 1275 to 1305. Another tomb belongs to local heroine Maria Avegno, who drowned trying to save the crew of the English steamship *Croesus* that sank here in 1855. A small museum in the abbey houses documents and items relating to the monks.

Another sight, best appreciated by divers or through the bathyscopes on boats is the bronze **Cristo degli Abissi** (Christ of the Depths), eight fathoms deep, set up in 1954 as a protector of all who work underwater.

The Golfo del Tigullio: Santa Margherita, Portofino and Rapallo

The Golfo del Tigullio, on the east of the promontory of Portofino, is just as lovely as its paradisiacal counterpart to the west – a steep coastal garden plunging into the sea scalloped out here and there with coves and beaches – and space for three of the Italian Riviera's most beautiful and glamorous resorts.

Santa Margherita Ligure

Santa Margherita, with its beautiful harbour and mild climate, was a popular 19th-century British winter hidy-hole; now 'Santa' becomes trendier by the year with its garden villas, beaches, boutiques and nightlife. Once two villages, the town became one in the 19th century and was named after **Santa Margherita d'Antiochia**, a rococo extravaganza full of 17th-century Italian and Flemish art. Near here, you can wander through the luxuriant Parco di **Villa Durazzo**. The villa, built just after 1560, is decorated with architectural frescoes and stuccoes, Murano chandeliers, chinoiseries and tapestries. Just below, towards the sea, the grand Baroque church of **San Giacomo di Corte** has frescoes by Nicolò Barabino. On the shore, near the ruins of the castle, the **Chiesa dei Cappuccini** contains one of Liguria's oldest sculptures: a 12th-century *Virgin Enthroned*.

Parco di Villa Durazzo
t 0185 205 449; villa open Tues–Sun 9.30–12.30 and 2.30–4.30 in winter, 9–6 in summer; adm; park open daily 9–7, till 5 in winter

The 9km stretch of the S227 to Portofino is one of the most beautiful on the coast, a meandering ribbon of asphalt roughly one-and-a-half cars wide. On the way it passes the enchanting Abbazia di San Girolamo at **La Cervara**. Founded in 1361, the abbey was visited by a host of medieval celebrities from Petrarch to St Catherine of Siena, and French king François I, unwillingly, when he was imprisoned here in 1525. In 1937 it became a private residence and has been carefully restored, along with its lovely monumental Italian gardens, the only ones of their kind surviving in Liguria, with pergolas and box hedges, and a rare old pepper tree. **Paraggi**, further along, is Portofino's beach – an enchanting patch of sand on a crystal-clear turquoise sea.

Abbazia di San Girolamo
toll-free t 800 652 110, www.cervara.it; guided tours Mar–Oct first and third Sun of the month at 10, 11 and 12; book; adm

Portofino

🐾 Portofino

At the end of the Second World War, a Nazi officer was ordered to blow up Portofino, and he had it all mined when the wife of Baron Alfons Von Schwarzenstein, residing in the Castello San Giorgio, talked him into disobeying his orders. He had to agree with her; it would be too sad. And she wasn't even German: she was Jeannie Watt from Glasgow.

She deserves a statue. One of Italy's most romantic nooks, Portofino has the looks and seclusion that long made it a favourite for yachties and paparazzi-shy celebrities. This exclusiveness still exists to a certain extent – although Portofino was linked, unwillingly, to the world by road, no new development has been allowed to come with it since 1935. And, although thousands pour in each weekend and every summer to people-watch in the exquisite *piazzetta* or walk in the cypress-studded hills, in the evening the residents of the hillside villas and fortunate guests of the handful of hotels descend to reclaim Portofino as their own.

Portofino was the Roman *Portus Delphini*, site of a *mithraeum* (a sanctuary dedicated to the Persian god Mithras, popular with Roman soldiers). The *mithraeum* was replaced by the church of **San Giorgio**, rebuilt in 1950 after war damage but still supposedly housing relics of the defrocked soldiers' saint George; as often as not there's a cat sleeping on or under the altar. And if she didn't get a statue, there is a memorial on the side of the church to Portofino's heroine, Jeannie Watt Von Mumm, who lies buried in the adjacent Protestant cemetery. Further up her former residence, the **Castello di San Giorgio** – built in the 1500s, converted into a residence in the 1890s by the British consul, Montague Yeats Brown, the 'discoverer' of Portofino, then reconverted into a castle – affords enchanting views of the little port. Another lovely walk, beyond the castle, is to Punta del Capo and the **Faro**, the old lighthouse, taking in magnificent views of the Gulf of Tigullio through the pines.

Castello di San Giorgio
open Wed–Mon 10–6, till 5 in winter; adm

Rapallo

Rapallo, in a marvellous setting at the innermost pocket of the Gulf of Tigullio, was another resort first appreciated by Brits in the 19th century, who basked in its mild year-round climate and bathed at its fairly good beach – genteel days still recalled along the **Lungomare Vittorio Veneto**, with its grand hotels and villas.

Rapallo counts among its blessing several things Portofino lacks: affordable hotels, the **Circolo Golf e Tennis**, with a picturesque 18-hole golf course under the ruined Abbazia di Valle Christi, indoor pool and riding stables. The new **Museo A. e C. Gaffoglio** in a former convent on Piazzale Libia contains the eclectic personal collection of Attilo Gaffoglio – goldwork and ivories, porcelain, and pieces by Fabergé. Rapallo's bijou **castle**, surrounded by the harbour's waters, was built after the notorious pirate Dragut destroyed Rapallo in the 1550s; it now holds exhibitions. Further along the shore, **Villa Tigullio** by the Parco Casale houses an international library and the **Museo del Merletto**, dedicated to the town's age-old art of lace-making, going back to the 16th century – one piece is 26ft long. If you want to take some home, visit **Emilio Gandolfi** in Piazza Cavour 1. Don't miss a ride on Rapallo's *funivia*, which ascends 7,707ft in seven minutes to the 16th-century **Santuario di Montallegro**, built where the Virgin appeared to a farmer, leaving a Byzantine icon. The striped façade is neogothic; inside there's a *pala* of the *Pietà* by Luca Cambiaso, and hundreds of *ex votos* left by grateful sailors. Any sinner can enjoy heavenly views of the Gulf of Paradise.

Rapallo was the home of Max Beerbohm, who lived in the Villino Chiaro and attracted a literary circle to the resort; it is also a favourite venue for conferences – the Treaty of Rapallo was signed at the **Villa Spinola** in 1920, setting the border between Italy and Yugoslavia and normalizing relations between Germany and the Soviet Union. The villa lies along the Santa Margherita road, not far from **San Michele di Pagana**, a hamlet with firework-popping festivals in July and September, and a church containing an excellent *Crucifixion* by Van Dyck and a *Nativity* by Luca Giordano.

Zoagli

Merging with Rapallo to the east, Zoagli was another casualty of the war and rebuilt after 1945, but it's no fashion victim; the town still produces handmade patterned velvets, silks and damasks just as it did in the Middle Ages, although now people prefer to use them for dressing their furniture. Two companies are open for visits: the **Seterie Cordani** and **Giuseppe Gaggioli**.

A path cut in the rock follows the shore from the beach, with lovely views over the gulf, which is home to another underwater statue, the **Madonna del Mare** by Marian Hastianatte (1996). Just

---

Circolo Golf e Tennis
Via G. Mameli 377,
t 0185 261 777

Museo A. e C. Gaffoglio
t 0185 234 497; open Tues, Wed, Fri and Sat 3–6.30, Sun 10–12; adm

Museo del Merletto
t 0185 63305; open Tues, Wed, Fri and Sat 3–6, Thurs 10–11.30, Sun open on request; adm

Emilio Gandolfi
www.gandolfilaces.com

Funivia
t 0185 52341; runs daily 9–12.30 and 2–6, or until 8 if there is the demand

Seterie Cordani
Via S. Pietro 21,
t 0185 259 141,
www.seterie cordani.com; open 9–6, closed Tues; in Nov and Dec Sun and hols 2–6 only; visit to looms by appointment

Giuseppe Gaggioli
Via Aurelia 208/a,
t 0185 259 057,
www.tessitura gaggioli.it; guided tours by appointment

10

Riviera di Levante | The Promontory of Portofino and Golfo del Tigullio: The Golfo del Tigullio

off the Via Aurelia towards Chiavari, the late 15th-century **Santuario della Madonna delle Grazie** shelters a Flemish Renaissance statue of the *Virgin* and some fine frescoes, especially a *Last Judgement* by Luca Cambiaso.

Where to Stay and Eat around Portofino

San Fruttuoso ✉ 16030

*Da Giovanni, Via San Fruttuoso 10, t 0185 770 047 (€€€). The only place to stay here: a small, charming hotel/**restaurant** with only seven rooms. *Closed Mon.*

Santa Margherita ✉ 16038

ⓘ Santa Margherita Ligure ›
Via XXV Aprile 2/h, t 0185 287 485, www.apttigullio. liguria.it

*****Imperiale Palace, Via Pagana 19, on the edge of town, t 0185 288 991, www.hotelimperiale.com (€€€€€). A villa of 1889, converted into a hotel in the early 1900s; in 1922, the Weimar Republic and Russia signed the Treaty of Rapallo in one of the marble- and gilt-encrusted public rooms, officially ending the First World War. Antiques litter the halls, public rooms and pricier bedrooms, and concerts are held in the music room some afternoons. There's a heated outdoor sea-water pool, fitness and beauty centre and sauna, a tropical garden, private beach, seafront terrace. The **restaurant** is rich and refined and leads onto a wonderful breakfast room overlooking the garden.

****Grand Hotel Miramare, Via Milite Ignoto 30, t 0185 287 013, www.grandhotelmiramare.it (€€€€€–€€€€). Where Laurence Olivier and Vivien Leigh honeymooned in 1947; a palatial, Liberty-style hotel from the early 1900s. Surrounded by a delightful garden, with a heated salt-water pool (and private beach across the road), it has lovely rooms, many with fine views of the gulf. During autumn and winter, cooking courses are available.

**Fasce, Via Luigi Bozzo 3, t 0185 286 435, www.hotelfasce.it (€€€). Homey and good for families, with fresh modern rooms, free bikes, modem plugs, parking and a small garden. Check the website for special offers. *Open Mar–Christmas.*

***La Vela, Corso N. Cuneo 21, t 0185 284 771, www.lavela.it (€€€–€€). A 19th-century castle villa a bit above town, a 10-minute walk from the centre, with a friendly, intimate atmosphere, roof terrace and sea views. Breakfast but no restaurant.

***Minerva, Via Maragliano 34/d, t 0185 286 073, www.hminerva.it (€€€–€€). A good-value, up-to-date hotel near the sea, with a good **restaurant** (open to non-guests).

***Conte Verde, Via Zara 1, t 0185 287 139, www.hotelconteverde.it (€€€–€€). A big white villa in the centre with a small terrace, garden and bar, plus a small gym (with jacuzzi) and bikes for guests. Breakfast, but no restaurant, although discounts for nearby restaurants are available.

**Europa, Via Trento 5, t 0185 287 187, www.hoteleuropa-sml.it (€€€–€€). Recently refurbished, central little family-run hotel close to the Villa Durazzo.

La Mela Secca B&B, Via Tre Scalini 30, up at S. Lorenzo della Costa, t 0185 286 655 (€€). En-suite rooms in an elegantly refurbished country house with sea views; meals made with farm ingredients on offer. *Two nights' minimum stay; no credit cards.*

La Stalla dei Frati, Via G. Pino 27, 3km up at Nozarego, t 0185 289 447 (€€€€). A narrow hairpinning road leads up to a villa with stupendous views. Excellent *antipasti, fettucini* and desserts. *Closed Mon, Tues lunch and Nov.*

Ardiciocca, Via Maragliano, t 0185 281 312 (€€€€). For the best pesto and *trenette* in Santa Margherita, and much more. *Closed Mon.*

Oca Bianca, Via XXV Aprile 21, t 0185 288 411 (€€€€). Sick of seafood? Not a mention of it on the menu of this little restaurant; come for a fat steak or lamb or even ostrich, but be sure to book. *Closed Mon, Tues–Thurs lunch and Jan–mid-Feb.*

(i) **Portofino** >
Via Roma 35,
t 0185 269 024,
www.apttigullio.
liguria.it

⭐ **Da Puny** >>

(i) **Rapallo** >>
Lungomare Vittorio
Veneto 7, t 0185 230 346,
www.apttigullio.
liguria.it

Portofino ✉ 16034

*****Splendido**, Viale Baratta 16, **t** 0185 267 801, *www.hotelsplendido. com* (€€€€€). The management believe they run the best hotel in Liguria, if not Italy, and few dare to argue. The views alone, of olive- and cypress-clad hills framing the town and the sea beyond, are worth the huge rates. Built in 1901, the updated bedrooms are sumptuous, the **restaurant** refined and the breakfast terrace delightful. Swim in the heated outdoor pool or go out in the hotel's speedboat. If you are still not impressed, the staff will point to their wall of fame, with signed photographs of Churchill, Groucho, Taylor and Burton, Bogart and Bacall, the Duke of Windsor and Wallis Simpson, Madonna and others who found the Splendido to their taste. *Half-board only. Closed Dec–Feb.*

****Splendido Mare**, Via Roma 2, **t** 0185 267 802 (€€€€€). The Spendido's sibling by the sea on the Piazza. Less grand, livelier and slightly cheaper with no half board but a delightful restaurant, the **Chuflay Bar** (€€€€). A shuttle service links the two hotels. *Closed Dec–Feb.*

****Nazionale**, Vico Dritto 3, **t** 0185 269 575, *www.nazionaleportofino.com* (€€€€€). Smack on the port, with a slightly faded charm. The best rooms have Venetian furniture and overlook the harbour. No restaurant.

****Piccolo**, Via Duca degli Abruzzi 31, **t** 0185 269 015 (€€€€€). Lovely villa-hotel on the sea, the only one with a private beach.

****San Giorgio**, Via del Fondaco 11, **t** 0185 26991, *www.portofinohsg.it* (€€€€€). Airy rooms with parquet floors. *Closed Nov–Feb.*

***Eden**, Vico Dritto 18, **t** 0185 269 091, *www.hoteledenportofino.com* (€€€€). Intimate, charming establishment in the centre, with a fine garden and good **restaurant** offering fish and Ligurian specialities.

Il Pitosforo, Molo Umberto I 9, **t** 0185 269 020 (€€€€). An experience. A tree grows out of the dining room, and one wall is lined with a collection of spirits from around the world. At 10pm all the lights are switched off to highlight the magical view of the port. *Book. Open eves only; closed Mon, Tues and Oct–Mar.*

Da Puny, Piazza Martiri dell'Olivetta 5, **t** 0185 269 037 (€€€€). Wonderful owner, delicious pasta and seafood for starters, and well-prepared main fish dishes, like sea bass in salt. *Book well in advance. No credit cards. Closed Thurs, and Jan.*

Taverna del Marinaio, Piazza Martiri dell'Olivetta 36, **t** 0185 269 103 (€€€). Relaxed and convivial, with tables under a portico. *Closed Tues.*

El Portico, Via Roma 21, **t** 0185 269 239 (€€€). For tasty pizza and pesto dishes.

Rapallo ✉ 16035

*****Excelsior Palace**, Via San Michele di Pagana 8, **t** 0185 230 666, *www. excelsiorpalace.thi.it* (€€€€€). Built in 1901 (when it housed modern Italy's first casino) and set on the cliffs overlooking both the Rapallo and Portofino bays, the Excelsior reopened in 2004 after a 20-year closure; it has an indoor and infinity pool, beach terraces and the **Eden Roc** restaurant (*closed Oct–May*) for candlelit dinners.

****Eurotel**, Via Aurelia Ponente 22, **t** 0185 60981, *www.eurotelrapallo.it* (€€€€). On the outskirts of town, with great views, large rooms with balconies, smart lounge areas, a **restaurant** and a heated outdoor pool (open 15 May–early Oct). *Free parking. Closed mid-Oct to mid-Mar.*

***Riviera**, Piazza IV Novembre 2, **t** 0185 50248, *www.hotelriviera rapallo.com* (€€€€–€€€). Opened in 1905 (and hosted Hemingway in 1923), this converted villa near the sea has been prettily remodelled; it has a popular **restaurant** in the front offering a gourmet Piedmontese menu (as well as traditional Ligurian fare) and a garden in the back. Special golfing holiday offers are available.

***Italia e Lido**, Lungomare Castello 1, **t** 0185 50492, *www.italiaelido.com* (€€€–€€). Handsome historic hotel on the seafront promenade, with a private beach and **restaurant**.

***Bandoni**, Via Marsala 24, **t** 0185 50423, *www.turismoinliguria.it* (€). Comfortable, simple hotel in the centre.

Osteria O Bansin, Via Venezia 105, t 0185 231 119 (€€). Since 1907, authentic osteria and wonderfully good, local food. *Closed Sun eve and Mon, Sun lunch in summer.*

U Giancu, up at S. Massimino 78, t 0185 260505 (€€€€–€€€). A few miles out of town up among the olive groves. A proper family restaurant where every cranny is filled with cartoon characters. Chef Fausto Onesto doesn't play around with the food, however – it is excellent; try one of his vegetable tarts. *Best to book. Open eves only; closed Wed.*

Zoagli ✉ 16030

★★★Zoagli, Piazza Stazione 5, t 0185 259 048, *www.hotelzoagli.it* (€€). Family-run B&B by the station, separated from the sea walk and beach by an underpass.

Entertainment and Nightlife around Portofino

In Portofino, the port-side **La Gritta** (with its barge-like extention into the sea), glamorous in the resort's studied, laid-back expensive style, has seen just about every celebrity under the sun since 1954.

For those with lighter wallets, Santa Margherita offers a greater selection. **Bar Colombo**, Via Pescino 13, has a beautiful Liberty-style interior. Ballroom dancing (*ballo liscio*) is big in Rapallo, at **Privilege**, Via Costaguta 6, and **S.M.S. Aurora**, Via Volta 21. The American bar **ZI Pier Café**, Via Avenaggi 17, also located in Rapallo, features live music on Friday nights.

Chiavari, Lavagna and Sestri Levante

At Chiavari, the coast flattens out for the last time on the Riviera di Levante. This was the stamping ground of the Fieschi family, which produced a pair of popes and the leader of the conspiracy against Andrea Doria, who might have succeeded if he hadn't fallen overboard in his heavy armour at the key moment, and drowned.

Chiavari

Atmospheric Chiavari was born on 19 October 1178 as a colony of Genoa, and laid out in a grid of porticoed streets. Once the capital of the Levante, and famed for its crafts – wooden and straw Chiavari chairs, and macramé fringes for towels and tablecloths (an art brought back by the town's sailors from the Middle East) – tourism is now the main earner, in spite of the train tracks between the town and its big sandy beach.

Life in Chiavari focuses on **Piazza Mazzini**, with a lively morning market, an old citadel tower and stern medieval palaces. A few streets away at Via Costaguta 4, the **Palazzo Rocca** was designed by Bartolomeo Bianco in 1629 and now hosts the **Museo Archeologico**, with artifacts from the nearby 8th-century BC necropolis that demonstrate trade links with the Phoenicians, Greeks and Egyptians, plus Etruscan pots and jewellery; it also houses the **Civica Galleria**, with Baroque paintings by Domenico Piola, Orazio De Ferrari, and furniture. The Greek temple façade of Chiavari's **cathedral** (1907) replaces an earlier version, built to house a painting of the *Virgin* (1493) by Benedetto Borzone that

Museo Archeologico
t 0185 320 829; open Tues–Sat and the 2nd and 4th Sun of each month 9–1.30

Civica Galleria
t 0185 308577; open Sat, Sun and hols 10–12 and 4–7

Museo Diocesano
*Piazza Dell'Orto 7, t 0185
59051; open Wed and
Sun 10–12; adm*

Caffè Defilla
*t 0185 309 823;
closed Mon*

was hung on a garden wall and immediately began working
miracles. It also has two fine sculptural groups by Anton Maria
Maragliano (the *Temptation of St Anthony* and *St Francis Receiving
the Stigmata*). Nearby, the **Museo Diocesano** has art from the
Abbazia di Cervara, Genoese Baroque art and a silk canopy made in
China in the late 1500s. Afterwards, treat yourself to an ice cream
or pastry at **Caffè Defilla**, founded in 1883, at Via Garibaldi 4.

Lavagna

Several bridges span the broad bed of the Entella to link Chiavari
to Lavagna; today the two towns can seem like one great traffic
jam, but in the Middle Ages they were quite distinct. Lavagna was
the fief of the Fieschi, a litigious family who began to play a
leading role in Genoa in the 12th century. Their fortunes soared
when Sinibaldo Fieschi became Pope Innocent IV (1243–54), the
arch-enemy of Emperor Frederick II Stupor Mundi. His nephew
Ottobono was elected pope in 1276 as Adrian V, and although he
only survived a month in office, Dante placed him in Purgatory
because he was Genoese. Innocent's brother, Opizzo Fieschi,
married the Sienese Countess Bianca dei Bianchi in 1230 in
Lavagna, and made such a splash by ordering a cake large enough
to provide a slice for each of his subjects that the party is annually
re-enacted every 14 August, climaxing in the eating of the 1,500kg
Torta dei Fieschi.

Lavagna's long beach has brought it much new building, but its
medieval core is intact. Its old crafts are still alive, apparent on
Thursdays, when the weekly market sells items in wood, iron and
slate (Lavagna has so much of the latter that it gave its name to
'blackboard' in Italian). The Torre Civica contains the **Collezione
Alloisio**, with archaeological odds and ends.

Collezione Alloisio
*t 0185 3671; open mid-
July–mid-Sept Tues–Sun
6.30–10.30pm; rest of
year by prior booking*

**Basilica di
San Salvatore
dei Fieschi**
*open 8.30–5.30,
6.30 in summer*

If his brother is remembered with a cake, Innocent IV is
remembered in the beautiful church he founded in 1244, the
Basilica di San Salvatore dei Fieschi, a mile or so up from Lavagna
by a vineyard. Romanesque with inklings of Gothic, it has an
enormous tower, a lovely marble rose window, and a striped
façade; the dimly lit interior is solemn and spiritual, bare of
decorations (except for a Renaissance fresco in the lunette over the
door, showing the Crucifixion with the Madonna, St John, Innocent
IV and Ottobono Fieschi). In the charming piazza by the church
stands the black-and-white-striped 12th-century **Fieschi palace**,
rebuilt after the Turks wrecked it in 1567.

The *Entroterra*: into the Fief of the Fieschi

Behind the busy coast, the *entroterra* remains a world apart, of
timeless farming hamlets in the Apennines – on the whole, more a
place to be than to see. From Chiavari, a winding road follows the

Abbazia di Borzone
open until dusk

Entella up to **Borzonasca**, a main centre, and beyond through olives and chestnuts to the **Abbazia di Borzone**, founded in this tranquil spot in the 12th century by Benedictines from San Colombano in Bobbio, Emilia. The present abbey was built by the Fieschi in 1244 over the ruins of a late Roman fortress; re-roofed in 1834, the tower, basilica and convent stand lonely by a giant cypress. The altar has a slate tabernacle of 1513.

The S586 winds up, skirting the **Parco dell'Aveto** on the Emilian border; the forests here were used by Genoa's shipbuilders, and cutting trees was strictly regulated by the 1500s. Regulations are still strict (much of the park is off limits), to the extent that, in recent years, even wolves have made a comeback. **Cabanne**, up the road, has become a modest summer resort; it belonged to one of Liguria's minor feudal families, the Della Cella. Their residence is opposite the church, which proudly houses two fine paintings purchased from Genoa's Santa Maria di Castello: the *Deposition* and *Resurrection*, attributed to Agostino Carracci and Giovanni Lanfranco. **Rezzoaglio**, 8km up the road, was another Della Cella property, and has a lovely medieval stone bridge.

At the village of **Magnasco**, you can detour south to the pretty little Lake Lame, or continue up to the mostly modern **Santo Stefano d'Aveto**, where inhabitants of the Riviera di Levante head for snow and a bit of skiing at 3,300ft. Santo Stefano's landmark is the ruined but still imposing 13th-century **Castello Malaspina**.

From Lavagna, if you continue above the Basilica dei Fieschi, you'll find the Ligurian village with the shortest name, **Ne**, and some good cheap restaurants. You can learn all about magnesium mining at the Gambatesa mine with **Geo Adventures**, complete with a ride on a genuine mining train into working galleries.

Geo Adventures
*t 0185 338 876,
www.miniera
gambatesa.it; tours
Feb–Nov Wed–Sun 9–5,
daily in Aug, closed 4,
24, 25, 31 Dec and 1 Jan;
book in advance; adm
exp*

Sestri Levante: Bays of Silence and Fables

The railroad delves inland from the coast here, leaving **Sestri Levante** with its huge palms and sandy beaches one of the happiest resorts on the Riviera di Levante. Roman *Segesta Tigulliorum*, it grew up at the junction of the Via Aurelia and the Via Aemilia Scauri. Its lovely, curving peninsula, called the Isola, once upon a time really was an islet and divides the lovely little **Bay of Silence** from what Hans Christian Andersen himself named the **Bay of Fables** during a stay in 1833, with a bigger sandy beach and more than its share of development. The private garden on the Isola belongs to the Hotel del Castello, but you can take a footpath to the 12th-century **Marconi tower** where, in 1934, Marconi experimented with ultra-short radio-wave transmissions and UHF and VHF 'blind' navigation. The peninsula also has the churches of **San Nicolò dell'Isola** (1151), with a Renaissance façade, and **Santa Caterina**, which was bombed in 1944; a statue of the saint stands in the ruins.

Down on the isthmus, **Piazza Matteotti** is the main crossroads, where the 17th-century Palazzo Durazzo Pallavicini houses the town hall, and the Baroque basilica of **Santa Maria di Nazareth** houses a 12th-century *Crucifix*. The **Galleria Rizzi**, by the Bay of Silence at Via Cappuccini 8, contains art by the Florentine, Emilian and Ligurian schools, including two 15th-century female wooden busts from Tuscany and works by Denis Calvaert and Sebastiano Ricci. Along picturesque Via XXV Aprile/Corso Colombo, the tall tower of the neogothic **Palazzo Fascie** advises, like the temple of Apollo at Delphi, *Conosci Te Stesso* ('Know thyself'); in the same vein, Sestri also has an inordinate number of machines offering to tell you your weight and horoscope. If Sestri's beaches are too busy, and they can be in summer, there's another just east at **Riva-Trigoso**, next to the shipyards.

The *comune* of Sestri encompasses the **Val Gromolo**, an area rich in minerals from gold and silver to copper and magnesium. **Libiola** was the centre for copper mining; a legacy of its geological wealth is an exceptionally colourful *risseu* pavement in front of the church, using black, white, brown and red pebbles.

Galleria Rizzi
t 0185 41300; open April–Oct Sun 10–1; May–Sept also Wed 4–7; July and Aug also Fri and Sat 9.30pm–11.30pm; adm

Activities around Chiavari, Lavagna and Sestri Levante

For rafting, canoeing or floating in rubber rings down the Vara, contact the **Ente Parco di Montemarcello**, t 0187 691 071, *www.parcomagra.it*.

Where to Stay and Eat around Chiavari, Lavagna and Sestri Levante

(i) **Chiavari >**
Corso Assarotti 1, t 0185 325 198, www.apttigullio. liguria.it

(★) **La Brinca >>**

(i) **Lavagna**
Piazza Torino, t 0185 395 070, www.apttigullio. liguria.it

Chiavari ✉ 16043

Lord Nelson Pub, Corso Valparaiso 25, t 0185 302 595 (€€€€). Don't let 'pub' fool you. Five suites upstairs have sea views and jacuzzis; there's a cellar filled with 16,000 bottles, a bar modelled on the HMS Victory and a gourmet restaurant, serving ravioli with smoked ricotta and shrimp, *dentice* with pine nuts, olives and potatoes, and exquisite desserts. *Closed Wed and 1–15 Nov.*

★★★Monte Rosa, Via M. Marinetti 6, t 0185 300 321, *www.hotelmonte rosa.com* (€€€–€€). A welcoming hotel in the historic centre since 1909, with a decent **restaurant** and shuttle to the airport or the port. Free bike hire.

★★★Zia Piera, Via Marina Giulia 25, t 0185 307 686 (€€). Modern, refurbished hotel right on the beach, with a big solarium by the sea.

Luchin, Via Bighetti 51, t 0185 301 063 (€). Classic trattoria with a blackboard menu, famous for its *farinata. Closed Sun.*

Ca' Peo, Via dei Caduti 80, Strada Panoramica, in Leivi, 6km up from Chiavari, t 0185 319 696, *www.capeo.it* (€€€€). Elegant octagonal dining room with views over the hills, and delicately prepared food, featuring ingredients like radicchio from Treviso and truffles from Alba. They also have two apartments and three suites in another building, if you don't want to drive back. *Booking essential. Closed Mon, Tues and Wed lunch and Nov.*

Ne ✉ 16040

La Brinca, Loc. Campo di Ne 58, t 0185 337 480 (€€€). One of Liguria's finest restaurants lies at the end of a little road through the forest from Ne specializing strictly in local recipes and olive oils. Wine list of over 1,500 bottles. *Reservations only. Closed Mon, and lunch exc Sat, Sun and hols.*

Antica Trattoria dei Mosto, Piazza dei Mosto 15/1, **t** 0185 337 502 (€€€). Early 19th-century inn on the road between the Riviera and Po, now an excellent restaurant serving home-made pasta and other dishes of the Valgraveglia. *Closed Wed and mid-Sept to mid-Oct.*

ⓘ **Sestri Levante >**
Piazza S. Antonio 10, t 0185 457 011, www.apttigullio. liguria.it

Sestri Levante ✉ 16039

****Villa Balbi**, Viale Rimembranza 1, **t** 0185 42941, *www.villabalbi.it* (€€€€€–€€€€). Stately palace on the sea, built in the 17th century and full of treasures: a library and a room decorated entirely with paintings of fish, oak-beamed bedrooms and antique-laden public rooms. Much of the original garden remains, including a camphor tree in the middle of the **restaurant**. It also has a pool and private beach. *Closed Nov–Mar.*

****Grand Hotel dei Castelli**, Via Penisola 26, **t** 0185 487 220, *www.hoteldeicastelli.it* (€€€€). Built in the 1920s at the tip of the Isola peninsula on the site of a Genoese castle, and constructed from the castle's stone. The views of both bays are magnificent, especially from the dining terrace. There's also a natural sea-water pool cut into the rock. *Closed Nov–Mar.*

****Miramare**, Via Cappellini 9, **t** 0185 480 855, *www.miramare sestrilevante.com* (€€€€). In an idyllic location on the Bay of Silence, with a decent terrace **restaurant** and its own beach; most rooms have sea views.

***Helvetia**, Via Cappuccini 43, **t** 0185 41175, *www.hotelhelvetia.it* (€€€€–€€€). Right on the Bay of Silence, a welcoming, cosy hotel with a large beach terrace and bar for

lazing. Breakfast buffet and free bikes for guests. *No pets. Three-day minimum stays.*

***Mira**, Viale Rimembranza 15, **t** 0185 41576, *www.hotelmira.com* (€€€–€€). Family-run hotel with rooms with a view and a **restaurant** serving an excellent *riso marinara. Closed Mon.*

*Villa Jolanda**, Via Pozzetto 15, **t** 0185 485 122, *www.villaiolanda.com* (€€). Good budget hotel; children very welcome.

Fiammenghilla Fieschi, Via Pestella 6, **t** 0185 481 041 (€€€€). Seafood and traditional Ligurian cuisine. A great place to try marinated swordfish, lobster, *focaccia* or *pansotti. Booking advisable. Open evenings only except Sun. Closed Mon and first 10 days of Feb and Nov.*

El Pescador, Via Pilade Queirdo 1, **t** 0185 42888 (€€€€). Excellent seafood fresh from the adjacent sea. *Closed Tues and mid-Dec–Feb.*

Polpo Mario, Via XXV Aprile 163, **t** 0185 480 203 (€€€). Cosy and popular with locals, with generous portions of good food. *Book. Closed Mon.*

Varese Ligure ✉ 19028

***Amici**, Via Garibaldi 80, **t** 0187 842 139 (€). Simple hotel and excellent **restaurant**, serving traditional dishes based on mostly organic ingredients. *Closed Wed except in summer.*

Il Pruno Selvatico, Loc. Groppo Marzo 70/c , **t** 0187 842 382 or mobile **t** 334 338 9691, *www.ilprunoselvatico.it* (€). Cosy, high-altitude *agriturismo* (35-minute drive to Sestri Levante), and meals of farm ingredients, if you book ahead. *Closed Dec–late Mar.*

The Val di Vara

There are two routes east from Sestri Levante to La Spezia. The first, by way of the Val di Vara, runs parallel to the coast along the River Vara (a favourite for white-water rafting). For millennia the road from points east of Genoa ran here, as does the *autostrada*, shunning the cliffs of the Cinque Terre. The ancient Ligurians had several *castellari* along the route; on houses along the valley you may see little rough stone heads with primitive faces (*testine apotropaiche*), used to keep evil away, similar to the *more de peira* in Piedmont (*see* p.265). On a more delicate level, the Val di Vara is famous for its *corzetti* (or *croxetti*), thin pasta discs stamped with arabesques or floral patterns, and served with pesto or a light sauce designed to accent the relief. Once a favourite dish of the Genoese nobility, they are almost too pretty to eat.

Varese Ligure

From Sestri a bus heads inland along the tortuous S523 to **Varese Ligure**, an organic farming and cheese-making centre, and chief town of the Val di Vara. Varese's strategic location (it lies below two mountain passes into Emilia) was behind a late 15th-century special offer by the Fieschi: they would donate the land and protect any merchant who built a house and shop in a ring around the market. Now known as the **Borgo Rotondo**, the sole entrance is protected by the Fieschi's 15th-century **castle**, a striking building with a beautiful slate roof. Nearby, the church of **SS. Teresa d'Avila e Filippo Neri** has an elegant façade of the 1700s and a painting by Gregorio De Ferrari. The road north of Varese towards the Passo di Cento is especially lovely and lush.

Downriver, off either side of the Vara Valley, picturesque hamlets snooze in the chestnut forests, half-forgotten places such as Groppo, Sesta Godano and Carro. Even **Cornice**, a panoramic medieval village in the main valley, is all but abandoned. **Brugnato** has a centre even odder than Varese's Borgo Rotondo, laid out like pincers, gripping the church of **SS. Pietro, Lorenzo and Colombano**. This has a strawberry parfait bell tower, built over a Palaeochristian necropolis, and a Benedictine abbey that flourished under the Lombards, whose abbots warred with the bishops of Luni until 1133 when they themselves were made bishops. A fresco inside shows San Colombano, the Irish founder of the great abbey at Bobbio in Emilia, a strong influence in this part of Liguria.

Further down the valley, fortified **Beverino**, a free *comune* since 1247, was an 'independent' island in the Genoese republic. The bell in its campanile was hung in 1492 and still rings. North, **Calice al Cornoviglio** is the capital of its own little valley, and has a **Castello Doria Malaspina** with a fat tower containing a little pinacoteca. To the south, **Pignone**, with a striking stone bridge, takes pride in growing the best onions in Liguria. The Pignone-Levanto mule path has been restored, for a lovely 17.5km trek to the coast.

Castello Doria
Malaspina
t 0187 936 309; open Mon, Wed, Fri 9–12, Sat and Sun 3.30–5.30

Sestri Levante to La Spezia and the Cinque Terre

While the Via Aurelia and *autostrada* delve inland, the Apennines and coastal tunnels begin in earnest east of Sestri; here the single-lane road tunnel to Moneglia, originally made for steam trains, is

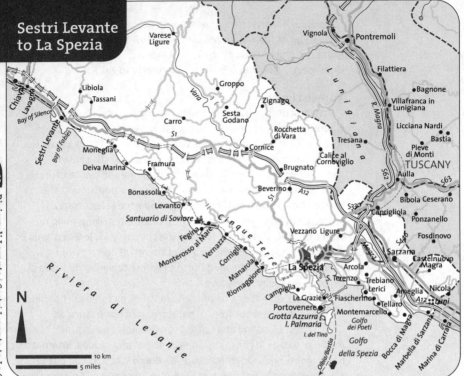

known as the 'Devil's Tube' for its driving thrills and the huge summer traffic jams as people wait for the signals to change. All the villages here have a certain drama, but the stunning Cinque Terre, as these five villages have been known since the Middle Ages, take the cake and the frosting too.

Moneglia, Deiva Marina and Levanto

Here and there the mountains admit sandy strands – one is at **Moneglia** (from the Latin *monellia*, or jewel) with a quiet beach framed by two medieval castles. Moneglia's 18th-century church, **Santa Croce**, has one of the most beautiful of all *risseu* pavements, made in 1822; inside there's a Byzantine cross that washed up on shore, an *Immacolata* by Maragliano, and a *Last Supper* by Luca Cambiaso, who was born here. Santa Croce's chain links were part of the chain that guarded the port of Pisa, a trophy given to Moneglia by Genoa for its help in the victory of Meloria in 1284. There's more art in the church of **San Giorgio** (rebuilt in 1704) on the west end of town: an *Adoration of the Magi*, by Luca Cambiaso, and a *St George* attributed to Rubens.

Deiva Marina is a conglomerate of hamlets: condos by the big beach and more traditional houses and camp sites on the hillside; towards **Framura** are the romantic ruins of a castle of the Da

Passano, destroyed by the Genoese in 1180. The road circles inland to **Costa**, where the striking medieval church of **San Martino de Muris** has stupendous views over the sea. San Martino has three pretty apses, a campanile made from a watchtower and a *Madonna* by Strozzi; the nearby oratory has a handsome Gothic door. Tiny **Framura**, next on the coast, has sandy beaches under the train tracks and a 9th-century Carolingian tower, one of the oldest buildings on the coast.

Bonassola

The road winds inland to descend to **Bonassola**, with fancy villas and a long beach. Back in the 16th century, when the inhabitants lived by fishing, they came up with one of the first forms of insurance in Italy – against being kidnapped by corsairs. The church of **Santa Caterina** is full of *ex votos* and a striking painting by Antonio Discovolo of the *Pious Women at the Foot of the Cross* (1924). The favourite thing to do at sunset is to walk out to the chapel of the Madonna della Punta on the cliff.

Levanto has the best beach in this area, a long sandy strand, and plenty of hotels – it's a favourite base for groups visiting the Cinque Terre. Originally a bailiwick of the Da Passano, it later became a free *comune*, and an ally of Genoa in 1229. The east end of the *centro storico* still has its medieval walls, the little **Castello di San Giorgio** and a **Torre dell'Orologio** of 1265 on top of a stair. The lovely **Loggia** (1256) overlooks central Piazza del Popolo, from where a narrow lane leads up to the 12th-century striped church of **Sant'Andrea**, with a handsome 18th-century rose window and a venerated 15th-century *Crucifixion*. Adjacent, the **Museo della Cultura Materiale** documents work and domestic life from pre-tourism days. Two churches up on Via S. Giacomo have beautiful 15th-century bas reliefs: **Santa Maria della Costa**, its door carved with *St George and the Dragon*, and the **Oratorio di San Giacomo**, with a relief of St James.

Museo della Cultura Materiale
Piazza Massola 4, t 0187 817 776; open June–Sept Tues–Sun 9pm–11pm or by appointment

To the west, the grid of the Borgo Nuovo was laid out in the 17th century, when Genoa made Levanto a local administrative centre; **Piazza Cavour**, in the centre, was once the cloister of a convent. On the road to Bonassola, the Renaissance **Convento dell'Annunziata** has good paintings (the *Miracle of St James* by Strozzi and a *St George* by Pier Francesco Sacchi) and serene cloisters.

Where to Stay and Eat from Moneglia to Levanto

Moneglia >
Corso L. Longhi 32, t 0185 490 576

Moneglia ✉ 16030

***Villa Edera**, Via Venino 12, t 0187 49291, www.villaedera.com (€€€€–€€€). Quiet hotel, 150m from the beach. Rooms are simple but comfortable, with views of the countryside. It also has two pools, a fitness room, gardens and a lovely **restaurant** featuring regional specialities and offering gluten-free meals. Minimum stay three nights. For something special, stay in the neighbouring early 19th-century **Castello di Monleone**, Via Venino 3 (€€€), a folly with its lovely garden full of statues;

(i) **Levanto >>**
Piazza Mazzini 4,
t 0187 808 125

(★) **Nazionale >>**

(i) **Deiva**
Marina >
Lungomare Colombo,
t 0187 815 858

it's a five-room B&B with many original fittings and painted ceilings.
***Piccolo**, Corso L. Longhi 19, t 0185 49374, *www.piccolohotel.it* (€€€–€€). Welcoming hotel with an indoor pool in front of the sea. *Half-board only, minimum stay three days. Closed Nov–Feb.*

Gian Maria, Corso L. Longhi 14, t 0185 49335, *www.albergogianmaria.it* (€€). A little hotel with comfortable, if small, rooms, with balconies.

Deiva Marina ✉ 19013
***Clelia**, Corso Italia 23, t 0187 82626, *www.clelia.it* (€€€–€€). Good for families – 50m from the beach, with a heated pool, playground, two **restaurants** and internet. *Closed Nov to mid-Feb.*
****Lido**, Loc. Fornaci 15, t 0187 815 997, *www.hotelristorantelido.com* (€€). Classic seaside hotel right on the beach, in the hamlet of Framura. Excellent seafood restaurant, too (*closed Nov–Easter and Sat–Sun*).

Bonassola ✉ 19011
***Delle Rose**, Via Garibaldi 8, t 0187 813 713, *www.hoteldellerose bonassola.it* (€€). Well-run, recently renovated family hotel a few steps from the beach; many rooms have sea views, and all have ceiling fans. *Closed Nov–Feb.*
***Moderna**, Via G. Daneri 81, t 0187 813 662, *www.pensionemoderna.it* (€€). Only 50m from the sea, a friendly

and family-run place with a certain old-fashioned charm, and a good garden restaurant.

Levanto ✉ 19015
Stella Maris, Corso Marconi 4, t 0187 808 258, *www.hotelstellamaris.it* (€€€€). The pricier rooms in this 18th-century palace have frescoes and antiques. The price includes a generous breakfast buffet.
***Nazionale**, Via Jacopo da Levanto 20, t 0187 808 102, *www.nazionale.it* (€€€). One of Levanto's oldest and nicest hotels, near the sea, with old-fashioned iron beds.
Villa Margherita B&B, Via Trento e Trieste 31, t 0187 807 212, *www. villamargherita.net* (€€€). Pretty rooms sleeping up to four people in an attractive villa and three gardens dating from 1906; internet and shuttle service to the station. *Closed Jan–Feb.*
Osteria Tumelin, Via D. Grillo 32, t 0187 808 379 (€€€€). Famous for its generous portions of seafood antipasti. *Closed Thurs except in summer and Jan.*
L'Oasi, Piazza Cavour, t 0187 800 856 (€€€). Wonderful pesto, beautiful seafood; be sure to book. *Closed Wed, Jan, Feb and mid-Nov–end Dec.*
Antica Trattoria Centro, Corso Italia 35, t 0187 808 157 (€€€). Excellent *zuppa di pesce* and other fishy treats, and homemade desserts. *Closed Tues.*

The Cinque Terre

(✪) **The Cinque Terre**

Southeast of Levanto, beyond the Punta Mesco, rises the startling vertical coast of the Cinque Terre, its five villages forming a unique ensemble: the concentrated essence of Liguria at its most tenacious. Fishing remains a livelihood, and, amazingly, wine-making – more than 7,000 kilometres of dry-stone terraces ('*cian*') corrugate the precipitous slopes, the labour of generations of men and women, forming one of Europe's most stunning 'artificial' landscapes, hanging over a cobalt blue sea. Once accessible only by sea or by cliff-skirting footpaths, the five villages have maintained much of their charm and character, even though they are far from being undiscovered. Declared a UNESCO World Heritage site in 1997, and a National Park and a Marine Protected Area in 1999, sustainable tourism is now the catchphrase here. University

Getting to and around the Cinque Terre

The easiest way to reach the Cinque Terre is by **train**. Each village has a station, a few minutes apart from each other, and the Cinque Terre National Park runs **electric buses** to the sanctuaries and other lofty places. The **Cinque Terre card** (*www.cinqueterre.com*), available at the stations, is good for one, two, three or seven days of unlimited train and bus travel between Levanto and La Spezia; prices start at €8 a day. Several **boat** lines (*www.navigazionegolfodeipoeti.it*) link La Spezia, Lerici, Portovenere and the Cinque Terre (*see* p.179). Avoid driving if you can. A narrow hairpinning **road** known as La Strada dei Santuari links the Cinque Terre, but distances are long and, once you arrive, parking is difficult at best – although you may find an expensive car park a long walk away. Nearest petrol stations are in Levanto and La Spezia.

You can, of course, most memorably visit the Cinque Terre by foot, on the gorgeous **coastal footpath** that extends all the way from Sestri Levante to Portovenere. The footpaths require a €3 ticket, unless you already have the Cinque Terre card.

students come in the summer to rebuild the *cian* and keep the paths clear. Even so the Cinque Terre have become too popular, perhaps, for their own good; recently the park was the pilot study in a 'Smart History' project for similar areas, to work out ways to maintain the area's integrity in the face of rising use.

Terra was a medieval term for a village, and dates from the refounding of the five; settled in Roman times, the inhabitants fled to the hills until the Saracens were chased away in the 11th century. Despite their impossible location, all the Cinque Terre were doing well enough in the Middle Ages to afford the local status symbol: a sculpted marble rose window for the parish church. Like all good Ligurian towns, each *terra* has a sanctuary high above, inevitably dedicated to the Madonna and inevitably affording astonishing views. Come, if you can, between March and May when the broom is in bloom and the walking a delight, or in September to watch the world's most vertical wine harvest, using specially designed rack monorail train cars to get the grapes up to the road (in the old days, the harvesters had to go down on ropes). The Cinque Terre's DOC white, tangy Vernaccia wines have been praised since the Middle Ages, when Petrarch called them 'most pleasing to Bacchus'; after dinner, try the villages' famous 17 per cent Sciacchetrà, a sweet wine made from raisins.

Westernmost **Monterosso al Mare** is the only Cinque Terre village with sandy beaches (two, in fact), and has the most in the way of hotels. The new half of town, Fegina, grew up by the train station, and is linked to the old by the seaside Via Fegina in ten minutes. A huge cement statue of Neptune known as **Il Gigante** (1910) guards the minute harbour, near the villa where Eugenio Montale (Nobel Prize winner in 1975) lived and wrote. The old town's hill is crowned with the **Convento dei Cappuccini** (1622), encompassing the medieval **Torre Aurora** ('Tower of the Dawn') and church of **San Francesco**, home to some surprisingly fine art for a small town: Strozzi's *La Veronica*, a *Crucifixion* by Van Dyck and two works by Luca Cambiaso; if the guardian is about, ask to visit the cloister to drink in the views. Down below in the *centro storico*, the striped church of **San Giovanni** has an exquisite marble rose window with lacy edges. You can take the bus up to the 18th-century **Sanctuary of Soviore**, built over an 8th-century church (remains under glass), with a doll-like Madonna on the altar. If you have the puff, don't miss the climb up to the breathtaking (literally) **Punta Mesco**.

From Monterosso, it's a momentary train ride, spectacular but nerve-wracking drive or strenuous hour-and-a-half cliff walk to the next *terra* and prettiest town of all, **Vernazza**, the 'Pearl of the Cinque Terre', founded by the Romans on a rocky spit and guarded by two Saracen towers, a striking vision from the footpath above. It is the only one of the five with a little port. Colourful fishermen's houses, many with cafés and restaurants, surround the seaside church, **Santa Margherita d'Antiochia**, built in 1318 on two levels, coyly turning its apse to the charming *piazzetta*.

The hour-and-a-half walk from Vernazza to **Corniglia** is the steepest, but the most beautiful of all the Cinque Terre inter-village paths. Corniglia, unlike the other *terre*, sits over 300ft above the sea and its train station (365 steps below). It has the longest (albeit pebbly and boulder-strewn) beach of the Cinque Terre, at Guvano. The parish church of **San Pietro** was Baroque but keeps its Gothic portal and lovely rose window. Wine-making is the main activity, but it's nothing new here; an amphora bearing its ancient name Cornelius was found at Pompeii. The wine cooperative is on the road to Manarola, at **Groppo**; in May, Corniglio holds a wine festival.

From Corniglia another hour's walk through splendid scenery leads to picture-postcard **Manarola**, its colourful houses piled like a vision on a great black rock by the sea, its colourful fishing boats hoisted up from the exposed 'port' to protect them from the winds. Founded in the 12th century, the walls of the outer houses follow the walls of a castle, demolished in 1273. The Gothic church of **San Lorenzo** has another superb rose window; the interior has been stripped of its Baroque foldirols, but its pebble mosaic was cemented over, too. For Christmas, the hill above is decorated with the biggest illuminated *presepe*, or Christmas crib, in the world, its figures all made out of recycled materials.

Manarola is linked to **Riomaggiore** by the most popular section of the footpath, the **Via dell'Amore** or Lovers' Lane, carved into the cliff – for the not terribly romantic reason of giving railworkers access to the track; to walk it, you need a valid Cinque Terre Card, *see* p.197). Founded in the 8th century by Greeks fleeing the iconoclasm, Riomaggiore is the most populous of the Cinque Terre (with 1,890 souls) and visitors crowd its lively cafés and rocky beaches. Its church, **San Giovanni Battista**, has a good 14th-century rose window, in a neogothic façade; inside there's a life-size wooden *Crucifixion* by Anton Maria Maragliano. Pretty paths go up to the ruins of the castle and to the spectacular viewpoint of the **Santuario di Montenero**, 1,120ft above the sea (there's also a path from the *strada panoramica*, or a rack railway, the *trenino del vino*, built to help the grape harvest). Legend has it that Riomaggiore's founders built a church here to house an icon painted by St Luke, later stolen by the Lombards; the current monastery dates from the 13th century. On the Monte Nero promontory, the **Torre Guardiola** is now a botany and birdlife centre.

Sports and Activities around the Cinque Terre

There are **dive centres** in Levanto (Cartura, **t** 0187 808 766, or Punta Mesco (Levanto), **t** 0187 807 055), Monterosso (Teseo Tesei, **t** 0187 818 122) and Riomaggiore (Coop. Sub 5 Terre, **t** 0187 920 742). The Levanto tourist office has information on local hiking paths.

ⓘ Cinque Terre National Park

headquarters is at Via Signorini 118, Riomaggiore, **t** *0187 760 000, www.parconazionale 5terre.it, and each village has a National Park tourist office*

Where to Stay and Eat around the Cinque Terre

In the Cinque Terre, many hotels, by necessity, are not far from the train tracks. Pack a pair of ear plugs. Also, as is so often the case along the Riviera, many hotels will insist on half-board terms at Easter and in summer. Many are also small, with only six or seven rooms, so booking well ahead is advised.

ⓘ Monterosso >

Via Fegina 40, **t** *0187 817 059*

Monterosso al Mare ✉ 19016

****Porto Roca, Via Corone 1, **t** 0187 817 502, *www.portoroca.it* (€€€€€). The most luxurious hotel in the Cinque Terre, set on the headland, with lovely sea views from all the rooms, and a superb terrace. Private beach a five-minute walk away. *Closed Nov–Mar.*

***Suisse-Bellevue, Loc. Minali 2, **t** 0187 818 065, *www.hotelsuisse bellevue.it* (€€€€). A good bet for motorists; a family-run hotel and **restaurant**, 20 minutes' walk (or take a taxi) from Fegina beach, in a garden with absolutely stunning views. *Closed Nov–Mar.*

***Cinque Terre, Via IV Novembre 21, **t** 0187 817 543, *www.hotelcinque*

ⓘ Vernazza >>

Via Roma 51, **t** *0187 812 533*

terre.com (€€€). Modern, with a private beach.

***Villa Adriana, Via IV Novembre 23, **t** 0187 818 109, *www.villaadriana.info* (€€€). Large and friendly hotel next door, with a pool and its own beach. *Closed Nov–last week of Mar.*

***Hotel degli Amici, Via Buranco 36, **t** 0187 817 544, *www.hotelamici.it* (€€€). Light and airy rooms, 150m from the beach, lemon garden and terrace and an excellent restaurant.

***Baia, Via Fegina 88, **t** 0187 817 512, *www.baiahotel.it* (€€€). Right on the water's edge, with light, airy rooms.

Santuario di Soviore, **t** 0187 817 385, *www.soviore.it* (€€). Peaceful monastic doubles and triples and restaurant.

La Cambusa, Via Roma 6, **t** 0187 817 546 (€€). In a 13th-century building, tasty seafood from ravioli to swordfish grilled with sun-dried tomatoes. Great house wine. *Closed Mon, Nov and mid-Jan–mid-Feb.*

Il Pirata, Via Molinelli 6, **t** 0187 817 536 (€€). Favourite spot for lunch by the port, with mostly Ligurian treats, plus French wines. *Book. Closed Thurs and mid-Jan–mid-Feb.*

La Lampara, Piazza Don Minzoni 4, **t** 0187 817 014 (€€€). Long-established chef-owned seafood restaurant with tables out in the pretty square. *Closed Wed and Nov.*

Micki, Via Fegina 104, **t** 0187 817 608 (€€). Cheerful and popular; seafood and pizzas from the wood oven. *Closed Tues.*

Il Frantoio, Via Gioberti, **t** 0187 818 333 (€). Monterosso's best snack bar – stop here for a slice of pizza, *farinata* or *focacce*.

Vernazza ✉ 19020

Pensione Sorriso, Via Gavino 4, **t 0187 812 224 (€€). Honest little inn.

ⓘ **Riomaggiore** >>
Piazza Rio Finale 26,
t *0187 920 633*

ⓘ **Corniglia** >
Via alla Stazione,
t *0187 812 523*

ⓘ **Manarola** >
Stazione, **t** *0187 760 511*

⊛ **Cappun-Magru** >>

***Barbara**, Piazza Marconi 30, **t** 0187 812 398 (€€). Basic rooms, overlooking the port.

Gianni Franzi, Piazza Marconi 5, **t** 0187 821 003 (€€). A climb, but beautiful views from the small rooms. The restaurant (€€) can be good or mediocre – it's pot luck. *Closed Wed and Jan–Mar.*

Gambero Rosso, Piazza Marconi 7, **t** 0187 812 265 (€€). Well-known **restaurant** partly carved out of the rock; try the *tegame di acciughe*, made with the Cinque Terre's anchovies. They also rent out **rooms** with lovely views. *Closed Mon except in summer and some weeks in winter.*

Corniglia ✉ 19020

Cecio, Via Serra 58, **t** 0187 812 043, *www.cecio5terre.com* (€). Basic rooms with views and a **restaurant**.

Osteria a Cantina de Mananan, Via Fieschi 117, **t** 0187 821 166 (€€). A husband and wife run this hole in the wall in an 18th-century wine cellar with no views, but it's usually packed for its excellent Ligurian food, home-made pasta and wines. *Book.*

Manarola ✉ 19010

***Marina Piccola**, Via Birolli 120, **t** 0187 920 103, *www.hotelmarina piccola.com* (€€€). A great place to get away from it all. Rooms have air con: the hotel is better than the annexe.

Arpaiu, Via Belvedere 196, **t** 340 687 9732 *www.arpaiu.com* (€€€). Rooms and a studio flat built on the foundations of the medieval tower, with a terrace and a constellation ceiling in the *cantina*.

***Il Saraceno**, in Volastra, **t** 0187 760 081, *www.thesaraceno.com* (€€). This is a good bet for motorists. Comfortable and quiet seven-room hotel with nice owners.

***Ca' d'Andrean**, Via Discovolo 101, **t** 0187 920 040, *www.cadandrean.it* (€€). Five minutes' walk from the centre, a villa with en-suite rooms, garden and bar. *Closed mid-Nov–Christmas.*

Ca' del Michelè, Via Pasubio 58, in Volastra, **t** 0187 760 552, *www.cadel michele.com* (€€). Up in the hills, a peaceful B&B with lovely views.

Il Porticciolo, Via Birolli 92, **t** 0187 920 083, *www.ilporticciolo5terre.com* (€€€). Good mixed seafood fry-up. They also offer **rooms** to rent. *Closed Wed and part of Nov.*

Riomaggiore ✉ 19017

Cinque Terre Locanda, Via De Battè, **t** 0187 760 538, *www.cinqueterre residence.com* (€€€€). Trendy and surrounded by greenery, each room a little house with a terrace, some with kitchenettes. *Closed Dec–Feb.*

Locanda Ca'dei Duxi, Via Pecunia 19, **t** 0187 920 036, *www.duxi.it* (€€€–€€). In the centre, this locanda in a 15th-century house has six colourful rooms suitable for families, as several have bunk beds. Breakfast is served in the former wine cellar. Check website for special deals.

****Villa Argentina**, Via A. De Gasperi 170, **t** 0187 920 213, *www.villargentina. com* (€€€). Arty hotel in a pretty corner, with a buffet breakfast that will give you the oomph to walk the Via dell'Amore. Lunch and dinner also available at €20 per person, per meal.

*****Due Gemelli**, Via Litoranea 1, **t** 0187 920 678, *www.duegemelli.it* (€€). A low-key choice, 5km from the centre at Campi, on the road from La Spezia overlooking the sea.

Locanda di Campi, Via Litoranea, **t** 0187 760 111, *www.borgodicampi.it* (€€). Apartments in a hamlet, to let by the week or weekend. *No credit cards. Closed Nov–Christmas, Jan and Feb.*

Cappun-Magru, Via Volestre 19, Loc. Groppo, on the Strada Panoramica, **t** 0187 920 563 (€€€). A romantic setting in a traditional house, presided over by a wonderful chef. *Open eves only and Sun lunch. Closed Mon and Tues.*

La Lanterna, Via San Giacomo 10, **t** 0187 920 589 (€€€). On a beautiful terrace, tuck into the best seafood in the Cinque Terre. The menu includes spaghetti with tuna roe or sea urchins. *Closed Tues except in summer.*

Ripa del Sole, Via de' Gasperi 282, **t** 0187 920143, *www.ripadelsole.it* (€€). Dine *al fresco* on the likes of tagliatelle with scampi and truffles, fish and good vegetarian fare; good wine list. *No credit cards. Closed Mon.*

La Spezia and Portovenere

Until the 19th century, La Spezia, despite its deep inlet and a name evoking spice, never gathered more than 5,000 souls to its bosom. Napoleon mentioned in passing that it might make a perfect naval base, an idea that Cavour pushed in the early days of the Risorgimento; there were even proposals to make La Spezia the new capital of Italy. Instead it became Italy's chief naval base, earning it a heavy bombing in the Second World War. Today, La Spezia presents a cheerful face to the world, standing at the head of the 'Gulf of Poets', framed by the rocky peninsula of Portovenere.

La Spezia

La Spezia may not be a big-league *città di arte*, but it does have three fine museums, and the tourist office offers a free guide in English called *Art Nouveau in La Spezia* to help you find some of its swisher 20th-century architecture. La Spezia's proper entrance is by sea, where it greets visitors with beautifully tended public gardens and heroic statues. Beyond lies a businesslike grid of streets planted with orange trees, patrolled by a busy army of meter maids, until hills, villas and gardens take over.

Piazza Chiodo, anchoring the southwest corner of the seafront, has a fancy bandstand which the city purchased at the Turin International Exhibition in 1866, the inspiration for its architectural adventures. The square is named for the engineer who designed the massive naval **Arsenale**, which has its main gate just over the moat; once open to visitors only on 19 March (the feast day of St Joseph, the patron of shipbuilders) and 4 December (feast of St Barbara), you may now chance upon a weekend tour or a weekday visit by asking at least three days in advance. Adjacent, the **Museo Tecnico Navale** has a maritime collection begun in 1560 by Emanuele Filiberto, with over a hundred models, relics from the Battle of Lepanto, figureheads, and a section on the *maiali*, 'pigs', Italy's secret weapon during the Second World War.

From Piazza Chiodo, Via Chiodo leads back to pedestrian-only Via Prione. The Art Deco **Teatro Civico** on the left was the symbol of 1930s La Spezia; further up on the left, in Piazza Beverini, is the black-and-white façade of the church of **Santa Maria Assunta**, refinished in 1954, and containing a beautiful terracotta *Coronation of the Virgin* by Andrea della Robbia and a *Martyrdom of St Bartholomew* by Luca Cambiaso.

Further up, at Via Prione 234, is La Spezia's big surprise, the **Museo Amedeo Lia**, a superb collection donated by the Lia family in 1995 and housed in the 17th-century convent of San Francesco da Paola. Give yourself at least two hours to take in the medieval and Renaissance enamels from Limoges, intricate ivories, bronzes,

Arsenale
t 0187 745627 on Mon–Fri 9–1; ask at the tourist office

Museo Tecnico Navale
Via Amendola 1, t 0187 770 750, www.museotecnico navale.it; open Mon–Sat 8–6.45, Sun 8–1; adm

Teatro Civico
Piazza Mentona 1, t 0187 733 098

Museo Amedeo Lia
t 0187 731 100, www.castagna.it/ musei/mal; open Tues–Sun 10–6; adm

Getting to and around La Spezia and Portovenere

Buses for Portovenere (every 15mins) and the rest of La Spezia province are run by the ATC, **t** 0187 522 511; departure points vary, so ask.

Boats are handy when roads clog up in the summer. From La Spezia, Navigazione Golfo dei Poeti (NGP), **t** 0187 732 987, *www.navigazionegolfodeipoeti.it*, sails to Lerici, Portovenere, the Cinque Terre and Genoa.

From La Spezia, Medmar Lauro **ferries** sail in summer to Porto Vecchio – services to Sardinia, Corsica and Tunis are currently suspended (office at Via San Bartolomeo Molo 48, **t** 0187 564 340).

gem-studded crosses and illuminated antiphonals – there's even one showing the Green Man. Upstairs, among the Greek and Roman art, is a striking 5th-century BC head of Dionysos; there are ancient and Renaissance bronzes, and 13th- and 14th-century paintings by Lippo di Benivieni, Daddi, Pietro Lorenzetti, Niccolò di Pietro Guerini, Barnaba da Modena and Matteo di Giovanni, and, from the next century, a glowing *Madonna and Child* by Giampetrino and sculptures by Francesco Laurana and Benedetto da Maiano. One scholar has recently attributed the collection's *St Jerome* (1433), long believed to be by Bicci di Lorenzo, to Masaccio.

The 16th century is represented by the likes of Tintoretto, a Pontormo *Self Portrait*, Sebastiano del Piombo's *Birth and Death of Adonis*, and portraits by Titian, Gentile Bellini, Veronese and Moroni. Lucas Cranach contributes with a jewel-like *St Catherine of Alexandria*, and there's also a dangerous-looking club-wielding *Madonna del Soccorso* by Sano.

From the 17th century, look for works by Salvatore Rosa, Pittoccetto, Castiglione, and bizarre '*Capriccio Archittonicos*' by Monsú Desiderio. Next comes Magnasco's *Soldiers by a Fireplace*, Venetian scenes by Guardi and a portrait of an Englishman by Sir Thomas Lawrence, who looks out of place but keeps a stiff upper lip. Upstairs are more bronzes, ancient and Venetian glass, objets d'art and a room of 17th-century still lifes, including Giandomenico Valentino's kitchens with copper pots.

Museo del Sigillo
t 0187 778 544, www.castagna.it/ musei/museodelsigillo/ index.htm; open Wed–Sun 10–12 and 4–7, Tues 4–7; adm

If that's not enough, next door, at No. 236, the **Museo del Sigillo** has the world's biggest collection of seals, from the 3rd millennium BC to Art Nouveau works by René Lalique.

Museo del Castello
Via XXVII Marzo, t 0187 751 142, www.castagna. it/musei/sangiorgio/ home.htm; open summer Wed–Mon 9.30–12.30 and 5–8, winter Wed–Mon 9.30– 12.30 and 2–5; adm

On the hill behind Via Prione, the Castello San Giorgio, begun in the late 14th century and last remodelled by Genoa in 1607, now the **Museo del Castello**, has an important collection of prehistoric finds from Palmaria, pre-Roman and Roman material from Luni (including a mosaic pavement of a Nereid riding a sea monster) and, best of all, statue steles from the 4th–3rd millennia BC that look uncannily like prehistoric spacemen (others are in Pontremoli, *see* p.210).

Museo Civico Ubaldo Formentini
Via Curtatone 9, t 0187 739 537; open Tues–Sat 8.30–1; adm

Returning to the lower town, there's one last museum, the **Museo Civico Ubaldo Formentini** and **Etnografico Podenzana**, with costumes, tools and more. Two streets south, at Via Colombo and

Via dei Mille, is the charming Art Deco **Palazzo del Ghiaccio** (1921) or ice house, decorated with penguins and polar bears. La Spezia's strangest building is one of the tallest, the **Grattacielo** (1927 or *Anno V*) at Via Veneto 11, whose architect should have been shot. Nearby squats La Spezia's pillbox cathedral, **Cristo Re** (1975).

South of La Spezia, off the road to Portovenere, two roads wind up to extraordinary viewpoints. **Biassa** offers huge panoramas over La Spezia and the Apuan Alps, near the ruined 12th-century **Castello di Corderone**, erected by the Genoese against trouble-some Pisa. Tiny **Campiglia**, up the second road, hangs like a balcony over the stupendously vertical landscapes of the **Tramonti**, a continuation of the Cinque Terre. Paths lead to Riomaggiore and the Madonna di Montenero, or down to Portovenere.

Portovenere

① Portovenere

Like heaven, Portovenere isn't easy to reach; the road from La Spezia is narrow and winding (you may prefer to take the boat). It passes by way of the pretty cove and tiny beaches of **Le Grazie**, home to the 15th-century church of Santa Maria delle Grazie, and the **Convento degli Olivetani**; both have good 16th-century frescoes by Nicolò Corso. If you ring ahead you can visit Le Grazie's Roman villa of **Varignano Vecchio** (1st century BC) and olive press, in a lovely setting over the sea.

Varignano Vecchio
*t 0187 790 307;
open mid-June–mid-
Sept 1.30–7.30; mid-
Sept–mid-June 9–3; free*

At the end of the road is **Portovenere**, the ancient *Portus Veneris*, or port of Venus, one of the most beautiful towns on the coast, with its orange, yellow and pink tower houses. Protected by a long promontory and three islets, it was on the frontlines in the Middle Ages, fortified by the Genoese to counter the Pisans, who had made a stronghold of Lerici across the gulf; the gate reads *Colonia Januensis 1113*, as the Genoese liked to think that 'Genoa' derived from Janus, the two-faced god of doors and the month of January. The tower to the left of the gate was added in 1606.

A protectress of fisherfolk, Venus had her temple at the tip of the promontory, until she was upstaged by Christianity's top fisher-man. The strange little striped church of **San Pietro**, with its loggetta and wall, was built in 1277, using a few colourful marble remains of a 6th-century predecessor. There are splendid views towards the Cinque Terre and cliffs of Muzzerone. The pretty cove below once held the Grotta Arpaia (until it collapsed in the 1930s), which provided the inspiration for Byron's *The Corsair*; a plaque in town celebrates his famous swim across the bay to Lerici.

Portovenere is Italy's champion kitty city, and the best thing to do is join the cats for a wander up through its narrow lanes and steep vaulted stairs. Aim for the lovely church of **San Lorenzo** (1130), built by the Genoese in only three years, with a bas-relief of Lawrence on his gridiron over the door. It shelters Portovenere's most precious relic, the *Madonna Bianca*, said to have floated to the town encased in a cedar log in the 13th century, a 15th-century marble ancona attributed to Mino da Fiesole, and, in the little **church museum**, Syrian and Byzantine ivory coffers from the 12th century and a 15th-century Flemish 'Pace' in silver and precious gems. A steep walk leads to the 16th-century Genoese **Castello Doria** and its marvellous views; inside there's an exhibition of photographs of the Cinque Terre and Gulf of Poets from 1870.

Church museum
t 0187 790 684;
open by request

Castello Doria
open Mon–Thurs
10–1 and 2–5,
Fri–Sun 11–6; adm

Excursion boats cross the channel to **Isola Palmaria** (now a nature reserve) to visit the local version of Capri's Grotta Azzurra, and to wander the paths that crisscross the islet over white cliffs and black marble quarries. Palmaria's land cave, the Grotta dei Colombi, yielded many of the Mesolithic finds in La Spezia's Museo del Castello. The smaller islet, **Tino**, has a lighthouse and the evocative ruins of an 8th-century **Abbazia di San Venerio**, once the address of the dragon-whacking hermit with the suspiciously venereal name; however, as it's a military zone, you can only visit on 13 September, his feast day. Even tinier **Tinetto**, a big rock in the sea, has a ruined Benedictine oratory from the 4th century.

Where to Stay and Eat in La Spezia and Portovenere

ⓘ **La Spezia** >
Viale Italia 5, t 0187 770 900, www.aptcinque terre.sp.it

La Spezia ✉ 19100

****Jolly**, Via XX Settembre 2, t 0187 739 555, *www.jollyhotels.it* (€€€€). La Spezia's finest accommodation. A modern and stylish member of the Italian chain, with views over the gulf.

***Firenze & Continentale**, Via Paleocapa 7, t 0187 713 210, *www.hotelfirenzecontinentale.it* (€€€). Recently refurbished and comfortable; near the station, so convenient for rail hops to the Cinque Terre. See website for special offers.

***Genova**, Via Fratelli Rosselli 84, t 0187 732 972, *www.hotelgenova.it* (€€€–€€). Just off the pedestrian precinct in the city centre, offering well-appointed rooms near the fruit and vegetable market.

Locanda del Prione, Via del Prione 152, t 333 177 6696, *www.locandadel prione.it* (€€). Spacious rooms in the vicinity of the Amedeo Lia museum.

***Flavia**, Vicolo dello Stagno 7, t 0187 736 060 (€). One of the best bargains, not far from the station.

5° Chilometro, Via Montalbano 1, t 0187 700 130 (€€€€). Elegant restaurant in a historic *palazzo*, offering a change from seafood, specializing in meats, mushrooms and truffles. *Open evenings only. Closed Tues and July.*

Toscana Da Dino, Via Cadorna 17, t 0187 736 157 (€€€€). Charming and unpretentious, with an excellent fixed-price menu. Outside tables in summer. *Closed Sun eve and Mon.*

Vicolo Interno, Via della Canonica 22, t 0187 23998 (€€€). Pleasant *osteria* near the market, so fish and vegetables are always fresh. Try the Monterosso anchovies. *Lunch only, also dinner Fri and Sat eve; closed Sun.*

Da Gianni, Corso Cavour 352, t 0187 717980 (€). One of the most traditional *osterias* in La Spezia – sit down and Gianni will reel off the choices on the fixed-price menu. *Lunch only.*

Caberet Voltaire, Via Napoli 92, t 0187 4607587 (€). Well-stocked wine bar with French and Italian cheeses, cold meats and more to keep you going. *Eves only; closed Sun and Aug.*

(i) Portovenere >

Piazza Bastreri 7,
t 0187 790 691,
www.portovenere.it

Portovenere ✉ 19025

****Grand Hotel Portovenere, Via Garibaldi 5, **t** 0187 792 610, *www.portovenerehotel.it* (€€€€–€€€€). In a 17th-century seaside Franciscan convent, with views across the gulf. The cells have been converted into stylish rooms; there's a fitness and beauty centre, and a restaurant with a panoramic terrace.

****Royal Sporting, Via dell'Ulivo 345, **t** 0187 790 326, *www.royalsporting. com* (€€€€€–€€€€). Large, modern Mediterranean-style hotel in a fantastic location; amenities include a salt-water pool, beach, garden, tennis and a car park. *Closed Nov–Mar.*

***Della Baia, Via Lungomare 111, in Le Grazie, **t** 0187 790 797, *www.baiahotel. com* (€€€€). Pristine rooms, internet access, **restaurant** and pool. *Half-board only in Aug.*

***Paradiso, Via Garibaldi 34, **t** 0187 790 612, *www.hotelportovenere.it* (€€€). Family-run hotel with lovely views from its seaside terrace, and cosy, well-equipped rooms.

La Casa del Pescatore, Isola Palmaria, **t** 0187 791 141, *www.palmariaisland. com* (€€€). Little B&B in a stone house, with a garden and terrace and lovely views back towards Portovenere. *Closed mid-Oct–Mar.*

Locanda Lorena, Via Cavour 4, Isola Palmaria, **t** 0187 792 370, *www.locandalorena.com* (€€€). Peaceful place to stay, in a historic building with a good restaurant. *Closed Feb–Nov.*

Genio, Piazza Bastreri 8, **t 0187 790 611 (€€). The cheapest rooms in town, and a nice little garden, too. *Closed 10 Jan–10 Feb.*

La Marina da Antonio, Piazza Marina 6, **t** 0187 790 686 (€€€€). Enjoy stuffed squid followed by creamy *pannacotta* with blackberry coulis, while watching the little ferries potter to Palmaria. *Closed Thurs and Nov.*

Da Iseo, Calata Doria 9, **t** 0187 790 610 (€€€). Portovenere's best-known restaurant offers a lovely setting and classic dishes; don't miss the delicious spaghetti with seafood. *Closed Wed and 10 Dec–10 Jan.*

La Pizzaccia, Via Cappellini 94–98, **t** 0187 792 722 (€€). Best place in Portovenere for a tasty slice of pizza or *farinata* or *torta di verdura. Closed Thurs and end Nov–end Feb.*

The Gulf of Poets and the Val di Magra

There is a legend that a sea monster, pursued by hunters, fled into this gulf, and clawed and scratched out all the coves and inlets along its shores in its mad efforts to escape. Enchantment lingered in everything the monster touched, bewitching all who set eyes on it; poets such as Petrarch, Shelley and Byron were especially vulnerable to its charms. Today, a bit of poetic imagination may be required to see past La Spezia's military installations and the *cementificazione* of the east gulf coast.

Lerici and Around

Fortunately, the sprawl and industry end abruptly at a tunnel: beyond opens the pretty bay of Lerici. The first place you'll come to is **San Terenzo**, the charming fishing village where Shelley, his wife Mary Wollstonecraft and her stepsister rented the white **Casa Magni** (not open to the public), bearing a suitably romantic plaque (in Italian): 'Upon this terrace, once protected by the shadow of an

Shelley goes Boating

After the Napoleonic interlude, Grand Tourists of all stripes began to drift back to Italy, including England's wayward poets Byron and Shelley, both of whom composed some of their finest verse under the Italian sun. Shelley wrote the 'Ode to the West Wind' and 'To a Skylark' in Tuscany, and 'In the Euganean Hills' in the Veneto.

Not all of Italy, however, agreed with Shelley as much as it suited Byron, who appalled expat society by slumming with the Venetians, and having one notorious affair after another – a grocer's daughter was as likely a target of his attentions as a countess. Shelley may have been expelled from Oxford for being an atheist, but he was never a traitor to his class. At one point he wrote home:

There are two Italies – one composed of the green earth and transparent sea, and the mighty ruins of ancient time, and the aereal mountains, and the warm and radiant atmosphere which is interfused through all things. The other consists of the Italians of the present day, their works and ways. The one is the most sublime and lovely contemplation that can be conceived by the imagination of man; the other is the most degraded, disgusting and odious. What do you think? Young women of rank actually eat – you will never guess what – garlick!

Shelley loved boating, and he loved Lerici Bay: 'My boat is swift and beautiful, and appears quite a vessel ... We drive along this delightful bay in the evening wind, under the summer moon, until earth appears another world ...' It was from here that he sailed in his schooner, the *Don Juan*, to meet Leigh Hunt at Livorno in 1822, only to shipwreck in a storm on his return and drown. He was just shy of his 30th birthday. His friends, including Hunt and Byron, cremated him, pagan style, on the beach, as described in ghastly detail by Edward Trelawney: 'The fire was so fierce as to produce a white heat on the iron, and to reduce its contents to grey ashes. The only portions that were not consumed were some fragments of bones, the jaw and the skull, but what surprised us all was that the heart remained entire.'

ancient oak tree, in July 1822, Mary Shelley and Jane Williams awaited with weeping anxiety the return of Percy Bysshe Shelley, who, sailing from Livorno in his fragile craft, had come to shore by sudden chance among the silences of the Elysian Isles.

Shelley Museum
t 0187 972 736; open daily 9–12 and 3–4; free

'O blessed shores, where Love, Liberty and Dreams have no chains.' A **Shelley Museum**, dedicated to Mary, in the 11th-century castle, has some of the Gothic atmosphere of her best-known work, *Frankenstein*.

Castello di San Giorgio
www.castellodilerici.it

Museo Geopaleontologico
t 0187 969 114; open 20 Oct–15 Mar Tues–Fri 10.30–12.30, Sat, Sun and hols 10.30–12.30 and 2.30–5.30; 16 Mar–30 June Tues–Sun and hols 10.30–1 and 2.30–6; 1 July–31 Aug Tues–Sun and hols 10.30–12.30 and 6.30–midnight; 1 Sept–19 Oct Tues–Sun and hols 10.30–1 and 2.30–6; adm

Beaches line the sheltered coves towards **Lerici**, the former Roman *Mons Ilici*. The town makes a bold sight, circling the skirts of the **Castello di San Giorgio**, the best-preserved castle on the Riviera, towering on its promontory over the busy marina. Genoa acquired Lerici as a bookend to Portovenere, but the Pisans seized it in 1241, built this castle, and held tight to it for 45 years before the Genoese got it back. Inside you'll find the Gothic chapel of **Sant'Anastasia** (1250) and a surprise – a multimedia **Museo Geopaleontologico**, evoking the dinosaurs who stomped about these parts 210 million years ago as well as earthquakes (including a virtual reality seismic experience). Below, the **Oratorio di San Rocco** in Corso Marconi was curiously turned back to front in 1524; it has a pair of Renaissance reliefs embedded in the bell tower and a painting by Fiasella. Near the end of Via Cavour, the 17th-century **San Francesco** has more Renaissance art and a marble triptych by

Domenico Gare (1529). A road from Lerici leads to pine-wooded **Serra** for lovely views over the gulf.

The best part of the eastern Gulf of Poets is south of Lerici (in summer take the bus: there's no place to park, and the beaches are packed), where a Roman shipwreck in transparent waters is the centrepiece of a **Parco Subacqueo Archeologico**. Further on is the tiny cove and beach of **Fiascherino**, where D.H. Lawrence and his Frieda lived in the 'Pink House' (1913–14). Beyond is the unspoiled, quintessentially Ligurian fishing hamlet of **Tellaro**, with its tall houses and pink Baroque church by the sea. If shellfish rules at Portovenere, Lerici and its bay is the land of the *polpo*, or octopus. In a letter, Lawrence recorded a local legend: one night the inhabitants of Tellaro awoke to the sound of the church bell ringing frantically, and ran over to see that the rope in the campanile had been seized by the tentacle of a giant octopus – just in time to warn them of a pirate raid.

Up the Val di Magra

A natural border between Liguria and Tuscany and the Po Valley, the Val di Magra region prickles like a hedgehog with castles from the bad old days when it was coveted by bishops, signori and the Republic of Genoa. Because of its in-between status, perhaps, few visitors ever see its attractive coast and unspoiled hill villages.

The Caprione promontory and the lower River Magra to the east were beloved by the Romans, and now form the **Parco Naturale Montemarcello-Magra**, incorporating Liguria's only wetlands. From Lerici, a scenic corniche road rises to the colourful hill town of **Montemarcello**, named after the Consul Marcellus, victor over the local Ligurians. Its rectangular plan reflects its origins as a Roman *castrum*, but it also has one of those perfect medieval Ligurian piazzas. The nearby summit of Monte Murlo offers views and Mediterranean flora in the **Orto Botanico di Montemarcello**. Another path goes to the white cliffs of **Punta Bianca** on the Caprione promontory.

Orto Botanico di Montemarcello
t 0187 691 071; guided tours only, telephone for hours

The road east winds down to where the Magra flows into the sea under the marbly Apuan Alps, at **Bocca di Magra**, a fishing village favoured as a summer resort after the war by Cesare Pavese, Marguerite Duras, Moravia, Pasolini, and Liguria's own Nobel laureate, Eugenio Montale. Now given over to tourism and boating under the parasol pines, a patrician Roman villa from the 2nd century BC excavated here suggests the Romans once swam and boated here, too. In summer, regular boats sail to the lovely beaches at Punta Bianca and Punta Corvo.

Roman villa
the municipio can arrange visits in summer, t 0187 609 221 or 010 27181

Heading back up the Magra, the first town is pretty hilltop **Ameglia**, the local gourmet capital. In 963, it became an imperial stronghold, belonging to the Count-Bishops of Luni, who did all they could to squash the local nobles, without much success; in 1380 the town was annexed to Genoa. Concentric streets encircle the 10th-century citadel; handsome slate portals adorn the older houses. A path from here leads to the 'Fairy Cave' (*Grotta delle Fate*), while up on the Montemarcello road the 12th-century **Monastero del Corvo** hosted Dante, who slept in as many places as George Washington; it houses a rare Romanesque 'Black Jesus' with Oriental features.

Upriver, **Trebiano** is another medieval hill town with a castle-belvedere, where the church has a 15th-century *Crucifixion* and a stoop made from a Roman altar. **Arcola**, further north, is a perfect example of a Ligurian hill town, built around the pentagonal tower (all that remains of the castle); the Piazza della Parrocchiale is one of the most delightful in Liguria, with a grand stair in an otherwise typical rural setting.

North, **Vezzano Ligure** has two centres, *Inferiore* and *Superiore*, both overlooking the Val di Magra. The lower town has a leafy square with lovely views; Vezzano Superiore, piled on a knob of a hill, has a similar square by the ruined castle, with views over the Magra and Vara valleys. The church of **SS. Prospero e Ciro** has a lovely pebble mosaic and more views, stretching for miles.

Ancient Luni: the Port of the Moon

Ancient Luni
t 0187 660 266; site and museum open Tues–Sun 8.30–7.30; adm

At Ameglia a bridge crosses over the Magra for Luni or *Portus Lunae*, a Roman colony founded on the border of Tuscany in 177 BC as a bulwark against the fierce Ligurians. The settlement, named after the moon – or the whiteness of the marble it exported – thrived in the 2nd century AD. Although later a bishopric and a busy Byzantine port, it eventually succumbed to the Lombards beginning in 643, but the real death knell was the silting up of its port. The bishop soon sought safer quarters up in Sarzana, and by the time Petrarch visited, Luni was in such a melancholy state that he used it to evoke the ephemeral nature of human things. Excavations have revealed a 2nd-century AD amphitheatre seating 5,000, the forum, houses (some with frescoes and mosaics), temples, and a Palaeochristian basilica; on site, the **Museo Nazionale di Luni** has statues, coins, jewellery, portraits and more.

Above Luni, **Nicola** is a charming little walled village with a spiral plan, in a beautiful bucolic setting. On Easter morning, men here play *manda*, an ancient game with a metal ball that symbolizes the end of the hunting season. Also here is **Ortonovo**, a similar village of concentric streets that was sold by Florence to Genoa in 1454; it

Museo Etnografico
t 0187 690 111; open by
appointment only; free

Enoteca
Regionale Ligure
t 0187 694 182

has a small **Museo Etnografico** in a wine press in the nearby hamlet of Casano. To the north, **Castelnuovo Magra** offers a change of pace, a town stretched over the crest of a hill with a **Malaspina castle** at one end. In 1306 Dante was here, brokering a peace treaty between the Malaspina (who ruled the upper Val di Magra and had given him shelter when he was exiled from Florence) and the bishop of Luni, an event re-enacted on the fourth Sunday of August. Castelnuovo's lavish church of **Santa Maria Maddalena** contains a superb *Crucifixion* by Brueghel the Younger. The cellars of the town hall house the **Enoteca Regionale Ligure**. This exhibits all the wines produced in the region – with special attention paid to those made in the Cinque Terre and Colli di Luni – and is where you can try Vementino dei Colli di Luni. There's a beach at **Fiumaretta di Ameglia**.

Sarzana

As Luni's fortunes declined, Sarzana thrived, taking over its powerful bishopric in 1204. Located on the Magra and on the Via Francigena, northern Europe's road to Rome, Sarzana attracted envious suitors: Pisa in 1284, Lucca in the early 14th century, Florence in 1486, and Genoa, which took it in 1562 and held on to it. Although bombed in the war, its historic centre survived, and forms a perfect backdrop for a huge antiques fair, the 'Soffitta in strada' (street attic) held on the first weekend in August.

The Florentines built quite a bit in Sarzana, including the **Palazzo Comunale** in Piazza Luni, designed by Giuliano da Maiano for Lorenzo de' Medici – although the Genoese obliterated it and built their own version in the 16th century, albeit with an elegant portico, decorated with coats of arms and marbles from ancient Luni. **Via Mazzini** (the old Via Francigena) is lined with palaces and tower houses, including one at No.28 that is said to have belonged to the Buonaparte family before they emigrated to Corsica in 1529. Nearby is Sarzana's oldest church, **Sant'Andrea** (11th century, remodelled in 1579) with a door framed by caryatids.

Further along, in Piazza Niccolò V (named after the great mid-15th-century Humanist Pope and founder of the Vatican library, a native of Sarzana) the **Cattedrale dell'Assunta** was rebuilt over the Gothic church of St Basil in 1474, and preserves the older church's marble rose window and tower. The sumptuous interior contains Master Guglielmo's *Crucifixion* of 1138, one of the oldest datable works of its kind in Italy, two beautiful marble polyptychs (1430s) by Leonardo Riccomanni of Lucca, paintings by native Domenico Fiasella ('Il Sarzana', 1589–1669) and the *Annunciation with Saints* (1720) by Giuseppe Maria Crespi. From here, Via Castrocani leads north to the church of **San Francesco**, with a 17th-century fresco

Cittadella
open Tues–Sun 5–8pm,
Sat and Sun also
9.30–12.30; adm

Fortezza di
Sarzanello
t 0187 622 080; open
Sept–Oct Fri 5–7, Sat,
Sun and hols 10–12
and 6–7; July and Aug
daily 10–12 and 5–7;
April–June Wed–Sun
3.30–7; Nov–Mar Sat,
Sun and hols 2.30–6;
guided visits every 30
mins; adm

Castello del
Piagnaro
t 0187 831 439; open
Tues–Sun 9–12 and 2–5,
till 7 in summer; adm

cycle on the life of the saint (including a depiction of Pope Nicholas V) and good sculptures, including the tomb of Guarnerio degli Antelminelli, the infant son of Castruccio Castracani (d. 1322), the likeable tyrant of Lucca, whose name means 'dog-castrator'.

Two forts defended Sarzana. The **Cittadella** in the centre was built by Lorenzo de'Medici, and now hosts special exhibitions. The **Fortezza di Sarzanello**, a mile to the east on Sarzanello Hill, was first recorded in 963, when Emperor Otto I gave it to the Bishop of Luni. In 1322, Castracani, as Vicar of the Emperor, rebuilt it; the Medici rebuilt it again in 1480s, and then the Genoese perfected it in 1502; from one angle, it resembles a giant steam iron. If you aren't in a hurry, take the scenic walk up from San Francesco, to drink in the surrounding views.

Luni lent its name to the nearby Lunigiana region of Tuscany: the town of **Pontremoli**, up the river Magra, has a fascinating collection of the Neolithic statue menhirs found in the region in the town's **Castello del Piagnaro**.

Where to Stay and Eat in the Gulf of Poets and the Val di Magra

San Terenzo ✉ 19036

Il Giglio, Via Garibaldi 16, **t 0187 970 805, *www.albergoilgiglio.com* (€€). On the left as you come into the village, with well-equipped rooms.

*Il Nettuno, Via Mantegazza 1, **t** 0187 971 093, *www.albergonettunolerici.it* (€). Another option along the seafront, with big rooms, some with balconies. *Open June–Sept only, half or full board; Aug full board only.*

(i) Lerici >
Via Biaggini 6,
t 0187 967 346

Lerici ✉ 19032

***Shelley & Delle Palme, Lungomare Biaggini 5, **t** 0187 968 204, *www.hotel shelley.it* (€€€). One of the most comfortable hotels on the 'Gulf of Poets'.

***Doria Park, Via Doria 2, **t** 0187 967 124, *www.doriaparkhotel.it* (€€€). Just over the headland; good **restaurant**, pretty views.

(★) Locanda
Miranda >>

Hotel del Golfo, Via Gerini 37, **t 0187 967 400, *www.hoteldelgolfo.com* (€€€). A less expensive hotel, by the tourist office.

***Byron, Via Biaggini 19, **t** 0187 967 104, *www.byronhotel.com* (€€€–€€).

Also a good choice, where smallish rooms are compensated for by views across the bay.

Due Corone, Calata Mazzini 14, **t** 0187 967 417 (€€€€). Award-winning restaurant near the port. Seafood is a speciality: try the *cocktail di antipasti mare* and *grigliata mista. Closed Tues exc in summer.*

La Pettegola, Lungomare Biaggini 4, **t** 0187 965 056 (€€). Fresh, seasonal cuisine by a chef who knows just what to do. *Eves only, also lunch Fri, Sat and Sun; closed Mon except in summer.*

La Piccola Oasi, Via Cavour 58, **t** 0187 964 588 (€). You need to book to get a table in this little restaurant, with simple, tasty local dishes. *Open eves only; closed Tues.*

Fiascherino/Tellaro ✉ 19030

***Il Nido, Via Fiascherino 75, **t** 0187 967 286, *www.hotelnido.com* (€€€€). A 'nest' in a lovely location on the cove of Fiascherino, with a relaxation area (jacuzzi, sauna, etc.), tiny private beach and great views.

***Locanda Miranda, Via Fiascherino 92, **t** 0187 968 130 (€€€). A little seven-room charmer on the corniche, with lovely sea views. The **restaurant** (€€€€) is one of the best in the area, serving fine dishes like prawn flan in white truffle sauce and fish gnocchi with pesto. *Half board only. Closed Mon.*

Montemarcello ✉ 19031

Il Gabbiano, Via della Pace 2, **t 0187 600 066 (€). On the hill at Punta Bianca, offering simple rooms with stunning panoramic views of the Apuan Alps and sea.

Pescarino, Via Borea 52, **t** 0187 601 388 (€€€€). Off the beaten track, in a log cabin. Try unusual dishes such as *triangolini di ortica con ricotta* (triangular ravioli made of young nettles) and *parmigiana di branzino*. *Book. Open eves only and weekend lunches; closed Mon and Tues exc in Aug.*

Dai Pironcelli, Via delle Mura 45, Montemarcello, **t** 0187 601 252 (€€€€). Dine by candlelight on the delicious, creative dishes based on the freshest ingredients. *Closed Wed and lunchtimes except Sun; June–Sept closed Sun lunch also.*

Bocca di Magra ✉ 19030

***Sette Archi, Via Fabbricotti 242, **t** 0187 609 017, *www.hotelsette archi.com* (€€€). Pretty hotel with bougainvillea-covered façade in the pedestrian zone, offering comfort as well as great views of the marbled mountains. You can moor your boat in front. *Closed Nov to mid-Mar.*

Monastero Santa Croce, Via S. Croce 30, **t 0187 60911, *www.monasterosanta croce.it* (€). Managed by Carmelites, immaculate rooms in a patrician villa dating from the early 1800s, set in a vast park. There's a rare 12th-century *Crucifixion* in the church.

Ameglia ✉ 19031

****Paracucchi Locanda dell'Angelo, at Ca' di Scabello, Viale XXV Aprile 60, **t** 0187 64391, *www.paracucchi locanda.it* (€€€€). The pioneer establishment: a slick hotel, a pool and a **restaurant**, founded by celebrity chef Angelo Paracucchi, now run by son Marco. Each dish is superb, often amazingly simple. *Closed Mon except in summer and Jan.*

***Locanda delle Tamerici, Via Litoranea 106, **t** 0187 64262, *www.locandadelletamerici.com*

(€€€€–€€€). Located by the sea at Fiumaretta, with seven adorable rooms and a flower-filled garden. The **restaurant** (€€€€) rivals Paracucchi's for its delicious seafood and vegetables. *Closed Mon and Tues lunch, 24 Dec–14 Jan and one week in Oct.*

Arcola ✉ 19021

Villa Ducci B&B, Via Nosedro 2, **t** 0187 982 918, *www.villaducci.net* (€€). Rooms in a 18th-century mansion; Italian or English breakfast served on the terrace. *Minimum stay two nights; no credit cards. Closed 10 Jan–30 Mar and 5 Nov–21 Dec.*

Nicola (Ortonovo) ✉ 19034

Da Fiorella, Via Case Sparse 5, **t** 0187 66857 (€€). Resolutely traditional *trattoria* serving traditional Ligurian or Italian dishes – chickpea soup and a wide choice of meat dishes, including game in season, plus gluten-free recipes. *Closed Thurs, Jan and Sept.*

Castelnuovo Magra ✉ 19030

Armanda, Piazza Garibaldi 6, **t** 0187 674 410 (€€€€). People make special trips just for the delicate stuffed lettuce in broth (*lattughe ripiene in brodo*), *cima* – an exquisite, delicate *torta* filled with courgette and artichoke hearts – and other authentic dishes. It's minute, so book. *Closed Wed, 24 Dec–15 Jan and one week in Sept.*

Il Mulino del Cibus, Fraz. Canale 46, **t** 0187 676 102 (€€€€). In an old, but still working mill, with a wide selection of wines and dishes to match, from cheese and salami to something more filling like lasagne or duck's breast in vinegar and honey. *Closed Mon.*

Osteria dei Sani, Via Torrione Testa Forte 11, **t** 0187 620 829, *www.osteria deisani.it* (€€). Vast choice of both fish and meat recipes, from local salami and ravioli to tasty seafood. Portions are huge, and there are some fantastic desserts. *Closed Tues.*

Sarzana ✉ 19038

****Al Sant'Andrea, Via Circonvallazione, Aurelie 34,

⭐ **Armanda** ≫

ⓘ **Ameglia** ›
Via XXV Aprile,
t 0187 600 524

ⓘ **Sarzana** ≫
Piazza San Giorgio,
t 0187 620 419

⭐ **Locanda delle Tamerici** ›

---

10 | Riviera di Levante | The Gulf of Poets and the Val di Magra: Up the Val di Magra

t 0187 621 491 (€€). Comfortable and convenient, near the *autostrada*.

Taverna Napoleone, Via Bonaparte 16, **t** 0187 627 974 (€€€€). Dine in a restored stable on refined dishes based on garden ingredients (such as ravioli with radicchio, aubergine tart) plus a few meat dishes. *Closed Wed lunch and Feb.*

Girarrosto da Paolo, Via dei Molini 388, **t** 0187 621 088 (€€). Old-fashioned family-run rural trattoria, of a dying breed. *Closed Wed.*

Pizzeria Bugliani, Piazza San Giorgio 20, **t** 0187 620 005, *www.bugliani.it* (€). In the centre, serving excellent pizza, *focacce* and *farinata* by the slice since 1946.

Turin

Detroit without the degradation; the absolutist capital of the Savoys; a stately, masculine Baroque city of porticoed avenues and royal squares; the home of the Holy Shroud, of Juventus, vermouth, an endearingly outrageous Mole and the centre of black magic in the Mediterranean – Piedmont's capital, Turin (Torino, pop. 900,000) is not your typical Italian city. Positioned midway between the pole and the equator, its winters are colder than Copenhagen's; its most renowned museum is Egyptian.

11

Don't miss

⭐ **A magnificent public museum**
Galleria Sabauda **p.236**

⭐ **An eye-catching synagogue**
Mole Antonelliana **p.231**

⭐ **A Versailles-inspired palace**
Palazzo Madama **p.224**

⭐ **Guarini's zigzagging masterpiece**
Cappella della Sacra Sindone **p.226**

⭐ **Modern art**
Galleria d'Arte Moderna **p.237**

See map overleaf

to Stazione Dora

S. Maria Ausiliatrice

VIA DON BOSCO

CORSO UMBRIA

VIA SACCARELLI

VIA SAN DONATO

VIA LUIGI CIBRARIO

VIA PIFFETTI

CORSO FRANCIA

VIA VASSALLI EANDI

VIA PRINCIPI D'ACAJA

VIA AVIGLIANA

VIA CAVALLI

CORSO VITTORIO EMANUELE II

VIA CARLO BOGGIO

CORSO PRINCIPE ODDONE

CORSO REGINA MARGHERITA

VIA COTTOLENGO

Porta Palazzo

PIAZZA DELLA REPUBBLICA

Museo delle Antichità

Porta Palatina

Teatro Romano

CORSO PR. EUGENIO

CORSO VALDOCCO

VIA C. GIULIO

SS. Sudario/ Museo della Sindone

VIA STA CHIARA

VIA STA CHIARA

VIA S. DOMENICO

VIA DEL CARMINE

PIAZZA STATUTO

CORSO S. MARTINO

VIA PASSALACQUA

VIA MANZONI

CORSO PALESTRO

VIA

BERTOLA

JUVARRA

Giardino Cittadella

VIA DELLA CONSOLATA

S. Consolata

PIAZZA EM. FILIBERTO

PIAZZA D. CONSOLATA

S. Domenico

DOMENICO

Palazzo Falletti di Barolo

PIAZZA D. SAVOIA

Church of the Carmine

PZA ARBARELLO

S. Maria di Piazza

VIA STA MARIA

VIA BLIGNY

VIA CORTE D'APPELLO

VIA GIUSEPPE GARIBALDI

SS. Martiri

VIA BARBAROUX

VIA MILANO

V. D. BASILICA

PZA S. GIOVANNI

LARGO IV MARZO

Palazzo di Città

Duomo

S. Lorenzo

Pal. Madama

Palazzo Reale

PIAZZETTA REALE

PIAZZA

CASTELLO

CORSO II FEBBRAIO

VIA XX

PIAZZA C. AUGUSTO

VIA SETTEMBRE

VIA ROMA

PIAZZA CARIGNANO

Stazione Porta Susa

PIAZZA XVIII DICEMBRE

Museo Civico Pietro Micca

VIA GUICCIARDINI

CORSO INGHILTERRA

CORSO BOLZANO

VIA VINZAGLIO

CORSO BOLZANO

VIA CERNAIA

Mastio della Cittadella

Museo Storico dell'Artiglieria

CORSO G. FERRARIS

PIAZZA SOLFERINO

Santa Teresa

VIA STA TERESA

Galleria S. Federico

VIA ALFIERI

VIA P.

VIA BERTOLA

Museo Egizio Gall. Sabauda

PIAZZA S. CARLO

Sta Cristina

S. Carlo

VIA S. FRANCESCO D'ASSISI

VIA MONTE DI PIETÀ

VIA P.

MICCA

VIA ROMA

VIA D. ARCIVESCOVADO

VIA ROMA

VIA GRAMSCI

CORSO G. MATTEOTTI

CORSO G. MATTEOTTI

VIA S. QUINTINO

VIA AVOGADRO

CORSO VITTORIO EMANUELE II

LARGO VITTORIO EMANUELE

CORSO RE UMBERTO I

PZA PALEOCAPA

PZA LAGRANG

PIAZZA CARLO FELICE

Bus Station

Galleria d'Arte Moderna

VIA V. VELA

MAGENTA

CORSO G. FERRARIS

Air Terminal

VIA SACCHI

Stazione Porta Nuova

VIA NIZZA

CORSO STATI UNITI

SLOVENIA

CROATIA

FRANCE

Turin

Corsica

Sardinia

Sicily

Don't miss

⭐ Galleria Sabauda **p.236**

⭐ Mole Antonelliana **p.231**

⭐ Palazzo Madama **p.224**

⭐ Cappella della Sacra Sindone **p.226**

⭐ Galleria d'Arte Moderna **p.237**

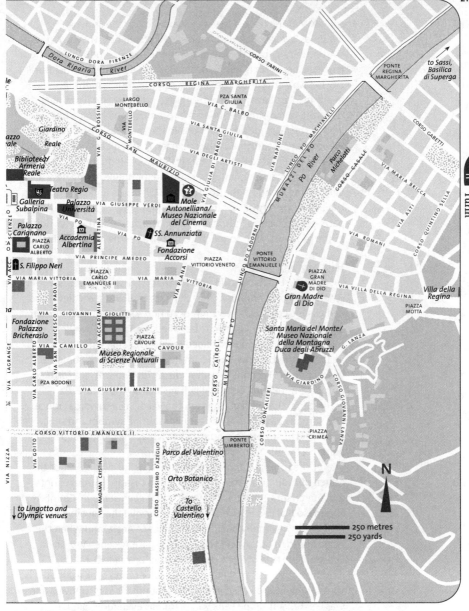

Turin straddles the Po, so close to its source that the water is almost clean. One of its nicknames is Grissinopoli ('breadstick-ville'). The story goes that in 1679, when the seven-year-old heir to the ducal throne Vittorio Amedeo II was suffering a life-threatening intestinal sickness, the doctor cured him by inventing easily digestible breadsticks (*grissini*). As an adult, Vittorio Amedeo went on to free Piedmont from French tutelage by stabbing

Louis XIV in the back, and was rewarded with the crown of Sardinia. 'We are all Italian thanks to a breadstick', they say in Turin.

After uniting Italy, then captaining the nation's industry for the past century, Turin is remaking itself into a dynamic, multicultural city in love with contemporary art, cinema, music, nightlife, food and drink. The Savoys' long struggle to put the capital of their little city state in the same league as Paris and Vienna left it a unique legacy: the fascinating collections in the museums, astonishing Baroque architecture, and over a dozen royal palaces in and outside the city, designated World Heritage Sites. Old industrial relics, beginning with Fiat's Lingotto plant, are finding exciting new uses. Since being awarded the 2006 Winter Olympics and after hosting the event, the city has been primping and building at a fiendish pace (*see* pp.220–3). 'Torino always on the move!' is the new slogan; at the moment, with so much going on, it seems like a whirlwind.

History

One thing that sets Turin apart is that its first 1,800 years – when every other major Italian city had its glowing medieval and Renaissance periods – were almost a non event. Originally *Taurasia*, a village of a Celto-Ligurian tribe called the Taurini ('dwellers at the foot of the mountain') it decided in 218 BC to side with Rome against Hannibal and was decimated for its troubles. Some 200 years later, the Romans rebuilt *Augusta Taurinorum* as a fortified outpost on their Via della Gallia Transalpina (the future Via Francigena) that passed through the Val di Susa towards France. The Romans gave the city its familiar taurine symbol and their usual grid of streets, in a quarter known as the Quadrilatero Romano, the kernel of all subsequent Turins.

After the Lombard and Frankish invasions, Turin was part of the March of Arduinica, later to be ruled by a bishop, then by counts and merchants, until c. 1280, when it was conquered by Count Tommaso II of the House of Savoy. For a while the Savoys shared Piedmont with their cousins, the Princes of Acaia, and when the Acaia line died out in 1417, the emperor gave Amedeo VIII 'The Peaceful' the title of Duke of Savoy. Amedeo made Turin the administrative seat of Piedmont (his career then took a curious turn, when he abdicated in 1434 in favour of his son Ludovico and was elected anti-Pope Felix V in 1439). His even more pious grandson Amedeo IX (d. 1472) was given all the Church lands around Turin by the pope in 1464 and was later beatified.

During the bitter wars between France and Spain, Turin was occupied by France (1536–62). Then, just when everyone thought that the Savoys were through, young, feisty 'Iron-headed' Duke Emanuele Filiberto came out of the woodwork to beat the French for Charles V. His transalpine lands restored, he moved his capital

Getting to Turin

By Air

Caselle International airport (t 011 567 6361, *www.aeroportoditorino.com*) is 16km north of Turin. Every 30mins a SADEM airport bus (t 011 300 0611, *www.sadem.it*) stops at the air terminal at Corso Vittorio Emanuele II 57 by Porta Nuova railway station, and it also stops at Porta Susa railway station. Buy tickets (€5.50) at the Turismo Torino e Provincia office in the arrivals hall, at bars near the bus stops, or on board (€1 extra). GTT trains (*www.gtt.to.it*) have a station 140m from the airport and run every 30mins to Turin's Dora railway station in 20mins; tickets – €3.40 one way, €6.20 return – include 70mins on Turin's buses – no.11 goes straight to the centre and Porta Nuova. Alternatively, this last service is included in the Torino/Piedmont card package.

By Rail

Turin's rail system is undergoing a revolution. The old main station, the **Porta Nuova**, will be replaced by **Porta Susa Station** in the west, to be linked up with the new metro line, the new Eurostar service from Geneva and high-speed trains to Novara and Milan and eventually Lyon. A third station, **Dora**, Via Giachino 10, serves the airport, Ciriè, Lanzo and Ceres.

By Coach

The terminal coach station is on Corso Vittorio Emanuele II 131/h, but many buses also stop near Porta Susa station. Buses serve towns in the province, Aosta's ski resorts as far as Chamonix, and Milan Malpensa airport along with many other destinations. Eurolines buses (t 055 357 110, *www.eurolines.it*) to London and other European capitals depart from that terminal as well. For further information on how to get there and getting around, see *www.regione.piemonte.it/ptplweb/index.do*.

Getting around Turin

Most of Turin's sights are within **walking** distance of each other in the historic centre, where cars have been banned. Distant sites, especially going south, can be reached by GTT **trams** and **buses**, supplemented at the beginning of 2006 by a **metro** (*www.metrotorino.it*), linking Porta Susa and Porta Nuova railway stations, and linking the former to Collegno (northwest), and Lingotto (south). Pick up a free transport map at the tourist office. Tickets are €1 (valid for 90mins), day passes €3.50. There is also a tourist bus that visits all the major sights and shopping areas that you can hop on and hop off at your convenience.

Parking in Turin is not impossible, but in the city centre you don't need a car, and traffic is restricted at certain times of day. You can hire a **bike** from Amici della Bicicletta, Via Vittorio Amedeo 28, t 011 561 3059. **Car hire** addresses in town include Avis, Corso Turati 37, by Porta Nuova Station, t 011 205 3547, *www.avisautonoleggio.it*; Maggiore, Porta Nuova Station, t 011 650 3013, *www.maggiore.it*; Hertz, Via Reiss Romoli 213, t 011 222 9605, *www.hertz.it*; Targarent, Corso Agnelli 220, t 011 003 1022, *www.targarent.it*.

Taxis queue in the main piazzas; for a radio taxi, t 011 5730 or t 011 5737.

from Chambéry to Turin, along with his dynasty's most important relic, the Holy Shroud.

Having served in the court of Spain, Emanuele Filiberto was determined to make old feudal Savoy-Piedmont into an absolutist centralized state on the French-Spanish model. In Turin, his first priority was to build a massive pentagonal citadel (of which only the Mastio survives), but his second ambition, inherited by his successors, was to make the city into a showcase. Under three chief architects, Ascanio Vittozzi (d. 1615), Carlo di Castellamonte and his son Amedeo (d. 1683), extensions were added to the Quadrilatero Romano, all with straight streets and geometric squares, many lined with arcades and homogeneous street fronts – beginning with Piazza Castello and the Contrada Nuova (Via Roma and Piazza San Carlo). The rest of Europe knew of Turin through engravings called the *Theatrum Saubadiae* (1682), the stage for the ambitions of the house of Savoy. Italians nicknamed the city 'Little Paris'.

The most dramatic production staged in the *Theatrum Saubadiae* occurred during the War of the Spanish Succession, when Louis XIV put his grandson Philip on the throne of Spain, a seat coveted by the Emperor of Austria for his own son. After first siding with France, Duke Vittorio Amedeo II realized he was more likely to pick up territorial gains from Austria (which then occupied most of northern Italy) and changed sides in 1703. Furious, Louis XIV vowed he'd destroy the Duke and invaded Piedmont, laying it waste, then concentrating in May 1706 on taking Turin, with an army of 44,000. In mid-June, Vittorio Amedeo rode off, promising to bring aid, leaving the city, with a population of *c.* 40,000, defended by 4,000 thinly stretched men. The outlook for Turin was grim: bombarded and threatened with famine, much of the summer-long siege was fought in the 14km of subterranean galleries under the citadel (*see* p.230–1). At the end, Vittorio Amedeo met up with his cousin, Prince Eugene of Savoy, General of the Habsburg armies (and later victor over the Turks at Belgrade and the subject of Josef Strauss's *Prinz Eugen March*) and defeated the French.

In the postwar shake-up, Vittorio Amedeo's reward for picking Austria was a crown (1714). The new king went down to inspect his realm of Sicily (which he had to exchange a few years later for poorer Sardinia) and there met the great architect Filippo Juvarra, whom he summoned to Turin to make the city into a royal capital.

In the mid-18th century, the population had more than doubled to 94,000. Yet Turin became the greyest of Italian capitals, its rulers rigidly protectionist and reactionary just when the rest of northern Italy began to wake up to the Enlightenment. Change came forcibly when Napoleon's General Joubert took the city in 1798, and sent Carlo Emanuele IV into exile on Sardinia. Piedmont was annexed to France as the *département* of Eridano (the ancient name of the Po), with Turin as capital. The city walls were dismantled, a bridge was built, but Napoleon's other projects stayed on the drawing board when Vittorio Emanuele I was restored in 1814, and set the clock back fifty years.

Thanks to the Congress of Vienna, this clock was ticking in a kingdom of Sardinia which now included the radicalized ex-Republic of Genoa. But change was in the air, even in grey Turin. In 1831, Carlo Alberto, Prince of Carignano, scion of a junior branch of the House of Savoy and a well-meaning liberal, inherited the throne and set about reforming the Kingdom of Sardinia, giving it a constitution (*Statuto*) that, among other things, guaranteed freedom of religion for the once-persecuted Waldensians.

Forced to abdicate in 1848 after starting and losing a war to Austria, Carlo Alberto was succeeded by his son Vittorio Emanuele II. Although known in the courts of Europe as 'King Buffoon' for his bluff coarse manner and skirt chasing, Vittorio Emanuele did have the wiliest of politicians as his prime minister. Count Camillo Benso di Cavour, a follower of John Adams, put Piedmont firmly on the capitalist path – a catch-up task in regards to northern Europe, but hastened along by public works, canal and railroad building, and the founding of a national bank (the future Bank of Italy). Cavour knew that a liberal economy required a liberal society and the new freedom of press, of teaching and of political association soon brought Turin a flood of political refugees from across Italy; the *caffè* were filled with talk and intrigue.

In 1861, Turin became the capital of the new kingdom of Italy. There were riots in 1865 when pressure from France forced the government to move a safer distance away, to Florence, and on to Rome – once the French occupation there ended. Yet the energies unleashed soon found a new outlet in making Turin the capital of Italian industry. It held Italy's first international fair in 1884 (there would be others, in 1902 and 1961), but the most notable date was 1899, when Giovanni Agnelli founded Turin's new dynasty, Fiat (Fabbrica Italiana Automobili Torino). His employees became Italy's first proletariat: Antonio Gramsci, the Sardinian philosopher and co-founder of the Italian Communist Party in Turin (1921), led the workers' factory councils in occupying the Fiat works at Mirafiori in what he hoped would become an Italian Petrograd. The failure taught him that Italians required a different solution, and made him fear that extremism in one form or another would be the end result; he was arrested in 1926 and died in Fascist custody in 1937. His influential *Notebooks* and *Letters from Prison* were later published by Turin's fabled leftist publisher, Einaudi.

The 1920s also brought Turin a wave of newcomers from rural Piedmont in search of jobs, although the Fascists did all they could to keep folks down on the farm. Riots and strikes in 1930, brought on by an unemployment rate of 25 per cent, were brutally dealt with. As factories turned to war production, Turin was bombed in 1942 (by the end of the war, 40 per cent of the city would be destroyed); workers revolted, and many took to the hills to fight the Germans when they occupied the city in 1943; the *partigiani* liberated Turin (30 April 1945) three days before the Allies arrived.

The post-war years were equally troubled. As Fiat geared up to produce its first economy cars (the classic 600 and 500), thousands of Italians – this time from the poorer south – came up to work in the factories, swelling the city's population. Paradoxically, although Turin liked to take most of the credit for Italy's unification, it also suffered the consequences, in bigotry and racism. Nor had conditions for workers improved; in the deepening discontent the Red Brigades – 'the armed instrument of class struggle' – were founded in the early 1970s on the factory floors of Milan and Turin. This initiated Italy's 'Years of Lead' (*Anni di Piombo*) of kidnappings and kneecappings of managers, politicians and journalists, actions at first supported among disgruntled workers, but much less so after the 1978 assassination of Christian Democrat leader Aldo Moro in Rome (by still unidentified perpetrators).

Behind all the sound and fury, Giovanni Agnelli's grandson, Gianni Agnelli (aided by the government in Rome) was busily turning Fiat into a huge conglomerate and making Italy a world economic power, attracting a new wave of immigrants to Turin – this time from Africa, Eastern Europe and China. Turin's economy is now changing. Heavy industry is declining; as government agreements restricting car imports into Italy expired, Fiat's former 60 per cent market share in Italy was cut in half, and today automobiles are now only a small part of Agnelli interests, inherited by Gianni's grandson John Elkan, who recently married the Milanese princess, Lavinia Borromeo. Meanwhile, Turin is changing direction yet again, rediscovering assets neglected during the industrial boom, looking towards hi-tech (one company, Alenia Spazio, provides parts for the international space station), communications and environmental technologies as well as contemporary art, food, culture, tourism, education and training (it is home to a university, polytechnic, the alternative Scuola Holden that teaches writing techniques, a UN training centre and the European Training Foundation), fashion (Borbonese, Superga, Invicta and Robe di Kappa are based here) and, of course, sport.

The New Turin: the 2006 Winter Olympics and Beyond

Just as in the Olympic cities of Barcelona and Athens, bagging the XX Winter Olympics (February 2006) and the Paralympic Games (March 2006) acted as a catalyst for an immense urban overhaul in Turin. The largest city ever to host the Winter Games, the intention was to put a special stamp on the games as the 'Piazza Olympics' celebrated as much in the city centre as on the pistes; medal ceremonies, for instance, took place in central Piazza Castello. There were local touches, too: the sleek Olympic torch was designed by the city's most prestigious design firm, Pininfarina.

Although not as big as the summer Olympics, the numbers still gave pause for thought: some 2,500 athletes from 84 countries, their 2,500 assistants, 2,300 IOC officials, 650 judges and referees and 10,000 media people attended the games, along with 6,000 guests of the official sponsors (two of the biggest, of course, were Fiat and the Agnelli-owned Instituto Bancario San Paolo) as well as more than a million spectators. There were 84 gold medals to be

N

5 km

2 miles

Chieri

Superga

Parco della Collina di Superga

Po River

SP7

Casale

Faculty of Law and Political Science

Faro della Victoria

Villa della Regina

CENTRAL TURIN

Palazzo Porta Nuova

Porta Nuova Stazione

Parco del Valentino

Moncalieri

Castello di Moncalieri

A6

Po River

CORSO MONCALIERI

UNITA D'ITALIA

CORSO

TRIESTE

VIA NIZZA

to Carignano

Dora Stazione Porta Dora

Parco della Spina (proposed route)

Viale della Spina

Piazza Statuto

CORSO NOVARA

CORSO PRINCIPE ODDONE

CORSO GIULIO CESARE

CORSO

VERCELLI

Politecnico

Stazione Porta Susa

Palazzo della Regione

A5

A4

CORSO BONINSEGNA

CORSO REGINA MARGHERITA

Churchof the Santo Volto

Stadio delle Alpi

Stura di Lanzo River

to Airport

Parco Regionale La Mandria

Venaria Reale

Collegno

Centro Culturale Stazione Porta Susa

OGR

BORGO SAN PAOLO

Olympic Stadium

Pilasport Olympic Village

Oval

LINGOTTO

Mirafiori

Palazzo di Caccia di Stupinigi

CORSO GROSSETO

CORSO SVIZZERA

CORSO FRANCIA

VIA SAN DONATO

CORSO REGINA MARGHERITA

CORSO VITTORIO EMANUELE II

CORSO PESCHIERA

CORSO TELESIO

VIA SAN PIETRO IN VINCOLI

VIA DE SANCTIS

VIA INFERNI

CORSO SALVEMINI

CORSO SEBASTOPOLI

CORSO UNIONE SOVIETICA

CORSO AGNELLI

VIA SETTEMBRINI

CORSO ALLAMANO

A32

A21

Dora Riparia River

Rivoli

Museo dell'Arte Contemporanea

Turin and Around

won in 15 different sports. Some 25,000 volunteers recruited from all over Italy made sure the 350 events ran smoothly.

Turin, host of all the 'non-gravity events' (except curling, which took place in Pinerolo) had the biggest of three Olympic villages for athletes (others were up at Bardonecchia and Sestriere) and seven media villages, scattered throughout the city. Alongside the games, the city hosted a massive Cultural Olympic programme: opera, dance, special art exhibits (concentrating on the body and sport), literary dinners, an Italian cinema retrospective, and ice sculptures and more in a Snow Show.

Key to many of the changes in Turin is the new **Crossrail System**, begun in 1986 and slated to be completed by 2009 at the cost of over 2 billion euros. Since the early 20th century the city has been divided east/west by rail lines; thanks to 15 kilometres of tunnels, this will be replaced by a six-lane tree-lined boulevard, **La Spina**, which will extend from the exit of the Milan–Turin *autostrada* all the way south to Corso Orbassano, with parks and large contemporary art installations along the way. Old factories and warehouses nearby are being converted to new uses, with an eye to integrating the city's industrial past into its future.

The main **Olympic district** was clustered around **Lingotto** (*see* p.239), the former Fiat factory, as media centre and international broadcasting headquarters for the games. Lingotto's former train station was replaced by the **Oval**, designed by London's HOK studio for Olympic speed-skating events; a **Palaghiaccio** in nearby Corso Tazzoli was used for speed- and figure-skating training during the Olympics, and is now Turin's municipal ice sport arena. Opening and closing ceremonies took place just west in the Piazza d'Armi park, in the **Olympic Stadium** – the refurbished Stadio Comunale, built in 1931 and the home of Turin's football clubs before the construction of the Stadio delle Alpi; it is now the permanent home of Torino FC. Ice-hockey pucks flew in the neighbouring 12,000-seat **Palasport** by Arata Isozaki; the **Palavela** of 1961 (given a smart makeover by Gae Aulenti), just east of Lingotto, hosted figure-skating events.

Transport was and still is a main concern. Italy's Motown is going green: it was the first city in Italy to put hydrogen-cell buses on the streets, and it had the first line of its **metro** completed in time for the Olympics; the system is to be extended from Rivoli to beyond Lingotto, scheduled to be completed by 2011. Turin's shambolic airport has been improved.

Other projects will change the way Turin works. Along Corso Bolzano the long futuristic glass arcade of a new **Stazione Porta Susa** by Agostino Magnaghi, complete with two skyscrapers, is destined to replace Porta Nuova as the city's main station. It will be served by a **high-speed train to Milan**, and eventually link to Lyon, part of the ambitious trans-European fast train line planned from Lisbon to Kiev. The vast train repair works (**OGR**) are being converted to provide an extension of Turin's Gallery of Modern Art, and have already doubled the size of Turin's **Polytechnic**.

Turin's first industry grew up along the Dora Riparia river, and here the brownfield site of the old Michelin plant and Fiat steel works is being redeveloped, along with a new Dora station. New housing is going up everywhere here, including nine towers that house a media village next to the new **Parco Dora commercial centre**. Nearby in Via Val della Torre 11, Turin's striking new cathedral, the **Church of the Santo Volto** designed by Mario Botta, was opened in December 2006. With a nave illuminated by a circle of eight towers transmitting natural light, it looks like no other; even the campanile is a former smokestack. Behind the altar, the holy face of the Turin Shroud has been reproduced with a pixellated effect, obtained thanks to a relief technique using small bricks. The new riverside **Dora Park** already hosts the **Environment Park**, housing small hi-tech and environmental firms, in the hope of seeding future jobs in the area, along with the **Multimedia Park** and a future centre of **Information and Communication Technology**, to be built on the site of the old Savigliano train works. Downstream along the Dora, by Corso Regina Margherita, the former Italgas works are being converted by Norman Foster into the university of Turin's **Faculty of Law and Political Science** (with another Olympic media village); the old tobacco factory, on Corso Regio Parco, will house the **Faculty of Psychology**. If you're interested in learning about the extraordinary transformation of run-down or formerly industrial areas of the town, the **Metropolitan Urban Centre** (in co-operation with the Architectural Society) organizes guided tours, leaving from the city centre.

Environment Park
www.envipark.com

Metropolitan Urban Centre
t 011 1975 1603, www.urban center.to.it; €5.

Turin saw the Olympics not as an end, but as a beginning of its proper place in the European Big Time. Already on the cards are the World Congress of Architecture (2008), the European Championships of Rhythmic Gymnastics (2008), the European Short Track Speed Skating Championships (2009) and the 150th anniversary of the Risorgimento (2011), when all the current building projects, fingers crossed, should be completed. In addition, Turin is currently a candidate for the Figure Skating Worldwide Champioships in 2010, Speed Skating in 2011 and World Chair Sledge Championships in 2011.

Piazza Castello: the Royal Command Centre

Turin was born ambitious. The huge **Piazza Castello** at its heart was laid out in 1587, with enough space for knightly tournaments, and since then it has seen many key events, not least of which was the invention of vermouth in 1786 by Benedetto Carpano (see the

Palazzo Madama

plaque at the corner of Via Viotti). The *castello* of the piazza's name, ornate **Palazzo Madama**, has a history as long as the city itself: it began as the fortified east gate of the Roman town, the Porta Decumana. Property of the Acaia princes in 1205, they enlarged the Roman towers just before their line died out in 1418 and their Savoy cousins took over. Emanuele Filiberto made it a showplace for his new capital; in the 17th century two 'Madame regents' chose to live here, hence its name. In 1718, Juvarra was given the task of doing up the old place, but of his plan, only the front bit was ever built, a beautiful, articulated Versailles-inspired façade with enormous windows and a bold array of columns, and a breathtaking hall and **staircase** that occupies the entire width of the palace, as glamorous as ever after a 19-year restoration. In December 2005, the palace's excellent **Museo Civico di Arte Antica** reopened after decades, allowing visitors once more to feast their eyes on its *Heures de Milan* by Jan Van Eyck and the superb *Portrait of a Man* (1476) by Antonello da Messina.

Museo Civico di Arte Antica
Piazza Castello, t 011 4433 501, www.palazzo madamatorino.it; open Tues–Sun 10–6, Sat 10–8; free on the first Tues of the month

The west end of Piazza Castello is closed by the **Teatro Regio**. When Turin moved up a notch to become a royal capital in 1713, Vittorio Amedeo's first concern was to build a theatre for a king. Completed in 1738, it was splendiferous by all accounts, although after a huge fire in 1936 only the façade survives – the innards all date from the 1970s, while the handsome forged iron gate, the *Odissea Musicale*, is by Umberto Mastoianni (1994). On the north side of Piazza Castello, the **Armeria Reale** was opened to the public by Carlo Alberto in 1837, to show off one of the world's finest collections of weapons and armour. Once part of the royal palace, access to the Armeria is by way of a monumental stair (1740) by Benedetto Alfieri: exhibits, arranged along Juvarra and Alfieri's grand Galleria Beaumont under frescoes on the *Life of Aeneas*, include a magnificent shield from the court of Henri II, the armour of Diego Felipe de Guzman, who stood 6ft 7in tall, a sword signed by Donatello but believed to be a forgery, Napoleon's sword and wooden horses, covered with the skins of the Savoys' favourite steeds, supporting their suits of armour. The adjacent **Biblioteca Reale** contains works by Leonardo da Vinci: a sketch of the angel of the Virgin of the Rocks, his *Codex on birds in flight* and a self-portrait in red ink, of an elderly magician weary of his own magic (*to see them, you need written permission from the library director*). Here, too, is the **Prefettura**, decorated with a relief of Columbus; for good luck, rub his little finger.

Armeria Reale
Piazza Castello 191, t 011 543 889, www.artito.arti.beni culturali.it; open Tues–Fri 9–2, Sat–Sun 1–7

The Palazzo Reale

Palazzo Reale
t 011 436 1455, www.ambienteto. arti.beniculturali.it; tours Tues–Sun from 8.30am, last at 7.30pm; adm; 1st floor closed for restoration until 2008

The Palazzo Reale is set back from Piazza Castello behind an iron gate framed by bronze **statues of the Dioscuri**, the twins Castor and Pollux. Begun in the late 16th century, this palace was the main residence of the Savoys until 1865, and you can take the tour to see how they lavished their subjects' taxes on heavy chandeliers and frescoes, few of which stand out. Highlights include the sumptuous Throne Room, Juvarra's Scala delle Forbici ('Scissors' Stair') and his lacquered Chinese cabinet, the lofty Swiss Hall with a massive painting of *Emanuele Filiberto alla battaglia di San Quintino* (1557) by Palma il Giovane, the lavish ballroom, and Carlo Alberto's Chinese vase collection. The Royal Gardens laid out in the 17th century by French garden genius André Le Nôtre, are a quiet oasis, with a monumental Triton fountain, and the Mole Antonelliana (*see* pp.231–2) peeking like an alien over the trees.

The royal chapel of **San Lorenzo** (1668–80) is one of Guarini's masterpieces, though you wouldn't know it by the façade: Guarini's original design, which would have linked the exterior and interior, never left the drawing board – it threatened to unsettle the order the Savoys strove to maintain in their capital; the sight of its stunning concave-convex octagonal drum, dome and lantern over the rooftops was already troubling enough. The interior is a dynamic, complex Baroque fantasia, culminating in a dome, which, supported on pendentives pierced by large Palladian windows,

Royal Gardens
entrance in Viale Luzio, behind Piazza Castello; when restoration of the Royal Palace is completed, it will be possible to access the Royal Gardens straight from the palace courtyard; open 9am–7pm

San Lorenzo
www.sanlorenzo. torino.it

City of Magic

Perhaps you've guessed by now: Turin isn't all that it seems. According to those in the know, it stands at the vortex of two mystical triangles: a black magic triangle (Turin, London and San Francisco) and a white magic one (Turin, Prague and Lyon). Around the city, 230 sculpted figures are said to represent aspects of the energy flowing out of this unique geometry. Not a few of these are gruesome masks designed to ward off evil; there's one for every window of the Royal Palace.

Most Torinese know that the gate of the Royal Palace, guarded since 1846 by the benign underworld deities Castor and Pollux, is the most magical spot in the city, where good vibrations flow. Underneath the Giardini Reali's Triton fountain, they say, lies Emanuele Filiberto's alchemy cave, where the Iron Head sought the philosopher's stone. He was (this is documented) a friend of Nostradamus, who visited Turin and predicted the birth of a son, Carlo Emanuele I, after giving the duke and his wife a 'magic oil'; he also predicted the year Carlo Emanuele would die, 'when a nine comes before a seven' (he died at the age of 69). In 1983, when the house where Nostradamus lodged on Via Michele Lessona burned down, a stone with a mysterious inscription was found in the garden wall, dated 1556: 'Nostradamus stayed here, where there is Paradise, Hell, Purgatory. I call myself Victory. Who honours me will have glory, who disdains me will know complete ruin.'

Some say it is the presence of the Shroud that attracts the forces of good and evil. Certainly the city's own magus, Gustavo Rol (1903–94), was a good Christian who discouraged belief in the occult. Son of a wealthy Turin banker, Rol was famous for mind-reading, painting watercolours without touching the paper, passing through solid walls, and reading books without taking them off the shelf. He called his gifts 'extraordinary possibilities', which he had since the age of 23, when he discovered 'a tremendous law that links the chromatic vibrations of the colour green with the sound of the fifth note on the musical scale and certain thermal vibrations: the secret of sublime consciousness.' He was consulted by Mussolini (and told him that Italy would lose the war and that he'd be shot), Charles de Gaulle (who told a minister afterwards to beware of Rol, because such a mind-reader could pick up French state secrets), Federico Fellini (who became a close friend), JFK and Ronald Reagan; for Albert Einstein he made a rose appear out of thin air. He never did anything for money, but never let himself be studied, either, describing himself merely as 'the gutter that channels water falling from the roof'.

seemingly floats, almost dematerialized, in streams of light and geometry. Guarini's aim as a priest may have been to suggest the mystery of heaven itself. Uniquely, as far as anyone knows, the architect himself said the inaugural mass.

The Duomo and the Cappella della Sacra Sindone

Duomo di San Giovanni
Piazza San Giovanni 2, t 011 436 1540; open Mon–Fri 7.30–12 and 3–7, Sat–Sun 8–12 and 3–7

Around the corner, just off Via XX Settembre, Turin's cathedral and only surviving Renaissance building, the **Duomo di San Giovanni** was designed by three dry Tuscans and given a bland façade. Juvarra worked on the bell tower in 1723 but even he could do it no favours. Inside, its best art is at the front: the 16th-century tomb of Anna de Créquy, with its five *pleurants* (mourners), and a polyptych of *SS. Crispin and Crispinian* (*c.* 1500) with 18 stories of the patron saints of shoemakers by Martino Spanzotti and Defendente Ferrari.

At the back of the Duomo, however, rises one of the most bizarre domes ever built, zigzagging up like a prickly, squat pine-cone pagoda. For what the Duomo lacks in presence it compensates for by possessing one of the most provocative relics of Christendom: the **Shroud of Turin**. Although Emanuele Filiberto intended to build a new church for the relic, his successors settled for a chapel the size of a church: the **Cappella della Sacra Sindone**, the inimitable Guarini's masterpiece, begun in 1668 and completed after his death in 1694. The lower tiers of the entablature were built by Amedeo di Castellamonte. On this uneventful base, Guarini subverted the expected, weaving a diaphanous conical dome of restless energy and dissonant patterns zigzagging ever upwards, suggesting infinity, reaching its climax in a dome that presages some of the wilder moments of Art Deco.

⭐ **Capella della Sacra Sindone**

In 1997, while the chapel was being restored, it and part of the Palazzo Reale went up in flames; although there were rumours of pagan militants, a hearing blamed negligence on the part of the restoration firm. A heroic fireman rescued the shroud, just before it was buried in burning debris. Nevertheless, the public displays of the shroud went on as planned in 1998 and 2000 and attracted millions of pilgrims; the next showing, however, won't take place until 2025. A copy is on display; the real thing is hidden under an altar in a side chapel, laid out flat behind protective glass. As for Guarini's chapel, studies on its original structure have been completed – with some rather surprising results – and the restoration, in the same style, using the same materials, is due to begin soon, and to be completed, perhaps, by 2009.

Near the Duomo's campanile are the ruins of the *cavea* of the **Roman theatre**, while across the piazza stands the Roman **Porta Palatina** (1st century AD), with its pair of tall 16-sided brick towers and a section of city wall. This gate, like Palazzo Madama, was transformed into a medieval castle, but here most of the additions have been stripped away. At the time of writing the whole area is being transformed into a **Parco Archeologico**; as the nearby buildings around Via della Basilica and Via Porta Palatine preserve the layout of an ancient Roman *insula* (block of flats) they are getting a facelift to reflect their past; one will soon be the four-star Hotel NH Santo Stefano. More of *Augusta Taurinorum* waits in the Museo di Antichità on Via XX Settembre 88/c: Greek and Roman reliefs, ceramics and sculpture, a throne from Luni, finds from Susa, and Lombard artefacts.

Museo di Antichità
t 011 521 1106,
www.museo
antichita.it;
open Tues–Sun
8.30–7.30; adm

The Holy Shroud of Turin

As arguably the most important relic in Christendom, the Shroud (or *sindone*) has been venerated by millions over the centuries. Since 1898, when the first photographs showed the faint image on the cloth was actually a photographic negative, it has also been the subject of intense studies; sindonology symposia now take place annually around the world, and interest shows no sign of abating, especially now that the famous 1988 carbon dating that pronounced it a forgery has been called into question (apparently the studies were done on a medieval patch).

The Shroud's story, pieced together by Ian Wilson in his *Shroud of Turin* (1978) reads like a novel. It starts with the story of the *Mandylion* (p.165), only here the portrait 'the True Likeness of Christ not made by human hands' is the one on the Shroud, folded so that only the face appeared (ancient fold marks suggest this was done). Evidence for this is in a document in the Vatican Library written in 944 by Gregory Referendarius, the archdeacon of Hagia Sophia in Constantinople, which describes the *Mandylion* as a full length image with bloodstains from a side wound. It was considered the most sacred relic in the Imperial collection, and the *Mandylions* now in Genoa and Rome are believed to have been painted copies of the face on the Shroud. Another source is French crusader Robert de Clari, who, in his *History Of Those Who Conquered Constantinople* written just after 1204, says Christ's burial linen was shown in its full length (raised as if from the tomb by means of a pulley device) in the imperial church of Santa Maria Blachernae. And he wrote that during the looting by the Crusaders the cloth vanished – for the next 153 years.

Wilson and others suspect that during those years the Shroud was in the custody of the Knights Templar, the mightiest and wealthiest organization of the day, who acted as bankers for the high and mighty. They were also famous for their secrecy, and in 1204 they were among the first inside the walls at Constantinople. What is known for certain is that when King Philip le Bel of France, who owed the Templars a huge sum of money, trumped up charges of heresy against them, in collusion with the French pope Clement V, one accusation, and one that many Templars admitted to, was that they worshipped 'a head'. Wilson believes these 'heads' were copies made of the face on the shroud, which may have been distributed to their various houses throughout Europe (one, in fact, was found in Temple Combe in Dorset in 1951). When King Philip finally disbanded the order, the last Grand Master, Jacques de Molay and Geoffrey de Charney, the Preceptor of Normandy of the Knights Templar, who refused to confess to the Inquisition, were burned at the stake in Paris in 1314.

De Charney, it seems, was able to smuggle the relic to his family for safekeeping, because the Shroud is next heard of in the possession of Geoffrey de Charney, a distant relative and the bravest knight of France, lord of the French village of Lirey. Charney apparently made a vow to build a church in Lirey to exhibit the relic, but died in the Battle of Poitiers defending King Jean le Bon in 1356. That year, however, the Shroud was documented for the first time in the west, when his widow and son, another Geoffrey de Charney, put it on exhibition. Although local bishops accused them of displaying a forgery, the de Charneys defied them, although for safekeeping they gave the Shroud to the Dukes of Savoy (1453). It was kept in Chambéry's Sainte Chapelle, where it just barely survived a fire in 1532 and was restored with patches. In 1587 Emanuele Filiberto brought it to Turin, where it has remained, except in times of danger – during the French siege of 1706, and in the Second World War. In 1983, when ex-King

Umberto II died in Portugal, he willed the Shroud to the Pope and his successors, on condition that it remain in Turin with the archbishop as its custodian.

In the summer of 2002, a controversial restoration of the relic by the diocese had many sindonologists fearing that further studies might be compromised. However, new findings have been coming in apace, most of them suggesting that a medieval forgery seems highly improbable. One fact that seems hardest to explain away is that the figure on the Shroud accurately portrays a crucifixion – nails through the wrists rather than through the hands, which could never have supported the weight of the body; a medieval forger would surely have depicted the nail wounds where medieval artists had always portrayed them. Forensic scientists believe it would have been impossible to forge the unique front and back impressions of a crucified man, with horrific wounds in all the places mentioned in the Bible. The button-like shapes on the closed eyes have been identified as coins issued in the reign of Pontius Pilate. The image comes out in three dimensions when plotted on 3D computer graphic programmes, again making a forgery unlikely. Pollen studies place it in the right place at the right time. An expert on ancient fabrics says that the herringbone weave was common in quality fabrics of ancient Judaea. Raymond Rogers, the chemist who debunked the 1988 carbon dating, showed that primitive linen woven and treated according to Pliny's description would have had a thin film of crude starch and soap on the outermost fibres, on which an image could have been imprinted by bodily amine vapours reacting with saccharides in the starch. This theory was supported in 2004, with the discovery of a second face imprint (superficial, in that nothing soaked through the linen) on the opposite end of the shroud that had long been hidden under a protective cloth. What is essential for the chemical theory, however, is that the body was removed from contact with the cloth before any further decomposition took place...the only sure thing is that the discussions will continue.

West of Piazza Castello: the Quadrilatero Romano

The streets west of Piazza Castello were the core of the Roman city, and today this grid of narrow streets, the Quadrilatero Romano, is full of trendy bars and restaurants. To the north, the quarter is flanked by the massive Piazza della Repubblica, the site of **Porta Palazzo**, Europe's largest open-air food market, with its swish new glass pentagonal **Mercato dell'Abbigliamento** for clothes by Massimiliano Fuksas (not yet open to the public), while in the little streets behind it, in the multi-ethnic Borgo Dora, the sprawling **Balôn** flea market takes place every Saturday. The Gran Balôn (Piazza Borgo Dore) is every second Sunday of the month, with 205 exhibitors.

Just south of Piazza della Repubblica, on Via Milano, the Gothic church of **San Domenico** was rebuilt in 1776 and redone in a medieval style in 1911, but preserves, in the chapel of the Madonna delle Grazie, fine frescoes from c.1350. To the west (take Via S. Chiara to Via Consolata) stands the **Santuario della Consolata** dedicated to the beloved Virgin protectress of Turin, an unusual church founded in the 11th century, the date of its campanile. Behind a neoclassical façade, it consists of two churches, a hexagon and an oval, knitted together by Guarini in 1678. Juvarra added the lavish high altar, incorporating a much-venerated 15th-century Greek icon of the Virgin; a room off the sacristy is packed full of ex votos. Piazza della Consolata's other shrine is **Al Bicerin**, founded in 1763 and owned by women since the day it opened.

Santuario
della Consolata
*Piazza della
Consolata,*
www.laconsolata.org

The Shroud, its history and scientific studies are covered in the Museo della Sindone, at Via San Domenico 28 in the crypt of the church of SS. Sudario (1735), headquarters of the confraternity dedicated to the Shroud. Its prize is the beautiful 16th-century reliquary that housed the rolled-up relic until 1998 (it's now kept flat, to prevent any new wrinkles). Juvarra's last work before leaving for Madrid, the magnificent **Church of the Carmine** (1732), on Via del Carmine 3, hides, behind a workmanlike façade of 1872, a beautiful barrel-vaulted interior lined by double rows of arches and open galleries above the chapels, the whole filled with a play of light and shadows. Next to this, an obelisk marks *palazzi*-filled Piazza Savoia; you can visit one, the Palazzo Falletti di Barolo (1692). Silvio Pellico (*see* p.267) served as the librarian and died here in 1854. His patron, the Marquise Giulia Falletti di Barolo, was a well-known philanthropist who often welcomed Cavour to her salons.

South of Piazza Savoia runs pedestrian-only **Via Garibaldi**, the *Decumanus* of the Roman city and now a popular street for a *passeggiata*, with its shops and bars. Its west end runs into arcaded **Piazza Statuto**, the supposed seat of black magic in Turin. The Romans, in their time, regarded the west as malevolent, as the setting sun represents the divide between day and night; it sits on the gate to hell, according to some, or on a more prosaic level, a manhole into the city's sewers. Certainly its **Monument to the Fréjus Tunnel**, commemorating a 19th-century engineering feat considered the equal to the digging of the Suez Canal, is more than a tad peculiar: on a tall pile of dark boulders excavated from the mountain, white figures, said to represent workers killed on the project, struggle to reach the beautiful bronze angel on top – none other than Lucifer, with the star on his head, looking down Via Garibaldi towards Piazza Castello and the equally star-topped statue of Pollux.

Corso Inghilterra marks the former extent of the walls; just west of Piazza Statuto is a neighbourhood that grew up after the city's *Esposizione di Arti Decorative e Industriali* in 1902, during Turin's love affair with Art Nouveau (or *Stile Liberty*). There are examples sprinkled throughout the district, especially along Corso Francia: the **Villino Raby** at No.8, the ornate **Casa Fenoglio** at the corner of Via Principi d'Acaja with Corso Francie, and the **Palazzo della Vittoria** at No.23.

Heading east on Via Garibaldi there are three little churches to visit. **SS. Martiri** at No.25 was built for the Jesuits by Pelligrino Tibaldi in 1577 and dedicated to the three guardians of Turin, Solutore, Avventore and Ottavio. It has a richly decorated interior and high altar by Juvarra. Some say the Holy Grail is hidden in Turin – hence the statue holding a goblet on the façade. To the right of the church, through an atrium, is the **Cappella della Pia**

Museo della Sindone
t 011 436 5832,
www.sindone.it; open
9–12 and 3–7; adm
includes audio guide

Palazzo Falletti di Barolo
Via delle Orfane 7, t 011 436 0311,
www.palazzobarolo.it;
open Mon and Wed 10–12 and 3–5, Fri 10–12, Sun 3.30–6.30; adm

---

11

Turin | West of Piazza Castello: the Quadrilatero Romano

Congregazione dei Banchieri e Mercanti (1692), with more lavish decoration and a mechanical perpetual calendar of 1835 in the sacristy. Via Botero from here leads shortly to Via Santa Maria and **Santa Maria di Piazza** (1751), Bernardo Vittone's most important work in the capital, its luminous little rococo gem of an interior hidden, as usual, behind a plain-Jane neoclassical façade.

Back on Via Garibaldi, the **Palazzo di Città** was built in the 17th century as Turin's city hall, overlooking the former Roman forum and medieval market square, and the original place of executions. Its statue of the 'Green Count' (named for his favourite colour) Amedeo VI shows him pummelling an unlucky knight; in 1362 Amedeo founded the Order of the Collar, now the Order of the Annunziata, and one of the oldest chivalric honours in existence.

The West End: Piazza Solferino, the Citadella and Museo Pietro Micca

In 1885, Turin's tidy Roman plan was disrupted when Via Pietro Micca was plowed diagonally from Piazza Castello to long narrow **Piazza Solferino**, formerly site of Turin's timber market. Piazza Solferino is another vortex of magic Turin, thanks to its **Angelic Fountain** (1930). The fountain was commissioned by the Fascist authorities to be placed near the cathedral, until the Church realized that its sculptor, Giovanni Riva, was a freemason, and surely filled his sculptures full of esoteric juju, so it ended up here. And ever since then people have come to analyse it for masonic secrets; those in the know say it represents the Gateway into Infinity. Another statue remains in situ, however – this is the 1887 **Monument of Fernando Duca di Genova**, son of Carlo Alberto, who fought in the Battle of La Bicocca, near Novara, at the end of the first, disastrous War of Independence. The sculptor, Balzico, chose to depict the very moment in battle when the horse was killed beneath the prince, rendered with the most exacting realism; in fact Balzico had a horse killed to capture its death throes. The square's **Teatro Alfieri**, was built in 1857 for equestrian events but now sticks to more typical dramas.

When Emanuele Filiberto moved the capital to Turin in 1563, his first task was to erect a mighty pentagonal fortress to defend it from the French. In 1857, when France had become an ally rather than a perennial threat, it was all pulled down, leaving only the Mastio, or donjon, at Corso Galileo Ferraris. This houses Turin's oldest museum (since 1731), the **Museo Storico Nazionale dell'Artiglieria** dedicated to the national artillery (closed for restoration until 2011).

Museo Civico
Pietro Micca
*t 011 546 317,
www.museopietro
micca.it; open
Tues–Sun 9–7; adm*

To the west, the **Museo Civico Pietro Micca** at Via Guicciardini 7/a commemorates the ex-citadel's greatest test: the French siege from 13 May to 7 September 1706 (*see* p.218). Vauban, Louis XIV's military engineer, had warned against attacking the citadel because of its treacherous subterranean anti-mine galleries linked to the massive outer defences, and indeed much of the siege took place there, in a battle of spades and wits between miners, as the French fought to penetrate the galleries, or flood them. At one point, when the French managed to enter a tunnel beneath the emergency gate, a miner, Pietro Micca, heard them coming and blew up a huge cache of powder, using, as time was short, a very short fuse, knowing he too would be blown to bits; 'his' stair, which you can visit, was only rediscovered in 1958. The museum has models and documents on the siege, and you can walk through the galleries where so much took place 300 years ago – some 14 kilometres of tunnels survive, a legacy unique in European cities.

East of Piazza Castello: The Mole Antonelliana and Cinema Museum

㉗ Mole Antonelliana and Cinema Museum
Via Montebello 20, t 011 8138 560–1, www.museocinema.it; lift operates Tues–Sun 10am–8pm, Sat 10am–11pm; museum open Tues–Sun 9–8, Sat 9am–11pm; adm

Although they didn't have a perfect record, the Savoys were more tolerant towards non-Catholics than many rulers in Europe. In 1430, Amedeo VIII had decreed laws protecting Jews; Emanuele Filiberto, in spite of papal frowns, had welcomed them to Turin. In 1848 Carlo Alberto signed his act of religious emancipation and in 1863 Turin's Jews commissioned Alessandro Antonelli to build a synagogue, which, because of its small plot, was to have plenty of height. A decade later, however, they ran out of money, and Antonelli, distraught at abandoning the project, asked the city to take it on, and re-dedicate it to Vittorio Emanuele II, in whose glory it should be allowed to grow like Topsy, an extra 400ft or so. Most cities would have said no, but Turin, which cut its milk teeth on the extravaganzas of Guarini and Juvarra, agreed.

Known ever since as the **Mole Antonelliana** ('Antonelli's massive bulk'), Turin's utterly unique 549ft landmark is a feat of engineering and aesthetics, harmonious and bizarre, made up of a vaguely Greek temple façade, topped by a colonnade and windows, a sloping glass pyramid, then a double-decker Greek temple, and a pinnacle crowned with a star that shines at night. If Turin is a city of magic, the Mole is its cosmic transmitter that picks up currents of energy and relays them throughout the city; others say it is a lightning rod for madness. At night when they're aglow, Mario Merz's red Fibonacci numbers on the dome, a permanent installation from the Luci d'Artista festival, add to the strangeness.

Inside the bulk, the wonderful interactive **Museo Nazionale del Cinema** is a must, especially if you've brought the kids (there are good explanations in English). Turin was the first capital of Italian cinema, home to a dozen studios before 1920, one of which produced the first Italian feature film, the three-hour *Cabiria* (1914) directed by Giovanni Pastrone. The collection begins with magic lanterns, shadow plays, very early animation and film clips (a man boxing a kangaroo and fairies prancing around a bonfire). Up in the belly of the Mole, under the baleful eye of the enthroned Moloch (a prop from *Cabiria*) you can spend hours watching films, projected on the huge screens in the centre and in a dozen witty little theatres along the sides: for the Surrealists, the seats are toilets; a big red bed is provided for viewing love scenes. In between there's a huge collection of posters and film memorabilia. A glass-walled lift up to the top offers a big view over Turin and the Alps.

Nearby, at Via Giulia di Barolo 9, you can see another of Antonelli's tall, narrow buildings, this one a house nicknamed the **Fetta di Polenta** or 'Slice of Polenta'.

Towards the River: Down Via Po

Porticoed **Via Po**, just south of the Mole, was part of the city's second expansion, laid out by Amedeo di Castellamonte in 1673 to lead down to the big river. There's another famous café here, **Fiorio** at Via Po 8, where Cavour used to plot his next move in the Risorgimento (today people tend to go for the *gelati*). The whole area is busy with students attending the University of Turin, an institution dating back to 1404, with its seat since 1720 at the **Palazzo Università**, Via Po 17; the courtyard has a plaque to Erasmus, the most renowned of its alumni. Many of the humanities students will soon have a new campus all their own, at the former Italgas works, designed by Norman Foster.

In the 1820s, Carlo Alberto moved the royal art school, the **Pinacoteca Albertina delle Belle Arti**, to its current headquarters just off Via Po. Its large gallery has works by Filippo Lippi (*Fathers of the Church*), Defendente Ferrari (*Nativity*), Luca Cambiaso (*Ascent to Calvary*), Martin van Heemskerck (*Last Judgement*), Mattia Preti (*Tasso in the Court of Ferrara*), a beautiful Flemish tapestry and an important collection of 60 drawings by Gaudenzio Ferrari.

Just south, Piazza Carlo Emanuele II (better known as **Piazza Carlina**) was laid out at the same time as Via Po, as another royal square, this time octagonal, to set off an equestrian statue of the eponymous duke. Not very popular (he was the one who ordered the massacre of the Waldensians in 1655), his piazza was squared after his death and his statue has been replaced by a **monument to Cavour** (1872). But the spot must be cursed: it is a strange, almost smutty statue of the man, wearing a smug smile and a toga (but minus his famous pince-nez) while 'Italy', buxom and undraped, kneels before him. Continuing south, at Via dell'Accademia Albertina and Via Giolitti, stands an imposing 17th-century hospital, the seat of the **Museo Regionale di Scienze Naturali**, founded in 1978 to unite the university's vast palaeontological, geological, zoological and botanical collections.

Fiorio
www.fioriocaffe gelateria.com

Pinacoteca Albertina delle Belle Arti
Via Accademia Albertina 8, t 011 817 7862, www.accademia albertina.torino.it; open Mon–Sat 10–6; adm

Museo Regionale di Scienze Naturali
t 011 432 6354, www. regione.piemonte.it/ museoscienzenaturali; open Wed–Mon 10–7; adm

Nietzsche on Turin: Beyond Good and Evil

Friedrich Nietzsche, always a solitary traveller, moved to some rented rooms in Turin in 1888, where he wrote his last works, *Twilight of the Idols*, *Ecce Homo* and *The Antichrist*, and the following letter: 'What a worthy and serious city! Not at all a metropolis, not at all modern, as I had feared: rather, it is a city of seventeenth-century royalty, which has but one commanding taste in all things, that of the court and the nobles... There is a unity of taste, down to the colours (the whole city is yellow or reddish brown). And for the feet as well as the eyes it is a classic spot! What safety, what sidewalks, not to mention the omnibus and the trams, which are miraculously arranged here! What solemn and earnest piazzas! And the palaces are built without pretension, the streets clean and well made – everything far more dignified than I expected! The most beautiful cafés I've ever seen. These arcades are necessary here, given the changeable weather: yet they are spacious, not at all oppressive. Evenings on the bridge over the Po: splendid! Beyond good and evil!' One wonders if Gustave Flaubert, who visited in 1845, meant the same thing, more succinctly, when he wrote, 'Turin is the most boring city in the world'.

Museo di Arti Decorative Fondazione Accorsi
t 011 812 9116, www.fondazione accorsi.it; guided tours on the hour Tues–Sun 10–1 and 2–6.30; adm

At Via Po 55, the **Museo di Arti Decorative Fondazione Accorsi** has a major hoard of decorative arts, the legacy of antiques dealer Pietro Accorsi – furniture, mostly from the 18th century, as well as paintings, porcelain and objets d'art, with a big dose of rococo. Via Po then flows into long porticoed **Piazza Vittorio Veneto**, originally conceived as a parade ground, and now free of its throng of parked cars as an underground lot has been created. Steps from the big piazza lead down to the **Murazzi**, the walls built along the river in 1830, where bars and clubs occupying the old boathouses and quays buzz by night; by day, the riverside paths are a favourite for walkers and cyclists, and there's a boathouse if you fancy a row. Here, too, you can embark on a cruise, getting on and off at will, on the Valentino or Valentina as far as Moncalieri and see how surprisingly wild and natural the Nile of Italy can be, even in the city limits.

Cruise
t 800 019 152 for hours, daily in summer, weekends and holidays only in winter; check before going as services can be suspended if the water levels are low; free with Torino+Piemonte Card

On the Right Bank: the Gran Madre di Dio and Villa della Regina

Piazza Vittorio Veneto was laid out to form a grand foyer to the **Vittorio Emanuele I bridge**, built by Napoleon but named for the king who returned to his capital from Sardinia when the coast was clear after Waterloo. The landmark on the far bank is an imitation Pantheon, the **Gran Madre di Dio church** (1831), built by the Savoys to celebrate their homecoming. In a city where every slight deviation from the orthodox is suspect, the church's unusual name, the 'Great Mother of God' is said to also refer to Egyptian Isis, the mother of Horus. In a niche to the left of the door, the statue of Faith holds a chalice identified as the Holy Grail, which those in the know say is in Turin, invisible and in permanent orbit around the Mole Antonelliana.

Villa della Regina
t 800 329 329, t 00 800 111 333 00 if calling from the UK, www.artito.arti.beni culturali.it; open weekends only

On the hill behind the church, on an axis with Piazza Castello and Via Po, stands the majestic **Villa della Regina** (Strada Santa Margherita 40), a UNESCO world heritage site. Built on a vineyard in 1615 by Cardinal Maurizio, son of Carlo Emanuele I, to house his literary Accademia Solinghi, the initial building was modelled on the Villa Aldobrandini at Frascati; it later became the favourite residence of Anne d'Orléans, queen of Vittorio Amedeo II. Over the centuries various architects, including Juvarra, added their two cents' worth to the villa and its gardens, integrating them in a wonderful theatrical whole with fountains, pavilions and a 'theatre of waters'. It reopened in 2006 following restoration.

Prominent just south of the Gran Madre di Dio, on the Monte dei Cappuccini, stands Ascanio Vitozzi's distinctive, centrally planned church of **Santa Maria del Monte**, begun in 1584, and given a tall octagonal drum by Carlo di Castellamonte in 1656; beautifully lit at night, it serves as a kind of beacon for the clubbers down at the Murazzi. The cloister houses the important and newly refurbished **Museo Nazionale della Montagna Duca degli Abruzzi** at Via Giardino 39, named in honour of the famous mountain climber Luigi of Savoy, Duke of the Abruzzi (d. 1942). The Club Alpino Italiano was founded in Turin in 1863, and begun the museum's collections on all aspects of the geography, flora and fauna and human activity in the mountains. There's a spectacular view of the Alps from the belvedere.

Museo Nazionale della Montagna Duca degli Abruzzi
t 011 660 4104; open Tues–Sun 9–7; adm

South of Piazza Castello: Down and Around Via Roma

Baroque Turin is laid out in a stately rhythm of squares and streets, lined with 18km of porticoes. On the south side of Piazza Castello, **Via Roma**, lined with the city's most exclusive boutiques, was laid out in 1620 as the main street in the Contrada Nuova, the first extension of the new capital of the Savoys. It had the first unified shop fronts in Italy (one of the things that made Turin look so 'Parisian' to other Italians) although these have mostly been lost in a 1937 remodelling by Marcello Piacentini.

Parallel to Via Roma, the glass-roofed **Galleria Subalpina**, linking Piazza Castello and Piazza Carlo Alberto, was built in 1874, at the dawn of the consumer age, when it was the height of fashion to stroll and window-shop for pretty things no one needed, stopping for a coffee at the lovely **Caffè Baratti & Milano**, decorated with marbles and reliefs. Nietzsche collapsed here while strolling in 1889, apparently after tearfully embracing a horse he felt had been mistreated by its owner, then went from a religious ecstasy into the insanity that filled the last decade of his life. 'A disconcerting number of writers, from Tasso to Rousseau, J.A. Symonds to Primo Levi, have become depressed or gone mad in Turin' (Lesley Chamberlain, *Nietzsche in Turin*).

Piazza Carlo Alberto is overlooked by the secondary neoclassical façade (the entrance to the palace stables) of the splendid **Palazzo Carignano** begun in 1679 by Guarino Guarini for the Savoia-

Carignano branch of the ducal family (descendants of the younger son of Emanuele Filiberto; Vittorio Emanuele II was born here). The main entrance faces Piazza Carignano, and it's a Baroque cracker: a bold undulating brick façade billowing like a wave, swelling around an elliptical core, although it is currently hidden behind scaffolding as the exterior and innards are both undergoing a complete restoration (check its status at *www.artito.arti.beniculturali.it*).

The palace is full of historical fossils: the reconstructed bedroom in Oporto where Carlo Alberto died in exile; Cavour's study; and the chamber of Piedmont's Subalpine Parliament preserved as it was during its final session in 1860 – all chandeliers, gilt and plush. Here its successor, the first Italian Parliament, proclaimed Vittorio Emanuele II King of Italy on 14 March 1861 and remained in session until the capital was moved to Florence in 1865 – before having a chance to use a second chamber especially built for it, completed only in 1870 (although it awaits, pristinely, in case the Italian government ever changes its mind about Rome and moves back

Museo Nazionale del Risorgimento Italiano
closed for restoration until the end of 2008

to Turin). Rooms on the *piano nobile* contain the **Museo Nazionale del Risorgimento Italiano**, one of the most important historical museums in Italy, covering the 1706 Siege of Turin to 1945, with a special emphasis on the Risorgimento: one of the highlights of the collection are the paintings illustrating episodes from that war.

Just south of Palazzo Carignano, on Via Accademia delle Scienze, a Corinthian temple façade distingushes Juvarra's **San Filippo Neri** (1715) – the biggest church in Turin. The style harks back to the baths of Rome and Alberti's Renaissance church of Sant'Andrea in Mantua, which Juvarra knew well. Turin keeps its greatest treasures nearby as well, in the monumental brick **Palazzo dell'Accademia delle Scienze**, a building begun in 1679 by Guarino Guarini as a Jesuit college. This is Guarini's most 'ordinary' building, although the façade is lively, with its rows of large windows growing more elaborate with each floor.

The Egyptian Museum

Egyptian Museum
Via Accademia delle Scienze 6, t 011 561 7776, www.museoegizio.it; open winter Tues–Sun 8.30–7.30; summer (11 Jun–9 Sept) 9.30–8.30; adm exp

This, the most important Egyptian collection in the world after Cairo, was begun as a cabinet of curios in 1628 by Carlo Emanuele I, who may well have been inspired by his alchemist father, Emanuele Filiberto. His passion for all things Egyptian was inherited by later Savoys, especially Carlo Felice, who acquired the collection of Piedmont native Bernardo Drovetti (the French consul-general of Egypt and a confidant of Mehmet Ali) and in 1824 opened the world's first Egyptian museum in Turin. Two 20th-century Italian expeditions added to the collections, and the museum played a major role in the Aswan Dam rescue digs. It was rewarded with one of the Aswan temples: the 15th-century BC rock-cut **Temple of Ellessya**, with a relief of Tuthmose III, now reconstructed on the ground floor – best seen in the early evening when the half-light highlights the reliefs.

The same floor houses an excellent collection of monumental sculpture, much of it from the temple of Ammon at Karnak, notably the 13th-century BC black granite Ramses II, the 15th-century BC Thothmes III and the sarcophagus of Ghemenef-Har-Bak, a vizier of the 26th Dynasty. Upstairs, the immense papyrus library was studied by Champollion after he cracked the Rosetta Stone, to complete his translation of hieroglyphics. Elsewhere you can spend hours wandering amid the essentials and the trivialities of ancient Egypt; there's a reconstruction of the 14th-century BC **tomb of the architect Khaiè and his wife Meriè** – even the bread and beans for their afterlife remain intact, along with some excellent paintings. Other rooms contain mummies in various stages of *déshabille* (the face of one, of a 45-year-old man named Harwa, has been intensely studied for two years by scientists, and recreated in clay). There are wooden models of boats and funerary processions, paintings, statuettes, jewellery, clothing and textiles – including some very rare painted pieces from pre-3000 BC. The basement has a segment of Turin's Roman walls and finds from the Gebelein, Assiut and Qau el Kebir sites excavated by the museum (1905–20). There are reconstructed tombs, painted sarcophagi and dozens of beautifully preserved wooden models: boats, kitchens, granaries, and servants performing everyday tasks.

The Galleria Sabauda

🅘 Galleria Sabauda
t 011 547 440, www.artito.arti. beniculturali.it; open Tues–Fri 8.30–2, Wed–Thurs 2–7.30; adm

On the top floors of the same palace, the magnificent **Galleria Sabauda** was created in 1832, when Carlo Alberto gathered over 350 paintings from his family's collections to create a French-style public museum covering the main schools. There are fine Florentine works: a *Madonna* by Beato Angelico, *Tobias and the Archangel* by Antonio and Piero del Pollaiuolo, and another *Tobias* by Filippino Lippi.

The Venetians are well represented by Mantegna (*Madonna and Saints*), Giovanni Bellini, Tintoretto, Titian and Veronese; other paintings are by Bergognone, Taddeo Gaddi, Il Sodoma and Piedmontese masters Jacques Iverny (a 15th-century triptych) and Gaudenzio Ferrari (*Crucifixion*). The Savoys liked Flemish and Dutch art, too: look for Jan Van Eyck's *St Francis*, Memling's drama-filled *Scenes from the Passion*, Van Dyck's beautiful *Children of Charles I*, popular scenes by Jan Brueghel, Rubens' *Deinira Tempted by the Fury*, *Portrait of a Doctor* by Jacobs Dirk, and Rembrandt's *Old Man Sleeping*. The French have their own room, with works by Poussin, Claude and Clouet.

Piazza San Carlo

Via Roma makes a beeline to 'Turin's Drawing Room', **Piazza San Carlo**, a theatrical 17th-century set piece by Carlo di Castellamonte, inspired by the royal squares in Paris and overlooked by the nearly twin façades of the churches **Santa Cristina** (1639) and **San Carlo** (begun in 1619) – Santa Cristina's, the fancier concave one on the left, is by Juvarra. Now liberated from a sea of parked cars, Carlo Marochetti's **equestrian statue of Duke Emanuele Filiberto** (1898) rules the piazza once again in all his glory, sheathing his sword after defeating the French at Saint-Quentin. When Turin's modern warriors, Juventus and Torino, triumph on the field, their fans dress him in their banners. The palaces lining the piazza are now offices, although one, the elegant 17th-century Palazzo Bricherasio, is used for exhibitions. Others house some of the city's oldest cafés; at the 19th-century Caffè Torino be sure to step (for luck) on the testicles of the bronze bull in the pavement before wallowing amid chandeliers and frescoed ceilings. Or try its elegant rival, the Caffè San Carlo, which first opened its doors in 1828.

> **Palazzo Bricherasio**
> Via Lagrange 20, t 011 571 1811, www.palazzo bricherasio.it; open Tues–Fri and Sun 3.30–10.30pm, Thurs and Sat 10.30am–10.30pm; adm
>
> **Caffè Torino**
> No.204, www. caffe-torino.it
>
> **Caffè San Carlo**
> No.156, www. caffesancarlo.it
>
> **Museo della Marionetta**
> t 011 530 238; open by appointment only; adm

Just west of Piazza San Carlo, the church of **Santa Teresa** was begun in 1642, in a flurry of Counter-Reformation piety; pop in to see Juvarra's Cappella della Sacra Famiglia in the right transept, his altar in the left transept, and the dramatic *Transvenerazione del cuore di Santa Teresa* in the apse, a painting attributed to Moncalvo. The Museo della Marionetta, in the Teatro Gianduja at Via S. Teresa 5, has a superb collection of stage memorabilia going back to the late 18th century and some 2,000 marionettes, many sculpted by the Lupi family and given wigs of real hair and eyes of Murano glass. Nearby, between Via Santa Teresa and Via Bertola, the glass-roofed **Galleria San Federico** is one of the most elegant corners of central Turin. It also houses a striking Art Deco cinema, currently closed for restoration.

Closing the south end of Via Roma, the elegant arcaded **Piazza Carlo Felice** has a garden of rare plants. And on the other side, through the gates and over Corso Vittorio Emanuele, stands the mastodonic **Stazione Porta Nuova**, Turin's main train station for years, on the verge of being dethroned by Porta Susa.

GAM – Galleria d'Arte Moderna e Contemporanea

> ⭐ **Galleria d'Arte Moderna e Contemporanea**
> Via Magenta 31, t 011 442 9628, www.gamtorino.it; open Tues–Sun 10–6; adm; free every first Tues of the month

In 1863, the city of Turin marked the changes wrought by the Risorgimento by establishing the first museum of modern art in Italy. It was bombed in 1942, and since 1959 the collection has been housed in this striking pavilion by Carlo Bassi and Goffredo Boschetti, completely renovated in 1993. Initially, the city only purchased works by Piedmontese artists from local shows, beginning with 19th-century neoclassical and Romantic painters, including the talented Massimo d'Azeglio, the Turin-born statesman of the Risorgimento, Antonio Fontanesi and Giuseppe Pellizza (notably the striking *Lo Specchio della Vita*). Later the purchasing criteria widened to Italian artists, in time for the gallery to bag masters such as Fattori, Balla, Boccioni, Modigliani, Carra, De Pisis, De Chirico, Morandi, Martini, Mafai, Severini, Burri, Guttoso, Messina and Fontana, and foreign painters such as Klee, Arp, Hartung, Chagall, Ernst, Picabia, Picasso, Chillida, Andy Warhol and many, many more.

More Art: the Borgo San Paolo

Turin's love affair with contemporary art has spread into the old working quarter of Borgo San Paolo, to the southwest, with Piazza Robilant as its centre (take bus 56 from Piazza Castello or 64 from Porta Nuova, or tram 10 from Porta Susa). Art galleries are springing up around a pair of foundations. The austere windowless **Fondazione Sandretto Re Rebaudengo** at Via Modane 16 keeps the Torinese abreast of the cutting edge of art thanks to its changing exhibitions on the latest avant-garde movements in visual and performance arts. In 2005, the **Fondazione Merz** opened its doors in the former Art Deco Lancia power plant at Via Limone 24. Dedicated to Mario Merz, the father of Arte Povera and called a modern alchemist for his ability to transform the meaning of objects, Merz also worked with the Fibonacci series as a way of representing organic growth, and is perhaps most known for his famous igloo installations, such as Turin's *Igloo Fontana* in Corso Mediterraneo, between Via Torricelli and Via Caboto. The foundation displays his works as well as changing exhibitions.

Fondazione Sandretto Re Rebaudengo
t 011 379 7600, www.fondsrr.org; open Tues–Sun 12–8, Thurs 12–11pm; adm; free Thurs 8–11pm

Fondazione Merz
t 011 1971 9437, www.fondazione merz.org; open Tues–Sun 11–7; adm

East of Porta Nuova: Parco del Valentino and the Car Museum

East of Porta Nuova, along the Po, stretches the **Parco del Valentino**, opened in the mid-19th century as one of the first public parks in Italy. It encompasses the **Castello del Valentino**, a pleasure palace overlooking the Po built by Emanuele Filiberto and redesigned in the 17th century for Vittorio Amedeo I's wife, the Madama Reale Cristina, daughter of Henri IV of France and a famous lover of chocolate, music and the Marchese Filippo d'Agliè. Inside, her splendid 17th-century décor is intact. The castle's **Orto Botanico**, founded in 1560, with 4,000 species of plant, fine old trees and a small lake, is a bit more accessible. But this isn't the only castle on the block. Turin built another one for its World's Fair, the Esposizione of 1884, in a mock medieval hamlet on the Po, the **Borgo e Rocca Medievale**. The houses are modelled on traditional Piedmont styles, while the castle, or Rocca, is made up of features

Orto Botanico
entrance Viale Mattioli 25, t 011 670 5985, www.bioveg. unito.it; open by appointment; adm

Borgo e Rocca Medievale
Viale Virgilio, t 011 443 1701, www.borgo medievaletorino.it; castle open Tues–Sun 9–7; adm; borgo open daily 9–7

from castles in Aosta and Piedmont, including copies of the frescoes at Manta (*see* p.267).

You would expect Turin to have a top car museum, and it does,

Museo Nazionale dell'Automobile
Corso Unità d'Italia 40, bus no.45 from Corso Marconi by Porta Nuova, t 011 677 666, www.museo auto.it; closed for restoration until end of 2008

further south in the **Museo Nazionale dell'Automobile Carlo Biscaretti di Ruffia**. It houses all the classics – Lancias, Maseratis, Alfa Romeos, Bugattis, Italas (made in Turin until 1934, including one that won the Peking–Paris marathon in 1907) and the first Fiats – as well as oddities like the asymmetrical 1948 Tarf 1.

Further along Corso Unità d'Italia, other halls built in 1961 for the Centenary of the Risorgimento Exhibition were refurbished for the Winter Olympics. The **Palazzo del Lavoro** (or Torino Esposizioni) by Pier Luigi Nervi, was restructured to host ice hockey, and the **Palavela** by Annibale and Giorgio Rigotti (1961), with its sloping hexagonal roof, which featured in the original *Italian Job* with Michael Caine, was renovated by Gae Aulenti to host the figure skating.

Lingotto and the Pinacoteca Giovanni e Marella Agnelli

Further south at Via Nizza 230, Fiat's **Lingotto** plant (1916) was the 'temple of modernity' in its time. Designed by Giacomo Mattè Trucco, it had the most sophisticated vertical assembly line in Europe, from the auto components manufactured on the ground floor to the finished vehicle ready to roll down the ramp on the fifth. Closed since 1983, the old factory has since been converted by Renzo Piano into a combination auditorium, exhibition and congress centre, shops, cinemas, hotel and heliport, with a suspended glass bubble on top for meetings and, the icing on the

Pinacoteca Giovanni e Marella Agnelli
Via Nizza 230, t 011 006 2008, www.pinacoteca-agnelli.it; open Tues–Sun 10–7; adm; audio guide available

cake, the **Pinacoteca Giovanni e Marella Agnelli**. The late Gianni Agnelli, 'Italy's uncrowned king', collected art even more diligently than starlets (Rita Hayworth and Anita Eckberg were among his conquests), and he commissioned Renzo Piano to build what Piano nicknamed the *Scrigno* ('jewel coffer') projecting over the roof, to house a small but select handful of the magnate's works by Balla – whose Futurist *Velocità Astratta* (1913) seems to evoke a speeding car – Matisse (seven lovely interiors), Renoir, Canaletto, Bellotto, Tiepolo, Modigliani, Picasso and a pair of dancers by Canova. Tram or bus nos.1 and 35 from Porta Nuova and 18 from Via Accademia Albertina go to Lingotto, but, if you come by taxi, ask to be taken up the Pinacoteca by way of the famous south ramp and kilometre-long rooftop test track where Michael Caine sends his Mini Coopers in *The Italian Job*.

Lingotto was also the epicentre of the Olympic district, and as a result, two early 20th-century industrial buildings just to the north along Via Nizza, the **Carpano e Pastificio Italiano**, have

11

Turin | Lingotto and the Pinacoteca Giovanni e Marella Agnelli

Football, Torinese Style

Mention Turin, and many immediately think of Juventus, the 'Old Lady'. Founded in 1897 by a group of teenagers sitting on a now immortal park bench in the city, by 1900 Juventus had won their first national championship; in 1903, through a mix-up, a factory in Nottingham sent them their now famous black and white striped jerseys, and a legend was born. The Agnelli clan first became involved in 1923, when Edoardo Agnelli, son of Fiat's founder, was elected president, a role later inherited by the late Gianni, and now by Giovanni Cobolli Gigli, a very experienced manager not linked to the football environment. For workers arriving in Turin from the south, supporting Juve became a rite of integration into the Italian mainstream: today the club claims 17 million supporters worldwide. After many years of victories in national and international competitions, in 2006 Juventus were involved in a massive scandal concerning phone calls by the former management allegedly trying to get favours from referees – a scandal that then spread to most of the Serie A teams, provoking intense debates throughout the nation. As a consequence, Juventus were relegated to Serie B, with a further deduction of nine points, and stripped of two trophies. After a complete change of management and under the chairmanship of Giovanni Cobolli Gigli, yet still sponsored by the Agnelli family, the team was back in Serie A at the time of writing.

Despite all this, Torino, or 'Toro', the side in burgundy, founded by Juve's disgruntled manager in 1906, is the local team, in spite of the huge success of their aristocratic rivals. Local writer Giovanni Arpino explains it this way: 'Juventus is a universal language, a football Esperanto. Torino is a dialect.' Toro's great moment came when they won five consecutive national titles (1943–49), in a decade when they were so good that, except for one player, Toro was the national team – until a dark and rainy 4 May 1949, a date branded on the city's soul, when all were killed when their plane crashed into the hill just behind the basilica on their return from a friendly match in Portugal. 'Only Fate could beat them,' is still the watchword, and the anniversary is celebrated by an annual pilgrimage to the monument marking the crash site. And on a now famous day in 2003 when Juventus were crowned champions yet again and Toro was regulated to Serie B, Turin witnessed 50,000 Toro fans in the street – not rioting or protesting as Italian fans are wont to do, but there to encourage their beloved side in what has become known as the *Marcia dell'Orgoglio Granata*, the 'March of the Burgundy Pride'.

AC Torino

Via Risalta 11, t 011 639 5091, www.ac-hotels.com

Città del Gusto Eataly

Via Nizza 230, int 14, t 011 950 6811, www.eataly.it; open Mon–Sun 10am–11.30pm

Sassi-Superga Rack Railway

t 011 576 4733; operates Mon–Fri 9–12 and 2–6, Sat, Sun and hols 9am–9pm

Basilica di Superga

t 011 899 7456, www.basilicadisuperga.com; open daily, check opening hours on the website as they vary for different attractions

been turned into a five-star hotel, the **AC Torino**, and the **Città del Gusto Eataly**, 'a gourmet food and wine regional park', a permanent offshoot of the very popular Salon del Gusto that takes place in even-numbered years at Lingotto.

Northeast of the Centre: Superga

You can drive, but public transport is more fun. Bus no.61 from Via Po or Porta Nuova, or tram no.15 from Piazza Castello will take you northeast along the Po to the recently restored **Sassi-Superga Rack Railway** built in 1884. It still uses cars from the 1930s for the 18-minute, 3km climb through the greenwood to the **Basilica di Superga**, enjoying what Le Corbusier called 'the world's most charming setting' at 2,205ft. Here Vittorio Amedeo II and Prince Eugene of Savoy, their armies united in September 1706 to succour Turin, went up to survey the French positions before the battle, and here Vittorio Amedeo vowed to build the Virgin a grand church if Turin were saved. In gratitude for his unexpected victory on 7 September (a date that is celebrated every year at Superga with a *Te Deum*), the duke – soon to be king – commissioned Juvarra to build the Mother of God an exceptional basilica and a pantheon for his dynasty. The result, inspired by Borromini's churches in Rome, is one of Juvarra's masterpieces. Two towers set in freestanding corner columns flank a deep neoclassical porch, while above rises an exceptionally lofty drum and dome.

The interior is luminous and serene, the great drum of the cupola supported on eight columns; the views from the lantern stretch to the Alps. Guided tours will take you to visit the Hall of the Popes, with portraits of all 265 pontiffs by anonymous painters (inspired by the mosaics in the basilica of San Paolo fuori le Mura in Rome) and down to visit the ornate **Royal Tombs**, starting with Vittorio Amedeo II and containing the remains of 60 other members of the House of Savoy. Note at the entrance the statue of St Michael conquering Satan – not the usual ugly devil but a handsome young man; another angel blithely holds Masonic symbols.

Football, of course, is Italy's other religion and Superga is also a pilgrimage site for fans remembering one of the worst tragedies that ever happened in the sport (*see* box, p.240).

Lantern
check opening hours on the internet; guided tours available; adm; handout in English

Chieri and Martini

If you have a car, you can take the scenic back road down from Superga to Pino Torinese and **Chieri**, an old town spared by the hills from being gobbled up by Turin. A fief of Turin's powerful 11th-century bishop Landolfo, it was one of several Guelph cities razed by Emperor Frederick Barbarossa in 1155, and came under the Savoys in 1418. Its pride is its handsome Gothic **Duomo** (1403–36), built over Landolfo's church; it has a rich portal with a high gable, and excellent art: a baptistry with early 15th-century frescoes on the *Passion of Christ* by Guglielmo Fantini, frescoes by the school of Jaquerio in the sixth chapel on the right and, in the transept, a Renaissance marble icon. To the right of the altar, the Cappella dei Gallieri has fine frescoes of 1418 and inlaid choir stalls of the same period. The crypt was part of Landolfo's church.

If James Bond were a pilgrim, however, he would aim straight for **Pessione**, 5km south of Chieri, to the **Museo Martini di Storia dell'Enologia** in Piazza Luigi Rossi 2. Alessandro Martini, Teofilo Sola and Luigi Rossi bought a vermouth distillery in Turin in 1863 and started exporting to America the following year, and moved out to Pessione to be closer to the rail line to Genoa. Located in the cellars of Martini's 18th-century headquarters, their wine museum, founded in 1961, claims to be the oldest in Europe and vividly recounts not only the story of their own firm, but also the history of wine-making from the time of the ancient Greeks and Etruscans to the present.

Museo Martini di Storia dell'Enologia
t 011 94191, www.martinimuseum.org; open Tues–Fri 2–5, Sat and Sun 9–12 and 2–5; closed Aug

ⓘ **Turin >**
Turismo Torino e
Provincia, Via Bogino 8,
t 011 535 181, www.
turismotorino.org;
open 9am–9pm

Porta Nuova;
open daily 9.30–7

Caselle Airport; open
daily 8am–11pm

Tourist Information in Turin

Turismo Torino e Provincia has an office in the city (*see* left) and is also at Porta Nuova Station and Caselle Airport. They offer the **Torino+ Piemonte Card**, offering entry to more than 160 cultural sites (museums, exhibitions, monuments, castles, fortresses and royal residences), travel on all public and tourist transport and discounts on car hire, theme parks, theatre tickets and tours. You can also get a discounted **ChocoPass**, which grants you tastings and discounts in historic cafés and *pasticcerie* in Turin. It is available for two, three, five and seven days, starting from €18, and is valid for an adult and a child under 12 years of age.
Turismo Torino e Provincia, *www.turismotorino.org/guided_tours.* Offers visitors a classic tour combining the city centre and the Egyptian museum, as well as many different themed tours.

Shopping in Turin

Turin's big-name designer shops are planted in **Via Roma**, while younger, less pricey boutiques (including the Juventus Store) are clustered along pedestrian-only **Via Garibaldi** and in the **Quadrilatero Romano**. The city is best known for its excellent food shops, many wonderfully old-fashioned: Via Lagrange and Via San Tommaso are good places to look. Looking for that special bottle of Barolo? Try **La Botte Gaia**, Via S. Massimo 2/l, which also does grappas and *digestivos*. Turin is the chocolate capital of Italy, famous for its *bonet* (chocolate and amaretto pudding) and *gianduia*, made with toasted ground hazelnuts (Nutella is the kid's form): try the little *gianduiotti* at **Peyrano** (*www.peyrano.com*), Corso Vittorio Emanuele II 76, Via Andrea Doria 4 or Corso Moncalieri 47; at **Guido Gobino** (*www.guidogobino.it*), Via Cagliari 15/b; or at **Confetteria Avvignano**, a historic monument at

Piazza Carlo Felice 50. A little less central but well worth the short trip is **Bruno Croci**, Via Principessa Clotilde 6a, an ancient chocolate workshop. Or buy sweets fit for a king: **Stratta** (*www.stratta1836.it*), founded in 1836 at Piazza San Carlo 191, supplied the House of Savoy. Turin claims Europe's largest open-air market, **Porta Palazzo** with 685 stands (Mon–Fri till 1.30, Sat till 6.30). For bargains, don't miss the **Balôn flea market** (*www.balon.it*), held every Saturday morning for over 150 years behind Porta Palazzo, and the higher-class **Gran Balôn**, every second Sunday of the month. For books in English, try **Hellas** (*www.hellas.it*), Via Bertola 6, t 011 546 941, or **Luxemburg** at Via C. Battisti 7.

Sports and Activities in Turin

The vast **Stadio delle Alpi**, home to **Juventus** and former home to **Torino** (*see* p.240), is currently closed for restoration. The Stadio Olimpico is hosting both teams in the meantime – take bus no.4 from Porta Nuova or no.10 from Porta Susa. Tickets are available online from *www.juventus.it* or *www.torinofc.it*.

Golf is big in Turin: the closest course is the 9-hole Golf Stupinigi, Corso Unione Sovietica 502, t 011 347 2640. There are two 18-hole courses in Carmagnola: I Girasoli, Via Pralormo 315, t 011 979 5088, *www.girasoligolf.it*, and Margherita, t 011 979 5113; and others north in Fiano: Royal Park Gold and Country Club, Rota Cerbiatta 24 (18 holes), t 011 923 5719, *www.royalparkgolf.it*, and the Circolo Golf Torino (36 holes), t 011 923 5440.

Where to Stay in Turin

Turin ✉ 10100

Turismo Torino e Provincia runs a free hotel- and B&B-finding service (contact them 48hrs in advance, t 011 535 181, *reshotel@turismotorino.org*). If you're visiting at the weekend and stay 2–3 nights, many hotels offer special discount packages, along with

Victoria >>

a Torino+Piemonte Card (*see* p.242). For further information on hotels and prices, see *www.turismotorino.org*.

Luxury (€€€€€)

*****Golden Palace Hotel, Via dell'Arcivescovado 18, **t** 011 551 2111, *www.thi.it*. A luxurious, contemporary hotel that consists of two geometric buildings, Golden One and Golden Two. It includes a pool with a relaxation area, spa, Turkish bath, fitness centre and free Internet access in the rooms.

*****Le Meridien Turin Art + Tech, Via Nizza 230, **t** 011 664 2000, *www.lemeridien-lingotto.it*. Minimalist, hip and cutting-edge high tech, Turin's first five-star hotel and its restaurant **Art + Café** were designed by Renzo Piano and Philippe Starck as a hotel in a hotel within the larger and nearly as plush ******Le Meridien** in Lingotto, Via Nizza 262. For fun, jog around the Fiat rooftop test track.

****Principi di Piemonte, Via Gobetti 15, **t** 011 551 151, *www.ata hotels.it/principi*. Always a favourite stop for celebrities and VIPs. Recently refurbished, a spa and wellness centre will soon be open to guests.

****Art Hotel Boston, Via Massena 70, **t** 011 500 359, *www.hotelboston torino.it*. Cool art hotel southwest of Porta Nuova: 'ethnic, pop, eccentric but always stylish and pampering'.

****Villa Sassi, Via Traforo di Pino 47, **t** 011 898 0556, *www.villasassi.com*. In a lovely park under the Basilica di Superga; atmospheric hotel in a 17th-century villa, with marble floors and Baroque fireplaces. It also has a fine **restaurant**, serving the classics. *Closed Aug.*

****Grand Hotel Sitea, Via Carlo Alberto 35, **t** 011 517 0171, *www.sitea.thi.it*. Where the Juventus team stay before a match, in a quiet street near the centre, with plush bedrooms and half-price deals at weekends. Its smart restaurant **Carignano** (€€€) is one of the best. *Closed Sat lunch.*

Very Expensive (€€€€)

****Victoria, Via Nino Costa 4, **t** 011 561 1909, *www.hotelvictoria-torino.com*. Near Piazza S. Carlo, a real gem – quiet, comfortable and enchanting, with no two rooms alike. Lovely breakfast served in a bright, airy room overlooking the garden. Features a spa offering massage and beauty treatments, plus a heated pool and steam bath.

Expensive (€€€)

***Genio, Corso Vittorio Emanuele II 47, **t** 011 650 5771, *www.hotelgenio.it*. By Porta Nuova, one of many Best Western hotels in Turin. Classic and comfortable, with internet portals in every room and buffet breakfast.

***Roma & Rocca Cavour, Piazza Carlo Felice 60, **t** 011 561 2772, *www.romarocca.it*. In the same family since 1854, with rooms ranging from the basic to lovely, with period furnishings. *Rates drop out of season.*

***Dogana Vecchia, Via Corte d'Appello 4, **t** 011 436 6752, *www.hoteldoganavecchia.com*. Charming and atmospheric, the oldest hotel in Turin, in business since the 18th century, and now beautifully restored.

***Luxor, Corso Stati Uniti 7, **t** 011 5620 777, *www.hotelluxor.it*. Located very near the centre and yet in a quiet and elegant area of the city.

***Piemontese, Via Berthollet 21, **t** 011 669 8191, *www.hotelpiemonte.it*. Just east of Porta Nuova station, handsome rooms in a late 19th-century building; buffet breakfast included. *Weekend discounts.*

B&B Ai Savoia, Via del Carmine 1b, **t mobile 0339 125 7711, *www. aisavoia.it*. Beautiful rooms in a *palazzo* of 1730 on a pedestrian street by the Quadrilatero Romano, with a delicious buffet breakfast.

Moderate (€€)

B&B Aprile, Via delle Orfane 19, **t 011 436 0114, *www.aprile.to.it*. Cosy rooms conveniently located near the shops, restaurants and nightlife in the Quadrilatero Romano.

Bologna, Corso Vittorio Emanuele II 60, **t** 011 5620191, *www.hotel bolognasrl.it*. Near the Porta Nuova railway station, a classy hotel located in an end-of-19th-century building.

Centro di Accoglienza Pellegrini Basilica di Superga, **t** 011 898 0083, *www.parrocchie.it/torino/basilicasuperga.hospitality.htm*. Monastic en-suite rooms in the 18th-century pilgrimage house next to the big basilica. Magnificent views, peace and quiet, and cheap trattorias nearby. Breakfast included. There's also a youth hostel with dorm beds (€).

Inexpensive (€)

Statuto, Via Principi d'Acaja 17, **t 011 434 4638. Plain but comfortable family-run hotel a few streets west of the Porta Susa station, just off Corso Francia. Buffet breakfast.

B&B Gilda, Via S. Bernardino 12, **t 011 375 241, *www.bbgilda.it*. South of the centre in the lively Borgo San Paolo, 15mins from the centre by public transport. Three rooms with shared bathroom.

*Mobledor, Via Acc. Albertina 1, **t** 011 888 445, *www.hotelmobledor.it*. Just off Via Po, offering simple but comfortable rooms decorated with murals, with shower and TV.

Ostello Torino, Via Alby 1, **t** 011 660 2939, *www.ostellotorino.it*. Youth hostel, near Piazza Crimea (bus no.52 from Porta Nuova), has decent rooms. *Closed 21 Dec–mid-Jan.*

Eating Out in Turin

Very Expensive (€€€€)

Del Cambio, Piazza Carignano 2, **t** 011 543 760. Legendary, plush nostalgia. The 'Exchange' opened in 1757 and the chandeliers, gilt mirrors, frescoes, red upholstery and even the costumes of the waiters haven't changed, nor has Cavour's corner, where he could keep an eye on the Palazzo Carignano. The old recipes have, however, been lightened up. The *agnolotti* are famous and the new *tartara di tonno* splendid. Other

classics are beef braised in Barolo and *finanziera* – Cavour's favourite. Fine wine list. *Closed Sun and Aug.*

La Barrique, Corso Dante 53, **t** 011 657 900. Near the corner of Via Nizza, midway between Stazione Porta Nuova and Lingotto, this restaurant is the showcase for one of Turin's young chefs, Stefano Gallo. Try the courgette flowers filled with fish wrapped in crispy pastella, the home-made bread and divine desserts. *Closed Sun and Mon and Aug.*

Vintage 1997, Piazza Solferino 16/h, **t** 011 535 948, *www.vintage1997.com*. Refined restaurant in a historic house, popular with local VIPs for its delicate fusion of Mediterranean and Piedmontese cuisine; excellent pasta and seafood, exquisite desserts and wines from around the world. *Closed Sat lunch and Sun.*

Locanda Mongreno, Strada Comunale Mongreno 50 (on the northeast edge of town, up Corso Casale), **t** 011 898 0417. Romantic and elegant, and outdoor tables in the summer. The food, prepared by Piercarlo Bussetti, lives up to the atmosphere, featuring the likes of *foie gras* served with berry sauce, gnocchi in an aubergine and fresh *tomino* sauce, sushi, and a bitter chocolate cake to die for. Great international cellar. *Closed Mon and two weeks in Aug.*

Al Gatto Nero, Corso Turati 14, **t** 011 590 414, *www.gattonero.it*. A Turin classic, where chef Andrea Vannelli has inherited his father's and grandfather's saucepans, and dishes out tasty Mediterranean cuisine. *Closed Sun, Aug.*

Antiche Sere, Via Cenischia 9, **t** 011 385 4347. Rated the most authentic trattoria in Turin. Excellent starters, including gnocchi in sausage *ragù*, traditional main courses and super *panna cotta*. Outdoors in summer. *Booking essential. Open eves only; closed Sun and 10 days mid-Aug.*

Expensive (€€€)

Al Garamond, Via Pomba 14, **t** 011 812 2781, *www.algaramond.it*. Gourmet haven in the centre, where homemade breads accompany

⭐ **Del Cambio >**

seafood, sturgeon *carpaccio* and *foie gras, broccoletti lasagnette* and succulent meats. *Closed Sat lunch, Sun, July.*

Tre Galline, Via Bellezia 37, **t** 011 436 6553. Traditional Piedmontese cuisine (*fritto misto, bolliti misti*, regional cheeses) with class in a 17th-century *palazzo* in the Quadrilatero Romano. *Closed Sun, and Mon lunch; in Aug open lunch only.*

Sotto La Mole, Via Montebello 9, **t** 011 817 9398. Intimate restaurant under the Mole Antonelliana, serving both Piedmontese classics and creative dishes such as chestnut gnocchi and capon in tomato and basil cream. *Open eves only; closed Wed, Jan and June.*

L'Oca Fola, Via Drovetti 6/g, **t** 011 433 7422. Near Corso Inghilterra, traditional-style Piedmontese trattoria serving tasty *bagna cauda, agnolotti al sugo di arrosto* and *bonet*. *Open eves only; closed Sun and three weeks in Aug.*

Solferino, Piazza Solferino 3, **t** 011 535 851. Piedmontese classics (including a delicious *fonduta* and truffles in season) at very good prices. *Closed Fri eve, Sat and Aug.*

Le Vitel Etonné, Via S. Francesco da Paola 4, **t** 011 812 4621, *www.levitel etonne.com*. Wine bar with a menu that changes daily, although it always has *vitello tonnato*, the dish that gives the place its name. *Open Tues–Fri 5pm–1am, Sat 10.30am–1am, Sun 10.30am–3.30pm; closed Mon.*

Tre Galli, Via Sant'Agostino 25/b, **t** 011 521 6027. Fashionable restaurant located in the Quadrilateral; serving delicious gnocchi with Castelmagno cheese and other Piedmontese classics; huge wine list. *Closed Sun.*

Arcadia, near Piazza Castello in the Galleria Subalpina, **t** 011 561 3898, *www.ristorantearcadia.com*. Popular Italian restaurant and sushi bar combo. *Closed Sun.*

Moderate (€€)

Valenza, just north of Piazza della Repubblica at Via Borgo Dora 39, **t** 011 521 3914. One of the last old-fashioned trattorias in Turin, a jolly place with filling *antipasti*, delicious *pasta e fagioli* and roast pork. *Closed Sun, Mon and Aug.*

Inexpensive (€)

Sfashion Cafè, Via Cesare Battisiti 1 (on Piazza Carlo Alberto and the Galleria Subalpina), **t** 011 516 0085, *www.sfashioncafe.com*. Popular bar and pizzeria with a huge choice of pizzas, using genuine *mozzarella di bufalo* and other prime raw materials. *Open till midnight.*

Dai Saletta, Via Belfiore 37, **t** 011 668 7867. Old-fashioned trattoria, serving up antipasti and other Piedmontese favourites. *Closed Sun and Aug.*

Cafés and Bars in Turin

Turin, with Italy's most historic bijou cafés, is a coffee-lover's dreamland. The java is excellent but so are the hot chocolate, cakes, ice cream and cocktail nibbles or *stuzzichini*, which are a culinary art form (*served 6–8pm*). Try **Baratti & Milano**, in Piazza Castello 29 near the Galleria Subalpina, largely unchanged since 1873; **Fiorio**, opened in 1780 at Via Po 8, and called the 'ponytail café' because of all the aristocrats who chinwagged there; the Art Nouveau **Caffè Platti**, Corso V. Emanuele II 72, opened in 1875 and rendezvous of intellectuals and the late Gianni Agnelli (*open till 9pm*); **Caffè Torino**, Piazza San Carlo 204, a favourite of movie stars and Savoia royalty for its cocktails; tiny **Al Bicerin**, at Piazza della Consolata 5 since 1763 and still serving *bicerin*, a melange of coffee, chocolate and milk that was Cavour's favourite; and the beautiful Art Nouveau **Mulassano**, Piazza Castello 15, from 1905, birth-place of *tramezzini* (little crustless sandwiches filled with goodies); **Lavazza**, at Via S. Tommaso 10, is the place where local coffee magnate Luigi Lavazza roasted his first beans.

Turin also has some great wine bars. **Caffè Elena**, in Piazza Vittorio

Veneto 5, was Nietzsche's favourite; **Da Bacco**, Via Madama Cristina 82/c, has lots of bottles and hot lunches; **Antica Enoteca del Borgo**, Via Monferrato 4, has over 700 labels and outdoor seating; **Smile Tree**, Piazza della Consolata 9/c, is a relaxed cocktail bar with good snacks.

Entertainment and Nightlife in Turin

There's always something to do in Turin; for information check listings in *La Stampa*, or visit the Vetrina per Torino booth at Piazza San Carlo 159, freephone **t** 800 015 475, open Mon–Sat 11–7, *www.turismotorino.org*. In March, chocolate is celebrated for nine days at the **CioccolaTò** festival (*www.cioccolato.com*). In July, **Traffic Torino** is a three-day free festival, drawing big-name musicians. **MITO** (formerly Settembre Musica) features concerts from symponies to jazz to ethnic music in the city's theatres and churches. The **Torino Film Festival** (*www.torinofilmfest. org*) in November is one of the most important in Italy, a showcase for up-and-coming directors of independent films; also in November, the city holds **Artissima**, the biggest contempary art fair in Italy (*www.artissima.it*). From mid-November to mid-January, the Luci d'Artista sees the centre city wonderfully illuminated by contemporary light installations.

The **Teatro Regio** in Piazza Castello stages ballet, concerts and opera throughout the year: **t** 011 881 5242, *www.teatroregio.torino.it*; others take place in the enormous state-of-the-art **Lingotto Auditorium** (*www.lingottomusica.it*). In even-numbered years in October, Slow Food's massive **Salone del Gusto** (*www.salonedelgusto.it*) takes place in Lingotto. The annual **Turin Book Fair** is held at Lingotto during the second week in May, *www.fieralibro.it*.

Turin has a very lively **night scene**. The **Quadrilatero Romano** is a good place to start with an aperitif before crossing Piazza della Repubblica to the **Balòn**, the old flea market area and **Via Borgo Dora**, now hopping with bars, restaurants and clubs; for clubs, try the old industrial area – the **Docks Dora** north of Stazione Dora and the **Murazzi** (former boat sheds along the Po) are the fulcrum of late-night fun in summer, when they spill out along the water (bring mosquito repellent); here **Dottor Sax**, **Jammin Club**, the **Beach** and **Bokhaos** are usually packed out. At the end of the night, everyone ends up at **Giancarlo's** (also known as the **Amici del Fiume** club). Traffic jams at 3am are common.

Gay-friendly nightspots include the popular **Centralino Club**, Via delle Rosine 13, with electronic sounds, or the quieter **Meaculpa**, Via Bertola 31, **Metropolis Club**, Via Principessa Clotilde 32, and Vineria Zi Barba; **Le Vedove Allegre** at Via Don Bosco 69 is a women-only pub.

Around Turin: a Garland of Pleasure Domes

See map, p221.

The Savoys, always eager to keep up with their Bourbon rivals in France, built a ring of magnificent residences around their capital, and in 1997 UNESCO made the lot of them a World Heritage Site. They are the focus of Turin's outskirts, but there's more. South of Superga, amid the hills (the *collina*) where the Agnellis and other élites have their homes, the beautiful Colle della Maddalena (2,526ft) is the site of the **Parco della Rimembranza**, a beautiful arboretum, planted with 15,000 trees dedicated to Turin's First World War dead and crowned by the **Faro della Victoria** (1928), by Edoardo Rubino – the largest cast bronze statue in the world at nearly 60ft tall.

Castello di Moncalieri
Piazza Baden Baden 4, bus no.67 from Porta Nuova, t 011 640 2883; open Thurs, Sat and Sun 9.30–12.30 and 2.15–6; adm

Just south of here, in **Moncalieri**, the Castello di Moncalieri overlooks busy Piazza Baden Baden. Its four sturdy towers date back to *c.*1200 and were converted into a palace by the Savoys beginning in 1619. There are three glittering royal apartments to visit, and there may be more to see once its occupants, a battalion of *carabinieri*, are moved out. For the Piedmontese, the palace is closely associated with the saintly Maria Clothilde, eldest daughter of Vittorio Emanuele II, who at age 16 was compelled to marry the dissipated, lascivious 37-year-old 'Plon Plon', Napoleon Jerome Bonaparte, cousin of Napoleon III, to make sure her father won the crown of Italy (neither was she the only beautiful young woman used to lure the French over; *see* p.287). After the Bonapartes fell from grace she ended up here and became famous for her works of charity. Also in Moncalieri, in Piazza Vittorio Emanuele, stands an arch of 1560, now known as the **Arco di Vittorio Emanuele II** and the Lombard Gothic church of **Santa Maria della Scala**, with a superb terracotta Pietà from the 1400s.

Stupinigi and Carignano

Palazzina di Caccia di Stupinigi
bus no.63 from Porto Nuova – stop is in Via Sacchi – to Piazzale Caio Mario, then cross this to get to bus no.41, 'Traiano stop' in Corso Giovanni Agnelli; t 011 358 1220; closed for restoration until the end of 2008

The Savoys' most beautiful royal palace was their last one, just southwest of the centre: the **Palazzina di Caccia di Stupinigi**. In 1729, Vittorio Amedeo II asked Juvarra to design an 'urban' hunting lodge, which he and his courtiers could visit without all the fuss of an overnight stay. Set at the head of broad Corso Unione Sovietica, lined with trees and stables, Juvarra's huge white rococo palace is a magnificent sight, with its swollen oval heart and radiant arms modelled on the cross of St Andrew and proud statue of a stag on the roof. The decoration, however, is enough to give a vegetarian nightmares: interminable hunts and trompe-l'œil scenes of their trophies on nearly every wall and ceiling; the exotic birds and Chinese legends in some rooms come as a relief after all the dead bunnies. The palace became a favourite residence of the Savoys, and they added apartments extending the arms of the cross. It was used as a furniture museum – until one night in February 2004 when daring burglars made off with all its finest pieces. Juvarra's superb salon in the centre, however, is unchanged, and was deemed lovely enough for royal wedding receptions and the ballroom scenes of King Vidor's film *War and Peace*.

If you have a car, you may want to head 15km south to **Carignano**, a sprawling town with a core of late medieval *palazzi* (along Via Vittorio Veneto) and fine Baroque and rococo churches: the curvaceous **Cattedrale dei SS. Giovanni Battista e Remigio** (1764) in the centre was designed by Benedetto Alfieri; **Santa Maria delle Grazie** (1667) in Piazza Carlo Alberto has a lovely façade and rich stuccoes within. Best of all, 5km southwest on the road to Vigone, is the little white **Santuario di Vallinotto** (1738), Piedmont native Bernardo Vittone's first building, and one of his best. A wealthy banker commissioned it as a chapel for his farm workers, and Vittone used the opportunity to demonstate his admiration for Guarini's geometrical play and Juvarra's classical stage sets. From the outside, hexagonal pagoda-like tiers rise, charming and unfussy; within, a Guarini-inspired but unique diaphanous dome and lantern are set on four different vaults (a rococo record), while the arches and chapels recall Juvarra's Carmine church in Turin, rearranged here to a central plan.

Rivoli and the Museo d'Arte Contemporanea

Rivoli, west of Turin, preserves the Savoy's **Castello di Rivoli** (Via Piazza Mafalda di Savoia), an 11th-century fort on a hill that was enlarged and converted by Juvarra and other architects into a huge palace, an overly ambitious one that was never completed. The family sold it to the municipal authorities in 1883 and, after languishing for a century, it reopened in 1984 as the **Museo d'Arte Contemporanea**. There are three floors, two dedicated to temporary exhibitions and one with the permanent collection; the enormous rooms, some with lingering bits of Juvarran bravura, are perfect for the minimalist and *Arte Povera* installations that predominate: the fluffy frescoed figures seem especially bemused by Maurizio Cattela's *Natura Morta* – an embalmed horse suspended from the ceiling.

Before moving to Turin, the Savoy Counts spent a good deal of time in Rivoli. The **Casa del Conte Verde** (the 'Green Count', Amedeo VI) on Via Fratelli Piol 8 with its portico may not really have belonged to him, but it's from the 15th century and now hosts special exhibitions.

Museo d'Arte Contemporanea
ask at the coach station for the direct shuttle bus to the museum; from Porta Susa, take the subway, get off at Fermi and take the shuttle bus, or get off at Paradiso and take bus no.36 to Rivoli; **t** *011 956 5222, www.castellodirivoli.it; open Tues–Thurs 10–5, Fri–Sun 10–9; adm exp*

Casa del Conte Verde
t *011 956 3020, www.casadel conteverde.it*

La Reggia di Venaria Reale
t *011 559 2211, www.lavenaria.it; open Tues–Sun 9–8, Fri 9–5, last entry 90mins before closing; adm*

Really Big Pleasure Palaces: La Reggia di Venaria Reale and La Mandria

Northwest of Turin, **La Reggia di Venaria Reale** was begun in 1660 by architect Amedeo di Castellamonte as Duke Carlo Emanuele II's answer to Versailles. Hunting and daunting the viewer were, as ever, the Savoy's main concerns: along with the palace, they built a planned Baroque village to wait on it, with a uniform main street aligned on La Venaria's grand axis. The oldest part of La Venaria, with its high mansard roof, looks the most 'French' of Turin's palaces. Over the decades, other architects, notably Juvarra, worked on the rococo addition, but it was never completed before the Savoys lost interest and moved on to the next palace, Stupinigi, leaving La Venaria as a barracks.

By the 1980s it was ready to collapse through neglect, and the 950,000 square metre complex underwent the biggest restoration project in Europe, destined to become a 'giant cultural container' by 2009; the monumental **stables** are already in use as a university, appropriately offering five-year courses in art and architecture restoration. The once famous gardens, destroyed in 1693 by the French, have been replanted with 17th-century-inspired *grandes allées*, pergolas, waterworks and labyrinths. Inside, guides will lead you through rooms with lavish stuccoes and frescoed ceilings to two beautiful works by Juvarra: the **chapel of St Hubert** and the cream-toned **Galleria Granole**, aka **Galleria di Diana**, a stunning, rhythmically luminous 272ft hall of windows. When the restoration is complete, part of the palace, the 'Teatro della Magnicenza', will be dedicated to La Venaria itself; there will be restaurants, an exhibition centre, craft shops and more. Most of Turin's palaces are reputedly haunted (as one might expect!) but the Venaria Reale has the best-known ghost, of Vittorio Amedeo II, who is said to prowl about holding a sword and candle, or, according to some, his famous breadstick. You can tell when he's about to appear – when you get a noseful of his favourite scent, bergamot.

A couple of kilometres up the road from the Venaria, and in contrast to all its artifice, is the 16,230-acre walled park of **La Mandria**, the Savoy hunting grounds but also where the kings raised their horses (cars are not allowed, but you can hire a bike by the entrance). In 1713, feeling short of a house, the Savoys added the brick **Borgo Castello de la Mandria**, with royal apartments, where Vittorio Emanuele II often stayed with his morganatic second wife, the Bella Rosina, far from the society who snubbed her (she was the daughter of a drummer). Decorated in the king's homey bourgeois taste, the rooms look as if the happy couple might return at any minute – even the grease spot from the king's head is preserved on the bedstead. When restoration work finishes here, there will be a five-star hotel, a youth hostel, a summer pool, a fitness centre, a restaurant, a market, and a 'landscape gallery' dedicated to humanity's relationship with nature. Farm buildings (*cascine*) are spread around La Mandria: one, known as **La Bizarria**, is shaped like a horse, and another, the **Cascina Rubbianetta**, will become a foundation dedicated to horses and their training, and to safeguard rare species. The park also encompasses rare native Po valley woodlands.

La Mandria
www.parcomandria.it

Borgo Castello de la Mandria
t 011 499 3381, www.parks.it/parco. mandria; guided tours Sun at 10.30, 11.30, 2.30 and 3.30, in summer also at 4.30; adm

Turin | Around Turin: a Garland of Pleasure Domes: La Reggia di Venaria Reale and La Mandria

Eating Out Outside Turin

⭐ Combal Zero >

Combal Zero, Piazza Mafaldo di Savoia in the Castello di Rivoli, **t** 011 956 5225, *www.combal.org* (€€€€). Cutting-edge cuisine in one of the region's most talked-about restaurants. Davide Scabin is perhaps Italy's ultimate food designer – after all, who else does cyber-eggs? *Closed Mon, Tues and Aug.*

Casa Casellae, Piazza Caselli 4, Chieri (To), **t** 011 9415 856, *www. casacasellae.it* (€€). A restaurant and B&B that was a 16th-century convent, then a private mansion. The main hall was restored in the 19th century, and it is possible to have a meal there, in a smaller room, or in the former cellar – and in the garden during summer. *Closed Mon.*

Piedmont

Trying to define Piedmont (Piemonte) in a few words is not unlike the blind men trying to describe the elephant. The name may mean 'foot of the mountains' but there are serious peaks here, too – 40 per cent of Piedmont is mountainous. No, no, our man in eastern Piedmont would say: it's flat, with rice paddies extending as far as the eye can see. It's industrial, sprawling and a big traffic jam, another might say. No, another could argue, it's so rural and woodsy you're lucky to see another car on the road. No, the man in Le Langhe and Monferrato would say, it's a hot destination, of vineyards and hills and arty hotels and fabulous restaurants. But no, on lakes Orta and Maggiore, it's all charming 19th-century villas and gardens. The truth is, Piedmont is all these things and more, a fabulous patchwork of sights and sounds.

12

Don't miss

⭐ **Lakeside towns and islands**
Lake Maggiore p.302

⭐ **A perching church**
Sacra di San Michele p.256

⭐ **Truffles, wine and castles**
Le Langhe and Asti p.276

⭐ **The Disneyland of the Counter-Reformation**
Varallo and Sacro Monte p.322

⭐ **An evocative Marquisate**
Saluzzo p.266

See map overleaf

Piedmont

SWITZERLAND

Don't miss

⭐ Lake Maggiore **p.302**

⭐ Sacra di San Michele **p.256**

⭐ Le Langhe and Asti **p.276**

⭐ Varallo and Sacro Monte **p.322**

⭐ Saluzzo **p.266**

pp.82–3

pp.176–7

FRANCE

PIEDMONT

LIGURIA

N

20 km

10 miles

SWITZERLAND

AUSTRIA

SLOVENIA

CROATIA

FRANCE

Corsica

Sardinia

Sicily

Locarno
Domodossola
Cannobio
Val Vigezzo
Val d'Ossola
Macugnaga
Toce
Lago Maggiore
Verbania
Stresa
Varese
Zermatt
Matterhorn
Monte Rosa
Cascata di Sesia
Rimella
Fobello
Omegna
Lago di Orto
A8
Breuil-Cervinia
Crépin
Alagna Valsesia
Riva Valdobbia
Sacro Monte
Varallo
Borgosesia
Arona
Gallarate
Chamonix
Bourg-Saint-Bernard
Saint-Oyen
Saint-Barthélemy
Saint Vincent
Gaby
Piedicavallo
Oasi Zegni
STRADA PANORAMICA ZEGNA
Romagnano Sesia
A26
Malpensa
Busto Arsizio
Plampincieux
Courmayeur
Flassin
Aosta
Santuario d'Oropa
Pont-Saint-Martin
Pollone
Valle Mosso
Biella
Oleggio
Mont Blanc
Pré-saint-Didier
La Thuile
Planaval
Val d'Aosta
A5
Cogne
Santuario di Graglia
Donato
Gaglianico Castle
Ivrea
Galliate
Ticino
Trecate
Novara
Vivetone
Vercelli
Vigevano
Bourg-Saint-Maurice
Parco Nazionale del Gran Paradiso
Noasca
Ceresole Reale
Forno Alpi Graie
Mondrone
Ceres
Lanzo Torinese
Valperga
Candia Canavese
Lago di Viverone
Roppolo Castle
San Nazzaro Sesia
Borgo Vercelli
Lignana
Val d'Isère
Modane
Novalesa
Ciaglione
Massif du Mont Cenis
Margone
Stura di Viù
Venaria Reale
Abbazia di Vezzolano
Casale Monferrato
Lomello
Valenza
Fréjus tunnel
Bardonecchia
Susa
Chiomonte
Exilles
Oulx
Sacra di S. Michele
Buttigliera
Rivoli Castle
TURIN (TORINO)
Chieri
Albugnano
Moncalvo
Vignale Monferrato
Alessandria
Tortona
Sansicario
Cesana Torinese
Sestriere
Fenestrelle
Stupinigi Castle
Moncalieri
Asti
Montegrosso d'Asti
Argentera
Torre Pellice
Pinerolo
Carignano
Carmagnola
Canale d'Alba
Nizza Monferrato
Novi Ligure
Villanova
Bobbio Pellice
Cavour
Racconigi
Bra
Barbaresco
Mango
Acqui Terme
Colle dell'Agnello
Piano del Re
Crissolo
Paesana
Alba
Grinzane Cavour
La Morra
Monte Viso
Savigliano
Saluzzo
Casteldelfino
Varaita
Levaldigi
Fossano
Bastia Mondovì
Ceva
GENOA (GENOVA)
Acceglio
Valle Maira
Pradleves
Castelmagno
Cuneo
Mondovì
Frabosa Soprana
Savona
Gulf of Genoa
Colle della Maddalena
Argentera
Demonte
Borgo San Dalmazzo
Vernante
Monte Matto
Valle Stura
Gesso
Vermenagna

Piedmont's great variety is its greatest attraction. Tremendous military forts bristle over the Alpine passes; in other places castles and towers rise from every hill with sweet fairytale precision. Piedmont can be medieval or splendidly Baroque, startlingly eccentric or avant-garde – no region in Italy has more contemporary art galleries. Yet in their own dialect the Piedmontese call themselves *bogianen*, those who never move. Or rather, like the wise old elephant, they don't move or change without good cause, and this is one of their greatest virtues.

West of Turin into the 'Olympic Mountains'

Some of the most spectacular scenery in Piedmont lies west of Turin in the upper Susa Valley, where mountain resorts of the 'Milky Way' (Sestiere, Sauze d'Oulx, Sansicario, Cesana, Claviere, etc. – *see www.neveitalia.it/ski/vialattea*) and others hosted the Alpine events in the 2006 Winter Olympics. Turn the clock back a thousand years, to the early 11th century, and instead you'd see pilgrims trundling along the Lyons–Turin branch of the Via Francigena, the many-branched path from Canterbury to Rome recalled by several outstanding churches and monasteries.

Turin to Susa: Sant'Antonio di Ranverso, Avigliana and San Michele

From Rivoli (*see* p.248), it's a short 5km west to **Buttigliera Alta** and the delightful abbey of **Sant'Antonio di Ranverso**, signposted just off the N25. Founded in 1188 by Count Umberto III, this was an important hospital for pilgrims and for succouring sufferers of St Anthony's fire, or ergotism. The church, next to a giant rock embedded with a column and St Anthony's Tau symbol, has a striking 15th-century Gothic façade, with three high gables and inside the best surviving frescoes (signed) by the early 15th-century court painter Giacomo Jaquerio – discovered under the plaster only in 1912: the turmoil-filled black-skied *Ascent to Calvary* in the sacristy is his masterpiece. A superb polyptych (1531) by Defendente Ferrari adorns the altar.

Sant'Antonio di Ranverso
t 011 936 7450,
www.mauriziano.it/
arte/frsetpatr.htm;
open Tues–Sun 9–12.30
and 3–5.30, last entry
5pm; adm

Avigliana, next west, was until 1965 famous for its Nobel dynamite works, built in 1872, the oldest in Italy. It was important in the Middle Ages, too: the old town sprawls around a picturesque medieval core and ruined **castle**, first built by King Arduino in the 10th century. Below, **Piazza Conte Rosso**, the old market square, is near the octagonal clock tower (1330) – the second public clock put on a tower in Italy, after the one in Saint Eustorgio, Milan – and 12th-century church of **San Giovanni**, with another fine altarpiece

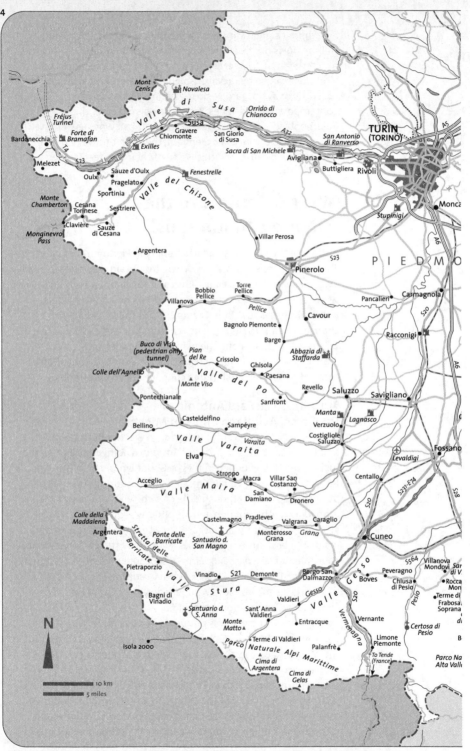

The 'Olympic Mountains' West of Turin, Southwest and Southeast Piedmont

Getting West of Turin and into the 'Olympic Mountains'

Trains from Turin to Modane/Chambéry via the Fréjus Tunnel go through the Valle di Susa; for the resorts, get off at Oulx, where there are connecting **buses**. Otherwise, frequent buses from Corso Vittorio Emanuele II 131/h in Turin go to Susa, Pinerolo, Sestriere and Claviere.

San Pietro
t 011 932 8300; open June–Oct Sat and Sun 9–12 and 3–6

㉒ Sacra di San Michele
t 011 939 130, www.sacradisan michele.com; open mid-Mar–mid-Oct Tues–Sat 9.30–12.30 and 2.30–6, Sun and hols 9.30–12.30 and 2.30–6.30; mid-Oct–mid-Mar Tues–Sat 9.30–12.30 and 2.30–5; last entry 30mins before closing; adm

Cappella del Conte
t 0122 622 640; open April–Oct Sun 3–6; other times by appointment; adm

of the *Birth of Christ* by Defendente Ferrari. Outside the oldest walls, the church of **San Pietro**, founded prior to 1000, was enlarged in the 14th and 15th centuries and adorned with Gothic terracotta cornices and pinnacles; inside are 14th- and 15th-century frescoes. Avigliana is closed in to the south by a pair of pretty glacier lakes.

The road between the lakes leads up in 14km to one of the most extraordinary churches in Italy, the **Sacra di San Michele** sitting on a 2,018ft pinnacle, atop 90ft of substructures, all gloriously lit up at night. The Lombards were the first to worship Michael here, and built and fortified the dams (*chiuse*) at the foot of the mountain where their king Desiderius was routed by Charlemagne in 773. In 983, the story goes, angels indicated to an Auvergnat Hugo de Montboissier that the mountain would be a great place for an abbey, and it soon became a beacon for pilgrims on the Via Francigena. Now occupied by Rosminian fathers, it is an uncanny place, for the esoterically minded a seal over a dragon's lair exactly midway between the equally strange Mont St-Michel in Normandy and Monte Sant'Angelo in the Gargano, on Italy's heel. After a kilometre hike up from the car park, the church proper is reached by way of the steep, rock-hewn **Scalone dei Morti**, the 'Staircase of the Dead', designed to test your mortality (its name really comes from the tombs of monks that once lined it). At the top is the wonderful **Porta dello Zodiaco** (*c.* 1120), carved by Master Niccolò, decorated with Cain and Abel, Samson, mermaids, mermen and other creatures who have nothing to do with any known zodiac. The **church**, rebuilt in the 12th century, has an irregular plan, some curious capitals and the tombs of the early princes of Savoy-Carignano, as well as a triptych by Defendente Ferrari.

Further west, **San Giorio di Susa** is marked by its hilltop castle, rebuilt after it was demolished by the French in 1691. One of its former owners, Count Lorenzetto Bertrandi, built a cemetery chapel in 1328, dedicated to his patron saint, Lawrence. Known as the **Cappella del Conte**, its fresco cycle has been recently restored, showing the lives of Christ and St Lawrence, and the medieval legend of the *Three Living and Three Dead Men*. Walk down and around to the back to see the surviving exterior frescoes, and the sacred pre-Christian rock the chapel is built on – as in Susa (*see* right) druids would come here to sacrifice victims to tell the future by the way the blood flowed. If you come on 23 April, you can join in the *Soppressione del feudatario* festival, celebrating the re-enactment of a victory of the locals over another count, who tried to enjoy his *droit de seigneur* once too often. Just north of San Giorio, at Chianocco, two paths lead into a beautiful steep canyon, the Orrido di Chianocco.

Susa and the Abbey of Novalesa

The atmospheric old town of Susa (Roman *Segusio*), on the banks of the rushing Dora Riparia, was the seat of the Gaulish chieftain Cottius. Cottius was the kind of fraternizing Gaul that Asterix and Obelix would have liked to slap around with a menhir, one who so admired the Romans that he erected the **Arco di Augusto** (above the modern Parco di Augusto) in the Emperor's honour. Augustus returned the compliment by making Cottius a prefect, and naming the Cottian Alps after him. Other remains of *Segusio* are nearby: the Terme Graziane, part of a 3rd-century **aqueduct** and a big rock, the **Coppelle**, engraved with canals, where the druids sacrificed and told the future by the path taken by the blood.

The **Castello della Contessa Adelaide di Susa** looms nearby; the great grand-daughter of Arduino il Glabrione, who chased the Saracens out of these parts, the Countess Adelaide was born here in c. 1012 and inherited all the lands from Ventimiglia to Ivrea. Widowed twice, she took Otho of Savoy, son of Umberto of the White Hands, as her third husband in 1045, uniting the two realms on either side of the Alps, and marking the beginning of the Savoys' 900-year career in Italy. One son, Oddone, became a powerful bishop of Asti; one daughter, Bertha, married Emperor Henry IV of Saxony, one of the protagonists in the great medieval war over the independence of the Church. When Henry was excommunicated by Pope Gregory VII, he crossed over the Mont Cenis Pass in the bitter winter of 1077 and met up with the pope at Canossa. The pope was protected by his powerful supporter, Countess Matilda of Tuscany; Adelaide accompanied Henry and helped negotiate a settlement with the pope that ended with Henry's famous public penance in the snow. The castle contains a quirky **Museo Civico** with everything from natural history to a medieval capital to a small Egyptian and esoteric collection.

Museo Civico
t 0122 622 694; open by request; adm

Incorporating part of the mighty Roman-medieval gate, the **Porta Savoia**, the **Duomo di San Giusto** (1020) stands in the shadow of its own massive tower; it has a *quattrocento* choir, the Flemish brass *Triptych of Rocciamelone* (1338), a polyptych by Bergognone and a rare 10th-century font. The excellent **Museo Diocesano**, by the riverside church of the Madonna del Ponte, has fine art: barbaric-looking Lombard reliquaries, a hieratic 12th-century bejewelled Madonna, and 18th-century saints by the 'Bousson sculptor' which resemble figures in Gauguin's Tahitian paintings. On the ground floor part of the original Via Francigena has been exposed.

Museo Diocesano
t 0122 622 640; open July–Sept Tues–Sun 9.30–12 and 3.30–7; Oct–June Sat and Sun 2.30–6.30, by appointment during the week; adm

12

Piedmont | West of Turin into the 'Olympic Mountains'

The modern road to the **Mont Cenis Pass** begins north of Susa; it has always been a favoured route into Italy, used by pilgrims to Rome and by Napoleon, who began the carriage road in 1808. Up here, along the original Via Francigena, the once-powerful **Abbazia di Novalesa** was founded as the first stop in Italy in 725 by the local Carolingian governor to help contain the Lombards on their side of the Alps; Charlemagne himself stayed here in 773. The abbey then had a famous library, and produced the 9th-century *Chronicon Novalicense*, a fascinating melange of fable and history written on a narrow 40ft scroll of parchment by an anonymous monk. Destroyed by the Saracens in 906, rebuilt, then abandoned, the church was rebuilt in 1710 and the abbey repopulated in the 1970s by four now elderly Benedictines who specialize in book restoration. Four detached medieval chapels survive, including **Sant'Eldrado**, with wonderful, never restored Byzantine-influenced 11th-century frescoes of the *Lives of the SS Eldrado and Nicholas*. According to legend, Eldrado, the mid-8th-century Abbot of Novalesa, had a special power over animals, and once when the local monks working in the fields were beset by swarms of snakes he commanded the snakes to follow him, and like the Pied Piper led them into a dark cavern and told them to stay there. Another time when Novalesa was suffering from famine, he brought forth a fountain of pure olive oil, but when the monks began to sell it for profit, he angrily turned the oil to water. The **Museo di Arte Sacra** in a chapel of the 16th-century church of Santo Stefano has an important collection of art and items dating back to Roman and Carolingian times, as well as paintings by the schools of Caravaggio, Daniele da Volterra and others, left here by Napoleon.

Abbazia di Novalesa
t 0122 653 210, www. abbazianovalesa.org; open Sat and Sun 9–11.30, guided tours at 10.30 and 4.30 during July and Aug weekdays; church only open Mon–Sat 9–12 and 3.30–5.30, Sun and hols 9–12

Museo di Arte Sacra
t 0122 622 640; open by appointment

The Upper Susa Valley: Big Forts, Big Resorts

West of Susa, the old road ascends steeply past the villages of **Gravere** and **Chiomonte**, the latter also the first of the valley's ski resorts. In 1984, during the building of the A32, at a site called **La Maddalena di Chiomonte**, roadworkers discovered the extensive remains of a Neolithic village of *c.* 4000 BC – what has been termed the 'Pompeii of the Alps'. Finds are in Chiomonte's **Museo La Maddalena Archeologico**. The next village, **Exilles**, lies under a huge, superbly positioned **fort** built after the devastating Saracen raid of 906. Rebuilt in the 19th century, restored after years of work in 2000 and now illuminated at night, it seems to spill over the hill like molten gold; inside are displays on Alpine troops and forts.

Oulx, a market town and rail junction at the crossroads of the upper valleys, is a good place to pick up the **Sentiero dei Franchi**, the path retracing the route of Charlemagne in 773. To the northwest lies **Bardonecchia**, one of the few ski stations in Piedmont served by rail. There are two *borgos*, one dating from the

Museo La Maddalena Archeologico
Via Avaná, Loc. La Maddalena, t 0124 651 799; from the museum, visitors can have access to the archaelogical park; guided tours are also available; open Feb–Nov Wed, Fri and Sat 9.30–5; 15 July–30 Aug Wed, Sat and Sun

Fort
t 0122 58270; open Tues–Sun 15 April–Sept 10–7; Oct–April 10–2; adm

Museo Civico
Via Des Geneys 6
t 0122 999 350; open
July–Aug Mon–Fri 3–7,
Sat–Sun 9.30–12.30 and
3–7; other times by
appointment

Museo Arte
Religiosa Alpina
t 0122 622 640,
www.centroculturale
diocesano.it; ring ahead

Forte di Bramafam
t 011 311 2458; open
May–June Mon–Sat
9.45–1 and 2–6;
July–Sept Sun 9.45–1
and 2–6; adm

19th century, below an atmospheric Borgo Vecchio of stone houses or *grangie*. Bardonecchia is famous for its traditional costumes, on display in the **Museo Civico**. The hamlet of **Melezet** was famous for its woodcarvers; examples and a fine polyptych of the *Annunciation* are in the **Museo Arte Religiosa Alpina**.

The new *borgo* of Bardonecchia grew up during the building of the **Fréjus Tunnel**, finished in 1871, cutting the ten-hour coach journey over the Mont Cenis Pass (taken by Caesar and his legions to conquer Gaul) to a half-an-hour by rail. It was a bad business for Marseille's shipping business, but a boon to Brindisi, which was now linked by rail to Calais (even this isn't fast enough: a new tunnel for the planned high-speed line between Lyon and Turin was begun in 2001). The **Fréjus road tunnel**, at 12.8km the second-longest road tunnel in Europe, opened in 1980. Near the entrance, the **Forte di Bramafam**, erected to protect the first rail tunnel, is slowly being restored by volunteers.

The Via Lattea: A Milky Way of Ski Resorts

Above Oulx, **Sauze d'Oulx** with its mountain **Sportina** is one of the liveliest ski resorts in the region, with plenty of action on and off the pistes. Set in a basin surrounded by forests, famed as the 'Balcony of the Alps', Italian skiing was born here in 1896, when Adolfo Kind donned his funny 'skate shoes' and went hurtling down the slopes. In the 1930s Fiat and Martini built summer holiday villages for their workers; in the 1950s winter skiing was added to their offerings, and Sauze has never looked back. It lies in the centre of the Via Lattea or 'Milky Way', a string of resorts (Sestriere, Sansicario, Cesana, Claviere and Montgenèvre in France) encompassing 600km of pistes; by purchasing a week's ski pass at one resort, you can spend a day at another. The mountains are also adored, in summer, by hikers and motorcyclists, some of whom attempt to scale Mount Chamberton, the highest point in Europe accessible by bike.

The Milky Way sweeps around the Upper Susa Valley to **Cesana Torinese**, home and origin of the name of the ancestors of Paul Cézanne, and its modern satellite **San Sicario**. Every July, Cesana

Carton Rapid Race
www.carton
rapidrace.it

hosts one of the nuttier Italian festivals, the **Carton Rapid Race**, in which contestants are given two hours to build their own boats out of cardboard boxes and tape to see which one survives the rapids of the Dora Riparia to reach the finish line. **Claviere**, next in the galaxy, was the pinnacle of ski fashion in the 1930s and is still a good resort for intermediate skiers who prefer their après-ski low key. Claviere is located just below the Monginevro/Montgenèvre pass, the Roman *Mons Janus*, favoured by Hannibal (perhaps), Julius Caesar (again), Petrarch, the first poet to love mountains (he wrote an ode to its beauty in 1353) and Napoleon (again), who built the road replacing the old mule track. The Roman god Janus had two faces, and his mountain does, too – Claviere on one face and French Montgenèvre on the other. In 1907 skiers here competed in the world's first international ski competition; even the local golf course straddles the frontier. Near the frontier post, you can drive, then hike, up to the last of the Susa Valley's hundred forts, the **Batteria Chaberton**, begun in 1898. Europe's highest fort at 10,269ft, served by its own cablecar, Chaberton was considered impregnable by Mussolini, only to be wrecked by the French in a day during the brief Battle of the Alps in 1940. Eight huge cannon towers, subterranean barracks and magazines remain.

Sestriere (6,676ft), the flashiest star of the Milky Way and Piedmont's most fashionable playground, was the first purpose-built ski resort in the world, built by 'Senator' Giovanni Agnelli and his sporty son Edoardo in the 1930s at a place known since Roman times as *Ad Petram Sistrariam* (100km from Turin); when Edoardo was killed in a plane crash in 1935, Giovanni built **San Edoardo**, a pseudo-Romanesque church of local stone in his memory, the bronze door sculpted with portraits of Edoardo's seven children; inside is a Via Crucis (1958) sculpted by Francesco Messina.

Much of the rest of Sestriere's architecture, including the two landmark cylindrical tower-hotels, may have all the charm of university dormitories, but the mountains are glorious, good enough for the 1997 World Championships and the 2006 Olympic downhill events. In summer, you can tee off at Europe's highest 18-hole golf course. Above Sestriere, **Sauze di Cesana** and **Grangesises** have traditional wooden Alpine houses; the wooded valley of **Argentiera** is a popular destination for cross-country skiers and hikers. Ten kilometres along the road to Fenestrelle, **Pragelato**, the newest member of the Milky Way, has a ski jump.

The Waldensian Valleys:
Valle del Chisone and Val Pellice

The Valle del Chisone and Val Pellice are steeped in history. Strategically located where the two meet, the big town of **Pinerolo** was coveted by the French, who captured it three times. Once, when they really meant to keep it, the great military architect Vauban rebuilt its citadel, but in the late 1600s the French realized they could no longer hold it and destroyed it. Its most famous inmate was the mysterious Man in the Iron Mask (1668–78), imprisoned by Louis XIV – one of some 85 theories has it that he was the doctor of Louis XIII, who knew the king couldn't produce heirs. There's a **monument** to him in Via Gabotto, and Pinerolo holds a festival in his honour in early October.

Sunday is the best day to visit Pinerolo, when its many small museums are open. In central Piazza Vittorio Veneto (which hosts big markets on Wednesday and Saturday) stands the handsome Baroque **Palazzo Vittone** (1743), built as a pilgrims' hospice by Bernardo Vittone; it now houses the local **Art Museum** at No.8 with 19th-century Piedmontese art and a **Museum of Natural Sciences**. Nearby on Via Duomo is the Gothic **Cattedrale di San Donato** (unkindly restored in the 1800s), with a 17th-century painting of St Michael chasing the rebellious angels, attributed by some to Rubens, and a fresco of St Thomas Aquinas; there's a **Museo Diocesano** in the bishop's palace at Via del Pino 49 with items from local churches and cartoons of the frescoes by Michele Baretta. Pinerolo was the seat of princes of Acaia, whose Palazzo dei Principi d'Acaja (1318) is set behind a loggia in Via Principi d'Acaja. On top of the oldest part of town, the Gothic church of **San Maurizio** retains a Romanesque campanile; inside are frescoes from the 1400s.

Pinerolo is home to an important study centre of prehistoric art: the **Museo d'Arte Preistorica**, dedicated to the cultural and physical evolution of humanity over the past five million years; they often have special exhibits in the Palazzo del Senato in Via Principi d'Acaja. This is also a very horsy town – its *Cavallerizza Caprilli* is the largest stable in Italy. The town hosts a series of international equestrian trials in summer; a former barracks in Viale Giolitti 5 houses the **Museo Storico della Cavalleria**, dedicated to the weapons, gear and uniforms of Italian and foreign cavalries. Pinerolo's sweet climate has earned it the nickname 'the Nice of Piedmont' and a new attraction: the **Parco Ornitologico Martinat**, on the road to San Pietro Val Lamina. Dedicated to the preservation and reproduction of endangered species, it boasts the world's

Art Museum and Museum of Natural Sciences
both open Sun 10.30–12 and 3.30–6

Museo Diocesano
t 0121 393 932; open Sun 10.30–12 and 4–6

Museo d'Arte Preistorica
Viale Giolitti 1, t 0121 794 382; open Sun 10.30–12 and 3.30–6

Museo Storico della Cavalleria
t 0121 376 344; open Tues–Thurs 9–11.30 and 2–4, Sun 10–12 and 3–6, or by request

Parco Ornitologico Martinat
t 0121 303 199, www.parcomartinat.it; open daily 10–6, till sunset in winter; adm exp

12 | Piedmont | West of Turin into the 'Olympic Mountains'

The Waldensians

The special history of the Valle del Chisone and Val Pellice begins with Peter Waldo (or Valdes) of Lyon, a wealthy merchant who in 1160 was at a feast when a guest suddenly dropped dead. This shocked Waldo into a religious conversion: yearning to return to the origins of the Church, he gave away all his possessions to preach the Bible and the virtues of poverty, but, unlike St Francis, who would later do the same, Waldo the proto-Protestant openly condemned the idea of priests (there are none among the Waldensians) and criticized the rampant corruption of the medieval Church ('No man can serve two masters, God and Mammon,' he said) and so was condemned as a heretic by a Lateran Council in 1184.

Those of his followers who escaped the subsequent massacres took refuge here, in Piedmont's secluded valleys, where the counts of Savoy allowed them to live, in spite of opposition from Rome. During the Reformation, however, they were persecuted for supporting Luther, especially under Carlo Emanuele II, who, at the urging of Louis XIV of France, sent military expeditions against them, killing many and forcing the Waldensians to take refuge in Geneva until 1698. Vittorio Amedeo II agreed to officially tolerate them, although in fact they had to wait until 17 February 1848, when Carlo Alberto granted civil rights to all his subjects – a day still celebrated with bonfires here. Still, true freedom of religion only came with the republican constitution of 1947. Today there are some 30,000 Waldensians in Italy, and most are concentrated in these valleys, where nearly every village has a simple, unostentatious building, a *tempio valdese*.

biggest aviary, over a thousand parrots, and other birds as well, reptiles and mammals.

If you're heading up the Val del Chisone towards Sestriere (*see* p.260) you'll pass **Villar Perosa**, the cradle of the Agnelli family, where Giovanni, the founder of FIAT, set up a ball-bearings factory, Riv, that was badly bombed along with the rest of the town in the war, but was rebuilt and now belongs to an alphabet soup of different companies; the Agnelli family still has a big 17th-century Baroque villa in town. Further along, it's hard to miss the **Forte di Fenestrelle**, 'Piedmont's Great Wall of China' built between 1728 and 1850 by the Savoys to defend their frontier against France. It consists of three mountain forts that are linked by an extraordinary 2km subterranean stair of 4,000 steps; to see it all (or some) book ahead for a long (7hrs), medium (3hrs) or a short (1hr) guided tour in Italian and wear sturdy shoes. Nearby is the majestic **Selva di Chambons**, an ancient larch forest; from its footpaths there are splendid views of the giant fortress.

South of Pinerolo in the Val Pellice, the somehow otherworldly town of **Torre Pellice** is the unofficial Waldensian capital. The **Museo Storico Valdese**, in a former boarding school, is run by the local Waldensian Foundation, and covers their history and daily life. But Torre isn't all history: there's contemporary art (Daniel Buren, Tony Cragg, Mario Merzon and many others) at the **Studio per l'Arte Contemporanea Tucci Russo**, founded in Turin in 1974 and relocated in a former mill here in 1994. That's not all: there's also the **Galleria Civica d'Arte Contemporanea** on Via D'Azeglio with a collection of post-war Italian art.

The upper valley is pretty around **Bobbio Pellice** and **Villanova**, which still has a flood embankment built with money sent by the Waldensians' great supporter Oliver Cromwell. South, **Cavour** is isolated on a plain celebrated for its spuds and apples, and is known for its biannual confab of *grassoni* (very big people). The town sits next to a curious rock, the **Rocca di Cavour**, with a medieval fort and rock engravings; the **Abbazia di Santa Maria**, just to the east, has the oldest altar in Piedmont in its crypt.

Forte di Fenestrelle
SAPAV buses from Pinerolo or Turin; t 0121 83600, www.fortedi fenestrelle.com; open Sept–May Thurs–Mon 9.30–1 and 2.30–5.30; June–Aug Mon–Sun 9.30–1 and 2.30–6; adm

Museo Storico Valdese
Via Beckwith 3, t 0121 932 179; open Feb–June and Sept–Nov Thurs, Sat and Sun 3–6; July–Aug Mon–Sun 4–7; adm

Studio per l'Arte Contemporanea Tucci Russo
Via Stamperia 9, t 0121 953 357, www.tuccirusso.com; open Thurs–Sun 10.30–12.30 and 4–7; adm

Galleria Civica d'Arte Contemporanea
t 0121 932 530; open Tues–Thurs 3.30–6.30, Sat 10.30–12.30 and 3–6.30

ⓘ **Susa >>**
Corso Inghilterra 39, t 0122 622 447

ⓘ **Avigliana >**
Piazza del Popolo 2, Corso Torino 6, t 011 932 8650

Where to Stay and Eat West of Turin and into the 'Olympic Mountains'

Avigliana ✉ 10051

Corona Grossa, Piazza Conte Rosso 38, t 011 932 8371 (€€). Old-fashioned place in the *centro storico*, specializing in seafood and mushrooms in season. *Closed Tues.*

Susa ✉ 10059

★★★Napoleon, Via Mazzini 44, t 0122 622 855, *www.hotelnapoleon.it* (€€€). The top place to stay, but don't expect unbridled luxury. It's unpretentious and friendly with the bare three-star essentials plus a gym.

Pizzeria Bella Napoli, Via XX Settembre 1, t 0122 622 203 (€). Reliable local favourite serving not only proper pizza but lots of seafood. *Closed Mon.*

ⓘ **Bardonecchia** ›
Viale Vittoria 44,
t 0122 99032

Bardonecchia ✉ 10052

****Des Geneys-Splendid**, Viale Einaudi 21, t 0122 99001, *www.hotel desgeneys.it* (€€€€). A tranquil setting in the trees and more character than many resort hotels.

****Bucaneve**, Viale della Vecchia 2, t 0122 999 332, *www.hotelbucaneve bardonecchia.it* (€€). At walking distance from the lifts, the 'snowdrop' is a large wooden chalet with ample rooms and that extra bit of warmth. *Half board. Closed mid-Sept–Nov.*

****La Quiete**, Viale San Francesco 26, t 0122 999 859, *www.hotellaquiete.it* (€€). As quiet as its name. Inside, it's warm and cosy, with good-sized rooms, some with balcony. *Full board in season.* Pets admitted.

ⓘ **Claviere** ››
Via Nazionale 30,
t 0122 878 856,
www.claviere.it

Oulx ✉ 10056

*****Cascina** Genzianella Residence, Via Cazettes 2, t 0122 832 119 (€€€). Old farmhouse on the edge of town, converted into woodsy self-catering flats available by the week; within easy driving distance of the slopes.

****Niblé**, Via R. Ghiotti 19 in Gad hamlet, t 0122 832 372, *www.italiaabc. it/h/nible* (€€). Cosy inn 1km from the centre, with a good trattoria.

Club Colombiere, Via Monterotta 23, t 0122 76323 (€). Good set menu and fantastic views.

ⓘ **Sestriere** ››
Via Louset 14,
t 0122 755 444,
www.sestriere.it

Sauze d'Oulx ✉ 10050

****Capricorno**, Case Sparse 21 in Le Clotes, t 0122 850 273, *www.chaletil capricorno.it* (€€€€). Intimate, quiet lodge. Elegant **restaurant**; book well in advance. *Half board. Closed May–mid-June and mid-Sept–Nov.*

****Relais des Alpes**, Piazza III Reggimento Alpini 24, t 0122 859 747, *www.gestioniabc.it* (€€€€). Good for nightlife, just off Sauze's main piazza, near the ski bus stop, with rooms and sauna. *Half board.*

*****Chalet Faure**, Via Chaberton 4, in the old town, t 0122 859 760, *www. faure.it* (€€€). Small, comfortable chalet with rustic-style rooms, as well as a welcoming spa in the basement – a treat after a day on the slopes.

*****Chalet Chez Nous**, Loc. Jouvenceaux 41, t 0122 859 782, *www.chaletcheznous.it* (€€€). Prettily

ⓘ **Sauze d'Oulx** ›
Piazza Assietta 18,
t 0122 858 009

restored, cosy chalet, offering 'B&B and motorcycle repair'. One of the few here open year round.

***Stella** Alpina, Via Miramonti 22–24, t 0122 858 731, *www.stellalpinahotel.it* (€€€). Good-value, English-run.

Del Borgo, Via Assietta 30, t 0122 858 318 (€€–€). Choose from 40 different kinds of pizza in a wood oven.

*Orso Bianco, up at Sportinia, t 0122 850 206, *www.gestioniabc.it* (€). Cheap and cheerful. *Half board.*

Claviere ✉ 10050

*****Pian del Sole**, Via Nationale 28, t 0122 878 085, *www.piandelsole.com* (€€€€). Intimate hotel 100m from the ski lifts; eight rooms with mod cons, including DVD players.

Gran Bouc, Via Nazionale 24/a, t 0122 878 830, *www.granbouc.it* (€€€). The local favourite for après-ski – good Piedmontese cuisine. *Closed Wed in low season, May and Nov.*

Sestriere ✉ 10058

****Grand Hotel Sestriere**, Via Assietta 1, t 0122 76476, *www.grand hotelsestriere.it* (€€€€€). Elegant hotel, with an indoor pool, fitness centre, billiards room, spacious rooms and a good **restaurant** with an enormous wine list. *Open Dec–April and summer.*

****Fraitevino**, Piazza Fraiteve 3 bis, t 0122 76022, *www.hotelilfraitevino.it* (€€€€€). Hotel with splendid views, located near the old *funivia* station.

****Du Col**, Via Pinerolo 12, t 0122 76990 (€€€€). Modern, friendly, with great views; convenient for the slopes, restaurants and nightlife.

*****Sud-Ovest**, Via Monterotta 17, t 0122 755 222, *www.hotel.sud-ovest.it* (€€€€). Quiet hotel with rooms and two-bed flats, and a good **restaurant**. Free mountain bike use in summer. *Open Dec–April, July and Aug.*

*****Miramonti**, Via Cesana 3, t 0122 755 333, *www.miramontisestriere.com* (€€€€). Short walk from the centre, good family-run hotel and **restaurant**.

Enoteca Tre Rubinetti, Piazza Agnelli 4/b, t 0122 77397 (€€). Gourmet wine bar with a French touch; try the *bagna cauda. Closed Sat and Sun.*

Osteria Barabba, Piazzale Fraiteve 2, t 0122 76402 (€€). Lively wine bar with good food, drawing a wide international clientele.

Pinky's, Piazza Fraiteve 5, **t** 0122 76441 (€). Popular après-ski bar and pizzeria. *Closed May, Oct and Thurs.*

(i) **Pinerolo >**
Viale Giolitti 7/9,
t *0121 795 589*

(★) **Flipot >>**

Pinerolo ✉ 10064

***Locanda della Maison Verte, Via Rossi 34, north of Pinerolo in Cantalupa, **t** 0121 354 610, *www. maisonvertehotel.it* (€€€–€€). A 19th-century farmhouse in the woods; comfortable rooms at a herbalist spa with a pool and a **restaurant**.

***Regina, Piazza Barbieri 22, **t** 0121 322 157, *www.albergoregina.net* (€€). Warm and welcoming hotel/restaurant, now run by the third generation of the Rissolo family.

Agriturismo Turina, Strada Tagliarea 16, at Bricherasio (6km south of Pinerolo), **t** 0121 59257, *www.agri turismo-turina.it* (€). In a panoramic spot, a fruit farm with four apartments sleeping 2–4. The farm/*agriturismo* also has its own **restaurant** (fruit a speciality since the family owning it has specialized in the culture of kiwi fruit). *Three-day minimum stay in high season.*

(★) **Taverna degli Acaja >**

Taverna degli Acaja, Corso Torino 106, **t** 0121 794 727, *www.tavernadegli acaja.it* (€€€€). Picturesque place serving a limited but excellent choice of tasty mountain dishes with a gourmet touch, followed by a sumptuous cheeseboard. *Closed Sun, Mon lunch and 3 weeks of Aug.*

Torre Pellice ✉ 10066

****Gilly, Corso Lombardini 1, **t** 0121 932 477, *www.hotelgilly.it* (€€€). A classic hotel offering big rooms, with a lovely garden, covered pool and sauna. The **restaurant** (€€) is good, too, serving the likes of venison pâté

with blueberry sauce. *Discounts for cyclists. Closed Jan.*

Villagio Crumière, Piazza Jervis, just up in Villar Pellice, **t 0121 930 623 (€). Little hotel at the local felt factory founded in 1904, with a museum and a good **restaurant** (€€). The chef trained at Flipot. Good fixed-price menus. *Closed Mon; temporarily closed at time of writing.*

Flipot, Corso Gramsci 17, **t** 0121 91236 (€€€). Flipot is Piedmontese for Philip, who founded the first inn here. Atmospheric place that in the hands of chef Walter Eynard is now the last word in traditional but highly personal French/Italian cuisine. People make special trips out of Turin just to eat here; there are over 1,000 labels in the wine cellar, so it's advisable to book ahead. *Closed Mon and Tues.*

Cavour ✉ 10061

Palazzo Malingri, Via Palazzo at Bagnolo Piemonte 23 (✉ 12031), 6km west of Cavour, **t** 0175 391 394, *www.castellodibagnolo.it* (€€€€€). Self-catering flats sleeping 2–5 in the 18th-century farmhouses on the grounds of an 11th-century feudal estate. The later palace sits among gorgeous gardens of bamboos, azaleas, rhododendrons and hydrangeas. *Minimum stay two nights except July–Aug.*

***Locanda La Posta, Via dei Fossi 4, **t** 0121 69989, *www.locandalaposta.it* (€€€). A former 17th-century staging post, this has been an inn since 1782. There are lovely views towards Monviso and the Rocca di Cavour, and rooms are furnished with period pieces. They also have a good **restaurant**: try the *agnolotti* and *fritto misto alla piemontese* (€30). *Closed Fri and 25 July–10 Aug.*

Southwest Piedmont: the Marquisate of Saluzzo

The courtly, Occitan-speaking Marquisate of Saluzzo (the western half of the modern province of Cuneo) was founded in 1142, shone in the 15th century, and lost its independence (and its last marquis, to poison) in 1548. In 1601, Carlo Emanuele I, after failing to reconquer Geneva, picked it up from France in exchange for Bresse,

Bugey and Gex. Today, people in the valleys of Saluzzo still speak the *lenga d'oc*, the language of the troubadours, and remember when their marquises granted them a good deal of autonomy. But memories are long here – *more de peira* (stone heads) embellish the portals of the houses and churches, an atavistic relic from the night of time, when the heads of enemies or deified heroes were hung like trophies on Celtic temples.

Carmagnola to Stroppo

South from Turin

Until the Savoys lapped it up, **Carmagnola**, 27km south of Turin, was an outpost of the Marquisate of Saluzzo. If you've ever studied the French Revolution, the name may ring a bell: local minstrels composed the *Carmagnole* about an early 15th-century *condottiere* from the town, although how the song made Danton's hit parade, with very different lyrics, is anyone's guess. The marquis' 15th-century residence, the **Casa Cavassa**, is in porticoed Via Valorba; the other thing to do is stroll along the banks of the Po. East of Carmagnola, at **Casanova**, the Cistercian abbey church of **Santa Maria** is one of the earliest Gothic buildings in Piedmont. To the west, towards **Pancalieri**, the crop is mint – acres of it; local shops sell it in a variety of essences and liqueurs.

Further south, **Racconigi**, once the Savoys' chief silk-making town, has its **Castello di Racconigi**, rebuilt in 1676 for Prince Tommaso di Savoia-Carignano by Guarino Guarini, and refurbished in 1842; highlights are a Chinese apartment, rooms frescoed with gods, Carlo Alberto's art collection, Sav and his neogothic model farm. Behind the castle extends a lovely **park** laid out by the French landscape architect André Le Nôtre, and a romantic English garden, with ancient trees, a lake and special stork oasis.

Castello di Racconigi
t 0172 84005, www. ilcastellodiracconigi.it; open Tues–Sun 8.30–7.30; adm

Park
can be visited 25 Mar–4 Nov Tues–Sun 10–7; ticket office closes at 6pm

Savigliano and Fossano

Savigliano, further south, was an important medieval *comune*, and in 1559 it was a candidate for the new Savoy capital, before Emanuele Filiberto settled on Turin; the locals, not sore losers, built a **triumphal arch** anyway in their central Piazza Santarosa. Birthplace of the astronomer G.V. Schiaparelli (1835–1910), of Martian canal fame, Savigliano has a bijou little **Teatro Milanollo** (1835) and two swish **palaces**. The first, the late-Renaissance **Palazzo Muratori Cravetta** has a frescoed courtyard, a stair with a splendid coffered ceiling, and beautiful gardens once used as a theatre. The second, the Baroque **Palazzo Taffini d'Acceglio**, has rococo rooms and frescoes in its Aula Regia, on the military exploits

Palazzo Muratori Cravetta
t 0172 717 185; open 10–12.30 and 2–6 by appointment; adm

Palazzo Taffini d'Acceglio
t 0172 717 185; open 10–12.30 and 2–6 by appointment at the Cassa di Risformio of Serigliano; adm

Museo Ferroviario Piemontese
t 0172 31192, www.museoferroviario piemontese.com; open Thurs 2.30–5.30, Sat and Sun 10–12 and 2.30–5.30; adm

Castello dei Principi d'Acaja
t 0172 61976; open Sept–June Mon, Tues, Thurs, Fri 2–7, Wed 8.30–12 and 2–7, Sat 9–12; Aug Mon, Tues, Thurs, Fri 2–7, Wed 8.30–12 and 2–7

Slow Fly
t mobile 335 8307 972, www.slowfly.it

⭐ **Saluzzo**

of Vittorio Amedeo I. The **Museo Ferroviario Piemontese** is dedicated to trains.

Fossano, another industrial town with an old core, wants to make you laugh in early July, at the Fossano Funny Festival. When Fossano passed to the Acaia princes in 1314, they built the massive brick **Castello dei Principi d'Acaja**, which in 1560–62 housed Emanuele Filiberto and his court. His son Carlo Emanuele I commissioned its frescoes of crests and emblems by Giovanni Caracca in the 1590s; the castle is also proud of its collection of 19th-century military postcards. The little airport of **Levaldigi** to the west has Italy's only school for hot-air balloonists, and it's rare, on a fine day, not to see a balloon floating over the hills; hour-long flights over the vineyards of Le Langhe are offered by **Slow Fly**.

Saluzzo, the 'Little Siena of the Alps'

Mellow old **Saluzzo** is one of those Italian towns out of time, famed in an old French story that Boccaccio used to conclude his *Decameron*: of the Marquis Gualtieri, who mentally tortured his lowly born wife, Patient Griselda, a story translated by Petrarch into Latin and borrowed by Chaucer. It doesn't seem quite fair – historically the rulers of Saluzzo were among the least tyrannical of all Italian Renaissance *signori*. Nor has a lot happened since their day, and the lanes of Saluzzo's historic centre as well as the surrounding castles and churches all have tangible memories of their golden days.

Corso Italia, now the main street of Saluzzo, follows the medieval walls. For reasons of space, the **Cattedrale** (1491–1501) was built here; like many Piedmontese late Gothic churches it has a main portal framed in a tall gable; inside, there's a beautiful polyptych (just left of the Baroque high altar) by Hans Clemer, a native of Burgundy who worked in Saluzzo in the late 1400s, and a Renaissance tomb in the ambulatory. Near the cathedral, the **Porta Santa Maria** is one of several gates leading up into the medieval city, along **Via Volta**, lined with shadowy porticoes and leading to the **Birthplace of Silvio Pellico** at Piazza dei Mondagli 5 (now the tourist office). Nearby, at Via dell'Annunziata 1/B, a 16th-century monastery houses the prestigious **Scuola di Alto Perfezionamento Musicale**, dedicated to perfecting musical techniques and the latest technology.

Scuola di Alto Perfezionamento Musicale
t 0175 47031, www.scuolaapm.it; ring ahead to visit Mon–Fri 9–1 and 2.30–6.30

Torre Civica
t 0175 42117; open Mar–Sept Thurs–Sun 9.30–12.30 and 2.30–6.30; Oct–Feb weekends only, same hours; adm

From here the steep, cobbled **Salita Castello** leads up past lovely Renaissance buildings and the angel-topped **Torre Civica** (1462), with views over the medieval roofs as far as Monte Rosa. At the top, the Castiglia (1280) was the residence of the marquises but was much altered to serve as a prison, a role it played until 1992. Its **Fontana della Drancia** recalls the aqueduct built by Ludovico II that brought running water to Saluzzo.

The Gentle Patriot

A key figure in the Risorgimento, Silvio Pellico (1789–1854) moved to Milan at the age of 20. There he met the top patriotic authors of the day, Ugo Foscolo and Alessandro Manzoni, and wrote several plays, including *Francesca da Rimini*, performed in 1818 and translated by Byron. Shortly after, Pellico became a tutor for the children of Count Lambertenghi, a leading opponent of the Austrians then ruling Milan, and when Lambertenghi founded a literary journal, Pellico edited it. In 1820, the Austrians accused him of belonging to the secret society of the Carbonari and, after a perfunctory trial, condemned him to death, although this was commuted into imprisonment with hard labour at Spielberg in Moravia. In 1830, Pellico was released and, broken by the hardships, spent the rest of his life as the librarian of the Marquise Giulia Falletti di Barolo, shunning the fame brought by *Le Mie Prigioni* ('My Prisons') – his prison diary – which was soon read throughout Europe. The book was a watershed in public opinion: Pellico's unaffected prose, his gentle resigned spirit, and homely detail (one of the best-loved accounts is how he trained a spider to eat from his hand) were said to have hurt Austria more than any military defeat ever could.

Back by the Torre Civica, the church of **San Giovanni** and its Romanesque-Gothic *campanile* (the cockerel on top recalls Saluzzo's close ties to France) date back to 1330. Frescoes by Pietro da Saluzzo from the next century decorate the nave by the stair, and behind the high altar the pretty Burgundian-Gothic **Cappella dei Marchesi** houses the tomb of Saluzzo's greatest marquis, Ludovico II (d. 1503) with his motto 'Noch–Noch' – not an early appreciation for knock-knock jokes, but German for 'More and More'. The beautiful choir stalls are from Sant'Antonio di Ranverso.

On the same Via S. Giovanni, the charming 15th-century Casa Cavassa, once home to the Vicar-General of Saluzzo, was restored in the 1880s as the **Museo Civico,** with Renaissance furnishings and a splendid altarpiece of the *Madonna della Misericordia* (1499) by Hans Clemer, who also painted the grisailles of Hercules on the ground floor. Here and there you'll see the Cavassa family's rather alarming motto, *Droit Quoi qu'il Soit* ('Forward at any cost'). Further down Via S. Giovanni, the *quattrocento* church of **San Bernardo**, with a Baroque front, sits among the aristocratic *palazzi*; just below is a belvedere, with views to Monviso.

Museo Civico
t 0175 41455; open April–Sept 10–1 and 2–6; Oct–Mar Thurs–Sun 10–1 and 2–5

Castles near Saluzzo: Manta and Lagnasco

Castello di Manta
t 0175 87822, www. fondoambiente.it; open Mar–Sept Tues–Sun 10–6; Feb and Oct–early Dec till 5; adm

The marquises had a favourite residence at the **Castello di Manta**, 4km south. Here, more than anywhere, you can get a feel for the polished court of Saluzzo, especially in the exquisite courtly frescoes (1420s) in the Sala Baronale. The subject is derived from an epic poem, *Le Libre du Chevalier Errant*, by the Marquis Tommaso III and commissioned by his natural son Valerano, who inherited the castle. A rare copy of the manuscript in the Bibliothèque Nationale in Paris shows the same scene, of nine elegant heroes and nine heroines, here nearly life-sized and in all likelihood portraits of the marquises and their wives. On the opposite wall, a seductive *Fountain of Youth* by the same painter is one of the finest depictions of that favourite court fantasy. Southeast of Saluzzo

Castello di Lagnasco
t 0175 72101; open Mar–July and Sept–Oct, ring ahead for times; adm

in **Lagnasco**, there's more at the Castello di Lagnasco built in 1100 with two strong towers. In 1560, its lord, Benedetto Tapparelli d'Azeglio, inspired by the artistic fancies going on in Saluzzo, converted it into a proper residence, adding a Renaissance courtyard, a unique Salone degli Scudi, decorated with a frieze of 167 coats of arms of the noble houses of Savoy, stucco ceilings and delightful trompe l'œil frescoes on mythological scenes.

Alpine Saluzzo: Up the Po Valley

These Occitan-speaking valleys are rich in little frescoed churches, many of which have been beautifully restored in recent years. The apple-growing **Valle del Po**, now a nature reserve, was an important route to France, and **Revello** was fortified early on by the marquises. Their palace, once the favourite of the Marchioness Margherita di Foix-Béarn, the second wife of Ludovico II, is now the *Municipio*, but you can visit the Cappella Marchionale (1519), which

Cappella Marchionale
ring ahead, t 0175 257 687

Margherita had frescoed with portraits of the marquises and a Leonardoesque *Last Supper*. Revello's 15th-century **Collegiata dell'Assunta**, founded by Ludovico II, has an elegant marble portal by Matteo Sanmicheli (1534), a unique Renaissance work for Piedmont; inside are three 16th-century polyptychs by Hans Clemer and Pascale Oddone. To the northeast, the Abbazia di Staffarda

Abbazia di Staffarda
t 0175 273 215; open April–Oct Tues–Sun 8.30–12.30 and 2.30–5.30; Nov–Mar Tues–Sun 8.30–12.30 and 1.30–4.30; adm

was founded in 1135 by the Marquis Manfredi I; the austere Cistercian church houses a majestic retablo by Oddone and a sculpted pulpit. You can visit the 13th-century cloister, pilgrims' inn and market, where the monks sold their produce.

Sanfront, further up the Po Valley, is a picturesque village under steep Mombracco, the mountain home of innumerable fairies or witches in local lore. Its old quartzite mines and the ghost hamlet of **Balma Boves** are located up under a huge overhanging rock, a half hour's walk above Robella; near this is the Rocca la Casna, with prehistoric incisions. According to tradition, when Charlemagne exiled Desiderius, the last Lombard king of Italy in 774, he took refuge in **Ghisola**, an ancient hamlet near **Paesana**. The little resort of **Crissolo** lies under the striking pyramid of Monviso, 'the Stone King', at 12,600ft the highest peak in the Cottian Alps. Crissolo is

Grotta del Rio Martino
torch essential, wellies and helmet advisable

the base for visits to the Grotta del Rio Martino and its 140ft waterfall, a short walk up from the village and the lovely **Pian del Re** (9,455ft), where a plaque marks the sparkling source of Italy's longest river. Above Pian del Re, you can walk through the first Alpine tunnel ever: the 246ft **Buco di Viso**, dug in 1480 by Marquis Ludovico II – a remarkable feat of engineering to facilitate mule-bound trade between Saluzzo and France (best done in summer; bring a torch and a helmet if possible). The Col de la Traversette, above Pian del Re, may have been used by even bigger freight – Hannibal's elephants.

More Alpine Saluzzo: the Varaita and Maira Valleys

South of Manta, **Costigliole Saluzzo** has three castles (the Castellotto, the Castello Rosso and the Castello Reynaudi), one of which is now a hotel (*see* p.270); the *Municipio* is housed in a rare secular work by Vittone, the **Palazzo Giriodi** (1740), which you can visit by request. Here you take a lovely detour into the luxuriant **Valle Varaita**, an Occitan-speaking valley that has retained many of its old traditions. One of these is woodworking: since 1954 craftsmen in **Piasco** have made Victor Salvi harps; a **Victor Salvi museum** designed by Dario Castellino and dedicated to three centuries of harps, with a listening library is in the works. In **Sampeyre**, manufacturer of ironwork and eiderdowns, the church of SS. Pietro e Paolo has good 15th-century frescoes by the Biazaci brothers. Every five years at Carnival (next in 2012), Sampeyre celebrates the Baio, a 1,000-year-old pageant celebrating the expulsion of the Saracens, in which 300 men participate, some playing women's roles, with brightly ribboned hats. Another village, **Casteldelfino**, recalls in its name that it was the capital of the Dauphin's Cisalpine lands in 1300; in good weather you can continue into France, through the ski resort of **Pontechianale** over the **Colle dell'Agnello**. The other road west of Casteldelfino leads to **Bellino** and its hamlets, where 32 sundials (1735–1934) and stone heads decorate the houses. The road ends near the monolithic **Rocca Senghi**, accessible to climbers by means of a *via ferrata* (iron way) or a muletrack. The stars blaze at night here in clear skies; at the time of writing an observatory is under construction.

The **Valle Maira**, next south, is known for its lush orchards, and for its democratic local governments in feudal times. It begins at **Dronero**, which boasts an attractive stone bridge of 1428, an octagonal grain market and the **Museo Civico Mallé**, Via IV Novembre 54 (temporary entrance at Via Valmala 9), holding an eclectic collection of decorative arts, photos and prints. Dronero's Espaci Occitan has a **Museo Son de Lenga** dedicated to the Occitan language and culture in Europe. Nearby **Villar San Costanzo** is an old, old place where the church of **San Pietro in Vincoli** has a crypt of 1091, a survivor of a long-gone Benedictine abbey; one chapel has charming frescoes on the Golden Legend by Pietro da Saluzzo (known as the 'Master of Villar' until his name was discovered under the plaster). A second church, Romanesque **San Costanzo al Monte**, marks the martyrdom of San Costanzo under Diocletian, and has a few 8th-century Lombard sculptures and good capitals from the 12th century, too. Near Villar San Costanzo, you can stroll among the **Ciciu** ('puppets'), vaguely humanoid standing rocks up to 26ft high, wearing stone caps left by glaciers – an especially haunting sight under a full moon.

Palazzo Giriodi
see www.castellia
perti.it for details

Victor Salvi museum
t 0175 270 511,
www.victorsalvi
foundation.com, for
current status – at time
of writing, open
Wed–Sun 10–1 and
2–5; adm

Museo Civico Mallé
t 0171 909 329,
www.museomalle.it;
open Sun 2.30–7; adm

Museo Son de Lenga
Via Val Maiza 19,
t 0171 904 075; www.
espaci-occitan.org,
open Tues–Fri 9–12
and 2.30–5; museum
Sun 2.30–6, till 3 in
winter; adm

San Pietro in Vincoli
t 0171 902 432; open
Tues–Sun 9–12

12

Piedmont | Southwest Piedmont: the Marquisate of Saluzzo: Carmagnola to Stroppo

San Peyre
for visits call Le Terre del Marchesato,
t 0175 240 352

Assunta
t 0171 997 986; pick up the keys at the Convitto Seprimo in front of the church

Further up the valley, **Stroppo** has remarkable frescoes by the 'Master of Stroppo' in its 12th-century church of San Peyre, beautifully isolated on a spur. In **Elva**, where houses are dispersed in a gorge-lined valley, people were famous for their unusual vocation – travelling around Italy and buying women's hair, which they would sort and weave into skeins to sell to wig-makers in France and England. Elva's church of the Assunta was built in the 1400s but decorated with curious sculptures straight out of the Middle Ages, and an important fresco cycle, culminating in a majestic *Crucifixion* by Hans Clemer. The upper Valle Maira, around Acceglio, is unspoiled; there are lovely hikes, especially to the Cascate Stroppia and the lake of Nove Colori ('nine colours').

Where to Stay and Eat from Carmagnola to Stroppo

(i) Carmagnola >
Piazza Manzoni 10,
t 011 972 4238, www.
carmagnolaturismo.it

Carmagnola ✉ 10022

Agriturismo Cascina Montebarco, Via Poirino 650, Fraz. Casanova, 7km east of Carmagnola, t 011 979 5051, *www.agriturismomontebarco.it* (€). A traditional Po Valley farm with a courtyard; self-contained apartments sleep 2–3. Bicycle hire available.

(★) La
Carmagnole >

La Carmagnole, Via Chiffi 31, t 011 971 2673 (€€€€). Lovely restaurant in a 17th-century Piedmontese mansion, featuring dishes tailor-made for each customer based on the freshest of ingredients, such as pheasant *galantine* in Sauternes, or *osso buco* and *porcini* mushrooms in cream. The desserts and wines are exceptional. The chef, Renato Dominici, is a professor at the Università di Scienze Gastronomiche at Pollenzo. *By reservation only. Open eves and Sun lunch; closed Mon and 20 days in Aug.*

Savigliano ✉ 12038

Antica Osteria dell'Orsa, Piazza Battisti 5, t 0172 717 606 (€€€). Welcoming place in the centre, serving home-made pasta and tender beef dishes. *Eves only; closed Wed, Jan.*

(★) Castello
Rosso >>

(i) Saluzzo >
Piazzetta dei Mondagli 5,
t 0175 46710

Saluzzo/Manta ✉ 12037

***Griselda**, Corso XXVII Aprile 13, t 0175 47484, *www.hotelgriselda.it* (€€€). Modern hotel overlooking the historic centre, with parking.

***Astor**, Piazza Garibaldi 39, t 0175 45506, *www.mtrade.com/astor* (€€).

Modern and functional, on the edge of the historic centre.

Persico, Vicolo Mercati 10, t 0175 41213, *www.albergopersico.net* (€€). A bohemian hotel (complete with resident artist), with comfortable if slightly oddly furnished rooms. The good **restaurant** (€) serves a tasty boar stew. *Closed Mon.*

La Gargotta del Pellico, Piazzetta dei Mondagli 5, t 0175 46833 (€€€). Good restaurant in the birthplace of Silvio Pellico. Try the quail in pastry, or the *raviolini* with marjoram and mushroom butter. *Book. Closed Tues, and at lunch.*

L'Ostu dij Baloss, Via Gualtieri 38, t 0175 248 618, *www.ostudijbaloss.it* (€€€). In a wonderfully atmospheric 17th-century house in the historic centre, delicious, imaginative food based on fine-quality ingredients. Good-value fixed-price menus. *Closed Sun, and Mon lunch.*

La Piola del Barbon, Via Garibaldi 190, Manta, t 0175 88088 (€€€). Popular old place, serving resolutely traditional dishes of the area – definitely not for vegetarians. *Closed Tues eve and Wed.*

Costigliole Saluzzo ✉ 12037

****Castello Rosso**, Via Ammiraglio Reynaudi 5, t 0175 230 030, *www.castellorosso.com* (€€€€). A 16th-century castle in an English park, with large, luxurious rooms, period furniture and Murano chandeliers. Amenities include a beauty centre, a pool with a retractable roof, and a good **restaurant** (€€€).

Sampeyre ☒ 12020
***Monte Nebin**, Via Cavour 26,
t 0175 977 112, *www.hotelmonte
nebin.it* (€€). Large, modern base for
mountain visits, with a bouncy castle
playground for the kids and a classic
Italian restaurant (*closed Wed*).

Stroppo ☒ 12020
Locanda Occitana Alla Napoleonica,
Fraz. Bassura, t 0171 999 277, *www.
locandanapoleonica.it* (€€). Four
antique-furnished rooms are housed

in a stone hayloft, and there's a good
restaurant with a €26 set-price menu.
*Closed Tues, and Wed (exc in summer),
10 days in Dec and 10 days in June.*

Lou Sarvanot, Via Nazionale 64,
Fraz. Bassura, t 0171 999 159 (€€€).
Tiny and popular place to dine, not
only for the charm of the setting,
but also for the tasty cheese-based
menu *degustazione* which changes
from week to week. *Open Fri eve,
Sat, Sun and hols lunch and dinner;
closed Jan.*

Cuneo and the Alpi Marittime

A pleasant provincial capital of gardens and wide boulevards,
Cuneo stands at the confluence of the Gesso and Stura rivers on a
lofty wedge (*cuneo*), accessible to trains via the city's landmark
Soleri viaduct, built in the early 1930s. Cuneo's nickname, the City
of the Seven Sieges, comes from the pesky French (1542, 1557, 1639,
1641, 1691, 1744 and 1799). Mostly rebuilt in the 19th century, Cuneo
is arranged around its vast Turin-style **Piazza Galimberti**, site of a
market every Tuesday. In Piazza G. V. Virginio, the church of **San
Francesco** (1227) has a marble portal from 1481; its cloister now
houses the **Museo Civico** with a small collection of Piedmontese
art, and prehistoric to medieval artifacts. At the crossroads of the
roads to Turin and Saluzzo, **Villa Tornaforte** was a monastery,
converted into a stately home in the 1800s; admission includes its
beautiful park, which is an ecological oasis.

Cuneo, too, has its valleys, the closest of which is the chestnut-
forested **Valle Grana**. Pietro da Saluzzo left some frescoes in the
Cappella di San Bernardo, just outside the 'capital' **Valgrana**; some
of his first and liveliest works are further west, in the plain 15th-
century **Cappella di San Sebastiano** by the cemetery of Occitan-
speaking **Monterosso Grana**. In Monterosso's hamlet, Santa Lucia
di Coumboscuro has a small **Museo Etnografico di Coumboscuro**
dedicated to local wool, cheese, hemp and wood industries, and a
school hoping to revive furniture-making and weaving. **Pradleves** is
a small resort, while, further up, **Castelmagno** lends its name to the
valley's 'king of cheeses'. A little **Museo del Lavoro**, Via Giordano e
Marino in Fraz. Chiappi has a large collection of old tools, in a
house of 1684. A serpentine road leads up to the striking 15th-
century **Santuario di San Magno** set in the mountains on a spot
long holy to the ancient Celts and Romans (an altar dedicated to
Mars is embedded in the wall) and dedicated to the 8th-century
alpine missionary Magno. Surrounded by a panoramic gallery, the
Cappella Allemandi has more frescoes by Pietro da Saluzzo.

Museo Civico
*entrance Via Santa
Maria 10/a, t 0171 634
175; open Tues–Sat
8.30–1 and 2.30–5.30,
Sun 3–7; adm*

Villa Tornaforte
*Fraz. Madonna
dell'Olmo, t 0171 412
664, www.castelli
aperti.it; adm*

**Museo Etnografico
di Coumboscuro**
*t 0171 98707; open
9–12 and 2–7*

Museo del Lavoro
*t 0171 986 370; open
end June–Aug 8–12
and 2–6, otherwise
by request*

**Santuario di
San Magno**
*t 0171 986 178; open
Sun and hols June–Sept;
daily July and Aug*

Getting around Cuneo and the Alpi Marittime

Cuneo's **airport, t** 0172 741 500–558, *www.aeroporto.cuneo.it*, 20km north at Levaldigi, has links to Rome, Bucharest and Tirana, and summer flights to Olbia, Split, Ibiza, Gerona and Bastia. Cuneo is linked by **rail** with Turin via Saluzzo, and with Genoa via Ceva and Mondovì. You can also take one of Italy's most spectacular railways to Limone Piemonte and Ventimiglia – 96km of track with 81 tunnels.

Into the Parco Naturale delle Alpi Marittime and Limone Piemonte

Although just up from the Riviera, the lofty Maritime Alps have made this southwest corner of Piedmont something of a best-kept secret. The French influence is strong, and the difficulty of access has also meant that traditions have lingered. One is the early December *Fiera Fredda* (Cold Fair) in Borgo San Dalmazzo, a market established by Emanuele Filiberto, where the local snails hold pride of place. The town is named after another martyr, Dalmatius, and the Romanesque church of the once powerful abbey built over his tomb is curiously framed in an unfinished Baroque façade, although it still has a crypt dating back to the 5th century.

Fiera Fredda
www.fierafredda.it

A trio of valleys convene at Borgo San Dalmazzo. The longest, the **Valle Stura**, is a botanical paradise for its rare flowers. A major route of salt merchants and armies (Pompey, the Saracens, Charles d'Anjou and François I were here), its chief town is medieval **Demonte**, with pretty porticoed lanes and a church of San Donato with a fresco of the Battle of Lepanto. Only a tower and ruins remain of its once mighty **Fortezza di Consolata**, destroyed by Napoleon in 1796. Further up the valley, Carlo Alberto built a huge fort to replace it at **Vinadio** at the cost of half the village, although the king personally intervened to save the pretty Romanesque Gothic church of **San Fiorenzo**. At Vinadio you can turn off for the highest church in Europe, the 6,676ft **Santuario di Sant'Anna** set up in the 1300s as a hospice and rebuilt in the 17th century, now a pilgrimage destination (*open June–Sept*). Further up the Valle Stura, the sulphurous **Bagni di Vinadio**, famous since Roman times, now have high-tech spa facilities. At **Pietraporzio** begins the **Stretta delle Barricate**, a ravine closed in by sheer walls. **Argentera**, the last and highest *comune*, is a cool summer resort. From May to mid-October you can continue up the hairpinning road to the **Colle della Maddalena** into France, lined with pastures and flowers, the realm of the valley's sturdy mountain sheep, *pecora sambucana*.

Vinadio
t 0171 959 151; *open June–Oct Thurs–Sat 2.30–7, Sun 10–7; mid-July–Sept also Mon, Tues and Wed 2.30–7; adm*

Santuario di Sant'Anna
t 0171 959 125, *www.santuariosantanna.it*

Bagni di Vinadio
open all year Mon–Sun 8.30–10.30; caves free, otherwise adm

The Valle Gesso leads into the heart of the Maritime Alps, pre-global warming the southernmost to have snow all year round. Three peaks – Argentera, Gelas and Matto – at over 10,000ft, encompassed in the **Parco delle Alpi Marittime**, are seamlessly linked with the Côte d'Azur's Parc National du Mercantour. Lofty altitudes so close to the sea bring plenty of rain and make the area

Parco delle Alpi Marittime
www.parks.it/parco.alpi.marittime

Terme di Valdieri
t 0171 971 067,
www.termedivaldieri.it;
open June–Sept; adm

Valderia
open early June–mid-Sept 9–12 and 2–6; adm

exceptionally rich in flora and fauna; even wolves have returned, without even being asked. The Parco encompasses the Valle Gesso, and the old summer spa of dukes and kings, **Terme di Valdieri** with hot sulphur caves and a unique algae called 'muffe' (Ulva labyrinthiformis), used to treat rheumatism. It has a botanic garden, **Valderia**, hosting 400 of the 2,600 species of local flora that grow in these parts.

Vittorio Emanuele II built two Swiss chalets here, one used for his dalliances with the Bella Rosina, as well as a hunting lodge up at the lovely **Piano del Valasco**, a lovely big meadow with larches and waterfalls, an hour's walk from Terme. East of Mount Argentera, a second branch of the valley leads to **Entracque** and its *frazione* **San Giacomo** further south, with another Savoy hunting lodge in the beech woods, and a path up to the lovely Piano del Rasur, where marmots and chamois frolic. San Giacomo is the site of the world's biggest turbine-pumps, supplying a generating station built in the

Enel Information Centre
t 0171 978 811

mountain; at the **Enel Information Centre** you can visit a model and take a little train into the station to watch it at work.

South of Borgo San Dalmazzo, the **Valle Vermenagna**, sliced by the SS20 and the Cuneo–Ventimiglia railway, is steep and wooded. From the little resort of **Vernante** (proud to be 'the only village in Italy where the houses are covered with Pinocchio frescoes'), an 8km side road leads up to **Palanfrè**, a traditional village; from here in an hour you can walk a circuit through an enchanting ancient beech forest, in a lush microclimate where over 650 different trees and flowers thrive. Back in Valle Vermenagna, **Limone Piemonte** is a delightfully old-fashioned winter sports centre, with skiing usually until Easter, and very popular with the skiers from the Riviera and Côte d'Azur – it's only an hour's drive from Nice. Its citrusy name derives from *leimon*, Greek for meadow, one of the town's most charming features. The old town clusters around the Gothic church of **San Pietro in Vincoli**, which houses a hodgepodge of frescoes, carvings and commemorative plaques.

Museo della Resistenza
Via Mazzini 4,
t 0171 735 554; open Thurs 3–6, otherwise by request; free

Museo Naturalistico
t 0171 738 123; open Tues–Sun 9–12 and 2–6, closed Mon; ring to check opening times

The next valley east, the **Valle del Pesio**, has **Chiusa di Pesio** as its capital; during the Second World War it was a seat of the Resistance, documented in the **Museo della Resistenza**. The **Certosa di Pesio**, founded in 1173 and dominated by an oversized cloister, was abandoned after Napoleon, but since 1934 has been housing brothers of the Istituto Missioni Consolate and their **Museo Naturalistico**, with items from Latin America and West Africa; it has the only Resistance cemetery in Italy, set up in 1946. The road rises to the **Parco Alta Valle Pesio**, with karstic formations and pine forests, under Mount Marguareis. In May and June, when the snows melt, don't miss the hour-and-a-half walk up to the Pis del Pesio, a spectacular 100ft jet of water shooting from the cliff wall, which resembles just what it sounds like.

⭐ **Al Rododendro** >>

ⓘ **Cuneo** >
Via Vittorio Amedeo
II 8/a, **t** 0171 690 217,
www.cuneoholiday.com

ⓘ **Parco Alpi Marittime**
www.parks.it/parco.
alpi.marittime. Visitors'
centres are at Terme di
Valdieri, **t** 0171 97208
(summer), Vernante,
t 0171 920 220 (all year)
and Entracque, **t** 0171
978 616 (summer only)

ⓘ **Limone Piemonte** >>
Via Roma 30, **t** 0171
925 280, www.limone
piemonte.it

⭐ **Agriturismo La Commenda** >

Where to Stay and Eat in Cuneo and the Alpi Marittime

Cuneo ✉ 12100

****Principe**, Piazza Duccio Galimberti 5, **t** 0171 693 355, www.hotel-principe.it (€€€€). Since 1932 one of the town's best hotels, right in the centre.

****Lovera Palace**, Via Roma 37, **t** 0171 690 420 (€€€). Elegant hotel in the centre that once hosted King François I of France, which now offers a fitness centre, tours and cooking lessons in its Michelin-starred restaurant, the **Delle Antiche Contrade** (€€€€), located at Via Savigliano 11, **t** 0171 480488, www.antichecontrade.it. Closed Sun eve and Mon.

***Ligure**, Via Savigliano 11/a, **t** 0171 681 942 (€€€€). In the oldest quarter, itself a bit old and worn at the edges, but brightened with old-fashioned courtesy. **Restaurant** serving tasty meals of home-made pasta and roast meat or trout. Closed Jan. Restaurant closed Sun eve and Mon.

Osteria della Chiocciola, Via Fossano 1, **t** 0171 66277 (€€€). Serves traditional Piedmontese fare, including mouthwatering agnolotti del plin (stuffed with meat and vegetables), duck, and rabbit with olives. Closed Sun, 15 days in Jan and 1 week in Aug.

Boves/Peveragno (south of Cuneo) ✉ 12100

Agriturismo La Commenda, Loc. S. Margherita 16, Peveragno, **t** 0171 385 351, www.paginegialle.it/cascinala commenda (€). A great place to recharge your batteries; rooms with kitchenettes and a jacuzzi in a peaceful farmhouse in a lovely setting. Sumptuous farm-grown breakfasts, and a trattoria nearby.

Al Rododendro, Loc. San Giacomo, Boves, **t** 0171 380 372 (€€€€). For a special treat, head 13km south of Cuneo to Boves, where you'll find the atelier of Maria Barale, one of Italy's top female chefs. Her leek soup, truffles with eggs, and ravioli di gallina are renowned across Piedmont. Book. Closed Sun eve, Mon and some of June.

Pradleves (Valle Grana) ✉ 12100

***Tre Verghe d'Oro**, Via IV Novembre 129, **t** 0171 986 116 (€). In the Cunean valleys there are many rustic places to stay and eat. Try this old-fashioned inn, in which the restaurant serves gnocchi al Castelmagno and other mountain specialities (€€). Hotel closed Jan; restaurant closed Tues.

Vernante (north of Limone) ✉ 12019

****Nazionale**, Via Cavour 60, **t** 0171 920 181, www.albergonazionale.it (€€). Family-run since 1896, a great base for visiting the mountains; rooms have all been refurbished including internet connections. Good **restaurant**, and special web offers.

Limone Piemonte ✉ 12015

****Le Ginestre**, Via Nizza 68, **t** 0171 927 596, www.hotelginestre.com (€€). Small, cosy and conveniently near the slopes, with beautiful views, bar and **restaurant**.

Lu Taz, Via S. Maurizio 5, **t** 348 444 6062 (€€€). In a stone house in the woods 1km out of town, where traditional rib-sticking Piedmontese dishes are prepared with flair. Book. Closed Tues, 2 weeks in June and 1 week in Nov.

Mondovì and the Monregalese

Lively, unpretentious Mondovì was founded rather late by Italian standards – in 1198 – by three villages united against the Bishop of Asti. The bishop wasn't having it, though, and destroyed the town in 1231; it was rebuilt and changed hands several times, before coming under the Savoys in 1418. At the base of the hill, **Breo** is Mondovì's commercial centre, where the city's symbol, the 'Moor', sounds the hours on the church of **SS Pietro e Paolo** (1489), convenient for people waiting next door in the train station. A funicular goes up to **Piazza**, the oldest part of town, built around the attractive, asymmetrical **Piazza Maggiore**, where the **Chiesa della Missione** (1675–1733) adds an elegant Baroque touch, its vault afloat with 17th-century trompe-l'œil figures by Andrea Pozzo. Mondovì native Francesco Gallo (1672–1750) was one of the busiest architects of his day; although he lacked the imagination of his rival Juvarra, he left his home town a **cathedral** with a chapel dedicated to Universal Suffrage, a notion introduced in Italy by five-times prime minister Giovanni Giolitti, another native of Mondovì. In 1472 Mondovì printed the first book in Piedmont, recalled in a large collection of antique printing presses in the new **Museo Civico della Stampa**. Don't miss the views from the 13th-century **Torre del Belvedere** with its unusual clock.

On the plain just east of Mondovì, the huge sanctuary in **Vicoforte** makes a startling sight. Here, the story goes, a hunter accidentally shot a rustic image of the Virgin instead of a deer. In 1596 the Savoys began a church on the spot and in the early 1700s Francesco Gallo crowned it with the world's biggest elliptical dome, rising 240ft from the church floor. A bit further east, at **San Michele Mondovì**, the **Cappella della Madonna della Neve** has unusual frescoes of 1403, showing the City of Heaven, works of mercy, and Hell with a cavalcade of vices. North of Mondovì (on the N28d), **Bastia Mondovì's** 11th–15th-century **San Fiorenzo** has 51 late-Gothic Provençal frescoed scenes of Vices and Virtues, stories of the lives of Jesus and Mary by several hands.

In the mountains to the south, **Villanova Mondovì** is crowned by the **Confraternita di Santa Croce** (1755), one of Bernardo Vittone's masterpieces, where he uses his famous inverted squinch in the vault to seamlessly turn a square into an octagon. **Roccaforte Mondovì** is a cheerful village, its homes and shops covered with frescoes by local talent. Just west, amid chestnut groves, the trendy spa of **Terme di Lurisia** was 'discovered' by Marie Curie in 1918 when she came to study its exceptional minerals and radioactivity; the bottled stuff from its Fonte Santa Barbara is New York City's favourite Italian water. It has a small ski station, and there's another one east of Roccaforte, at **Frabosa Soprana**, which is also the site of the spectacular **Grotte di Bossea**, one of the most interesting cave systems in Italy, with beautiful stalactite formations and eccentrics, an underground river and lakes and a waterfall, and a skeleton of a prehistoric bear; a lab is dedicated to the cave's fauna, including the endemic pseudo-scorpion. Even stranger than that is the installation by the Viennese art group Gelatin on the slopes above the ski resort of **Artesina** to the south: a 200ft pink rabbit stuffed toy, set to remain until 2025.

Chiesa della Missione
open daily 7.30–7pm, till 9pm in summer

Cathedral
t 0174 41549; open daily 7.30–12 and 3–7, till 9 in summer

Museo Civico della Stampa
Via della Misericordia 3, t 0174 559 256; open April–Oct Sat–Sun 3–6.30, or by appointment; adm

Torre del Belvedere
t 0174 40389; open mid-Sept–Oct and April–mid-June Sun 3–6.30, other days by appointment; mid-June–mid-Sept Tues–Sun 3–6.30; adm

Vicoforte
t 0174 565 611

San Fiorenzo
contact the Comune, t 0174 60112, or the Pro Loco, t 0174 60178

Terme di Lurisia
t 0174 683 421, www.lurisia.it; open all year except for the Fangoterapia and Balneoterapia sections

Grotte di Bossea
t 0174 349 240; www.grottedibossea.it; guided tours all year – ring to check times, but usually Mon–Sat 10, 11.30, 3 and 4.30 and Sun 10, 11.30, 2.30, 4 and 5.30; adm; dress warmly

Where to Stay and Eat in Mondovì and the Monregalese

(i) **Mondovì** >
Via Vico 2, t 0174 47428

(i) **Ormea**
Via Ormea,
t 0174 392 157

Mondovì ✉ 12084

***Nuovo Park**, Via Delvecchio 2,
t 0174 46666, www.parkhotelmondovi.
it (€€). Comfortable modern hotel, in
the new part of town, set in a park,
with good views.

***Portici**, Piazza Carlo Emanuele 47,
t 0174 563 980, www.hotelportici.com
(€€). Atmospheric hotel in the
porticoes around the mighty basilica.
Rooms have been nicely renovated.

Marchese d'Ormea, Via Carassone
8, t 0174 552 540 (€€€). Charming
trattoria that uses seasonal
ingredients: gnocchi with *fines
herbes* is a speciality. Theme
evenings on various Piedmontese
classics in autumn. *Closed Sun
eve and Mon.*

Montaldo di Mondovì ✉ 12080

Corsaglia, Via Corsaglia 27,
t 0174 349 109 (€). Hotel/restaurant
offering a taste of yesteryear near
the Bossea caves; menus combine
some Ligurian dishes with
mountain cuisine.

San Bernardo
t 0174 81101

**Castello Reale
di Casotto**
t 0174 351 131; open
daily 9–12 and
2–6; adm

Trains follow the upper Tanaro south as far as Ormea, by way of
Garessio, a picturesque collection of hamlets, with ski slopes, a golf
course and cures at **San Bernardo**, source of 'the lightest water in
the world'. Picturesque houses dot Via Cavour, and the old parish
church has a campanile with a garlic-bulb roof. Between Garessio
and **Pamparato** to the north, the **Castello Reale di Casotto**, built
over an 11th-century Certosa, is not the luckiest of buildings; it
burned down in 1380 and twice in the 1500s. In the early 1700s
Francesco Gallo and Bernardo Vittone rebuilt it again. Napoleon's
troops sacked it, Carlo Alberto purchased it, and it became a
favourite of his son Vittorio Emanuele II.

Ormea is a picturesque medieval town with wrought-iron
balconies and an old town gate, incorporated into a bell tower, and
contemporary statues carved in the local black marble. Its ruined
castle was a nest of Saracen corsairs in the 10th and 11th centuries,
when they controlled the coast.

South of Turin: Roero and Le Langhe

Castles
see the tourist offices
or www.castelliaperti.it

For many visitors, Roero and Le Langhe are the 'real' Piedmont,
cradle of Slow Food and some of Italy's most exquisite wines,
truffles and cheeses. Often compared to Tuscany, pale hills and
ridges are robed in vines producing Barolo, Barbera, Dolcetto and
Nebbio and crowned by walled villages and castles, a reminder that
this was once fiercely disputed territory. Now knife and fork have
replaced sword and cannon, and invaders are welcome in some of
Italy's most charming country hotels and *agriturismos*. Autumn
is high season, when freshly harvested truffles perfume the
restaurants and a barrage of festivals celebrate the good things of
the earth. But spring is lovely, too, and from late May to late October
many otherwise locked-up **castles** open their doors to the public.

Bra, Slow Capital of the Universe, and the Roero

Bra (the memorable name comes from *braida*, the planting of vines in wide rows so grain could be sown in between) was founded *c.* 1000 as a Guelph stronghold by inhabitants of Roman *Pollentia* (*see* below) and became, in 1552, a loyal subject of the Savoys. Today headquarters of Slow Food (*see* pp.49–50), it is also, as of 1999, a founding member of what has been called 'Neo-Humanism', the League of Slow Cities which has now spread worldwide, promoting a more reflective way of life, biodiversity, sound environmental policies, sustainability, trees, local produce (as in the organic fruit and vegetables served in Bra's school lunches), as little noise and as few cars as possible. In September, in odd-numbered years, Bra hosts **Cheese**, the world's most prestigious cheese fair (*see www.cheese.slowfood.com*). At other times, visit Bra's legendary cheese shop, **Giolito**.

Bra's long arcaded Corso Garibaldi (known as the 'Ala' or wing) ends in the delightful main Piazza Caduti della Libertà, overlooked by the church of **Sant'Andrea** (1682) with a lavish façade of 1830. Three museums beckon. In the curious Gothic **Palazzo Traversa** on Via Parpera 4 is the **Museo Civico di Archeologia**, with Roman odds and ends from *Pollentia*. The **Museo Civico Craveri** is devoted to flora and fauna, both local and from the Congo, Sahara, Mexico and Brazil, collected by the Craveri brothers. A third museum, the private **Quasi per Gioco**, inside the Cultural Centre Giovanni Arpino, has a charming collection of antique toys. At the bottom of Via Barbacane stands one of Bernardo Vittone's masterpieces: the tall quadrifoil church of **Santa Chiara** (1742), with a delightful rococo interior of high Juvarrian arches and a dome with two shells – the outer one, viewed through 'windows', depicts heaven and its saintly population. Today it hosts some music festivals, thanks to its wonderful acoustics. Bra's landmark is a curious little octagonal villa overlooking the town, the **Zizzola**, where local witches are rumoured to have held their Black Sabbath meetings.

Roman *Pollentia* is now **Pollenzo**, a *frazione* of Bra on the River Tanaro. A rich textile manufacturer, it has the ruins of a circular funerary monument, forum, theatre and amphitheatre (with seating for 17,000). A village grew up in its ellipse and in 1842 Carlo Alberto added a neogothic castle-farm, the **Agenzia Sabauda**, to promote local agriculture, and a Gothic Revival church, **San Vittore**, to provide for spiritual needs. It contains a surprise: a real Gothic choir, stolen by Napoleon's troops from the Abbey of Staffarda. In October 2004, the Agenzia Sabauda opened its latest venture, the **Università di Scienze Gastronomiche**, the world's first university of

Giolito
Via Montegrappa 6,
t 0172 412 920

Sant'Andrea
t 0172 413 764

Museo Civico di Archeologia
t 0172 423 880; open Oct–Aug Tues–Thurs 3–6; also 2nd Sat and Sun of the month 10–12 and 3–6

Museo Civico Craveri
Via Craveri 15,
t 0172 412 010; open Tues–Sun 3–6

Quasi per Gioco
Via Guole 45, t 0172 426 035; open Mon–Fri 4–6.30 and Sun 10–12.30 and 3–6.30 by appointment; adm

Santa Chiara
t 0172 413 148

Pollenzo
guided visits and information from Agenzia di Pollenzo, Piazza Vittorio Emanuele II 13, t 0172 458 416, www.agenzia dipollenzo.com

Università di Scienze Gastronomiche
www.unisg.it

Getting to and around Bra

Bra, Cherasco and Alba are all linked by **rail** from Turin, and also have good **bus** connections to Cuneo. Local buses (*www.comune.torino.it/gtt/intercomunale*) are adequate but you'll wish you had a car or bike.

taste, sponsored by Slow Food. Three-year courses are offered in gastronomy and agricultural ecology, plus specialist degrees and masters in gastronomic sciences and food culture; the complex includes a hotel, restaurant and a wine 'bank'. Just east of Pollenzo, **Santa Vittoria d'Alba** has spectacular views over the hills.

South of Bra, atmospheric **Cherasco**, where times seems to have stopped in 1940, is not to be outdone in slowness – it's proud to be the 'Italian capital of snails' and home to an international institute of *Elicicoltura* (snail raising). It was founded by the city of Alba on a chessboard grid in 1243 on a ridge at the confluence of the Tanaro and Stura di Demonte, as a strategic outpost to confound rival Asti; it is proud to have witnessed the signing of seven peace treaties in its history and today is well known for its antique fairs in April, May (ceramics and glass), July (books), September, October (toys) and December. Main Via Vittorio Emanuele II, dotted with medieval houses (and the 19th-century **Confetteria Barbero**, famous for exquisite *baci di Cherasco* made of hazelnuts coated in bitter chocolate), is closed off by two arches, a sparkling white **Arco Trionfale** on the north end, celebrating triumph over the plague of 1630, the southern one unfinished. In between, the **Torre Civica** has a rare Baroque clock showing the phases of the moon; behind this, at Via dell'Ospedale 40, the **Museo Civico**, in the 17th-century Palazzo Gotti di Salerano, has coins and Roman finds, although the frescoes on wisdom by Sebastiano Taricco (1681) steal the show. The Romanesque church of **San Pietro** has a façade and porch decorated with majolica and sculpted heads. Just south, the **Palazzo Salmatoris** (1616), now used for special exhibitions, hosted the *Savoys* (and the Shroud) during the plague of 1630, and Napoleon after he conquered Piedmont in a ten-day blitzkrieg in 1796; it was here that he signed the armistice with the delegates of Vittorio Amedeo III. A wonderful street lined with ancient plane trees, the Viale dei Plantani, leads from the south arch to the Visconti **castle**, a handsome residence built in 1348 when Cherasco briefly belonged to them.

Elicicoltura
www.lumache-elici.com

Confetteria Barbero
at No.74, **t** *0172 488 373; closed Wed*

Museo Civico
t 0172 489 101; open Mar–Dec, Sat 9.30–12.30, Sun and hols 9.30–12.30 and 3–6.30

Where to Stay and Eat in and around Bra

(i) **Bra** >
Piazza Caduii della Libertà, **t** *0172 430 185,*
www.comune.bra.cn.it

Bra ✉ 12042
★★★Badellino, Piazza XX Settembre 4, 3.8km from the centre by the A20 Marene interchange, **t** 0172 439 050,

www.ristorantealbergobadellino.it (€€). Friendly, family-run hotel with **restaurant** – try the local sausage and the peppers with anchovies.
Osteria del Boccondivino, Via Mendicità 14, **t** 0172 425 674, *www.boccondivinoslow.it* (€€€). Founding Slow Food member back in

1984, serving delicious renditions of local dishes and exquisite wines in its three dining rooms, next to Italy's Slow Food HQ. *Closed Sun and Mon.*

Pollenzo ✉ 12060

****Albergo dell'Agenzia**, Via Fossano 21, t 0172 458 600, *www.albergo agenzia.it* (€€€€€–€€€€). Sharing the neogothic quadrangle of the University of Gastronomic Sciences, with fine rooms and fitness pool, jacuzzi and steam bath. The complex includes the **Slow Food Wine bank** and **Guido a Pollenzo**, t 0172 458 422, *www.guidoristorante.it* (€€€€). Run by the sons of the legendary chef Guido of Costigliole. Classic Piedmontese cuisine and seafood. *Book.*

***La Corte Albertina**, Via Amedeo di Savoia 8, t 0172 458 410, *www.lacorte albertina.it* (€€€). Charming hotel of 26 rooms, each different and decorated with period furnishings, a wine store, and an excellent **restaurant** (*reservations mandatory*), featuring authentic local dishes on a €36 *menu degustazione. Restaurant closed Wed.*

Cherasco ✉ 12062

Al Cardinal Mazzarino, Via S. Pietro 48, t 0172 488 364, *www.cardinal mazzarino.com* (€€€€). The welcoming Nucci and Flavio Russo run two perfect guest suites in their small 'palace', with plenty of extras thrown in. *Restaurant open Thurs, Fri, Mon and Tues eves only and Sat–Sun at lunch.*

Antica Corona Reale, Via Fossano 13, at Cervere, 9km southwest of Cherasco, t 0172 474 132 (€€€). Renowned restaurant (founded in 1835) where award-winning chef Gian Piero Vivalda uses only the finest *foie gras*, white truffles, Cherasco snails, and so on to produce culinary masterpieces. *Closed Tues eve, Wed, Aug and 26 Dec–10 Jan.*

Operti 1772 da Fausto, Via Vitt. Emanuele 103, t 0172 487 048, *www.operti1772.it* (€€€). The fief of young chef Fausto Carrara, interested in the history of cooking, as well as developing his own recipes. Snail lovers will love his 'snail menu' but there's much much more, including a hazelnut *torta* without flour or butter. Superlative wine cellar. *Closed Tues.*

Rosa Rossa, Via S. Pietro 31, t 0172 488 133 (€€€). Warm and welcoming *osteria* in the centre, with tasty pasta dishes and the local snails. *Closed Wed, Thurs and Aug.*

Santa Vittoria d'Alba ✉ 12069

****Castello Santa Vittoria**, Via Cagna 4, t 0172 478 198, *www.santavittoria. org* (€€€). Beautiful rooms in a castle, many with balconies, a panoramic pool and an excellent **restaurant**. The same people also run the stylish **Agriturismo Valdispiso**, Via S. Rolfi 5, t 0172 478 198, a former property of the House of Savoy set amid vines at the foot of the castle, with three rooms and three apartments.

(★) Castello Santa Vittoria >>

(i) Cherasco >
Via Vitt. Emanuele 79, t 0172 489 101, www.cherasco 2000.com.

12

Piedmont | South of Turin: Roero and Le Langhe: Alba

Alba: World Capital of White Truffles

Alba, once the splendid Roman city of *Alba Pompeia*, now the capital of white truffles and hazelnuts, is an austere medieval city of narrow lanes and brick towers (like Asti, it once had a hundred of these, but now gets by with three), all scented by the chocolatey aromas wafting from the **Ferrero chocolate factory**, set up in Alba in the 1940s. For the real ambrosia, come on a Saturday in September–November to visit the pungent **Truffle Market**, which takes place under a giant tent off main Via Maestra.

Alba produced a good Renaissance painter, Macrino d'Alba, whose *Vergine Incoronata* (1501) hangs in the council chamber of the **Palazzo Comunale**, along with the *Piccolo Concerto* by Mattia Preti; another Macrino, a *Nativity* of 1508, hangs in the church of **San Giovanni**. The stalwart 14th-century brick **Duomo** has seen

Ferrero chocolate factory
guided visits with qualified guides every day at 10, 2.30 and 4pm; contact Consorzio Turistico Langhe Monferrato Roero, Piazza Risorgimento 2, t 0173 366 328, www.turismodoc.it/ escursioni-tour/visita-ad-alba.asp

Museo Civico Eusebio

t 0173 292 473; open Tues–Fri 3–6, Sat and Sun 9.30–12.30 and 3–6; adm

 Le Langhe and Asti

Grinzane Cavour

t 0173 262 159 to book a guided tour, www. grinzane.it; open Sept–mid-Nov Mon– Sun 10–12.30 and 2.30–6.30; Feb–Aug and Dec Wed–Mon, same hours; adm

Castello di Roddi

t 0173 363 480; open May–Oct Sun 11–1 and 2–5.30 or by appointment, adm

Ratti Wine Museum

t 0173 50185; call ahead to visit, or send an email to info@renatoratti.com

Cappella del Barolo

visits should be booked on t 0173 282 582 or email visit@ ceretto.com; usually at 10am and 3pm; adm

Castello Falletti

t 0173 56277, www. baroloworld.it; open Fri–Wed 10–12.30 and 3–6.30; closed Jan; adm

numerous renovations, but still has choir stalls, inlaid with still lifes and city scenes in 1500 by Bernardino Fossato, and a huge *Crucifixion*, an *ex voto* from the plague of 1630. At Via Vittorio Emanuele II 19, the **Museo Civico Eusebio** contains artifacts, coins and *stele* from *Alba Pompeia*. Traditionally a bitter enemy of Asti, Alba is now content to send up its old rival in a donkey *palio* the first Sunday in October, kicking off the truffle season; ever since a local restaurateur, Giacomo Morra, sent a 2.5kg white truffle to Harry Truman in 1951, publicity and razzmatazz has not been lacking. But Alba can be serious: its Resistance fighters defended the 'Free Republic of Alba' from the Germans for 23 days in 1944.

Into Le Langhe: Grinzane Cavour and Barolo

'Le Langhe' are ridges, and around Alba they are scattered with villages, castles and *enoteche* waiting to introduce you to the region's famous wines (if you want to visit the vineyards themselves, you usually need to book; the tourist offices have details). South of Alba, the *enoteca* at **Grinzane Cavour** is in the striking castle that Cavour called home when he served as village mayor. Now the seat of the *Premio Grinzane*, one of Italy's most prestigious literary prizes, it also has a restaurant and a museum dedicated to wine, folklore, and Cavour. In November it holds a charity truffle auction, broadcast live to New York and Los Angeles; in 2004, the largest one went to a New York restaurateur for $41,000, per ounce over six times the price of gold. A member of another famous family, a nephew of the Renaissance humanist Pico della Mirandola, owned the 13th-century **Castello di Roddi** north of Grinzane with medieval prisons and kitchens. The name comes from *Campi Raudii*, where the Romans in *c.* 100 BC won a victory over the barbarians, who are nevertheless remembered in the names of two great wines, Barbera and Barbaresco.

South, **La Morra** is the belvedere of Le Langhe, for visiting the former Abbazia dell'Annunziata, now the **Ratti Wine Museum** – not as funny as it sounds; after all, it was at La Morra that Julius Caesar stopped to try the wine, and was so impressed that he paused in his accounts of conquest to mention it. A deconsecrated church at Brunate La Morra is now the very colourful **Cappella del Barolo**, the result of a deal made by wine growers Bruno and Marcello Ceretto with American artists Sol LeWitt and David Tremlett, who painted it in return for a constant supply of Barolo.

Barolo itself, further south, is a little hill village surrounded by vines, with an *enoteca* of the 'wine of kings, and king of wines' in the 16th-century **Castello Falletti**. François I liked Barolo so much he imported it to France; the last Marquise, Giulia (*see* p.267), famously sent King Carlo Alberto, when he merely asked for a taste, 325 barrels of her finest, one for every day of the year – minus the 40 days of Lent. There are guided tours of the other rooms, including a wine museum and the library purchased for the castle by Silvio Pellico (see p.267).

At pretty **Serralunga d'Alba** (east as the crow flies, squiggling back and forth as the car drives) you still need to use the drawbridge to enter another of the family's castles, the impressively vertical **Castello Falletti di Barolo** of 1340. Many of its defensive features are intact, along with a frescoed corner in the banquet hall, so diners could say their Hail Marys and get back to the main business at the table.

Castello Falletti di Barolo
t 0173 613 358; guided tours Tues–Sun summer 9–12 and 2–6; winter 10–12 and 2–5

Alta Langa

Further south lies the mountainous Alta Langa, where nearly every hill town enjoys enchanting views. **Dogliani**, one of the larger towns, is noted for its production of Dolcetto, the star of the *enoteca* in the old cellars of the town hall. It is also proud of two native sons, Domenico Ghigliano, inventor of sulphur matches (or *zolfanelli*) and the eccentric mid-19th-century architect Giovanni Battista Schellino, who left the town 14 eclectic Rosary chapels leading to his monumental gate to the cemetery (1867). In **Farigliano**, just southwest, Giuseppe Occelli has led the way in preserving the old rare cheeses of Piedmont at his **Occelli Agrinatura**. **Murazzano**, southeast, is a striking hill town under a medieval tower, all that survives of its castle. It also has the **Parco Safari delle Langhe**, a 5km circuit to drive with lions and tigers, zebras and hippos, and an aquarium and reptilarium.

Occelli Agrinatura
Via Stazione 5, www.occelli.it

Parco Safari delle Langhe
t 0173 791 142, www.parcosafari.com; open Mar–Oct Wed–Mon 10–12 and 2–6, Sun and hols 9.30–6.30; Feb and Nov only Sun; adm exp, no credit cards – cash only

In the Middle Ages several 'salt roads' passed through here to the coast; **Cortemilia** (the Roman *Cohors Aemilia*, founded in 118 BC) grew up around one of these, until the Genoese cut off its trade in the 16th century. Medieval *borgos* on either bank of the Bormida make up Cortemilia: Borgo San Michele has evocative ruins of its castle and the Pasticceria Canobbio in Piazza Molinari 1, a shrine for hazelnut lovers. Prettiest is the 12th-century **Madonna della Pieve**, with a stone triptych, just outside town. If you continue up the Bormida towards Savona, you can stop in the little churches at **Levice**, **Prunetto** and **Monesiglio** to see their Gothic frescoes, but the best frescoes are at **Saliceto** near the Ligurian border, in **San Martino di Lignera**. Saliceto was destroyed by the Saracens and rebuilt by the Del Carretto, whose castle stands opposite the 16th-century church of **San Lorenzo**, one of the finest Renaissance buildings in Piedmont.

East and North of Alba: Barbera and Barberesco

Castello dei Marchesi di Busca
t 0141 89291; open Mar–Dec Wed–Sun 10.30–7; closed Jan and Feb

More castles and fine wines await east of Alba: at **Mango** an *enoteca* specializing in Moscato is in the big Baroque **Castello dei Marchesi di Busca**, built by the Gonzaga but a property of the

Museo Arti e Mestieri di un Tempo
Piazza Maggiore Hope 1, t 0141 979 021; open Tues–Sat 3–7; adm

Enoteca
t 0173 635 251; open Thurs–Tues 9.30–6, Sun 9.30–1 and 2.30–6, closed Wed

Castello Reale di Guarene
t 0173 611 101, www.castellodiguarene. com; guided tours Sun and hols in May and 23 Sept–25 Nov 10–12 and 2.30–5.30; adm

Fondazione Sandretto Re Rebaudengo
t 011 379 7600, www. fondsrr.org/fond.html; open Sun 2–7, ring ahead during weekdays to book; adm

Museo della Culture del Gesso
t 0173 66311; open May–Oct Sun 11–12.30 and 3–6, or by reservation; adm

Castello Reale di Carlo Felice
t 0173 58103, www. comune.govone.cn.it; open April–June and Sept–Oct Sun 10–12 and 3–6 July and Aug till 7; other months by reservation; adm

ⓘ **Alba** >
Piazza Risorgimento 2, t 0173 35833, www.langheroero.it

★ **Locanda del Pilone** >

Savoys after 1714. North of Alba, Barbera is the star of the *enoteca* and superb restaurant in **Canale d'Alba**, Via Roma 57 (*see* p.284). Or go back in time: the castle of **Cisterna d'Asti** just north of Canale holds the **Museo Arti e Mestieri di un Tempo**, which houses an excellent ethnographic collection in an 11th-century building.

Northeast of Alba lies the zone of the 'Prince of wines', named after **Barbaresco**, a tiny village founded in *c.* 1000 with a landmark 12th-century **tower** high over the Tanaro, accessible only by way of a stair hanging over the river; the eponymous *enoteca* is in the deconsecrated church of San Donato at Via Torino 8/a. One of the most charming Barberesco hill villages, **Neive**, has a castle from the same era and a fair sprinkling of delightful Piedmontese Baroque, as well as the area's best hotels and restaurants.

Near Barbaresco, **Guarene d'Alba** lies under its lordly **Castello Reale di Guarene**, one of the great 18th-century residences in Piedmont, designed by Count Giacinto Roero, who based his design on Juvarra's grand style; it also has a beautiful formal garden. Another residence, the 18th-century **Palazzo Re Rebaudengo** in Piazza del Municipio, was remodelled in 1997 by its owner, Turin collector Patrizia Sandretto, as an exhibition space for her **Fondazione Sandretto Re Rebaudengo** (*see* p.238), dedicated to contemporary art, with a permanent collection and special exhibitions. **Magliano Alfieri**, just north, has a splendid Baroque castle, where Asti's poet Vittorio Alfieri often sojourned; it now hosts the **Museo della Culture del Gesso**, dedicated to stuccoed ceilings, concentrating on the 16th and 17th centuries; in the centre of town, the **Museo di Arti** on Via Alfieri 4 (same hours) explains how the stucco masters did it.

At **Govone**, further north, there's another fancy castle to see – the **Castello Reale di Carlo Felice**, now the Palazzo Comunale, started as a medieval fort, and was given its elegant Baroque façade and grand stair by Guarino Guarini. One owner, Count Ottavio Solaro, employed the young Jean-Jacques Rousseau here in 1730. Purchased by the Savoys in 1792, it was a favourite of Carlo Felice, who added the telamons from the *Venaria Reale*, frescoed the ballroom and decorated rooms with rare Chinese wallpaper.

Where to Stay and Eat in and around Alba

Alba ✉ 12051

★★★**Locanda del Pilone**, Fraz. Madonna di Como 34, t 0173 366 616, *www. locandadelpilone.com* (€€€€). Romantic rooms and a superb restaurant in the vaulted cellars, from the home-made bread through the delicious mountain-inspired cuisine to the giant cheese cart. *Closed Tues and Wed lunch, and most of Jan and Aug.*

Palazzo Finati, Via Vernazza 8, t 0173 366 324, *www.palazzofinati.it* (€€€€). A gem in the centre: rooms and breakfast in a 19th-century *palazzo*, full of elegant touches – including frescoed bathroom ceilings.

Villa La Favorita, at Altavilla 12, 1km from Alba, t mobile 338 4715 005, *www.villalafavorita.it* (€€€).

Agriturismo on a wine and organic fruit estate, with charming rooms, great breakfast and English-speaking owner who offers cookery classes.

(★) **Castello di Verduno** >>

***Savona, Via Roma 1, **t** 0173 440 440, *www.hotelsavona.com* (€€€). Recently refurbished hotel (vintage 1863) in the centre of town with very stylish, comfortable rooms, as well as a **restaurant** and bar.

Casa Scaparone, 2km from Alba at Loc. Scaparone 8, **t** 0173 33946, *www.casa scaparone.it* (€€). Five rooms on a farm going back to 1874, with bikes and carriage riding, as well as an excellent **restaurant** (*open eves Thurs–Sat, and all day Sun*) serving the farm's own produce, meats, cheeses and wines. *Open Fri eve, Sat and Sun, other days by appointment. Closed Jan.*

La Meridana Ca Reine, at Loc. Altavilla 9, 1km from Alba, **t** 0173 440 112 (€€). B&B and self-catering flats in a Liberty-style villa overlooking vines, with pool, billiards and bikes to hire. Friendly owner speaks English and can organize truffle hunts in season. *No credit cards.*

***Ideal Rooms, Via Ognissanti 26, **t** 0173 282 858 (€€–€). En suite B&B with air-conditioned rooms, just outside the *centro storico*; parking.

Locanda del Barbaresco, 4km from Alba at Fraz. S. Rocco Seno d'Elvio 2, **t** 0173 366 734 or **t** mobile 0333 86 95 428, *www.locandadelbarbaresco.it* (€). Rooms in a Liberty-style villa in the country, and there's also a bar; the owner, Elio Sabena, is an experienced guide and can organize walks and mountain-bike trips through the vines. *Closed Mon.*

Osteria dell'Arco, Piazza Savona 5, **t** 0173 363 974 (€€€€). Small and cosy with an excellent-value menu including tarragon risotto and stuffed guinea fowl. *Closed Sun and Mon.*

Enoclub, Piazza Savona 2, **t** 0173 33994 (€€€€). Atmospheric place with a cellar atmosphere; a great place for risotto. *Closed Mon, Sun eve between mid-July and mid-Aug.*

Grinzane Cavour ✉ 12060

Nonna Genia, 2km from the centre at Loc. Borzone 1, **t** 0172 262 410 (€). Satisfying Langhe cuisine – get the works with an excellent value €25 fixed-price menu. *Eves only; closed Wed and Thurs.*

La Morra/Verduno ✉ 12064

Castello di Verduno, Via Umberto I 9, Verduno, **t** 0172 470 125, *www.castello diverduno.com* (€€€€–€€€). Stay amid luxuriant gardens in Carlo Alberto's 17th-century castle – in a wing designed by the great Juvarra or its outbuildings, and dine on *tajarin* and hazelnut torte. *Closed Dec–Feb. Restaurant open eves only, lunch as well Sat–Sun. Closed Wed.*

***Corte Gondina, Via Roma 100, La Morra, **t** 0173 509 781, *www.corte gondina.it* (€€€). In a historic family house, 14 rooms with antiques and most mod cons.

Belvedere, Piazza Castello 5, La Morra, **t** 0173 50190, *www.belvederelamorra.it* (€€€€). Stupendous views and *agnolotti del plin ai tre arrosti*; also a good place to try *finanziera*, and mushroom and truffle dishes in autumn. *Closed Sun eve and Mon.*

Osteria Veglio, Fraz. Annunziata 9, La Morra, **t** 0173 509 341, *www.osteria veglio.com* (€€€€). Elegant *osteria* in an old farm house amid the vineyards, where the emphasis on only the freshest quality ingredients has made it a Slow Food favourite; great wine list, too. *Closed Tues and Wed lunch.*

Cantina Gagliardo, Via Serra dei Turchi 88, Fraz. Santa Maria, La Morra, **t** 0173 500 663 (€€€). Excellent home cooking to complement the wines in a lovely setting in the vines. *Closed Wed and part of Aug.*

Barolo ✉ 12060

Del Buon Padre, Via delle Viole 30, just east at Vergne, **t 0173 56192 (€). Peaceful rooms, good Piedmontese cuisine and divine wines. *Closed Wed, last 2 weeks of July, 1 Aug, 26 Dec–Jan. No credit cards.*

Agriturismo Le Viole, Via delle Viole 14, Fraz Vergne, **t** 0173 56259, *www.leviole. it* (€). Seven new rooms on a wine estate. *No credit cards.*

Locanda nel Borgo Antico, Via Boschetti 4, **t** 0173 56355, *www. locandanelborgo.com* (€€€€). In a romantic sophisticated setting, well-prepared traditional dishes of Le

(★) All'Enoteca >>

(★) Antinè >>

(★) Villa Beccaris >

Langhe and a superb hazelnut *tortino* to go with your bottle (and there's more than just Barolo). *Closed Tues, Wed lunch, 27 Dec–16 Jan and last 2 weeks of Aug.*

La Cantinella, Via Acquagelata 46, t 0173 56267 (€€). Classic Piedmontese dishes in a classic trattoria. *Closed Mon eve and Tues.*

Serralunga d'Alba ✉ 12050

Foresteria delle Vigne, Via Alba 15, t 0173 626 191, *www.villacontessa rosa.com* (€€€). Stay in the *foresteria* of the fabled Tenimenti di Barolo e Fontanafredda, set in an ancient park – once owned by Vittorio Emanuele II's wife, the Bella Rosina. The restaurant (**Villa Contessa Rosa**, €€€€) in the cellar showcases local cuisine and the estate's wines. *Booking obligatory. Closed Wed, and Sun eve.*

Monforte d'Alba ✉ 12064

***Villa Beccaris**, Via Bava Beccaris 1, t 0173 78158, *www.villabeccaris.it* (€€€€€–€€€€). Built in 1700, a lovely hilltop villa in a park with an *enoteca* full of Barolo. Very stylish rooms, all different, and with views.

Trattoria della Posta, Fraz. Santa Anna, t 0173 78120 (€€€€). Run by the same family since 1875, and as true to tradition as ever, with special mushroom and truffle menus in season. *Closed Thurs, and Fri lunch, Feb–1 Aug, 26 Dec–Jan. No credit cards.*

Cortemilia ✉ 12074

Villa San Carlo, Corso Divisioni Alpine 41, t 0173 81546, *www.hotelsancarlo.it* (€€€–€€). Award-winning hotel and restaurant with a pool. Cookery and wine courses available; bikes available to work off the calories.

Cravanzana ✉ 12050

Da Maurizio, Via S. Rocco 16, t 0173 855 019, *ristorantedamaurizio.it* (€€). Hotel in business since 1902; the excellent restaurant is the main thing here – fine views and lovely seasonal menu, with excellent meats and cheeses. *Closed Wed.*

Canale d'Alba ✉ 12043

Agriturismo Cascina Vrona, Fraz. Sant'Anna 6, Monteu Roero (4km from Canale), t 0173 90629, *www.cascina*

vrona.it (€). In the heart of the Roero, a working farm with comfortable rooms and delicious food; lunch €23 without wine. Bikes to hire and chance to tour the local vineyards in a horse-drawn wagon. *Restaurant always open eves, lunch on Fri, Sat and Sun.*

All'Enoteca, Via Roma 57, t 0173 95857, *www.davidepalluda.it* (€€€€). Superb restaurant above the Roera wine shop, the realm of one of Italy's best young chefs, Davide Palluda. *Book. Closed Wed, Thurs lunch, Jan and Aug.*

Barbaresco ✉ 12050

***Vecchio Tre Stelle**, Via Rio Sordo 13, t 0173 638 192, *www.vecchiotrestelle.it* (€€€). Comfortable hotel and elegant restaurant that serves a mix of creative and traditional dishes. *Closed Tues, 26–Dec–15 Jan and part of July.*

Antinè, Via Torino 34a, t 0173 635 294 (€€€€). Friendly, intimate and superb – it's often rated the very best in Piedmont. Save room for the exquisite *panna cotta*. Tiny, so book well in advance. *Closed Wed, 27 Dec–25 Jan and 10–25 Aug.*

Neive ✉ 12052

Palazzo De Maria, t 0173 677 558, *www.countryholiday.it/palazzode maria* (€€€). Beautiful B&B in a 16th-century villa in a park with a pool and Finnish sauna; the owners are keen bridge players and will take on all comers. *Closed New Year to Easter.*

***La Contea**, Piazza Cocito 8, t 0173 671 126 *www.la-contea.it* (€€). Little *palazzo* converted by Claudia and Tonino Verro into an inn and great restaurant; they also run the wine shop across the square, **Al Nido della Cinciallegra**. *Closed late Jan–mid-Mar.*

La Luna nel Pozzo, Piazza Italia 23, t 0173 67098, *www.lalunanelpozzo-neive.it* (€€€€). Sophisticated creative cuisine based on the finest ingredients, including four kinds of bread baked daily from stone ground flour. *Closed Tues eve and Wed.*

Magliano Alfieri ✉ 12050

Cascina del Cornale, just off the Alba-Asti road, t 0173 66669, *www. cornale.it* (€€€). A co-op featuring organic foods from Piedmont and

Liguria with a big restaurant that uses only strictly seasonal produce. There's even that rarity in these parts: a vegetarian menu, plus menus for those with food allergies (on request). *Restaurant open for lunch only and by booking for dinner, excluding Sun. Closed Wed.*

Priocca ✉ 12040

Il Centro, Via Umberto I, t 0173 616 112, *www.ristoranteilcentro.com* (€€€€). Near the Castello di Govone, a fine restaurant serving dishes such as *fritto misto alla piemontese*, prepared as it should be by a self-taught chef. *Closed Tues.*

Asti and Monferrato

Hills of vines and truffled woodlands roll on east of Le Langhe into the lands of Asti and the Marquisate of Monferrato. In medieval times both fought with their neighbours as cheerfully as any place in Italy, so expect plenty of castles, but there's fine art, too, at Asti, Acqui Terme and Casale, and particularly at the Romanesque abbey at Vezzolano. On the whole, people come here for a rarefied rural experience or to soak in the spa at Acqui, to take in the festivals, and just drink, eat and be merry.

Asti

⭐ Le Langhe and Asti

Overlooking the Tanaro, **Asti** (the Roman *Hasta Pompeia*) is a proud city that grew rich transporting the spices of the Orient to Europe; it was a free *comune* by 1095, and by the end of the 1200s it was known as the City of a Hundred Towers (it actually had 120), inhabited by bankers – at the time some 3,000 Astigiani, or one out of six, were lending money to Northern Europeans at extortionate rates. Fiercely independent, Asti declined after 1525, when Charles V punished it for supporting France by giving it to the Savoys. But Asti never liked being bossed; when no one was looking, in 1797, it had one last fling of independence, declaring itself a Republic for a few months.

Asti gave Italy one of its great poets and playwrights, Vittorio Alfieri (1749–1803), as passionate and eccentric as the city itself, who left town as a young man, ran off with the young wife of the not-so-bonnie Prince Charlie in Florence, and never returned. Nevertheless, Asti has named everything it could after him, including its main street, Corso Alfieri. At its east end stands the

San Pietro in Consavia
t 0141 353 072; open Tues–Sun 9–12 and 3–6

15th-century church and baptistry of **San Pietro in Consavia**, part of a priory of the Knights of St John, decorated with worn reliefs of sea serpents. It has an intriguing 12th-century octagonal **Rotonda** modelled after the Holy Sepulchre, supported by eight thick columns with cubic capitals, and the **Museo Archeologico** in the cloister with palaeontological, Neolithic to Roman finds and a small Egyptian collection. Heading west, the Corso passes by triangular **Piazza Alfieri**, just north of the Campo del Palio, scene of Asti's beloved Palio (*see* p.286). Just west of Piazza Alfieri and south of the Corso, the attractive Romanesque-Gothic **Collegiata di San Secondo** (the patron saint of punters who bet to place) was built over the 6th-century crypt where the martyred saint was buried. In the left aisle there are good 15th-century paintings, an anonymous Nativity and a polyptych by Renaissance painter Gandolfino da Roreto. The first chapel on the right holds the *carroccio* (in medieval times they were stored in churches).

Jews were first documented in Asti back in 812, and played a key role in the city's medieval prosperity. In 1723, Vittorio Amedeo II ordered them to live in a ghetto between Via Aliberti and Via Ottolenghi; the neoclassical **Synagogue**, just off the Corso at Via Ottolenghi 8, has some beautiful woodwork and a little museum. Asti's surviving medieval towers loom over the rooftops – the elegant 144ft **Torre Troyana** (also known as the clock tower, Torre dell'Orologio) across the Corso has the oldest bell in Piedmont, great views, and stands next to a wonderfully loopy fountain, with a giant embracing a pipe sticking out of the ground. Further down the Corso, there's the **Torre Comentina**, with the swallow-tail merlins of the Ghibellines, and the **Torre de Regibus**.

Vittorio Alfieri was born in the **Palazzo Alfieri**, built by his architect cousin Benedetto Alfieri at Corso Alfieri 375. The palazzo has a small museum to the poet. In the basement of the neighbouring Liceo Classico, Corso Alfieri 365/a, you can visit the 8th-century **Crypt of Sant'Anastasio**, founded according to legend by the Lombard King Liutprando, and other intriguing stone bits from the past in the **museum**. Memories of Asti's brief republican

Synagogue
t 0141 59003; open by request Sept–July daily except Sat and Jewish holidays

Torre Troyana
Piazza Medici, t 0141 399 489; open April–Oct Sat and Sun 10–1 and 4–7

Palazzo Alfieri
t 0141 538 284; closed for restoration

Museum
t 0141 437 454; open summer Tues–Sun 10–1 and 4–7; winter Tues–Sun 3–6; adm

Italy's Oldest Horse Race

Forget Siena. Italy's first documented *palio* dates back to 1275, when, while besieging Alba, the cheeky Astigiani held a horse race around Alba's walls tearing up their vines and orchards. From then on this daredevil bareback race was run back home in the streets and squares of Asti, until 1935, when Mussolini declared that only Siena could have a 'Palio' and that Asti would have to find another name for its event; Asti, deeply miffed, refused to have any race at all until it was revived in 1967.

There are plenty of events in the ten days leading up to the Palio – banquets, pranks on opponents, attempts to work magic, a Thursday *palio* of the *sbandieratori* (the flag throwers), a Saturday *palio* of first-time jockeys. The main event begins on the afternoon of the third Sunday in September with the *corteo*, a procession of the 21 competing neighbourhoods and *comuni* – a total 1,200 Astigiani in superb medieval costume, all representing a different aspect of the city's history, in a 700-year-old fresco come to life (there's a competitive spirit among tailors as well). At the end comes the *carroccio*, a replica of the medieval ox-drawn cart that Asti, like other *comuni*, used to take into battle with their banner, an altar, and their bishop praying for victory. This bears the much-desired first prize, the *palio* itself, a velvet banner painted each year by a different artist with symbols of the city and its patron, San Secondo. When all are in position in Piazza Alfieri (wooden barricades and tons of sand are laid for the event), the Captain of the Palio makes the ritual announcement to the mayor, that men, horses and insignia are ready, and the mayor sends them off with: 'Go, and may San Secondo help you.' Three heats are run with seven horses each; nine run in the *finale*, where luck and cunning count as much as speed. This is followed by flag tossing, and then the awarding of prizes: the banner, a purse of silver coins, spurs, a chicken, a rosette – and for last place, an anchovy with a lettuce.

moment in 1797, and 19th-century paintings and sculptures are in the **Pinacoteca Civica** in the Palazzo Mazzetti, Corso Alfieri 375.

Pinacoteca Civica
t 0141 594 791; closed for restoration at the time of writing

Two streets back from the Palazzo Alfieri rises Asti's fine Gothic **Cathedral of San Giovanni** (1309–54), decorated with the racy red-and-white chequered pattern popular in the city, and a beautiful porch of 1470. The interior, covered with Baroque frescoes, has good paintings by Gandolfino da Roreto and Moncalvo, and terracotta statues of the *Pietà* of 1502. The third chapel on the left has a retro *Marriage of the Virgin* by Gandolfino and a pillar with a painting of Sant'Aventino, patron saint of headaches; on 4 February the afflicted would come and hold the saint's relics against their heads. Nearby, the **Archivio Storico Comunale**, in the 16th-century Palazzo Mazzola at Via Cardinal Massaia 5, houses the remarkable illuminated *Codex Astensis de Malabayla*, encompassing some 991 documents from 1065 to 1353, and an exhibit on the Palio.

Archivio Storico Comunale
t 0141 399 339; open Mon–Fri 9–1, Tues and Thurs also 3.30–5.30, ring to check opening times; adm

If you return to Corso Alfieri and continue down Via Mazzini, you'll find one of Asti's finest Renaissance buildings, the **Palazzo Malabayla**. The Corso ends by the **Torre Rossa**, a Roman tower from the 1st century AD, with a 16-sided base and a chequerboard crown; in 119 San Secondo was imprisoned there. Part of the medieval walls are visible near the Baroque church of **Santa Caterina**. And beyond that is a ring of sprawl – Asti is one of the few places in Piedmont with a growing economy, not counting the 60 million bottles of Asti Spumante it produces a year. One business is tapestries at the **Arazzeria Scassa**, which specializes in adapting works by the likes of Dalì, Ernst and Kandinsky, at Via dell'Arazzeria 60; it also has a small museum. Beyond the sprawl, 4km northeast of Asti, the Madonna di Viatosto is a pretty Romanesque-Gothic chapel, with frescoes and great views over the hills to the Alps.

Arazzeria Scassa
t 0141 271 352, www.arazzerias cassa.com; free guided tours on request

South of Asti

There's a castle in every town; the one at **Costigliole d'Asti**, east of the Tanaro, dates from the 11th century, was dolled up in the 19th century, and is now the seat of the **Italian Culinary Institute for Foreigners**. Long before it was filled with eager chefs, this was the residence of Cavour's remarkably beautiful cousin, Virginia Oldoini, Countess of Castiglione, who had a fling at age 18 with Vittorio Emanuele before taking her cousin's hints and doing her patriotic duty – by becoming 'first mistress' to Napoleon III, whispering sweet nothings in his ear about Italian unification; those in the know called her 'Notre Dame de Cavour'. As French aid was vital for securing Italy's freedom from the Austrians, she probably deserves at least a commemorative stamp.

Italian Culinary Institute for Foreigners
Piazza Vittorio Emanuele II 10, t 0141 962 171, www.icif.com

Canelli, built in tiers of tufa under its castle, is the capital of Asti Spumante, with four historic cellars. One, the Cantine Contratto, on Via G.B. Giuliani 56, has a museum, a subterranean 105ft 'cathedral'

Cantine Contratto
t 0141 823 349, www.contratto.it; visits and tastings by appointment

of wine so evocative there's a movement to have it listed as a World Heritage Site; in spring it hosts a series of concerts. Take care if you come to Canelli the third weekend of June, when the city re-enacts the siege of 1619; tourists need a *tiletto* – a special pass – to get through enemy lines.

For fantastic views, climb to the top of the tall white cupola of the peculiar early 20th-century **Santuario dei Caffi**, just outside **Cassinasco**; the interior is packed with *ex votos*. **Nizza Monferrato**, northeast of Canelli, grows the best cardoons for *bagna cauda*, and has the excellent wine and ethnographic **Museo Bersano**, celebrated for its collection of four centuries of wine labels.

Santuario dei Caffi
t 0141 851 123, afternoons only

Museo Bersano
opposite the train station at Piazza Dante 10, t 0141 721 273; open by request

Acqui Terme

Acqui Terme
www.termedi acqui.info

In Imperial times, the Roman elite came to soak away their aches and pains in the hot sulphuric waters of *Acquae Statiellae*, now the mellow old town of **Acqui Terme**. It was ruled by a powerful bishop until 1185, when it became a free *comune* which in turn became part of Monferrato in 1278. The old spa has now been put back on the map – in central **Piazza Italia**, a fountain of water nymphs now celebrates the city's pride and joy.

To the east, Acqui's Romanesque **cathedral** (1067) has a good campanile, three spectacular apses, and a marble doorway of 1481, decorated with reliefs of the *Assumption of the Virgin* and *Doctors of the Church*. Inside, five naves contain a late Renaissance pulpit and high altar, a *Crucifix* carved from a single elephant's tusk, and a picturesque crypt contains the sarcophagus of San Guido, Acqui's patron. The best picture hangs in the Sala del Capitolo: a triptych featuring the *Virgin of Montserrat* (*c*. 1480) by the great Spanish painter Bartolomè Bermejo. From here Via Domenico Barone leads to the recently rearranged **Museo Civico Archeologico**, which occupies the half-ruined 11th-century **Castello dei Paleologi**, containing a prehistoric collection, mosaics, a large marble fountain discovered under the Piazza della Bollente and other finds from recent excavations in the same spot (a theatre was found on the hill just above), and grave goods from the Roman necropoli; the castle garden is a reserve for birds and small mammals.

Museo Civico Archeologico
Via Morelli 2, t 0144 57555; open Wed–Sat 9.30–12.30 and 3.30–6.30, Sun 3.30–6.30; adm

Acqui has more than its share of good restaurants, and holds frequent temporary exhibitions in the **Palazzo Robellini** at Piazza Levi 12 and the *enoteca* of the **Brachetto d'Acqui**, but the most memorable sight, especially in winter, is the **Bollente**, a spring that bubbles up 500 litres a minute at 75°C in an octagonal neoclassical pavilion, belching a cloud of steam. Over the River Bormida, in the Bagni district, four arches of a **Roman aqueduct** leapfrog near the Antiche Terme. This area may soon lose its dumpy look: once finished there will be a super glassed-in spa and skyscraper hotel – one of the last projects by the late Japanese architect Kenzo Tange.

Brachetto d'Acqui
t 0144 322 142

North of Asti: Basso Monferrato and the Abbazia di Vezzolano

Hilly green Basso Monferrato is one of the most beautiful corners of Piedmont, and has for its keepsakes Romanesque churches; finding these little gems can add a pleasant challenge to pootling around the countryside. Northwest of Asti, and 2km north of **Montechiaro**, one of these jewels is the 12th-century **SS. Nazario e Celso**, zebra-striped with red brick and dark tufa stone, with a sculpted portal and colourful cornice. At tiny **Cortazzone**, southwest of Montechiaro, sturdy **San Secondo** has three little naves and apses, carved capitals and, on the south side, among the geometric motifs, something you rarely see on a church: a couple making love. **Montiglio**, north of Montechiaro, has two Romanesque churches: **San Lorenzo**, now the cemetery chapel, and the **Cappella di Sant'Andrea**, in the castle park, with the most extensive 13th-century fresco cycle in Piedmont. Little roads wind up to the pretty medieval town of **Cocconato** and, further north on the Po, **Cavagnolo Po** has the delightful 11th-century church of **Santa Fede**, with a sculpted French portal, a reminder that it was founded by the great French abbey of St Foy at Conques.

If you only have time for one church, however, make it the remarkable **Abbazia di Santa Maria di Vezzolano** right next to **Albugnano**, 'the balcony of Monferrato'. Founded in 773 by Charlemagne (or so they say), the church has a façade from the 12th century, adorned with blind arcades, reliefs and sculpture. Inside there's a surprise: a magnificent 13th-century French *jubé* in green stone, covered with painted high reliefs of the *Four Evangelists* and the *Deposition, Assumption and Coronation of the Virgin*, while below a highly animated band of 35 patriarchs, the royal ancestors of Mary, sit in a row, their names draped over their chests like beauty contestants. On the high altar, a 15th-century triptych shows the Virgin and Child worshipped by Charles VIII of France, while the apse contains beautiful reliefs of the *Annunciation* from *c.* 1180 and a capital showing a musician, perhaps Orpheus. The cloister has a delightful hodgepodge of columns and 13th- and 14th-century frescoes, including one of the favourite post-Black Death legends of *The Three Living and the Three Dead* (three young knights meet a hermit who takes them to a chapel, where they see their future decomposing selves); the artist depicts the fear felt by their rearing horse.

North of Asti towards Casale, **Montemagno** is an attractive medieval town famous for its bread, with twelve narrow lanes circling out from the Ghibelline (i.e. swallowtailed) battlements of a **fort** begun around the year 1000 and 'Born on a site as irregular and crooked as a friar's head', according to the inscription in the castle's atrium. There are lovely views from the beautiful ruins of

Abbazia di Santa Maria di Vezzolano
t 011 992 0607; open Tues–Sun 9–12.30 and 2–6.30, till 5 in winter

12
Piedmont | South of Turin: Roero and Le Langhe: Asti and Monferrato

the Romanesque church of **SS. Vittore e Corona** (11th century) located by the town cemetery.

Moncalvo, with 3,500 inhabitants, is the smallest 'city' in Italy. It gave its name ('Il Moncalvo') to the painter Guglielmo Caccia (1568–1625), whose works fill the Gothic church of **San Francesco**; there's also a pretty Gothic house in Via Testafochi and a spectacular view of the countryside from Piazza Carlo Alberto. To the east, **Grazzano Badoglio's** church of **SS. Vittore e Corona** has the tomb of Aleramo, the first Marquis of Monferrato. North of Moncalvo, the **Sacro Monte di Crea** (*see* p.319), founded in 1589, has 23 chapels in a lovely setting, devoted to the Rosary and the life of St Eusebius, culminating in a *Paradiso* with an explosion of putti and saints. In Crea's **basilica**, where a 13th-century Madonna holds pride of place, there are frescoes in the chapel on the right on the life of Santa Margherita, with portraits of Monferrato nobles, including the Marquis Guglielmo VIII. Southeast of Moncalvo, little **Vignale Monferrato** hosts a dance festival in summer and has Monferrato's *enoteca* in the 15th-century Palazzo Callori; don't miss the view over a sea of vine-clad hills.

Sacro Monte di Crea
t 0141 927 120; open April–May Sun and hols 2.30–5; June Sat, Sun and hols 2.30–5; July Sat, Sun and hols 3–6.30; Aug Mon–Sat 3–6.30, Sun 10–12.30 and 3–6.30

Enoteca
Piazza del Popolo, t 0142 933 243; open Feb–Dec Mon–Fri 9–1 and 1.30–4.30, Sat and Sun 10–12 and 3–7

Casale Monferrato

Casale Monferrato is Italy's biggest producer of cement. Once, however, this fine little city on the Po held the more glamorous title of capital of Monferrato. It traces its origins back to Emperor Otto I, who made Aleramo first marquis in 988. Emperor Frederick Barbarossa gave the marquisate to his uncle Guglielmo, making Casale such a hotbed of Ghibelline sentiment that in 1215 Milan, Vercelli and Alessandria united to destroy it; his grandson Frederick II 'Stupor Mundi' rebuilt it. In 1305 the title of marquis was inherited by the Paleologi, cousins to the Byzantine emperors, who made Casale their capital in 1464. In 1536 the title passed through the marriage of Margherita Paleologa to the Gonzaga of Mantua, then to the Savoys in 1713.

The arms of Margherita Paleologa are over the gate of the **Castello dei Paleologi**, built in the mid-1300s and much altered since; when the Savoys picked it up, its citadel became a barracks, although it saw battle again when the Austrians attacked in 1849. From here Via Saffi leads past the brick **Torre Civica**, begun in the 11th century, to Piazza Mazzini, with its equestrian **monument to King Carlo Alberto**, who doesn't look entirely happy in his Roman togs; Casale was grateful to him for building the first bridge over the Po. Via Duomo leads back from here to the cathedral of **Sant'Evasio**. The Lombard King Liutprando ordered a huge church built here on the site of Evasio's martyrdom, and the result was consecrated by Pope Pascal II in 1107. Although reworked in the 1800s, it preserves a truly remarkable **narthex**, which would look at home in Constantinople – the origin, in fact, of the 11th-century gilded and crystal-studded *Crucifix* suspended over the altar; it hung in the cathedral of rival Alessandria until the Casalese stole it in 1404. When the church was restored, its mosaic floors were put on the walls of the ambulatory; St Evasio's remains (once stolen in turn by the Alessandrians) lie in an 18th-century chapel on the right.

Under the Gonzaga, Monferrato was an important safe haven for Jews; Casale's plain-looking **Synagogue** (1595) at Vicolo S. Olper 44 hides a magnificent 18th-century gold and stucco interior; it also has a **Jewish museum**, with an excellent collection of religious and historical items. Nearby at Via Cavour 5, in the former Convento di Santa Croce (frescoed by Moncalvo), the **Museo Civico** has an archaeological section, paintings, ceramics, sculptures and 130 plaster works by symbolist sculptor Leonardo Bistolfi, born in Casale in 1859. Further down the Po, **Valenza** is the 'city of jewellers', where 1,300 workshops claim to produce one out of four pieces you see in any shop around the world (there are some 50 shops in town, too, if you're a bracelet short); there's a **Permanent Exhibition of Goldsmiths' Art** in the Istituto Gemmologica Italiano in Piazza Don Minzoni.

Synagogue
take Via Roma south of Piazza Mazzini,
t *0142 71807; open Sept–Dec and Feb–July Sun 10–12 and 3–5; closed Nov–Feb and Aug*

Museo Civico
t *0142 444 249; open Sat and Sun 10.30–1 and 3–6.30 or by request; adm*

12

Piedmont | South of Turin: Roero and Le Langhe: Asti and Monferrato

Festivals and Events in Asti

The last three weekends in September in Asti start with the **Festival delle Sagre**, when people parade in 19th-century costumes, and recreate old cooking and working practices, along with plenty of feasting. This is followed by the **Palio** (*see* p.286) and the Douja d'Or wine fair, followed the next weekend by the **Arti e Mercanti**, a recreation of the medieval economy and market of Asti. To stand at the Palio is free; for more, see the website, *www.palio.asti.it.*

🌟 Gener Neuv >>

ⓘ Asti >
Piazza Alfieri 29,
t *0141 530 357,*
www.terredasti.it

Where to Stay and Eat North and South of Asti

Asti ✉ 14100

★★★Reale, Piazza Alfieri 6, **t** 0141 530 240, *http://hotelristorantereale.it* (€€€). Founded in 1793; Garibaldi stayed in one of the spacious rooms enjoying the best position in town, all with balconies over the Palio square.

★★★Aleramo, Via E. Filiberto 13, **t** 0141 595 661, *www.hotel.aleramo.it*

(€€€€–€€€). Excellent hotel, recently renovated. The top two floors enjoy superb views over the rooftops.

★★★Hasta, Valle Benedetta 25, **t** 0141 213 312, *www.hastahotel.com* (€€€–€€). Just outside Asti, tranquil and cosy, with tennis courts and a garden. It also has a good **restaurant**.

Villa Sampaguita, 2km from Asti at Bricco Cravera, Valleandona 117, **t** 0141 295 802, *www.villasampaguita.com* (€€€–€€). Comfortable B&B on a wine estate. The owners also organize excursions in the region. *Minimum stay 3 nights. Closed Dec–Feb.*

★★Cavour, Piazza Marconi 18, **t** 0141 530 222 (€€). Pleasant, popular, near the station.

Gener Neuv, Lungo Tanaro dei Pescatori 4, **t** 0141 557 270, *www.generneuv.it* (€€€€). On the river, the realm of a masterful self-taught chef; her cuisine is based on Piedmontese traditions, but is imaginative; the *finanziera* is excellent. The desserts are light and beautiful to behold. Great local and international wines. *Book. Closed Aug, Sun and Mon eve.*

L'Angolo del Beato, Via Guttuari 12, **t** 0141 531 668, *www.angolodelbeato.it*

(€€€). In a medieval buidling, feast on solid Piedmontese home cooking: excellent *finanziera del re* and €42 *menu degustazione*. *Closed Sun and most of Aug.*

Da Aldo, Via Giobert 8, **t** 0141 354 905 (€€€). In the *centro storico*, traditional Piedmontese classics. *Closed Thurs.*

Tacabanda, Via al Teatro Alfieri 5, **t** 0141 530 999 (€€). *Enoteca* with an enormous choice of bottles (especially Barbera), serving tasty meals and *spuntini* (snacks). *Closed Mon.*

Francese, Via dei Cappellai 15, **t** 0141 592 321 (€). Asti's best pizzeria/ trattoria, with a good wine cellar. *Closed Wed and Aug.*

Tigliole d'Asti ✉ 14016

★★★Ca' Vittoria, Via Roma 14, **t** 0141 667 713, *www.cavittoria.it* (€€€€). Luxurious rooms in a restored 18th-century manor with a lovely garden and pool, and Michelin-starred *cucina del territorio* revisited in the **restaurant**, made with home-grown vegetables and herbs. *Closed Sun eve and Mon.*

Costigliole d'Asti ✉ 14055

Collavini, on the Asti–Nizza Monferrato road, Strada Traniera 24, **t** 0141 966 440 (€€€€). Excellent seasonal cuisine and good wine cellar. *Closed Tues eve and Wed.*

Isola d'Asti ✉ 14057

★★★Il Cascinalenuovo, Asti–Alba road 15, **t** 0141 958 166, *www.ilcascinale nuovo.it* (€€€). Fifteen rooms set in a serene park by a pool, and a gourmet **restaurant** owned by the Ferretto family, where Walter combines long-forgotten recipes with innovative flair. *Closed Sun eve and Mon. Hotel closed 15 days in Aug and June.*

★★★Castello di Villa, Via Bausola 2 at Villa, **t** 0141 958 006, *www.castello divilla.it* (€€€€). An 18th-century castle, stylishly refurbished; the spacious bedrooms have views over the vines. Pool and wine cellar, and mountain bikes available.

Canelli ✉ 14053

Agriturismo La Casa in Collina, Regione S. Antonio 30, **t** 0141 822 827, *www.casaincollina.com* (€€€). Six fine rooms on the Amero family's estate.

Agriturismo La Luna e i Falò, Regione Aie 37, **t** 0141 831 643 (€). 'The Moon and the Bonfires', named after Cesare Pavese's novel about Le Langhe, has rooms in a villa, and six even nicer ones in a garden guesthouse. Superb dinners by reservation (open to non-guests), washed down by the house's own wine. *Closed Dec–Feb.*

San Marco, Via Alba 136, **t** 0141 823 544, *www.sanmarcoristorante.it* (€€€€). Base of star chef Mariuccia Ferrero, a student of historical recipes and desserts, which she adapts marvellously to modern tastes. *Closed Tues eve, Wed, 20 July–mid-Aug and 10 days between Jan and Feb.*

Calosso ✉ 14052

La Crota de Calos, Via Cairoli 7, **t** 0141 853 232 (€€). The local *enoteca* of Calosso wines and a restaurant – a wonderful, friendly place to while away a day eating and drinking. *Closed Wed.*

Nizza Monferrato ✉ 14049

Cascina Christiana, Strada S. Michele 24, **t** 0141 725 100, *www.cascina christiana.com* (€€). Barbera d'Asti Winery and B&B and self-catering in an early 19th-century estate with a stunning infinity pool.

La Signora in Rosso, Via Crova 2, **t** 0141 793350, *www.signorainrosso.com* (€€). Charming 'new generation' bar next to the Barbera d'Asti *enoteca*; great *antipasti* and simple but excellent dishes to accompany your chosen bottle. *Eves only, also lunch on Sat and Sun; closed Mon and Tues.*

Mombaruzzo ✉ 14046

La Villa Hotel, Fraz. Casalotto, **t** 0141 793 890, *www.lavillahotel.net* (€€€€). Chris and Nicola Norton gave up corporate jobs in the UK to turn this 17th-century villa overlooking the hills and vines into an idyllic guesthouse with a pretty pool and garden. Lavish rooms furnished with eclectic but choice antiques and all mod cons, plus a fine restaurant, a lounge with a fireplace and a tasting room.

Santo Stefano Belbo ✉ 12058

★★★★★Relais San Maurizio, Loc. San Maurizio 39, **t** 0141 841 900, *www. relaissanmaurizio.it* (€€€€€). In a garden above vine-clad hills, a 17th-century convent converted into a villa and restored as the most starred country hotel in Piedmont; many bedrooms, in the former cells, have sitting areas and fireplaces. It has a Michelin-starred **restaurant** (*closed Tues and Wed lunch*), named after the legendary Guido da Costigliole and run by his widow and Luca Zecchin, and a wine-therapy spa, **Caudalie**, run by Bertrand and Mathilde Thomas, founders of the first Caudalie spa in Bordeaux in 1990. *Hotel closed 8 Jan–Feb.*

Osteria dal Gal Vestì, Via Pavese 18, t 0141 843 379, *www.osteriadalgalvesti.com* (€€€€). Delightful restaurant/*enoteca* in the birthplace of Cesare Pavese, with a big summer terrace and authentic dishes; try the exquisite *tajarin alla monferrina*. *Book. Closed Mon and Tues and at lunch except Sat–Sun.*

(i) **Acqui Terme** >
Via M. Ferraris,
t 0144 322 142

Acqui Terme ✉ 15011

****Grand Hotel Nuove Terme**, Piazza Italia, t 0144 58555, *www.antichedimore.com* (€€€€). In the heart of town, over a hundred years old and radically refurbished. Great place to indulge in the water or mud cure, in the three pools (hot, tepid and cold), replicating an ancient Roman bath.

***Talice Radicati**, Piazza Conciliazione 12, t 0144 328 611, *www.antichedimore.com* (€€€€). Elegant rooms in a 15th-century *palazzo*, all different, some with kitchenettes, with all mod cons, plus a wine bar, the **Taverna degli Artisti**.

***Ariston**, Piazza Matteotti 13, t 0144 322 996, *www.hotelariston.net* (€€). Centrally located, modern hotel.

Relais dell'Osso, Via dei Dottori 5, t 0144 56877, *www.osso.it* (€€). Four luminous new rooms, in a 16th-century *palazzo*.

***San Marco**, Via Ghione Franco 5, t 0144 322 456 (€). Family run and one of the best deals in town. *Closed Christmas and late July.*

Pisterna, Via Scatilazzi 15, t 0144 325 114, *www.pisterna.it* (€€€€). Fragrant, beautifully prepared traditional-innovative cuisine by Walter Ferretto in an elegant designer setting. *Open eves only and Sun lunch.*

Cappello, outside town at Strada Visone 62, t 0144 356 340 (€€€). Delightful, imaginative dishes on a €31 *menu degustazione*; also fixed-priced lunches. *Book. Closed Tues, Wed, second half of July and 10 days in Jan.*

La Curia, Via alla Bollente 72, t 0144 356 049, *www.enotecalacuria.com* (€€€). Lively *enoteca* with the best cellar in town and dishes that match. *Closed Mon.*

I Caffi, Via Verdi Angolo Vicolo del Voltone, t 0144 325 206, *www.icaffi.it* (€€€€–€, depending on menu). Two rooms and excellent seasonal local dishes. *Closed Sun, Wed, hols, 15 days in Aug and 15 days after Christmas.*

Da Bigat, Via Mazzini 30, t 0144 324 283 (€). Famous for its hearty Ligurian *farinata*, and local specialities, including Roccaverano cheese. *No credit cards. Closed Sun eve, Wed, second halves of Feb and June.*

Albugnano ✉ 14020

Monastero del Rul, Loc. Vezzolano 57, t 011 992 2031, *www.monasterodelrul.com* (€€). Lovely B&B of character in an old farmhouse, rebuilt out of original materials, located on a hill surrounded by woods and vines. The English-speaking owner knows the area well and can show you where to walk, bike or ride; delicious farm-fresh breakfasts and dinners by request.

Cocconato d'Asti ✉ 14023

***Vecchio Castagno**, Strada Cocconato 1, Loc. Maroero, t 0141 907 095, *www.cannondoro.it* (€€€). Beautiful rooms, garden and a pool. *Minimum four night stay.*

***Cannon d'Oro**, Piazza Cavour 21, t 0141 907 794, *www.cannondoro.it/albergo.htm* (€€). Set atop one of Monferrato's highest hills, this restaurant is renowned for classic dishes and lovely setting: wild mushroom salad, gnocchi, tasty *bollito misto*, and home-made desserts. *Closed Mon eve and Tues.*

Montemagno ✉ 14030

La Braja, Via S. Giovanni Bosco 11, t 0141 653 925, *www.labraja.it* (€€€€). Classy family-run restaurant, serving delicious home-made pasta and lamb dishes. *Closed Mon and Tues.*

① Casale
Monferrato >>
*Piazza Castello (in a
kiosk),* t 0142 444 330

Moncalvo and around ✉ 14036

****Locanda del Sant'Uffizio**, Strada Sant'Uffizio 1, just south at Cioccaro di Penango, Strada Sant'Uffizio 1, t 0141 916 292, *www.thi.it/hotels/locanda-del-sant-uffizio/hotel.html* (€€€€€). The 17th-century seat of the Inquisition, and now a luxurious spot for romantic getaways. Rooms furnished with antiques look out over a charming Italian garden and pool; great **restaurant**. *Closed Jan.*

Locanda del Melograno, Corso Regina Margherita 38, t 0141 917 599, *www.locandadelmelograno.com* (€€). Opened in 2005; nine lovely bedrooms and big breakfasts in an old *palazzo*, with some very pretty views.

La Bella Rosin, Piazza Vittorio Emanuele II 3, t 0141 916 098 (€€€). Attractive *enoteca* and trattoria with dishes highlighting local ingredients – try the *gnocchi al Castelmagno. Closed Mon and end of Jan.*

Casale Monferrato ✉ 15033

****Candiani**, Via Candiani d'Olivola 36, t 0142 418 728, *www.hotelcandiani.com* (€€€). Mid-sized hotel of character, restored using authentic Art Nouveau furnishings; excellent restaurant, **La Torre** (*www.ristorante-latorre.it*) that the Turinese and Milanese drive out of their way to patronize for its delicacies based on fresh ingredients from the immediate environs, such as risotto with crayfish, spinach-filled tortelli, or breast of duck. *Closed Tues eve, Wed and Aug.*

***Principe**, Via Cavour 55, t 0142 452 019, *www.principehotel.net* (€€). Typical rooms in an old *palazzo* in the *centro storico.*

La Vineria del Munfrà, Via Lanza 10, t 0142 461 416 (€). Friendly wine bar-restaurant that stays open late. *Closed Mon and Jan.*

Piedmont's Far Southeastern Corner

At the crossroads between Genoa and Lombardy, Piedmont's far southeastern corner has seen more than its share of fierce battles. Wine is important here, too, and cycling something of an obsession, especially at Novi.

Alessandria and the Battle of Marengo

Alessandria was founded in 1168 by disgruntled nobles from Ghibelline Monferrato, who opposed Frederick Barbarossa, and emptied four villages to form a new Guelph town named after his arch enemy, Pope Alexander III. Barbarossa duly besieged them (1175), but they survived, so they say, thanks to a cow, which they fattened on their last grains, then paraded on the walls; Barbarossa saw how well off they were and lifted the siege (the emperor also had business elsewhere). Although Casale Monferrato was put in Alessandria's province, to this day the two towns don't see eye to eye; the town of Alessandria jealously guards an ornamental cockerel it stole from Casale in 1225.

Artistically, at any rate, it has been Alessandria's misfortune to occupy a strategic spot; when the Savoys picked it up in 1707, they destroyed its finest civic and lay buildings on the left bank of the Tanaro to build their **Cittadella**, still awaiting restoration and a new use. In 1803, the city's huge medieval cathedral was knocked down by Napoleon to create **Piazza della Libertà** as a parade ground for

Marengo and its Chicken

Napoleon never ate before a battle, believing it dulled his wits, and this was one battle where he needed them all. In 1800, when the Austrians were making a comeback in Lombardy, Napoleon made a brilliant quick crossing over the Great St Bernard Pass to teach them a lesson. When he reached the Austrian army at Marengo, he spread his forces thinly across the plain to prevent any of the enemy from escaping, confident they were too cowed by his reputation to attack. But at dawn on 14 June 1800 they did, under General Melas. Boney at first didn't take the attack seriously, but soon realized that he was in hot water; messengers were sent to recall the two divisions he had sent to outflank the Austrians, while he battled for hours against a vastly superior army. General Desaix then arrived in the nick of time, and told Napoleon he may have lost one battle here, but there was still time to win another, and led the counterattack that cost his life, but won the day. The Austrians fled.

In the confusion, Napoleon had left his commissary far behind, but his cook Dunand was at his side. As the battle wound down, Dunand knew he needed to concoct something for his famished boss, but it seemed as if dinner would be as improvised as the battle: all the foraging party could find was an old chicken, a few crayfish, three eggs, four tomatoes, a bit of oil and a frying pan; Dunand cut it all up with his sabre, cooked it, and chicken Marengo was born. Napoleon thought it was excellent and demanded the dish after every battle. When Dunand tried to improve it by leaving out the crayfish (as most cooks do today), Napoleon was furious; he was superstitious, and sure that the chicken and crayfish together brought him luck.

San Francesco
Via Cavour 39, t 0131 234 794; open Fri–Sun 3–7; adm; currently closed for restoration

Museo Civico
t 0131 262 913; open Sept–July Sat and Sun 4–7; adm

Museo Etnografico C'era una Volta
t 0131 40030, www. museogambarina.it; open Mon–Tues and Thurs–Sat 9–12 and 4–7, Sun 4–7, Wed 9–12; adm

Museo Francesco Janniello
Via Guasco 142, t 0131 222 374; open Mon–Sat 9–12 and 3–6

Hat museum
Via Cavour 84, t 0131 252 260; open Sat and Sun 4–7 and by appointment at other times; adm

his troops; today it's a big car park lined with civic buildings and a **post office** of 1932, decorated with mosaic friezes on the glories of the *Posta Italiana* by Gino Severini. The replacement neoclassical **cathedral** just down Via Parma has the second tallest **campanile** (347ft) in Italy, after Cremona; inside, the cupola is decorated with the patron saints of the 24 cities of the Lombard League that thumbed their noses at Barbarossa (Italians, as you've probably realized by now, have elephantine memories). The 15th-century Gothic **Santa Maria di Castello**, off Via dei Guasco, north of Piazza della Libertà, has a fine 17th-century choir.

Alessandria has its share of museums. In 1971, a remarkable cycle of 15 late 14th-century frescoes was discovered in a tower in Frugarolo, with themes inspired by the Arthurian legends; detached and restored, they are on display in the **Stanze di Artù** in the convent of **San Francesco**, converted in the 19th century to serve as a military hospital. The **Museo Civico**, in the 18th-century Palazzo Cuttica at Via Parma 1 has archaeological finds, corals and miniatures, prints, Flemish tapestries and paintings. Life in the 18th and 19th centuries is the subject of the **Museo Etnografico C'era una Volta** ('Once Upon a Time') in Piazza della Gambarina 1; the **Museo Francesco Janniello** has keys, iron, fossils and Robespierre's guillotine. For all that, Alessandria is best known as home to the maker of the world's best hats, **Borsalino**, founded by Giuseppe Borsalino in 1857; the old factory has a **hat museum**.

Just south of Alessandria, Napoleon thumped the Austrians in what he considered the greatest battle of his career at **Marengo** (*see* box, above). In the village of **Spinetto Marengo**, the Villa Cataldi, built in 1847 over the inn where Napoleon slept, contains

Museum of the Battle of Marengo
t 0131 216 344; open daily 8–12 and 2–5 by appt, currently closed for restoration; adm

Casa Natale di Pio V
Piazza Castelvecchio, t 0131 299 342; ring for a free visit

Museo Vasariano
t 0131 299 410; under restoration at the time of writing

the **Museum of the Battle of Marengo**, with weapons, helmets and plans. Enthusiastic re-enactments of the battle are held on the second Sunday in June in even-numbered years.

Another 6km south, **Bosco Marengo** was the birthplace of Antonio Ghislieri, better known as Pius V (1566–72), whose papacy saw the great naval victory of the Christian allies over the Turks at Lepanto. You can visit his birthplace, the **Casa Natale di Pio V**, and the church he built, **Santa Croce**, to house his **tomb**. This is a masterpiece of green marble – but an empty one, as the Romans interred him in Santa Maria Maggiore. The Tuscan biographer-painter Giorgio Vasari painted a *Last Judgement* and scenes for the altar, some of which are in the church's **Museo Vasariano**.

Around Alessandria

Southwest of Alessandria, **Castellazzo Bormida** has a Virgin at its *ex voto*-filled **Santuario della Madonna della Creta**, who was proclaimed patroness of 'centaurs', as Italians call motorcycle riders, by Pius XII in 1947; since that year the town has held an annual three-day motorcycle fest during the second weekend in July, complete with the blessing of the *centauri* by the bishop of Alessandria. Further south, **Sezzadio** was an important Lombard town, where the Lombard king Liutprando founded an oratory to

Santa Giustina
Via Badia 53; open by appointment daily Nov–Mar 9–5.30, April–Oct 9–8

Santa Giustina in the 8th century. In 1030 it was rebuilt by the Marquis Oberto and, although converted into a silo in Napoleonic times, colourful frescoes from the 15th and 16th centuries have survived, as well as Oberto's mosaic floor in the crypt.

Ovada, a truffle and wine town further south, was part of Monferrato until 1216, when the Genoese muscled in; its church of the **Assunta** has an early work of Luca Giordano (*Santa Teresa*) and the *trecento* church of **Sant'Antonio** in Via S. Antonio 17 contains the **Museo Paleolontologico Giulio Maini** with fossils from the region, including an ancestor of the crab discovered by Giulio Maini. The road east towards Gavi (*see* right) takes in pretty country: the oldest tower of the **Castello di Tagliolo Monferrato** was built by the Genoese in the 10th century against the Saracens and now belongs to a wine estate. Further east, **Lerma** is a charming hill town with a bijou **Castello Spinola**, rebuilt in 1499 and still in the Spinola family.

Museo Paleolontologico Giulio Maini
t 0143 81774; open Oct–May Fri 9–12; otherwise Sat 3–6, Sun 10–12; guided visits every first Sun of the month – contact tourist info, t 0143 821 043

Castello di Tagliolo Monferrato
t 0143 89195, www.castelloditagliolo.com; guided tours by appointment; adm

East of Alessandria, **Tortona** has been a transport hub ever since it was the Roman *Julia Dertona*, on the Genoa–Piacenza *Via Postumia*. It was a powerful *comune* in the Middle Ages, standing side by side with Milan against Barbarossa. Its two older churches, the white 16th-century **Duomo** and the 14th-century **Santa Maria Canale**, at the bottom of Via Verdi, are full of minor works of art. A startling 46ft bronze Madonna keeps an eye on Tortona from the 200ft tower of the **Basilica della Madonna della Guardia**, begun in

1926 by the Blessed Luigi Orione, founder of the Piccola Opera della Divina Providenza, and consecrated by John Paul II in 1991. Tortona still has a sprinkling of Roman remains, including the **Necropoli Monumentale** and part of the city walls, north of town at Fitteria.

The name of **Novi Ligure**, a town on the main route to Genoa, recalls its age-old links with Liguria, still reflected in its dialect, cuisine and *palazzi* (*the tourist office offers a free map, picking them out*). In Via G.C. Abba, the **Basilica di Santa Maria Maddalena** has a remarkable Flemish *Calvary* of life-sized painted wooden statues, and a terracotta *Deposition*, both from the late 1500s. Novi produced a remarkable number of great cyclists, including Costante Giradengo and Fausto Coppi, celebrated in the **Museo dei Campionissimi**, with everything you wanted to know about Italian cycling including a model of the bicycle designed by Leonardo.

Some villages in the nearby Val Borbera were only joined to Piedmont in 1815, such as white-wine producing **Gavi**, where the mighty **Forte di Gavi** guards the road to the coast. The ancient Ligurians had a fort here in the 2nd century BC, rebuilt over the years by the Byzantines, Franks, Saracens and Genoese; in the 16th century it was enlarged by the Guasco counts of Alessandria to its current state, capable of housing 900 men, who were probably bored most of the time but enjoyed splendid views. Also in Gavi, don't miss the Romanesque church of **San Giacomo** with a delightful 12th-century *Last Supper* over the door. East, on the road to Serravalle Scrivia, you can visit the ancient Roman colony of *Libarna*, founded in the 2nd century AD on the Via Postumia but completely abandoned by the 7th century.

Basilica di Santa Maria Maddalena
to visit, t 0143 70015

Museo dei Campionissimi
t 0143 322 634; open Fri 3–8, Sat and Sun 10–8, till 7 in winter; adm

Forte di Gavi
t 0143 642 679; open Nov–April Tues–Sun 9.30–3.30; May–Oct Tues–Thurs 9.30–5.30, Fri–Sun 9.30–6.30; adm; undergoing restoration at time of writing and some parts cannot be visited

Libarna
t 0114 347 954; ring ahead to visit; adm

Where to Stay and Eat in the Far Southeast of Piedmont

(i) **Alessandria >**
Piazza Santa Maria di Castello 14, t 0131 288 095, www.alexala.it

Alessandria ✉ 15100

****Mercure Alessandria**, Via Cavour 32, t 0131 517 171, www.mercure.com (€€€). The most comfortable hotel, plus a fine restaurant, **Alli Due Buoi Rossi** (€€€€), serving Piedmontese specialities and a gluten-free menu. *Closed Sun eve and Mon.*

****Domus**, Via T. Castellani 12, t 0131 43305, www.hoteldomus-al.com (€€€). Central, with small, modern rooms.

***Rex**, Via S. Francesco d'Assisi 48/a, t 0131 252 297 (€). Bright and modern.

La Fermata, Via Vochieri 120, t 0131 617 508, www.lafermata-al.it (€€€€). Just west of town, before the bridge, in an old *palazzo* where chef owner Riccardo Aiachini creates the province's most memorable dishes. *Closed Sat lunch and Sun.*

Il Grappolo, Via Casale 28, t 0131 253 217 (€€€€). Smart, modern restaurant in a 19th-century *palazzo*, with a fine selection of local wines. *Closed Mon and Tues eves.*

Enoteca Gusto, Via Cesare Lombroso 17, t 0131 441 141 (€€). In the centre; wine shop with a restaurant, serving cold meats, cheeses and tasty pasta and meats. *Open 6–midnight. Closed Sun, Jan and Aug.*

Bosco Marengo ✉ 15062

Locanda dell'Olmo, Piazza Mercato 7/8, t 0131 299 186, www.locanda dellolmo.it (€€€). Intimate little place serving Alessandrian specialities, strictly according to season. *Booking essential. Closed Mon, Tues eve, Aug and 27 Dec–5 Jan.*

Ovada ✉ 15076

Villa Schella, Via per Molare, t 0143 80324, *www.villaschella.com* (€€€). Very charming B&B in the outbuilding of a 19th-century farm, in a lovely old park with a pool. Cookery classes, bikes to hire; riding, tennis, and an 18-hole golf course 10km away. *No credit cards. Open Easter to mid-Nov.*

Tortona ✉ 15078

****Villa Giulia, on the Alessandria road, t 0131 862 396, *www.villagiulia-hotel.com* (€€). Twelve rooms in an old country house with elegant furnishings.

Tastevin, Via Fracchia 16, t 0131 815 099 (€€). Elegant place, a huge assortment of wines and seasonal dishes to match. *Closed Tues and half of Aug.*

ⓘ **Novi Ligure >**
Viale dei Campionissimi 2,
t 0143 72585

Novi Ligure ✉ 15067

***Corona, near the station at Corso Marengo 11, t 0143 322 364, *www.albergodellacorona.it* (€€€). Refined 18th-century palace, and home to the city's best **restaurant**, serving light, memorable dishes with a Ligurian touch; try the duck with citrus fruits. *Closed part of Jan and Aug.*

Villa La Marchesa, Via Gavi 87, t 0143 743 362, *www.tenutalamarchesa.it* (€€€). Charming antique-furnished rooms in a 17th-century building on a Gavi wine estate. Tasting tours of the wine cellars and the estate are offered (*by previous booking only*) €12 pp.

Agriturismo Cascina degli Ulivi, Strada Mazzola 14, 3km from Novi Ligure, t 0143 744 598, *www.cascinadegli ulivi.it* (€). Four rooms on an organic farm in a lovely setting, with half-board terms available. Delicious cooking in the **restaurant** (€); *open to all on Fri, Sat and Sun by reservation.*

Gavi ✉ 15066

****L'Ostelliere, Fraz. Monterotondo 56, t 0143 607 801 *www.ostelliere.it* (€€€€€–€€€€). Rooms and suites of classic rustic charm in a 17th-century farmhouse, overlooking the vines of the Villa Sparina, which bottles a Gavi di Gavi rated as one of the top white wines in the world. The restaurant, **La Gallina**, t 0143 685 132, *www.montero tondoresort.com/gallina* (€€€€), serves excellent Piedmontese and Mediterranean dishes. *Closed Wed and mid-Nov–Feb.*

Northeast of Turin: Vercelli, Novara and Rice

Northeast of Turin, Vercelli and Novara were part of Lombardy until the Savoys peeled them away from the occupying Austrians in 1738, in return for backing the right horse in the War of the Austrian Succession; both, especially Novara, still have a very Lombard feel, and monuments from their glory days as free *comuni*. They had money, too: rice was introduced in Sicily by the Arabs, and it grew here like kudzu. Today 60 per cent of the rice produced in Europe comes from Vercelli and Novara's seemingly endless patchwork of fields, divided by hundreds of canals dug in the 15th century.

For a long time this rice was a jealously guarded monopoly, but when Thomas Jefferson was in Piedmont in 1787, he managed to smuggle out a couple of bags of it and took them to South Carolina – the beginning of the American rice industry. In summer, when the rice paddies are flooded, they reflect the clouds and sunset in an irregular chequerboard of mirrors, a landscape bordering on the abstract: desolate, melancholy and beautiful.

Getting to and around Vercelli and Novara

Trains from Turin are frequent; a fast train links Turin and Novara in only 20 minutes. Novara has frequent links to Lakes Orta and Maggiore and beyond, and **buses** to nearby Malpensa airport, t 0321 472 647.

Vercelli

Vercelli, on the banks of the River Sesia, started off as *Wer-Celt*, founded in 600 BC by the Salii Gauls. An important Roman town, it became a *comune* in the 13th century, when it knew its greatest prosperity. In the 16th century it produced a fine school of painters, even though the most brilliant one, Il Sodoma (born in 1477), escaped to more promising territory in Tuscany. Even so, as a minor 'city of art', Vercelli is an old, atmospheric place. If you have only an hour between trains you can take in its chief marvel, the **Basilica di Sant'Andrea**, which looms up opposite the station. The basilica was begun in 1219 by Cardinal Guala Bicchieri, the papal legate sent to England to avert civil war after the death of King John and to support the future King Henry III, then a minor, during the ratification of the Magna Carta. To thank Bicchieri for his aid, Henry III gave him the Abbey of St Andrew in Chesterton, near Cambridge, which the cardinal bestowed on Vercelli. Part of the revenue went to finance a new St Andrew's, in Vercelli. Completed nine years later, the basilica, though basically Romanesque, is famous in Italian architectural history as one of the first to display signs of the new Gothic style from the Île de France; it whispers in Sant'Andrea's twin bell towers, the flying buttresses, the vaulting in the nave and floor plan of the church. The change of materials halfway up the façade gives it the jaunty incongruity of a 1960s half-timbered station wagon. The three Romanesque portals have sculpted lunettes; in the majestic interior, emphasized by the simple red and white decoration, note the choir stalls, decorated with intarsia still lifes and city views (1513), and the Gothic tomb of the Abbot Tommaso Gallo (d. 1246). The cloister, with its cluster columns and sculptural details, offers the best view of the unusual cupola. The campanile was added in 1407.

Vercelli's grand 16th-century **cathedral** is just behind, in Piazza Sant'Eusebio; of the original Romanesque construction only the bell tower remains. It has a precious silver Crucifix from the year 1000 and an octagonal chapel with the tomb of the holiest member of the House of Savoy, the Blessed Amedeo IX, who died in Vercelli in 1472. Priceless codices, including the 'Vercelli Book' of 11th-century Anglo-Saxon poems, probably left here by Cardinal Bicchieri and used by scholars to study the origins of English, are displayed in the **Museo del Tesoro del Duomo** in the Bishop's Palace, Piazza D'Angennes 5.

Museo del Tesoro del Duomo
t 0161 51650; open Sept–July Wed 9–12, Sat 9–12 and 3–6, Sun 3–6

From the cathedral, Via Duomo leads past the **Castello d'Amedeo** (to the left, behind Santa Maria Maggiore) to Via Gioberti and Via Borgogna, site of the **Museo Francesco Borgogna**, the second most important gallery in Piedmont after the Sabauda in Turin, featuring paintings by Vercelli natives (Il Sodoma, Bernardo Lanino, Gaudenzio and Defendente Ferrari) and works by Titian, Palma il Vecchio and Luini, as well as some by Dutch and Flemish artists.

Via Borgogna gives onto Vercelli's main Corso Libertà; if the door is open at No.204, look in at the lovely courtyard of the 15th-century **Palazzo Centori**. From here, go down Via Cagna/Via S. Cristoforo, where the church of **San Cristoforo** conserves excellent frescoes (1529–33) by Gaudenzio Ferrari, including his masterpiece, the *Madonna of the Oranges*. Big, porticoed **Piazza Cavour** is just north of Corso Libertà, and just north of the piazza, at Via Verdi 30, archaeological and historical relics fill the **Museo Camillo Leone**, spread between a 15th-century house (with charming frescoes) and a Baroque palace. Off the west end of Corso Libertà, in Piazza Zumaglini, rice prices are decided in the Rice Exchange, or **Borsa del Riso**; here, too, is the national rice board headquarters. To learn more, visit a rice farm, just southwest of Vercelli at **Lignana**; the **Cascina Venerìa** has been in business since 1789, and featured in the Italian neorealist classic, Giuseppe De Santis' *Riso Amaro* (1948), along with nearly 800 farm workers.

Museo Francesco Borgogna
t 0161 252 776, www.museoborgogna.it; open Tues–Fri 3–5.30, Sat and Sun 10–12.30; Jan–May also Sun 2–6, but ring ahead; closed two weeks in Aug; adm

Museo Camillo Leone
t 0161 253 204; open Tues–Thurs and Sat 3–5.30, Sun 10–12 and 3–6; adm

Cascina Venerìa
t 0161 314 233, www.cascinaveneria.it; open Mon–Fri by appointment only

Novara

Novara, Piedmont's second and most Lombard city, became a *municipium* under Julius Caesar, and to this day the main streets laid out by the Romans, the cobbled Corso Cavour (the *cardo*) and Corso Italia (the *decumanus*), are its soul, lined with tearooms and fashionable shops. **Roman walls** have been dug up at the north end of Corso Cavour, and if you turn down Via G. Ferrari from here, you'll soon be face-to-face with Novara's landmark, the 396ft dome of **San Gaudenzio**, which you've probably already spotted anyway: it's visible for miles from the surrounding plains. The church, dedicated to Novara's first bishop and patron, was begun in 1577 by Pellegrino Tibaldi, while the bold dome was added by the amazing Antonelli (of Turin's Mole fame), who was born near Novara and finished it the year he died, 1888. The shining figure of Jesus on top of the spire seems to poke the very sky; an eccentric 18th-century *campanile* makes a handsome companion piece. Inside, San Gaudenzio lies in a raised crypt, topped by a Baroque altar; look for a polyptych by Gaudenzio Ferrari in the Cappella Nazari.

Nearby, the **Museo di Storia Naturale Faraggiana Ferrandi** has had a facelift to better set off its collection of stuffed birds and

Museo di Storia Naturale Faraggiana Ferrandi
Via G. Ferrari 13, t 0321 370 2755; open Tues–Sat 9–1 or 10–1 in summer and 2.30–6, Sun 9–6, till 7 in summer

animals gathered from around the world, and an ethnographic collection from Somalia, Eritrea and Ethiopia.

Corso Italia to the south has Novara's **Broletto**, a picturesque complex of four buildings, built and rebuilt between the 12th and 18th centuries. Once the seat of city government, it now houses the **Museo Novarese di Arte e Storia**, with paintings and frescoes from the 1400s on and archaeological bits from the province, including armour found in the tombs of Lombard warriors, and the **Museo Lapidario del Broletto**, with a collection of Roman altars and boundary stones from ancient Suno.

Through the Broletto courtyard stands the **Duomo**, rebuilt in the 1860s by Antonelli. This time, instead of building tall, he built one of the widest doorways in Europe (38ft by 19ft). He also preserved parts of the Romanesque cathedral, including the campanile, the **Cappella di San Siro** (open by request) with important frescoes of c. 1180 of the *Life of San Siro* and a *Christ in Majesty*, and a large **mosaic** pavement in the chancel showing Adam, Eve and the Serpent and four rivers flowing from Paradise. Paintings by Gaudenzio Ferrari and the Vercelli school, and a series of 16th-century Flemish tapestries on the *Life of Solomon* decorate the nave. The **Baptistry** dates back to the 5th century, and contains frescoes of the *Apocalypse*, added 500 years later, discovered only in 1959 and considered among the most important pre-Romanesque paintings in Italy. The 15th-century cloister in Vicolo Canonica contains the **Museo Lapidario del Duomo**, with Celtic and Roman stelae and a 3rd-century AD relief of a ship casting off. At the end of the street, beyond the handsome 19th-century **Teatro Coccia**, stands the austere 14th-century **Castello Visconti-Sforzesco**, seat of Novara's Milanese rulers.

Around Novara

Any cows you may see around Novara are busy making the base ingredient for gorgonzola, a cheese first documented in the 9th century. Besides gorgonzola, the busy towns of the plain have a few things to see: **Galliate**, just east, has an imposing **Castello** rebuilt in 1476 by the Duke Galeazzo Maria Sforza and where, according to legend, Leonardo da Vinci designed a secret room in the 1490s to hide the fabulous treasure of Ludovico il Moro (the prototype for Shakespeare's Prospero), which was never found after the duke died in a French prison; rumour has it that it hides behind an incongruous brick, if you want to look. One tower contains art by Angelo Bozzola, who was born in Galliate in 1921. Galliate's parish church has a tall campanile, with an unroofed bell; another church, the **Santuario del Varallino**, was designed by Pellegrino Tibaldi, who took his inspiration from the Sacro Monte at Varallo (*see* p.323); there are ten chapels filled with painted terracotta

Museo Novarese di Arte e Storia
t 0321 623 021; open Tues–Sun 9–12 and 3–6, 4–7 in summer; currently undergoing restoration and visitable by appointment only, t 0321 370 2755

Museo Lapidario del Broletto
t 0321 623 021; open daily 7.30–7.30

Baptistry
open Sat and Sun 3–6

Museo Lapidario del Duomo
t 0321 661 661; open by request; adm

Castello
t 0321 800 763 to book a guided tour, usually every Sun mid-Mar–June; adm

12 Piedmont | Northeast of Turin: Novara

Where to Stay and Eat in Vercelli and Novara

ⓘ **Vercelli >**
Viale Garibaldi 90,
t 0161 58002,
www.atlvalsesia
vercelli.it

⭐ **Osteria Cascina dei Fiori >**

ⓘ **Novara >**
Baluardo Quintino
Sella 40, t 0321 394 059,
www.turismonovara.it

Vercelli ✉ 13100

***Il Giardinetto**, Via L. Sereno 3,
t 0161 257 230, www.hrgiardinetto.com
(€€). Modern rooms and a **restaurant**
(€€€€) rated by many the best in
town. Closed Mon and Aug.

Osteria Cascina dei Fiori, Via Regione
Forte, over the Sesia in Borgo Vercelli,
t 0161 32827 (€€€€). Seriously good
food (but definitely not for
vegetarians) served in a charming
country house, run by two couples, by
a rice paddy; try Vercelli's classic
panissa (rice cooked with white beans,
tomatoes, onions and bacon). Closed
Sun, Mon, Thurs lunch, Jan and July.

Novara ✉ 28100

****Italia**, Via Solaroli 8/10, t 0321 399
316, www.panciolihotels.it (€€€€).
Central and elegant, modern and
comfortable, it also claims one of the

best **restaurants** (€€€€) in Novara,
with good rice dishes and surprises
like chicken curry.

***Parmigiano**, Via dei Cattaneo 4/6,
t 0321 623 231, www.parmigiano.
novara.com (€€€). An old façade
conceals a sparkling modern interior
with simple rooms and an excellent
restaurant (€).

*Stazione**, Viale Manzoni 4/c, t 0321
623 256 (€€). Budget-friendly, simple,
en-suite rooms next to the train
station, in easy walking distance of
the centre.

Tantris, Via P. Lombardo 35,
Lumellogno, t 0312 469 156 (€€€€).
Wonderful creative cuisine based on
the harmony of flavours of top-quality
ingredients. Closed Sun eve and Mon.

Tri Scalin, Via Sottile 25, off Via
Paganini, t 0321 623 247 (€€€). The
shrine of Novarese cuisine. The food –
the local salame della duja, risotto al
Barolo or pasta e fagioli – is excellent.
Closed Sat lunch, Sun and Aug.

figures and paintings by Lorenzo Peracino (d. 1790), whose
masterpiece is the great whirlwind of paradise in the dome. The
River Ticino, dividing Piedmont from Lombardy, is now a nature
reserve, a haunt of storks and otters.

West of Novara, overlooking the Sesia, **San Nazzaro Sesia** has an
impressive fortified abbey founded in 1040, of which the massive
campanile and walls survive; the church was rebuilt in the 15th
century, and has a pretty terracotta portal; inside are frescoes on
the life of St Benedict. The hills to the north are Novara's wine-
growing region. Here, **Oleggio** has an excellent **Museo Civico
Etnografico,** with 35 rooms of displays of items from 1850 to 1950,
and just outside town the cemetery church of **San Michele**, with
rare 11th-century frescoes.

**Museo Civico
Etnografico**
Piazza Bertotti 2,
t 0321 91429; open
Sat 3–5.30, Mon–Fri
by request

Lake Maggiore

 Lake Maggiore
Winding majestically for 65km between Piedmont and Lombardy,
its northern quarter lost in the Swiss Alps, Lake Maggiore is large
enough to create its own Mediterranean microclimate. The
Romans called it Lacus Verbanus, for the verbena that grows on its
shores. The lords of the lake, however, have always been Milanese;
the Della Torre, then the Visconti (1314), who granted lands to the
Borromei beginning in 1439. They still, in fact, own the fishing
rights and the three jewel-like Borromean Islands in the Golfo

Getting to and around Lake Maggiore

Trains from Milan, Turin and Novara to Domodossola stop at both Arona and Stresa. Stresa is also linked by train to Orta. **Buses** connecting Maggiore to Orta run from the Stresa and Arona stations, and from Verbania to Omegna. Others serve all the villages along the western shore of the lake.

By far the best way to see the lake is by boat: **Navigazione Lago Maggiore**, t 0322 233 200, *www.navigazionelaghi.it*, runs **steamers** and fast services to all corners of the lake, with most frequent services in the central area, between Stresa, Baveno, Verbania, Pallanza, Laveno and the Borromean Islands. **Car ferries** run year-round between Intra and Laveno.

Borromeo. Although, for reasons of space, we only include Maggiore's western, Piedmontese shore, it has most of the lake's star attractions.

From the South: Arona to Baveno

Southern Lake Maggiore's reedy lagoons and woodlands, now the **Parco dei Lagoni di Mercurago**, were a favourite stomping ground of Neolithic Italians who lived in houses on stilts. There must be something good in the grass, too, judging by the thoroughbred horses raised in the environs; you can hire one to explore the park's trails. If you have kids, there's a **Safari Park** 10km south at Pombia, with everything from water slides to giant fibreglass dinosaurs, and two flesh-and-blood white lions.

Maggiore's waters deepen at **Arona**, which looks across the water to the Borromean castle at Angera. In cobbled Piazza del Popolo, the 15th-century **Casa del Podestà** has a handsome portico, and in Piazza San Graziano you can visit the **Museo Archeologico**, with items from the prehistoric lake settlement up to the Middle Ages. Upper Arona has two fine churches: Renaissance **Santa Maria**, where the Borromeo chapel contains a lovely polyptych of 1511 by Gaudenzio Ferrari, and **SS. Martiri**, with 16th-century stained glass, and paintings by Bergognone and Palma Giovane.

The **Castle of Arona**, wrecked by Napoleon and now a park, was the birthplace of Charles Borromeo (1538–84). Nephew of Pius IV, Charles instigated the decade-long Council of Trent that launched the Counter-Reformation. When he was canonized in 1610, his cousin and successor Cardinal Federico Borromeo commemorated him in Arona with a church and a statue designed by Cerano, covered with copper sheets, known as **San Carlone**, a strikingly ugly 115ft colossus, completed in 1697 after 84 years of work. It shows Charles blessing the lake with the codex of the Council of Trent under his arm – New York may have its Statue of Liberty; Maggiore's is devoted to Religious Conformity. For a queer sensation walk up the steep steps through his hollow viscera to look out over the lake through his eyes. Facing Arona on the other side and overlooking the southern part of Lake Maggiore, the

Safari Park
t 0321 956 431, www.safaripark.it; open Jan, Feb and Nov daily 10–4; Mar and Oct Mon–Fri 10–6, Sat, Sun and hols 9–7; April–Sept daily 9–7; 1–24 Dec open Sat, Sun and hols, closed 25 Dec, 26–31 Dec open daily 10–4; adm exp

Museo Archeologico
t 0322 48294; open Tues and Thurs 10–12, Sat and Sun 3.30–6.30; adm

San Carlone
t 0322 249 669; open mid-Mar–Oct 9–12.30 and 2–6.30; other months Sat and Sun only; Dec only Sun and 8th 9–12.30 and 2–4.30; closed Jan–Feb; adm; may not be suitable for children under 9

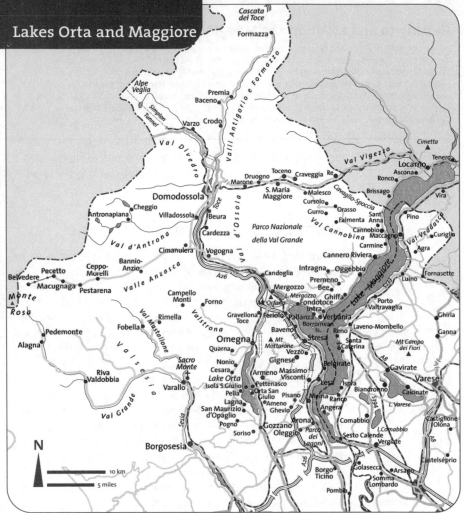

Museo della Bambola e della Moda Infantile *open mid-Mar–mid-Oct 9–5.30; adm*

Castle or Rocca Borromeo of Angera is a rare example of a medieval fortified building completely preserved. In addition to the local history, the Rocca hosts the Museo della Bambola e della Moda Infantile (Museum of the Doll and of Newborn Fashion), one of the most important in Europe .

From Arona to Stresa

Two roads link Arona to Stresa: the panoramic upper road through the villages of the **Colle Vergante**, and the main road hugging the lake shore. **Meina**, on the shore, has a sprinkling of neoclassical villas from the 18th century, when the lake first became fashionable. From here you can turn off for **Ghevio** and **Silvera**, charming villages immersed in the green of the hills of

Vergante, and **Massino Visconti**, with its 13th-century castle and church. The shore road continues to **Lesa**, a little resort with a well-preserved Romanesque church, **San Sebastiano** (1035). The lake really opens up at **Belgirate**, with a pretty square, the 15th-century frescoed church of **Santa Marta** and the **Villa Carlotta** (now a hotel), a favourite retreat of Italy's intellectuals in the 1800s.

Stresa, the 'Pearl of Verbano'

Beautifully positioned overlooking the Borromean Islands, under the majestic peak of Mottarone, Stresa is Maggiore's most beautiful town, bursting with flowers and sprinkled with villas. A holiday resort since the 19th century, famous for its mild climate, it soared in popularity after the construction of the Simplon Tunnel in 1906; Hemingway used its **Grand Hôtel des Iles Borromées** as Frederick Henry's refuge from war in *A Farewell to Arms*. Triangular **Piazza Cadorna**, shaded by age-old plane trees, is Stresa's social centre, its number of habitués swollen by participants in international congresses. Two of Stresa's villas are open to the public. **Villa Pallavicino** was built in 1855 for Queen Margherita and King Umberto I. The subsequent owners planted the now majestic sequoias, ginkgos and other trees, and laid out the colourful gardens and lawns where animals roam freely – llamas, kangaroos and zebras. At the **Villa Ducale** (1771), once the property of Catholic philosopher Antonio Rosmini (d. 1855), besides the gardens, there's a museum on his life.

From Stresa you can ascend **Monte Mottarone** (4,920ft), via the cable car in Carciano di Stresa. The views are famous, on one of those legendarily clear days taking in all seven major Italian lakes, and you can also visit the **Giardino Alpinia** with over 1,000 species of plants; or visit **Gignese**, where the **Museo dell'Ombrello e del Parasol** recalls the manufacture and history of umbrellas and walking sticks, with some 1,500 examples. Once you reach the **Parco del Mottarone** and the Strada Panoramica La Borromea, there's a toll: the Borromei paved it, so you pay for it.

The Borromean Islands

Frequent boats from Stresa or Baveno sail to the three Borromean Islands. If you want to make a day of it, all have restaurants, but don't expect many gourmet thrills.

Closest to Stresa, **Isola Bella** was a scattering of bare rocks until the 17th century, when Count Carlo III Borromeo decided to make it a garden in the form of a ship for his wife Isabella (hence 'Isola Bella'). Engineer Angelo Crivelli, in charge of designing this pretty present, built ten terraces to form a pyramidal 'poop deck', to create the architectural perspectives beloved by Baroque theatre. Carlo's son Vitaliano VI (d. 1670) added the **palace**, completed by the

---

Villa Pallavicino
t 0323 32407, www.
parcozoopallavicino.it;
open mid-Mar–Oct
9–6; adm

Villa Ducale
t 0323 30091; open
Mon–Fri 9–12 and 3–6

Monte Mottarone
t 0323 30295, www.
stresa-mottarone.it,
for schedules

Giardino Alpinia
t 0323 30295, www.
giardinoalpinia.it; open
April–Oct Tues–Sun 9–6

**Museo
dell'Ombrello
e del Parasol**
Via Golf Panorama 2,
t 0323 89622; open
April–Sept Tues–Sun
10–12 and 3–6; adm

Isola Bella
t 0323 932483, www.
borromeoturismo.it;
open end Mar–end Oct
daily 9–5.30; adm exp

---

12 Piedmont | Lake Maggiore: From the South: Arona to Baveno

Borromei according to the original plans only in 1959 and filled it with art by Annibale Carracci, Luca Giordano, Pannini, Zuccarelli, Cerano, Tiepolo and Pietro Mulier, 'Il Tempesta' (d. 1701), who in spite of his stormy nickname was a long-time guest of the family. The room in which Napoleon slept in August 1797 is done up in the Directory style in his honour, while the music room, with its antique instruments, hosted the 1935 Stresa Conference, at which Italy, Britain and France met to decide what to do in the face of Hitler's rearmament – a sad sequel to the pact signed at Locarno ten years earlier – but did nothing. The **Tapestry Gallery** has six 16th-century Flemish tapestries featuring the Borromean emblems, the three rings (symbol of unity between the three great Milanese families – Borromeo, Sforza and Visconti), the Visconti serpent swallowing a baby, and the unicorn, a statue of which also holds pride of place in the gardens, which are filled with grapefruit and bitter orange, orchids, azaleas, rhododendrons, carnivorous plants, and a 200-year-old camphor tree. Six mosaic **grottoes** by the lake offer relief from the sun and vaguely queasy feelings you may get from so much grand kitsch.

Isola Madre
t 0323 31261; open end Mar–end Oct 9–5.30; adm exp, joint adm possible with Isola Bella

As an antidote, visit the delightful **Isola Madre**, which the Borromei opened to the public in 1978. Here they planted a luxuriant botanical garden, dominated by Europe's largest Kashmir cypress. On its best days, few places are more conducive to languor, at least until one of the isle's bold parrots or peacocks tries to stare you out. The 16th-century villa, with its charming rococo rooms, was often used by the family, and contains their rather remarkable collection of antique puppet theatres and marionettes, including a stage set of Dante's *Inferno*. The Borromei's third island, **Isola dei Pescatori**, has an almost too quaint fishing village; their smallest islet, **San Giovanni** by Pallanza, has a villa once owned by Toscanini.

Baveno

Baveno is Stresa's quieter sister, linked by a beautiful, villa-lined road. Known for its quarries (Milan's Galleria Vittorio Emanuele, the Basilica of St Paul's in Rome and the Columbus monument in New York all started here), it first made the society pages in 1879, when Queen Victoria spent a summer at the Villa Clara, now Castello Branca. Opera composers followed, first Wagner, and then Umberto Giordano, who composed his *Fedora* – the first opera to call for bicycles on stage – in his Villa Fedora. Although the interior was baroqued, Baveno's 11th-century church of **Santi Gervasio e Protasio** has its original façade (note the Roman inscriptions on the blocks reused in the front) and a charming little octagonal baptistry from the 5th century.

Sports and Activities from Arona to Baveno

With its many parks and reserves, Lake Maggiore's banks are ideal for **trekking**; ask the local tourist offices for itineraries and see *www.illago maggiore.com*. There are three **golf courses**: Alpino, 9 holes, **t** 0323 20642, *www.golfalpino.it*, in Vezzo; Des Iles Borromées, in a fine Alpine setting, 18 holes, **t** 0323 929 285, *www.golfdes ilesborromees.it*, in Brovello Campugnino; and Piandisole, 9 holes, at the entry of the Val Grande Park, **t** 0323 587 100, *www.golfpiandisole.it*, in Via Alla Prueta 1, Premeno.

Festivals in Stresa

Settimane Musicali di Stresa, *late Aug–early Sept*. Orchestras from around the world descend on Stresa. For information, *see www.settimane musicali.net*.

Where to Stay and Eat from Arona to Baveno

(i) Arona >
Piazzale Duca d'Aosta,
t 0322 243 601

Arona ✉ 28041

Campagna, 4km from the centre at Campagna, Via Vergante 12, **t** 0322 57294 (€€€€). Welcoming trattoria serving food from Lombardy and Piedmont; delicious home-made pasta and constantly changing menu of *secondi*. *Closed Mon eve, Tues, mid-June and mid-Nov.*

(i) Beligirate >
Via Mazzini,
t 0322 7494

Beligirate ✉ 28832

Villa dal Pozzo d'Annone, Strada Sempione 5, **t** 0322 7255, *www.villadalpozzodannone.com* (€€€€€). Aristocratic villa on the lake, set in a superb garden with a waterfall and rare plants, all oozing 19th-century atmosphere. Recently the **Borgo Ottocentesco**, a group of fishers' cottages in the 12-acre villa park, have been converted into rooms and a bistro wine bar. There's a beach and boat mooring, gym and pool; Turkish bath has extra fees. *Villa open Easter–Oct, Borgo open all year.*

(i) Stresa >
Via Canonica 3,
t 0323 30150, www.
distrettolaghi.it

Stresa ✉ 28838

*****Des Iles Borromées, Corso Umberto I 67, **t** 0323 938 938,

www.borromees.it (€€€€€). Opened in 1861; stylish in both its dazzling belle époque furnishings and mod cons. Overlooking the islands and a garden, the hotel has two pools, beach, tennis, helipad, gym and a *Centro Benessere* .

****Regina Palace, Corso Umberto I 29, **t** 0323 936 936, *www.regina-palace.it* (€€€€€). A lovely, bow-shaped Liberty-style palace, in a large park, which conserves its original decor in the halls. Heated pool, tennis, Turkish bath, gym, beach and splendid views.

****Milan au Lac, Piazza Marconi 9, **t** 0323 31190, *www.milansperanza.it* (€€€€). Another lake-front hotel; large rooms, many with balconies. If sent to the modern sister hotel Speranza next door, ask for a top-floor lake-front room, or room no.606. Tennis, pool and a garage. *Closed Nov–Mar.*

****La Palma, Corso Umberto I 33, **t** 0323 32401, *www.hlapalma.it* (€€€€). Recently refurbished rooms in a quiet spot on the lake, beautiful pool and private beach; free garage parking and fine **restaurant**.

***Primavera, Via Cavour 39, **t** 0323 31286, *www.stresahotels.net/ primavera* (€€€). Friendly, stylish hotel in the pedestrian zone.

***Du Parc, Via Gignous 1, **t** 0323 30335, *www.duparc.it* (€€€). A charming family-run hotel in a period villa set in its own beautiful park, 300m from the lake. The hotel also has two-star rooms in its annexe in the gardens. *Closed Nov–Mar.*

Fiorentino, Via Anna Maria Bolongaro 9, **t 0323 30254, *www.hotel fiorentino.it* (€€). Simple, central, family-run, with a nice restaurant.

*La Locanda, Via Leopardi 19, close to the Mottarone cable car, **t** 0323 31176, *www.stresa.net/hotel/lalocanda* (€). Quiet, family-run: all rooms are en suite and comfortable, and most have a balcony.

Piedmontese, Via Mazzini 25, **t** 0323 30235 (€€€€). Find a table in the garden to tuck into the divine spaghetti with melted onions, basil and pecorino, and the excellent fish dishes. *Closed Mon, Dec and Jan.*

The Irish Pub, Via P. Margherita 9, **t** 0323 31054. A Stresa institution for the past 28 years.

Borromean Islands ✉ 28838

***Verbano**, Via Ugo Ara 2, Isola dei Pescatori, t 0323 30408, *www.hotel verbano.it* (€€€€). A lovely place to stay, as well as a chance to see the island after most have left, with a good **restaurant** where a romantic location and views compensate for the service. Small beach. Pets admitted. *Closed 7 Jan–Feb.*

ⓘ **Baveno** ▸
*Piazza D. Alighieri 14,
t 0323 924 632*

Baveno ✉ 28831

****Lido Palace**, SS Sempione 30, t 0323 924 444, *www.lidopalace.com* (€€€€). A beautiful park surrounds this 18th-century palace overlooking the Borromean Islands. Many extras, including a pool, tennis and private beach. *Closed mid-Jan–mid-Mar.*

***Carillon**, Via Nazionale del Sempione 2, Feriolo, t 0323 28115, *www.hotelcarillon.it* (€€€). On the north edge of town, on the beach. Nice rooms are all lake-front with balconies; the same family runs the nearby **Serenella** (*www.hotelseren ella.it*), with a summer garden, serving

home-made pasta and risotto, lake fish or meat. *Closed Wed, Jan and Feb.*

***Beau Rivage**, Viale della Vittoria 36, t 0323 924 534, *www.wel.it/beaurivage* (€€). On the lake front overlooking the Borromean Islands, family-run hotel with parking, a nice garden, a **restaurant** (€€), old-style furniture and atmosphere on the ground floor; the top-floor suites (€€€€) are lovely. *Closed late Oct to mid-Mar.*

****Elvezia**, Via Monte Grappa 15, t 0323 924 106, *www.elveziahotel.it* (€€). The charming Monica and Marco run this bright hotel up by the church, with a little garden and parking. Pets admitted. *Closed Dec–Feb and May.*

***Al Campanile**, Via Monte Grappa 16, t 0323 922 377 (€€). In the centre, basic rooms in a pretty villa in a lush garden and a **restaurant**.

****Villa Ruscello**, Via Sempione 64, t 0323 923 006, *www.villaruscello.it* (€). Garden villa run by three friendly siblings, with smallish rooms but lovely lake views, parking and a beach.

Verbania and Maggiore's Northwest Shore

Verbania: Pallanza and Intra

In 1939 Mussolini united three towns, Pallanza, Suna and Intra, and christened the whole **Verbania** as part of his campaign to revive Roman names; in 1994 it became a provincial capital. Over the bridge from Baveno, near the road to Mergozzo (*see* p.312), **Fondotoce** is the site of the new **Tecnoparco del Lago** designed by Aldo Rossi with a World's Fair flair and ambitions of shaking Maggiore out of its slumbers. **Pallanza**, the pretty centre of Verbania, was long a resort and has a Bramante-inspired church, the **Madonna di Campagna** up Viale Azari. It sports a gazebo-like arcaded drum and a Romanesque campanile; the lavish interior has good 15th-century frescoes by Gerolamo Lanino.

In the centre of Pallanza, the 17th-century Palazzo Viani-Dugnani houses the **Museo del Paesaggio** with items from the proto-Celtic necropolis at Ornavasso, frescoes, landscapes and scenes painted in the area such as *The Diggers* (1890) by Arnaldo Ferraguti. One section is devoted to photographs, another to casts and sculptures by Arturo Martini, Giulio Branca (from Cannobio), and Paolo Troubetzkoy (born in Intra of Russian parents). Religious artefacts,

Tecnoparco del Lago
www.tecnoparco.it

Museo del Paesaggio
Via Ruga 44, t 0323 502 418; open April–Oct Tues–Sun 10–12 and 3.30–6.30; adm

Palazzo Biumi Innocenti
t 0323 556 621; same hours, but open all year

with more than 5,000 *ex votos*, are housed in the nearby **Palazzo Biumi Innocenti**, where you can also find photographs documenting the history of Lake Maggiore.

Beautiful villas and gardens, an eclectic showcase of 19th-century and early 20th-century styles, dot Pallanza's **Castagnola promontory**. Here you'll find the glory of Verbania, the gardens of the **Villa Taranto**. In 1931, Scots Captain Neil McEacharn purchased a derelict villa and renamed it in honour of his ancestor, a MacDonald made Duke of Taranto by Napoleon. McEacharn had one of the world's greenest thumbs, and pockets deep enough to travel around the world seven times gathering 20,000 varieties of exotic plants, which 100 gardeners helped him to acclimatize and plant in 16 very tidy hectares, with ponds, woods and fountains. McEacharn died in 1964 and was buried in a chapel in the gardens, which he left to the Italian state; the villa is now the Verbania prefecture.

Villa Taranto
t 0323 556 667, www.villataranto.it; open late Mar–Oct daily 8.30–6.30; adm exp

The tourist office organizes visits to the eclectic Anglo-Italian gardens of the nearby **Villa San Remigio**: these, too, were a labour of love – of Sofia Browne, a painter, and her poet husband, the Marquis Silvio Della Valle di Casanova – arranged into gardens of memory, sadness, whispers, delight and joy. The villa is named after the asymmetrical Romanesque bombonnière of a **church** at the top of the promontory, with frescoes from the 13th century. Another house, the lakeside **Villa Giulia** with its distinctive exedra on the roof, was built in 1847 by Bernardino Branca, inventor of the popular *digestivo* Fernet Branca, and is now used for conferences.

Villa San Remigio
t 0323 503 249; open Mar–Sept Sat and Sun from 10.30am by prior booking only

Intra is Verbania's industrial and business quarter, with a ferry across to Laveno. Buses serve the woodsy holiday towns in the hinterland: **Arizzano**, **Bee** and most importantly **Premeno**, overlooking Maggiore and the Alps, with skiing and a golf course up at **Pian Cavallone** (5,131ft), which has views almost as good as those from Mottarone. At Intragna you can pick up trails into the **Parco Nazionale della Val Grande**, Italy's largest wilderness area.

Parco Nazionale della Val Grande
t 0323 557 960, www.parcovalgrande.it; pick up maps at the tourist office

Back on the lake, north of Intra, **Ghiffa** is pleasant and quiet. Here you can uncover the history of felt hats in the old Panizza hat factory, Italy's most renowned brand after Borsalino, now the **Museo del Cappello**. Up in Ghiffa's suburb of Ronco lies the **Sacro Monte SS. Trinità**, another late 17th-century Counter-Reformation devotional trip (*see* p.319), this one an idea of St Charles Borromeo, although only three chapels were ever finished. The main church (1617) has a very curious fresco of the Trinity, showing three beardless blessing Jesuses in a row. The surrounding woodlands are part of a nature reserve, and there are several marked paths, including an archaeological one past prehistoric rock engravings. Further north, the 15th-century **Oratorio di Cadessino** at **Oggebbio** is a national monument for its frescoes of the same period, and **Cannero Riviera** is a quiet resort, set amid glossy citrus groves. It

Museo del Cappello
Corso Belvedere 279, t 0323 59174; open April–Oct Sat and Sun 3.30–6.30

Sacro Monte SS. Trinità
t 0323 59870; visits by prior appointment only

faces two intensely picturesque islets, the **Castelli di Cannero**, once strongholds of the five brothers Mazzarditi, fierce pirates defeated in 1414 by Filippo Maria Visconti: he razed the castles, and on their ruins Ludovico Borromeo built a tower and castle (1521) that seem to emerge straight out of the water. They can't be visited for security reasons, but some proposals have been made to restore them, preserving their original structure. Further north, **Carmine** is overlooked by the equally romantic Romanesque church of **San Gottardo**, set on a rocky spur.

Cannobio and the Val Cannobina

Cannobio, with a wide sandy beach, is an ancient town with steep, medieval streets, and a monument honouring local Giovanni Branca (d. 1645), inventor of the steam turbine. Cannobio's churches adhere to the Milanese Ambrosian Rite, revived by Borromeo in an effort to promote local pride. Much of this religious fervour is concentrated by the lake in the Bramante-inspired **Santuario della Pietà**, built to house a miraculous painting on parchment of the *Dead Christ*; the altarpiece by Gaudenzio Ferrari of *Christ on the Road to Calvary* is one of his finest. On Sundays a huge market takes over the lake front.

Santuario della Pietà
t 0323 71255, www. santuariosantapieta.it; open 7.30–12 and 2–7

From Cannobio, the wild, sparsely populated **Val Cannobina** rises up to meet the Val Vigezzo and Domodossola. Just 2km from Cannobio you can hire canoes to explore the dramatic **Orrido di Sant'Anna**, a narrow gorge ending in a placid swimming hole, a favourite for scuba divers, overlooked by a church built in 1631 by the Cannobians in gratitude for being spared from the then-raging plague. Further up the valley, hamlets of stone houses make up **Cavaglio-Spoccia**, where the valley's first road, the Via Borromeo, crosses old mossy bridges. **Falmenta**, a tiny village on the other side of the valley, has among its black stone houses a church with a rare wooden altarpiece, crowded with small figures, from the 1300s. The next village, **Gurro**, has retained its medieval centre and has in its town hall a little **Museo Etnografico della Val Cannobina** of local customs. **Orasso** has a 13th-century *Visitazione* church, and a lovely altarpiece in the 15th-century church, San Materno.

Museo Etnografico della Val Cannobina
t 0323 76100, www. museogurro.it; open mid-June–mid-Sept daily 10–12.30 and 1.30–5; mid-Sept–mid-Nov and mid-April–mid-June Sat, Sun and hols 10–12.30 and 1.30–5; adm

Where to Stay and Eat in Verbania and on Maggiore's Northwest Shore

(i) **Verbania-Pallanza >**
Corso Zanitello 6/8, t 0323 503 249, www. verbania-turismo.it

Verbania-Pallanza ✉ 28922

****Grand Hotel Majestic, Via Vittorio Veneto 32, t 0323 509 711, *www.grand hotelmajestic.it* (€€€€€–€€€€). Grand old hotel on the lake, with plenty of amenities – indoor pool, bikes, tennis, park and beach. Suites 4 and 6 are the best. Spa, pool, fitness centre and tennis court. *Closed Nov–Mar.*

****Ancora, Corso Mameli 65, Intra, t 0323 53951, *www.hotelancora.it* (€€€€). Small lake-front hotel, with elegant interiors and good food.

***Hotel Aquadolce, Via Cietti 1, Lungolago, t 0323 505 418, *www.*

hotelaquadolce.it (€€€). Carefully restored 19th-century building offering 13 rooms with wi-fi access, satellite TV and all comforts.

*Villa Tilde, Via Vittorio Veneto 63, t 0323 503 805 (€€). Old lake-front villa, just off Pallanza's centre; enjoys a lovely quiet position and a superb view.

Ostello Villa Congreve, Via alle Rose 7, t 0323 501 648 (€). Pallanza's nice youth hostel is to be found in a villa up on the road to the botanical gardens of Villa Taranto. *Open Mar–Oct.*

Milano, Corso Zanitello 2, t 0323 556 816 (€€€€). The best place to eat in Pallanza, in an old lake-front villa, with dining out on the terrace for a romantic evening. Wonderful *antipasti* and lake fish. *Closed Mon eve and Tues and mid-Jan–mid-Feb.*

Osteria del Castello, Via Piazza Castello 9, Intra, t 0323 516 579 (€€). Weekly changing menu, with some tasty lake-fish dishes, and a good choice of wines. *Closed Sun.*

Ghiffa ✉ 28823

***Ghiffa, Corso Belvedere 88, t 0323 59285, www.hotelghiffa.com (€€€€–€€€). This hotel maintains the charm of its aristocratic past in the dining room, with huge windows overlooking the lake. Rooms are modern, except no.114. Nice garden, pool and private beach and good **restaurant**.

*Park Paradiso, Via G. Marconi 20, t 0323 59548 (€€€). A grand old hotel above Ghiffa in a lush terraced garden with beautiful views of the lake, it has plenty of faded 19th-century character, but not in the bedrooms. The dining room still has its original Liberty décor. Partially covered pool. *No credit cards.*

Cannero Riviera ✉ 28821

****Cannero, Piazza Re Umberto I 2, t 0323 788 046, www.hotelcannero. com (€€). An 18th-century villa opened as a hotel in 1902, with balconies overlooking the lake, pool, tennis, and a garage. The annexe enjoys three-sided views of the lake, and offers a multilingual library. Free boats and bikes for guests; motorboats for hire. *Closed Nov to mid-Mar.*

**La Rondinella, Via Sacchetti 50, t 0323 788 098, www.hotel-la-rondinella.it (€€). Rooms and apartments sleeping up to four in a Liberty-style villa from the 1930s in a panoramic spot, with a scenic garden terrace and private beach. *Half board.*

*Miralago, Via delle Magnolie 13, t 0323 788 282 (€). Simple, with views and shared bathrooms. *Closed Dec–Feb.*

Cannobio ✉ 28822

***Del Lago, Via Nazionale 2, Carmine inferiore, 1.5km from Cannobio, t 0323 70595, www.enotecalago.com (€€€). Rooms with balconies over the lake, a private beach and wine shop, and one of the most romantic **restaurants** on the lake, with only eight tables. Try the risotto with saffron, zucchini and mussels, or duck breast with honey-roasted sesame seeds. *Closed Tues, Wed lunch and Nov–Mar.*

***Pironi, Via Marconi 35, t 0323 70624 or 0323 70149 in winter, www.pironihotel.it (€€€€). Occupies a frescoed 15th-century palace, in the historic centre, that is shaped like the Flatiron building in New York. The rooms are all different in shape and furniture, and furnished with antiques; book room no.12 for a romantic frescoed balcony all to yourself. *Closed Nov–Feb.*

***Il Portico, Piazza Santuario 2, t 0323 70598, www.hotelilportico.com (€€). Under the porticoes by the lake; another classy, if more staid, choice. Stylish rooms but sadly with no lake view; they overlook a quiet courtyard and the bell tower. The **restaurant**, however, has a lovely terrace on the lake (*June–Sept*). *Closed Nov–Feb.*

***Antica Stallera, Via P. Zaccheo 7, t 0323 71595, www.anticastallera.com (€€). One of the oldest inns in the area dating from 1650; the renovated rooms are comfortable. It also has a nice **restaurant** in the courtyard.

Lo Scalo, Piazza Vittorio Emanuele III 32, t 0323 71480, www.loscalo.com (€€€€). Sit on the pretty, porticoed terrace on the lake, and dine on traditional and *recherché* Piedmontese recipes and home-made breads. *Closed Mon, Tues lunch and Jan–Feb.*

ⓘ **Cannobio >>**
Viale Vittorio Veneto 4, t 0323 71212, www.cannobio.net

ⓘ **Cannero Riviera >**
Via Roma 37, t 0323 788 943, www.cannero.it

12

Piedmont | Lake Maggiore: Verbania and Maggiore's Northwest Shore

North of the Lakes: the Lower Ossola Valleys

Unspoiled, and mostly unnoticed by visitors whizzing down the motorway to more Mediterranean delights, the seven Ossola valleys cut deep into the Alps, sculpted by the moody River Toce, its tributaries and waterfalls, surrounded by snowcapped peaks. Nowadays the valleys are visited for their pistes, their forests and rustic hospitality, their famous cured meats and salami, and Alpine lakelets so blue they hurt.

Lake Mergozzo and the Valle Anzasca

West of Verbania, the road passes into the shadow of the mighty granite dome of Mount Orfano, which the locals are slowly whittling away to make flowerpots. Orfano in its turn guards an orphan lake, the small but deep **Lake Mergozzo**, which formed an arm of Lake Maggiore until the 9th century, when sediment from the Toce plugged it, a loss compensated for by the fact that Mergozzo is now one of the cleanest lakes in Europe, surrounded by soothing deep forests. Between the mountain and lake, the hamlet of **Montorfano** has the striking granite Romanesque church of **San Giovanni**, with a 12th-century statue of the Madonna and a 5th-century baptismal font. The lake's main town, **Mergozzo**, has been a quiet place ever since it lost its role as a transit centre with the construction of the Simplon tunnel. It has a castle, a 12th-century church made of Orfano granite, Santa Marta, and by the lake, one of the oldest elm trees in Italy, its trunk nearly hollow with age. Little **Candoglia** is synonymous with the quarry that for six centuries has been worked for the pink and white marble that built Milan cathedral; two Imperial Roman necropoli yielded the finds exposed in the Antiquarium in Via Roma 8.

Mergozzo is the gateway to the numerous Ossola valleys. The first, splitting off to the west, the enchanting **Valle Anzasca**, rises straight towards the tremendous east face of Monte Rosa. Among the woods and vineyards, look for **Cimamulera**, where one of the oldest horse chestnut trees in Italy grows next to the church. The slate roofs of tiny **Colombetti** huddle under a lofty cliff; **Bannio Anzino**, the 'capital' of the valley, has a 1st-century BC Gallo-Roman necropolis, and in its parish church a life-sized, 16th-century bronze *Christ* from Flanders. At **Ceppo Morelli** the vertiginous bridge over the Anza traditionally divides the valley's Latin population from the Walser. Beyond Ceppo the road plunges through a gorge to the old Walser mining town of **Pestarena**; until recently the Valle Anzasca had Italy's largest gold deposits, extracted from galleries that extended for 40km underground.

Santa Marta
ring the tourist office for the key,
t 0323 800 935

Antiquarium
t 0323 80101; open by request

Getting to the Lower Ossola Valleys

The Ossola Valleys are served by **bus** from Domodossola. For Macugnaga, take the **train** to Piedimulera or Domodossola and the connecting Comazzi **bus**, **t** 0324 240 333, *www.comazzibus.com*, which also runs a summer service (Tues–Sun) from Varese via Lake Maggiore (Laveno/Intra).

Casa Museo Walser
*Via Monterosa 232,
t 0323 65440; open
June and 1st week of
Sept Sat and Sun
3.30–6.30; July–Aug
daily 3.30–6.30, Sat and
Sun in Aug also 10–12;
26 Dec–6 Jan 3.30–5.30;
at other times call Carla
Bettineschi on t 0324
65230; adm*

Museo della Miniera d'Oro della Guia
*t 0324 65570,
www.minieradoro.it;
open June–mid-Sept
daily 9–11.30 and
2–5.30, other times ring
for appointment; adm*

Antronapiana
*see www.vcoinbus.it
for timetables*

The various hamlets that comprise **Macugnaga**, the Valle Anzasca's popular mountain resort, seem tiny under the 15,305ft 'cathedral of stone and ice' of **Monte Rosa**. Macugnaga is a charming old-fashioned place popular with families, beginner and intermediate skiers. It has some 40km of ski runs, a dozen ski lifts and a chair lift that operates in the summer to the magnificent **Belvedere**, which has views over the local glacier, as well as a *funivia* to the **Passo Monte Moro** (9,410ft). Fearless climbers come to attempt the Himalayan east flank of Monte Rosa, one of the most dangerous ascents in the Alps. Local Walser traditions are recalled in the **Casa Museo Walser** in the hamlet of Borca. To learn about local goldmining, the **Museo della Miniera d'Oro della Guia**, also at Borca, offers visits into a gold mine that was opened in 1710 (*dress warmly; it can be visited by disabled people too*). Macugnaga also has a monumental tree, in this case a huge, ancient lime.

North of the Valle Anzasca, the pretty **Val d'Antrona** is famed for its trout fishing and old-fashioned ways: the older women still wear traditional costumes and make Venetian lace. The valley begins at **Villadossola**, with a Romanesque church, **San Bartolomeo**, containing a fine 16th-century altarpiece. From here catch a bus to **Antronapiana**, a village near the lakelet of Antrona, created when a landslide buried half of Antronapiana in 1642. The north branch of the valley winds up to **Cheggio**, a small resort with another lake.

Sports and Activities in the Lower Ossola Valleys

Apart from **skiing**, **snowboarding** and **ice skating**, Macugnaga offers mountain sports such as **heli-ski** (off-piste descent of Monte Rosa to Swiss resorts), **paragliding** (from Monte Moro) and **ice-waterfall-climbing**. For a guide, **t** 0324 65170.

Where to Stay and Eat in the Lower Ossola Valleys

(i) Mergozzo >
*Corso Roma 20,
t 0323 800 935,
www.mergozzo.it/
turismo*

Mergozzo ✉ 28802
★★★Due Palme, Via Pallanza 1, **t** 0323 80112, *www.hotelduepalme.it* (€€€).

Maintains a faded charm, and has a pretty front terrace lorded over by a whistling parrot; the *gnocchi all'Ossalana* in the **restaurant** (€€) are equally noteworthy. Private beach. The same owners run an annexe, **Bettina**, in the centre (no lake view, but quiet).

★★★Piccolo Lago, Via Turati 87 in Fondotoce, **t** 0323 586 792, *www.piccololago.it* (€€€). Twelve modern rooms in a wooden chalet-like building, with lake views and individual terraces, plus a garden, private beach and a pool. *Closed 20 Dec–10 Feb*. Best known for its **restaurant** (€€€€), where chef Marco Sacco prepares dishes such as *agnolotti* stuffed with artichokes and prawns, delicate wild salmon smoked with juniper, or lake fish with a fondue of the local cheese,

Bettlematt; over 600 wines and spirits. *Closed Mon except June–Sept.*

***La Quartina**, Via Pallanza 20, t 0323 80118, *www.laquartina.com* (€€€). A warm, family-run hotel situated right on the lake, with a solarium, slightly spoilt by the rather overcrowded public beach it shares with the neighbouring camp site. Rooms 1 and 3 have their own terraces overlooking the lake. Excellent **restaurant** (€€€€), too. *Closed Mon, Jan and Feb.*

Macugnaga ✉ 28876
***Zumstein**, Via Monte Rosa 84, t 0324 65118 (€€€). The largest, most luxurious choice, **a** big chalet with attractive rooms with satellite TV, views of Monte Rosa, sauna and **restaurant**. *Closed May, Oct and Nov.*

***Flora**, Piazza Municipio 1, t 0324 65037, *albergoflora.com* (€€). On the main square, with pleasant, comfortable rooms. Some furnished flats also available to rent by the week or month.

***Signal**, Via Pecetto 18, t 0324 65142 (€€). Family-run hotel in a lovely setting at Pecetto hamlet, with a good **restaurant** that is popular with UK skiers. The ski bus stops just outside.

ⓘ **Macugnaga** >
Piazza Municipio,
t 0324 65119,
www.macugnaga.eu

Domodossola and the Upper Ossola Valleys

After his victory at Marengo, Napoleon, to facilitate meddling in Italy, built the first transalpine highway from Geneva to Domodossola over the Simplon Pass (Passo del Sempione), a major engineering feat completed in 1805. Exactly 100 years later the even more remarkable Simplon rail tunnel was completed – at the time the longest in the world, at 19.8km. The improved communications didn't help the Nazis, however, when the inhabitants booted them out in 1944 and formed an independent republic that lasted 40 days – one of the most significant acts of the Italian Resistance.

Domodossola

Domodossola, best known these days as the largest town in Italy beginning with the letter D, has a compact, car-swamped historic centre called the **Motta**, whose pretty trapezoid-shaped **Piazza Mercato** has 15th-century porticoes where a market is still held every Saturday. A few steps away, the old church of **SS. Gervasio e Protasio** was rebuilt in the 18th century, but conserves a Baroque porch and a Romanesque architrave carved with the *Dream of Constantine*, informing the emperor that he would conquer under the sign of the cross.

Opposite the church, the Renaissance Palazzo Silva houses the **Museo Civico G. Galletti** containing Etruscan and Roman finds from a 3rd-century AD necropolis in the Val Cannobina, Egyptian mummy bits and costumes; a **second section**, at Via Rosmini 20, is dedicated to natural history, coins, African ethnography, the construction of the Simplon tunnel and the Peruvian Jorge Chavez, the first man to fly over the Alps (29 September 1910), only to die in a crash near Domodossola. In 1944, the adjacent **Palazzo di Città** was the seat of the 40-day Repubblica Partigiana dell'Ossola.

Museo Civico
G. Galletti
t 0324 249 001;
currently visitable on
request; adm

Second section
visiting conditions as
above; at time of
writing temporarily
housed in the
Municipio-Section
Culture as it waits for
the Palazzo San
Francesco to be restored

Getting to and around Domodossola and the Upper Ossola Valleys

Domodossola and the other towns along the Toce can be reached by **train** or **bus** from Lake Maggiore or Lake Orta; the other Ossola valleys are served by bus from Domodossola (*www.vcoinbus.it*).

A narrow-gauge electric **railway** deliciously named SSIF-FART makes the scenic 1½-hour journey between Domodossola and Locarno on Lake Maggiore through the Val Vigezzo and Swiss Centovalli, serving all the villages on the way; for information, **t** 0324 242 055.

Buses to the valleys depart from the FS station, Piazza Matteotti in Domodossola, **t** 0324 240 333, *www.comazzibus.com*. To alleviate traffic in the Val Vigezzo, a summer service, Prontobus, will pick you up if you book by noon the previous day, **t** 0324 93565.

Via Mattarella leads up the Colle della Mattarella (marked by a big cross) and the 11th-century church of **San Quirico**, with a relief of a Celtic god in the wall. Above is a ruined castle, where two Capuchin friars founded the **Sacro Monte Calvario** in 1656, with 15 Baroque chapels dedicated to the Via Crucis; unfortunately the first and best one exploded in 1830, when it was used to store gunpowder. Domodossola has its own ski station 10km away called **Domobianca** or, if you're weighed down by polenta, relax at the hot springs at **Bognanco** just up the next valley to the west.

Sacro Monte Calvario
t 0324 241 976; open daily till dusk except May and Sept

Domobianca
t 0324 44352, www.domobianca.it

Bognanco
t 0324 234 109; open June–Sept

The Val Vigezzo

East of Domodossola begins the Val Vigezzo, where romantic woodlands, rolling hills and velvet pastures inspired enough minor artists to earn it the name 'the Valley of Painters'. The valley also had a knack for producing useful emigrants; one 18th-century artist, Giuseppe Borgnis, ended up painting country homes in Buckinghamshire. In the same century two emigrants to Germany formulated the first *acqua di colonia*, or cologne. Another family, the Mattei, emigrated to Holland in 1600 and accidentally invented snuff when they bought a storm-wrecked cargo vessel and found that the casks of rum had soaked into the bales of tobacco; at first despondent, they later discovered that the rum had imparted a wonderful fragrance to the tobacco and sold it as a novelty that soon became the rage.

The valley was also famous for chimney sweeps, one of whom, the story goes, saved a king of France: while cleaning the Louvre chimneys he overheard traitors conspiring against the baby king, Louis XIII, and warned the regent, Maria de' Medici. Since that time sweeps, who used to be banned from trading in France, have become industrious and rich. Another version claims a different reward: the local chimney sweeps were made royal jewellers, and remained so long enough to make a funerary cap for Louis XIV, now kept in Craveggia's church.

The Val Vigezzo's first village, **Druogno**, has pretty frescoed chapels scattered through its hamlets, crowned with stone roofs. **Santa Maria Maggiore**, the main town, is built around the 18th-century church; once Santa Maria had enough souls to fill its grand rococo interior, before they emigrated to become dockers in Livorno. Those who became chimney sweeps are honoured in the little **Museo dello Spazzacamino**; in September the town holds a sweeps' competition. The **Scuola di Belle Arti** is dedicated to local painters Carlo Fornara and Enrico Cavalli; some of their best works over the years are on display in the **Pinacoteca Rossetti Valentini**. Buses from Santa Maria go north up to **Toceno**, with pretty views and a Roman necropolis, and to **Craveggia**, birthplace of Giuseppe Borgnis, who left the valley's finest frescoes in the church.

Continuing up the Val Vigezzo, **Malesco** is a picturesque, higgledy-piggledy old village with a visitor centre for the rugged **Parco Nazionale della Val Grande**, the largest wilderness area in Italy; the former prefecture houses the **Museo Archeologico della Pietra Ollare** with archaeological finds and special exhibitions. At Malesco you can turn off on a narrow road that will keep you in second gear as it descends the Val Cannobina (*see* p.310) to Lake Maggiore. Further up the Val Vigezzo, **Re** had a chapel with a crude painting of the Madonna on the wall. In 1494 the village idiot threw a stone at it, striking the Virgin on the forehead and causing it to bleed profusely. The bleeding Madonna still has thousands of devotees: a ghastly neogothic Byzantine **Santuario della Madonna del Sangue** was built in 1922, over the previous (and still existing) chapel, filled with sincere, home-made *ex votos*.

Museo dello Spazzacamino
t 0324 95091; open July–mid Sept daily 10–12 and 4–6; ring ahead to check times and book visit; adm

Pinacoteca Rossetti Valentini
t 0329 6505 494; open July–Sept daily 10–12 and 3.30–7.30, other times by request; adm

Parco Nazionale della Val Grande
www.parcoval grande.it

Museo Archeologico della Pietra Ollare
open July–mid-Sept daily 10–12 and 4–6, Sat 8.30pm–10pm

Santuario della Madonna del Sangue
t 0324 97016

North of Domodossola

The **Val Divedro**, along the Simplon road, is as austere as the Val Vigezzo is gentle. Inhabited since the cows came home in the Mesolithic era (7000 BC), it teems with legends of dragons and elves. But nature is the main attraction, especially the **Alpe Veglia**, a high Alpine basin amid little lakes – including the Lago delle Streghe, named for the witches who haunt it. North towards the San Giacomo Pass, the road rises through the spectacular scenery of the **Valli Antigorio e Formazzo**, valleys along the River Toce settled by the Walser in the 13th century. Their charming scattered

The Walser

German speakers from the Swiss Valais, the Walser were shepherds who crossed the Alps beginning in around the year 1200, and colonized the high altitudes of Italy that no one else wanted, from the Ossola valleys to the Val di Gressoney in Aosta. To survive here, they evolved a special way of life, in hardy self-sufficient hamlets, building their three-storey wooden houses close together to save land, the roofs meeting to create snow-free paths. Each hamlet had a chapel, a windmill and an oven, where bread was baked once a year, communally, then allowed to go stale on special racks under the ceiling until it was rock hard; they would then chisel bits off and soften them in milk, broth or water. The living room, kitchen and stables were on the ground floor, heating the bedrooms on the first floor; the hayloft on the top also acted as insulation. Furniture was sparse. In their isolation (they remained practically autonomous until the 18th century), the Walser preserved a medieval German dialect known as *titsch*. Now German linguists come here to study the last 1,500 speakers.

villages are planted with vines and figs, and the valley's spa, **Crodo**, is famous in Italy for bottling a soft drink called Crodino, as well as iron-laced mineral water. Further north, Baceno's parish church, **San Gaudenzio** (11th–16th century) is the best in the Valle d'Ossola; it has a fine front portal and a cartwheel window, 16th-century Swiss stained glass and a magnificent gilded altarpiece of 1526.

In **Premia**, you can visit the **Orridi**, steep gorges sliced by the River Toce. You can reach an evocatively empty old Walser settlement, **Salecchio**, by foot from Antillone; **Formazza**, further up, is a pretty, still lived-in Walser community, with sturdy wooden houses. At the end of the road is one of the most breathtaking waterfalls in all the Alps, a thundering 985ft veil of mist, the **Cascata del Toce**. At other times, like all of Italy's best waterfalls, its bounding, splashing energy spins hydroelectric turbines.

Cascata del Toce
visitable June–July Sun 9–6 and Tues and Thurs 11–1, Aug daily 9–3.30, last 10 days of Aug Tues and Thurs 11–1

Piedmont | Lake Maggiore: Domodossola and the Upper Ossola Valleys

Where to Stay and Eat in Domodossola and the Upper Ossola Valleys

ⓘ **Domodossola >**
Piazza Matteotti 24, t 0324 248 265, www.prodomodossola.it

ⓘ **Santa Maria Maggiore >>**
Piazza Risorgimento 28, t 0324 95091, www.consorzioturistico-vigezzo.com

ⓘ **Parco Nazionale della Val Grande**
t 0323 557 960, www.parcovalgrande.it

ⓘ **Malesco >>**
Via Ospedale 1, t 0324 929 901

Domodossola ✉ 28845
***Corona**, Via Marconi 8, t 0324 242 114, www.coronahotel.net (€€€). The most stylish hotel in town has very comfortable rooms, with good views from the top-floor back rooms. The restaurant serves local and international dishes.

***Motel Europa**, Via Siberia 1/a, 4km south on the N33, t 0324 481 032 (€€). Comfortable enough; all bedrooms have private bathroom and TV.

Piemonte da Sciolla, Piazza Convenzione 4, t 0324 242 633 (€€€€). Central location, and recommended for its regional dishes such as polenta with milk and poppyseeds, *cuchela* (made with potatoes and flat beans, slowly cooked in an oven), and good home-made desserts. Participates in a local gourmet event that advertises local products and cuisine – special menu available. *Closed Wed, late Aug–mid-Sept and 15 days in Jan.* They also have a few basic rooms (€).

Druogno ✉ 28853
***Boschetto**, Via Pasquaro 18, t 0324 93554, www.albergoboschetto.com (€€). Family-run hotel by the ski slopes, with summer skiing on grass, a kids' playground and a good *pizzeria*

that also serves polenta and other traditional fare.

***Stella Alpina**, Via Domodossola 13, t 0324 93593, www.stellaalpinahotel.com (€€). The most comfortable hotel in the village, but close to the road.

Santa Maria Maggiore ✉ 28857
***Miramonti**, Piazzale Diaz 3, t 0324 95013, www.almiramonti.com (€€€). You can sleep up near the station here, in the hotel proper, or preferably at the cosy chalet with flowery balconies. Dine by candlelight at the **restaurant** (€€; *closed Tues or Wed, call to check*) on local dishes and the local *digestivo*. *Closed Nov.*

***Delle Alpi**, Via Luigi Cadorna 1, opposite the entrance of the pedestrian centre, t 0324 94290 (€€). Another family-run hotel with a nice front terrace.

La Jazza, Via La Jazza 4, before the entrance to town, t 0324 94471 (€€). Has a garden and cheaper rooms without bath.

Le Colonne, Via Benefattori 7, t 0324 94893, (€€). Creative cuisine in an 18th-century building, with tables around the columns; try the foie gras. *Closed Wed out of season.*

Malesco ✉ 28854
***Alpino**, Via al Piano 61, Zornasco, t 0324 95118, www.hotelalpino.org (€€). Moderate-sized, with comfortable rooms, a pool, a pub and a gym.

⭐ **Edelweiss >>**

*****Lo Scoiattolo**, Piazza Brindicci Bonzani 7, **t** 0324 97009 (€). In an old building overlooking the square in nearby Villette, a charming village full of sundials (there are 20 painted on the walls). Rooms are basic, bathrooms are communal, but nos.9 and 12 have views. *Open April–Oct and winter on request.*

Crodo ✉ **28862**
*****Edelweiss**, Fraz. Viceno 7, **t** 0324 618 791, *www.albergoedelweiss.com* (€€). Wonderful, serene family-run hotel, with an indoor pool, Jacuzzi, gym and sauna and an excellent **restaurant** (€€€€) where you can try a range of Ossola cold meats. *Closed Wed exc in summer; also parts of Nov and Jan.*

Lake Orta

Lake Orta (the *Lacus Cusius* of the Romans) stretches a mere 13km at its longest point. But what it lacks in volume it compensates for with an exceptional dose of charm: a lake 'made to the measure-ments of man', according to Honoré de Balzac, that can be encompassed by a glance. Nietzsche, not a man to fall in love, did so on its soft green shores. He didn't get the girl, but the world got *Thus Spake Zarathustra*.

The shimmering opal waters of Lake Orta are enchanting in the moonlight, and in the centre they hold a magical isle, illuminated on summer nights to glow like a fairytale castle in the dark. On a more mundane level, Orta's villages produce bathroom taps, saxophones, coffeepots and chefs; so many come from Armeno that the second Sunday each November it holds an annual reunion of cooks and waiters and there is a small **Museo degli Alberghieri**, for people working in the hotel and catering industries.

Museo degli Alberghieri
Via dei Prati 3; open mid-June–mid-Sept Fri–Sun 10–12 and 2.30–5.30

Orta San Giulio, its Island and its Sacro Monte

Blithe on its own garden peninsula, the lake's 'capital', Orta San Giulio, is a fetching little town of old houses and pretty churches. Lanes too narrow for cars all lead into charming, convivial lakeside **Piazza Motta**, Orta's 'drawing room' and a delightful place to linger, with its centrepiece the bijou **Palazzotto** (1582), once seat of the lake authorities and now hosting exhibitions. A lovely walk, the **Lungolago**, starts at the bottom of Via Motta, following the villas and gardens of the shore to Via Panoramica by the tourist office.

Orta looks out to the mystical little **Isola San Giulio**; when the lake is calm and misty, it often seems to float dreamily between the water and sky. Appropriately it was inhabited by dragons – at least before 390, when Giulio, a Greek preacher and church founder, showed up and asked to be rowed to the island. When the terrified locals refused, Giulio spread his cloak and windsurfed across. He sent the dragons packing, then built the precursor to the island's basilica by yoking a team of wolves to his cart – a feat good enough to make him the patron saint of builders. His wolf-assisted **Basilica** was rebuilt for the first time in *c.* 1000. The

Isola San Giulio
*island open to visitors in summer 9–6; winter 9–12 and 2–5; **t** 333 6050 288 for info*

Basilica
t 0322 90156; open daily 9.30–12.15 and 2–6.45, till 5.45 in winter; Mon closed until 11

Getting to and around Lake Orta

The lakeside resorts of Orta San Giulio, Pettenasco and Omegna are all easily reached from Turin on **trains** that are heading north to Domodossola.

Orta is also easy to reach from Lake Maggiore: **buses** run from Stresa to Orta, from Arona to Orta via Borgomanero, and from Verbania to Omegna (**t** 0321 391 601, *www.comazzibus.com*).

Navigazione Lago d'Orta, **t** 0322 844 862, provides a **boat** service between the lake's ports and to Isola San Giulio from Orta's Piazza Motta every 15–20 minutes; the alternative is to take a **taxi-boat**, or hire your own boat and row yourself.

---

startling black marble **pulpit** dates from this period, showing Giulio in relief, wearily leaning on his sword after chasing the dragons, along with symbols of the Evangelists – the Lion of St Mark looks like a sphinx grinning over a slice of *pizza al taglio* – while a griffin and crocodile fight it out in the corner. There are 15th-century frescoes by Gaudenzio Ferrari and his school (note the *Story of San Giulio* in the left aisle) and a marble sarcophagus belonging to the Lombard Duke Meinulphus, who had betrayed the island to the Franks and was beheaded by King Agilulf; his decapitated skeleton was duly found inside in 1697. The vertebrae from Giulio's dragons are no longer visible, but you can see what's left of the saint in a glass casket. A few villas and San Giulio's Bendictine convent occupies most of the island – the nuns specialize in tapestry restoration, while the abbess is behind the admonishments to spiritual reflection that encircle the island's

Festival Cusiano
www.amicimusica cocito.it

'Way of Silence'. The isle's Villa Tallone hosts the **Festival Cusiano** in June each year, when groups in costume play ancient music.

Sacro Monte
t 0322 911 960; www. sacromonteorta.it; park always open, chapels open daily summer 9–6.30; winter 9–4.30

Orta is framed by sacred places; a road winds up the promontory behind town to its chapel-covered acropolis or **Sacro Monte**. Begun in 1591 and dedicated to Italy's patron, St Francis, this is a masterpiece of the genre (*see* box, below): 21 slate-roofed chapels spiral to the top of the hill; in each, life-sized statues in 17th-century costume enact an important event in Francis' life – 376

12 Piedmont | Lake Orta

Sacro Monti, or Little Theatres for the Soul

During a visit to the Holy Land, Caimi, a Franciscan friar, was so moved that he was inspired to build an ideal holy city on the hill, a *Sacro Monte*, reproducing Biblical sites for the folks back home. His dream inspired Gaudenzio Ferrari who, calling upon the Franciscan tradition of Christmas cribs and medieval passion plays, designed a series of chapels, each containing life-size statues with frescoed backdrops – the precursor of those dioramas you see in natural history museums or Disneyland. Each chapel is numbered, starting with Adam and Eve (with God the Father suspended overhead in a basket of clouds, like Oz about to float away from the Emerald City).

With the advent of the Counter-Reformation and its desire to make the faith more tangible, immediate and emotive, the Sacro Monte caught the fancy of the pope's grand vizier, Carlo Borromeo, who saw it as a chance to promote the cults of Mary, the Rosary and the saints – the very aspects of Catholicism most beleaguered by the Protestants. His enthusiasm was tempered, however, by the insistence that the Church maintain strict control over every aspect of the work, to keep even the slightest tinge of heresy from infecting the desired response to each scene; Varallo's Sacro Monte, for instance, had to be completely reworked to toe the line.

figures and 900 frescoes in all, contributed by various artists over two centuries. The setting is delicious, with views over Isola San Giulio, enjoyed by a pleasant bar and restaurant. While here, spare a thought for shy, awkward Nietzsche who, beguiled by the nightingales of Sacro Monte, fell head over heels for Lou Salomé, his Russian poet travelling companion. He boldly advanced; she, surprised, retreated. He never tried love again.

Around Lake Orta

It doesn't take long to drive around the 'grey pearl in a green casket', as Balzac called Lake Orta, and there's certainly no reason to hurry. At nearby **Legro** you can have a look at the 24 murals painted by European artists, based on films shot on the lake (including King Vidor's *Farewell to Arms*). Just north of Orta town, **Pettenasco** is a perfect place to meditate (it hosts yoga courses – *see www.ompio.org*). It has one of several locations of the Ecomuseo Cusius dedicated to Orta's industries, this one dedicated to wood turning .

Ecomuseo Cusius
t 0323 819 622, www.lagodorta.net/eco museo; open Tues–Sun 9–12.30 and 2–6

Villas and vantage points are scattered in the hills above, along with **Armeno**, the town of chefs, from where you can continue to Mottarone (*see* p.305). **Miasino** has a beautiful Baroque church of **San Rocco**. **Ameno**, further south, has a fine Romanesque church with frescoes. The painter Antonio Calderara (1903–78) lived in a 17th-century villa in nearby **Vacciago**, and left his collection of art from the 1950s and '60s in the **Collezione Calderara**. But his own paintings are the most memorable: landscapes which capture Orta better than any photograph. South of Ameno, two paths marked with Stations of the Cross lead up Monte Mesma (nature reserve) to its enchanting Franciscan **Convento Monte Mesma**, built in 1619.

Collezione Calderara
t 0322 998 192, www. fondazionecalderara.it; open mid-May–mid-Oct Tues–Sun 10–12 and 3–6; at other times ring t 0273 262 001

At the south end of Orta, **Gozzano** is overlooked by the 82ft **Torre di Buccione** (a 15-minute walk through a chestnut wood, starting from the Miasino road), all the remains of a once-extensive citadel that defended the entire lake, built by the Romans in the 4th century and rebuilt in the 11th; its bells were loud enough to warn all the lake communities in times of danger. Gozzano's **Villa Junker** has a fine garden and there are two tiny beaches. And one of Italy's top restaurants, Al Sorriso, is close by.

Convento Monte Mesma
t 0322 998 108; open summer Tues, Thurs and Sun 3–5; winter Sun 3–4.30; from May 2007 the façade and cloisters are being refurbished – call to check

A bit up from Gozzano, on Orta's west shore, the church of the **Madonna di Luzzara** has 15th–16th-century frescoes. While here, you can learn about your bathroom tap, in **San Maurizio d'Opaglio**, where the Museo del Rubinetto is devoted to nothing else. Behind San Maurizio, on a majestic granite outcrop, the 18th-century Santuario della Madonna del Sasso has grand views as far as Liguria's Appenines and the western Alps, a dome frescoed with trompe l'œil windows and angels, and a beautiful 16th-century *Pietà* on the altar, by Fermo Stella.

Museo del Rubinetto
t 0323 89622; open mid-June–mid-Sept Fri–Sun 2.30–7; other times by appointment

Santuario della Madonna del Sasso
t 0322 981 177

Northernmost **Omegna** (Roman *Vomenia*) is the birthplace of Italian fablist Gianni Rodari; it's also where the likes of Alessi, Bialetti and Lagostina make pots and pans, coffeepots and pressure cookers, all subject of a special museum of art and industry and shop, **Forum Omegna**. The kids may like a look in at the nearby **Parco della Fantasia**, dedicated to Rodari's imagination. Omegna's centre is pleasant, especially where Piazza del Municipio gives onto a bridge spanning Orta's 'drain', the **Nigoglia** – the only river in Italy to flow towards the Alps.

From Omegna, a road curls in ringlets through chestnut forests to **Quarna Sotto**, where wind instruments have been big business for over 150 years; you can learn how they make clarinets, bassoons, oboes, saxophones, flutes and horns in the **Museo Etnografico e dello Strumento Musicale a Fiato**. Further up, **Quarna Sopra** has spectacular views and a summer music festival.

A second valley radiating from Omegna, the **Valstrona**, is less spectacular and the road narrow and steep, but **Forno** is a fine little place where dogs sleep in the street; it has a **Raccolta d'Arte Sacra** in the parish church with an interesting collection of *ex votos* sent by immigrants; **Campello Monti**, the last hamlet, is a good place to walk off too many tortellini.

Forum Omegna
Parco Maulini 1, t 0323 866 141, www. forumomegna.org; open Tues–Sat 9–12.30 and 2.30–6, Sun 3–6.30; adm for guided tours, otherwise free

Museo Etnografico e dello Strumento Musicale a Fiato
Via Roma, t 0323 826 368; open mid-June– mid-Sept Tues–Sun 10–12 and 4–6; other months by request; adm

Raccolta d'Arte Sacra
t 0323 885 101; open all year by request

12
Piedmont | Lake Orta

Festivals around Lake Orta

Festa di San Vito is held during the last week of August. Omegna's patron saint is fêted with a market and evening concerts by Italian pop stars, and culminates in a religious procession and blessing of the lake (*Sat*), antique car and motorcycle racing and fireworks (*Sun*).

Sports and Activities around Lake Orta

For **sailing**, try Circolo Vela Orta, at Imolo hamlet, t 0322 905 672, *www. circolovelaorta.it*. Beaches suitable for children are Lido di Buccione (Gozzano), and in Omegna and Pella.

Where to Stay and Eat around Lake Orta

ⓘ **Orta San Giulio >**
Via Panoramica, t 0322 905 614

★ **Villa Crespi >**

Orta San Giulio ✉ 28016

★★★★**Villa Crespi**, Via G. Fava 18, t 0322 911 902, *www.lagodortahotels.com* (€€€€€). A Moorish folly built in 1880 by a cotton magnate, painstakingly restored. All rooms have canopied beds, marble baths and Jacuzzis, and the hotel also has a sauna, steam bath and fitness area. The elegant **restaurant** (€€€€) is equalled by the ravishing dishes prepared by top chef Antonino Cannavacciuolo, a sophisticated mix of Mediterranean and Alpine flavours. *Closed Tues, Wed lunch, Jan and Feb.*

★★★★**San Rocco**, Via Gippini 11, t 0322 911 977, *www.hotelsanrocco.it* (€€€€€). Down in Orta's historic centre, San Rocco is a former 17th-century monastery with a pretty garden and heated outdoor pool right on the water, and one of the town's best **restaurants**, which has three Michelin stars. In August it hosts a series of jazz and classical music concerts.

★★★**La Bussola**, Via Panoramica 24, t 0322 911 913, *www.orta.net/bussola* (€€€). Set back on a quiet hill, with a magnificent panorama over the lake; pretty garden with a pool and a good **restaurant**. *Closed Nov. Half board only during weekends and in summer.*

★★★**Orta**, Piazza Motta 1, t 0322 90253, *www.hotelorta.it* (€€€). Since 1864,

(i) **Omegna**
Piazza XXIV Aprile 17,
t 0323 867 235, www.
proloco.omegna.vb.it

(★) **Al Sorriso >>**

(✪) **Varallo and
Sacro Monte**

brimming over with old-fashioned Italian character, and run by the same family for over a century, with big rooms and a charming dining terrace.
***La Contrada dei Monti**, Via Contrada dei Monti 10, **t** 0322 905 114, *www.orta.net/lacontradadeimonti* (€€€). Charming hotel in Orta's centre. Rooms are individually furnished and overlook quiet inner courtyards or the side streets of the centre.
***Leon d'Oro**, Piazza Motta 42, **t** 0322 911 991, *www.orta.net/leondoro* (€€€€–€€€). In 1882, Nietzsche and Lou Salomé spent their love-troubled week here, and to this day the lake terrace and bar are especially amenable to such breaks from philosophy. Rooms are small but immaculate and recently renovated; *à la carte* **restaurant** (€€€). *Closed Jan.*
***Santa Caterina**, Via Marconi 10, **t** 0322 915 865, *www.orta.net/s.caterina* (€€€–€€). A peaceful hotel of character overlooking the town. Family rooms available.
****Piccolo Hotel Olina**, Via Olina 40, **t** 0322 532 656, *www.orta.net/olina* (€€). Simple rooms and an elegant **restaurant** (€€€) offering specialities such as lake fish, and meat cooked in stone pots. *Closed Wed. Book.*

Pettenasco ✉ 28028
****L'Approdo**, Corso Roma 80, **t** 0323 89346, *www.lagodortahotels.com* (€€€€). Family-friendly, with a big garden on the lake and all mod cons – heated pool, tennis, sauna, private mooring and boats.
***Giardinetto**, Via Provinciale 1, **t** 0323 89118, *www.charmerelax.it* (€€€€). A member of the Charme and Relax group, a friendly family hotel and apartments, with pool, private beach and water sports, and an excellent **restaurant** (€€€€) serving

locally cured meats, perch fillets on fresh salad, and guinea-fowl pasta. *Open Easter–end Oct.*

Soriso (above Gozzano) ✉ 28024
***Al Sorriso**, Via Roma 18, **t** 0322 983 228, *www.alsorriso.com* (€€€€). Set among trees overlooking the lake, charming rooms and Michelin three-star **restaurant** to die for. Self-taught Luisa Valazza is one of the very best chefs in Italy and her elegant dining room has become an international gourmet shrine for its lacquered guinea fowl with rhododendron honey. Around €130 a head or more. *Closed Mon, Tues, Jan and Aug.*

Borgomanero ✉ 28021
Pinocchio, Via Matteotti 147, **t** 0322 82273, *www.ristorantepinocchio.it* (€€€€). Elegant family-run restaurant with a garden terrace, serving Piedmontese dishes with flair and excellent value for money. Children's menu available. Booking advisable. *Closed Mon, and Tues lunch.*

Omegna and Around ✉ 28026
****Vittoria**, Via Zanoia 37, **t** 0323 62237, *www.alberghilagodorta.it* (€€). Family-run: ten tidy rooms, all with bath and TV, and a reasonably priced **restaurant** (*closed Sat*).
****Belvedere**, Via Belvedere 8, Quarna Sopra, 7km up a winding road from Omegna, **t** 0323 826 198 (€€). Simple rooms but lives up to its name with enchanting bird's-eye views over Orta; also a garden solarium.
***Leone**, Via IV Novembre 9, Forno di Valstrona, **t** 0323 885 112, *www.albergo delleone.it* (€). Run by the same family for over 150 years, peaceful, cute and cosy. The **restaurant** (€€€) serves typical local dishes. *No credit cards. Closed Tues, Wed and Nov–April.*

West of Lake Orta: Varallo and Biella

The Valsesia, Varallo and the Original Sacro Monte

Before irrigating Vercelli's rice paddies, the Sesia froths and tumbles to the delight of white-water rafters as it descends through the **Valsesia**, the 'greenest valley in Italy'. The lower valley, however, is all business, mostly wool and textiles; the landmark at

Getting around West of Lake Orta

The main rail and **road** approach to the Valsesia is from Novara (if coming from Turin, change at Romagnano); **trains** go as far as Varallo, where you can catch a **bus** up to Alagna (*www.atlvalsesiavercelli.it*). Vercelli, Novara and Turin have trains to Biella (1 hour), a base for **buses** into the Alpine valleys and to Oropa (departing from the train station, t 015 840 8117, *www.atl.biella.it*).

Borgosesia, the biggest town, is a statue of Mary and her lambs in a roundabout.

The steep wooded slopes begin to get dramatic at **Varallo**, a friendly town which wears its patina of age well. Varallo has a good **Pinacoteca**, with works by the Vercelli school, sharing space with the Natural History Museum in the **Palace of Museums**. In the centre, the church of **San Gaudenzio**, artistically piled on top of a stair, houses a polyptych showing the Madonna dressed in local lace, by Gaudenzio Ferrari, a native of the Valsesia. His statue stands in front of the convent church of **Santa Maria delle Grazie**, which has an entire magnificent wall of his work, the *21 Scenes from the Life of Christ* (1513); even at that late date, note how some elements, such as the Roman armour, are raised – a frequent feature of Gothic art.

Palace of Museums
t 0163 51424; open
Tues–Fri 10.30–12.30
and 2.30–6; adm

Santa Maria delle Grazie
t 0163 51112;
closed 12–3

Sacro Monte
t 0163 51131, www.
santuari.it/varallo;
open Mon–Sun 8.30–12
and 2–6; reached by
road or funivia(open
summer 9–6;
winter 9–7); adm

Sacro Monte is Varallo's five-star attraction. There are dozens of other *Sacri Monti*; many, like this one, in beautiful settings, but this is the original, founded in 1491 by the Blessed Bernardo Caimi (*see* box, p.319). Sacro Monte's 50 chapels each contain a 3-d Biblical scene with 800 life-sized wood and terracotta statues with real hair (the oldest by Gaudenzio Ferrari) and 4,000 painted figures in the background, in a sincere if slightly nutty extravaganza. The chapels featuring Christ's Passion are clustered, city-like, in the **Piazza del Tempio**: this includes the oldest one, San Sepolcro (no. 43), based on Caimi's memory of Christ's tomb; bizarrely Caimi's own skull grins from the doorway. The **Basilica** itself provides the final flourish with a mass of exploding gilded Baroque, the choir featuring 145 sculpted figures and 500 frescoed children in heaven's vortex, while the crypt (the *scurolo*, or 'dark place') is covered in heart-rending tributes to dead children.

Lace museum
Via Rizetti 25, t 0163
55124; open by request
during the opening
hours of the
municipal offices

North of Varallo, the **Val Mastallone**, of deep ravines and Alpine scenery, was settled, like much of the Valsesia, by the Walser (*see* p.316). Lace-making is an old tradition: **Fobello** has a small lace museum in its town hall; **Rimella** has a lovely nucleus of traditional wood and stone houses at San Gottardo and the **Museo G.B. Filippa**, a collection of curiosities assembled by a local while fighting in the Napoleonic wars.

Museo G.B. Filippa
t 0163 55203; open
July–Aug Sat 3–6, Sun
10–12.30 and 3–6, or
by request

In the main **Val Grande**, **Riva Valdobbia** enjoys views of mighty Monte Rosa and a church with exterior frescoes of the *Last Judgement* and a giant *St Christopher* (1597). A number of trails begin here, including one over the **Colle Valdobbia** to Aosta's Val di

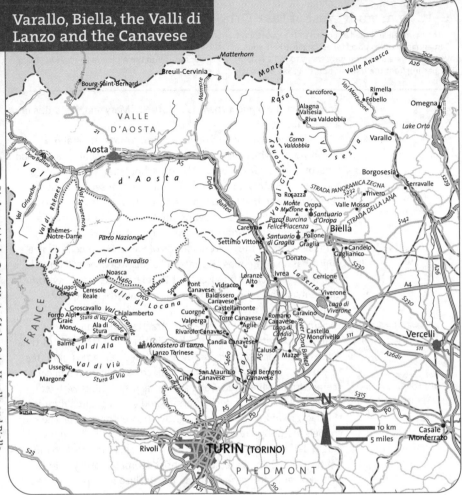

Gressoney. **Alagna**, the last town in the valley, has the best preserved Walser hamlets in Italy, in a truly beautiful setting, famous in winter for its off-piste skiing and snowboarding. In charming **Pedemonte**, 3km from Alagna, one of their houses built in 1628 is now an excellent **Walser Museum**. Don't miss Alagna's parish church with its intricate wood altar and frescoes.

Walser Museum
t 0163 922 998,
www.alagnacultura.it;
open Sept–June Sat, Sun
and hols 2–6; July daily
2–6, Sat and Sun also
10–12; Aug daily 10–12
and 2–6; adm

Biella: City of Cashmere

Biella was for centuries a fief of Vercelli's powerful bishop. In the 19th century, so many mills (*lanifici*) were built along the river Cervo that it was nicknamed 'Italy's Manchester'. These mills still supply the big design houses in Milan and Florence, at least with cashmere (which requires a highly skilled labour force), although silk and, increasingly, wool, have moved to low-wage countries in

Eastern Europe and Asia. A new industrial research centre designed by Gae Aulenti, who is Biella's most famous resident, hopes to invent techniques that will keep the city on the map.

Social life in **Biella Piano** is focused along pretty cobbled **Via Italia**. Along this is Piazza Duomo with a little **baptistry**, built in the late 10th century out of Roman blocks, with a Roman relief over the door (*to visit, enquire in the cathedral*). The campanile is from the same period, while the adjacent **Cattedrale di Santo Stefano** was begun in 1402 and has a 15th-century choir inlaid with scenes of fruit trees and labourers. To the left of the altar, by the old entrance, a *Sunday Christ* fresco (*c.*1470) shows Jesus surreally attacked by hoes, hammers, rakes, scissors and other tools – a reminder of what it was forbidden to take up on the Sabbath day. Once popular throughout Europe, the image was prohibited by the Council of Trent; this is one of the few to survive.

Nearby, in Via G. Ferrero, the elegant triple-naved basilica of **San Sebastiano** (1504) was built by Sebastiano Ferrero, a local who ran the finances of Duke Ludovico in Milan and worked on building Leonardo's canals. A beautifully preserved Renaissance interior hides behind a 19th-century façade, housing works by the Vercelli school – the best is Bernardino Lanino's *Assumption* (1543) in the right nave – and a unique inlaid choir embedded with 12th-century enamels from Limoge. Ferrero's descendants, the Marquises Lamarmora, produced four brothers who held important posts in the Risorgimento; the wife of prime minister Alfonso Lamarmora has a striking Victorian tomb in the right nave. The cloister houses the **Museo del Territorio**, containing everything from an unwrapped mummy and artefacts of local industries to art by Bernardino Lanino, Chagall, Magritte, Mirò, Yves Tanguy, and more.

Atmospheric, aristocratic upper **Biella Piazzo**, enjoying fine views over the city, was founded in 1160 by the Bishop of Vercelli; to encourage other swells to move up with him he granted Piazzo the right to administer justice, hold a market and slaughter animals. Since 1885, it has been linked to Piano by a jaunty little **funicular**. Follow the porticoes into handsome main Piazza Cisterna to Piazzo's grandest residence, the 17th-century **Palazzo Ferrero Lamarmora**, built by the descendants of Sebastiano Ferro. The palace has a charming frescoed and stuccoed interior; one room shows all the family castles and a view of Biella *c.* 1650.

North of the centre, by the river, the old Lanificio Trombetto found a new use in 1994 as the **Fondazione M. Pistoletto**, a space for exhibitions and shows. Nearby at the restaurant of the **Menabrea Brewery**, you can also taste some of the world's best lager, brewed here since 1846. Made in small quantities, it's hard to find outside Biella; there is also a little museum with photos, old advertising and the brewery's many awards.

Museo del Territorio
t 015 252 9345,
www.museodelterri
torio.biella.it; open Tues
10–1, Wed 11–3, Thurs
3–7, Fri 3–10, Sat and
Sun 10–12 and 3–7

Funicular
open daily 7am–
midnight, Fri and Sat till
2am; pay at the top

Palazzo Ferrero Lamarmora
t 015 352 533; open for
exhibitions or by
appointment

Fondazione M. Pistoletto
Via Serralunga 27,
t 015 28400, www.
cittadellarte.it; open
Dec–May Sat and Sun
11–8; times still being
decided for other
months – ring to check

Menabrea Brewery
Via Ramella
Germanin 4, t 015 252
2320, www.birramena
brea.com; closed Sun,
and Mon otherwise
open Tues–Fri 7pm–
1am, Sat 7pm–2am

12

Piedmont | Lake Orta: West of Lake Orta: Varallo and Biella

Around Biella and the Santuario di Oropa

On the map, the environs of Biella look like a plate of spaghetti, all squiggly valley roads between the mountains, where signs often let the bewildered motorist down. More than 50 factory outlets, most selling cashmere, are in the vicinity: the very keen can find most of them along the **Strada della Lana** from Biella to Valle Mosso and Borgosesia. Others come to jump: Exploring Bungee, at the Ponte Colossous, one of the world's highest jumps (500ft), is just north of Valle Mosso at **Veglio**; there's also an **Adventure Park** in the deeply wooded valley. Five kilometres south of Biella, there's a stately 16th-century castle at **Gaglianico**, and 5km southeast, at **Candelo**, you can visit a perfectly preserved 14th-century walled **Ricetto** ('shelter'), where the inhabitants of Candelo would store their farm produce and wine and take refuge in times of danger.

Just northwest of Biella, the lovely **Parco Burcina Felice Piacenza**, at **Pollone**, is famous for its rhododendrons and azaleas, which burst into a dazzling pageant of colour in May. The park was founded in 1850 by a wool magnate, Giovanni Piacenza, who made frequent trips to England, but the current result is the work of his son Felice, who donated it to the city of Biella in 1935. North of here, in a pretty mountain hollow, is the **Santuario di Oropa**, the oldest and most venerated shrine in Piedmont and the biggest Marian shrine in the Alps. Legend has it that Oropa was founded in the 4th century by St Eusebius, Bishop of Vercelli, when he took refuge here from the persecutions, with a black *Madonna and Child* carved by St Luke that he brought back from Jerusalem (never mind that art historians say it's 12th century) and which now holds pride of place in the **Basilica Antica** (rebuilt in 1600). The sanctuary also has a huge **New Basilica** with an altar topped by a *cibreo* by Giò Ponti, three vast quadrangles, restaurants, cafés and scores of *ex votos* attesting to the powers of the *Vergine Bruna*. The most precious, as well as historical items, are in the **Museo dei Tesori**, which also includes the Savoy royal apartments. Below the sanctuary there's a **Sacro Monte** with 19 chapels, 12 dedicated to the life of Mary (1620–1720), seven to Oropa itself. A *funivia* ascends 7,661ft **Monte Mucrone**, popular for hiking in summer and skiing in winter. Near the lower station is the **Oropa Botanical Garden**.

The sanctuary road continues north into the **Oasi Zegna**, a nature reserve that is crisscrossed by the **Strada Panoramica Zegna** (aka the SS232), which winds east from Rosazza to Trivero. The Oasi has spectacular views of Monte Rosa. Among entomologists, it's famous as the home of a rare golden beetle (*Caravus olympiae sella*). Some paths trace the routes of a famously bad monk, heretic and *bandito*, Fra Dolcino, who molested passers-by here in 1306.

West of Biella, roads twist up to another popular shrine, the Baroque **Santuario di Graglia**, dedicated to Our Lady of Loreto, with

---

Strada della Lana
Wool Road, www. docbi.it/stradalana.htm

Adventure Park
www.parco avventura.it ,visit www.bungee.it

Ricetto
always visitable, t 015 253 4118

Parco Burcina Felice Piacenza
t 015 256 3007, www. parcoburcina.piemonte. it; open daily 8.30–dusk; guided tours April–June

Santuario di Oropa
t 015 255 51200, www. santuariodioropa.it; open July–Aug Tues–Sun 10–12.30 and 2.30–5.30; Sept–June Sat and Sun 10–12.30 and 2.30–5.30

Funivia
t 015 245 5929

Oasi Zegna
www.oasizegna.com

Santuario di Graglia
open May–Sept daily 7–10pm; Oct–April daily 9–6

four Sacro Monte chapels – a bit of a comedown for the founder, who planned to build a hundred chapels, at the peak of Piedmont's *Sacro Monte* mania. A sign marks the spot of the 'Hendecasyllabic echo' over the Valle Elvo – any eleven syllables you say here will be perfectly repeated.

Southwest, at **Donato**, begins a district of steep wooded moranic ridges called **La Serra** stretching towards Ivrea. Oaks, chestnuts, birch and vines grow here in Arcadian harmony, dotted with unspoiled villages. At **Vermogno**, however, you can visit one of the strangest landscapes in Piedmont – the **Riserva Naturale della Bessa**, 10 square kilometres of stones, dug up between the 2nd and 1st centuries BC by thousands of Ictimuli Celts for their Roman masters, in one of the world's biggest open-cast gold mines; the highest pile is over 70ft. **Cerrione**, just south, is topped by a 13th-century castle, a rendezvous for the Resistance, bombed by the Nazis and now a ruin.

Enoteca della Serra
t 0161 98501; open April–Sept Thurs 3–7, Fri–Sun 9.30–12 and 3–7; Oct–6 Jan and mid-Feb–Mar Fri, Sat and Sun 9.30–12 and 3–6.30; closed 7 Jan–mid-Feb

At the end of La Serra lies the **Lago di Viverone**, an unglamorous but relaxing place to camp, swim or mess about on a boat. The **Castello di Roppolo** enjoys a lovely setting over the lake and houses the Enoteca della Serra , which emphasizes the lesser-known wines from eastern Piedmont. It has a restaurant and a ghost: Bernardo Valperga di Mazzè, who in 1459 was walled up alive by the castle owner, Ludovico Valperga, his brother in arms but rival in love; his armed skeleton was found in the 19th century.

ⓘ **Alagna >>**
Piazza Grober 1, t 0163 922 988 (Oct and hols open weekends and hols only)

ⓘ **Varallo >**
Corso Roma 38, t 0163 564 404, www. atlvalsesiavercelli.it

★ **Monte Rosa >**

ⓘ **Biella >>**
Piazza V. Veneto 3, t 015 351 128, www. atl.biella.it

Where to Stay and Eat West of Lake Orta

Varallo ✉ 13019

***Vecchio Albergo Sacro Monte**, Sacro Monte 14, t 0163 542 545, www. laproxima.it/albergo-smonte (€€). Built in 1594 to house artists, it has pretty rooms, lovely views, a good **restaurant** (€€). Closed Nov–Feb and Mon.

Casa del Pellegrino, Sacro Monte, t 0163 564 458 (€€). Built around the chapel of the Last Supper; more basic.

*Monte Rosa, Via Regaldi 4, t 0163 51100, www.albergomonterosa.it (€€). A wonderful little family-run hotel. Large old-fashioned rooms, with balconies and views. No credit cards. Pets admitted.

Il Ghiottone, Loc. Chiesa 2, Vocca (7km up the N299), t 0163 560 911 (€€€€). Warm, welcoming restaurant decorated with local art, featuring trout from the Sesia. Eves only, but lunch Sat, Sun and Aug; closed Wed.

Alagna ✉ 13021

***Monte Rosa**, Piazza Alberghi 2, t 0163 923 209, www.hotelmonterosa-alagna.it (€€€). Refurbished hotel of 1850 with modern, cosy rooms and a good **restaurant**. Closed mid-May to mid-June, and Oct–mid-Nov.

***Pension Genzianella**, Fraz. Centro 33, t 0163 923 205, www.pensione genzianella.com (€€€). Modern, friendly, and near the cableway.

***Mirella**, Fraz. Bonda, t 0163 922 965 (€€€–€€). Delightful residence over a cake shop. Each room is equipped with a kitchenette.

Carcoforo ✉ 13026

Scoiattolo, Via Casa del Ponte 3/b, t 0163 95612 (€€€€). Elegant restaur-ant hidden up the Alto Val Sesia in a tiny Walser hamlet. Booking advisable. Closed Mon and Tues except in Aug.

Biella ✉ 13900

****Augustus**, Via Italia 54, t 015 27554, www.augustus.it (€€€). A no-

nonsense business hotel with comfortable rooms; also offers tours of the area and cashmere shops.

****Astoria**, Viale Roma 9, **t** 015 402 750, *www.astoriabiella.com* (€€). Biella's grandest hotel specializes in 'sober elegance'; also very good value.

***Europa**, Viale Trossi 7/d, **t** 015 849 7120, *www.hoteleuropa-bi.com* (€€). Big bright rooms near the train station; breakfast and parking included in the price.

La Taverna del Ricetto, inside the Ricetto, Via Rua, Candelo, 5km east of Biella, **t** 015 253 6066, *www.lataverna delricetto.it* (€€€€). In the very heart of a medieval village, traditional cuisine from Biella and surroundings. Musical evenings on Fridays (*aperitivo* followed by a one-hour concert, then dinner). *Closed Mon and Tues lunch.*

Il Patio, Via Oremo 14, Pollone, **t** 015 61568 (€€€€). Elegant restaurant serving elegant cuisine, including some unusual local dishes. *Closed Mon, Tues, 15 days in Jan and Aug.*

Il Baracca, Via Sant'Eusebio 12, **t** 015 21941 (€€). In an 18th-century *palazzo*, the oldest place to dine in Biella, serving treats like *bagna cauda*, *salame della duja*, rice dishes and *bolliti misti*. *Booking advisable.* No credit cards. *Closed Sat and Sun.*

Oropa ✉ 13813

Santuario di Oropa, **t** 015 2555 1200, *www.santuariodioropa.com* (€€–€). You don't have to be a pilgrim to stay in the big quadrangles; 350 rooms ranging from the monastic to suites, furnished with antiques.

Magnano ✉ 13887

***Le Betulle**, Regione Valcarozza 2, by the Golf Club Biella, **t** 015 679 151, *www.golfhotelbetulle.it* (€€€). Comfortable rooms in a woodland setting, plus an award-winning 18-hole course.

North of Turin: Valli di Lanzo and the Canavese

As the really big Alps beckon just up the road in Aosta, these pretty valleys tend to be overlooked. The upper Lanzo valleys, however, have been popular weekend escape hatches for the Torinese for over a century, while the Canavese, an attractive region of lakes, rocky outcrops and amphitheatres sculpted by glaciers, has some of the gourmet prestige of Le Langhe, but at much kinder prices. Castles crown nearly every hill; in pre-telegraph days, they say the Savoys could send a message from Chambéry to Turin in two hours, signalling with fires or flags from the towers.

The Valli di Lanzo

The Lanzo valleys first began to attract wealthy tourists from Turin in the 1890s, and here and there you can see their summer Liberty-style villas. Faster roads and cars have since made the lower valley a bedroom suburb of Turin. Beyond Turin's airport at Caselle, **San Maurizio Canavese** is an industrial town, with a National Monument in its 11th-century cemetery church, full of 16th-century frescoes. **Ciriè** has an attractive *centro storico* and **cathedral**, built in the 14th century with a gabled portal decorated with terracotta reliefs; inside there's a polyptych by Giuseppe Giovenone, a 13th-century Byzantine crucifix, and an oval altarpiece of the *Madonna del Popolo* by Defendente Ferrari. Just north of town, towards San

Getting North of Turin

Trains on a regional line head north from the Dora staton in Turin into the Valli di Lanzo, as far as Ceres, and to Cuorgné. Main FS trains from Turin to Aosta stop at Ivrea, where you pick up **buses** for the Canavese (*www.sadem.it* and *www.comune.torino.it/gtt*).

Carlo, there's an 11th-century church, **Santa Maria di Spinerano**, with good 15th-century frescoes.

Lanzo Torinese has a pretty medieval core, and is a base for excursions into the upper valleys. Its most famous monument is the **Ponte del Diavolo** (1378), spanning the River Stura with its soaring single arch; as with many startling medieval bridges the architect was said to be the devil himself. The gate in the middle was added in 1564, in case plague broke out on the other side of the river. Close by, note the 'Giant's Kettles' left by passing glaciers. Six kilometres north, at Monastero, the **Santuario di Sant'Ignazio** (1725) is one of Vittone's simpler models, but enjoys a lovely setting.

The southernmost of the Lanzo's three valleys, the **Val di Viù**, is narrow and windy, and popular with weekend ramblers. Huge meadows open up at **Usseglio**, where the economy once depended on cobalt mining and the old church has a Roman altar to Heracles embedded in its façade.

The railway from Turin peters out at **Ceres**, a summer resort at the fork of two pretty valleys; its little **Museo delle Genti delle Valli di Lanzo** has displays on local people and customs, and on the nails they used to forge and sell all across Italy. Up the steep wooded **Val di Ala**, **Ala di Stura** is the main town, not far from **Mondrone**, where a short path leads to a splendid gorge, resounding with the rushing waters of the Stura; there's also a lovely waterfall by the small ski resort of **Balme**, at the top of the valley. The wider and greener **Val Grande** has curious mushroom-shaped rocks near **Chialamberto** and a 135ft monolith, the Bec Ceresin, wider at the top than at the bottom, at **Groscavallo**. The last village, **Forno Alpi Graie**, is a good base for mountain walks.

Museo delle Genti delle Valli di Lanzo
t 333 482 5771; open Nov–Mar 1st and 3rd Sun of the month 3–6 by appointment; adm

North of Turin: the Canavese

In the free-for-all 9th century, the Canavese was the Marquisate of Ivrea, whose masters would be king of Italy. The first was Berenguer II, a nasty piece of work who kidnapped Adelaide, the widow of the previous king; he was crowned in 950, but had to pay homage to Holy Roman Emperor Otto I, who rescued and married Adelaide, then captured Berenguer, leaving him to die in a German prison. The Canavese prefer Arduino, who had some big-time enemies: chief among them Warmondo, the powerful bishop of Ivrea, who had two important allies, the Holy Roman Emperor Otto III, and Otto's tutor, Gerbert of Aurillac, a scholar and alumnus of the Muslim schools of Toledo, who became Pope Sylvester II, and who was so clever the Romans thought he was a wizard. In 1002, at the death of Otto III, the nobles who had hated the emperor's pro-clerical policy crowned Arduino king of Italy in Pavia, in spite of Sylvester's condemnation, striking a blow for secular independence.

If you're in a hurry, the A5 from Turin will take you to Ivrea in half an hour; if you're not, take the Volpiano exit for **San Benigno Canavese**, where four 17th-century sundials on Via Miaglia keep, surprisingly, French, Italian, canonical and Babylonian time. San Benigno's once wealthy **Abbazia di Fruttaria** was founded in 1003 by Arduino's family; when the king abdicated in 1014 he became a monk here, and died the following year 'in the odour of sanctity'. In 1749, the abbey was sumptuously rebuilt by Bernardo Vittone, but archaeologists have had a dig under the floor, bringing to light the foundations of the original abbey and its lively mosaic floors.

To the northeast, the pretty **Lake of Candia** is the centre of a nature reserve, guarded by a 14th-century castle and surrounded by vineyards producing the Canavese's finest wines, white Erbaluce and sweet Passito di Caluso. Hire a rowing boat at the **Ristorante Lido**, and visit the **Castello di Mazzè** set at a height between the lake and the Dora Baltea river. In 175 BC, the Romans built a fort here, and in 1316, when the emperor granted the lands to the Counts of Valperga, descendants of Arduino, they built the 'little castle' which stands next to a much larger one, rebuilt in 1840. The interiors are lavish and, in a string of underground chambers made up of a Celtic temple, Roman cisterns and medieval prisons, there's a **museum of torture** with the ingenious instruments used by the Spanish Inquisition and elsewhere (sponsored by Amnesty International). You can also visit the **Bosco Parco**, a half-wild private reserve running down to the river, or stay like a count in the suite.

The Counts of Valperga had another castle to the north, across the Dora Baltea by Caravino. This **Castello di Masino** has superb views over the Canavese and was their chief residence for more than ten centuries, although it had to be rebuilt after the Savoys destroyed it in 1459. Now owned by FAI, the Italian National Trust, the castle has some 30 lavishly decorated rooms from ballroom to billiards room, some frescoed with scenes of Arduino's life. In the chapel, an urn contains Arduino's remains, stolen in 1764 from the Castello di Agliè by its mistress, the Countess Cristina, and given to her lover, Count Francesco Valperga di Masino. Throughout the castle note the hemp leaf motif (the name Canavese comes from *canapa*, or cannabis), and the decorations made in a kind of rice paste stucco, according to a lost recipe. The castle has a fine sweeping English park.

That's not all. From Mazzè, you can head west to Cigliano, and north to the medieval **Castello Moncrivello**, furnished with antiques; in the 15th century this was the favourite residence of

Abbazia di Fruttaria
t 011 988 0487; open mid-April–9 July and Sept–Oct Sun 3–5.30; Jan–Mar and Nov–Dec Sun by appointment only; closed 10 July–Aug

Castello di Mazzè
t 011 983 5250, www.castellodimazze.it; open Sun and hols 2.30–5.30; in Mar–Sept also 10–12; closed Mon–Sat plus Dec and Jan; always ring ahead as times may change; park open Mar–Aug from 10am; adm

Bosco Parco
open Feb–Nov Sat, Sun and hols 2.30–5.30

Castello di Masino
t 0125 778 100; open Mar–Sept Tues–Sun 10–6; closed late Dec–Jan; adm exp

Castello Moncrivello
t 0165 401 175, www.castellodimoncrivello.it

Amedeo IX and his wife Jolande, sister of French king Louis XI, with views towards Vercelli. And north of this is **Castello di Borgomasino**, now a hotel (*see* p.335) but once owned by the vassals of Monferrato, the rivals of the Savoys; it was rebuilt in 1860 but nevertheless shelters some ancient bits and frescoed ceilings.

Ivrea: Old and New

Straddling the Dora Baltea river, Ivrea is a busy and likeable city founded by the Salassians, the toughest of Celtic tribes in Cisalpine Gaul. Their gold mines lured the Romans, who conquered them and renamed the city *Eporedia*; by 397 it was the seat of a bishop, and later a Lombard duke. The little city reached its peak of influence as the capital of a Marquisate under Berenguer II and Arduino; a plaque observing the millennium of Arduino's coronation as king of Italy in 1002, placed on the recently restored **Duomo** at the top of town, would not have pleased the cathedral's builder and Arduino's excommunicator, Bishop Warmondo. In spite of neoclassical remodelling, Warmondo's tower and **crypt** have survived, the latter with Roman columns and a Roman sarcophagus. Ivrea was the seat of a **scriptorium** in the 7th–9th centuries, where books were copied, although the best one in the nearby **Biblioteca Capitolare** in the Seminario Maggiore is the bishop's own beautifully illustrated codex, the Sacramentarium Episcopi Warmundi, which records, among other things, his furious curses directed at Arduino. A Byzantine ivory coffer holds Warmondo's remains, and outside, under a portico, is a **mosaic** relocated here from the old cathedral choir, showing Philosophy, Dialectic, Geometry and Arithmetic.

Biblioteca Capitolare
t 0125 47957; ring for opening hours

12 Piedmont | North of Turin: Valli di Lanzo and the Canavese

---

When City Squares Run with Orange Juice

Medieval Ivrea, like most Italian cities, not only quarrelled with its neighbours but was divided into rival neighbourhoods, whose swains never said no to a punch-up. But twice they united to burn down the castle of foreign-imposed tyrants, Raineri di Biandrate in 1194 and Gugliemo of Monferrato in 1266. Over the years, these two became one in the popular mind. A brave Miller's Daughter was somehow added to the story; the tyrant was said to have demanded her favours on her wedding night, only she cut off his head. The story became part of the city's carnival.

In 1808, the then-French rulers of the city, dismayed at the anarchy and fighting that went along with carnival, chose local notables to enforce the peace, dressing them in the uniforms of the French army: hence the current figures of the Napoleonic General and his staff, who accompany the Miller's Daughter, dressed like the French Marianne in a red Phrygian cap, the *Berretto Frigi*. Children recalled the story of the tyrant she beheaded by carrying little swords with oranges impaled on the end.

Oranges first appeared in the 19th century, when bystanders began to playfully toss them at the parades. This soon degenerated into anarchy, until the current rules were set up after the Second World War, establishing three days of orange battles (Sunday, Monday and Tuesday), pitting 30 teams on horse-drawn carts against some 3,500 *arancieri* (orange hurlers) on foot, all in bright costumes. Some 400 tons of surplus oranges are brought up from the south for the occasion, paid for by the participants. Visitors can join in, but if you'd prefer just to watch, buy a *Berretto Frigi* at one of the stands, marking you as an official non-combatant in the fruity fray.

Castello
t 0125 44415; open May–mid-Oct Sat 2–6 groups only, Sun 10–12 and 3–6.30; adm; some areas closed for restoration

Museo Civico
at Piazza Ottinetti 18; open by appointment only, t 0125 410 311

Museo a Cielo Aperto dell'Architettura Moderna
visitor centre on Via Jervis 26; open for guided tours, t 0125 43206

Behind the cathedral loom the four tall towers of the **Castello**, built by the 'Green Count' Amedeo VI in 1358 when Ivrea passed to the Savoys; the main tower blew up in 1676 when it was struck by lightning. Ivrea also has a good **Museo Civico** with archaeological finds, detached frescoes and Japanese art.

Ivrea has long been synonymous with the Olivetti family and their office machine company, founded in 1909. In August 2003, however, Olivetti merged with Telecom Italia and no longer exists. Ivrea's Olivetti legacy is remembered in the company's old buildings in the **Museo a Cielo Aperto dell'Architettura Moderna**, an 'open-air museum' along Via Jervis on the riverbank. These former Olivetti buildings encompass the church of **San Bernardino**, with fine 15th-century frescoes on the *Life of Jesus* by Martino Spanzotti. On this same bank of the river, the medieval neighbourhood **Borghetto** is fun for a drink or dinner.

And Now for Something Completely Different: Damanhur

Southwest of Ivrea is Damanhur, Piedmont's New Age utopia, not on any map but near **Baldissero Canavese**. Damanhur was founded in 1977 by esoteric author Oberto Airaudi, who used Chinese geomancy to choose this very spot, where three 'synchronic' lines of energy are said to intersect. When they become citizens, Damanhurians (besides the 800 plus here, there are over 8,000 members worldwide) take double animal-plant names (e.g. Wolf Oak) and live in a confederation of four energy self-sufficient communities, with their own currency (pegged to the euro), schools, newspaper, publishing house, businesses and political movement, Con Te, which is very prominent in the local council. Couples marry for a year at a time, renewable if they so choose (most do). Their houses are painted with giant flowers; their fields are decorated with stones arranged into giant spirals.

Temple of Humankind
t 0124 512 226, www.damanhur.info

In Damanhur, you can visit an open-air temple with statues of Egyptian gods, but to get into their extraordinary **Temple of Humankind**, you need to get in touch with them . Begun in 1978, the temple was excavated entirely by hand, 240ft into the bowels of the earth, its rooms lavishly decorated with stained glass, frescoes, statues and so on like a fairy-tale Hall of the Mountain King. It was a secret until 1992, when a disaffected member blabbed, causing all sorts of trouble over building permits and zoning, until the Italian National Arts Superintendency stepped in and declared it a collective work of art. In 2003 Damanhur purchased the old Olivetti factory at **Vidracco**, founded on the ideals of bringing work to the mountains, rather than forcing people to move or commute; now called **Damanhur Crea**, it's used for art workshops and as an organic food shop for local farmers.

Castellamonte and Agliè

The rest of Canavese is more Old than New Age, but there are a few surprises. For instance, **Torre Canavese**, south of Damanhur, has since 1990 turned itself each summer into an outdoor museum of art by painters from the former Soviet Union and the Canavese. **Castellamonte**, just west, has been making ceramics since the Bronze Age, and is now known for its arty pieces, pots and traditional ceramic woodstoves. In 1842, the town commissioned Alessandro Antonelli to build a new parish church in central Piazza Martiri della Libertà, next to its still-standing Romanesque campanile, and Antonelli, who never had a puny thought in his life, designed a huge round one that had to be abandoned after three years for lack of funds. Even so his big ring of walls, the **Rotonda Antonelliana**, has become Castellamonte's landmark; it embraces the town's big August **Ceramica** show, held since 1961.

Castello Ducale d'Agliè
t 0124 330 102; open Tues–Sun 8.30–7.30; park open May–Nov; adm

In **Agliè**, southeast of Castellamonte, the imposing **Castello Ducale d'Agliè** dates from 1141, but in 1642 Count Filippo San Martino di Agliè had court architect Amedeo di Castellamonte convert it into a splendid Baroque palace to host his lover, the Madama Reale Cristina. The Savoys purchased it in 1764, and redecorated it yet again as a home for a second son, the Duca del Chiablese; a fourth refurbishing occurred under Carlo Felice in the early 19th century. Most of the furniture is gone, but the English-Italian gardens are lovely and feature an enormous 18th-century horseshoe fountain.

Castello Malgrà
t 0124 26725; open for guided tours May–Oct, Sat 3–6.30, Sun 10–12 and 3–6.30; adm

Rivarolo Canavese, 5km southwest, is the site of the recently restored **Castello Malgrà** built in the 14th century by the Counts of San Martino, cousins of the Valperga clan and extended several times afterwards, and restored in the 1800s; there are some curious frescoes to the portico and a big drawbridge.

The Alta Canavese: Cuorgnè to Gran Paradiso National Park

Museo Archeologico dell'Alto Canavese
t 0124 651 799; open Mon–Fri 9–4, Sat 10–4

Castle
t 0124 617 146; open last Sun of each month 4–6, also Sat and Sun in July and Aug

West of Castellamonte, **Cuorgnè**, famous for copperware since the Middle Ages, has a cluster of medieval buildings, especially the so-called **Casa di Re Arduino** (although it dates from the 14th century). Arduino is remembered in a medieval tournament each May; yet older residents are remembered in the Palazzo del Comune's **Museo Archeologico dell'Alto Canavese** with finds from Neolithic to Lombard times. Just south, **Valperga** has an attractive castle, built in 980 by Arduino's father, added to over the centuries and now used as a rest home. The castle's chapel of **San Giorgio** has remarkable frescoes, dated 1300–1500.

From Cuorgnè, the N460 follows the Valle Orco to **Pont Canavese**, a Roman town at the junction with the Valle Soana, dotted with two of Arduino's towers; one of Pont's tiny hamlets, **Borgata Raje** is an unspoiled example of a typical medieval Alpine village. The Valle Soana leads into the **Parco Nazionale del Gran Paradiso**, which Piedmont shares with Aosta. Gran Paradiso was the favourite hunting reserve of Vittorio Emanuele II, and donated in 1919 to the state by his grandson Vittorio Emanuele III; there's a park visitors' centre at **Ronco** in the Valle Soana, dedicated to the chamois that are easily spotted here – if not in the mountains, on local menus.

Back in the main Valle di Locana, the **Castello di Sparone**, 5km from Pont, was Arduino's impregnable stronghold. His coronation as king was enough to bring down the army of Emperor Henry II, the ally of Warmondo, and Arduino was forced to retreat here. Henry had himself crowned king of Italy in 1004, even though Arduino refused to surrender his castle and claims; for two years the Imperial army besieged him here before returning to Germany empty-handed. The scenery becomes splendid towards **Noasca**, with its waterfall and park visitor centre, and majestic at **Ceresole Reale**, where the peaks of Gran Paradiso rise around the meadows and long artificial lake, a favourite of windsurfers. **Ceresole's visitor centre** is dedicated to the National Park's totem, the *stambecco* (ibex), a wild goat with long, ridged horns so hunted that by 1945 only 420 remained, all in the confines of Gran Paradiso. Since then their numbers have ballooned, allowing them to be reintroduced across the Alps. The park is crisscrossed by mule paths laid out for Vittorio Emanuele II's hunts (the 'Reale' in Ceresole's name was granted by the king in 1862 to thank the inhabitants for giving him their hunting rights); many paths have been repaired for walkers.

Noasca
t 0124 901 070

Ceresole's visitor centre
t 0124 953 187; open during summer and the main festivities

North of Ivrea to Aosta: Settimo Vittone and Carema

As the Dora Baltea river funnels out of the high altitudes of Aosta, it passes through a granite valley tiered with Nebbiolo vines, majestically supported on stone pillars and trellises known as *tupiun*, and dotted with medieval castles – and palm and olive trees. This area, in fact, has one of the most delicious microclimates in Piedmont: **Settimo Vittone** is famous for its herbs (especially the delicate *ajucche*, that grows nowhere else, and is even good in ice cream). Lovely paths snake over the hills; roads wind up to hidden restaurants. In the 9th century Ansgarda, repudiated wife of the Frankish king Louis the Stutterer and a paternal aunt of Arduino, spent her last days in a castle on a rocky spur over the valley and was buried, or so they say, in the sarcophagus in front of the 11th-century church of **San Lorenzo**. Only vestiges remain of the castle but San Lorenzo, restored by FAI, is a gem, linked by a corridor to the 9th-century baptistry. Inside are fascinating frescoes by several hands – rare depictions of the pregnant Virgin (an image banned by the Council of Trent) and St Christopher holding a palm instead

San Lorenzo
open Sat and Sun 3–6

Cantina dei Produttori di Nebbiolo di Carema
Via Nazionale 32,
t 0125 811 160

of baby Jesus, and a Last Supper that looks like a proper *menu degustazione* rather than the usual sparse fare depicted by painters.

The granite sucks in the sun during the day and releases the heat in the cool evenings, the secret of the lovely red wines of **Carema**; the little roadside **Cantina dei Produttori di Nebbiolo di Carema** offers tastings and bottles for half the price you'll pay in Turin.

Where to Stay and Eat North of Turin

Cirìè ✉ 10073

Dolce Stil Novo, Via San Pietro 71, t 011 921 1110, *www.dolcestilnovo.com* (€€€€). Handsome restaurant in an early 19th-century house, where Alfredo Russo has won just about all the awards as the Pied Piper of the New Italian Style. Nearly all ingredients are grown in the restaurant's own organic garden. *Closed Mon, Tues–Sat lunch, Sun eve.*

(i) **Lanzo Torinese** >
Via Umberto I 9, t 0123 28080, www.canavese-vallilanzo.it

Lanzo Torinese ✉ 10074

★★★Piemonte, Via Umberto I 23, t 0123 320 108, *www.hotelristorante piemonte.it* (€€). Comfortable and central, with a **restaurant**.

Rifugio Agriturismo Salvin, at Alpe Salvin, Monastero di Lanzo, t 0123 27205, *www.rifugiosalvin.it* (€). Italian/English-run refuge and farm, with cows and goats, plenty of activities for children; full or half board available. *Closed Jan–Mar.*

(★) **Castello di Borgomasino** >>

Groscavallo ✉ 10070

★Setugrino, Corso Roma 10 in Pialpetta, t 0123 81016 (€). Simple rooms and trattoria, serving delicious *antipasti*, game dishes and excellent cheeses. *Closed Tues from Sept–June and Oct.*

(i) **Ivrea** >>
Corso Vercelli 1, t 0125 618 131, www.canavese-vallilanzo.it

Candia ✉ 10010

★★★Residenza del Lago, Via Roma 48, t 011 983 4885, *www.residenzadelago.it* (€€). A farm attractively restored as a hotel; some bedrooms have vaulted brick ceilings. The **restaurant** (*closed Fri*) serves tasty *tench*.

(★) **Castello San Giuseppe** >>

Caluso (near Mazzè) ✉ 10014

Gardenia, Corso Torino 9, t 011 983 2249 (€€€€). One of the best restaurants in the Canavese, where French-born chef Mariangela Susigan

prepares elegant regional dishes with flair. *Closed Thurs, and Fri lunch.*

Romano Canavese ✉ 10090

★★★★Relais Villa Matilde, Viale Marconi 29, t 0125 639 290, *www.sinahotels. com* (€€€€€). Between Turin and Ivrea, 18th-century villa with a lovely park built for the Bishop of Ivrea, converted into a stylish hotel with contemporary furnishings. Large pool, tennis and new health spa. Beautiful **restaurant** in the former stables.

Caravino ✉ 10010

Il Ristoro, Via Castello 1 (right under the Castello di Masino), t 0125 778 486 (€€€). A talented young chef serves up delicious dishes made from the local potatoes, cheeses, and other fresh fare, either on a pretty terrace or in a rustic dining room. *Open at lunch and dinner by reservation. Closed Mon and mid-Dec–31 Jan.*

Borgomasino ✉ 10031

Castello di Borgomasino (south of Masino), Via Bonfiglio 2, t 0125 770 181, *www.castellodiborgomasino.it* (€€€). In a charming park, a romantic B&B in a castle with a tower begun a thousand years ago. The rooms come with parquet floors and fireplaces and antiques. Bike hire available. *Closed 12 Nov–10 Feb.*

Ivrea ✉ 10015

★★★★Castello di Pavone, just south at Pavone Canavese, t 0125 672 111, *www.castellodipavone.com* (€€€€). A superb medieval castle, reputed to bring good luck to anyone who sojourns here; atmospheric rooms and restaurant, popular for weddings.

★★★★Castello San Giuseppe, 5.5km northeast at Chiaverano, t 0125 424 370, *www.castellosangiuseppe.it* (€€€€). On a hill encircled by lakes, set in a beautiful garden, a convent converted into a mansion in the 17th century, once a favourite retreat of actress Eleanora Duse. It has lovely romantic rooms, period furnishings and a gorgeous **restaurant** (open eves only and popular for weddings).

***La Villa**, Via Torino 334, **t** 0125 631 696, *www.ivrealavilla.com* (€€€). Pleasant little hotel on the main street at the south end of town, with easy parking.

Agriturismo La Perulina, Via S. Pietro Martire 35 (on the north side of Lake Sirio), **t** 0125 45222, *www.laperulina.it* (€). Four rooms and a camping ground on a honey and fruit farm. Mountain bikes and canoes, too.

Aquila Antica, Via G. Gozzano 37, in the 'Croazia' district, **t** 0125 641 364 (€€€). Good traditional dishes in a traditional setting, featuring tasty Piedmontese *antipasti*, hearty pasta, and some seafood dishes. Also organizes themed gourmet evenings. *Closed Sun and Aug.*

Loranzè Alto (west of Ivrea) ✉ 10010

La Foreseria, Via S. Rocco 8, **t** 0125 669 065, *www.la-foresteria.com* (€€). Attractive B&B with six rooms in an early 18th-century convent, with its own little chapel.

Cuorgnè ✉ 10082

***Astoria**, Via Don Minzoni 15, **t** 0124 666 001, *www.astoria-damauro.it* (€€). The hotel, located in the centre, is just adequate. The restaurant, **Da Mauro** (€€€€), really shines, however, in its traditional seasonal dishes. *Closed Sun eve and Mon lunch.*

Ceresole Reale ✉ 10080

Chalet del Lago, Pian della Balma 10, **t 0124 953 128 (€€). A little hotel, down by the lake, that is well known for its rustic restaurant, serving a range of tasty dishes such as rabbit marinated in basil and walnut oil, and polenta with mushrooms. *Closed Oct–April.*

Settimo Vittone ✉ 10010

L'Ospitalità del Castello, Piazza Conte Rinaldo 7, **t** 348 452 7017, *www.lospitalitadelcastello.it* (€). Next to S. Lorenzo, in the old castle walls, a charming three-room B&B with charming owners. *Closed Nov.*

Dell'Angelo, Via Marconi 6, in the centre, **t** 0125 658 453 (€€). Easy to find, and good for *zuppa di ajucche* and *polenta grassa*, washed down with the local Nebiolo. *Closed Wed and end July–mid-Aug*

La Baracca , Fraz. Cornaley 68, **t** 0125 658 109 (€). Hidden in the hills, up a very narrow road, old-fashioned place with the best *all ajucche* menu (*April–May*), and *suet gris* (polenta with cheese, bacon and herbs). Ring ahead for directions. *Closed Mon, and 3 weeks in Jan and Feb.*

Carema ✉ 10010

Ramo Verde, Via Torino 42, **t** 0125 811 327 (€€€€). It may not look too promising from the outside, but inside there is a fine trattoria, serving delicious *agnolotti* and a *torta Novecento* for dessert. *Closed Sat and Sun lunch and Mon.*

Valle d'Aosta

At Pont-St-Martin, the one and only road from the rest of Italy enters the Valle d'Aosta – its highest, smallest (3,267 sq km) and least populous (118,000 inhabitants) region. It resembles a mighty leaf, with a main vein (the Dora Baltea Valley) and 13 smaller valley veins branching off in all directions. Rimmed by the highest mountains in Europe – Mont Blanc (15,780ft), Monte Rosa (15,200ft), the Matterhorn (Cervino, 14,690ft) and Gran Paradiso (13,402ft) – the Valle d'Aosta is one of Europe's most spectacular and popular summer and winter playgrounds, dotted with lakes and serenaded by rushing streams. Emerald meadows lie beneath great swathes of woodlands, with hills and gorges defended by fairytale castles.

13

Don't miss

⭐ The 'Rome of the Alps'
Aosta **p.345**

⭐ A vertiginous cable car
Courmayeur–Chamonix –Mont Blanc **p.354**

⭐ Charming courtly frescoes
Castello di Issogne **p.342**

⭐ A spectacular National Park
Cogne and Gran Paradiso **p.351**

⭐ A fairytale castle
Castello di Fenis **p.344**

See map overleaf

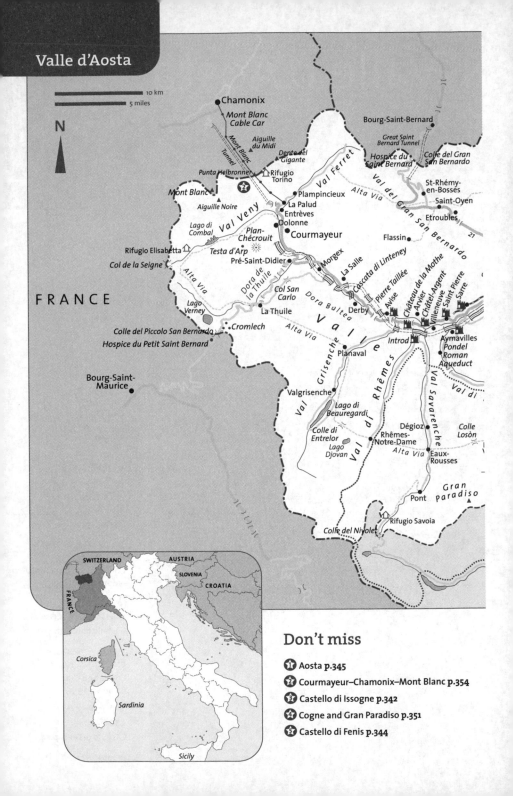

Valle d'Aosta

10 km
5 miles

N

Chamonix
Mont Blanc
Cable Car

Bourg-Saint-Bernard

Great Saint
Bernard Tunnel

Aiguille
du Midi

Dente del
Gigante

Mont Blanc
Tunnel

Hospice du
Saint Bernard

Colle del Gran
San Bernardo

Punta Helbronner

Rifugio
Torino

St-Rhémy-
en-Bossès

Mont Blanc

Plampincieux

Alta Via

Saint-Oyen

Aiguille Noire

La Palud
Entrèves
Dolonne

Val del Gran San Bernardo

Etroubles

Lago di
Combal

Plan-
Chécrouit

Courmayeur

Flassin

21

Rifugio Elisabetta

Testa d'Arp

Pré-Saint-Didier

Morgex

La Salle

Cascata di Linteney

Val Veny

Col de la Seigne

Dora de
la Thuile

Pierre Taillée

Château de la Mothe

Saint Pierre

Sarre

Lago
Verney

Col San
Carlo

Dora Baltea

Avise

Arvier

Châtel-Argent

Villeneuve

FRANCE

La Thuile

Derby

Valle

Aymavilles
Pondel
Roman
Aqueduct

Colle del Piccolo San Bernardo
Hospice du Petit Saint Bernard

Cromlech

Alta Via

Introd

Val Grisenche

Planaval

Val di Rhêmes

Val Savarenche

Val di

Bourg-Saint-
Maurice

Valgrisenche

Lago di
Beauregardi

Dégioz

Colle
Losòn

Colle di
Entrelor

Lago
Djovan

Rhêmes-
Notre-Dame

Alta Via

Eaux-
Rousses

Gran
paradiso

Pont

Rifugio Savoia

Colle del Nivolet

SWITZERLAND   AUSTRIA

SLOVENIA

FRANCE

CROATIA

Corsica

Sardinia

Sicily

Don't miss

① Aosta p.345

② Courmayeur–Chamonix–Mont Blanc p.354

③ Castello di Issogne p.342

④ Cogne and Gran Paradiso p.351

⑤ Castello di Fenis p.344

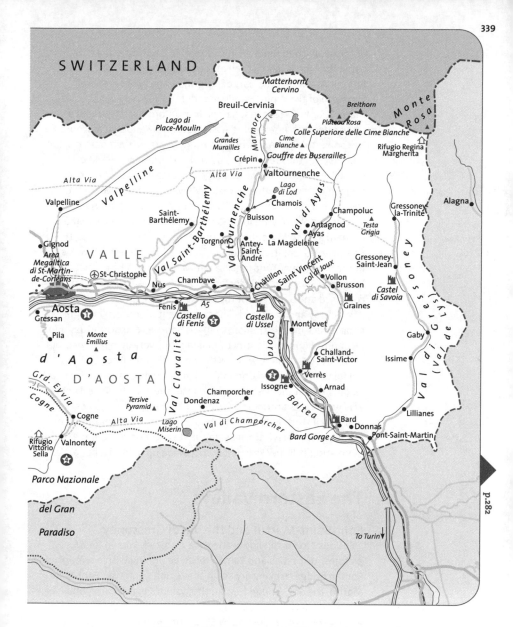

Although it now seems out of the way, Aosta was for centuries one of Europe's most important crossroads, thanks to the Great and Little St Bernard passes over the Alps. Hospices, bridges and roads were a big concern – and castles, from where local lords could exact tolls from travellers. These passes were used in Neolithic times, but the earliest inhabitants known to history were the tough Salassian Celts, who in 143 BC were in the way of Roman determination to build an inland road to Gaul. After the Romans came the Franks in 575, then in the post-Carolingian divisions of Europe, Aosta became part of Burgundy, and spoke French. Umberto of the White Hands, founder of the Savoy dynasty, was made Count of Aosta in 1032, and in 1191 Tommaso I granted a *Charte des franchises* giving Aosta autonomy under its viscounts – the powerful Challant family for many years – a system that would endure until the French Revolution. In 1561, Emanuele Filiberto made French the official language of Aosta in place of Latin. As merchants moved into the main valley, Italian took over in the towns, and stayed there; the two groups rarely intermarried.

After Napoleon (who in 1800 raced his army over the Great St Bernard Pass to Marengo) and the restoration of the Savoys, the Valle d'Aosta lost its autonomy. After the Risorgimento, it was stuck in the province of Turin, and Italian was declared the official language. Most rural Valdostani couldn't speak it; the economy collapsed and a quarter of the population emigrated. The building of a railway and new roads and the advent of tourism brought people back into the region; by 1936 there were 16,000. Mussolini recognized Aosta's identity by making it its very own province, but then infuriated many with his Italian-only cultural policy. A Valdostano Liberation Committee led by Emile Chanoux played a leading role in the Resistance, and after the war, the Valle d'Aosta was granted its autonomy, further enhanced in 1971 by laws granting it fiscal autonomy. Although officially bilingual, Italian, thanks to the television, now dominates. A good percentage of the population still speaks a patois, too, made up of local languages.

The Eastern Valleys

Pont-Saint-Martin and the Val di Gressoney

Besides Alpine splendour, the Valle d'Aosta is known for its picturesque castles and Roman relics, beginning with a remarkable **Roman bridge** (1st century BC) at the region's gateway, **Pont-Saint-Martin**. The only bridge to span the Lys until 1831, local legend has it that the devil built it, in exchange for the first soul to wander across – only to be cheated by St Martin, who sent a dog over at dawn. A neogothic folly, the **Castello di Baraing** on the hill is now a community centre; below, slopes serrated with terraces are adorned with columns supporting the high trellis of Nebbiolo vines that make Carema and Donnaz, two of Aosta's finest wines.

At Pont-Saint-Martin, the main valley meets the **Val di Gressoney**, which, after a steep ascent, meanders gracefully in big meadows up to the glaciers of Monte Rosa. In the 13th century, German-speaking Walser (*see* p.316) settled much of the valley, building pretty villages as wholesome as Heidi, their sturdy traditional Alpine chalets and balconies bursting with pots of geraniums.

At **Issime**, the façade of the church of San Giacomo Maggiore has a large fresco of sinners taking their licks in the *Last Judgement* (1698) as a warning to passers-by; if it's open, pop in to see a splendid gilded statue of St Barbara. Stone houses predominate at **Gaby**, 4km further on, an island of Occitan-speakers amid the German amid the French amid the Italian. Further up, pretty **Gressoney-Saint-Jean**, on a lake by the Lys glacier, is the site of the

Castel di Savoia
t 0125 355 396; open Mon–Fri 10–12 and 1.30–5.30, Sat–Sun 10–12 and 1.30–6.30; max 20 people at a time every 30mins; adm

neogothic **Castel di Savoia**, built by Queen Margherita, widow of Umberto, who loved the mountains; the furnishings are mostly Art Nouveau. From May to September you can stroll through the castle's lovely Alpine rock garden. There's also an

Alpenfaunamuseum
t 0125 355 406; open daily 9–12.30 and 3–6.30, closed Wed out of season; adm

Alpenfaunamuseum founded by Walser Baron Beck-Pecocz and dedicated to local fauna, hunting trophies, especially large and unusual antlers and hunting rifles. Further up, **Gressoney-la-Trinité**, a low-key but increasingly trendy spot to enjoy the snow, is synonymous with **Monte Rosa**, Europe's second-tallest peak (the name rosa derives not from a pinkish tint but from the old Valdostano word for ice). It boasts **Monterosa Ski**, the Valle d'Aosta's largest resort, with lift links to ski into Champoluc (*see* p.342) or Alagna (*see* p.324), and the highest shelter in Europe, the

Rifugio della Regina Margherita
t 0163 91039; open end June–mid-Sept

Rifugio della Regina Margherita at 14,957ft, with huge views into the Gressoney valley and Valsesia, where if you book ahead you can sleep in the mountaineering Queen's bed.

Up the Main Valley to Verrès and Issogne

From Pont-Saint-Martin, the main Dora Valley road continues to **Donnas**, running parallel to an impressive stretch of the original Roman road, hewn 200m into the rock, passing under an ancient

Fortress of Bard
t 0125 833 811; open Aug daily 10–8; Sept–July Tues–Fri 10–6, Sat–Sun 10–7; adm

gateway. Just beyond, the gloomy **Fortress of Bard**, linked by covered passages, rises on its promontory over a picturesque medieval hamlet. In 1800, Napoleon slipped past in the dead of night, spreading the road with sacking and straw to muffle the noise, then turned around and razed the original medieval castle. The current fort was rebuilt by Carlo Felice; a 20-year-old lieutenant named Camillo Cavour served there for eight months in 1831 – enough to convince him that a military career wasn't for him.

Bard marks the narrow entrance into the **Val di Champorcher**, one of the least visited valleys, with unspoiled villages; the women of **Champorcher** have recently revived its age-old hemp industry, and you can watch them weave it during working hours at **La Lavorazione del Canapa**. There are winter sports among the pines at **Chardonney** and up at **Dondenaz**, from where Vittorio Emanuele II built a hunting road to Cogne; you can walk up it in 90 minutes to pretty **Lago Miserin**.

13 Valle d'Aosta | The Eastern Valleys

St Martin
t 0125 966 116; open by request

Picturesque **Arnad**, up the main valley from Bard, has medieval houses and an 11th-century Romanesque church of **St Martin**, with a superb portal and wooden choirs and statues, and an excellent collection of art. Then comes **Verrès**, defended by the massive cube of the **Castello di Verrès**. Begun in 1390 by Ybelt de Challant, Captain General of Piedmont, this is 'one of the mightiest manors ever built by a vassal in a sovereign state'. Each side measures nearly 100ft. Delicate windows relieve the mass of the 8ft-thick walls; inside are a monumental stair and huge fireplaces.

Castello di Verrès
t 0125 929 067; open 1 Mar–30 June and 1–30 Sept daily 9–6.30; 1 July–31 Aug 9–7.30; max 50 people at a time every 30mins; adm

🔟 **Castello di Issogne**
t 0125 929 373; open for guided tours July and Aug 9–7.30; Mar–June and Sept 9–6.30; Oct–Feb Thurs–Tues 10–12 and 1.30–4.30, Sun and hols till 5.30; check in advance; adm

Yblet's nearby **Castello di Issogne** may look plain, but his less austere heirs, in particular De Challant, Prior of Sant'Orso in Aosta, called in the early Renaissance decorators. The cruciform garden was laid out as a symbol of heaven; the courtyard has lunettes frescoed with scenes of daily life in c. 1500 (the apothecary's, the butcher's, a grocer's) symbolizing good government. With a unique iron pomegranate fountain in the centre, a wedding gift from Georges de Challant to Count Filiberto, the whole cries out for a few dallying knights and ladies fair. Note, too, the centuries of grafitti carved by the Challants' guests – enough to give the modern hostess nightmares. The lavish baronial hall has a fresco cycle of landscapes and hunting scenes and a *Judgement of Paris*, inspired by Botticelli but not quite getting it right. One room was set aside for the king of France (just in case he should call), with fleurs-de-lys and a 15th-century canopied bed. Abandoned for decades, the castle was purchased in 1872 by painter Vittorio Avondo, who restored it, then donated it all to the state.

Val di Ayas to Champoluc

Thickly forested with pines and chestnuts, the **Val di Ayas** winds north of Verrès towards Monte Rosa. The Challants hailed from the hamlets at **Challand-Saint-Victor**; their striking 11th-century **Castello de Graines** (restored in the early 1900s, and visitable though still in ruins) sits high on its rock at Arcesaz. The 12th-century parish church of **St Victor** contains a fine collection of art from the chapels in the area. From **Brusson** you can take a chairlift up to the miniature mountain lakes under **Punta Valfredda** or take the good but windy road to the **Col di Joux**; at the top the entire Valle d'Aosta lies at your feet. Here too the 'fountain of Napoleon' where Bonaparte, about to fall into the hands of an Austrian patrol, managed to give them the slip when they stopped to drink the excellent water. The road, continues down to St-Vincent.

St Victor
t 0125 929 093; open in summer Mon–Sun 9–11.30 and 3–7; in winter Mon–Sun 9–11.30 and 3–6

Ayas is a *comune* of hamlets. **Vollon** is famous for its enormous 17th-century *rascade*, a traditional Valdostano wooden grain barn. Up at **Antagnod**, the church of **St-Martin** (1497) has a magnificent gilded Baroque altar, that incorporates medieval statues, and a 16th-century treasure. **Champoluc**, the most important hamlet, is a

St-Martin
t 0125 306 629; call for opening times and information

pleasant mountain town and largely unspoiled resort, and good for families; it shares the vast Monterosa ski complex with Gressoney-la-Trinité and has lifts to the slopes of **Testa Grigia** ('Grey Head'; 10,875ft), overlooking a tremendous sea of peaks.

Saint Vincent and Châtillon

Back in the main valley, at Montjovet, the landmark is the 10th-century **Castello di St Germain** sitting high on a rocky spur above the river. Next up, **St Vincent**, 'Riviera of the Alps', has been a spa since the late 18th century, and now boasts Europe's largest casino opened in 1947, the Casino de la Vallée, where the likes of Ray Charles and Ella Fitzgerald have performed in the past. A funicular goes up to the spa of the Fons Salutis built in 1900, where you can imbibe the famous water – a tonic for the liver, or almost anything that ails you. Near the base of the funicular, the 11th-century church of **San Vincenzo** was built over the baths of a Roman villa; inside are frescoes on the life of the fire-eating Saint Vincent Ferrer, and the Passion and a Museo Parrocchiale with a good collection of medieval and Rennaissance sacred art from the area. Another important museum in St Vincent is the Museo di Mineralogia e Paleontologia, the only one of its kind in Valle d'Aosta. In it are kept 650 crystal pieces from all over the world and a special exhibit on the minerals of the region, as well as 170 fossil specimens. The road continues to the Valle d'Aosta's second city, industrial **Châtillon**, a major crossroads since antiquity. It has two castles: one in town, the Castello Passerin d'Entrèves, is still inhabited and has a pretty 18th-century park open to the public, and one 5km south, the mighty Castello di Ussel, built in 1350 and beautifully lit up at night; donated in 1983 to the region by its last owner, Baron Marcel Bich – inventor of the Bic pen, whose ancestors came from Châtillon – it hosts changing exhibitions on the Valle d'Aosta.

Under the Matterhorn: the Valtournenche and Breuil-Cervinia

The 27km **Valtournenche** is Italy's picture window on the most easily recognizable of all the Alps – the majestic rakish pyramid of the Matterhorn. The first small resort, **Antey-Saint-André**, has a healthy, mild climate, which first attracted inhabitants in the Bronze Age; the campanile of its church was originally a castle tower. To the west, Torgnon has an excellent little museum of 15th-and 16th-century wooden sculpture in its parish church. East of Antey-St-André at **La Magdeleine**, a pretty path links eight old water mills; a few are still working, grinding the flour to make the Valle d'Aosta's distinctive black bread. Cable cars from **Buisson** ascend to the lovely old hamlet of Chamois – you can't get there by car; from here a chair lift continues up to the green banks of the

Casino de la Vallée
t 0166 5221; open daily except 24 Dec 3pm–3am, varying slightly depending on the room; Mon–Thurs free, Fri–Sun and hols adm of €3, free or very cheap with a 'Fortune Card', available from hotels and tourist information offices; bring your passport

Fons Salutis
open April–Nov 7am–1pm

Museo Parrocchiale
t 0166 512 350; open daily 9–6

Museo di Mineralogia e Paleontologia
Via Chanoux, t 0166 512 596; usually open Aug plus 26 Dec–6 Jan daily 10–12.30 and 4–7.30

Castello Passerin d'Entrèves
open mid-Mar–mid-Nov Tues–Sun 8–6

Castello di Ussel
t 0166 563 747; open late June–mid-Oct daily 9–7, last entry 6.30; adm

Torgnon
to visit, ring the priest, t 0166 540 241

Chamois cable car
t 0166 519 890, www.montecervino.it; every half-hour 7–1 and 3–8 plus one-way trips at 1.50, 2.15, 2.35, 9, 10 and 10.25pm; adm

Lago di Lod. Flowery **Valtournenche**, the valley capital, stands in tiers along the road. Many of its sons were Matterhorn guides – memorial plaques in the church square are a grim reminder of the dangers they faced. From Valtournenche you can get a cable car up the **Cime Bianche**, or take a walk along the **Gouffre des Buserailles**, a narrow gorge, waterfall and three glacial potholes, 3km up the road from Valtournenche.

Gouffre des Buserailles
usually open June–Sept

In 1934, the road was extended north to the big resort built by Mussolini, **Breuil-Cervinia**. The setting, with the Matterhorn to the north, the Grandes Murailles to the west and the Fruggen massif to the east, is truly grand, and the roadside **Lac Bleu** mirrors them prettily. Devoted heart and soul to the mountains, with the best snowfall record of any resort in Italy, it's very popular, with over 200km of ski runs, ice skating, bobsledding and ice hockey. For more thrills, a cable car and chairlift continue up **Piccolo Cervino/Klein Matterhorn** (12,739ft), from where pistes continue down 22km Valtournenche, a descent so lengthy that the KL time trials for the world speed record are held here. In the summer, Breuil is the base for ascents of the **Matterhorn/Cervino** (14,691ft), a feat first achieved from this side in 1867; the most precipitous passages are now fitted out with permanent ropes. Other excursions include the hike from Plateau Rosa over the Colle Superiore delle Cime Bianche, either to emerald Lago Goillet and its view over the Val d'Ayas, or to the top of the **Breithorn** (13,684ft).

Up the Main Valley: the Castello di Fenis

Vines line the valley west of Châtillon; in **Chambave** they make a prized muscat, Passito di Chambave, and in **Nus**, north of the *autostrada*, they make malvasia. In nearby **Fenis**, the Challants built their fairy-tale **Castello di Fenis** in the 1100s. It reached its present form in the early 1400s, fell into ruin and was perhaps a bit too keenly restored, at least for purists, in the 1920s and '30s. The kitchen has a chimney big enough to smoke an ox; other rooms contain an assortment of antiques. The baronial hall and delightful courtyard have International Gothic frescoes of *c.* 1425 by an artist close to Giacomo Jaquerio: there are *St George and the Dragon*, *Our Lady of Mercy* and a series of sages, each holding up a motto.

★ Castello di Fenis
t 0165 764 263; open Oct–Feb Wed–Mon 10–12.30 and 1.30–4.30, till 5.30 Sat, Sun and hols; Mar–June and Sept daily 9–7; July–Aug 9–8; adm

From Nus you can visit two remote valleys – the **Val Clavalité**, with the striking Punta Tersiva at its head, or the **Val Saint-Barthélemy**, with its scattered houses – or continue 13km to Aosta.

ⓘ Pont Saint-Martin >
Via Circonvallazione 30, t 0125 804 843, www.laporta dellavallee.com

ⓘ Gressoney-Saint-Jean >>
Villa Deslex, Lyskamm Walg 8, t 0125 355 185, www.aiatmonte rosawalser.it

Where to Stay and Eat in the Eastern Valleys

Pont-Saint-Martin ✉ 11026
***Ponte Romano**, Piazza IV Novembre 14, **t** 0125 804 329, *www.hotelponteromano.it* (€€). Basic hotel by the Roman bridge.

Gressoney-Saint-Jean ✉ 11025
***Gran Baita**, Fraz Gresmatten, Strada Castello Savoia 26, **t** 0125 356 441, *www.hotelgranbaita.it* (€€€–€€).

ⓘ **St Vincent >>**
Via Roma 62, t 0166 512 239, www.saint vincentvda.it

Rebuilt Walser house by the castle, with a ski bus in winter, and free green fees in summer.

****Lo Scoiattolo**, Gressoney-la-Trinité, Loc. Tache 6, **t** 0125 366 313, *www. htlscoiattolo.com* (€€). Charming little hotel with a good **restaurant** – the owner is a good chef.

Capanna Carla, Loc. Tschaval, Gressoney-la-Trinité, **t** 0125 366 130 (€€€–€€). The best eating establishment here, a lovely place with wonderful Valdostano cuisine. *Closed Mon exc in summer.*

Verrès ✉ 11029

****Da Pierre**, Via Martorey 73, **t** 0125 929 376, *www.dapierre.com* (€€€€). Classy and comfortable rooms and fine dining. Try the *agnolotti alla savoiarda* and venison in blueberry sauce. *Cheaper rates available for half board. Closed Tues.*

Grand Gourmet, Via Giardini 25/a, **t** 0125 921 080 (€€€). Specializes in Mediterraean dishes, seafood and desserts. *Closed Mon.*

ⓘ **Breuil-Cervinia >>**
Via Guido Rey 17, t 0166 949 136, www.montecervino.it

ⓘ **Ayas-Champoluc >**
Via Varasc 16, t 0125 307 113, www.aiat monterosa.com

Ayas-Champoluc ✉ 11020

****Castor**, Via Ramey 2, **t** 0125 307 117, *www.hotelcastor.it* (€€€€). In the centre of Champoluc, big chalet with breathtaking views of Monte Rosa, panelled rooms with all mod cons, and a nice **restaurant** (€€). Very family-friendly: the English-Italian owners have three kids and lots of canaries. *Closed mid-April–end June, Oct and Nov.*

****Petit Tournalin**, Loc. Villy-Frachey 2, **t** 0125 307 530, *www.hotelpetit tournalin.it* (€€). Big rooms in a quiet setting, off the main road a few minutes from Champoluc centre.

Goil, Loc. Alpe Goil, **t** 0125 306 370 (€). An *agriturismo* in an enchanting setting with three simple rooms and

traditional meals. Be sure to book. *Open July, Aug, all hols and weekends.*

Le Petit Coq, Loc. Frachey, **t** 0125 307 997 (€€€). Cosy place serving the Aosta classics and a delicious *pierrade*. *Book. Closed Tues.*

St Vincent ✉ 11027

*****Grand Hotel Billia**, Viale Piemonte 72, **t** 0166 5231, *www.grandhotel billia.com* (€€€€€). Grand Liberty-style hotel of 1907, built for the water cure – today just as many check in to get soaked at its roulette tables. Spa, pool, tennis courts and a park.

****Elena**, Via Biavaz 2, **t** 0166 512 140, *www.hotelelena.be* (€€). Large pleasant rooms with balconies and good views. Its only drawback is its proximity to a church with bells.

Breuil-Cervinia ✉ 11021

*****Hermitage**, Strada del Cristallo, **t** 0166 948 998, *www.hotelhermitage. com* (€€€€€). A romantic mountain oasis offering every comfort, including a beauty farm, plus an elegant **restaurant** (€€€€). *Closed May–June and Sept–Nov.*

***Les Neiges d'Antan**, Loc. Crêt 10, **t** 0166 948 775, *www.lesneigesdantan. it* (€€€€). The **restaurant** (€€€€) serves a great traditional meal of salt beef, polenta, cheeses, Valdostano wines and home-made desserts. *Closed May–June.*

****Edelweiss**, Via Guido Rey 18, **t** 0166 949 078, *www.matterhorn.it* (€€€). Central, family-run and cosy; good food and the best cocktails in the Valle d'Aosta.

Maison de Saussure, Via Abbé Gorret 20, **t** 0166 948 259 (€€€€). Excellent traditional food in an intimate setting. *Book.*

Etoile, **t** 0166 940 220 (€€). Cosy, right on the slopes; a favourite for lunch.

Aosta: the 'Rome of the Alps'

⭐ **Aosta**

Aosta, the region's capital and crossroads, has an enchanting setting: on clear mornings a ring of mountains wraps the little city in a total, shimmering blueness, while their bright snows join the clouds to form a magic circle high above. They overlook a city whose street plan has changed little since 23 BC, when the Romans founded it as *Augusta Praetoria* at the confluence of the Buthier

Getting to and around Aosta

Aosta's **airport** Corrado Gex is east at St Christophe and has direct flights from Cuneo and Rome on Airvallée, **t** 0165 303 303, *www.airvallee.com*. **Trains** from Turin via Ivrea or Milan (via Chivasso) continue west as far as Pré-Saint-Didier (*www.trenitalia.it*). SAVDA **buses, t** 0165 361 244, *www.savda.it*, leave from the corner of Corso Vittorio and Emanuele II 131 in Turin for Aosta, and continue as far as Courmayeur; they also go directly to Aosta from Turin airport, **t** 011 300 0623. SAVDA run daily bus services from Milan's Garibaldi station and Malpensa airport to Aosta. Buses go to all the main villages in the region, and to Bourg-St-Maurice, Chambéry, Chamonix, Annecy and Grenoble in France; see *www.regione.vda.it/trasporti* for information on timetables and fares.

---

torrent and the Dora Baltea, but only after they finally subdued the diehard Salassian Gauls. After the Romans left, it went into decline until the early 11th century, when it became a seat of ecclesiastical and feudal power, visited by all who came over the Great or Little Saint Bernard passes. Today the city remains a major crossroads, of sorts; on 29 September, thousands of cows descend on it from their hundred days in the high Alpine pastures in the *Desarpa*.

If you approach Aosta from the east by way of Corso Ivrea, you can walk over a little **Roman bridge** spanning the former bed of the Buthier. These days the river has moved 100m west, just before the **Arco di Augusto**, Aosta's symbol, erected when the city was founded to celebrate Augustus' victory over the Salassians. A Crucifix called the **Saint-Vout** (now a copy) was suspended in the centre of the arch after a flood in the 15th century; the roof was added in 1716 to keep out the rain and snow. The arch marks the start of Aosta's pedestrian main street, **Via Sant'Anselmo**, the Roman *decumanus*, now awash with stuffed Saint Bernards and garish bottles of Alpine elixirs. Aosta's most famous son, St Anselm, Archbishop of Canterbury, Doctor of the Church and the founder of Scholasticism, was born in 1033 at No.66.

Collegiata di SS. Pietro e Orso

Collegiata di SS. Pietro e Orso
t 0165 262 026; open daily

Turn right on Via Sant'Orso for one of the jewels of Aosta: the Romanesque-Gothic **Collegiata di SS. Pietro e Orso** founded in the late 10th century outside the town walls, over the tomb of Aosta's patron saint, Orso or Ursus, a 6th-century Irishman who came here preaching against Arian heretics. Legend has it that Orso made and distributed wooden clogs to the needy, and he is celebrated every 30–31 January, when the city holds one of the oldest continuous fairs in Europe, the **Sant'Orso Fair**, dating back to the year 1000, where a thousand artisans from across the region fill the city to show their wares, from ladders and *grolle* to fine sculpture. Music, costumes, folklore, food and wine-tasting in the snow are part of the fun, culminating in an all-night party, the *Veillà*, on the 30th, drawing tens of thousands of visitors.

In the 1100s, a massive isolated campanile and cloister were added, and the complex took its current form in 1510 under its wealthy prior, Georges de Challant, who built the priory, added the high gable over the door, decorated the apse, and restored the cloister; an enormous 480-year-old lime (linden) tree in the little square is another landmark. High up in the central nave are rare Ottonian frescoes from *c.* 1015 of *Jesus and the Apostles*. The crypt is supported by Roman columns; in the apse, the stained glass and exceptionally lively choir, sculpted with 144 figures, were added under Prior Georges. Recently, in the centre of the choir, a 12th-century mosaic pavement was discovered in excellent condition, with the palindromic words of the famous magic square in a circle (SATOR AREPO TENET OPERA ROTAS) around a man wrestling with a lion. The cloister, one of the most delightful in northern Italy, has columns topped by 40 marble capitals sculpted with Biblical scenes, the life of St Orso, animals and foliage. Across the lane lie

Basilica di San Lorenzo
t 0165 238 127; open daily Mar–June and Sept 9–7; July and Aug 10–8; Oct–Feb 10–5

the excavations of the **Basilica di San Lorenzo**, built in the 6th century and destroyed in the 9th. Via Sant'Anselmo is closed off by the mighty double arches of the Roman **Porta Praetoria**; over 10ft of the gate is now buried under the street. Adjacent is the square **Torre dei Signori di Quart**, a 12th-century tower house belonging to the family that collected tolls for the bishop; it now houses exhibition spaces. To the right, Via Baillage leads back along the Roman walls to the stout medieval **Torre Fromage**, built by the Casei family, whose name means 'cheese'; it, too, now holds changing exhibitions. It overlooks the **Roman Theatre** begun in the

Roman Theatre
t 349 643 6018; open Oct and Feb daily 9–6.30; Nov–Jan 9–5 except 25 Dec and 1 Jan; Mar and Sept 9–7; April–Aug 9–8; last entry 30mins before closing time

early 1st century AD – firm proof that there was culture even in the highest Alps. It had a permanent roof, and was enlarged over time to seat 4,000, making it one of largest of its kind to survive in Europe; an impressive 82ft façade, sections of seats in the *cavea* and part of the *scena* remain. Originally a covered portico linked the theatre to the ancient low-brow entertainment centre, the Claudian-era 20,000-seat **Amphitheatre**, now part of the convent

Santa Caterina
t 0165 262 149 to visit

of **Santa Caterina**. Nearby, in the northwest corner of the Roman walls, rises the 12th-century **Torre dei Balivi** of the Savoys.

The Cathedral and Roman Forum

Via Porta Praetoria from the gate continues into Aosta's central **Piazza Emilio Chanoux**, dedicated to Aosta's leader of the Resistance, who died in a Fascist prison in 1944; it has the city's elegant neoclassical **Hôtel de Ville** (1839), the town hall. Next to

Cattedrale
t 0125 300 222; guided tours every half hour July–Sept and Easter Christmas and Easter holidays 10–5.30, or by appointment; adm

this, take Via Hôtel-des-Etats and turn left for the **Cattedrale**, first built at the same time as Sant'Orso, its neoclassical façade and lunette hiding a Gothic cross-vaulted interior all reworked in the late 1400s by Georges de Challant. His remodelling hid the early 11th-century frescoes along the upper walls, by the same artists who painted Sant'Orso; rediscovered only in 1986, they have now been restored. The 23 stained-glass windows added by Challant are of Swiss workmanship, while the choir contains Inlaid 15th-century stalls and two mosaics, one a 12th-century *Labours of the Months*, the other a 14th-century scene featuring 'ferocious beasts' from Mesopotamia, the Tigris and Euphrates. The life-sized *Crucifixion* dates from 1395. In the ambulatory, the excellent **Museo del Tesoro** contains lovely old things: a Roman cameo, an ivory diptych of the Emperor Honorius from AD 406; the 13th-century effigy of Count Tommaso II of Savoy, and in the choir, exquisite reliquaries and expressive Gothic saints sculpted in wood, a Valdostano speciality.

Museo del Tesoro
t 0165 40413; open Tues–Sun 8.30–10, 10.45–1.30 and 3–5.30 or by appointment; adm

The Cathedral Place Jean XXIII was part of the **Roman Forum** much of which was lost in later rebuilding, although excavations have revealed the original 4th-century cathedral, the baths, foundations of a temple under the **Casa Arcidiaconale** and a striking **Crypto-portico**, a twin-naved underground gallery, three sides of a 302ft by 285ft quadrangle. No one knows what went on here – guesses are it had a sacred purpose, or was used to store grain, or offered a place to cool off on hot days. From here, Via S. Bernard de Menthon leads into Piazza Roncas, named after Aosta's most beautiful Renaissance building, the **Palazzo Roncas** (1606), later seat of the Savoy administration. Piazza Roncas also has the excellent **Museo Archeologico Regionale** housing Neolithic steles, a bust of Jupiter found at the Little St Bernard Pass, an excellent coin collection, a ceremonial breastplate for a horse (3rd century AD), remains of the Roman city and more. Two blocks north, at Via Martinet 16, the church of **Santo Stefano** has a façade painted in the 1600s with pictures of saints and, inside, a giant statue of St Christopher sculpted in 1450 from the trunk of a single tree.

Roman Forum
t 0165 31166; open 9–7 by prior appointment

Museo Archeologico Regionale
t 0165 31572; open daily 9–7, 25 Dec and 1 Jan 3–7; adm

To the west extends a nearly intact portion of the Roman wall, with the 11th-century cylindrical **Tour Neuve**. Following the walls south, there's another medieval tower, the crenellated Torre del Lebbroso, which earned its sad name from a family of lepers who were incarcerated here from 1733 until the last person died in 1803. Other sections of the walls remain in the south, along with the 13th-century **Torre di Bramafam**, and the Roman **Torre Pailleron**.

Torre del Lebbroso
open for exhibitions Tues–Sun 9.30–12.30 and 2.30–6.30

Just north of the centre, off Via Roma in the Consolata neighbourhood, the late Republican **Roman Villa of the Consulate** with baths and geometric mosaic floors was discovered in the

Roman Villa of the Consulate
max 25 people at a time, call t 335 798 1505; open Wed and Fri 9–1

When Queens Butt Heads

The Valdostani have a sport all their own called the *Bataille de Reines*, the 'Battle of Queens', but they aren't playing chess: the queens are sturdy black or brown Valdostano heifers, who during their summer transhumance to the mountains would square off with the top cows from other herds to determine who was queen of the meadow and get first pick of the sweetest grass and herbs. This involves a good deal of staring, pawing with hooves, and then boom! heads collide in a serious but bloodless test of strength and cussedness. Their owners held their first organized 'battle' in 1859. Now local contests take place all summer, with much betting on the outcome, and in October the winners meet in Aosta town for the finals to decide whose cow is the queen of queens.

Area funeraria fuori porta decumana
open every first Wed of month 2–6

1970s. West of the centre, along Corso Battaglione, the **Area funeraria fuori porta decumana** has recently been excavated, with 4th-century AD tombs and the ruins of a palaeochristian basilica.

Around Aosta: Mountains and Megaliths

Pila has the city's nearest skiing, 20km south by road, but easy to reach thanks to a *funivia* from near **Aosta's train station**. Chairlifts from Pila to the **Col di Chamolé** (7,546ft) and **Couis 1** (9,028ft) operate from the end of June until the beginning of September, making it easy to explore the trails and lakes around **Monte Emilius** (11,677ft). If you're driving, stop at **Gressan**, 4km up from Aosta, to see its 12th-century **parish church**, with frescoes of 1463 by Giacomino d'Ivrea.

Funivia
t 0165 521 148

Aosta's train station
www.pila.it; the cable car from Aosta–Pila will be closed from 31 Mar 2008 for works

The big news in local archaeology, however, was the discovery in 1969 of a Neolithic cult centre (*c.* 3000–2100 BC) on the western edge of Aosta. The **Area Megalitica di St-Martin-de-Corléans** by the church of the same name extends over 2½ acres. Occupied for millennia, the first people on the scene are believed to have been migrants from Anatolia, who set up alignments of stakes, left 40 anthropomorphic statue-steles (nearly all male, and nearly all broken by later arrivals) and who buried their chiefs in large stone tombs, under dolmens, and in a covered alley (they had a necropolis of cist tombs for the hoi polloi near Quart). One curious thing they did was ritually sow human teeth – reminiscent of the Greek myth of Cadmus of Thebes. A huge glass roof is being built over the site, which should open to the public in 2008.

North of Aosta: Gran San Bernardo

The **Valpelline** north of Aosta is best known for its dam and hydroelectric plant but cheese lovers may want to visit to learn about Aosta's *totem fontina* at the **Centre de Visite de Valpelline** at Frissoniere. In summer, two buses a day go up the Great St Bernard Valley, the road affording splendid vistas back towards Aosta itself. On the way the village of **Gignod** has, as usual, a castle, this one from the 1200s; the adjacent church of **Sant'Ilario** has good 15th-century frescoes and a little **Museo Parrocchiale** with wooden statues. **Etroubles**, further up, is the main resort, and **Saint-Oyen** is a quieter holiday centre, with skiing at Flassin. After the tunnel turn-off, above the last village, **St-Rhémy-en-Bosses**, a large **statue of Saint Bernard** honouring the patron of the Alps marks the **Great Saint Bernard Pass** (8,113ft; *closed Oct–May*). The lake here has one bank in Italy, the other in Switzerland. Before Bernard, the pass was known as *Summus Poeninus*, after a temple of Jupiter Poeninus. Neolithic shepherds, Celts, Romans, Emperors from Charlemagne to Barbarossa, pilgrims and merchants once passed here on a regular basis; in 1800 Napoleon frogmarched 40,000 troops over

Centre de Visite de Valpelline
t 0165 73309; open in summer daily 8.30–12.30 and 2.30–6.30, Sat and Sun 9–12 and 3–6; in winter Mon–Fri only 9–12 and 2.30–5.30

Museo Parrocchiale
t 0165 56004; open 8am–8pm

to defeat the Austrians at Marengo (*see* p.294). Part of the ancient **Roman road** is still visible.

Just over the Swiss border (*bring passports*), the legendary Hospice was founded in 1050 by St Bernard, then archdeacon of Aosta, to minister to weary travellers. To help find people lost in the heavy snows, the resident canons developed their famous hardy dogs; magnificent specimens abound, happily mugging for the cameras. The church has the tomb of General Louis-Charles Desaix, hero of Marengo, paid for by a grateful Napoleon, and a rich treasure, including a 13th-century bust of St Bernard; the **museum** has archaeological finds, several relating to the cult of Jupiter.

Hospice
t 0041 277 871 236,
www.gsbernard.ch;
open July and Aug
8–7; June and
Sept 9–5; adm

Museum
open July–Aug 9–7;
June and Sept 9–12 and
1–6; Oct–May on
request; adm

Sports and Activities in Aosta

For a mountain guide, contact the **Unione Valdostana Guide d'Alta Montagna**, Via Monte Emilius 13, **t** 0165 40939, *www.interguide.it*. Aosta's **air club, t** 0165 262 442, *www.aecaosta.it*, offers gliding, parachuting, hang-gliding and lessons on how to land small planes on glaciers; to go **hot-air ballooning** over Europe's highest mountains, contact Nello Charbonnier Mongolfiere, **t** 0165 765 525, *www.mongolfiere.it*. From the end of June until the beginning of August, a festival of classical music takes place, *www.aostaclassica.it*.

Where to Stay and Eat in Aosta

Aosta ✉ 11100

****Milleluci**, 1km from Aosta at Loc. Porossan Roppoz, 15, **t** 0165 235 278, *www.hotelmilleluci.com* (€€€€). A romantic old converted farmhouse overlooking the city; its name, 'the Thousand Lights', describes the view over Aosta by night. Outdoor pool, Turkish bath, jacuzzi and solarium.

****Europe**, Via Ribitel 8, **t** 0165 236 363, *www.ethotels.com/hoteleurope.html* (€€€€–€€€). An excellent, friendly hotel in the centre, with a fine **restaurant** and piano bar.

***Bus**, Via Malherbes 18/a, **t** 0165 43645, *www.hotelbus.it* (€€€– €€). Oddly named relic of the 1960s, in a quiet street off Via Aubert (with some parking). Adequate rooms, and a good **restaurant** (€).

ⓘ **Aosta >**
Piazza Emilio
Chanoux 45, t 0165 236
627, www.aiataosta.
com. For regional info,
see www.regione.
vda.it/turismo

⭐ **Praetoria >>**

***Rayon de Soleil**, above Aosta in Saraillon, Viale Gran San Bernardo, **t** 0165 262 247, *www.rayondesoleil.it* (€€). Convenient if you're driving; a pleasant, medium-sized hotel, with fine views, garden and pool.

****Monte Emilius**, Via G. Carrel 11, **t** 0165 230 068 (€). Next to the station, a gem of a hotel with some large, high-ceilinged Art-Decoish rooms with balconies and lovely/ terrible views of mountains/railway tracks. The **restaurant** is also good.

Agriturismo La Ferme, Regione Chabloz 18 (2km from Aosta), **t** 0165 551 647 (€). Three apartments in a traditional chalet on a fruit farm, sleeping up to five. *Four-day minimum stay. Open all year.*

Vecchio Ristoro da Alfio e Katia, Via Tourneuve 4, **t** 0165 33238 (€€€€). Elegant, intimate, housed in a 12th-century windmill that functioned until only a few years ago. The hot *antipasti*, smoked trout and salmon, and an especially good selection of local cheeses are all excellent. Booking advisable. *Closed Sun, and Mon lunch, 1–10 Nov and June.*

Vecchia Aosta, Piazza Porte Pretoriane 4, **t** 0165 361 186 (€€€). Well-prepared Italian classics, with outdoor tables in the square. *Closed Wed except in summer and Nov.*

Praetoria, Via Sant'Anselmo 9, **t** 0165 44356 (€€€). Wonderful and popular family-run trattoria serving simple but perfect dishes such as *pasta e fagioli*, suckling pig and apple pie. *Closed Thurs.*

Degli Artisti, Via Maillet 5, **t** 0165 40960 (€€€). A local favourite, serving classics like *seupa vapellenentse*, walnut gnocchi, roasted goose and *polenta grassa*, with a good house wine. *Closed Mon.*

La Cave, Via Challand 34, **t** 0165 44164 (€€). Located just off Via Aubert, a popular place to nibble the evening

away on wine by the glass, cheese, salads, smoked salmon and other treats. *Closed Sun.*

Le Grand Paradis, Via Sant'Anselmo 121, **t** 0165 44047 (€). Good wine bar, next to a serious wine shop.

The Western Valleys

Val di Cogne and Gran Paradiso National Park

😊 **Cogne and Gran Paradiso**

Castello Reale di Sarre
t 0165 257 539; open Mar–June and Sept 9–6.30; July and Aug 9–7.30; Oct–Feb Tues–Sat 10–12 and 1.30–4.30, Sun 10–12 and 1.30–5.30; adm

Museo Regionale di Scienze Naturali
t 0165 903 485; open daily June–July 10–6; 1–20 Aug 9–6; entry every hour; adm

Sarriod de la Tour
t 0165 904 689; open daily Mar–June and Sept 10–6; July and Aug 10–7; Oct–Feb Wed–Mon 10–12.30 and 1.30–5, Sun 1.30–6; guided visits only, max 25 people at a time; adm

Museo Minerario
t 0165 749 264, www.grand-paradis.it; open 23 June–9 Sept, Thurs–Tues 11–7; adm

Cooperative Dentellières de Cogne
t 0165 749 282

Paradisia
t 0165 74147; open June and Sept 10–5.30; July–Aug 10–6.30; adm

Before turning south to Cogne, there are more castles to see west of Aosta, beginning by the *autostrada* exit, with the solemn 13th-century **Castello Reale di Sarre** rebuilt in the 18th century. Vittorio Emanuele II and Umberto I, who spent every spare moment hunting, used it as a lodge, and filled it with trophies bagged in the surroundings; other rooms are full of memorabilia of the Savoys in Aosta. Two castles guard the village of **Saint Pierre**: one, set above the Romanesque church and campanile, with four picturesque baby towers added in the 19th century, now houses the **Museo Regionale di Scienze Naturali**, dedicated to Aosta's flora, fauna and minerals. The other castle, perched on a rock over the village, is **Sarriod de la Tour** (1393) with some of its original frescoes and other decorative bits inside, along with special exhibitions.

Beginning at Saint Pierre, the **Val di Cogne** stretches south towards the blunt peak of **Gran Paradiso** (13,323ft), the highest mountain entirely in Italy. Rich magnetite mines were the valley's mainstay and fed the steel mill in Aosta until 1979; tourism, its current bread and butter, began in earnest with the opening of the national park in 1922. The mouth of the valley is defended by another stunning castle, the **Castello di Aymavilles** (*closed for restoration*), built by the Challants, although its four round towers date from the 18th century. A few minutes further up, at **Pondel** (Pont d'Ael), a road descends to the Grand Eyvia gorge, spanned by a tall **aqueduct** in perfect nick, built, according to its inscription, in 3 BC for the exclusive use of two wealthy Romans.

The road continues through forested ravines and lush valleys to **Cogne**, an attractive resort beautifully set next to a vast meadow, the Prateria Sant'Orso. Cogne's former life as a mining town is commemorated with a cast-iron fountain of 1819 in front of the town hall and the **Museo Minerario** in the old mining hamlet of Boutillères; there's even talk of restoring the mining train that brought the ore to Aosta. In the 16th century, nuns from Cluny are said to have introduced bobbin lace to Cogne, and the local style is similar to Venetian, on display at the **Cooperative Dentellières de Cogne**, at Via Dr Grappein 50. The flowers and lichens are spectacular from late June to mid-July – especially in the Alpine garden **Paradisia**, in **Valnontey**, 2.5km up the road. Another hamlet

Getting around the Western Valleys

Trains go up the valley as far as Pré-Saint-Didier, where you can pick up a **bus** for Courmayeur or La Thuile. The 11.6km **Mont Blanc tunnel** links Courmayeur and Chamonix (France); car tolls are €32.30 single, €40.30 return.

near Cogne, **Lillaz,** has three pretty waterfalls a 10-minute walk from the road. To get on top of things take the *funivia* up to 6,889ft

Montzeuc
t 0165 74008; closed May, June, Oct and Nov, opens 3rd week of June: 23 June–9 Sept 9–12 and 2–5.30, 4–19 Aug 9–5; adm

Montzeuc for the lovely views and to walk one of its nature circuits. Cogne is the main gateway to the **Parco Nazionale del Gran Paradiso** (*see* p.333). The tourist office can provide maps and advice on paths, from flattish meanders to lung-bursting hikes. One of the easiest starts in Valnontey and continues up the river towards the glaciers. One of the most spectacular is up to the **Rifugio Vittorio**

Rifugio Vittorio Sella
t 0125 366 113

Sella (8,478ft), a trip into the vale of **Losòn,** where ibex and chamois frolic now that the refuge is no longer a royal hunting lodge.

The western reaches of the park – the lush, unspoiled **Val Savarenche** and the **Val di Rhêmes** – may be reached from Villeneuve (*see* below) on the main Dora Valley road, passing by way of the castle of **Introd** (13th-century, rebuilt 1910); the late John Paul II used to come to nearby Les Combes for his holidays, preferring the mountains to Castel Gandolfo; here the **Maison**

Maison Bruil
t 0165 920 623

Bruil, a 17th-century complex, has been converted into a centre for the study of EU mountain issues, and has frequent exhibitions. In the Val Savarenche, the ideal basè is **Eaux-Rousses,** from where you can pick up the Alta Via, the high mountain path around Aosta, which will take you east to the Rifugio Vittorio Sella (2½ hours), or west to **Lake Djovan** for the **Entrelor Pass.** The Valsavarenche road ends at **Pont,** the base for ascents of **Gran Paradiso** and the **Nivolet**

Rifugio Savoia
t 0165 94141, in winter t 0165 95272

Pass (8,569ft), site of yet another royal hunting lodge, the **Rifugio Savoia**; from here you can descend to Ceresole Reale. In the parallel Val de Rhêmes, the old village of **Rhêmes-Notre-Dame** has a visitors' centre dedicated to the lammergeyer, the largest bird in Europe; after vanishing from Paradiso, it has recently returned.

Up the Main Valley: Villeneuve to Pré-Saint-Didier

With the opening of the Aosta–Courmayeur–Mont Blanc *autostrada*, people tend to zoom through this rugged area, where every medieval Tom, Dick and Harry built a castle. **Villeneuve** is sprawled under the ruined 12th-century **Châtel-Argent,** while the next town, **Arvier,** sits under the slightly later **Château de la Mothe** and makes the Valle d'Aosta's famous *Vin de l'Enfer,* the Wine of Hell, named not after any brimstone aftertaste but for the heat that bounces back from the rocks onto the vines, ripening the grapes. Here a road forks for the wild and rocky **Val Grisenche,** where traditional wool weaving has yet to die out. The main villages, **Planaval** and **Valgrisenche,** have the **Rutor Glacier** for a backdrop, while just beyond towers the Beauregard dam (1957). Anyone interested in textiles should visit Valgrisenche's **Cooperativa 'Les Tisserands'** to watch them make the local speciality, 'drap', a thick hand-woven cloth used for upholstering.

Cooperativa 'Les Tisserands'
t 0165 97163

Back in the main valley, **Avise** is a charming village with two medieval castles at the foot of a gorge and the remains of the Roman road cut into the rock (the **Pierre Taillée**). Just past Avise you'll catch your first glimpse of Mont Blanc. Above the road to the left, **Derby** has a fine collection of fortified medieval houses and an impressive waterfall, the **Cascata di Linteney**. To the right of the road the landmark is the 13th-century **Châtelard tower** in **La Salle**.

Medieval **Morgex** was an administrative centre; its parish church of **S. Maria Assunta** preserves a Gothic portal and frescoes of 1492; the vines that grow around here are the highest in Europe. Just beyond, **Pré-Saint-Didier**, the last train station in Aosta, lies at the confluence of the Dora de la Thuile and Dora Baltea; it has warm arsenic-laced springs that are used for skin complaints.

Up to Piccolo San Bernardo

From Pré-Saint-Didier, the road winds up the **Little Saint Bernard Valley**, threading forests and dizzily skirting the ravine of the Dora de la Thuile. The valley's one town, **La Thuile**, was an old mining centre and is now a busy but not overcrowded resort, with unsurpassed skiing on the slopes of Chaz Dura. Three waterfalls spill from the Rutor glacier, a two-hour walk away. In summer, drive up to the **Col San Carlo** for a view taking in 150 peaks, just under the **Testa d'Arp**, with an azure lake under Mont Blanc.

Above La Thuile, Mont Blanc also forms a stunning backdrop to **Lake Verney**, a mirror in a setting of emerald meadows. Further up, the **Little Saint Bernard Pass** (7,178ft; *open June–Oct*) was the main link between France and Aosta before the Mont Blanc tunnel. The pass is marked by a **statue of Saint Bernard** on a column, replacing a statue of Jupiter that was demolished as pagan faldirol by the same Bernard. Older than either religion is the nearby **cromlech**, a Neolithic or Bronze Age circle made of 44 stones. Just over the French frontier, the ancient **Hospice du Petit Saint Bernard** was founded c. 1000, even before Saint Bernard, with the same purpose of sheltering travellers. Bombed during the Second World War, it was ceded to France, then abandoned until 1993, when reconstruction began again; it now contains a **Museum of the History of the Pass**. In 1897, the Abbot Pierre Chanous planted an Alpine botanical garden here, **La Chanousia**, reopened in 1967.

Museum of the History of the Pass
open July–Aug daily 9.30–12.30 and 2–6

La Chanousia
t 0033 479 074 332, www.chanousia.org; open beg July–3rd Sun of Sept daily 9–7; guided visits 15 July–30 Aug starting at 10am

Courmayeur and Mont Blanc

Courmayeur is that rare bird: a top ski resort that is also a charming old town, one that grew up around silver mines and a spa visited since the 18th century. Old cobbled streets are lined with boutiques and restaurants. lying at the foot of the 'Roof of Europe', 15,771ft Mont Blanc and a dozen other peaks, the skiing is superb, especially off piste, such as the famous 20km Vallée Blanche run from Punta Helbronner all the way to Chamonix and slopes from Cresta d'Arp and Cresta Youla. The main lifts to **Chécrouit-Val Veny** are within walking distance of town.

Courmayeur also offers magnificent cross-country skiing in the lower valley, a huge indoor ice-skating rink and an indoor pool: in summer there is a rock-climbing school, golf on the highest course in Europe, tennis, riding, hang-gliding, fishing and spectacular walks, with some 20 Alpine refuges. At Strada Villair 2, the Museo Alpino has items relating to the local guides.

La Palud, just north of Courmayeur near the medieval fortress-village of **Entrèves**, is the base for one of the most thrilling journeys anywhere: the five-stage **Funivie Mont Blanc**, the longest system of cable cars in the world, waiting to whisk you up and over the glaciers of Mont Blanc to Chamonix in the summer – an unforgettable trip, especially if you're lucky enough to catch the big mountain without its veil of mist (*packages include return by bus via the Mont Blanc tunnel*). All year round you can ascend to the **Pavillion du Mont Frety** (6,988ft), with a restaurant and the Giardino Alpino Saussurea, the highest botanical garden in Europe, then continue to the **Rifugio Torino** (11,073ft) or **Punta Helbronner** (11,358ft), offering a magnificent 360° view over the Alps and the **Mostra Permanente dei Cristalli**, devoted to crystals and minerals found on Mont Blanc. From June to October, the *telecabina* continues vertiginously over Mont Blanc's glaciers to the Aiguille du Midi (12,604ft), and from there down to Chamonix. Whenever you go, douse yourself in sunscreen and wrap up warmly.

In summer, there's an outdoor swimming pool up at the **Plan-Chécrouit**; from there you can walk to **Mont Chétif**, the peak just before Mont Blanc, offering tremendous views into the mighty abyss of the **Aiguille Noire**. Two gorgeous valleys run in opposite directions from Entrèves. The beautifully forested **Val Veny** to the south has a road up to the **Rifugio Elisabetta**; from there, it's a three-hour walk up to the **Col de la Seigne** on the French border, with fabulous views in either direction. The **Val Ferret** to the north of Entrèves is enchanting and serene, and filled with meadows, trout streams and the finest cross-country walks; there is accommodation in **Plampincieux**, a quiet resort in the pines.

Museo Alpino
t 0165 842 064; open Thurs–Tues 9–12 and 4–7

⚡ Funivie Mont Blanc
t 0165 89925; www.montebianco.com

Giardino Alpino Saussurea
t 333 446 2959, www.saussurea.net; open July–Sept daily 9–4.30, in Aug as long as the cable car is operational; adm

Rifugio Torino
t 340 227 0121

Rifugio Elisabetta
t 0165 844 080

Sports and Events in the Western Valleys

Ask the tourist office in Cogne about excursions up to Vittorio Sella

(*see also www.pila.it,* t 0165 521 045). For **white-water rafting**, contact Morgex & Valsesia Rafting, in Morgex, t 0165 800 088, *www.rafting.it*. The Mountain Guides of Courmayeur, t 0165 842 064, *www.guidecour mayeur.com*, will take you **heli-skiing**, **ice-climbing**, **snowshoeing**, and more; in summer they lead **climbing**, **trekking** and **canyoning** excursions.

Courmayeur holds the massive **Celtica music festival** (*www.celticavda. org*) in late June/early July.

Where to Stay and Eat in the Western Valleys

Saint Pierre ⊠ 11010

La Tour, SS 26, Via Piccolo San Bernardo 16, t 0165 903 808 (€€€€). Elegant dishes such as *foie gras* with new pears and guinea fowl with truffles. *Closed Tues and Wed*.

La Thuile ⊠ 11013

****Planibel Hotel and Apartments**, Fraz. Entrèves 156, t 0165 884 541, *www.tivigest.com* (€€€€€). Large complex with basic rooms, right at the base of the lifts. Also has an indoor pool. *Closed May–mid-June and mid-Sept–Nov*.

La Bricole, Loc. Entrèves 60, t 0165 884 149 (€€€). Good traditional food and home-made pasta. *Closed Mon*.

Cogne ⊠ 11012

****Bellevue**, Rue Grand Paradis 22, t 0165 74825, *www.hotelbellevue.it* (€€€€€). Open since 1925 with majestic views of the big meadow. Fine **restaurants**, including one dedicated to mountain cheese, as well as a spa, where you can bathe in wine, milk and honey or even hay. *Closed Nov to Christmas hols*.

****Sant'Orso**, Via Bourgeois 2, t 0165 74821, *www.cognevacanze.com* (€€). Also enjoys splendid views, at more affordable prices, and has an excellent **restaurant**. Rooms for disabled guests available. *Minimum three night stay. Closed April and Oct–Nov*.

Lou Ressignon, Via des Mines 22, t 0165 74034 (€€). Serves good, honest Valdostano specialities in an attractive chalet: chamois in civet with polenta, for instance. *Closed Mon eve and Tues out of season*.

Brasserie du Bon Bec, Via Bourgeois 72, t 0165 749 288 (€€€–€€). Cosy place serving big meaty grills, *pierrades* and

fondues, and an extensive wine list. *Book. Closed Mon*.

Les Pertzes, Via Grappein 93, t 0165 749 227 (€€). Brasserie-cum-wine and snack bar, with 800 different bottles from around the world in the *cantina*. *Closed Tues, Wed*.

Courmayeur ⊠ 11013

****Romantik Hotel Villa Novecento**, Viale Monte Bianco 64, t 0165 843 000, *www.villanovecento.it* (€€€€€). Charming, central, very atmospheric hotel from the early 1900s, packed full of antiques; there's a good **restaurant** (€€€€), and a fitness centre with Turkish bath and jacuzzi. *Closed May and Oct–Nov*.

****Royal e Golf**, Via Roma 87, t 0165 831 611, *www.royalegolf.com* (€€€€). May look a little lopsided from outside, but inside the facilities and service are as balanced as you could wish. The views, especially from the **restaurant**, are fantastic. Indoor pool. *Half board mandatory. Closed May–June and Sept–Nov*.

***Del Viale**, Viale Monte Bianco 74, t 0165 846 712, *www.hoteldelviale.com* (€€€€). Handsome family-run chalet with views, and a cosy lobby and **restaurant** with open fires. Most rooms have a balcony or sun terrace.

***Croux**, Via Croux 8, t 0165 846 735, *www.hotelcroux.it* (€€€). In the centre of town, with outstanding views and mod cons, sauna and steam baths. *Breakfast included. Closed mid-April–May and Nov*.

***Bouton d'Or**, SS26 No.10, t 0165 846 729, *www.hotelboutondor.it* (€€€). Friendly and central B&B, with cosy rooms; some have balconies with views of Mont Blanc.

Venezia, Strada Villette 2, t 0165 842 461 (€). Large rooms with great views.

Pierre Alexis, Via G. Marconi 50/a t 0165 843 517 (€€€€–€€€). Courmayeur's oldest restaurant provides the town's finest dining; in season try the hunter's menu for two. *Closed Mon*.

Le Vieux Pommier, Piazzale Monte Bianco 25, t 0165 842 281 (€€). A favourite with a rustic hyper-Alpine interior and solid Valdostano cuisine. They also have **rooms**. *Closed Mon*.

ⓘ **Courmayeur >>**
Piazzale Monte Bianco 13, t 0165 842 060, www.aiat-monte-bianco-com

ⓘ **Cogne >**
Via Bourgeois 34, t 0165 74040, www.cogne.org

13

Valle d'Aosta | The Western Valleys

⭐ Maison de Filippo >>

Leone Rosso, Via Roma 73, t 0165 846 726 (€€). Good for filling *fonduta*, fish and vegetarian dishes.

La Palud/Entrèves ✉ 11013

***Auberge de la Maison**, Via Passerin d'Entrèves, t 0165 869 811, *www. aubergemaison.it* (€€€€–€€€). Handsome new boutique hotel, run by the same family as the Maison de Filippo. **Restaurant** (€€€€) enjoys a spectacular view of Mont Blanc.

***Astoria**, Strada La Palud 23, Entrèves, t 0165 869 740, *www.hotel astoriacourmayeur.com*, (€€€). Stylish rooms and lots of après-ski action on weekends downstairs, plus free minibus shuttles to Courmayeur.

***Dente del Gigante**, Strada La Palud 42, Entrèves, t 0165 89145, *www.dente delgigante.com* (€€€). Pleasant hotel with a good **restaurant** (€€€€). *Closed Oct–Nov and May–end of June.*

***La Brenva**, Strada La Palud 12, Entrèves, t 0165 869 780 (€€). A Savoy royal hunting lodge that has been a hotel since 1897. The décor has changed little since then, although the amenities are up-to-date.

**Funivia, Via San Bernardo 2, La Palud, t 0165 89924, *www.hotel funivia.com* (€€). Big rooms, modern bathrooms, old wooden furniture and priceless views. *In winter, stays are by the week. Closed May, Oct and Nov.*

Pré de Pascal, Val Veny, t 0165 842 719, *www.predepascal.com* (€). Rooms (summer only) and little **restaurant** in a historic *alpeggio*.

Maison de Filippo, Entrèves 8, t 0165 869 797, *www.lamaison.com* (€€€€). The ultimate Alpine blow-out since 1965; the unique €45 menu offers 30 dishes from *antipasti* to ravioli stuffed with *porcini* mushrooms, fondue, trout or game, and a *grand dessert finale. Book. Closed Tues, June and Nov.*

La Clotze, Loc. Planpincieux Nord in Val Ferret, t 0165 869 720, *www. laclotze.com* (€€€€). Family restaurant serving fresh seasonal dishes, along with a huge cheese and wine selection. *Closed Wed, Tues lunch, mid-May–mid-June, mid-Sept–mid-Oct.*

Language

The fathers of modern Italian were Dante, Manzoni and television. Each played its part in creating a national language from an infinity of regional and local dialects; the Florentine Dante, the first to write in the vernacular, did much to put the Tuscan dialect into the foreground of Italian literature. Manzoni's revolutionary novel, *I Promessi Sposi*, heightened national consciousness by using an everyday language all could understand in the 19th century. Television in the last few decades has performed an even more spectacular linguistic unification; many Italians still speak a dialect at home though.

Perhaps because they are so busy learning their own beautiful but grammatically complex language, Italians are not especially apt at learning others. English lessons, however, have been the rage for years, and at most hotels and restaurants there will be someone who speaks some English.

Note that in the big northern cities, the informal way of addressing someone as you, *tu*, is widely used; the more formal *lei* or *voi* is commonly used in provincial districts.

Pronunciation

Italian words are pronounced phonetically. Every vowel and consonant except 'h' is sounded. The stress usually (but not always!) falls on the penultimate syllable. Accents indicate if it falls on the last syllable (as in *città*); accents serve no other purpose, except to distinguish between *e* (and) and *è* (is).

Consonants

Consonants are the same as in English, with the following exceptions:

C when followed by an 'e' or 'i', is pronounced like the English 'ch' (*cinque* thus becomes cheenquay).

G is also soft before 'i' or 'e' as in *gira*, or jee-rah.

Z is pronounced like 'ts'.

Look out too for the following consonant combinations:

Sc before the vowels 'i' or 'e' become like the English 'sh' as in *sci*, pronounced 'shee'.

Ch is pronouced like a 'k', as in *Chianti*, 'kee-an-tee'.

Gn is pronounced as 'nya' (thus *bagno* is pronounced ban-yo).

Gli is pronounced like the middle of the word *million* (so *Castiglione* is pronounced Ca-steel-yoh-nay).

Vowels

A is pronounced as in English *father*.

E when unstressed is pronounced like 'a' in *fate*; when stressed it can be the same or like the 'e' in *pet*.

I is like the 'i' in *machine*.

O has two sounds, 'o' as in *hope* when unstressed, and 'o' as in *rock* when stressed.

U is pronounced like the 'u' in *June*.

Useful Words and Phrases

yes *sì*
no *no*
I don't know *Non (lo) so*
I don't understand (Italian) *Non capisco (l'italiano)*
Does someone here speak English? *C'è qualcuno qui che parla inglese?*
Speak slowly *Parla lentamente*
Could you help me? *Potrebbe aiutarmi?*
Help! *Aiuto!*
Please *Per favore*
Thank you (very much) *Grazie (molte/mille)*
You're welcome *Prego*
All right *Va bene*
Excuse me *Permesso/Mi scusi*
I'm sorry *Mi dispiace*
Nothing *Niente*
How are you? *Come sta/stai?*
What is your name? *Come si chiama?/ ti chiami?*

Hello *Salve* or *ciao* (both informal)/ *Buongiorno* (formal)
Good morning *Buongiorno*
Good afternoon/evening *Buonasera*
Goodnight *Buonanotte*
Goodbye *ArrivederLa* (formal), *Arrivederci/Ciao* (informal)
What? *Che?*
Who? *Chi?*
Where? *Dove?*
When? *Quando?*
Why? *Perché?*
How? *Come?*
I am tired *Sono stanco*
I feel unwell *Mi sento male*
good *buono*
bad *cattivo*
well *bene*
badly *male*
hot *caldo*
cold *freddo*
slow *lento*
fast *rapido*
up *su*
down *giù*
big *grande*
small *piccolo*
here *qui*
there *lì*
too (excessively) *troppo*
lots/a lot *molto*
OK *d'accordo*
Is that OK with you? *ti* (formal: *le*) *va bene?*
That's OK, thanks *Va bene così, grazie*
address *l'indirizzo*

Time

What time is it? *Che ore sono?*
day *giorno*
week *settimana*
month *mese*
morning *mattina*
afternoon *pomeriggio*
evening *sera*
yesterday *ieri*
today *oggi*
tomorrow *domani*
It is too early/late *È troppo presto/tardi*
spring *la primavera*
summer *l'estate*
autumn *l'autunno*
winter *l'inverno*

Months

January *gennaio*
February *febbraio*
March *marzo*
April *aprile*
May *maggio*
June *giugno*
July *luglio*
August *agosto*
September *settembre*
October *ottobre*
November *novembre*
December *dicembre*

Days

Monday *lunedì*
Tuesday *martedì*
Wednesday *mercoledì*
Thursday *giovedì*
Friday *venerdì*
Saturday *sabato*
Sunday *domenica*

Numbers

one *uno/una*
two *due*
three *tre*
four *quattro*
five *cinque*
six *sei*
seven *sette*
eight *otto*
nine *nove*
ten *dieci*
eleven *undici*
twelve *dodici*
thirteen *tredici*
fourteen *quattordici*
fifteen *quindici*
sixteen *sedici*
seventeen *diciassette*
eighteen *diciotto*
nineteen *diciannove*
twenty *venti*
twenty-one *ventuno*
thirty *trenta*
forty *quaranta*
fifty *cinquanta*
sixty *sessanta*
seventy *settanta*

eighty *ottanta*
ninety *novanta*
hundred *cento*
one hundred and one *centuno*
two hundred *duecento*
one thousand *mille*
two thousand *duemila*
million *milione*

Transport

airport *aeroporto*
bus stop *fermata*
bus/coach *autobus*
railway station *stazione ferroviaria*
train *treno*
platform *binario*
taxi *tassì/taxi*
one ticket to xxx *un biglietto per xxx*
one way *semplice/andata*
return *andata e ritorno*
first/second class *prima/seconda classe*
I want to go to... *Desidero andare a...*
How can I get to...? *Come posso andare a...?*
Do you stop at...? *Si ferma a...?*
Where is...? *Dov'è/Dove sono...?*
From where does it leave? *Da dove parte?*
How far is it to...? *Quanto siamo lontani da...?*
When does the next ... leave? *Quando parte
il prossimo...?*
How long does the trip take? *Quanto tempo
dura il viaggio?*
How much is the fare? *Quant'è il biglietto?*
near *vicino*
far *lontano*
left *sinistra*
right *destra*
straight ahead *sempre diritto*
north/south/east/west *nord/sud/est/ovest*
crossroads *bivio*
street *strada*
road *via*
square *piazza*
petrol *benzina*
diesel *gasolio*
breakdown *guasto*
driving licence *patente di guida*
speed *velocità*
parking *parcheggio*
no parking *sosta vietata*
narrow *stretto*
bridge *ponte*

toll *pedaggio*
slow down *rallentare*

Shopping, Services, Sightseeing

I would like... *Vorrei...*
How much is it? *Quanto costa?*
open *aperto*
closed *chiuso*
cheap *a buon prezzo*
expensive *caro*
bank *banca*
entrance *ingresso*
exit *uscita*
hospital *ospedale*
money *soldi*
credit card *carta di credito*
newspaper *giornale*
pharmacy *farmacia*
police station *commissariato*
policeman *poliziotto*
post office *ufficio postale*
shop *negozio*
supermarket *supermercato*
WC *toilette/bagno/servizi*
men *Signori/Uomini*
women *Signore/Donne*

Useful Hotel Vocabulary

I'd like a double room, please *Vorrei
una camera doppia (matrimoniale),
per favore*
I'd like a single room *Vorrei una camera
singola*
...with/without bath *...con/senza bagno*
...for two nights *...per due notti*
We are leaving tomorrow morning *Partiamo
domani mattina*
There isn't (aren't) any hot water, soap,
light, toilet paper, towels *Manca/Mancano
acqua calda, sapone, luce, carta igienica,
asciugamani*
May I pay by credit card? *Posso pagare con
carta di credito?*
Is breakfast included? *È compresa la prima
colazione?*
What time do you serve breakfast? *A che ora
è la colazione?*
How do I get to the town centre? *Come
posso raggiungere il centro città?*

Glossary

Basilica: a rectangular building, usually divided into three aisles by rows of columns. In Rome this was the common form for law courts and other public buildings, and Roman Christians adapted it for their early churches

Campanile: a bell tower

Camposanto: a cemetery

Carrugi: narrow Ligurian alleys

Cartoon: the preliminary sketch for a fresco or tapestry

Castellari: ancient Ligurian fortified settlements, often on hilltops

Castrum: a Roman military camp, always nearly rectangular, with straight streets and gates at the cardinal points. Later the Romans founded or refounded cities in this form, and hundreds of these survive today

Centro Storico: historic centre

Comune: commune, or commonwealth, referring to the governments of the free cities of the Middle Ages. Today it denotes any local government, from the Comune di Roma down to the smallest village

Condottiere: the leader of a band of mercenaries in late medieval and Renaissance times

Confraternity: a religious lay brotherhood, often serving as a neighbourhood mutual aid and burial society, or following some specific charitable work (Michelangelo, for example, belonged to one that cared for condemned prisoners in Rome)

Cortile: inner atrium or courtyard of a palace

Duomo: cathedral

Entroterra: the Ligurian hinterland; each coastal town has its *entroterra*

Forum: the central square of a Roman town, with its most important temples and public buildings. The word means 'outside', as the original Roman Forum was outside the first city walls

Fresco: wall painting, the most important Italian medium of art since Etruscan times.

First the artist draws the sinopia on the wall. This is then covered with plaster, but only a little at a time, as the paint must be on the plaster before it dries. Leonardo da Vinci's attempts to find shortcuts ensured that little of his work would survive

Ghibellines: one of the two great medieval parties, the supporters of the Holy Roman Emperors

Guelphs (*see* Ghibellines): the other great political faction of medieval Italy, supporters of the Pope

Lungomare: seaside; also a name given to a coastal road

Palazzo: not just a palace, but any large, important building

Passeggiata: promenade

Pieve: a parish church, especially in the north

Podestà: a mayor or governor from outside a *comune*, usually chosen by the emperor or overlord; sometimes a factionalized city would itself invite a *podestà* in for a period to sort itself out

Polyptych: an altarpiece composed of more than three panels

Presepio: a Christmas crib

Putti: flocks of plaster cherubs with rosy cheeks that infested Baroque Italy

Quadratura: trompe l'œil architectural settings, popular in Mannerist and Baroque time, and something of a speciality of artists from Bologna

Risseu: a figurative black-and-white pebble mosaic, often in a sagrato of a church

Sagrato: a specially marked holy area or parvis just outside a church

Scuola: the headquarters of a confraternity or guild, usually adjacent to a church

Sinopia: the layout of a fresco, etched by the artist on the wall before the plaster is applied. Often these are works of art in their own right

Triptych: a painting, especially an altarpiece, in three sections

Further Reading

Ashley, Maureen, *Touring In Wine Country: Northwest Italy* (Mitchell Beazley, 1997). Practical guide to the best of the vineyards.

Chamberlain, Lesley, *Nietzsche in Turin: An Intimate Biography* (St Martin's Press, 1997). Beautifully evokes the complex, often misunderstood philosopher's last year in Turin, his work and thought.

Columbus, Christopher, *The Book of Prophecies*. Edited by Christopher Columbus (University of California, 1996). When he returned from his Third Voyage in chains, the Admiral compiled this peculiar list of Biblical writings, prophecies and medieval theology in a manuscript, in the hopes of justifying himself and preserving his rights.

Downie, David and Harris, Alison, *Enchanted Liguria* (Rizzoli, 1997). Hard to find these days but worth looking out for: a lushly illustrated and in-depth look at what makes the history, architecture, culture and food of this rather insular region unique.

Hawes, Annie, *Extra Virgin: Amongst the Olive Groves of Liguria* (Penguin, 2001). Funny, down-to-earth account of two young Englishwomen making a go of it in the Ligurian *entroterra*. The sequel *Ripe for Picking* (Penguin, 2003) is just as good.

Hibbert, Christopher, *Garibaldi and his Enemies* (Penguin, 1987). The whole sorry tale of the noble, if deeply flawed hero, regarded by the Italians of the day as a second Jesus Christ, while the politicians schemed, used and disowned him; the tale is told by a master.

Kramer, Matt, *A Passion for Piedmont: Italy's Most Glorious Regional Table* (Cookbooks, 1997). Hymn to Piedmont's wine and cuisine and recipes by a well-known American wine critic who spent a year in the region.

De Madariaga, Salvador, *Christopher Columbus* (Greenwood, 1979). Translated from Spanish, the intriguing if largely unsubstantiated theory that Columbus was Jewish.

Petrini, Carlo, ed. *Slow Food* (Grub Street, 2003). A collection of articles from *Slow* magazine on the fundamentals of the movement. Also *Slow Food: The Case for Taste* (Columbia University, 2003), with a foreword by American culinary guru Alice Waters. A summing up of viewpoints by Petrini and others who have worked with Slow Food over the years.

Plotkin, Fred, *Recipes from Paradise* (Little Brown, 1999). Some 200 wonderful recipes from Liguria, details about the wine and fond anecdotes by a food lover who lived there.

Sardi, Roland, *Mazzini* (Praeger, 1996). Full-length biography of Genoa's great revolutionary, and an in-depth exploration of his precocious ideals.

Smith, Denis Mack, *Garibaldi: A Great Life in Brief* (Greenwood, 1982) and *Mazzini* (Yale, 1994). Biographies by one of the best authors on modern Italian history.

Tagliattini, Maurizio, The Discovery of North America (not yet published). Read his chapter 10 on Columbus on the web at *http://muweb.millersville.edu/~columbus/tag liattini.html*.

Trevelyan, G.M., *Garibaldi and the Making of Italy* (Greenwood, 1982). Classic tales of the Risorgimento.

Wilson, Ian and Schwortz, Barrie *The Turin Shroud: Unshrouding the Mystery* (Michael O'Mara Books, 2000). Excellent pictures and a compilation of current evidence, some of which suggests that the Shroud may actually be from the right time and place.

Wittkower, Rudolf, *Art and Architecture in Italy 1600–1750* (Pelican, 1992). The classic on Italian Baroque; good for putting the architectural glories of Genoa and Turin in context.

Index

Main page references are in **bold**. Page references to maps are in *italics*.

abbeys
  Borzone 190
  Fruttaria 330
  Novalesa 258
  San Girolamo 184
  San Venerio 204
  Santa Maria 262
  Santa Maria di Vezzolano 289
  Sant'Antonio di Ranverso 253
  Staffarda 268
Acqui Terme **288**, 293
Agliè 333
Agnelli family 219, 239, 260, 262
agriturismo 73
Airole 87
Ala di Stura 329
Alagna **324**, 327
Alassio 113–15
Alba **279–80**, 282–3
Albaro 168
Albenga **116–17**, 120
Albisola Superiore 134–5
Albissola Marina **134**, 137
Albugnano **289**, 293
Alessandria **294–5**, 297
Alpe Veglia 316
Alpi Marittime 272–4
Alpicella 137
Altare 133
Ameglia **208**, 211
Amino 320
Andagna 102
Andora 111
Andora Castello 112
Andora Marina 111–12
Antagnod 342
Antey-Saint-André 343
Antronapiana 313
Aosta **345–9**, 350–1
Apricale **89**, 90–1
Arab invasions 22
Arcola **208**, 211
Arenzano **137**, 138
Argentera 272
Argentiera 260
Arizzano 309
Arma di Taggia **101**, 104
Armeno 320
Arnad 342
Arona **303–4**, 307
art and architecture **32–6**

Arte Povera 36
Artesina 275
Arvier 352
Asti **285–7**, 291–2
Austrians 150, 295–6
Avegno 179
Avigliana **253–6**, 262
Avise 353
Ayas-Champoluc **342–3**, 345

Badalucco **102**, 104
Bagni di Vinadio 272
Baiardo **98–9**, 101
Baldissero Canavese 332
Balestrino 123
Balma Boves 268
Balme 329
Balzi Rossi caves 20, **86**
banks 67–8, 78
Bannio Anzino 312
Barbaresco 58, **282**, 284
barbarian invasions 21–2
Barbarossa 22, 294
Bardineto 123
Bardino Nuovo 123
Bardonecchia **258–9**, 263
Barolo 58, **280–1**, 283–4
Baroque 34–6
Bastia Mondovì 275
Bataille de Reines 348
Batteria Chaberton 260
Baveno **306**, 308
Bay of Fables 190
Bay of Silence 190
bear cults 121, **122**
Bee 309
Beerbohm, Max 185
Belgirate **305**, 307
Bellino 269
Bergeggi **127–8**, 129
Berio, Luciano 107
Bestagno 109
Beverino 193
Biassa 203
bicycles 72, 79
Biella **324–5**, *324*, 327–8
Bobbio Pellice 262
Bocca di Magra **207**, 211
Boccadasse 168
Boccanegra, Simone 145–6
bocce 79

Bocchetta di Altare di Cadibona 133
Bogliasco **178–9**, 181
Bognanco 315
Bolzaneto 173
Bonassola **195**, 196
Borca 313
Bordighera **91–2**, 94–5
Borgata Raje 334
Borgio Verezzi 124–5
Borgo Foce 106
Borgo Marino 106
Borgomanero 322
Borgomaro 109
Borgomasino 335
Borgosesia 323
Borromean Islands **305–6**, 308
Borzonasca 190
Borzone abbey 190
Bosco Marengo **296**, 297
Bosco Parco 330
Boves 274
Bra **277**, 278–9
Brachetto 59
Bramaterra 59
Breithorn 344
Breuil-Cervinia **344**, 345
Brugnato 193
Brusson 342
Buco di Viso 268
Buggio 90
Buisson 343
buses and coaches 69, 71
Bussana Vecchia 99
Buttigliera Alta 253
Byron, Lord 206
Byzantines 21, 22, 146

Cabanne 190
Calice al Cornoviglio 193
Calizzano **123**, 124
Calosso 292
Caluso 335
Calvino, Italo 96
Camogli **180–2**
Campello Monti 321
Campiglia 203
camping 73–4
Campochiesa 118–19
Camporosso 88
Canale d'Alba 284
Canavese 324, 328–36

Candelo 326
Candia **330**, 335
Candoglia 312
Canelli **287–8**, 292
Cannero Riviera **309–10**, 311
Cannobio **310**, 311
Caravino 330
Carcoforo 327
Carema 59, **335**, 336
Carignano 248
Carmagnola **265**, 270
Carmine 310
cars 69–70, 71–2
Casale Monferrato **290–1**, 294
Casanova 265
Cascata di Linteney 353
Cascate del Toce 317
Casella 164, **173–4**
Cassini, Gian Domenico 93–4
Castel Vittorio 89–90
Casteldelfino 269
Castellamonte 333
Castellazzo Bormida 296
Castello d'Albertis 166
Castello di Aymavilles 351
Castello di Baraing 340
Castello Borgomasino 331
Castello di Corderone 203
Castello di Issogne 342
Castello di Lagnasco 268
Castello della Lucertola 89
Castello Malaspina 190
Castello di Manta 267
Castello di Masino 330
Castello di Mazzè 330
Castello Moncrivello 330–1
Castello della Pietra 174
Castello Reale di Casotto 276
Castello Reale di Sarre 351
Castello di Roddi 280
Castello di Roppolo 327
Castello di St Germain 343
Castello di Sparone 334
Castelmagno 271
Castelnuovo Magra **209**, 211
Castelvecchio di Rocca Barbena 120
Cathars 93
Cavaglio-Spoccia 310
Cavagnolo Po 289
Cavour **262**, 264
Celle Ligure 135–6
Ceppo Morelli 312
Ceres 329
Ceresole Reale **334**, 336
Ceriale 121
Ceriana 99
Cerrione 327
Cervo **111**, 112
Cesana Torinese 259
Chaberton 260
Challand-Saint-Victor 342
Chambave 344
Chamois 343–4
Champoluc **342–3**, 345

Champorcher 341
Charles V, Emperor 24, 148
Châtillon 343
Chécrouit-Val Veny 354
cheeses 57
Cheggio 313
chemists 77
Cherasco **278**, 279
Chialamberto 329
Chiavari **188–9**, 191
Chieri 241
Chiomonte 258
Chiusavecchia 109
Cicagna 180
Ciciu 269
Cimamulera 312
Cinque Terre 196–200
Cipressa 104–5
Ciriè **328–9**, 335
Civezza 105
Claviere **259–60**, 263
climate 64
coaches and buses 69, 71
Cocconato **289**, 293
Cogne **351**, 355
Cogoleto 137
Coldirodi 94
Colla di Langàn 90
Colla Micheri 112
Colle dell'Agnello 269
Colle della Maddalena 272
Colle di Melogno 123
Colle di Nava 119
Colle d'Oggia 108
Colle Valdobbia 323–4
Colle Vergante 304
Colombetti 312
Columbus, Christopher **38–42**, 137, 179–80
consulates 66
Convento Monte Mesma 320
Cornice 193
Corniglia **198**, 200
Cornigliano 167
Corso degli Inglesi 98
Cortazzone 289
Cortemilia **281**, 284
Cortese 59
Costa 195
Costigliole d'Asti **287**, 292
Costigliole Saluzzo **269**, 270
Courmayeur **353–4**, 355–6
Cravanzana 284
Craveggia 316
Crissolo 268
Cristo degli Abissi 183
Crodo **317**, 318
Crusades 22, 144
Cuneo **271**, 274
Cuorgnè **333**, 336

Damanhur 332
Deiva Marina **194**, 196
Demonte 272

Derby 353
Diano Borello 111
Diano Castello 110–11
Diano Marina **110**, 112–13
disabled travellers 67
Doctor Antonio 27
Dogliani 281
Dolceacqua **88**, 90
Dolcedo 108
Domobianca 315
Domodossola **314–15**, 317
Donato 327
Dondenaz 341
Donnas 341
Doria, Admiral Lamba 144
Doria, Admiral Lucian 146
Doria, Andrea 107, **147–8**
Doria, Gian Andrea 149
Dronero 269
Druogno **315–16**, 317

Eaux-Rousses 352
EHIC cards 67
Elva 270
embassies 66, 76
emergencies 76, 77
Entracque 273
Entrèves **354**, 356
Erbaluce 59
Eremo del Deserto 137
Etroubles 349
Exilles 258

Falmenta 310
Fanghetto 87
Farigliano 281
Fascism 28–9
Favale di Malvaro 180
Fenis 344
festivals 65
Fiascherino **207**, 210–11
Fiera Fredda 272
Fieschi family 189
Finale Ligure **125**, 128
Finale Pia **125**, 128–9
Finaleborgo **125–6**, 128
First Crusade 22, 144
First World War 28
Fiumaretta di Ameglia 209
Fobello 323
Fondotoce 308
food and drink **52–62**
football 79, 240
Formazza 317
Forno 321
Forno Alpi Graie 329
Forte di Bramafam 259
Forte di Fenestrelle 262
Fortezza di Consolata 272
Fossano 266
Frabosa Soprana 275
Framura 194–5
Frederick I Hohenstaufen (Barbarossa) 22, 294

Freisa 59
Fréjus Tunnel 229, 259
Fruttaria abbey 330

Gaby 341
Gaglianico 326
Galliate 301–2
Garessio 276
Garibaldi, Giuseppe 26–7, **42–7**
Garlenda **118**, 120–1
Gattinara 59
Gattorno 179
Gavi 59, **297**, 298
Genoa 29–30, *140–1*, **142–74**, *174*
  Albergo dei Poveri 153
  Aquarium 163–4
  art and architecture 32
  Bar Beto 158
  Barbarossa walls 157
  Basilica della SS. Annunziate del
    Vastato 152–3
  Bigo 163
  Bolla 163
  Campetto 161
  Cappella di San Giovanni
    Battista 160
  Casa di Colombo 157
  Casa di Mazzini 153
  Casella 164
  Castelletto 155
  Circonvallazione
    a Monte 164
  Città dei Bambini 163
  Cloister of Sant'Andrea 157
  Duomo di San Lorenzo 160
  eating out 171–3
  Galeone Neptune 163
  Gesù 160
  getting to and around 145
  history 22–3, 24–5, **142–51**
  Klainguti 161
  La Commenda 151
  Lanterna 151–2
  Largo della Zecca 153
  Loggia a Mare 151
  Loggia dei Mercanti 162
  Mackenzie Castle 164
  Mercato Orientale 157
  museums and galleries
    Accademia Ligustica di Belle
      Arti 156
    Antartide 164
    Archeologico Ligure 167–8
    Arte Contemporanea 157
    Arte Orientale 155–6
    Culture del Mondo 166
    Diocesano 160
    Fabrorum della Filigrana 161
    Galata-Museo del Mare 164
    Galleria Mazzini 156
    Galleria Nazionale di Palazzo
      Reale 152
    Galleria Nazionale di Palazzo
      Spinola 162–3

Genoa (*cont'd*)
  museums and galleries (*cont'd*)
    Lanterna 152
    Luzzati 163
    Natural History 157
    Navale di Pegli 167
    Risorgimento 153
    Santa Maria di Castello 159
    Sant'Agostino 158
    Tesoro della Cattedrale 160
  Nostra Signora della
    Consolazione 157
  Palazzo Reale 152
  Palazzo Spinola 162–3
  Piazza Banchi 162
  Piazza Corvetto 156
  Piazza Dante 157
  Piazza De Ferrari 156
  Piazza delle Fontane Marose 155
  Piazza Manin 164
  Piazza Matteotti 159–60
  Piazza San Matteo 160–1
  Piazza Sarzano 158
  Piazza della Vittoria 157
  Ponte Andre Doria 151
  Ponte Monumentale 157
  Ponte Parodi 164
  Porta Siberia 163
  Porta Soprana 157
  Portal of San Giovanni 160
  Porto Antico 163–4
  Quartiere del Molo 163
  Righi 153
  Romanengo 161
  San Bartolomeo degli Armeni
    164–5
  San Donato 158
  San Filippo Neri 153
  San Giorgio 159
  San Giovanni di Prè 151
  San Luca 162
  San Marco 163
  San Matteo 161
  San Pietro della Porta 162
  San Siro 153
  San Torpete 159
  Sant'Agostino 158
  Santa Maria Assunta in
    Carignano 157
  Santa Maria di Castello 159
  Santa Maria della Cella 166
  Santa Marta 156
  SS. Cosma e Damiano 159
  SS. Vittore e Carlo 152
  Santo Stefano 157
  shopping 169
  sports and activities 169
  Staglieno Cemetery 166
  Stazione Marittima 151
  Stazione Principe 151
  Strada della Mura 164
  Teatro Carlo Felice 156
  Torre degli Ebriaci 159
  tourist information 169

Genoa (*cont'd*)
  Trenino de Casella 164
  Via Balbi 152
  Via Garibaldi 154–5
  Via Luccoli 161
  Via San Bernardo 158–9
  Via San Luca 162
  Via Sotto Ripa 162
  Via XX Settembre 156–7
  Villa Croce 157
  Villa Imperiale de Terralba 166
  Villetta di Negro 155
  where to stay 169–71
Ghemme 59
Ghevio 304
Ghibellines 22–3
Ghiffa **309**, 311
Ghisola 268
Giannini, Amedeo Pietro 180
Giardino Alpinia 305
Giardino Esotico Pallanca 94
Gignese 305
Gignod 349
Giulio, Saint 318, 319
Giustenice 124
Gola di Gouta 89
golf 79, 137
Golfo del Tigullio 182–8
Govone 282
Gozzano 320
Gran Paradiso 334, 351–2
Grangesises 260
Gravere 258
Great St Bernard Pass 349–50
Gressan 349
Gressoney-Saint-Jean **341**, 344–5
Gressoney-la-Trinité 341
Grignolino 59
Grinzane Cavour **280**, 283
Groppo 198
Groscavallo **329**, 335
Grotta delle Arene Candide 126
Grotta della Bàsura 121–2
Grotta del Colombo 122
Grotta del Rio Martino 268
Grotta di Santa Lucia 122
Grotte di Bossea 275
Grotte di Toirano 121
Grotte di Verezzi 124
Grotto del Caviglione 86
Guarene d'Alba 282
Guelphs 22–3
Gulf of Diano 110–13
Gulf of Paradise *178*, 178–82
Gulf of Poets 205–12
Gurro 310

Hanbury Gardens 86–7
history **20–30**
Imperia **105–6**, 109–10
Intra 309
Introd 352
Isola d'Asti 292
Isola Bella 305–6

Isola Madre 306
Isola Palmaria 204
Isola dei Pescatori 306
Isolabona 89
Issime 341
Ivrea **331–2**, 335–6

Julius II, Pope 131
Juventus 240

La Cervara 184
La Magdeleine 343
La Mandria 249
La Morra **280**, 283
La Palud **354**, 356
La Reggia di Venaria Reale 248–9
La Salle 353
La Spezia **201–3**, 204
La Thuile **353**, 355
Lagnasco 268
Laigueglia **112**, 113
lakes
    Candia 330
    Maggiore 302–11, *304*
    Mergozzo **312**, 313–14
    Miserin 341
    Orta *304*, 318–22
    Viverone 327
language **357–8**
    menu reader 60–2
Lanzo Torinese **329**, 335
Lavagna 189
Le Caravelle 121
Le Langhe 276–85
Legro 320
Lercari, Megollo 146
Lerici **206–7**, 210
Lerma 296
Lesa 305
Levaldigi 266
Levanto **195**, 196
Levice 281
Libiola 191
Lignana 300
Ligurians 20
Lillaz 352
Limone Piemonte **273**, 274
Linguéglietta 105
Little Saint Bernard Valley 353
Loano **123**, 124
Lombards 21
Loranzè Alto 336
Losòn 352
Lucinasco 109
Lungomare Europa 137
Luni 208

Macugnaga **313**, 314
Maggiore 302–11, *304*
Magliano Alfieri **282**, 284–5
Magnano 328
Magnasco 190
Malesco **316**, 317–18
Manarola **198**, 200

Mango 281–2
Mannerism 33–4
Manta 267
Marassi 166
Marconi tower 190
Marengo, battle of 295–6
Mariani, Pompeo 92
markets 78–9
Marquisate of Saluzzo 264–71
Massino Visconti 305
Matterhorn 344
Mazzini, Giuseppe 26, **42–7**
Melezet 259
Meloria, battle of 144
Mergozzo **312**, 313–14
Miasino 320
Millesimo 133
Molini di Triora **102–3**, 104
Moltedo 108
Mombaruzzo 292
Monastero del Corvo 208
Moncalieri 247
Moncalvo **290**, 294
Mondovì **274–5**, 276
Mondrone 329
Moneglia **194**, 195–6
Monesi 119
Monesiglio 281
Monforte d'Alba 284
Mont Blanc 354
Mont Cenis Pass 258
Montaldo di Mondovì 276
Montalto Ligure 102
Monte Beigua 135
Monte Bignone 98
Monte Fasce 179
Monte Mottarone 305
Monte Mucrone 326
Monte di Portofino 182
Monte Rosa 313, 341
Monte Toraggio 90
Monte Ursino 127
Montebruno 174
Montechiaro 289
Montegrazie 108
Montemagno **289–90**, 293
Montemarcello **207**, 211
Monterosso Grana 271
Monterosso al Mare **197–8**, 199
Montiglio 289
Montorfano 312
Morgex 353
Mortola Inferiore 86
Mulinetti 179
Multedo 167
Murazzano 281
Mussolini, Benito 29

Napoleon Bonaparte 25–6, 132, 150, 295–6
national holidays 77
nature reserves
    Alpi Liguri 90
    Alpi Marittime 272–3

nature reserves (*cont'd*)
    Alta Valle Pesio 273
    Aveto 190
    Bessa 327
    Burcina Felice Piacenza 326
    Gran Paradiso 334, 351–2
    Lagoni di Mercurago 303
    Manie 126
    Monte Beigua 135
    Montemarcello-Magra 207
    Mottarone 305
    Piana Crixia 133
    Portofino 182
    Subacqueo Archeologico 207
    Val Grande 309
Ne **190**, 191–2
Neironi 180
Neive **282**, 284
Nervi 168–9
Nicola **208**, 211
Nietzsche, Friedrich 233
Nigoglia 321
Nizza Monferrato 292
Noasca 334
Noli **127–8**, 129
Novalesa 258
Novara **300–1**, 302
Novi Ligure **297**, 298
Nus 344

Oasi Zegna 326
Oggebbio 309
Oleggio 302
Olivetta-San Michele 87
Olympic Mountains 253–64, *254–5*
Omegna **321**, 322
Oneglia 107–8
Orasso 310
Ormea 276
Oropa **326**, 328
Orrido di Sant'Anna 310
Orta San Giulio **318–20**, 321–2
Ortonovo **208–9**, 211
Ortovero 119
Ospedaletti **94**, 95
Ossola valleys 312–18
Otto the Great 22
Oulx **258**, 263
Ovada **296**, 298

Paesana 268
Palanfrè 273
palio 286
Pallanza **308–9**, 310–11
palone elastico 79
Pamparato 276
Pancalieri 265
Paraggi 184
Parasio 106
parco naturale see nature reserves
Passito di Caluso 59, 330
Passo del Faiallo 135
Passo della Guardia 103
Passo Monte Moro 313

Pedemonte 324
Pegli 167–8
Pellico, Silvio 267
Perinaldo 93–4
Perino del Vaga 33–4
Perti 126
Pessione 241
Pestarena 312
Pettenasco **320**, 322
Pian Cavallone 309
Pian del Re 268
Piano del Valasco 273
Piasco 269
Piazza Matteotti 191
Piedmont 252, **253–336**
  food and drink 55–9
Pietra Ligure **123–4**, 181
Pietrabruna 105
Pietraporzio 272
Pieve Ligure 179
Pieve di Teco 119
Pigna **89**, 91
Pignone 193
Pila 349
Pinerolo **260–2**, 264
Pius V, Pope 296
Pius VII, Pope 132
Plampincieux 354
Planaval 352
Po Valley 268
Pogli 119
Pollenzo **277–8**, 279
Pollone 326
Pondel 351
Pont Canavese 333–4
Pont-Saint-Martin **340**, 344
Ponte delle Fate 126
Ponte San Ludovico 87
Pontechianale 269
Pontedassio 108–9
Pontremoli 210
Pornassio 119
Porto Maurizio 106
Portofino **184**, 187
Portofino Vetta 182
Portovenere **203–4**, 205
Pradleves **271**, 274
Pragelato 260
Pré-Saint-Didier 353
Premeno 309
Priocca 285
Prunetto 281
Punta Chiappa 182

Quarna Sopra 321
Quarna Sotto 321
Quarto dei Mille 168
Quiliano 134

Racconigi 265
Ranzo 119
Rapallo **185**, 187–8
Re 316
Realdo 103

Recco **179**, 181
refuges 79–80, 90, 341, 352
Renaissance 32–3
Revello 268
Rezzoaglio 190
Rhêmes-Notre-Dame 352
Rimella 323
Riomaggiore **198–9**, 200
Risorgimento 26–7, **46**
Riva Ligure 104
Riva Trigoso 191
Riva Valdobbia 323–4
Rivarolo Canavese 333
Riviera dei Fiori *84*, 84–104
Riviera di Levante *176–7*,
  177–212, *194*
Riviera degli Olivi *84*, 104–13, *107*
Riviera delle Palme 113–25
Riviera di Ponente *82–3*, 84–138, *136*
Rivoli 248
Rocca Senghi 269
Roccaforte Mondovì 275
Rocchetta Nervina 89
rococo art and architecture 34–6
Roddi 280
Roero 59, **276**
Romano Canavese 335
Romans 20–1, 32
Ronco 334
Ronco Scrivia 173
Rovere 111
Ruffini, Giovanni 27, 102
Ruta 182

Sacra di San Michele 256
Sacro Monti **319–20**, 323
Saint-Oyen 349
Saint-Pierre **351**, 355
St-Rhémy-en-Bosses 349
St Vincent **343**, 345
Salecchio 317
Saliceto 281
Saluzzo 264–71
Sampeyre **269**, 271
Sampierdarena 166
San Bartolomeo al Mare 111
San Bartolomeo degli Armeni 164–5
San Benigno Canavese 330
San Bernardo 276
San Fruttuoso **182–3**, 186
San Fruttuoso (Genoa) 166
San Giorio di Susa 256–7
San Giovanni 306
San Girolamo 184
San Lazzaro Reale 109
San Lorenzo al Mare 105
San Martino di Lignera 281
San Maurizio Canavese 328
San Maurizio d'Opaglio 320
San Michele Mondovì 275
San Nazzaro Sesia 302
San Pietro dei Monti 123
San Remo **95–8**, 100–1
San Romolo 98

San Sicario 259
San Siro di Struppa 174
San Terenzo **205–6**, 210
San Venerio 204
sanctuaries
  Graglia 326–7
  Maddalena 109
  Madonna del Sangue 316
  Madonna del Sasso 320
  Madonna delle Grazie 89, 186
  Madonna della Guardia 108, 173
  Madonna della Rovere 111
  Madonnetta 165
  Montenero 199
  Nostra Signora delle Grazie 108
  Oropa 326
  Sacro Cuore 99
  San Magno 271
  Sant'Anna 272
  Sant'Ignazio 329
Sanfront 268
Sant'Antonio di Ranverso 253
Santa Margherita Ligure **183**, 186
Santa Maria Maggiore **315–16**, 317
Santa Maria di Vezzolano 289
Sant'Olcese 173
Santa Vittoria d'Alba **278**, 279
Santo Stefano **104**, 109
Santo Stefano d'Aveto 190
Santo Stefano Belbo 292–3
Sarriod de la Tour 351
Sarzana **209–10**, 211–12
Sauze di Cesana 260
Sauze d'Oulx **259**, 263
Savigliano **265–6**, 270
Savona 129–34
Savoy counts 23–4
Seborga 92–3
Second World War 29
Serralunga d'Alba **281**, 284
Sestri Levante **190**, 192
Sestri Ponente 167
Sestriere **260**, 263–4
Settimo Vittone **334–5**, 336
Sezzadio 296
Shelley, Percy Bysshe 206
Silvera 304
Slow Food movement 30, **49–50**
Sori 179
Soriso 322
Sportina 259
Spotorno **127**, 129
Staffarda abbey 268
Stresa **305**, 307
Stroppo **270**, 271
Stupinigi 247
Susa **257**, 262
Susa valley 258–60

Taggia **101–2**, 104
Tellaro **207**, 210–11
Terme di Lurisia 275
Terme di Valdieri 273
Terrarossa Colombo 179–80

Testico 112
Tiglieto 135
Tigliole d'Asti 292
Tinetto 204
Toirano 121–3
Torgnon 343
Torre Canavese 333
Torre Guardiola 199
Torre Pellice **262**, 264
Torri Superiore 87
Torriglia 174
Tortona **296–7**, 298
tourist information 65–6
trains 69, 70–1
Tramonti 203
travel
  entry formalities 66–7
  getting around 70–2
  getting there 68–70
  when to go 64
Trebiano 208
Triora **103**, 104
truffles 56, 279, 280
Turin *214–15*, **215–46**, *221*
  Al Bicerin 229
  Armeria Reale 224
  Biblioteca Reale 224
  Borgo e Rocca Medioevale 238–9
  Borgo San Paolo 238
  Cavour monument 232
  Church of the Carmine 229
  Citadella 230–1
  Dora Park 223
  Duomo 226
  eating out **244–6**, 250
  entertainment 246
  getting to and around 217, 222–3
  Gran Madre di Dio 233
  history 28, **216–20**
  Lingotto 239
  markets 228
  Mole Antonelliana 231
  museums and galleries
    Antichità 227
    Arti Decorative 233
    Automobile 239
    Cinema 231–2
    Egyptian 235–6
    Fondazione Merz 238
    Fondazione Sandretto Re
      Rebaudengo 238
    Marionetta 237
    modern art (GAM) 36, **237–8**
    Montagna Duca degli
      Abruzzi 234
    Pietro Micca 230–1
    Pinacoteca Giovanni e Marella
      Agnelli 239
    Risorgimento 235
    Sabauda 236
    Scienzi Naturali 232
    Sindone 229
  Palazzina di Caccia di
    Stupinigi 247

Turin (*cont'd*)
  Palazzo Reale 224–6
  Parco Archeologico 227
  Parco della Rimembranza 247
  Parco del Valentino 238–9
  Piazza Castello 223–6
  Piazza San Carlo 237
  Piazza Solferino 230–1
  Piazza Vittorio Veneto 233
  Pinacoteca Albertina delle Belle
    Arti 232
  Porta Palatina 226–7
  Prefettura 224
  Quadrilatero Romano 228–30
  Royal Tombs 241
  San Carlo 237
  San Domenico 228
  San Filippo Neri 235
  Santa Cristina 237
  Santa Maria del Monte 234
  Santa Maria di Piazza 230
  Santa Teresa 237
  SS. Martiri 229–30
  Santo Volto 223
  Santuario della Consolata 228
  Superga 240–1
  Teatro Regio 224
  tourist information 242
  University 223
  Via Po 232–3
  Via Roma 234–5
  Villa della Regina 233–4
  Vittorio Emanuele I bridge 233
  where to stay 242–4
Turin Shroud 225, 226, **227–8**

Urbe 135
Uscio **179**, 181
Usseglio 329

Vacciago 320
Vado Ligure **128**, 129
Val d'Antrona 313
Val Cannobina 310
Val Divedro 316
Val Fontanabuona 179
Val Grande 329
Val di Gressoney 340–1
Val Gromolo 191
Val di Magra 207–12
Val Mastallone 323
Val Nervia 87–8
Val Polcevera 173
Val Roja 87
Val di Vara 192–3
Val Veny 354
Val Vigezzo 315–16
Val di Viù 329
Valderia 273
Valgrana 271
Valgrisenche 352–3
Valle Anzasca 312
Valle d'Aosta *338–9*, **339–56**
Valle Argentina 101–4

Valle del Chisone 260–4
Valle Gesso 272–3
Valle Maira 269
Valle Pellice 260–4
Valle del Pesio 273
Valle Stura 272
Valle Vermenagna 273
Vallecrosia 92
Valli Antigorio e Formazzo 316–17
Valli di Lanzo *324*, 328–36
Valnontey 351
Valpelline 349
Valperga 333
Valsesia 322–3
Valstrona 321
Valtournenche 343, 344
Varallo **323**, *324*, 327
Varazze **136–7**, 138
Varese Ligure 192, **193**
Varigotti **126**, 129
Veglio 326
Venaria Reale 248–9
Venice 144, 146
Ventimiglia **85–6**, 90
Verbania **308–9**, 310–11
Vercelli **299–300**, 302
Verdeggia 103
Verduno 283
Vermogno 327
Vernante **273**, 274
Vernazza **198**, 199–200
Verrès **342**, 345
Vessalico 119
Vezzano Ligure 208
Via Crucis 98
Via Julia Augusta 87
Vicoforte 275
Villa Faraldi 111
Villa San Sebastiano 109
Villadossola 313
village architecture 48–9, *49*
Villanova 262
Villanova d'Albenga 117–18
Villanova Mondovì 275
Villar Perosa 262
Villar San Costanzo 269
Villeneuve 352
Vin de l'Enfer 59
Vinadio 272
Vittorio Emanuele II 27, 47
Viverone 327
Vobbia 174
Vollon 342

Waldensians 261
Walsers 313, **316**, 324
whale watching 109, 133
where to stay 72–4
wine 55, 58–9
witches 103

Zoagli **185–6**, 188
Zuccarello 119–20

About the Updater

Gabriella Cursoli is a keen and curiosity-filled traveller. Her background in history and the arts supports and nourishes her interest in different places, people and cultures. After almost six years spent in London, she has now moved to Milan, where she works as an editor, updater and translator.

5th edition published 2008

Cadogan Guides is an imprint of
New Holland Publishers (UK) Ltd
London • Cape Town • Sydney • Auckland

New Holland Publishers (UK) Ltd	80 McKenzie Street	Unit 1, 66 Gibbes Street	218 Lake Road
Garfield House	Cape Town 8001	Chatswood, NSW 2067	Northcote
86–88 Edgware Road	South Africa	Australia	Auckland
London W2 2EA			New Zealand

cadogan@nhpub.co.uk
www.cadoganguides.com
t +44 (0) 20 7724 7773

Distributed in the United States by Globe Pequot, Connecticut

Cover photographs: © Brenda Tharp/Corbis; © Hall/PhotoCuisine/Corbis
Photo essay photographs © Kicca Tommasi, except p.14 (top) © Italian Tourist Board
Maps © Cadogan Guides, drawn by Maidenhead Cartographic Services Ltd
Cover and photo essay design: Sarah Rianhard-Gardner
Editor: Sarah Goulding
Proofreading: Dominique Shead
Indexing: Isobel McLean

Printed in Italy by Legoprint
A catalogue record for this book is available from the British Library

ISBN: 978-1-86011-391-8

Italian Riviera and Piedmont touring atlas

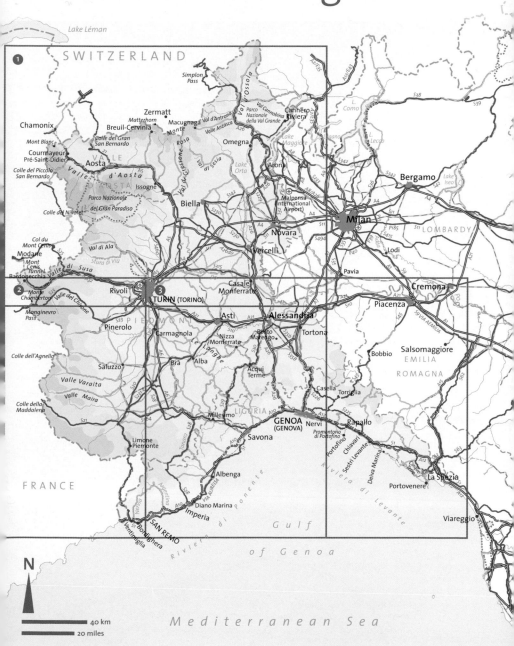

Brig

Simplon
Pass

Val Divedro

Antigorio

SWITZERLAND

Val Vigezzo

Locarno

Ascona

Vira

Domodossola

S. Maria
Maggiore

Pino L. Maggiore

Antronapiana

Villadossola

Parco Nazionale
della Val Grande

Cannobio

Musignano

rmatt

Trarego Viggiona

Maccagno

Cannero Riviera

A26

Intragna

Luino

Lugano

Mt Brè

L.
Lugano

Monte

Aurano

Miazina

Premeno

Germignaga

Ponte Tresa

Rimella

Cascata di Sesia

Val Mastallone

Fobello

L. Miazina

Verbania

S33

Arcumeggia

Rosa

Alagna
Valsesia

Gressoney-
la-Trinité

Riva Valdobbia

Omegna

Pallanza

Stresa

Cittiglio

Campo
dei Fiori

Santa
Caterina

Gressoney-
Saint-Jean

Sacro Monte

Mt
Mottarone

Vezzo

Gavirate

Varese

Valsesia

Nonio
Cesara

Lake Orta

Cesa

Varallo

Pella

Meina

S394

Gaby

nes

Isola S. Giulio

Orta San
Giulio

Angera

Varese

ime

Piedicavallo

Borgosesia

Arona

Comabbio

Comabbio

A8

Rosazza

STRADA PANORAMICA ZEGNA

S232

Serravalle

Borgo
Ticino

Gallarate

S233

A9

Monte
Mucrone

Oropa

Trivero

Valle Mosso

STRADA DELLA LANA

Romagnano Sesia

A26

Busto Arsizio

A8/A26

Parco Burcina
Felice Piacenza

S142

Malpensa
(International Airport)

Legnano

Pollone

Biella

LOMBARDY

S33

Graglia
Donato

Candelo
Gaglianico

S32

Donato

Gaglianico
Castle

S230

Ivrea

La serra

Cerrione

A4

A4

S11

Lago di
Viverone

Viverone

S230

Novara

Magenta

S11

Cassinetta di
Lugagnano

Caravino

Ticino

S11

Abblategrasso

S494

ese

Lago di
Candia

Canavese

A26dir

Vercelli

Mazzè

S11

Vigevano

nigno Canavese

Gambolò

S315

Battea

Po

Abbazia di
Vezzolano

Lomellina

Garlasco

A7

(RINO)

Albugnano

Casale
Monferrato

Lomello

Moncalvo

A1

hieri

Valenza

A21

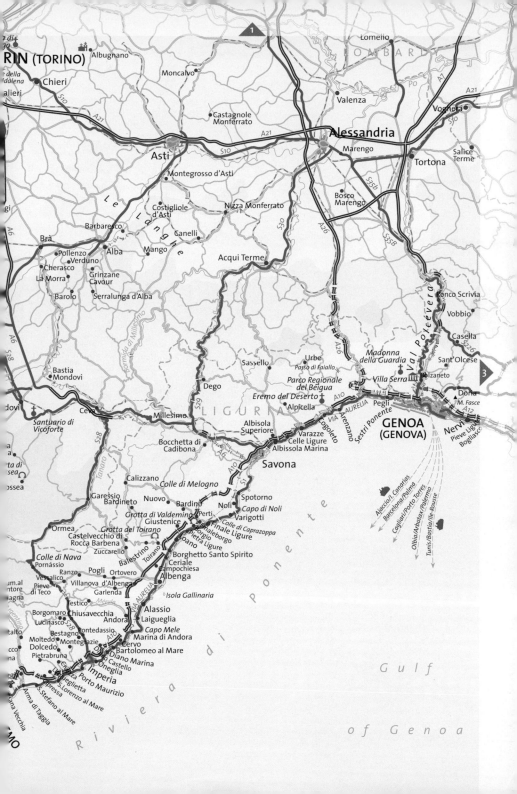

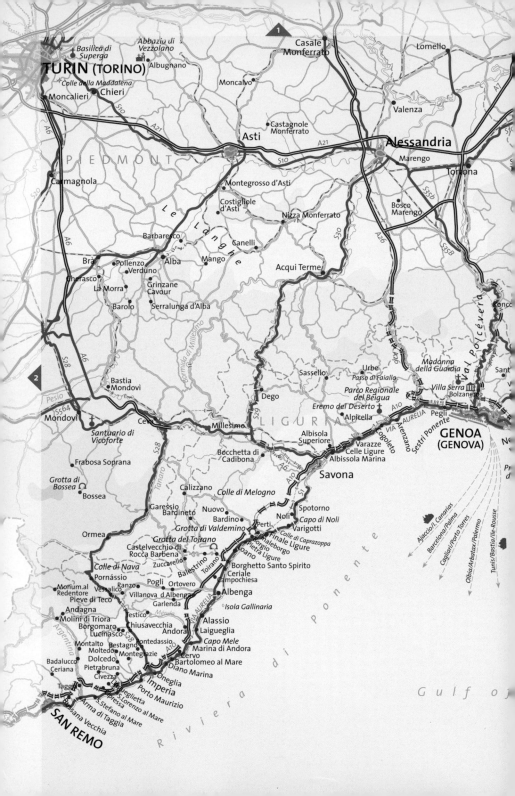

CADOGANguides ISLANDS

'Not for beach
and bar tourists,
but for real travellers'
Observer

Corsica • Crete • Greek Islands • Madeira
• Malta • Sardinia • Sicily